Standing up for a Sustainable World

For those who stood up and particularly for Georgina Mace

Standing up for a Sustainable World

Voices of Change

Edited by

Claude Henry

Professor of Sustainable Development, Sciences Po, France

Johan Rockström

Director, Potsdam Institute for Climate Impact Research (PIK); Professor in Earth System Science, University of Potsdam, Germany

Nicholas Stern

IG Patel Professor of Economics and Government and Chair, Grantham Research Institute, London School of Economics, UK

Edward Elgar
PUBLISHING

Cheltenham, UK • Northampton, MA, USA

Published by
Edward Elgar Publishing Limited
The Lypiatts
15 Lansdown Road
Cheltenham
Glos GL50 2JA
UK

Edward Elgar Publishing, Inc.
William Pratt House
9 Dewey Court
Northampton
Massachusetts 01060
USA

A catalogue record for this book
is available from the British Library

Library of Congress Control Number: 2020950121

This book is available electronically in the **Elgar**online
Economics subject collection
http://dx.doi.org/10.4337/9781800371781

Printed on elemental chlorine free (ECF)
recycled paper containing 30% Post-Consumer Waste

ISBN 978 1 80037 177 4 (cased)
ISBN 978 1 80037 178 1 (eBook)
ISBN 978 1 80037 179 8 (paperback)
Printed and bound in the USA

Contents

Contributors

Monica Araya is the Transport Lead within the COP26 Climate Champions Team. Her work focuses on accelerating the transition to zero-emission road transportation with a strong focus on coalition building and demand acceleration. She has founded several initiatives in Latin America to engage leaders in government, business and civil society, including Costa Rica Limpia. She has a doctorate in Environmental Management from Yale University and hosts a podcast on climate, technology and science.

Asmeret Asefaw Berhe is Professor of Soil Biogeochemistry and Falasco Chair in Earth Sciences at University of California, Merced. She graduated from Asmara University, Eritrea and received her PhD from UC Berkeley. Professor Berhe is a soil scientist and leader on scientific issues involving soil, climate change, and equity, diversity and inclusion in higher education. She is a member of the inaugural class of the New Voices in Science, Engineering, and Medicine and Past Chair of the US National Committee on Soil Science at the National Academies of Science, Engineering, and Medicine.

Michel Berry has been Research Director at the Centre National de la Recherche Scientifique (CNRS) (1981–2008), Director of the Centre de Recherche en Gestion at École Polytechnique (1975–91), founder and editor-in-chief of the journal *Gérer et Comprendre* (1985–2015), member of the International Programs Committee, American Academy of Management (1994–2002), and is founder and director of the École de Paris du management (1993–present).

Antoine Bizien, **Elsa Deville** and **Lucas Dubois** are three students at École Polytechnique. They were able to join this prestigious engineering school after two years of intensive classes in maths and physics. They got to know each other as neighbours on campus and through their weekly boxing matches! They chose to get involved in the school's sustainable development association in their desire to understand and commit to ecological issues. This breeding ground was conducive to the emergence of a reflection on their role as students and future workers.

Dominique Bureau works at the French Ministry for Ecological and Inclusive Transition. He currently chairs its Economic Council for Sustainable

Development and its Green Tax Commission. He is also Chairman of the French Authority for Official Statistics and a lecturer at the École Polytechnique, in charge of the steering committee of the Chair for Sustainable Development.

Camila Bustos graduated from Brown University with honours in Environmental Studies and International Relations, where she studied international climate change policy. After university, she worked as a researcher at Colombian-based NGO Dejusticia, researching issues related to business and human rights, climate-induced displacement, and the human rights movement. She is a 2019 Paul & Daisy Soros Fellow and a second-year law student at Yale Law School. Camila is interested in working at the intersection of climate change and human rights litigation.

Bobby Chan, this long-haired, music-loving environmental lawyer, leads one of the world's most effective direct-action eco-vigilante organizations. Inspired by their Catholic faith, he and a dozen other colleagues enforce conservation laws that usually go ignored by local police, environmental officers and coastguards. They confiscate chainsaws from loggers, boats from illegal fishermen and guns from poachers. Several of his friends have died in this campaign, but he believes that radical action is essential.

Susan Clayton is Whitmore-Williams Professor of Psychology at the College of Wooster in Ohio. She has written or edited six books, including *Psychology and Climate Change* (2018). Her PhD in Social Psychology is from Yale University. Her research focuses on the human relationship with nature, how it is socially constructed, and how it can be utilized to promote environmental conservation. She is a lead author on the upcoming Sixth Assessment Report from the Intergovernmental Panel on Climate Change.

Philippe Cury is a senior scientist at the Institut de Recherche pour le Développement (IRD), France, working in marine ecology. He is the President of the Scientific Council of the Monaco Institute of Oceanography. He has been working in Senegal, Côte d'Ivoire, California, South Africa and France to analyse the effect of climate on fisheries and how to implement the ecosystem approach to fisheries. He has published more than 150 articles in the main international journals and has received several scientific achievements and awards.

Anneliese Depoux leads the Centre Virchow-Villermé, a French-German research centre for Public Health, with a branch in Paris – Université de Paris – and another one in Berlin – Charité Universitätsmedizin. The Centre has pioneered work on the health impacts of climate change and is widely recognized as a European hub for research on this emerging topic. Dr Depoux is herself a leading voice in the communication of these issues to the general public: she founded the 4C-Health research consortium to foster this approach, and she is a member of *The Lancet* Countdown initiative, the Centre des Politiques de la Terre, and the Global Consortium on Climate and Health Education at Columbia University.

Catharina Dyvik is an associate at SYSTEMIQ and Programme Manager of the Blended Finance Taskforce, which seeks to accelerate mobilization of investment for emerging markets' sustainable and resilient infrastructure. She is co-author of a number of Taskforce publications such as *Better Finance, Better World* and *Infra 3.0: Better Infrastructure, Better World*. Prior to joining SYSTEMIQ, she worked for six years at the European Bank for Reconstruction and Development in various roles and geographies, focusing primarily on the financing of environmental improvement projects as well as energy and resource efficiency. She is currently advising a number of financial institutions on sustainable finance.

Both artists, musicians and activists, **Birhan Erkutlu** and **Tuğba Günal** gave up an urban consumer life and moved into the forests of Antalya, where they built a home from natural materials. Their creative and brave opposition to a cascade of hydro-electric dams led to the creation of a new protected area. Living their values, they have become symbols of environmental defence at a time when the Turkish government has ramped up infrastructure projects.

Gabriela Eslava-Bejarano is a lawyer from the Universidad de Los Andes, with minors in Journalism and Literature. She has worked as a political and legal advisor at Colombia's Congress, where she focused on environmental justice policy-making. She has also worked as a researcher at the NGO Dejusticia, where she led litigation cases on climate change and participation in environmental matters. She is currently studying for Master of Public Administration in Development Practice at Columbia University, USA. She is interested in developing economic tools for environmental protection.

François Gemenne is a specialist in environmental geopolitics and migration dynamics at the University of Liège, where he is a Fonds de la Recherche Scientifique (FNRS) senior research associate and the Director of the Hugo Observatory. He also heads the Observatory on Defence and Climate of the French Ministry of Defence. He also lectures on climate change and migration policies in various universities, including Sciences Po Paris and the Free University of Brussels. As a lead author for the Intergovernmental Panel on Climate Change (IPCC), his research deals with environmental and migration governance.

Alain Grandjean is a graduate of École Polytechnique and ENSAE Paris, and holds a PhD in Environmental Economics. He is co-founder and partner of

Carbone 4, a climate strategy consulting firm. He is Chairman of the Nicolas Hulot Foundation. He has co-chaired several official missions and is co-author of several books and hosts the blog 'Chroniques de l'anthropocène'.

Genevieve Guenther is the founding director of End Climate Silence and affiliate faculty at the Tishman Environment and Design Center at The New School in New York City.

Emmanuel Guérin is the Executive Director for International Affairs at the European Climate Foundation. Emmanuel also serves as the Director of the International Climate Politics Hub. Before joining the ECF, he worked for the French Foreign Affairs Ministry, as Special Advisor to France's Climate Change Ambassador and led the drafting team for the Paris Agreement. Emmanuel taught and researched at Sciences Po, Columbia University, and the London School of Economics.

Sophie Handford is the founder of School Strike 4 Climate NZ and coordinated the movement alongside others during its first year. She graduated from Kāpiti College in 2018 and has now gone on to become New Zealand's youngest elected council member on the Kāpiti Coast District Council. She is determined to be able to say she has done everything in her power to create a more beautiful world for generations to come.

Geoffrey Heal is a professor at Columbia Business School, noted for his work on environmental and resource economics and economic theory. He chairs the board of the Coalition for Rainforest Nations, is a member of the board of the Union of Concerned Scientists, sits on the advisory board of the Environmental Defense Fund and is a member of the National Academy of Sciences. He has written 18 books. His latest, *Endangered Economies*, sets out the economic case for environmental conservation.

Stephen B. Heintz is President and CEO of the Rockefeller Brothers Fund (RBF). He set the path to align the Fund's financial investments with its mission, resulting in its 2014 divestment from fossil fuels. Heintz has devoted his career to strengthening democracy. He serves as a co-chair of the American Academy of Arts and Sciences Commission on the Practice of Democratic Citizenship. Before joining the RBF, Heintz co-founded Dēmos and served as Executive Vice-President and COO for the EastWest Institute.

Physicist turned economist, **Claude Henry** is Professor of Sustainable Development at Sciences Po, Paris. He is President of the Scientific Council of Institut du Développement Durable et des Relations Internationales (IDDRI), Paris. He has previously been at Columbia University as Adjunct Professor in the School of International and Public Affairs, and at École Polytechnique as Head of Research in Economics, and as Professor of Public and Environmental

Economics; he has taught in the same fields at Université de Lausanne. He is co-author with Laurence Tubiana of *Earth at Risk: Natural Capital and the Quest for Sustainability*, published by Columbia University Press. He has served for five years on the Conseil d'Analyse Économique in Prime Minister Lionel Jospin's office.

Alice C. Hill is the David M. Rubenstein Senior Fellow for Energy and Environment Climate Change Policy at the Council on Foreign Relations. Hill previously served as Special Assistant to President Barack Obama and Senior Director for Resilience on the National Security Council staff. Earlier in her career, she was a judge and prosecutor in California. She serves on the boards of the Environmental Defense Fund and Munich Re Group's US-based companies. She is the recipient of Yale University's Public Voices Fellowship on the Climate Crisis and co-author of *Building a Resilient Tomorrow*.

Research Director (Emeritus) at the Commissariat à l'Énergie Atomique et aux Énergies Alternatives (CEA), **Jean Jouzel** is an expert in climate and glaciology. He was vice-chair of the Scientific Working Group of the Intergovernmental Panel on Climate Change (IPCC) from 2002 to 2015. He was awarded the Centre National de la Recherche Scientifique (CNRS) Gold Medal in 2002 and the Vetlesen Prize in 2012. He is a foreign member of the US National Academy of Sciences and a member of the French Academy of Sciences. Since 2010, he has been a member of the Economic, Social and Environmental Council, the third assembly in France.

Ma Jun is Chairman of the Green Finance Committee of the China Society for Finance and Banking, member of the People's Bank of China's Monetary Policy Committee, and Chair of the Supervisory Workstream of the Central Banks' and Supervisors' Network for Greening the Financial System.

Alessia Lefébure (PhD) is Vice-Dean of the French School for Public Health (EHESP), in charge of Academic Affairs. She previously ran the Columbia University Alliance, a joint initiative for innovation in global research and education. Adjunct Professor at Sciences Po Rennes, she taught at Columbia University in New York, Sciences Po Paris and Tsinghua University in Beijing. A sociologist by training, and an internationally recognized expert in global education, she is a member of the Board of the Red Cross Foundation.

Georgina M. Mace, DBE FRS, was Professor of Biodiversity and Ecosystems and Director of the Centre for Biodiversity and Environment Research (CBER) at University College London. Her research interests have been in measuring the trends and consequences of biodiversity loss and ecosystem change. She contributed to the Millennium Ecosystem Assessment, the UK National Ecosystem Assessment, the IPCC and IPBES. She was a member of the UK Government's first Natural Capital Committee and of the Adaptation Committee of the UK Climate Change Committee. She completed her chapter in this book a few weeks before her death on September 19, 2020.

Raven Maeder is a Law and Environmental Studies student at Victoria University of Wellington, and was a national coordinator of School Strike 4 Climate NZ in 2019. Raven has been involved in mobilizing young people for action on climate change and against fossil fuel development in her communities since she was 14. Through her studies and activism, Raven hopes to hone her skills as an advocate for intergenerational and environmental justice, and ultimately contribute to the transition to a more environmentally, socially and economically sustainable world for all.

Edward Maibach is a Distinguished University Professor at George Mason University and Director of Mason's Center for Climate Change Communication. He is a public health professional (MPH, San Diego State University, 1983) and communication scientist (PhD, Stanford, 1990) who has worked in universities (Emory and George Washington University), the private sector (Worldwide Director of Social Marketing, Porter Novelli) and government (Associate Director, National Cancer Institute). In 2018, he was made a Fellow of the American Association for the Advancement of Science.

Michael E. Mann is Distinguished Professor and Earth System Science Center (ESSC) Director at Penn State. He has received numerous awards including the EGU Hans Oeschger Medal, the American Association for the Advancement of Science (AAAS) Public Engagement with Science Award and the Tyler Prize. He made *Bloomberg News*'s list of 50 most influential people in 2013 and has authored more than 200 publications, and four books including *Dire Predictions*, *The Hockey Stick and the Climate Wars*, *The Madhouse Effect*, and *The Tantrum that Saved the World*.

William "Bill" McKibben is an author, environmentalist, and activist. He graduated from Harvard College. He is Schumann Distinguished Scholar at Middlebury College, VT. In 1988, he wrote *The End of Nature*, the first book in the US for a common audience about global warming; he is the author of many other books. He is a co-founder and Senior Advisor at 350.org, an international climate campaign that works in 188 countries.

Marjan Minnesma, LLM, MA, MBA, studied business administration, philosophy and (international) law. She worked with the Dutch government, NGOs, and for ten years, at different universities. Together with her co-director, Professor Rotmans, at the Institute for Transitions (Drift) at the Erasmus University Rotterdam, she founded the Urgenda Foundation. Marjan has been named one of the 20 most influential persons in the Netherlands.

In 2015, she was declared a 'leading global thinker' by the authoritative American magazine *Foreign Policy*.

David R. Montgomery is a MacArthur Fellow and Professor of Geomorphology at the University of Washington. He studies landscape evolution and the effects of geological processes on ecological systems and human societies. An author of award-winning popular-science books, he has been featured in documentary films, network and cable news, and on a wide variety of TV and radio programmes. His books have been translated into nine languages.

Patti Moore is a JD (Doctor of Jurisprudence) candidate at Vanderbilt Law School, specializing in environmental law and the effects of both public and private governance on our changing climate. She has received Vanderbilt Awards for Scholastic Excellence for her work in legal writing and her research on the feasibility of a carbon label in the fashion industry. Her current research centres on creating a model supply chain contract with a focus on supplier sustainability.

Hilda Flavia Nakabuye is a young African climate and environmental rights activist, founder and organizer of Fridays For Future Uganda. She is one of the leading figures in the environmental movement in Africa; she was among the climate activists who attended the C40 World Mayors Summit in 2019 as well as the COP25 in Madrid. She misses classes at Kampala International University every Friday to strike for a safe environment with a view to rallying government, corporate organizations and communities to take climate action. She leads a lake-shore clean-up activity on Lake Victoria to beat plastic pollution.

Luisa Neubauer is one of the co-organizers of Fridays For Future and the most prominent representative of the German movement in the media. She works for various NGOs on topics such as climate protection, intergenerational justice and is acting against poverty. In 2018, she met the Swedish pupil Greta Thunberg at the UN climate conference and was one of four German delegates to the G7 youth summit in Canada. At the end of 2019, she took part in the climate conference in Madrid, together with Greta Thunberg and other activists. In early 2020, she attended the World Economic Forum in Davos. In January 2020, Luisa Neubauer and Fridays For Future protested against Siemens's participation in the planned Australian hard coal mine Carmichael. Luisa Neubauer completed a bachelor's degree in Geography in 2019. She is currently studying for a master's degree in Resource Analysis and Management at the Georg August University in Göttingen. Together with Alexander Repenning, she published the book *From the End of the Climate Crisis – A Story of Our Future* in 2019.

Sadrach Nirere is a young Ugandan climate activist and social entrepreneur with a commitment to social, economic and environmental causes. He is knowledgeable about climate change communication, sustainability and development. He is a connoisseur-level learner at the World Bank, with a Bachelor of International Business and a Diploma in Sustainable Business. As a native of an agricultural rural district, Sadrach witnessed how climate breakdown is crippling his region and, for this reason, he is co-founder and coordinator of Africa's largest Fridays For Future movement.

Danny Noonan is a climate change lawyer, campaigner and scholar. He was the Global Program Coordinator at Our Children's Trust from 2018 to 2020, where he worked to support youth-led climate legal actions in countries throughout the world, and steered the successful development and launch of lawsuits in Canada and Mexico. He is a co-founder and team member of Breach Collective, a climate justice organization based in the United States. He holds a Bachelor of International and Global Studies from the University of Sydney and a JD (Doctor of Jurisprudence) from Sydney Law School.

Adenike Titilope Oladosu is a young Nigerian climate activist, eco-feminist, and the initiator of the Fridays For Future movement in Nigeria. She graduated in Agriculture Economics from the Makurdi University of Agriculture. She specializes in equality, security and peace building across Africa, especially in the Lake Chad region. In 2019, she attended COP25 in Madrid, where she gave an address about climate change in Africa and how it affects lives.

Concern for her child led **Phyllis Omido**, Goldman Prize-winning activist, to expose the dire pollution being discharged from a battery-recycling factory into a poor local community in Mombasa. Using science and politics to press her case, she has defied death threats and forced the closure of the plant. Omido is now leading the campaign for courts to recognize the human right to a healthy environment.

Jeremy Oppenheim, founder of SYSTEMIQ and Chair of the Blended Finance Taskforce, is lead author of New Climate Economy's *Better Growth, Better Climate* and co-lead author of Food and Land Use Commission's *Growing Better: 10 Critical Transitions to Transform Food and Land Use*. He acts as advisor to multiple governments, asset managers, development banks, companies and foundations on system transformation, energy policy, green investment and resource productivity. Previously, Jeremy worked for 24 years for McKinsey, serving leading companies across finance, consumer goods, technology, healthcare and energy.

Ridhima Pandey is a 12-year-old environment activist and student in lower secondary education, India. Her father Dinesh Pandey is an environment activist and wildlifer and her mother Vinita Pandey is working in Uttarakhand – the state where they live – forest department. She filed a petition in March 2017 against the Government of India in the National Green Tribunal (NGT), asserting that the Indian government has failed to fulfil its duties of protecting the future of the coming generations.

Daniel Pauly, who is French and Canadian, studied fisheries science in Germany and spent much of his career in the tropics, notably in Philippines. Since 1994, he has been a Professor of Fisheries at the University of British Columbia, where he directs the Sea Around Us project, devoted to studying, documenting and mitigating the impact of fisheries on marine ecosystems. The concepts, methods and software he developed are documented in over 1000 widely cited publications, and have led to his receiving multiple scientific awards.

Ye Qi is Director of the Institute of Public Policy at Hong Kong University of Science and Technology, and Professor of Environmental Policy and Management at Tsinghua University's School of Public Policy and Management. From April 2014 to January 2019, he was Senior Fellow at the Brookings Institution and the Director of Brookings-Tsinghua Center for Public Policy. Ye Qi received his PhD in Environmental Science in 1994 from the State University of New York College of Environmental Science and Forestry.

Pippo Ranci is Principal Advisor in the Florence School of Regulation, European University Institute, Florence, where he was director (2004–08). He was Professor of Economic Policy at the Università Cattolica in Milan (1973–2014), President of the Italian Regulatory Authority for Electricity and Gas (1996–2003), often a consultant to the Italian government (1972–93), Vice-President of the Council of European Energy Regulators (2000–03), and member of the Board of Appeal, Agency for the Cooperation of Energy Regulators (2011–15).

Johan Rockström is one of the scholars at the frontier of global sustainability science. He is a Professor in Earth System Science at the University of Potsdam, the Director of the Potsdam Institute for Climate Impact Research (PIK), and the co-chair of Future Earth and chief scientist of Conservation International. He is the Editor-in-Chief of the journal *Global Sustainability* by Cambridge University Press, was the founding director of the Stockholm Resilience Centre, and leads the science behind the planetary boundaries framework.

Valentina Rozo-Ángel holds a Master of Economics from the Universidad de los Andes, Colombia, where she also earned a BA in Economics and

Business Administration. She worked as a researcher in the litigation team at Colombian-based NGO Dejusticia, providing scientific and quantitative evidence. Valentina is currently the analytics' team coordinator at the Truth Commission in Colombia. She is interested in the use of data science for the promotion of human rights.

Gökşen Şahin is a project manager at Climate Action Network (CAN) Europe who worked with the families on the front line of the climate crisis taking the European Union to court in the historic People's Climate Case. Previously, she worked with Turkish NGOs and grassroot movements to phase out coal in the country and create a Turkish NGO network focusing on climate policies. As a fierce defender of independent media, she has produced environmental radio shows at Turkey's only independent radio, Open Radio (Acik Radyo), to provide a space for local environmental defenders.

Michael Sharp is a barrister practising in New Zealand, specializing in Māori indigenous law, climate change and administrative law issues. He has postgraduate degrees in law from the London School of Economics and Political Science and the University of Waikato. Michael contributes articles to academic publications and is involved in a number of pro bono law initiatives.

A fierce advocate for the rights of Amazon forest people and nature, **Maria do Socorro Costa Silva** – Dona Socorro, as she is best known – leads opposition to the world's biggest alumina refinery outside China. It is located in Bacarena, Pará, Brazil – the most deadly state for environmental defenders in the most murderous country in the world. Several of her colleagues have been assassinated, but she continues to campaign for the Amazon to have more powerful political representation and a more central role in the world.

Nicole Smith, FCIArb and FAMINZ (Arb), is a barrister practising in New Zealand, specializing in arbitration and dispute resolution, sitting as an arbitrator and adjudicator and also acting as an advocate in New Zealand-based and international arbitrations. She is also a UK solicitor and a partner in a UK law firm (Keystone Law). Nicole focuses on cross-border disputes in relation to trade, construction, finance, energy and environmental and climate change issues.

Nicholas Stern is IG Patel Professor of Economics and Government and Chair of the Grantham Research Institute at London School of Economics. He was Chief Economist at both the European Bank for Reconstruction and Development (1994–99) and the World Bank (2000–03). He was Head of the UK Government Economic Service 2003–07, and led the Stern Review on the economics of climate change. He was knighted for services to economics (2004), made a life peer (2007), and appointed Companion of Honour for services to economics, international relations and tackling climate change in 2017. He is a Fellow of the Royal Society and of the British Academy and was president of the British Academy 2013–17. His latest books are *How Lives Change: Palanpur, India and Development Economics* (with Himanshu and Peter Lanjouw, OUP, 2018) and *Why Are We Waiting? The Logic, Urgency and Promise of Tackling Climate Change* (MIT Press, 2015). He is a member of the High-Level Advisory Group for COP26 of the United Nations Framework Convention on Climate Change (UNFCCC).

Thomas Sterner is Professor of Environmental Economics at the University of Gothenburg, Sweden. He was elected Visiting Professor at the Collège de France in 2015–16, and Chief Economist at the US-based Environmental Defense Fund in 2012–13. The main focus of his work is on the design and application of environmental policy instruments and he has published over 120 articles in refereed journals, authored or edited some 20 books, and many book chapters, official reports and journalistic articles.

Charlotte Taylor is a policy analyst and research advisor to Professor Stern at the Grantham Research Institute on Climate Change and the Environment at the London School of Economics. She has research interests in the economics of climate change and economic development and growth.

Tania Te Whenua (Tuhoe, Whakatohea) is the principal of Te Whenua Law and Consulting, specializing in Māori and Treaty of Waitangi matters. Tania acts on a number of matters of national importance, including for the New Zealand Council of Trade Unions and the Public Service Association in regard to inequities facing Māori women in employment. Tania was recently appointed a Local Government Development Contributions Commissioner to hear disputes regarding housing development contributions that impact access to housing for Māori.

Marie Toussaint is a French lawyer in international environmental law. After getting involved in the movement End Ecocide on Earth, she created the NGO Notre Affaire à Tous and initiated the French climate litigation action 'L'Affaire du Siècle'. She is now a Green Member of the European Parliament, where she works for climate and environmental justice.

Sébastien Treyer is the Executive Director of IDDRI, the Institute for Sustainable Development and International Relations, an independent policy research institute based at Sciences Po, Paris. He graduated from École Polytechnique and AgroParisTech, and completed a PhD in Environment Management. He is a specialist in foresight for public policies and international negotiations on sustainable development; he chairs the Scientific and

Technical Committee of the French Global Environment Facility (FFEM) and is a member of the Lead Faculty of the Earth System Governance Network.

Laurence Tubiana is CEO of the European Climate Foundation (ECF). In addition, she is the Chair of the Board of Governors at the French Development Agency (AFD). Before joining the ECF, Laurence was France's Climate Change Ambassador and Special Representative for COP21, and as such a key architect of the landmark Paris Agreement. Following COP21, she was appointed High Level Champion for Climate Action by the UN. Laurence brings decades of expertise and experience in climate change, energy, agriculture and sustainable development, working across government, think tanks, NGOs and academia. Throughout the years, Laurence has held several academic positions, including as a Professor and Scientific Director for the International Development and Environmental Studies Master degrees at Sciences Po, Paris; and Professor of International Affairs at Columbia University, New York.

Katrien van der Heyden is a sociologist with a Master of International Politics and a Master of Gender Studies. She works as an independent consultant, project manager, trainer and evaluator. Her main topics are gender, climate change and diversity.

In over 20 years as a foreign correspondent, **Jonathan Watts** has covered nuclear disasters, earthquakes, tsunamis and gang wars, but all pale in significance compared to the collapse of the world's natural life support systems. From pollution in China to deforestation in Brazil, he has reported on the environmental front line for more than a decade and now specializes in this area. As editor of the part of the book on 'Defenders', he finds hope in courageous activists guarding their land and our Earth.

Anuna De Wever Van der Heyden is a Belgian climate activist who started the Fridays For Future movement in Belgium (Youth for Climate) and led youth for 22 consecutive weeks to strike in Brussels. She organized a climate panel composed of Belgian scientists who wrote a Belgian climate plan and became the symbolic face of a generation of young activists in Belgium.

Erik Woodward is a JD (Doctor of Jurisprudence) candidate at New York University School of Law, where he studies public international law as it relates to climate change governance and policy. Prior to law school he was focusing on soft-law approaches that low-lying island states can utilize to preserve their sovereignty in the context of sea-level rise. He is passionate about designing and implementing just international adaptation and mitigation strategies to the climate crisis.

Xiaofan Zhao is an assistant professor in the Division of Public Policy at Hong Kong University of Science and Technology (HKUST). Before joining HKUST, she was a postdoctoral fellow at the School of Public Policy and Management, Tsinghua University. She earned a Bachelor of Science in environmental engineering (with honours and with distinction) and a Master of Science in management science and engineering, both from Stanford University. She holds a doctoral degree in public administration from Tsinghua University.

Preface: a collective book project – the last chance? Voluntary actors in an ecological and economic transition

The world has, on some key dimensions, made extraordinary progress since the end of World War II: output per head has quadrupled; poverty, in terms of incomes, has been dramatically reduced; life expectancy has increased by around 30 years. However, the extraordinary growth has come at colossal environmental cost and the world is now in a deeply dangerous position with a very narrow window for action. Our biodiversity has been brutally damaged, our oceans have been fundamentally altered and marine life is in great danger, our forests have been ravaged, our air and water have been profoundly polluted, and our climate is gravely threatened in ways that could cause immense harm to lives and livelihoods across the world, lasting for centuries. Time is short. If we fail to act decisively in this decade, the damage to our climate, oceans and biodiversity is likely to be irreversible. This is our last chance to save the planet as we know it.

This book is about and by those who have not only understood those threats but become witness to them, and confronted them, often at great costs to themselves. The forces against them are systemic. And the individuals or organizations they have to take on are powerful, and often ruthless and malevolent. The most celebrated pronouncement in economics – Adam Smith's on the "invisible hand": "By pursuing his own interest he frequently promotes that of society more effectually than when he really intends to promote it" (Smith, 1776) – today sounds desperately outdated. Instead of a competitive market, where providers meet consumers' demands, we have at the core of the economy a nexus of dominant firms – private oligopolistic in Western countries, state-owned or state-controlled in China, cronyist in Russia, Iran and other developing countries – pursuing their own goals of profit and power, mostly indifferent to the welfare of the people, particularly inimical to their health and the environment within which they live. They are feeding the exorbitant financial returns expected by shareholders, or by any sort of people in control, by systematically destroying the natural capital – biodiversity, air, water, soil, climate – without which life on earth is doomed to collapse.

The book is also about and by those who have seen ways forward to a much better development path for human well-being, security and dignity. We can raise living standards and fight poverty across the world at the same time as creating a much safer and more attractive environment. Their momentum is building. The old polluting forces are somewhat weakening. But our future is in the balance. This book is an attempt to share their voices, vision and hope and thus help to tilt the balance their way.

The evidence on the scale and urgency of the threats is overwhelming. There should be no doubt that we are facing global systems challenges across multiple dimensions crucial to our well-being. There has been a flood of scientific warnings, illustrated in the following examples.

The 2019 *Aqueduct Water Risk Atlas* (published by the Water Resources Institute) identifies 17 countries, which are home to a quarter of the world's population, facing "extremely high water stress, close to day zero conditions when the taps run dry" (Hofste, Reig and Schleifer, 2019). India and Pakistan are among them. Countries and regions – the Yellow River basin, for instance – depending on dwindling Himalayan or Andean glaciers for their water, are on the edge, as are the Southwestern United States, Mexico and Central America, as well as countries around the Mediterranean Sea.

This severe water predicament is closely connected to global warming. 'The Intergovernmental Panel on Climate Change (IPCC) in 2018, when comparing 1.5°C and 2°C (increases in global mean temperature above pre-industrial levels), highlighted that the proportion of the global population exposed to severe heat at least once every five years is more than 2.5 times greater (Dosio et al., 2018) and the proportion of vertebrate and plant species that lose at least half of their bioclimatic range is double (Warren et al., 2018). There is strong evidence that exceeding 2°C will result in large biomes on Earth collapsing, such as coral reefs and tropical forests, and that going even beyond implies that "warming could activate important tipping elements, raising the temperature further to activate other tipping elements in a domino-like cascade that could take the Earth System to even higher temperatures" (Steffen et al., 2018, p. 8254). This describes a road to unbearable conditions of life on Earth: "In the absence of migration, one third of the global population is projected to experience a mean annual temperature greater than 29°C, currently found in only 0.8% of the Earth's land surface, mostly concentrated in the Sahara" (Xu et al., 2020, p. 11350). Giant redwoods in Sequoia National Park, California, are already having enough. They were supposed to live for another 500 to 1000 years. The combination of drought stress, fire damage and overall warming, have made them vulnerable, for the first time as far back as we can know, to bark beetles infestations. "That's not how giant sequoias die", laments Dr Christy Brigham, chief biologist of Sequoia and King's Canyon National Parks (Childs, 2020). A stern health warning was recently formulated by the

2019 Lancet Countdown on health and climate change: "A business as usual trajectory will result in a fundamentally altered world. The life of every child born today will be profoundly affected by climate change" (Watts et al., 2019).

The combination of climate change and loss of biodiversity will, in particular, result in repeated releases of pathogens. As tropical forests and other ecosystems rich in biodiversity are being subject to increasing damage, hidden reservoirs of unknown pathogens are exposed; displaced wild animals bring the pathogens to humans; birds that hitherto had been separated are now meeting, with the likelihood of new viruses developing. Another critical reservoir is the Arctic permafrost. As it thaws, a variety of pathogens emerge from long hibernation; the infection of members of the Siberian Nenets indigenous community from an unearthed reindeer carcass is a warning shot. Some of the pathogens to come could well be still more unpleasant than Covid-19 – children will not always be spared, as the Nenets discovered.

Global warming and virus spillovers from animals to humans are tightly connected to food production. As concluded by the UN Food and Agriculture Organization (FAO) in April 2019, in *State of the World's Biodiversity for Food and Agriculture* (FAO, 2019, p. xxxviii), "key ecosystems that deliver numerous services essential to food and agriculture are declining rapidly", and as climate change moves relentlessly, the world's food supply is under severe threat. It does not help that, while 3 billion people currently suffer from land degradation, yet more fertile soil is being lost at a rate of 24 billion tonnes a year worldwide. We risk being confronted with both significantly decreased food availability and significantly increased population.

All components of natural capital – biodiversity, air, water, soil, climate – are crumbling under human pressures. Under such extreme threats, many might give up. However, the contributors to this book have embraced the spirit of the Prins van Oranje, who said (in French) when the Netherlands, of which he was head of State, was invaded by mighty and brutal armies under King Felipe II of Spain: "Il n'est pas nécessaire d'espérer pour entreprendre ni de réussir pour persévérer" (One need not hope in order to undertake nor succeed in order to persevere). And they have gone further than bearing witness. They have also followed the inspiration of Bob Marley, "Get up, stand up, stand up for your rights". Who are they and what are their achievements?

DEFENDERS

They are community leaders, organizers of mass protests or of campaigns unveiling pollution, land grabs, deforestation. They are rangers, farmers, teachers, artists. They face land invaders, loggers, poachers, dam builders, mining operators, drug traffickers, corrupt public authorities, death squads. They live in and around the Amazon, Congo or Southeast Asia forests; in

East and Central African savannahs; in various Indian states; in the islands of the Coral Triangle across the Philippines and Indonesia; in Central American villages; in the plains of Dakota, USA; in Queensland, Australia, and so on.

Every year they are murdered by the hundreds. Nevertheless, their numbers are growing. *The Guardian* newspaper, and in particular Jonathan Watts, who popularized the name Defenders, regularly publishes information about them.

LITIGANTS

They are also active in many places – Australia, Colombia, China, European Union, India, New Zealand, Philippines, South Africa, Uganda, United States, appealing in the courts of justice to show that public authorities are failing, both themselves and the generations to come, by neglecting the common natural capital, the climate in particular, or even by acting as accomplices of rogue firms or gangs responsible for far-reaching damages.

Some are rather young, as befits front-line victims of the looming disasters. In the US, 21 students aged 11 to 22, from ten different states, are suing the federal government over immediate and future damages due to climate change denial or negligence. Likewise, a group of 25 young people in Colombia filed a suit against the state for failing to stop deforestation in the Amazon basin; the Supreme Court ruled in their favour. And in 2017, then nine-year-old Ridhima Pandey challenged the federal government in India's Supreme Court.

A claim that has been brought against New Zealand's government illustrates the potential for Māori communities, in their capacity as traditional guardians of the natural environment, to bring claims against governments for failing to properly tackle environmental issues. Their action resonates far beyond New Zealand's frontiers.

COMING GENERATIONS ON THE FRONT LINE

Another student, Greta Thunberg from Sweden, at age 15 started a different type of action, not in courts but in schools. What is the point of children going to school if they have no future? What is the point of them learning sciences if people in positions of responsibility refuse to listen to scientists? Millions of students have taken part – on Fridays, hence the name of their movement Fridays For Future (FFF) – in school strikes for the climate, throughout 130 countries. The FFF leaders in several countries – Belgium, Germany, New Zealand, Nigeria, Uganda – reflect on their experiences here. Often, they find inspiration and support from a remarkable organization, 350.org, the founder of which William "Bill" McKibben describes the origins, the methods and the prospects.

Students graduating from "elite" universities used to take plush jobs with bright futures in prosperous firms. For many among them that is no longer the case; they seek compatibility between professional prospects and deeply felt ecological concerns, to the point of making firms anxious about their capacity for recruiting the best candidates. For certain employers, particularly those with activities that are fundamentally detrimental to the environment and to the climate in particular, that capacity to compete for talent is seriously dented.

ENTREPRENEURS

They pioneer ways of producing, storing and consuming energy without killing life on earth and damaging the climate, and of devising and disseminating new materials to save resources. Of growing and producing safe food without wiping out biological diversity and polluting to death bodies of water and the soil itself. Of profitably managing forests and ocean resources without exhausting them. Of renovating cities to make them more resilient, more efficient, less destructive and more hospitable. Of particular significance is the role that visionary and determined social entrepreneurs, local and regional leaders, can play in bringing their communities forward on paths for ecological and economic transition.

INVESTORS

Aware of the climate risks, they rebalance their portfolios away from high carbon footprint (e.g., coal, oil, cement) towards assets positively associated with the transition to a decarbonized economy (e.g., renewable energy providers, producers of efficient materials). Pioneers such as the Wallace Global Fund and the Rockefeller Brothers Fund have kickstarted this movement for responsible investors, which, since 2014, has gained strong momentum. Major financial management companies, such as BlackRock and Allianz, have made strong climate commitments and so too have major banks, such as HSBC and Standard Chartered. We will, of course, find out about delivery. Increasingly, investors are recognizing that it is the dirty activities of the last century that are risky and in decline, and that it is the clean investments of the twenty-first century that are likely to prosper.

When an investor has rebalanced her portfolio in this way, she is motivated to support those public policies that enhance the value of her new investments – for example, stricter carbon pricing policies. In this sense, private interests and natural capital-friendly public policies might come to converge.

So-called green bonds, and other instruments for financing transition-oriented activities, are emitted and traded under various forms. Their scope is fast growing, particularly in China and in the European Union. Their healthy development is conditional on the formulation and implementation of appropriate public policies and regulations, but their existence and expansion help drive such policies.

COMMUNICATORS

Effective communicators are vital in order to amplify and disseminate the messages from policy-makers and from scientists, all the more so as such messages are not easy to convey and as time is short. President Franklin Delano Roosevelt was able to explain and convince a majority to approve his policies, however unfamiliar these looked initially. Explaining how to shift to a more sustainable development path is no less vital than explaining how to exit from the Great Depression; it requires the same qualities of coherence, clarity and conviction.

In the fields of science and technology, Professor Richard Feynman was not only an outstanding pedagogue in his physics classes, he was also supremely able to guide non-specialists through seemingly impenetrable thickets of scientific and technical complexities. This he showed as a member of the Rogers Commission that was investigating the circumstances of the explosion of the space shuttle *Challenger* in 1986. After having properly reconfigured the chain of failures that led to the explosion, he pleaded effectively for more exacting remedies than the other members of the Commission and some NASA executives would have liked; he enlisted a public following nobody had anticipated. Like Roosevelt, he showed both an ability to relate to his fellow human beings and a strong sense of kindness. Richard Feynman embodied the perfect role model for today's scientists who are confronting scepticism, apathy and, increasingly, despair about the condition of the planet. Several among them, who have proved they are up to the task, explain here how that proves possible.

These are inspiring stories. However, do they have the potential to grow, to coalesce and to force a profound transformation in society and economy, in spite of formidable obstacles? In *L'Ancien Régime et la Révolution, Livre III* (1856), Alexis de Tocqueville shows how, in the second half of the eighteenth century, mushrooming new visions and actions converged to overthrow a 1000-year-old French Ancien Régime and generate a new order, despite seemingly insuperable obstacles. Nowadays we observe a similar pattern with the – still fragile – perspective of another, potentially broader, revolution. Time, however, is severely constrained.

Before laying down the actors' accounts – what the defenders, litigants, leaders of coming generations, entrepreneurs, investors, communicators, have to say – the first part of the book begins with a section gathering relevant, concise background papers in earth sciences, psychology, economics and politics. In Section 2, Costa Rica and Sweden, two countries that are more advanced on paths to ecological and economic transition deserve special presentations; so do the giants, China and the US, who are struggling in different ways with these issues. This first part of the book closes with an assessment of international cooperation and governance, with special reference to the Paris Agreement.

There are many truly outstanding people 'standing up for a sustainable planet' that are not included in the actors' accounts. Indeed many, such as David Attenborough and Jane Goodall, have been 'standing up' for still longer than any of the editors, authors or actors featured in this book, while at the same time inspiring and encouraging others to do the same, whether that be through high-profile documentary narration or community initiatives like the Jane Goodall Institute's TACARE and Roots & Shoots programmes. This book showcases a multitude of individuals who have made exceptional contributions to the protection of our planet, but there are numerous others responsible for pioneering work across the globe that have paved the way for following generations of environmentalists: Davi Kopenawa, Wangari Maathai and Chandi Prasad Bhatt being outstanding examples.

REFERENCES

Childs, J.W. (2020), "Giant sequoias falling victim to climate change, study says", *Weather.com*, 23 January, accessed 8 August 2020 at https://weather.com/news/news/2020-01-23-sequoias-dying-climate-change-drought-beetles.

Dosio, A., L. Mentaschi, E.M. Fischer and K. Wyser (2018), "Extreme heat waves under 1.5°C and 2°C global warming", *Environmental Research Letters*, **13** (5), 054006.

Food and Agriculture Organization (FAO) (2019), *The State of the World's Biodiversity for Food and Agriculture*, edited by J. Bélanger and D. Pillings, Rome: FAO Commission on Genetic Resources for Food and Agriculture Assessments.

Hofste, R.W., P. Reig and L. Schleifer (2019), "17 countries, home to one-quarter of the world's population, face extremely high water stress", *WRI.org*, 6 August [blog], accessed 8 August 2020 at https://www.wri.org/blog/2019/08/17-countries-home-one-quarter-world-population-face-extremely-high-water-stress.

Smith, A. (1776), *An Inquiry Into the Nature and Causes of the Wealth of Nations*, London: W. Strahan and T. Cadell, in the Strand.

Steffen, W., J. Rockström and K. Richardson et al. (2018), "Trajectories of the Earth System in the Anthropocene", *Proceedings of the National Academy of Science*, **115** (33), 8252–9.

Tocqueville, A. de (1856 [1866]), *L'Ancien Régime et la Révolution, Livre III*, 7th edition, Paris: Michel Lévy.

Warren, R., J. Price and E. Graham et al. (2018), "The projected effect on insects, vertebrates, and plants of limiting global warming to 1.5°C rather than 2°C", *Science*, **360** (6390), 791–5.

Watts, N., M. Amann and N. Arnell et al. (2019), "The 2019 report of The Lancet Countdown on health and climate change: ensuring that the health of a child born today is not defined by a changing climate", **394** (10211), 1836–78, accessed

8 August 2020 at https://www.thelancet.com/journals/lancet/article/PIIS0140 -6736(19)32596-6/fulltext.

Xu, C., T.A. Kohler and T.M. Lenton et al. (2020), "Future of the human climate niche", *Proceedings of the National Academy of Sciences*, **117** (21), 11350–55.

Acknowledgements

Claude Henry initiated the idea for this book and asked Johan Rockström and Nicholas Stern to join him as scientific editors. It is well known that Alexandre Dumas' Three Musketeers were in fact four brave companions; that d'Artagnan belonged to another regiment was irrelevant. During the preparation of this book, along with the three editors, Jonathan Watts has been the fourth companion. When presented with the initial project he immediately saw its potential. He then took the entire responsibility for Part II: Defenders. He suggested some possible authors for other parts of the book; they have become actual authors. Throughout, he provided imaginative ideas to enhance the scope and substance of the book.

Marie Toussaint and Pippo Ranci quickly embraced the significance of the project. Marie Toussaint defined what Part III: Litigants should look like and persuaded the promotors of highly significant cases to discuss them in the book. Pippo Ranci's experience as an academic, a regulator and an entrepreneur has been invaluable to structuring and strengthening Part V: Entrepreneurs.

There was no part of the book on Communicators in the initial project, a serious lacuna that Gavin Schmidt, director of the NASA Goddard Institute for Space Studies, identified. He then pointed to remedies that helped organize Part VII as it appears in the book.

Having taken part in the preparation of one of the papers in Part V: Entrepreneurs, Jean-Michel Trochet chose not to be mentioned as an author. Our thanks go to him and to all authors who participated out of conviction and scientific interest, and without any other form of remuneration.

We are very grateful to Stephanie Hartley and the editors at Edward Elgar Publishing for their guidance and encouragement. This book would not have been possible, as an open access Edward Elgar Publishing book, if it had not been for the generous contributions from the Institute for Sustainable Development and International Relations, École Polytechnique, LSE and PIK. Should there be any surpluses from this book, they will be given to appropriate charitable foundations.

At the Institute for Sustainable Development and International Relations and École Polytechnique, Claude Henry is grateful to Sébastien Treyer and Dominique Bureau for insightful contributions to the project and for arranging financial support to the offer of an open access electronic version of the book.

Johan Rockström thanks PIK colleagues for insightful dialogues on the role of science in social transformations, and is grateful for support on text editing and fact checking by student assistants Aylin Mengi and Merle Quade, and final editing by research analysts Maria Martin and Lila Warszawski.

At LSE, Nicholas Stern is grateful to Charlotte Taylor and Kerrie Quirk for guidance and assistance and to the Economic and Social Research Council (via the Centre for Climate Change and Economic Policy) and the Grantham Foundation for financial support.

PART I

Introduction

Section 1   Scientific backgrounds

1. Science, society and a sustainable future

Johan Rockström and Nicholas Stern

The global turbulence triggered by the COVID-19 (coronavirus) pandemic, with abrupt impacts on human lives and widespread deaths, coupled with the fastest and largest downturn of the global economy since World War II, has placed many countries under war-like conditions. On 16 March 2020, President Macron declares that France is at war. On 18 March, President Trump labels himself as a war-time president combating the coronavirus, and on 25 March, PM Narendra Modi announces a 21-day lockdown of India. These are expressions of a state of emergency; a global fight against an abrupt threat to societal stability. And world citizens rose to the challenge, adapting and accepting weeks of quarantine, draconian regulations and surveillance and disruptions of daily lives. In many countries, notwithstanding huge increases in public spending, we see an abrupt loss of jobs, with large risks of long-term damage to economies around the world, particularly severe for developing countries that also face capital flight, declining remittances and falling commodity prices.

A few months before the coronavirus outbreak, the scientific community established the Earth Commission, an independent "IPCC for Earth", with the scientific task of assessing the safe guardrails for a stable planet.[1] This initiative is led by Future Earth, the global network of researchers and institutions that have provided a significant part of the scientific evidence that the human pressures on Earth are now so large they define a new geological epoch, the Anthropocene. That we today need to call on science to determine a safe operating space on Earth is a reflection of another interconnected emergency: *the imminent risk of destabilizing the entire planet.*

The entire Earth system is threatened by further destruction of biodiversity, the degrading of our land, forests and oceans, polluting air and water, destabilizing the climate and general devastation of our natural capital. Together they can undermine or destroy the basis for our livelihoods, where and how we can live – indeed, whether many can survive. If these forces are not managed much better, if we do not find better ways of producing and consuming, integrating adaptive capacity and flexibility – that is, resilience – in our social and environmental fabric, the consequences could be catastrophic, with widespread loss of life, great movements of people and the likelihood of severe and extended conflict. We are all threatened, but it is the poorest who are hit earliest and hardest.

The scientific community has been warning for many years, not only of the risk of crossing dangerous tipping points on Earth that may trigger unstoppable global warming – like irreversible melting of the Greenland ice sheet, thawing of Siberian permafrost or the slowdown of heat circulation in the Atlantic ocean (AMOC)[2] – but also of the risks of social–environmental interactions triggering abrupt shocks with large-scale impacts on communities and economies across the world (Homer-Dixon et al., 2015). These include the rising frequency over the past 20 years of outbreaks of zoonotic diseases – for example, Ebola, SARS, MERS and COVID-19, which are a result of the complex interactions of globalized networks of travel and trade, high human density of living, particularly in urban environments, and risky behaviour by human societies (such as wet wildlife markets), colliding with dramatic ecological habitat change due to deforestation and global warming, pushing wild species closer to humans, and, with climate change, changing patterns of migration of birds, implying new interactions (IPBES, 2019; Johnson et al., 2020; Shapiro and McAdams, 2018).

The evidence points in one direction – that the coronavirus crisis is a manifestation of the social and ecological vulnerabilities in the Anthropocene – and it provides ample support for the need to move quickly and decisively to bend the global curves of greenhouse gas emissions and to slow and halt the undermining of the natural ecosystems on Earth rapidly, in only one generation (the coming 20–30 years). In so doing we can transform our world to prosperity and equity within the safe operating space on a stable and resilient planet. At the same time, the Anthropocene also means, now that humanity is the dominant force of change on Earth, that we can collectively determine the future for all. Science, technology and innovation, if they can be guided and put to service in the appropriate direction, can be the means of achieving the sustainable, equitable and resilient future for both people and the planet that so many seek. Societies and economies must change too, including in the ways we work, live and interact and the governance we create.

The scientific support for the compelling need to "grasp our last chance" for climate action and for protecting and enhancing our natural capital of all kinds is overwhelming. Not only in terms of assessing the global risks we face – if we follow our current business-as-usual trajectory we are likely to crash through the 1.5°C ceiling by around 2040 or before and 2°C by 2050 or soon thereafter – but also in terms of providing an unprecedented clarity on the safe pathway the world must follow: the latest Intergovernmental Panel on Climate Change (IPCC) assessment (SR1.5) shows that global emissions of CO_2 must start bending in 2020 and be cut globally by half in the coming ten years (until 2030) and reach net zero by 2050, to have a reasonable chance of staying well below 2°C of global warming (compared to pre-industrial global mean temperature) (IPCC, 2018). This requires a global transformation across all sectors of society, from food production to energy supply, transport, construction and production of consumer goods. We are talking about a system-wide transformation that encompasses technology, innovation, governance, finance, business models, equity, values and behavioural change.

The call for the scientific community is surely "loud and clear", across academic disciplines, to work together advancing insights and solutions through interdisciplinary research collaboration. Of critical importance is a closer integration of research on political economy, finance and governance, with Earth system science and climate impact research. Economic policies should build resilience rather than build in brittleness. They should integrate externalities and capture the true risk landscape of fat-tail (high-impact and higher-than-comfortable probability) tipping points. These are policies that can also provide for more equitable distribution of well-being, both within and across generations. The failure to construct such policies has, in large measure, followed from an absence of understanding of how ecosystems work, a short-sighted and narrow view of objectives, and a neglect to address market failure. We can create sound policies, but we must deepen our economic understanding.

Similarly, the world needs to rapidly understand the governance implications of collectively stabilizing not only the warming of oceans and the atmosphere, but also the stability of big biomes, like the boreal forests and rainforests, ice sheets and wetlands, coral reef systems and peat lands. The agenda, of how to govern the global commons within planetary boundaries, can be pursued only through interdisciplinary science between political science and earth system research. And putting such governance into action will require political will within and across communities and nations and enlightened leadership, both of which can be fostered by a deeper understanding of the scientific issues, including the social science.

Making the digital revolution, biotechnology and advances in artificial intelligence work for a stabilized climate, a healthy biosphere and a just future for all is one of the major challenges over the coming decades. In a world of 10 billion people, where all citizens have the same right to a good life, one of our grand challenges is how to manage the remaining carbon and ecological space on Earth, wisely and equitably.

These are some of the frontiers of global sustainability science. As we show in this book, grasping our "last chance" for climate action and natural capital in pace and scale with the scientific necessity, will be possible only if stakeholders in society rise together to these challenges. Those who are indeed rising to these challenges include the *defenders*, *litigants*, *youth*, *entrepreneurs*, *investors* and *communicators* of this book. As shown here, there is ample evidence of strong responses, solutions and actions. Unfortunately, they are all too often islands of success in an ocean of indifference at best and of resistance and ignorance at worst.

We believe that change at the pace and scale we need is indeed possible. The coronavirus crisis provides proof of our remarkable ability to rise collectively and rapidly in the face of a global threat. It also reminds us that we must anticipate risk much better than we have done in the past. For the planetary climate and biodiversity threat, we sit on ample evidence that the transformation to a zero-carbon future that protects and nurtures natural ecosystems is more attractive, on all fronts, in terms of the economy, jobs, health, and in terms of building resilience – that is, the capacity to deal with abrupt shocks and surprises in the future. The evidence is clear today that a zero-carbon future is a much better future for humanity, across the full dimensions of well-being. Indeed, the drive to zero carbon is the sustainable, inclusive and resilient growth story of the twenty-first century. In the short run, the necessary investments will increase demand and sharpen supply. In the medium term, we shall see (indeed, are already seeing) the drive to zero carbon bringing discovery, innovation, investment and growth. There is no medium- or long-term high-carbon growth story – an attempt would produce an environment so hostile that it would halt and reverse economic and social development. Further, the new way of producing, consuming and living can be more inclusive, full of new opportunities and bringing greater security in a world with stronger natural capital.

Scientifically, accelerating the path towards generating solutions and relevant insights can be accomplished through closer co-design and co-development of knowledge. Formulating questions and challenges together, between scientists and stakeholders from business, city mayors, policy-makers, community leaders, indigenous voices, provides a co-design of fast-tracking research to tackle urgent real-world problems. Co-developing knowledge, by connecting scientific methodologies of transparency, replicability and uncertainty, with user inter-phases and experience of local behaviour and preferences, coupled to citizen science and big data gathering on citizen knowledge, can further advance and accelerate the knowledge–action interplay on climate management and protection and enhancement of natural capital.

This is where we see the defenders, litigants, youth, entrepreneurs, investors and communicators, as many of the true "heroes of the zero-carbon transition", playing a critical role interacting with science, to generate responses, solutions and positive momentum towards sustainable zero-carbon societies. They understand both the issues and how societies can rise to the great challenges we now face.

An area where multi-stakeholder action is urgently needed is safeguarding biodiversity and managing ecosystems as critical carbon sinks and sources of human well-being and resilience. Natural ecosystems, on land and in oceans, today sequester (absorb) some 50 per cent of the global emissions of carbon dioxide from fossil-fuel burning and deforestation (Friedlingstein et al., 2019). This is the largest single "subsidy" to the world economy, provided "for free" by the planet. Approximately half this occurs on land, and the latest science shows worrying signs of gradual decline in the carbon sink capacity (Hubau et al., 2020) and uncertainty regarding future sink capacity as the planet gets warmer (IPCC, 2019), with terrestrial ecosystems under multiple pressures such as loss of forest habitats, lowered biomass growth due to increased severity in droughts, disease in forests such as bark beetle outbreaks on temperate forests in Canada, and increased forest fires as in the Amazon and the devastating 2019/20 forest fires in Australia. Further, land degradation diminishes the capture of carbon in the soil. These are indications of how biodiversity loss and degraded ecosystems lead to loss of Earth resilience, resulting in risks of amplified global warming as nature loses its capacity to "be our best friend" by dampening global warming.

Losing biodiversity also puts us in a weaker state in the face of shocks, like droughts and pandemics. According to the latest assessment, in the *State of the World's Biodiversity for Food and Agriculture* by the United Nations Food and Agriculture Organization (FAO, 2019), of the 6000 plant species humans have cultivated for food, just nine now account for two-thirds of all crop production. There are nearly 8000 local breeds of farm animals still in existence, but global livestock production is today based on only a handful of breeds. At least a quarter of all local breeds are now at risk of extinction. This shows a remarkable development towards monocultures and reliance for food security across the world on very few species. Globally, to put this in perspective, 94 per cent of all biological weight from living animals on Earth is today represented by us humans and our livestock (Bar-On, Phillips and Milo, 2018). Only 6 per cent is the remaining wildlife on Earth, which is in the midst of the sixth mass extinction of species, caused by another species – us (IPBES, 2019). The loss of the genetic diversity in world agriculture makes our food supply, and thereby our future, increasingly vulnerable.

Agriculture is also the largest driver behind deforestation, which reduces natural habitats for wildlife, resulting not only in loss of carbon sinks and ecosystem functions, like moisture recycling for rainfall, but also pushes wildlife out of their normal habitats, closer to human settlements, increasing the risk of zoonotic disease outbreak (Johnson et al., 2020).

The "super-year 2020", when climate action was to be solidified five years after the Paris Agreement, has abruptly turned into the shutdown year 2020, due to the coronavirus crisis. While the pandemic is a "fast" crisis and global warming a "slow" crisis, they are both planetary emergencies, which, moreover, are interconnected in the globalized world of the Anthropocene. Recovery after the pandemic will pose tremendous social-economic challenges and requires learning on how to build more resilient societies able to meet planetary health risks. We would argue that the transformations required for a successful outcome on holding the 2°C line on global warming (Sachs et al., 2019; TWI2050, 2018) – decarbonize the energy sector, halt biodiversity loss, shift the global food system from carbon source to sink, make the digital revolution work for sustainability, invest in health, wealth and education for all citizens – are integral also to the recovery from the coronavirus pandemic and to reach the UN Sustainable Development Goals. It all integrates into one system-wide agenda for health, equity and prosperity for all humans on Earth. Fundamentally, it requires actions on climate and sustainability to provide the well-being, wealth and resilience we seek and on the basis of which we can navigate our joint future in a world where adverse surprises increasingly form part of normality.

We may have lost some time on climate action in 2020, but we have learnt – the hard way – how important it is to build sustainable and resilient economies. We have learnt more about our common humanity and our fragility, about the husbanding of resources, how the world looks with less pollution, that collective action is possible, and that mobilizing human and financial capacities to tackle the great problems is indeed possible. Now is the time to show that we can take on the global climate and ecological crises. The new development path can be enormously attractive; going back to the old one would be profoundly dangerous.

NOTES

1. See "Earth Commission", accessed 8 August 2020 at https://futureearth.org/initiatives/earth-targets-initiatives/earth-commission/.
2. Atlantic meridional overturning circulation.

REFERENCES

Bar-on, Y.M., Phillips, R., and Milo, R. 2018. "The biomass distribution on Earth". *Proceedings of the National Academy of Sciences*, **115** (25), 6506–11.
Food and Agriculture Organization of the United Nations (FAO). 2019. *The State of the World's Biodiversity for Food and Agriculture*, edited by J. Bélanger and D. Pilling. Rome: FAO Commission on Genetic Resources for Food and Agriculture Assessments.
Friedlingstein, P., Jones, M.W. and O'Sullivan, M. et al. 2019. "Global carbon budget, 2019". *Earth System Science Data*, **11**, 1783–838.
Homer-Dixon, T., Walker, B. and Biggs, R. 2015. "Synchronous failure: the emerging causal architecture of global crisis". *Ecology and Society*, **20**(3), article 6.

Hubau, W., Lewis, S.L. and Phillips, O.L. et al. 2020. "Asynchronous carbon sink saturation in African and Amazonian tropical forests". *Nature*, **579**, 80–87.

Intergovernmental Panel on Climate Change (IPCC). 2018. "Summary for policymakers". In *Global Warming of 1.5°C: An IPCC Special Report*. Edited by V. Masson-Delmotte, P. Zhai and H.-O. Pörtner et al. Geneva: IPCC.

Intergovernmental Panel on Climate Change (IPCC). 2019. "Summary for policymakers". In *Climate Change and Land: An IPCC Special Report*. Edited by R. Shukla, J. Skea and E. Calvo Buendia. Geneva: IPCC.

Intergovernmental Science-Policy Platform on Biodiversity and Ecosystem Service (IPBES). 2019. *Global Assessment Report on Biodiversity and Ecosystem Services.* Edited by S. Brondizio, J. Settele and S. Díaz et al. Bonn: IPBES Secretariat.

Johnson, C.K., Hitchens, P.L. and Pandit, P.S. et al. 2020. "Global shifts in mammalian population trends reveal key predictors of virus spillover risk". *Proceedings of the Royal Society B: Biological Sciences*, **287** (1924), 20192736.

Sachs, J.D., Schmidt-Traub, G. and Mazzucato, M. et al. 2019. "Six transformations to achieve the Sustainable Development Goals". *Nature Sustainability*, **2**, 805–14.

Shapiro, L. and McAdams, H. 2018. "Technological change and global biological disequilibrium". In *Beyond Disruption: Technology's Challenge to Governance*. Edited by G.P. Shultz, J. Hoagland and J. Timbie. Stanford, CA: Hoover Institution Press.

The World in 2050 (TWI2050). 2018. *Transformations to Achieve the Sustainable Development Goals*. Laxenburg: International Institute for Applied Systems Analysis (IIASA).

2. Conservation psychology and climate change

Susan Clayton

As the project of this book indicates, the major question surrounding environmental change and degradation is no longer, "Is it happening?", but "What can people do about it?" This is frequently followed by the frustrated question, "Why aren't people doing anything (or doing enough) to address climate change?", or framed more positively, "What explains the people who are taking action?" With this as the foundation, it becomes clear that we need to consider what motivates or deters people from engaging in actions that protect the climate. Only by understanding these positive and negative factors can we create a social context in which barriers are reduced, facilitators are enhanced, and more people act in ways that protect the natural world.

The investigation into behavioral motivations is a fundamentally psychological question. Fortunately, psychologists are increasingly contributing to research and policy that is directed toward environmental challenges. Psychological research on sustainable behavior, examining some of the triggers of actions such as recycling or energy efficiency, has existed more or less since the 1950s. More recently, psychologists have emulated conservation biology by developing the field of conservation psychology: psychological research and theory directed toward understanding and promoting a healthy relationship between humans and the natural world (Clayton & Myers, 2015).

The relevance of psychology to sustainability is important to examine for what it says about the role of nature in our lives. Psychologists are deeply concerned with human behavior, and with understanding the motivators and facilitators of behavior in order to promote positive behavioral change. But psychologists are also concerned with human health and well-being, and we are beginning to understand the relevance of environmental health to human health. There has been a veritable explosion of research demonstrating not only the threat that climate change poses to human health, but also the positive benefits that can be obtained from exposure to a healthy natural environment. Thus, even for anyone short-sighted enough to claim that they don't care about the health of the environment, there are reasons for concern about environmental degradation.

Before looking more closely at the barriers and motivators underlying sustainable behavior, I will briefly summarize what research has shown about the significance of the environment to human well-being.

THE INTERDEPENDENCE OF HUMAN AND ENVIRONMENTAL HEALTH

In the early years of the climate movement, the principal icon was a polar bear on a melting glacier. Indeed, this is still one of the things people most associate with climate change. People were encouraged to empathize with the animals in order to create concern about the climate; there was little sense that self-interest should be enough to motivate people. Those days are past. Weather and climate events such as hurricanes, droughts, and wildfires, in combination with media coverage that at least sometimes links these events to climate change, have led to an increased awareness of human vulnerability. Recent assessment reports from the Intergovernmental Panel on Climate Change (IPCC) have included a section on human health impacts, and this topic will receive even more coverage in the Sixth Assessment Report, due out in 2022.

Health Impacts from Environmental Changes

Some of the ways in which environmental health affects human health are easy to envision. The contaminants associated with air, land, and water pollution can be absorbed by humans in ways that compromise physical health and sometimes intellectual capabilities. The extreme weather events associated with climate change threaten safety and well-being, both during the event and in the aftermath as people cope with the damage to shelter, the medical system, food and water supplies, and physical infrastructure. Environmental degradation can lead to food insecurity, and environmental changes can lead to the spread of insect-borne diseases such as Lyme disease and Zika.

Other physical threats are less obvious. For example, warmer temperatures, such as those accompanying climate change, are associated with increased ground-level ozone, a toxic air pollutant. Climate change is leading to more severe asthma and allergic reactions. When environmental changes make a place less suitable for human habitation, environmental migration results, putting the migrants at increased risk to physical safety not only during the migration itself but also, frequently, when they arrive at a new location, where they may not be welcomed by local inhabitants.

Even less attention is paid to the potential impacts of environmental changes on mental health. As with the physical impacts, some of these are fairly easy to recognize. Experiencing extreme weather events such as hurricanes, floods, or wildfires increases the risk of serious mental health problems such as post-traumatic stress disorder or depression. Drought has been linked to a significant increase in suicide, especially among farmers. More recently, accumulating evidence has connected a rise in temperature to increases in aggression, suicide, and mental health problems. Air pollution is also associated with psychological distress.

Some reporters, researchers, and therapists have begun to speculate about a more general threat to mental health associated with the perception of changes in the environment, using terms such as "eco-anxiety", "solastalgia", and "climate change distress". It is still too early to definitively characterize this response, but there is growing evidence that people are worried about environmental changes and that environmental degradation is a source of stress, anxiety, and sadness for many.

Positive Impacts of Nature

It is important, however, to also acknowledge the potential for the environment to positively affect people's health and well-being. Researchers have been investigating this topic for decades, but are becoming increasingly confident in the link between health and exposure to "green" or "blue" spaces (i.e., vegetation and water). Results from both correlational studies and controlled experiments have shown that exposure to green spaces can reduce stress, lower heart rate and blood pressure, lead to faster recovery from illness, and contribute to longevity. Cognitive performance and work productivity tend to be enhanced by the presence of green plants or a view of nature. People who live near green space have better physical and mental health. Thus, even for the few people who do not value nature, or for the larger percentage who prioritize human well-being over environmental well-being, there is a sufficient reason for taking action to protect and preserve a healthy environment.

BARRIERS TO ACTION

Given the powerful arguments in favor of environmental protection, why is it that so many fail to take action, and continue to behave in ways that contribute to environmental degradation? In addressing this question, we should first acknowledge that all of us – certainly all of us in the developed world – are participants in the problem. Even those of us who are trying to do the right thing are using fossil fuels and other non-renewable environmental resources, contributing to the loss of habitat for wild species, and contaminating the air, land, or water. This is to say that none of us can speak from a position of virtue from which we can point fingers at others who are acting badly. There are many fundamental barriers that, to a greater or lesser extent, inhibit all of us from behaving sustainably. Some of these are structural rather than psychological:

we may not have the means to act in the ways that we prefer. If I have to get to work and there is no public transportation, I will need to drive a car. At other times, people may simply not know that their behavior is problematic, or they may be unaware that there are behavioral alternatives. Or they may be aware of the problem, but not know how to engage in actions that help to address it.

In addition to inability and ignorance, a third powerful inhibitor of positive behavior needs to be recognized: inattention. In a vast proportion of the time, people take action without really thinking about what they are doing. They act out of habit, or by mimicking what other people are doing. They are not consciously considering the pros and cons of their behavioral choices. All of us are so caught up in the trivia of daily living that we may not stop to think about the larger questions and opportunities to behave in more meaningful ways.

These barriers occur before people even start to think about environmental issues. But I want to examine the reasons why, when people are aware of the possibility that their behavior has implications for environmental well-being, they still make the less sustainable choice. There are many obstacles standing in the way of sustainable action. I will describe them according to three categories: cognitive barriers, which make it difficult to think clearly about environmental problems such as climate change; emotional barriers, in which feelings about the topic inhibit a person from confronting it; and social barriers, in which one's relationships with other people interfere with the ability to respond effectively to the problems.

Cognitive Barriers

Our brains are not well equipped for thinking about environmental problems. We evolved in a context in which the problems we had to deal with were concrete and short term: finding food and shelter, mating, defending ourselves from adversaries. People didn't live long enough to worry about long-term problems, and this tendency to disregard the future still defines us today. Many if not most people put their long-term health at risk through poor eating habits, lack of exercise, and overindulgence in risky substances or behavior. They fail to set aside enough money for retirement, even when it is within their capability. They make decisions that ignore future consequences. Environmental problems mostly unfold slowly, so that the impacts are not likely to emerge for decades. When it comes to threats such as these, many people are inclined to put off addressing it, "think about that tomorrow", and hope that something happens – some new invention, perhaps – that will eliminate the need to respond to the problem.

Environmental problems are also complex. People find it easiest to understand causal relationships when the effect is not only close in time to the cause, but also at a similar scale and type. The elaborate networks that underlie the connection between driving a car, or eating meat, and consequences such as increased global temperatures or the extinction of species, are beyond the comprehension of many. The fact that cold weather can still occur even in the face of general global warming seems impossible for many political figures to understand. Systems thinking is required to fully grasp the connections among processes occurring at different levels and in different domains (behavioral, ecological, geophysical). Even though people may be capable of understanding these connections if they try, they may be too preoccupied with more pressing concerns to devote the cognitive effort.

Negative environmental consequences not only emerge slowly; their nature and timing are also uncertain. We have known about the potential for climate change since at least the 1950s (arguably earlier), but the models that describe the nature, scope, and timing of the impacts have been evolving over that time and are still imperfect. It is still difficult to attribute any single weather event to climate change, and no one can predict exactly how much rainfall will change, or sea level will increase, in a particular location at a specific point in time. This uncertainty makes it possible for people to feel as though "the jury is still out": the existence of climate change is still uncertain. Given a range of possible outcomes, and a poor understanding of probability, people may choose to believe that the outcomes will be minimal, despite the fact that serious outcomes are much more likely. Especially when powerful media and political figures continue to insist that there is no problem, it may seem like a legitimate option to agree with them.

Emotional Barriers

This brings us to the second set of barriers: emotional responses. The impact of cognitive barriers would not be as significant were it not that people have preferences about what to believe. Environmental problems are scary, and it is unpleasant to think about scary things. One option is merely to avoid thinking about them. Avoidance probably characterizes the response of most reasonably informed people: they know that bad environmental things are happening but manage to go about their lives without paying much attention to the fact. A more extreme option is denial – refusing to believe in things that we would prefer to believe are not true. Denial is a powerful and profound human capability. It allows people to stay functional rather than being paralyzed by fear, but it also prevents them from effectively responding to a problem.

Ironically, although an overly strong emotional response can create one kind of barrier, insufficient concern is another. Some people believe, falsely, that environmental changes do not threaten the things that they care about. Climate change seems psychologically distant to them, something that might affect future generations, polar bears, or even people in far-off countries – but not anything that will significantly affect them. For those people, apathy may be the biggest obstacle that is inhibiting them from sustainable behavior.

A third level of emotional barrier is slightly more complex: it is based on the threat to one's ideology or belief system. System justification refers to the need to defend the system by which one lives, which could include capitalism, a Western lifestyle, or a set of religious beliefs. If acknowledging a problem requires that a person deny the beliefs that are important to them, they will be strongly motivated to ignore the problem. So, when people are informed that climate change is caused by their way of life – a lifestyle that they have engaged in without reflection or evil intent, but one characterized by a high carbon footprint due to materialism and heavy use of fossil fuels – they would rather not cope with the guilt, along with the recalibration of their norms and standards that appears to be required. More specifically, people who have a political ideology that embraces capitalism and rejects government intervention may refuse to accept climate change if it appears to be incompatible with that position. Some of the most powerful ideologies are religious. The reality of climate change is seen as inconsistent with religious doctrine by some, who believe that God is in charge of the Earth and nothing that human beings do can interfere with God's plan. Even beyond this, some Christian groups point to the story of the Flood and God's supposed promise to Noah that such an event would never happen again. For these groups, worrying about flooding implies worrying that God would break his promise, something that would be incredible to them.

All three types of emotional barriers – denial, apathy and ideological defense – are illustrated by remarks to the October 2018 Oil and Money Conference by the CEO of Shell Oil. He said: "Shell's core business is and will be for the foreseeable future very much in oil and gas". What is required to keep global warming under $1.5°C$ "can be done in massive reforestation. Think of another Brazil in terms of rainforest". He apparently does not feel worried about the concept of climate change, because it does not seem to him to threaten what he most cares about: his business. Although he seems at some level to acknowledge that climate change is real, he is also engaged in a certain amount of denial, such that he has convinced himself that the problem does not require his company to take action. Finally, his devotion to business as usual is obvious.

Social Barriers

Some of these examples highlight the relevance of social factors. Ideologies, in particular, are typically associated with groups that define, maintain and encourage standards concerning the specific beliefs each ideology comprises. When a person belongs to a particular religious or political community, there may be significant pressure to conform to the group's position on climate change: incredulity, mockery, or shunning of people who dare to state a different position. In the absence of a supporting group, ideologies may crumble, or at least be more prone to redefinition. In general, the social context can promote or activate the barriers already described. Beyond this, however, there are two additional barriers, particularly powerful, that are created by the social context.

The first is collective or pluralistic ignorance: the failure to accurately perceive what is required in a situation because of over-reliance on social cues. In other words, we think that something is not an emergency, or action is not necessary, because when we look to others for guidance, we see that they are not taking action. This concept grew out of research by Latané and Darley (1968) on the "bystander effect": the fact that people often fail to provide help when they witness a situation in which help is needed. In a series of studies, Latané and Darley showed that people were more likely to help in an emergency, such as when smoke issued into a room or someone was apparently having an epileptic seizure, when they were alone rather than when they were in the presence of others. The researchers interpreted this as indicating that we look to others for cues about how to act, and what behavior is called for – is it an emergency? We are reluctant to deviate from a norm of inaction for fear of looking foolish. Collective ignorance refers to the failure of a group to accurately interpret the situation. Importantly, this phenomenon does not require that any individual tries to avoid acting, or to dissuade others from acting. Instead, the phenomenon emerges from the fact that everyone looks to everyone else, waiting for someone else to act first.

With regard to environmental problems, most people, at least in developed nations, have heard about the potential issues. But they look to their friends and their immediate social context, and see that most people do not appear alarmed and have not significantly changed their behavior. There may even be some stigma attached to those who have taken action, who are labelled as "hippies" or "extremists". So the typical person concludes that action, particularly radical action, is not called for and may even be socially sanctioned. The result is that most people reside in a state of collective ignorance about the scale of the problem and the changes that are required.

The second social barrier results when attitudes about environmental problems become associated with particular social groupings, so that people in one social group are expected to have a certain attitude toward the environment, and people in a different social group are expected to have a different attitude. Because social identity is so important, people adopt behaviors and attitudes that signal their identities, even when they actually have no real opinion or the attitudes are not consistent with their real beliefs and values. This has clearly happened with political parties, most strongly in the United States but also in a number of other countries around the world: parties on the political left call attention to environmental problems, while parties on the political right ignore them and in some cases deny their very existence. For example, US President Donald Trump has repeatedly called climate change a hoax.

There are several reasons why support for action to address environmental problems is more strongly associated with the political left than the political right. For one, conservative parties typically reject government interference in markets, which environmentalists typically advocate. At a more subtle level, conservatives tend to endorse slightly different values – such as respect for authority, and loyalty – than do liberals, who prioritize care and fairness. Research has found that environmental appeals often highlight "liberal" values such as care for the Earth; when appeals are reframed to emphasize "conservative" values, they get more support from the left. Finally, Al Gore was the opponent of the Republican presidential candidate George W. Bush in a fiercely contested and controversial race for the US presidency. Al Gore, founder of the Alliance for Climate Protection, also received a Nobel Prize for his efforts to communicate about climate change. For political reasons, many Republicans rejected not only Al Gore but also everything he was associated with. However, it is important to recognize that the link between political party and environmental concern is not inevitable. Many policies for environmental protection have been proposed and implemented by figures on the political right, in countries around the world. Patriotism, stewardship and fiscal responsibility, values that are championed by conservatives, can also be used to generate arguments for sustainability.

Interestingly, social polarization over environmental protection can also occur along class lines. Environmentalists are sometimes accused of being "elitists" who have no concern for the poor and working-class members of society; their policies are described (sometimes accurately) as increasing the financial hardship of those who are already struggling. This is illustrated with one of the slogans produced by the *mouvement des gilets jaunes* (yellow vests movement) in France when protesting against a projected carbon tax: *Pour les élites: la peur de la fin du monde. Pour nous: la peur des fins de mois* (For the elites: fear of the end of the world. For us: fear of the end of the month [when the money runs out]). However the social divisions run, the linkage between social identity and environmental attitudes forces one group to represent the opposition to environmental action, and characterizing the situation as "us vs them" makes it more difficult to work together as a society to come up with solutions.

MOTIVATING BEHAVIOR

Identifying the barriers to behavior helps to identify the ways to overcome them, and points toward opposing forces that can motivate environmentally protective action. I will discuss the sources of motivation in three categories, though many examples may be impossible to neatly categorize into just one of these areas. First, and often easiest to address, are aspects of the physical environment. Second, there are important social factors. Finally, there are individual characteristics that may be fostered or activated in order to motivate sustainable action.

The Physical Environment

Making changes in the physical environment is often the easiest, as well as the most effective, way to encourage more sustainable behavior. Because, as mentioned above, people often act without really thinking about what they are doing, they can be highly responsive to environmental cues and affordances – the behaviors that are enabled by the physical context. So, for example, people are significantly more likely to do things that are easy: to bicycle if there are bicycle lanes, to buy an electric car if there are charging stations. They are more likely to recycle if recycling containers are clearly marked and easily accessible. The visibility of recycling containers also matters; they should be in a well-lit location. Even the structure of the recycling container affects people's recycling competence; in one study, containers with distinctively shaped lids (e.g., with a slit for paper in one and a round hole in another) led to less contamination of recycling compared to no lids. Potentially even more effective are structural changes that do not require people to think at all: motion sensor lights that go off automatically after people leave a room; low-flow showerheads that reduce water use; energy efficiency standards, such as for automobiles or appliances, that are enacted at the level of product design rather than at the level of consumer choice.

   A possible drawback to these approaches can be if they arouse resentment. People don't like to feel that their behavior is being controlled by others, and if the structural constraints on their behavior are too obvious people may exert effort to regain personal control by acting less sustainably. So, for example, some people have adopted workarounds that allow them to increase the pressure in their showers. Another drawback is that modifications of the physical infrastructure may seem to absolve people of personal responsibility, so that they think that they don't have to worry about environmental sustainability because (for example) the government is taking care of it. Although changing features of the physical environment to encourage sustainable behavior is an important approach, it must be done sensitively and should not be the only way of promoting environmental concern.

Another way of modifying the physical environment, which makes more allowance for good individual intentions, is to give people feedback about their behavior and its impact. People may care about the environment but be unaware of the ways in which their actions are having a negative impact. Or they may want to reduce their energy use but have no idea how much energy they are currently using, and how different behavioral changes affect their overall usage. Individualized feedback, such as from energy or water meters, can give people the information they need to gauge their own efficiency. Many energy companies in the United States have increased their emphasis on providing customers with the ability to track their own energy usage from month to month. Some automobiles, too, allow drivers not only to see how much gas they have but to track how their fuel efficiency changes from moment to moment under different driving conditions. This type of feedback can then be paired with suggestions – for example, from the energy company or the automobile maker – about how efficiency could be improved with some simple behavioral changes, such as insulated shades for the house and proper tire inflation for the car.

Suggestions for sustainable behavior seem like a good idea, but they have to be framed in the right way (Markowitz & Guckian, 2018). Many well-intentioned messages are ignored. People are constantly bombarded with information, so messages need to stand out. They also need to have the right content. Information about environmental threats is typically not what is needed to get people to behave in a more sustainable way. The messages need to attract attention, perhaps through visual interest, and by utilizing interesting content that personalizes the issue and provides an emotionally compelling narrative. They may also need to provide information, but the most useful information may be descriptions of *how* to change behavior rather than *why*. People typically know that the natural environment is endangered, but they frequently don't know what they can do about it.

Messages can even inadvertently backfire – for example, by eliciting the resistance to behavioral control that was described above, or by suggesting that unsustainable behavior is normative. Some pro-environmental messages include a description of an unsustainable behavior choice that many people make: environments are degraded because of the large number of people who litter, or due to the unsustainable food choices that constitute the typical diet. Although these messages are designed to illustrate the need for more sustainable behavior, they also suggest that it is normal to behave unsustainably. Researchers have found that such messages may actually encourage people to make the unsustainable choice, presumably because "everyone is doing it".

The Social Environment

As the previous example illustrates, and as discussed earlier, the social environment exerts an extremely powerful influence on people's behavior. Fortunately, this influence can work to encourage as well as discourage sustainability. When sustainability is seen as socially valued, the desire to impress others can motivate people to demonstrate their pro-environmental credentials. A number of studies have shown that people are more likely to purchase "green" rather than conventional products when they care what other people think about them, and when they think that other people will see and value their green choices (Griskevicius, Tybur & Van den Bergh, 2010). Even more powerful is the simple knowledge that other people are behaving in sustainable ways. People are more likely to install solar panels if their neighbors have them, and more likely to engage in sustainable agricultural practices if their neighbors engage in them. Returning to the example of the energy company, research has shown that providing people with feedback not only about their own energy use but also about the energy use of their neighbors tends to reduce the energy use of people who are using more than others (Schultz et al., 2007).

This raises the question, what about those who are using less energy than their neighbors? Does giving them this feedback lead them to increase their energy use? Yes, but this tendency can be mitigated. There are two types of social norms, descriptive and prescriptive: descriptive norms describe what other people do, and prescriptive norms describe what other people value or think should be done. Both can be influential. When people see that others are using less energy, the descriptive and prescriptive norms align. When people see that others are using more energy, the descriptive norm suggests using more, and on average people do increase their energy use. But if, when people see that others are using more energy, they are reminded of the prescriptive norm – the desirability of using less energy – they do not increase their own usage.

A more direct way in which the social environment can encourage behavior is when people form groups. Regardless of the primary reason for joining a group, group membership has several potential benefits: not only does it increase the ability to effect change, it also provides social benefits that include companionship and a feeling of belonging, a group identity, a sense of meaning and purpose, and the positive emotional experiences that accompany shared group activities. Just consider the shared celebrations that follow successful group activism. In order to be happy, people have a common set of core needs, including the need for self-esteem, for belonging, and for a sense of meaning; all of these have the potential to be met by group engagement. In a virtuous cycle, these shared group experiences contribute to a group identity that then strengthens engagement with the group. And when people commit to a group, they are more strongly affected by group behavioral norms. If people join pro-environmental groups, whether they engage in political activism, direct environmental action (like community clean-ups), or simply conversation about shared environmental interests, the norms that emerge are likely to promote more sustainable behavior.

Environmental problems are fundamentally collective problems: individual behavior will rarely lead to meaningful change, and environmental action is usually directed toward benefiting the collective rather than individual self-interest. That means it is useful to consider the environmental problems as examples of public goods dilemmas: cases in which individuals, acting in their own self-interest, fail to preserve a public good and thus lead to a more negative outcome for everyone including themselves. Each fisher, for example, may be motivated to catch as many fish as possible, but if everyone behaves that way, the fish stock will collapse and no one will have enough. Each individual may be motivated to pollute the air without paying the cost of clean-up but if everyone does this the air will become toxic to all. There are solutions to such dilemmas, often involving some form of regulation, but individuals are most likely to act on behalf of the collective when they trust other members of the group, feel that they have shared goals, and are able to communicate with each other. A strong group identity – which could include a national identity – is likely to encourage this orientation toward collective well-being.

Individual Characteristics

It is clearly the case that some people are more environmentally engaged than others: some people are climate champions, raising the bar and showing others the kind of behaviors that are possible and necessary. What explains these outliers? No single individual can be reduced to a simple formula, but three personal characteristics are important predictors of environmental activism. One is simply environmental concern, which is greater among some people than others. A second is a strong sense of moral responsibility: the need to act in a way that is consistent with one's values. And a third might be described as the confidence to take action that deviates from the norm, even when the consequences are not fully known.

There is a great deal of research on environmental concern. Not surprisingly, people who value the environment are more concerned about threats to the environment. Value for the environment is associated with early significant experiences in nature; although it has been argued that people have an inherent tendency to enjoy nature, that tendency needs to be nurtured (Chawla, 1999). People who are unfamiliar with natural settings may find them uncomfortable or frightening, since they don't know what to expect or how to behave in those environments. Although adults can learn to love nature, experiences tend to be particularly influential for young children, who are still developing a sense of themselves and learning about their own abilities. Especially when in the company of significant adults, who can make the experience more meaningful and manageable for the child, experiences in natural environments can lead children to construct a self-identity that acknowledges interdependence with the natural world. This linking of identity with environmental issues makes environmental topics more personally relevant and is associated with pro-environmental behavior later in life.

Liking nature is important, but most people like nature. Taking action on behalf of the natural environment also requires a sense of personal responsibility. This, too, is associated with early experience. Although it is impossible to perfectly predict who will become an activist, people who are exposed to role models – often a parent – who demonstrate the importance of acting in support of one's beliefs, are more likely to internalize that sense of obligation to stand up for what they believe to be right. The role model doesn't have to be an environmental activist; it is the need to take action in support of one's beliefs that is learned by imitating others. However, role models are not the only influence on people's tendency to stand up for their beliefs. The personality trait of conscientiousness is also implicated, and research suggests that personality is in part affected by genetics.

Finally, activism may require a willingness to take actions that challenge the status quo. Doing what everyone else does is safe; even if it is the wrong action, there is usually no social risk in doing what others are already doing. Doing something different entails the possibility not only of social disapproval, but also of other negative consequences, unforeseen because the behavior is novel. Thus finding, and belonging to, a group of people who support environmental engagement is likely to increase pro-environmental behavior by reducing those risks. However, there are environmental activists who are willing to defy social norms entirely. Such activism is likely to be associated with a perception of personal efficacy, or the belief that one can effectively accomplish what one sets out to do.

CONCLUSION

We are facing unprecedented environmental changes. Individual action is necessary, not only because individual and household consumption of environmental resources accounts for a significant proportion of environmental impacts (think about private car use, discretionary air travel, and meat eating), but also because individuals' attitudinal support and behavioral adoption is necessary for public policies to be successfully implemented. Psychological research can help to understand people's responses – or lack of responses – to these environmental crises, and this understanding can encourage messaging and behavioral interventions that promote sustainability (Clayton & Manning, 2018).

In some ways, the inadequate response to the environmental crisis is understandable. People are not good at planning for the future, especially when it is uncertain. There are always more immediate concerns to capture attention. Social dynamics as well as inertia make it easy to continue with the status quo. But there is increasing recognition of the fundamental connections between human and environmental health, and the need to protect the environment is becoming increasingly clear. Most people agree that protecting the environment has an ethical component. Nearly everyone acknowledges that it is necessary for our well-being.

There have always been people who stand out from the crowd, whether it be the scientists who pointed out the possible impact of carbon emissions on climate back in the early twentieth century, the inventors and entrepreneurs who are committed to finding new ways of doing things, or the activists who persist in drawing attention to a message that people do not want to hear. What we need to do now is allow these outliers to create new norms: behavioral, attentional, but also moral. Just as there can be tipping points in environmental systems, a social tipping point can occur when a small group of people demonstrate the possibility of a societal transition.

REFERENCES

Chawla, L. (1999). Life paths into effective environmental action. *The Journal of Environmental Education, 31*(1), 15–26.

Clayton, S., & Manning, C. (Eds.) (2018). *Psychology and climate change: human perceptions, impacts, and responses*. San Diego, CA: Elsevier.

Clayton, S., & Myers, G. (2015). *Conservation psychology: understanding and promoting human care for nature* (2nd ed.). Oxford: Wiley-Blackwell.

Griskevicius, V., Tybur, J.M., & Van den Bergh, B. (2010). Going green to be seen: status, reputation, and conspicuous conservation. *Journal of Personality and Social Psychology, 98*(3), 392–404.

Latané, B., & Darley, J.M. (1968). Group inhibition of bystander intervention in emergencies. *Journal of Personality and Social Psychology, 10*(3), 215–21.

Markowitz, E.M., & Guckian, M.L. (2018). Climate change communication: challenges, insights, and opportunities. In S. Clayton & C. Manning (Eds.), *Psychology and climate change* (pp. 35–63). London/San Diego, CA: Academic Press.

Schultz, P.W., Nolan, J.M., & Cialdini, R.B. et al. (2007). The constructive, destructive, and reconstructive power of social norms. *Psychological Science, 18*(5), 429–34.

3. Capitalism and the curse of external effects

Claude Henry

Every child worldwide now faces existential threats from climate change and commercial pressures. (WHO, UNICEF and *The Lancet*, 2020)

I have found, in business in particular but also in politics, that when something is in your personal best interests, the ability of the mind to rationalize that that's the right thing is really quite extraordinary. I have seen it in others, and I have seen it in myself. (Senator Mitt Romney at President Trump's impeachment trial)

The most celebrated pronouncement in economics – Adam Smith's on the "invisible hand": "By pursuing his own interest he frequently promotes that of society more effectually than when he really intends to promote it" (Smith, 1776) – today looks as outdated as the Commandment: "Thou shalt not bear false witness" (Matthew 19:16–19).

Instead of a competitive market, where providers meet consumers' demands, we have at the core of the economy a nexus of dominant firms, the activities of which bring more harm than good: abusers deeply indifferent to the welfare of the people, particularly of their health and the environment in which they live, rather than providers of goods and services meeting their needs. To maintain their dominance, they cover up the harmful effects of their activities, they manipulate the relevant information – scientific knowledge in particular. In democracies they marshal their outsized wealth and power to subvert representative and administrative institutions, the legitimacy of which they hollow out, hence still increasing their domination. In authoritarian regimes, under various forms of state or crony capitalism, firms and public authorities are tightly interwoven; only to the extent they deem it necessary to "keep them happy" – that is, quiet – do they worry about ordinary people.

In "market capitalism", it's not market, it's capitalism as it functions today that is the culprit (see, for instance, Philippon, 2019a, 2019b).[1] Even worse are the Chinese version, the defunct Soviet one, and various forms of crony capitalism in developing countries. Mark Twain once said, when reporting about the "water wars" along the Colorado River: "Whiskey is for drinking, water is for fighting about". In this chapter we illustrate – mainly with references to natural capital, climate in particular, and to public health – another dichotomy: *Smith's market is for making production and exchange more efficient; contemporary capitalism is for looting, duping and dominating.* Economists' famed "external effects"[2] are pervading and corrupting the whole organism, they are feeding the exorbitant financial returns expected by shareholders, or by any sort of people in control. In every possible way, capitalism as it now functions is destroying life on Earth. As Robert Watson, former chair of the Intergovernmental Panel on Climate Change (IPCC) (1997–2002) and later on of the Intergovernmental Science-Policy Platform on Biodiversity and Ecosystem Services (IPBES) (2016–20), puts it:

> The continued loss of biodiversity is not only an environmental issue. It risks undermining the achievement of most of the UN Sustainable Development Goals. It is central to development, through food, water and energy security. It has significant economic value, which should be recognised in national accounting systems. It is a security issue as far as loss of natural resources, especially in developing countries, can lead to conflict. It is an ethical issue because loss of biodiversity hurts the poorest people, further exacerbating an already inequitable world. And it is also a moral issue, because we should not destroy the living planet. Why has that loss been ignored? (Watson, 2019)

Hereafter are elements of an answer.

CAPITALISM OF LOOTING

"Climate change is the result of the greatest market failure the world has ever seen" (Stern, 2007). Or equivalently: the ultimate external effect. External indeed in the sense of bypassed, deliberately.

Firms producing fossil fuels control proven reserves, the burning of which would generate about 2500–3000 Gt of CO_2 emissions – that is, more than four times the amount beyond which the increase in the Earth's mean temperature would exceed 1.5°C (IPCC, 2018). Warming could then "activate important tipping elements, raising the temperature further to activate other tipping elements in a domino-like cascade that could take the Earth System to even higher temperatures" (Steffen et al., 2018, p. 8254). Elementary precaution thus requires that the level of these reserves be frozen. It is not, it is expanding, and it is expanding at an accelerating pace.

The fire power of the five largest stock market-listed oil and gas companies is impressive. Their profits in 2018 (for them a rather good albeit not exceptional year) are respectively, according to Moody's Investors Service, $23 billion for Royal Dutch Shell, $21 billion for ExxonMobil, $18 billion for Chevron, $14 billion for Total and $13 billion for BP. It is thus quite easy for them to spend $200 million a year in covert lobbying operations meant to delay, skew, block policies aimed at mitigating climate change. They spend about the same amount, with great fanfare, on branding campaigns, suggesting they are diligently taking part in the fight against climate change (Collins, 2019). On April 8, 2019, Shell made an additional move, announcing a significant expansion of its greenwashing operations: $100 million will be allocated each year to investments "in natural ecosystems as part of a strategy to act on climate change" (Monbiot, 2019). ExxonMobil is a pillar of Stanford's Global Climate and Energy Project. The late David Koch (see the "Capitalism of Influence and Dominance" section below) was a Life Member of the MIT Board. In 2019, at last, BP's fake humanism was pushed back by the Royal Shakespeare Company's decision to dispense with its donations. Financially these actions absorb only a tiny fraction of the resources that the companies muster; they are obviously not jeopardizing exploration and production projects. Nevertheless, they provide enough ammunition to successfully manipulate politicians, regulators and media, and to deceive the general public. Blowing smoke screens in these ways, it must be acknowledged, is, however, a far cry from stripping university charters of the right to free thinking, a recent Chinese move extending totalitarianism that "not only forbids you to express – even to think – certain thoughts, but dictates what you *shall* think" (Orwell, 1941; original emphasis). It is nevertheless an unwelcome, to say the least, contribution to the confusion that impedes the confrontation of looming environmental catastrophes.

With profits in 2018 amounting to $110 billion, Saudi Aramco is in a class of its own. Moody's doesn't provide equally reliable figures for the Chinese, Russian, and other, state-controlled companies; however, the size of their contributions to public budgets is a good indicator of their strength. Altogether – and also including coal companies, especially those active in Asia – since the December 2015 climate agreement approved in Paris, they have massively increased already massive investments in exploration and extraction of fossil fuels. Financing these ventures has not been a problem, as they could rely not only on their profits, but also on unflinching public subsidies and on loans – they are among the main beneficiaries of the prevailing ultra-low interest rates – and participations from global banks, amounting to more than $1 trillion (BankTrack et al., 2019), not including another $500 billion (about 40 percent from Chinese banks) to coal projects.

Bribing disbursements are mere slivers from these enormous amounts. They are nevertheless of strategic importance for the companies: they are control levers on corrupt governments along the processes of negotiating and implementing highly profitable exploration and extraction contracts. Referring to the government of Equatorial Guinea, among the most corrupt ones, Rachel Maddow (2019, p. 356) writes: "So long as nasty, authoritarian strongmen like Teodoro Obiang didn't start making untoward new demands on oil and gas producers, and they honored ExxonMobil's bottom line imperatives – the 'sanctity of contract' – all was cool".

Teodoro Obiang Nguema Mbasogo has been President of the Republic of Equatorial Guinea since 1979, regularly re-elected with more than 90 percent of the votes. He has avoided "untoward new demands" above the $25 billion that the oil and gas companies – mainly Marathon Oil, Noble Energy and in a dominant position ExxonMobil – have been channeling since 2019 towards him and members of his family and of his clique, without jeopardizing the profitability of their investments. During this decade, ordinary Guineans (about 1.4 million in 2020) got even poorer than they were before the oil era, with less access to drinking water, to health services and to education, and suffering from worsening malnutrition and infant mortality.

The situation in Equatorial Guinea appears as an extreme case of the *resource curse*; it is, for example, rare for a strongman to be accused by the UN Commission of Human Rights of directly overseeing torture of opponents. Nevertheless, it is a manifestation of a general pattern: for oil companies operating in developing countries it is optimal, as far as the smoothness of their operations and the size of their profits are concerned, to concentrate financial transfers on corrupt minorities that firmly control their respective countries; in this respect, countries like Angola, Guyana, Kazakhstan, Nigeria, Peru, along with Equatorial Guinea, proved particularly "cool". It is a key component of oil companies' business model; hence the furious reactions against Section 1504 of the Dodd-Frank Act.

After the Act – meant to reform regulation of the US financial sector, and of some other business practices – was passed by Congress in 2010, US oil companies led by the American Petroleum Institute and by ExxonMobil, respectively their professional association and their natural leader, started a guerrilla war to obstruct the implementation of Section 1504 of the Act, which:

> requires the SEC (Securities and Exchange Commission) to issue final rules that require each resource extraction issuer to include in an annual report…information relating to any payment made by the resource extraction issuer, a subsidiary of the resource extraction issuer, or an entity under its control, to a foreign government… for the purpose of the commercial development of oil, natural gas, or minerals… Foreign government means a foreign government, a department, agency, or instrumentality of a foreign government, or a company owned by a foreign government. (SEC, n.d.)

For six years companies succeeded in keeping Section 1504 in limbo, by making the most of the opportunities for appeal that the US judicial system offers. Then came Donald Trump and a Republican-dominated Senate; together they wasted no time in killing Section 1504. The main Senate executor has been James Inhofe, Republican of Oklahoma, also known as a vociferous denier of climate science – a coherent scenario.

BOX 3.1   BASKING IN OIL

We are about to take another major step in the development of promising oil and gas fields in the Arctic. (Vladimir Putin, inauguration of the first Rosneft-ExxonMobil drilling platform in the Kara Sea, Sochi, August 9, 2014; Maddow, 2019, p. 269)

In April 2019, we announced a significant discovery at the Blacktip prospect in the Perdido Corridor within the deep-water US Gulf of Mexico. This and other drilling successes in the US Gulf of Mexico highlight the potential of this area. (Shell, 2019)

We are very pleased with this first significant oil discovery made just after our entry into Block 58 offshore Surinam. (Kevin McLachlan, Senior Vice-President of Exploration, Paris, January 7, 2020; see Total, 2020)

Chevron has upped its Permian Basin (Texas) resource estimate to more than 21 billion barrels of oil equivalent, more than double the company's estimate just three years ago (Jay Johnson, Executive Vice-President of Exploration and Production at Chevron, Annual Security Analyst Meeting, New York, March 3, 2020; see Spencer and Greenhalgh, 2020).

Either all that oil cited in Box 3.1 remains in the ground, and the prospect is a broad financial crisis, or it is extracted and burnt, which amounts to a crime against humanity.

The race is accelerating, closer and closer to a cliff. Will a jump over a financial cliff – that is, the crisis contemplated by Governor of the Bank of England, Mark Carney, when it becomes clear that the reserves, on which the companies' high market valuations are based, are mere stranded assets, an enormous financial bubble will burst (see the Part VI of this book: "Investors") – derail the race before a fatal climate tipping point is reached?

The firms' hypocrisy about these prospects matches their unflinching exclusive quest for profit and growth. Ben van Beurden, CEO of Shell, has set a new standard in hypocrisy. In his remarks to the October 2018 Oil & Money Conference, he said: "Shell's core business is and will be for the foreseeable future very much in oil and gas". What is required to keep global warming under 1.5°C "can be done in massive reforestation. Think of another Brazil in terms of rainforest" (Redd-Monitor, 2019). Is it possible that he was not aware that the real Brazil is controlled by people for whom the Amazon forest is a nuisance, an obstacle against development as they see it – that is, agrobusiness, logging and mining activities, involving Brazilian and foreign firms like McDonald's, Burger King, KFC, AngloAmerican, Mineraçao Rio do Norte, Norsk Hydro, Rio Tinto, Vale and so on? Mining companies are no less brutal than fossil-fuel ones, killing large numbers of people in accidents that could and should have been avoided, and routinely having scores of indigenous activists murdered and, as the case may be, supporting lawyers and journalists as well (Souter et al., 2017). Jair Bolsonaro, president of Brazil since January 1, 2019, hates the indigenous inhabitants of the forest even more than he hates the trees; he sees them as *Untermenschen*[3] who, as he once said, "smell, are undereducated and don't speak our language" (see in Part V, "Entrepreneurs", Chapter 44 of this book, the story of some of these so-called *Untermenschen*). He thinks the Holocaust can be forgiven, as he said at a meeting with evangelical leaders on April 13, 2019. He thus might also think that he would be forgiven for transposing into the Amazon forest Hitler's *Endlösung der Judenfrage*.[4] Capitalism is not averse to that kind of playmate.

As far as coal is concerned, public and private Chinese institutions run the show, in ways that are, to say the least, beneficial neither to the climate nor to the countries where they operate. As Mohamed Adow, Christian Aid's head of climate policy for Africa, puts it: "It is deeply unfair for China to get Africa hooked on fossil fuels and debt when it comes to building Africa's infrastructure, while China is starting to adopt clean, cheap technologies of the 21st century" (Watts, 2019).

Indeed, while China is lessening its dependence on coal – mainly aiming at alleviating the pollution of air and water within the country – engineering firms and banks, mostly state-owned, are making up for lost business at home by frantically expanding into other countries, partly under the umbrella of the Belt and Road Initiative. More than 100 GW of coal-fired capacity of electricity production have recently been completed or are under development in 23 countries. During the 2000–09 decade, state banks have provided loans and participations for a total amount of $49 billion (Global Development Policy Center, 2020). An emblematic case is the 600 MW power plant inaugurated in April 2019 at Tharparkar, Sindh Province, Pakistan. A nearby opencast mine has been established to provide coal – low grade and severely polluting – in a country where miners are exposed to working conditions among the harshest worldwide. The choice is all the more significant as there are in the same province favorable wind corridors as well as abundant sunshine.

Far away from Africa and South Asia, powerful political and economic Chinese actors are pushing, along with Russian and US counterparts,[5] for the transformation of the Arctic region from a natural asset, the protection of which is essential to the balance of the planet, into a pool of non-renewable resources to be systematically tapped, in particular those very fossil fuels whose use must on the contrary be drastically scaled down. The Chinese approach amounts to doubling down on transforming the Arctic from a shield into a relentless engine of climate change, with huge quantities of methane ready to be released from melting permafrost, in excess of the soaring quantities of methane that the fossil-fuel industry worldwide routinely leaks or intentionally releases in the atmosphere. The atmospheric concentration of methane, which is a far more potent GHG than CO_2 – by a factor 72 over 20 years and 21 over 100 years, this difference resulting from the fact that CO_2 remains for far longer periods in the atmosphere – has already doubled since the beginning of the Industrial Revolution (Hmiel, 2020).

Climate is not the sole victim of fossil-fuel-based capitalism. From extraction to end uses, fossil fuels are leaving trails of destruction. Oil has devastated – polluting and poisoning water and soil beyond repair – the Niger delta and the Ecuadorian Amazon forest, a number of coastal settlements and ecosystems, and has destroyed large tracts of the Alberta boreal forest and vital ecosystems on the Xing Kiang plateau. Damage from coal is even broader. Assessing the situation in India, Mayuri Chabukdhara (2019, p. 87) writes: "Environmental challenges [due to coal] include large scale landscape damage, soil erosion, loss of forest ecosystem and wildlife habitat, air, water and soil pollution". This is not specific to India; worldwide, coal has destroyed lives and natural capital on par with world wars.

In tropical rainforests, not only in the Amazon basin, capitalism is leaving other trails of looting and destruction. In Asia, tropical forests also fare badly; capitalism, making the most of public authorities' weaknesses, is again the engine. These forests extend from India to Malaysia, Indonesia and Papua New Guinea. They are exploited and burnt – generating thick air pollution in Southeast Asia and bringing black carbon to the Eastern Himalaya mountains, hence accelerating the melting of the glaciers – to the point that their very existence is in balance. In most places public authorities are no match – often being bribed – for international logging and paper mills companies selling the products in China, Japan, India, and so on; nor for agribusinesses converting natural forests into palm oil plantations to meet the increasing demands of food companies for their popular brands all over the world. In Indonesia and Malaysia, there are projects for producing and selling more "green" diesel, from more palm oil, hence more deforestation. The ultimate culprits are the American, Asian and European companies involved, and their customers, along with the numerous banks that finance the destructive activities. "Forest & Finance", a report from the community group TuK Indonesia and the Dutch consultancy Profundo (Forests & Finance, n.d.; see also Rainforest Action Network [RAN], 2020), shows that financial institutions (mainly China Development Bank, HSBC, JPMorgan, Mizuho Financial, and three Indonesian banks) provided more than $38 billion worth of commercial loans and underwriting facilities to 50 companies implicated in deforestation in the Asia-Pacific region, from 2010 to 2015, in four sectors: palm oil, pulp, rubber and tropical timber. If the present trends are maintained – and there are not many credible counterweights – most of the Southeast Asia rainforests will be gone by mid-century, and with them a rich and original biodiversity as well as the carbon stored in trees and in soil.

Most frightening: the reservoirs of, mainly unknown, pathogens previously kept away in the depths of the forests will be exposed. As Wilcox and Ellis (2006, p. 12) observed some time ago: "Today, both deforestation and emerging infectious diseases remain largely associated with tropical regions but have impacts that extend globally". And not all these new diseases will be as restrained as COVID-19: they will kill children no less than adults. The most frequent mediators between emerging pathogens and humans are wild animals that have been disturbed by human actions. It is shown in Kreuder-Johnson et al. (2020) that it is the very actions that threaten wildlife species' survival – first of all ecosystem destruction and all modes of consuming animal bodies, or in many instances just parts of them – that also enable the transmission of viruses from animals to humans.[6]

The threats to boreal forests are no doubt less pressing. Nevertheless, they are more serious than generally recognized. In Canadian boreal forests, logging companies are operating in ways that are not up to the country's pretense to care for nature and the environment. The rate of deforestation is far higher than officially acknowledged. And, viciously, after a zone has been exploited, massive scars (all sorts of infrastructure built for the logging operations) are left over; they make regenerations of the trees all the more difficult (Wildlands League, 2019).

South Atlantic waters fronting the western coast of Africa offer a striking example of pillage of natural capital by powerful foreign firms, mainly from Asia. They send fleets of fishing ships equipped with the most efficient catching devices. Among these ships are those of the state-owned China National Fisheries Corporation, the exactions of which – notably robbing the livelihood of traditional African fishers – are not in tune with the spirit of cooperation that China pretends to display in Africa. They recently outsourced practices not uncommon inside China: abduction of those who stand in the way. An example: Ghana has appointed observers on fishing vessels whose mission is to detect violations of fisheries law; some have disappeared from the country. Africans are not the sole victims of Chinese fishing companies. Under the protection of armed Chinese Coast Guard vessels, they plunder parts of the Indonesian exclusive economic zone in the South China Sea. Chinese powerful trawlers not only take the fish, they destroy essential life-supporting ecosystems by scraping the bottom of the sea. The Indonesian central government shies away from confronting China, close neighbor and largest trading partner.

The seabed is also under threat. In 2001, Russia made the first claim of sovereignty on a portion of seabed, specifically on a portion of the Arctic seabed. Since then, 83 countries followed suit, making claims on a total of 37 million km². However, it is in the vast extent of ocean under international jurisdiction that the richest prizes of rare earths, metal nodules and other valuable minerals are to be found. The UN International Seabed Authority (ISA) is in charge of regulating the mining activities soon to be launched; later this year (2020), ISA intends to publish a Mining Code as a reference for regulation. Several companies – in particular, Canadian, Chinese and German ones – are already licensed and ready to start operations as soon as the Code is published, with scant concern for so-called external effects: "mining licenses [have been] granted prior to a consensus on how to mitigate environmental impacts of mining", due to which all flora and fauna living in the ocean depths will suffer (Jouffray et al., 2020, p. 48). This is not well known, which doesn't mean it isn't of great significance: "The deep sea is a vast, pristine and largely unexplored area, with rich biodiversity and biophysical systems which are as diverse and dynamic as terrestrial ones, but far more expansive. These systems support key processes in carbon sequestration which in turn affect global carbon cycles and climate regulation" (Howard et al., 2020, p. 4).

Limited experiments on the seabed suggest what those impacts might be. They are described as follows in a paper published in *Nature*: "As the collectors move across the sea floor, they would stir up large clouds of soft sediment that would disperse, possibly for thousands of kilometres, before eventually resettling. At high densities, sediment plumes can bury and smother animals on the sea floor… Once the nodules have been collected, they'll be shunted up a kilometres-long tube to a large surface support vessel which will sort out millions of nodules a day and return the waste sediments to the sea, creating yet another plume" (Hefferman, 2019, p. 468). Having devastated the upper layers of the oceans, capitalism is now aiming at the depths.

CAPITALISM OF DECEIT

In Akerlof's (1970) seminal model that illustrates the consequences of information asymmetry on the functioning of markets, the largest profit is made by sellers of "lemons" (i.e., bad used cars) when lemons and "peaches" (i.e., good used cars) cannot be distinguished on the market, provided the latter has not collapsed. Similarly, as political scientists Noemi Oreskes and Erik Conway (2010) put it in the introduction to their book *Merchants of Doubt*, which is the classical reference on the subject: "Call it the Tobacco Strategy. Its target was science, and so it relied heavily on scientists – with guidance from industry lawyers and public relations experts – willing to hold the rifle and pull the trigger" (p. 6).

In the 1950s and 1960s, more and more epidemiological studies were produced that documented the health hazards associated with smoking. The American producers of tobacco, American Tobacco, Benson & Hedges, Philip Morris, R.J. Reynolds, US Tobacco, and so on, organized a powerful counteroffensive through a common organism called the Tobacco Industry Research Committee. The Committee's task was to sponsor and promote research focusing on the imperfections of the epidemiological studies – exaggerating them when deemed expedient – and on possible alternative origins for the health hazards associated with smoking. A seemingly scientific institution was created to plan and coordinate this defensive research. Its links with the tobacco industry remained concealed from the public, and its name projected a highly respected image: the Alexis de Tocqueville Institution (François de la Rochefoucauld (1664 [2012], No. 218) would see here another *"hommage du vice à la vertu"*[7]). Professor Fred Seitz, a scientist with an impressive résumé (distinguished solid state physicist, president for seven years of the National Academy of Sciences, then for ten years of the Rockefeller University, from which he retired in 1979), was in 1976 put in charge of the research program financed by the tobacco industry at the Alexis de Tocqueville Institution. They sponsored both good cars (for example, Stanley Prusiner's research on the pathogenic action of mutated prions in the brain) and bad cars (spurious statistical studies to put in doubt the validity of epidemiological studies); such a mix reinforced the credibility of the operation. A lot of disguised bad cars were sold, and it lasted a long time. The first condemnation of tobacco firms at national level came as late as 2006; based on the Racketeer Influenced and Corrupt Organization Act, it was indeed infamous, but it didn't erase half a century of deceit and exceptional profits on the back of millions of avoidable individual tragedies.

The main instruments and methods designed for the defense of the tobacco industry have been adapted to the conduct of what became known as "climate wars" (see Michael Mann's account in Chapter 60 in Part VII: "Communicators"). In particular, the logistics are structured along the same lines, articulating the following actors:

- Behind the scene, powerful firms (directly or through industry associations) motivated by strong industrial and financial interests. They are more diversified than in the tobacco case, and include ExxonMobil, BP, Shell, Peabody, the National Mining Association, Ford, General Motors, Koch Industries, and so on.
- On the scene, fake scientific institutions, established from scratch and financed by the above firms. They have multiplied, always with names that make them look respectable: American Council on Science and Health, Friends of Science, Greening Earth Society, Natural Resources Stewardship Project, the Advancement of Sound Science Coalition, and so on.
- Scientists, and others, organized and supported within these institutions. First the old guard from tobacco, still eager to fight and to bask in the

limelight of the TV talk shows; despite having their scientifically productive life well behind them, they cannot bow out. Then newcomers
like meteorologist Richard Lindzen (a member of the National Academy
of Sciences) and astrophysicist Sallie Baliunas (highly regarded for her
scientific achievements, then spreading the good word that the real culprit
for climate change is the sun). All these are scientists, but they are joined
by people who are essentially lobbyists, media operators and manipulators.
The most prominent are Mark Moreno (who also coordinated the operation
"Swift Boat Veterans for Truth" that successfully put in doubt John Kerry's
record in Vietnam), Steven Malloy (known as "junk science" commentator
on Murdoch's Fox News Channel), and Frank Luntz (Republican pollster
whose "Straight talk memo" played a remarkable role in the 2004 electoral
campaign).[8] On the contrary, scientists working inside companies like
Exxon and Peabody, who were aware of serious risks associated with
climate change, have been silenced; these companies are now charged
with misrepresenting the issues to stockholders and regulators. In 1981, an
internal Exxon memo, later on revealed in a lawsuit process, warns that "it
is distinctly possible that CO2 emissions from the company's 50-year plan
will later produce effects which will indeed be catastrophic, at least for
a substantial fraction of the earth population".

Elaborate methods have been tested and refined, reminiscent of Plato's
Gorgias: "Socrates: You are saying, Gorgias, that the rhetorician will have
greater powers of persuasion than the physician even in a matter of health".
Indeed, these methods make the most of:

- *Common sense:* "How can you tell me that they have any idea what climate
  is going to be like 100 years from now if they can't tell me what the weather
  is going to be like in four months, or even next week?" (Timothy Ball, from
  Friends of Science, interviewed on August 12, 2006, by a journalist of the
  Toronto *Globe and Mail*; see Montgomery, 2006).
- *Doggedness:* "They promoted claims that had already been refuted in the
  scientific literature, and the media became complicit as they reported these
  claims as if they were parts of an ongoing scientific debate" (critique formulated by Oreskes and Conway, 2010, p. 241).
- *Unequal rules:* "Because scientists are so quick to acknowledge when
  something is not exactly correct, the attackers have won many apologies,
  corrections or reinterpretations, which they have used to argue that all of
  climate science is frail and uncertain" (Hoggan, 2009, p. 131).
- *Balance:* "It seems to demand that journalists present competing points of
  view on a scientific question as though they have equal scientific weight,
  when actually they do not" (Boykoff and Boykoff, 2003, p. 127). This is

particularly pernicious: a scientific result becomes a mere opinion, to be debated against a different opinion.

The sponsors' investments paid off. According to the Pew Research Center: in 2006, 79 percent of the Americans thought that "there is solid evidence the Earth is warming" and 50 percent that it was "because of human activity". In 2010, the corresponding figures were respectively 53 percent and 34 percent. Since then, recuperation has been slow, hindered by entrenched prejudices. In Book 2 of Virgil's *Aeneid*, Aeneas tells Queen Dido the story of Troy's last days: "Blind with frenzy, we site the accursed creature on top of our sacred citadel. Then Cassandra, who, by the god's decree, is never to be believed by Trojans, reveals our future fate by her lips". In America, Apollo's decree has morphed into ExxonMobil's (and the like) decree.

The chemical industry has been, for decades, no less successful in persuading, indeed duping, farmers, experts, politicians and the general public, that only industrial agriculture based on their products is able to ensure worldwide food security, and that this unique performance is worth a few inconveniences, despite evidence pointing otherwise (see IPCC, 2019; IPBES, 2019 and Chapter 61 by David Montgomery in Part VII: "Communicators").

Bending the truth by all possible means has been a constant strategy of the firms producing pesticides, while the tragedy was swelling, of insect and bird disappearance from entire regions dominated by industrial agriculture. Tragedy, indeed: "If insects were to vanish, the environment would collapse into chaos" (Edward O. Wilson, the famous Harvard biologist dubbed the father of biodiversity; see Sverdrup-Thygeson, 2019). "The fates of humans and insects intertwine, especially through the medium of plants", write a group of 25 biologists in Samways et al. (2020, n.p.).

Consider, for instance, pollinators. Bees play a prominent, albeit far from exclusive, role in pollination. During the last 15 years, beekeepers have noticed a severe decline in bee populations – in particular, sudden implosions of entire colonies. During the last five years, decline turned to collapse in some key rural regions in the USA, in Europe and in Asia. The causes of the phenomenon have proved difficult to investigate scientifically. Two studies reported in *Science* (Stokstad, 2012) have significantly enhanced the credibility of the following explanation: while general factors like the impoverishment of the ecosystems in rural regions are highly detrimental to bees – factors that the industry blew up out of proportion – there are also specific factors, the effect of which better corresponds to the brutality of the phenomenon – factors that the industry strenuously minimized. The scientific results reported mainly point to the extensive use in industrial agriculture of pesticides, in particular a class of pesticides called neonicotinoids. These are not particularly toxic to mammals, a good argument to have them authorized by regulators, albeit an argument that neglects the concealed (at the time market access permission was sought) fact that they are highly toxic to all sorts of insects. Even when they are not directly lethal, they act on the nervous system of insects in ways that indirectly provoke individual and collective deaths: sublethal doses of neonicotinoids damage bees' memories, their ability to forage, and their ability to navigate back to their hives (Siviter et al., 2018); the production of queens is also drastically inhibited. And pesticides weaken the defenses against the damaging effects from the actions of fungi, parasites like mites, and viruses.

Damage is by no means confined to honeybees, as is convincingly shown in a broad review investigating a great number of species and places (Soroye, Newbold and Kerr, 2020). For bumble bees, the situation is made worse by their recently observed susceptibility to temperature increases (Sanchez Bayo and Wyckhuys, 2019). Without bumble bees the pollination of wildflowers will be seriously compromised. So much for Shakespeare's sonnets.

The situation is mind-boggling: pollinators act as mediators in ecosystems whose sustainability is dependent upon this very mediation. The economic values involved are vastly superior to the profits made from producing and selling the offending pesticides. Notwithstanding that neither market nor regulatory mechanisms came and corrected these "imbalances", an international regulation institution is nominally in charge but it is controlled by the pesticides oligopoly in ways that make the case a classic of regulatory capture and regulation impotence, as discussed in the next section.

Before proceeding to the next section, it is worth reminding ourselves of the deadliest deceit in the history of the US pharmaceutical industry. The mass marketing of powerful opioids as routine painkillers, with the complicity (generously compensated) of tens of thousands of MDs, as well as of the regulator (Food and Drug Administration), is a monument of deceit. Entrusted with keeping American people in as good health as possible, the pharmaceutical industry has in fact addicted millions to hard drugs and killed hundreds of thousands (McGreal, 2019). One might think that deceit on a large scale in matters of public health would not resurface for some years; it did in 2018, showing how ingrained it is in contemporary American capitalism.

In 2007, two graduate students in product design at Stanford University started a company called Ploom, with the objective of producing an e-cigarette that, in their own words, would be "a lot less dangerous to smokers and could be enjoyable". Released in 2010, the Ploom Model 1 Vaporizer, despite its attractive design, languished on the market; it didn't feel a really enjoyable experience.

During the second semester of 2017, Ploom, rebranded as Juul Labs, put on the market a product, simply called Juul, that almost immediately lifted its fortunes to stratospheric levels; by the end of 2018 Juul Labs was valued at $38 billion, at the time overtaking Ford Motor Co. on Wall Street. The secret?

An innovative e-cigarette feeling both powerful and smooth in nicotine, the perfect enjoyable hit that had been sought after for ten years, designed as the "iPhone" of e-cigarettes.

Juul's self-proclaimed mission was to provide adult regular smokers with a safe and attractive substitute to ordinary cigarettes. In fact, it mainly targeted, attracted and addicted non-smokers, in particular teenagers. Despite the legal prohibitions on the sale of e-cigarettes to minors, "juuling" quickly became a high-school craze, to the point of reversing a declining trend in youth use of nicotine products; over 25 percent of teenagers reported using Juul more than ten times a month, most of them unaware of the dangers they were facing. Lawsuits are currently piling in, from:

- parents of hundreds of thousands of children;
- school districts across the US, for misrepresenting the nicotine content of the products, marketing to children and endangering their health;
- counties and states, for systematic and widely successful campaigns to attract teenagers to e-cigarettes engineered to sustain addiction.

This indeed is capitalism for which the main engine of temporary financial successes is deceit.

CAPITALISM OF INFLUENCE AND DOMINANCE

Lobbying and pressurizing lawmakers, either at Congress in Washington, or across US state legislatures, is permanent and ubiquitous, bringing rich rewards to the corporations that hire the lobbyists. Here are two spectacular instances: driving the Texas legislature to vote in 2019 for the Texas Critical Infrastructure Protection Act, and, at federal level, politically killing a member of the House, for having introduced a carbon tax proposal, and using it as a warning to deter any legislative initiative in favor of the climate.

Oil and gas companies operating in Texas, BP, Chevron, ConocoPhillips, ExxonMobil, Shell and various fracking operators, have conspired with Texan lawmakers, the majority of whom are Republican and staunch climatoskeptics, to have a law passed that contains extraordinary measures aiming at hitting people or groups acting in defense of environment: if convinced of obstructing or damaging energy facilities, in particular pipelines, they would be liable to prison sentences of up to ten years and to fines of up to $500 000. Other Midwestern States have followed suit. For fossil-fuel companies and regional politicians, the rationale is simple and compelling: in order to have their interests protected, they want potential perturbators terrorized. The Trump administration is extending a helping hand, with an executive order giving dispensation to major projects, pipelines in particular, from environmental review. That will help the Keystone XL pipeline (XLK) being built despite all objections and oppositions. When built, XLK will bring heavy oil extracted from tar sands in the Canadian province of Alberta – extracting, refining and burning this stuff is even more damaging for the environment and the climate than processing and burning coal – to facilities along the Gulf of Mexico. Till recently, judicial decisions as well as actions by tens of thousands of protesters have made it impossible to start works on the ground. Then COVID-19 entered the picture and lockdowns kept protesters away. For the promoters of the project the opportunity was too good to be missed. During the last days of March 2020, ignoring lockdowns, they brought in workers from across the US, effectively taking advantage of the pandemics to advance their interests (McKibben, 2020). This industry tolerates no barrier against their interests; they refuse to recognize public interest, even at its most fundamental.

For the Koch brothers, Charles and David, owners of Koch Industries (circa $110 billion of annual turnover in a variety of fossil-fuel businesses), fighting "climate change alarmism" and "moves to socialized healthcare" (they advocate scrapping Medicare and Medicaid) were priorities. When in 2009 Bob Inglis, Republican member for South Carolina of the House in Washington, proposed a bill introducing a carbon tax, the Kochs promoted a Tea Party activist against him, orchestrating and financing (as part of annual donations to the Tea Party that culminated at $17.5 million in 2010) a ruthless campaign, that proved successful, as Inglis was not re-elected at the 2010 mid-term election. That sent a very explicit message to Republicans in Congress and contributed to the Obama administration's failure to have any meaningful climate bill passed. The Kochs were systematic in the defense of their businesses and ideological interests: they systematically lobbied undecided state legislatures in opposing measures supporting renewables (Leonard, 2019). The 2018 campaign to stop a carbon tax proposition in Washington State was conducted in the same spirit by a coalition of fossil-fuel companies. The proposition was voted down.

Apart from China – lobbying and bribing are common lubricants in dealings with and within the Chinese Communist Party – the US is the industrialized country where lobbying is most prevalent. However, others are not immune – the EU for instance. Legal texts are being prepared at EU level for remedying pollution in rivers, lakes and wetlands, in order to bring them into "good ecological condition" by 2027. In order to derail the proposed legislation, lobbyists from the mining, chemical and agriculture sectors exercise maximum pressure on the Member States where firms in these sectors are particularly active; they have already enlisted the governments of Belgium, Germany and the Netherlands. A fierce battle is looming with the European Parliament, expected to oppose diluting the proposed legislation, and among governments of the Member States. It would seem that, on such an issue of clear public interest, there is no room for a battle; capitalism and its lobbyists think and act otherwise.

Several pesticides – atrazine, propisochlor, permethrin, and so on – have been banned from use in the EU since the beginning of the century; they had been proved too dangerous for both environment and public health. However, banned from use didn't imply banned from production feeding (highly profitable) sales in various African countries; the extent of the damage to public health and the environment is revealed at the Pesticide Politics in Africa conference (2019). A law passed by the French Parliament in October 2018 put an end to this "discrepancy", at least as far as France is concerned; it forbids producing, storing and transporting products banned from use in Europe. Since then the legislative and executive branches, up to the presidency, are targets of intense lobbying, meant to obstruct the implementation of the law. For the likes of Syngenta, Bayer, BASF, and so on, which produce the banned pesticides, Africans' well-being doesn't carry much weight. In financial terms, this is rational: highly hazardous pesticides, as they are called in the WHO-FAO nomenclature (WHO-FAO, 2018), make up more than half the total sales of pesticides in developing countries, and a third of the combined revenue, worldwide, of the five companies that dominate the market (these estimations are based on the data gathered by Phillips McDougall, crop science industry experts).

When agents from an industry penetrate an institution that is supposed to protect the environment and public health, to the point of occupying key executive or scientific positions within this institution, they are able to manipulate facts and rules in the interests of the industry. The nominations of two former fossil-fuel lobbyists, Andrew Wheeler, also former chief counsel to James Inhofe, the most outspoken climatoskeptic US Senator, as administrator – that is, head – of the Environmental Protection Agency; and of David Bernhardt, notorious in particular for having represented Wetlands Water District, in seeking to "un-do court-imposed protection for endangered salmon in Sacramento-San Joaquin delta", as US Secretary of the Interior (with authority on the no longer so well protected National Parks) are extreme cases, at least within democracies. However, they illuminate a trend in perversity resulting in "Death by a thousand cuts. It is not one issue, it's just across the board", according to historian Douglas Brinkley (Rice University, Austin, TX) – for example, weakening fuel-efficiency standards for new cars; ignoring mercury water pollution; lifting controls on methane emissions from flares and leaks in oil and gas production and transport; leasing protected public lands to fossil fuel companies; and sabotaging national and international efforts at reducing CO_2 emissions. Another case comes from the sugar industry, as a broad scientific investigation has shown (Kearns, Glantz and Schmidt, 2015; Kearns, Schmidt and Glantz, 2016); it has contributed to make the US a world champion of obesity and diabetes (Moss, 2014). Building on their successes, lobbyists have expanded their networks into emerging economies where, according to Laura A. Schmidt, Professor of Health Policy at the School of Medicine, University of California at San Francisco, "the health infrastructure is less established and populations may be less informed about health hazards. If corporations can get in on the ground floor, they can shape the narratives and policies around unhealthy products" (cited in Jacobs, 2019). They can get in with disguised intermediaries, one of the most prominent ones being the International Life Sciences Institute. With about 400 affiliated corporations from the food and pharmaceutical industries, it is present in 17 countries and expanding. In India it has convinced the federal government to postpone *sine die* legislation requiring warning labels on processed foods with excessive fat, salt and sugar content (Jacobs, 2019). In China, sharing offices and staff with the Centers for Disease Control and Prevention, it succeeded in diverting prevention from dietary measures towards the promotion of physical activities, the positive effects of which are severely curtailed by the continuing predominance of unhealthy foods. In Brazil, the Institute has colonized the seats nominally reserved to academics in various committees or panels of experts (ibid.). These are examples of how firms dominating a vital sector of economic activity consolidate and expand their domination by infiltrating regulatory institutions.

In 1998, the European Parliament adopted a resolution calling upon the European Commission to tackle the problems raised by the proliferation of endocrine disruptors (EDs). Numerous synthetic chemicals – about 1000(?), it is impossible to know exactly as new chemicals are not adequately tested before being brought to the market – interfere with the hormonal system, disrupting production and transmission of hormones, as well as execution of messages received within the body, hence the name "endocrine disruptors" (Diamanti-Kandarakis, 2009; Mnif et al., 2011). It is no surprise that they have severe health effects, even causing damage to babies in the mother's womb. It took the Commission ten years to have a scientific report published (Kortenkamp et al., 2011). This report systematically assessed the dangers associated with the EDs and recommended appropriate regulatory control.

The concerned industry reacted swiftly, with guns pointed at the European Commission. The Commission was due to propose by December 2013 regulatory criteria informed by the Kortenkamp report. DG Env (Directorate General for the Environment) was in charge, and a broad meeting was convened at the Commission on June 7, 2013, to review the work in progress. It was disrupted by an email from Bayer Crop Sciences to the Commission General Secretariat, requiring an economic impact assessment before proceeding to regulation criteria; the economic impact would primarily be an evaluation of the impact on the activity of the industry. The meeting fell apart. Six years later there is still no regulatory framework in place. In the meantime, independent economic assessments have been provided: "EDC [endocrine-disrupting chemical] exposures in Europe contribute substantially to neurobehavioral deficits and diseases, with a high probability of > €150 billion costs/year" (Bellanger et al., 2015, p. 1256). The US corresponding figure, according to Attina (2016), is $340 billion – that is, 2.3 percent of GDP. However, in the US, regulating EDs has not even been seriously contemplated.

CONCLUSION

In July 2007, when the financial subprime crisis was raging, Charles "Chunk" Prince, then CEO of Citigroup, famously uttered: "As long as the music is playing, you have got to get up and dance". Here also, as long as the familiar political, economic and financial music is playing, the fossil-fuel companies, the mining companies, the chemical "*Konzerns*", pharma firms, and so on, keep dancing. Dominant capitalism, under its various guises, cannot be stopped from destroying the essential natural capital our planet offers, and the conditions of almost all forms of life, ours in particular. It certainly cannot morph into a vehicle of the ecological and economic transition.

That doesn't imply that entrepreneurship has no future. It thrives in Costa Rica and Sweden, where entrepreneurs of all sizes play key roles in the transitions underway in these two pioneering countries (see Chapters 4 and 5 by respectively Monica Araya and Thomas Sterner in Part I: "Introduction"). In many other countries there also are entrepreneurs who work at driving transitions (see Part V: "Entrepreneurs" and also Henry and Tubiana, 2017). Nevertheless, on the unsustainable path on which dominant capitalism keeps accelerating, all worthwhile initiatives will be wiped away, as will the rest of us. We cannot survive under such dominant capitalism; it must be dismantled, or it is the planet- and life-support systems that will be dismantled (see the World Economic Forum's *Global Risks Report 2020*). Indeed, all components of natural capital – biodiversity, air, water, soil, climate – are currently crumbling, progressively leading to a condition of political, economic, social and moral decomposition, ultimately extending to Hannah Arendt's (1963) "banality of evil", worse than in today's Somalia or Venezuela. It is a matter of extreme urgency, for three main reasons:

- Ecological implosion is around the corner.
- Over the last four decades, inequalities have exploded all over the world (Atkinson, 2015, Piketty, 2014), even in Western Europe, albeit to a lesser extent than elsewhere; they make the immediate effects – not to mention the future ones – of climate change and other degradations of the natural

capital definitely unbearable for those at the bottom, and the bottom is deep and thick.

• Capitalism is entering a phase when scientific and technological development produces overwhelming tools for manipulation, psychological and social anesthesia, surveillance and harassment, of the majority by an increasingly dominant minority.

"Somebody must do the job", remarked President John Kennedy. Who is available for the job here? Young people who fear for their future and older people who fear for their children and for their money. A fast-growing number of young people refuse the no-future fatality, hence refuse to go and work for companies that keep killing the future; they prefer to join those that are innovating for a sustainable future (see Part IV: "Coming Generations on the Front Line"). A fast-growing number of older people divest from the killers and invest in sustainability oriented businesses (see Part VI: "Investors"). Time has thus come for public authorities to confront the ultimate choice: go on cozying up to the deadly dancers or break the curse and lead on the way to survival.

NOTES

1. "A powerful system of lobbying and campaign finance is largely responsible for the growing monopolization of the US economy" (Philippon, 2019b).
2. In Qiu Xiaolong's novel *Don't Cry Tai Lake*, Chief Inspector Chen Cao clearly grasps what external effects can be:

    Look at them. Paper mills, dyeing factories, chemical companies, and what not. In the last twenty years or so, those plants have sprung up like bamboo shoots after the rain. Sure, there's a city environmental office, but it exists only for appearance sake. Some of the factories are equipped with wastewater processing facilities, but they generally choose not to operate those facilities. The cost of doing so would wipe out their profits. So, they continue to dump waste into the lake in spite of the worsening crisis. (Qiu, 2012, p. 29)

    By dumping waste, they consume valuable resources, for free: no economic mechanism, pricing, for instance, sanctions their actions. These actions are thefts of valuable resources, but environmental officers are zombies, hence there isn't any legal sanction either. The detrimental effects on the lake are external to both economic and legal mechanisms. Such *external effects* are ubiquitous, as Geoff Heal came to discover:

    > As many in my profession do, I first saw external effects as the exception rather than the rule, and as cute textbook examples rather than what they actually are: effects that rule the world, the norm rather than the exception. (Heal, 2017, p. 15)

3. Literally, "inferior people".
4. The Final Solution to the Jewish Question.
5. Meet oil sharks in Maddow (2019), Chapter 14, Igor Ivanovich Sechin and Rex Wayne Tillerson – that is, Rosneft and ExxonMobil – assaulting the Arctic Sea (see also Box 3.1 above).
6. Humans are not the sole victims of pandemics. For instance: amphibians are disappearing from the surface of the Earth, hit by the combined attacks of various pathogens and toxic fungi; after having killed more than 1 million olive trees

in Southern Italy, bacterium *Xylella fastidiosa* is spreading to the other main Mediterranean olive oil-producing countries, a kind of "Terminator" that method-ically devastates orchard after orchard.

7.   That is, if vice hides behind hypocrisy, it's a nod to virtue.
8.   "Voters believe that there is no consensus about global warming within the scientific community. Should the public come to believe that the scientific issues are settled, their views about global warming will change accordingly. Therefore, you need to continue to make the lack of scientific certainty a primary issue in the debate" (Burkeman, 2003).

REFERENCES

Akerlof, G. (1970), "The market for lemons: quality uncertainty and the market mech-anism", *Quarterly Journal of Economics*, **84**, 488–500.

Arendt, H. (1963), *A Report on the Banality of Evil*, New York: Viking Press.

Atkinson, A.B. (2015), *Inequality – What Can Be Done?*, Cambridge, MA: Harvard University Press.

Attina, T.M. (2016), "Exposure to endocrine-disrupting chemicals in the USA: a population-based disease burden and cost analysis", *The Lancet: Diabetes and Endocrinology*, **4** (12), 996–1003.

BankTrack, Rainforest Action Network and Sierra Club et al. (2019), *Banking on Climate Change, Fossil Fuel Report Card 2019*, accessed August 9, 2020 at https://www.banktrack.org/download/banking_on_climate_change_2019_fossil_fuel_finance_report_card/banking_on_climate_change_2019.pdf.

Bellanger, M., B. Demeneix and P. Grandjean et al. (2015), "Neurobehavioral deficits, diseases, and associated costs of exposure to endocrine disrupting chemicals in the European Union", *The Journal of Clinical Endocrinology and Metabolism*, **100**, 1256–66.

Boykoff, B. and J. Boykoff (2004), "Balance as bias: global warming and the US pres-tige press", *Global Environmental Change*, **14**, 125–36.

Burkeman, O. (2003), "Memo exposes Bush's green new strategy", *The Guardian*, March 4, accessed August 9, 2020 at https://www.theguardian.com/environment/2003/mar/04/usnews.climatechange.

Chabukdhara, M. (2016), "Coal mining in Northeast India: an overview of environ-mental issues and treatment approaches", *International Journal of Coal Science and Technology*, **3**, 87–96.

Collins, E. (2019), *Big Oil's Real Agenda on Climate Change*, London: InfluenceMap.

de la Rochefoucauld, F. (1664 [2012]), *Maximes de la Rochefoucauld: Premier Texte Imprimé à la Haye en 1664*, Lexington, KY: Ulan Press.

Diamanti-Kandarakis, E., J.-P. Bourguignon and L.C. Giudice et al. (2009), "Endocrine-disrupting chemicals: an Endocrine Society scientific statement", *Endocrine Reviews*, **30** (4), 293–342.

Forests & Finance (n.d.) [website], accessed August 26, 2020 at https://forestsandfinance.org/.

Global Development Policy Center (2020), "China's Global Energy Finance" [data-base], Boston University.

Heal, G.M. (2016), *Endangered Economies: How the Neglect of Nature Threatens Our Prosperity*, New York: Columbia University Press.

Hefferman, O. (2019), "Seabed mining is coming – bringing mineral riches and fears of epic extinctions", *Nature*, **571** (7766), 465–68.

Henry, C. and L. Tubiana (2017), *Earth at Risk: Natural Capital and the Quest for Sustainability*, New York: Columbia University Press.

Hmiel, B., V.V. Petrenko and M.N. Dyonisius et al. (2020), "Preindustrial $^{14}CH4$ indicates greater anthropogenic fossil CH_4 emissions", *Nature*, **578** (7795), 409–12.

Hoggan, J. (2009), *Climate Cover-up: The Crusade to Deny Global Warming*, Vancouver: Greystone Books.

Howard, P., G. Parker and N. Jenner et al. (2020), *An Assessment of the Risks and Impacts of Seabed Mining on Marine Ecosystems: Executive Summary*, Cambridge, UK: Fauna & Flora International.

Intergovernmental Panel on Climate Change (IPCC) (2018), *Global Warming of 1.5°C*, Special Report, United Nations, October.

Intergovernmental Panel on Climate Change (IPCC) (2019), *Climate Change and Land*, Special Report, United Nations, August.

Intergovernmental Science-Policy Platform on Biodiversity and Ecosystem Services (IPBES) (2019), *Global Assessment Report on Biodiversity and Ecosystem Services*, United Nations, May.

Jacobs, A. (2019), "A shadowy industry group shapes food policy around the world", *The New York Times*, September 16, accessed August 10, 2020 at https://www.nytimes.com/2019/09/16/health/ilsi-food-policy-india-brazil-china.html.

Jouffray, J.-B., R. Blasiak and A.V. Norstrom et al. (2020), "The blue acceleration: the trajectory of human expansion into the ocean", *One Earth*, **2** (1), 43–54.

Kearns, C.E., S.A. Glantz and L.A. Schmidt (2015), "Sugar industry influence on the scientific agenda of the National Institute of Dental Research's National Caries Program: a historical analysis of internal documents", *PLoS Medicine*, **12** (3), e1001798.

Kearns, C.E., L.A. Schmidt and S.A. Glautz (2016), "Sugar industry and coronary heart disease research – a historical analysis of internal industry documents", *JAMA Internal Medicine*, **176** (11), 1680–85.

Kortenkamp, A., O. Martin and M. Faust et al. (2011), *State of the Art Assessment of Endocrine Disruptors*, Final Report to the European Commission, December 23.

Kreuder-Johnson, C., P.L. Hitchens and P.S. Pandit et al. (2020), "Global shifts in mammalian population trends reveal key predictors of virus spillover risk", *Proceedings of the Royal Society B: Biological Sciences*, **287** (1924), 201922736.

Leonard, C. (2019), *Kochland: The Secret History of Koch Industries and Corporate Power in America*, New York: Simon & Schuster.

Maddow, R. (2019), *Blowout: Corrupted Democracy, Rogue State Russia, and the Richest, Most Destructive Industry on Earth*, New York: Crown/Penguin Random House.

McGreal, C. (2019), *American Overdose – The Opioids Tragedy in Three Acts*, New York: Public Affairs.

McKibben, B. (2020), "Big Oil is using the coronavirus pandemic to push through the Keystone XL pipeline", *The Guardian*, April 5.

Mnif, W., A. Hassine and A. Bouaziz et al. (2011), "Effects of endocrine disruptor pesticides: a review", *International Journal of Environmental Resources and Public Health*, **8**, 2265–303.

Monbiot, G. (2019), "Shell is not a green saviour. It's a planetary death machine", *The Guardian*, June 26.

Montgomery, C. (2006), "Mr. Cool: nurturing doubt about climate change is big business", *Globe and Mail*, Toronto, August 12, accessed August 9, 2020 at https://web.archive.org/web/20110503192157/http://www.charlesmontgomery.ca/mrcool.html.

Moss, M. (2014), *Salt, Sugar, Fat – How the Food Giants Hooked Us*, New York: Random House.

Oreskes, N. and E. Conway (2010), *Merchants of Doubt*, New York: Bloomsbury Press.

Orwell, G. (1941), "Literature and totalitarianism", *Listener* [BBC radio broadcast], 21 May, accessed 9 August 2020 at https://www.orwell.ru/library/articles/totalitarianism/english/e_lat.

Pesticide Politics in Africa (2019), "The Arusha Call for Action on Pesticides Conference", Tropical Pesticides Research Institute, Arusha, Tanzania, May 31.

Picketty, T. (2014), *Capital in the Twenty-First Century*, Cambridge, MA: Harvard University Press.

Rainforest Action Network (2020), "Indonesia: on the frontlines of deforestation", in *Keep Forests Standing: Exposing Brands and Banks Driving Deforestation* (pp. 12–18), accessed August 26 at https://www.ran.org/wp-content/uploads/2020/03/RAN_Keep_Forests_Standing_vWEB.pdf.

Philippon, T. (2019a), *The Great Reversal: How America Gave Up on Free Markets*, Cambridge, MA: Belknap Press.

Philippon, T. (2019b), "Monopolies cost Americans $300 a month. We are no longer the land of the free markets", *The Guardian*, November 13.

Qiu, X. (2012), *Don't Cry, Tai Lake*, New York: St. Martin's Press.

Redd Monitor (2019), "Shell boss says 'Another Brazil in terms of rainforest' is needed to address climate change. Meanwhile, Shell continues to profit from fossil fuels", accessed August 9, 2020 at https://redd-monitor.org/2019/03/22/shell-boss-says-another-brazil-in-terms-of-rainforest-needed-to-address-climate-change-meanwhile-shell-continues-to-profit-from-fossil-fuels/.

Samways, M.J., P.S. Barton, K. Birkhofer and F. Chichorro (2020), "Solutions for humanity on how to conserve insects", *Biological Conservation*, **242**, 108427.

Sanchez-Bayo, F. and K. Wyckhuys (2019), "Worldwide decline of the entomofauna: a review of its drivers", *Biological Conservation*, **232**, 8–27.

Securities and Exchange Commission (SEC) (n.d.), "Section 1504: Dodd Frank Wall Street Reform Act", accessed August 26, 2020 at https://www.sec.gov/comments/s7-42-10/s74210-92.pdf.

Shell (2019), *Energy for a Better Future: Annual Report and Accounts 2019*, accessed August 9, 2020 at https://reports.shell.com/annual-report/2019/.

Siviter, H., J. Koricheva, M. Brown and E. Leadbeater (2018), "Quantifying the impact of pesticides on learning and memory in bees", *Journal of Applied Ecology*, **55** (6), 2812–21.

Smith, A. (1776), *An Inquiry into the Nature and Causes of the Wealth of Nations*, London: W. Strahan and T. Cadell, in the Strand.

Soroye, P., T. Newbold and J. Kerr (2020), "Climate change contributes to widespread declines among bumble bees among continents", *Science*, **367**, 685–8.

Souter, L.J., D. Herrera and D.J. Barrett et al. (2017), "Mining drives extensive deforestation in the Brazilian Amazon", *Nature Communications*, **8** (1), article 1013.

Steffen, W., J. Rockström and K. Richardson et al. (2018), "Trajectories of the Earth System in the Anthropocene", *Proceedings of the National Academy of Science*, **115** (33), 8252–9.

Stern, N. (2007), "Climate change, ethics and the economics of the global deal", Royal Economic Society annual public lecture, University of Manchester, *VoxEU.org*, 30 November, accessed August 9, 2020 at https://voxeu.org/article/climate-change -ethics-and-economics.

Spencer, S. and K. Greenhalgh (2020), "Chevron ups Permian Basin resource estimate to over 21 billion boe, double 2017 estimate", *S&PGlobal.org*, March 3, accessed August 9, 2020 at https://www.spglobal.com/platts/en/market-insights/latest-news/ natural-gas/030320-chevron-ups-permian-basin-resource-estimate-to-over-21-bil -boe-double-2017-estimate.

Stokstad, E. (2012), "Field research on bees raises concern about low-dose pesticides", *Science*, **335**, 1555–6.

Sverdrup-Thygeson, A. (2019), *Extraordinary Insects: Weird. Wonderful. Indispensable. The Ones Who Run Our World*, London: Mudlark/HarperCollins.

Total (2020), "Suriname: Total and Apache make significant discovery in Block 58" [press release], January 7, accessed August 9, 2020 at https://www.total.com/media/ news/press-releases/suriname-total-and-apache-make-significant-discovery-block -58.

Watson, R. (2019), "Biodiversity touches every aspect of our lives – so why has its loss been ignored?", *The Guardian*, September 19.

Watts, J. (2019), "Belt and Road Summit puts spotlight on Chinese coal funding", *The Guardian*, April 25.

World Economic Forum (WEF) (2020), *The Global Risks Report 2020*, accessed August 9, 2020 at http://www3.weforum.org/docs/WEF_Global_Risk_Report_2020 .pdf.

World Health Organization & Food and Agriculture Organization of the United Nations (WHO-FAO) (2018), *Global Situation of Pesticide Management in Agriculture and Public Health*, annual report.

World Health Organization (WHO), United Nations Children's Fund (UNICEF) and *The Lancet* (2020), "A future for the world's children?", *The Lancet Commissions*, **395** (10224), 605–58.

Wilcox, B.A. and B. Ellis (2006), "Forests and emerging infectious diseases of humans", *Unasylva*, **57** (224), 11–18.

Wildlands League (2019), *Boreal Logging Scars*, December 4, accessed August 9, 2020 at https://wildlandsleague.org/media/LOGGING-SCARS-FINAL-Dec2019 -Exec-Summary.pdf.

Section 2

Setting the scene

4. Costa Rica as pioneer of a green social contract

Monica Araya

INTRODUCTION

As society aims to combat climate change and inequality, Costa Rica offers the rare story of a small country that has over the years made bold decisions to address environmental and social problems. This chapter first outlines these bold choices and the significance of their legacy today as the country pursues a green economy with zero emissions, resilient and fair. Good public policies have made a difference, but local environmental activists have also played a pivotal role at key moments. Thanks to their efforts, Costa Rica reversed the decision to support oil-drilling plans by a US company, open-pit gold mining by a Canadian company and to build an oil refinery as part of a loan from China. Costa Rican civil society has also played a pioneering role in the promotion of zero-emissions electric mobility.

The chapter also looks at early efforts to promote carbon neutrality and why the Paris Agreement helped reset the button in Costa Rica by encouraging a framework for deeper decarbonization, not just carbon neutrality that is achieved through forest offsets that compensate previous emissions. The process leading to the Paris Agreement of 2015 helped Costa Rica rethink its national targets, opened the process for public discussion and engage a variety of stakeholders.

The third section focuses on the current developments. It looks at the efforts to make decarbonization a pillar of the narrative and governmental plans – both the National Development Plan and the National Decarbonization Plan to 2050. It looks at the logic of the National Decarbonization Plan and at how it integrates fairness and inclusiveness. The final section offers a brief reflection.

A HISTORY OF BOLD DECISIONS

Costa Rica's story of making bold decisions over the years could be instructive in the debate of how to win support for a greener and more inclusive economy.

The country made transformative decisions in the 1940s that opened the door for making bold choices later. Although Costa Rica is celebrated for protecting biodiversity and running on renewable electricity, the bold ideas that set the country on a distinct trajectory focused on protecting and investing in people, which in turn provided the political stability needed to make bold decisions, later on, to protect nature and pursue carbon neutrality.

Social Progress and Green Growth

The audacious decision to abolish the army in Costa Rica in 1948 – in a region where the military have had so much clout – freed up fiscal resources that went to social welfare and, perhaps even more important, having no army spared Costa Ricans from traumatic armed conflicts that have harmed so many Latin Americans over the years. Before that decision, social legislation had given workers a set of "social guarantees" in 1943, which included a critical right: universal access to free healthcare. This visionary approach to legislation protected workers from potential abuses from economic elites. One hundred years earlier, access to free public education had been guaranteed as well. Costa Rica was one of the first countries to grant education rights to women. Today, by constitutional obligation, the country must invest 8 percent of GDP in public education. Many of these social victories shaped the society. Today, with so much debate around inequality, amid social protests, Costa Rica's early investment in a social contract is a central part of the story.

Another bold decision was made in the 1970s: to invest in forest protection by creating a system of national parks. The timing of this decision is curious because it was made right when the logic of conquering nature for the sake of development and industrialization prevailed in the then-called "Third World". By the 1980s and early 1990s, cattle ranching had become a driver of deforestation. The mid-1990s marked a watershed because Costa Rica managed to reverse deforestation while growing the population and the economy. A system of payment for environmental services was pioneered to compensate owners of farms for not cutting trees and for preserving ecosystem services, such as watershed protection. Being the first country to reverse tropical deforestation shaped an enduring political narrative of green growth in which environmental protection and growth were not seen as clashing goals.

Today, Costa Rica runs on nearly 100 percent renewable electricity. Non-fossil-fuel power generation goes back several decades. Technically, economically and psychologically – this attribute has been a launching pad for going further in other sectors – for example, transportation. Because nearly 100 percent of the electricity comes from five renewable sources – hydropower, geothermal, wind, biomass and sun – Costa Rica is ideal for electric mobility (see the final section). In 2019, the state-owned utility discontinued plans to build the last hydropower dam, thus closing an era of hydropower investments. A major focus on diversity has been underway, with strong emphasis on geo-thermal and wind generation, which today represent 15 percent and 12 percent of power generation, respectively. Renewable electricity has also become a pillar of a green-economy discourse combining of elements of identity – "the country of renewable energy".

This rationale of differentiation – Costa Rica as a green economy with social stability – has been beneficial to attract tourism and generate income. In a small country of 5 million people, tourism has a direct contribution to the gross domestic product (GDP) of about 6.5 percent (the indirect contribution is 8 percent).

Bold Activism

Despite positive developments, tensions have emerged as in any other country. Over the years, some politicians have tried to put Costa Rica on a less green pathway. It is important to underscore the role that activism played whenever the country was at the brink of making mistakes. Three controversial proposals were made over a decade between 2002 and 2013: (1) to open Costa Rica for oil drilling; (2) to grant rights for gold mining; and (3) to take a loan from China to co-operate a $1.5 billion oil refinery.

The dream of prosperity through oil wealth and mining has never left some sectors in Costa Rica that view social and environmental regulations as expensive burdens that make Costa Rica more expensive for business compared to others in Central America. Often these voices promote a more traditional, dirtier, approach to growth – such as oil and gas as well as mining. Environmentalists have stopped these projects. Bold activists and conserva-tionists should be recognized for fighting politicians that have betrayed the vision of green economy with a respectable social contract. At times, life for activists and whistleblowers in Costa Rica has been difficult and a few even lost their lives. Environmentalism between 2001 and 2013 saved Costa Rica from making "U-turns" on environmental issues.

First, the country has had a moratorium on oil exploration and drilling since the 2002. This is the direct result of an environmental coalition of activists and experts. Although this ban on drilling is not law, it has survived five adminis-trations from three political parties: the Chinchilla administration (2010–14) extended it in 2011 with Executive Order 36693; the Solis administration (2014–18) extended it to 2021. In February 2019, President Alvarado extended the moratorium to 31 December of 2050 through Executive Order 41578.

Second, the country does not support mining activities. In November 2010, environmental activists helped overturn the push for gold mining by President Oscar Arias (2006–10) who had passed an executive order declaring the project in the "national interest". A tribunal stopped the project and ordered the company to compensate Costa Rica for the environmental impacts caused during the exploration. For the first time, a country in Latin America blocked future open-pit mineral mining: Congress adjusted the mineral law to prevent similar cases in the future.

Finally, in June 2013, activists, legal experts and Congress representatives also succeeded in making the government reverse its decision to take a loan from China to jointly own an oil refinery. Costa Rican experts from various backgrounds – law, economics, climate – argued the case against the governmental plans and lobbied against the loan: ethical concerns, constitutional reasons, and environmental concerns – including its contradiction to Costa Rica's narrative around green growth. The final blow came from an independent body in June 2013– the National Comptroller Office – when it rejected the project and the president had no green light to take a loan. The project was at a standstill for months and the following administration agreed to terminate it for good.

CARBON NEUTRALITY: PARIS AGREEMENT AS "GAME CHANGER"

On the road to the UN Climate Change Conference in Copenhagen, "COP15", in 2009, Costa Rica announced a goal to become carbon neutral. This vision took many by surprise and was announced without an execution plan. There was no clear pathway to achieve this aspirational goal and this period of bold vision with uncertainty culminated with the process leading to the UN Climate Change Conference in Paris, "COP21" in 2015. This is because each country was expected to have a plan and submit it as a contribution to the international community. Put simply, the logic of Paris Agreement helped Costa Rica put its house in order.

Carbon Neutrality Prior to Paris

Prior to Paris, Costa Rica had embraced "carbon neutrality" – which was the right instinct – at a time when other developing countries did not want to reduce their emissions. Back then, the Kyoto Protocol provided the international rules of engagement: only developed countries were obliged to cut emissions.

Costa Rica went alone and presented this vision at the COP15 in Copenhagen. The foundation underpinning carbon neutrality was acceptable at the time because no one was doing it and there was no simple way of achieving it. But the problem was that it was too heavily oriented toward the use of "carbon offsets" – which dominated the thinking back then. Costa Rica encouraged companies to reduce their environmental footprint and to "neutralize" emissions by supporting sustainable forest projects. The main legacy from those early days was the positive approach to climate action – countries wanted to be certified as "carbon neutral" – in contrast with corporate approaches in other economies that present climate action as a burden to profits. The most concrete legacy from that phase was the delivery of the world's "carbon-neutral coffee" since 2011. Pioneered by a rural cooperative of over 900 coffee farmers, Coopedota has evolved into an internationally recognized organization. Today the Ministry of Agriculture runs a project for the sector that is inspired by its early actions.

Paris Reset the Button in Costa Rica

The climate policy button was then reset on the road to Paris. The preparation for COP21 in Paris inspired several consultations to discuss the logic and scope of the national contribution to the Paris Agreement, and a more far-reaching approach by opening up a new debate on ways to achieve *absolute* reductions of greenhouse gases – for example, the need for an electric train – as opposed to previous debates that had operated under a more narrow logic of carbon offsets.

Costa Rica's Paris target was set as follows: to cut 25 percent of its greenhouse gas emissions to 2012 levels, which means a 44 percent emissions reduction compared to the business-as-usual scenario. The target received good international assessments, becoming one of the few countries in the developing world to offer an absolute reduction according to the global initiative, Climate Action Tracker. Today, the target is under revision to ensure it is aligned with the 1.5°C temperature imperative of the Paris Agreement. Another positive legacy from the process leading to the Paris Agreement was the creation of two councils on climate change: one made up of citizens and the other made up of scientists.

The road to Paris also energized civil society in Costa Rica. In June 2015, the first-ever consultation with Costa Rican citizens took place on climate change, organized by Costa Rica Limpia and the international organization World Wide Views, and bringing together citizens from the seven provinces. The results were shared with the Ministry of Environment and Energy as it prepared for COP21. Prior to the Paris Agreement, the citizen dimension had been absent from debates around carbon neutrality.

In addition to the debates around Paris and the new national reduction target, in 2015 public consultations were also carried out for the first time to provide feedback for the new National Energy Plan (2015–30). It included measures for power generation, efficiency, renewables and fuels. For the first time it integrated goals for transportation – the largest emitter in Costa Rica. For the first time, the Energy Plan set objectives to clean up fleets, public transit and promote much cleaner fuels.

Since 2015, the need to invest in sustainable transportation has gained prominence in the national debate. The Paris Agreement gave impetus to local advocates and Congress representatives to kickstart a debate around electrification of transportation, and this would culminate with the Congressional approval of the zero-emissions electric mobility law at the end of 2017. New work of a coalition of advocates, experts and representatives in Congress focused on decarbonization of transportation between 2016 and 2018 with a view to take decarbonization to the next level: why not become the first country to go fossil free? Box 4.1 illustrates key developments that set the regulatory framework as well as examples of efforts to engage citizens in the shift to fossil-free transportation.

BOX 4.1   DECARBONIZATION IN REAL LIFE: ENGAGING THE PUBLIC IN ZERO EMISSION ELECTRIC MOBILITY

Law 9518 provides incentives to zero-emission electric mobility of all types: cars, buses, motorbikes and e-bikes. The incentives apply to zero-emission battery electric transport as well as fuel-cell electric vehicles. It asks the state-owned utility to deploy infrastructure for charging battery electric vehicles by 2020 and to pass additional regulations and standards that are needed to execute the law. A National Plan for Electric Transport, Executive Order 41579 was published in February 2019 to set the basic rules for the deployment of electric vehicle infrastructure, tax benefits for cars and spare parts. The Plan also sets regulations to facilitate future manufacturing and assembly of electric vehicles in Costa Rica.

An electric mobility national commissioner was appointed in 2019 to coordinate governmental activities around e-mobility and engage with the private sector and users. To help bring the ministry on board, in February 2019, the Ministers of Environment and Energy and of Public Works and Transportation signed a sectoral agreement for the transportation sector to work together in the implementation of policies to reduce 4 Mt of CO_2 equivalent by 2050. The measures include public transport and to promote active modes of transportation such as biking and walking, as well as cargo logistics.

Most public charging in Costa Rica is free. In the first phase, about 100 public, semi-fast chargers are in place and about 34 fast chargers are to be in place by 2020. The public-service regulator set up the fee for fast-charging electric vehicles: 183 Costa Rican colones per kWh (approximately

US$0.32).

Several initiatives aim to increase the demand for electric mobility, both public and private. An electric bus pilot project will run three battery-electric buses in 2020 and the utility and Chinese vehicle and battery manufacturer, BYD, are already testing one bus in the capital. A private-sector company is testing a hydrogen bus in Guanacaste province. The feasibility study of a new electric train for great metropolitan area is underway.

Active efforts are in place to stimulate demand for electric vehicles as well: the state-owned utility acquired 100 electric cars. The postal service has started to electrify its fleet of 348 motorbikes. The national insurance company gives a 15 percent discount to electric vehicles. The first electric route for tourists was launched in Monteverde, Puntarenas by community organizers.

Costa Rica Limpia and the Costa Rican Association of Electric Mobility have played an active role in promoting a fossil-free vision for the country by working with Congresswoman Marcela Guerrero who led the legislative process, by breaking myths about the technology, educating public opinion and journalists, and by developing partnerships with the utility and the private sector. They have pioneered the concept of citizen festivals to promote electric mobility since 2017.

A PLAN TO 2050: A GREENER AND MORE INCLUSIVE SOCIETY

The political case for decarbonization entered a bolder phase in Costa Rica in 2018–20. First, in January 2018, when President Solís (2014–18) signed the new electric mobility law. That sent two powerful signals: one was that climate advocacy worked – the law had been conceived and pushed from the bottom up; it was not the Central Government's initiative – and the second was that incentives for electric mobility by law put Costa Rica in a leadership position because Law 9518 – providing incentives for all forms of electric mobility – was the first legislation of its kind in Latin America.

Second, in May 2018, the new president, Carlos Alvarado (2018–22), made international headlines with his inaugural speech by integrating the aspirational narrative of "becoming one of the first countries, if not the first one, to get rid of fossil fuels". This positioned Costa Rica as a country punching above its weight.

Third, in December 2018, the Alvarado administration presented the National Development Plan with its five pillars: economic growth, increasing employment, reducing poverty, decarbonizing the economy and reducing inequality. For each area, the Plan establishes specific indicators that will be used to report progress each year.

Fourth, the National Decarbonization Plan to 2050 was launched in February of 2019, followed by a citizen fair on decarbonization. This will provide a roadmap for each sector and responds to the Paris Agreement invitation to have mid-century decarbonization strategies by 2020. Costa Rica became one of the first developing countries to have such a strategy. The technical work took place between June 2018 and January 2019, including sectoral consultations. This economy-wide Plan organizes ten transformation routes along four clusters:

(1)   transport & sustainable mobility: (a) public transportation; (b) fleets & passenger cars; and (c) freight;
(2)   energy, green buildings & industry: (d) power sector; (e) buildings; and (f) industry;
(3)   integrated waste management: (g) waste management;
(4)   agriculture, land-use change & nature-based solutions: (h) agriculture; (i) livestock; and (j) biodiversity.

All the actions are organized around three periods: Beginning (2018–22), Inflection[1] (2023–30) and Massive Deployment (2031–50), with the focus of the current administration on the first phase.

From a sectoral perspective, cluster number one is critical because most of the emissions come from burning gasoline and diesel for transportation. The current approach to transportation is unsustainable, costing around $691 million a year due to congestion, $177 million due to poor air quality, $112 million due to noise and $17 million due to carbon pollution. This is only in the great metropolitan area – where nearly 60 percent of the population lives.

Beyond Emissions: Fairness, Inclusion and Human Rights

Because the transformation of the economy requires structural changes, the Plan complements sectoral routes with cross-cutting strategies in eight areas. This includes, for example, a green reform of the fiscal system, digitalization strategies and in-depth institutional reforms – for example, of the state-owned refinery.

The Plan aims to make Costa Rica a pioneer in the implementation of the Paris Agreement. However, the vision goes beyond a narrow logic of "emission cuts". It aims to build an economy that is green, with zero emissions and resilient but also fair. Costa Rica needs to reduce inequality in a country where about 21 percent of the population is poor. Efforts to green the economy need to be designed in a way that does not punish the socially vulnerable communities.

The Plan calls for the assessment of impacts from the measures to decarbonize each sector. It asks for the identification of the impacts of the measures on workers, because heavy impacts could decrease the political viability of decarbonization measures. Understanding the effects of the Plan on the labor market is crucial, according to the Plan, for the development of strategies for the "just transition" of Costa Rican workers. The Ministry of Labor will undertake this work, including the identification of best international practices on "just transition".

Human rights have also become an important priority for climate policy in Costa Rica: the importance of human rights was included in the national contribution to the Paris Agreement and it is one of the cross-cutting strategies of the Decarbonization Plan ("Inclusion, human rights and gender equality"). Some of the measures that it pursues are: encouraging gender parity and the integration of the National Institute for Women in climate governance, and promoting human rights and gender parity in international fora.

Costa Rica has been a champion of the "Regional Agreement on Access to Information, Public Participation and Justice in Environmental Matters in Latin America and the Caribbean", known as the Escazú Agreement. Signed in March 2018, in Escazú, Costa Rica, it is the first in the world containing specific provisions on environmental and human rights defenders. The first meeting of the signatories took place in San José, Costa Rica in October 2019. Given that Latin America is the region where many environmental defenders are murdered, this is a groundbreaking treaty.

FINAL WORDS: TOWARD A GREEN SOCIAL CONTRACT

How to build a green economy while reducing inequality? This is the defining question of our time and Costa Rica is pioneering both in social and environmental policies. This chapter has provided elements of the effort to combine these policies around a plan to 2050 that was approved in 2019 in response to the Paris Agreement on climate change.

Latin America is extremely vulnerable to climate change and highly unequal. The historical protests in Chile in October of 2019 – with the subsequent suspension of the UN Climate Conference, COP25, in Santiago – marked a watershed in the international community, especially in Latin America. Now more than ever, a big shift is needed to connect the dots and pursue agendas that aim to protect both people and nature.

This chapter has shown that the pioneering efforts to forge a social contract have paid off. The abolition of the army shaped a mindset that favored taking a "road less travelled". These political decisions from 1940s left a legacy that was favorable, it has been argued, to the promotion of environmental objectives in the 1970s and 1990s.

This decade, the most ambitious political vision – and plan – aims to make Costa Rica one of the world's first carbon-neutral countries withing a framework of fairness. The National Decarbonization Plan to 2050 offers transformative routes for all the sectors of the economy and includes a broader set of strategies involving inclusiveness, just transition, human rights and gender equality.

The execution of the Plan faces many challenges – for example, it entails a deep transformation of the fiscal architecture and a massive mobilization of financial resources. The Costa Rican experience will be a laboratory for the world not only in terms of decarbonization but also especially in terms of *fair* decarbonization. If execution goes well, the story of Costa Rica could inspire others to enable a new generation of bold, green social contracts in this defining decade for both the climate and inequality agendas.

NOTE

1.   An inflection in the emissions trajectory.

BIBLIOGRAPHY

Araya, M. (2016), "A small country with big ideas to get rid of fossil fuels", *TED Talks* [video], August 15, accessed May 1, 2020 at https://www.ted.com/talks/monica _araya_a_small_country_with_big_ideas_to_get_rid_of_fossil_fuels?language=en.

Araya, M. and Rodríguez, C.M. (2018), "The latest science must not paralyze us", *Project-syndicate.org*, October 8, accessed January 15, 2020 at https://www.project -syndicate.org/commentary/ipcc-report-dire-new-climate-change-conclusions-by -monica-araya-and-carlos-manuel-rodriguez-1-2018-10?barrier=accesspaylog.

Asamblea Legislativa (2018), *Ley 9518 de Incentivos al Transporte Eléctrico*, accessed January 15, 2020 at http://extwprlegs1.fao.org/docs/pdf/cos177932.pdf.

BBC (2010), "Costa Rica: fallo suspende proyecto de minería a cielo abierto", November 25, accessed May 1, 2020 at https://www.bbc.com/mundo/noticias/2010/ 11/101124_costa_rica_juicio_mineria_cielo_abierto_amab.

Birkenberg, A. and Birner, R. (2018), "The world's first carbon neutral coffee: lessons on certification and innovation from a pioneer case in Costa Rica", *Journal of Cleaner Production*, 189, 485–501.

Burgess, M. (2019), "Ad Astra strengthens H2 infrastructure in Costa Rica", *Gas World*, April 25, accessed March 1, 2020 at http://www.adastrarocket.com/pressReleases/ 2019/20190820-AdAstra-Aethera.pdf.

Central Bank of Costa Rica (2018), "Cuenta Satélite de Turismo", accessed January 15, 2020 at https://www.bccr.fi.cr/seccion-indicadores-economicos/cuenta-sat%C3 %A9lite-de-turismo.

Climate Action Tracker (2019), "Costa Rica", accessed 20 January 2019 at https:// climateactiontracker.org/countries/costa-rica/current-policy-projections/.

Dengo, M.E. (2001), *Educación Costarricense*, San José: EUNED.
EFE (2019), "Costa Rica extiende al año 2050 la moratoria para la exploración y explotación petrolera", February 25, accessed January 15, 2020 at https://www.efe.com/efe/america/economia/costa-rica-extiende-al-ano-2050-la-moratoria-para-exploracion-y-explotacion-petrolera/20000011-3908528.
Estrategia y Negocios (2018), "Grupo Q vende 100 autos eléctricos al ICE en Costa Rica", December 8, accessed May 1, 2020 at https://www.estrategiaynegocios.net/empresasymanagement/1240353-330/grupo-q-vende-100-autos-el%C3%A9ctricos-al-ice-en-costa-rica December 8.
Government of Costa Rica (2010), "Nota Verbal de la Embajada de Costa Rica en Alemania para la Secretaria de la convención Marco de Cambio Climático de las Naciones Unidas", January 29, accessed August 2019 at https://unfccc.int/files/meetings/cop_15/copenhagen_accord/application/pdf/costaricacphaccord_app2_2.pdf.
Government of Costa Rica (2019a), *National Decarbonization Plan 2018–2050*, San José, February.
Government of Costa Rica (2019b), *National Plan for Electric Transportation*, San José, February.
Parnell, J. (2013), "Costa Rica sacks climate advisor for criticising China oil loan", *Climatechangenews.com*, June 19, accessed March 1, 2020 at https://www.climatechangenews.com/2013/06/19/costa-rica-sacks-climate-advisor-for-criticising-china-oil-loan/.
Rodríguez, E. (1995), *Voces del 43*, San José: EUNED.
Silva, M. (1989), "La educación de la mujer en Costa Rica durante el siglo XIX", *Revista de Historia*, No. 20, accessed January 15 at https://www.revistas.una.ac.cr/index.php/historia/article/view/3265.
Soto, M. (2015), "Ciudadanos de Costa Rica opinaron en consulta mundial sobre el clima" *La Nación*, June 7, accessed January 15, 2020 at https://www.nacion.com/ciencia/medio-ambiente/ciudadanos-de-costa-rica-opinaron-en-consulta-mundial-sobre-clima/IH76D2ECYJEUFO3MSFNPAMRERA/story/.
Utgard, B. and Araya, M. (2017), "Electrifying emerging markets: the case of Costa Rica", paper presented at EVS30 Symposium Stuttgart, Germany, October 9–11, accessed March 1, 2020 at https://www.researchgate.net/publication/320434099_Electrifying_emerging_markets_the_case_of_Costa_Rica.

5.   The carbon tax in Sweden

Thomas Sterner

INTRODUCTION

To have a reasonable chance of avoiding the worst effects of climate change, the level of carbon dioxide (CO_2) in the atmosphere needs to be stabilized as soon as possible. This basically means that the whole world must stop emitting carbon completely within the space of less than two generations. For the rich and developed countries, it is reasonable to demand more, leaving a little more room for the poorest countries to adapt a little more slowly. A suitable goal would be decarbonization by 2050. It also happens to be the official goal in Sweden for 2045 and luckily, there is some degree of unity around this goal even though the environmentalists would like to set the date to 2040 and the conservatives maybe 2050 or 2060.

The crucial question is, of course, how is this to be done? Activists often focus on demanding percentage reductions, plans or laws. There is, however, no guarantee that these instruments have any effect. A price of carbon is different. It takes effect automatically in a market economy. Societies are complex and there are numerous policy instruments at various levels. This ranges from the European Community with its plans and its instruments (in particular, the EU Emissions Trading Scheme for climate permits for large industry) to the level of municipalities that plan and permit industries and other economic activities at the local level. Sweden has followed in the footsteps of the United Kingdom in implementing climate legislation and planning (Government Offices, 2008). It has followed Germany in subsidizing renewables, but the most striking feature of Swedish policy is the carbon tax.

Economists often put much emphasis on carbon taxation as the prime instrument of climate policy. One of the reasons for this is that in a market economy, affecting the price of a good or resource will typically be (1) the most effective way of changing resource allocation, and also it is (2) the most all-encompassing, and (3) the most compatible with consumer and producer sovereignty. Let me start with the last of these points. In reverse order:

3. To achieve decarbonization, many everyday choices have to be affected: how and where we build our houses, how we commute to work, what we wear and what we eat. But instead of telling everyone what to eat, how long to shower and whether to go by bike or by (electric) car, we just set the price of carbon – which affect the prices of gasoline, fuel oil, electricity, metals, cars and so on – and then let people make their own individual choices based on their preferences, health, age and other circumstances. Thanks to the price of carbon these individual decisions will automatically take account of the need to quickly phase out carbon and provide incentives for producers and entrepreneurs to find new ways of satisfying consumer demand in a more sustainable manner.

2. We also have the engineering approach. We tell the car companies to build more energy-efficient cars. Sweden has started ambitious and exciting projects in collaboration between the state and business to develop carbon-free steel and carbon-free cement. These are exciting and ambitious projects but at the end of the day, we still need a price on carbon. Otherwise, people will think of NEW ways to burn fossil fuels – new products ranging from anything like heating pools in the winter to the senseless so-called "mining" of bitcoins that now accounts for so much electricity that it requires numerous mega-sized power plants to produce. Thus, to set a price on carbon would be the most efficient tool to encompass a broad set of products and disincentivize the use of fossil fuels.

1. By respecting consumer sovereignty, incentivizing new technology and by covering as many uses as possible, carbon pricing tends to achieve emission reductions much more cheaply than through mandated programs in which government just tells firms and consumers what to do.

Experts argue what the optimal level of a carbon tax should be, and estimates start at about €50/ton of CO_2 (see, e.g., Edenhofer et al., 2019). Only one or two countries come close to this and the country with the highest tax, which has been imposed for a substantial time, is Sweden, with a tax of above €100/ ton. The carbon tax was introduced in 1991 at a rate corresponding to SEK250 (€24) per ton of fossil carbon dioxide and has gradually been increased (see Swedish Government, 1994). In 2019 it was SEK 1180 (€115).[1] By increasing the tax level gradually and in a stepwise manner, households and businesses have had time to adapt, which has improved the political feasibility of tax increases. The CO_2 tax and the use of revenues is determined following general Swedish national budgetary rules (Swedish Government, 2009). A central element is not to earmark tax revenues, but instead the spending of the tax revenues is decided in the normal, annual, national budget process. People wonder about what measures have been taken to address, inter alia, distributional consequences of CO_2 taxation. The truth is that there are few obvious answers to this question. On the other hand, Sweden is well known as being one of the countries that already has an unusually even income distribution and very active state programs to complement the market for various social programs. When industries close, the famous active labor market policies are used to retrain workers. In this case, there were very significant programs to insulate large apartment buildings already in the 1970s and 1980s as a response to the oil crises. Other examples of complementary policies include public transport and "public heating" – in other words, centralized district heating that provides very cheap heating to a majority of the population.

As mentioned, there is uncertainty about the optimal tax level and indeed there are people who think a tax may not be enough to do the job, but since so few countries have tried, Sweden with its unusually long history of a high carbon tax provides an interesting case study.

As is to be expected, once the tax is in place it has the effect of leading Swedish agents to economize in various ways on carbon emissions. Although we will see that there are some interesting details, exceptions, and some difficulties in definitively pinning down the effect, we show that in broad terms carbon intensity has fallen as expected. In most respects the carbon tax has worked smoothly and not triggered more opposition or discussion than other taxes, maybe even to the contrary. The bigger question marks are over why it was possible to introduce it in Sweden and how readily this experience can be transferred to other countries. We try therefore to give a broad background that suggests some explanations as to why this tax reform was possible in Sweden when it has been so elusive elsewhere.

A BRIEF CONTEXT IN TERMS OF GEOGRAPHY, POLITICS, RESOURCES AND HISTORY

The introduction of carbon taxes in Sweden should be seen within a historical context that focuses in particular on its resource base and its tax system. We start with the latter. Sweden has been a high-tax country for a long time. The Social Democrats had uninterrupted power for about half a century until 1976. The party supports provision of social welfare funded by progressive taxation, which largely shaped the Swedish tax system during the party's time in power. In the 1930s, taxes rose sharply and in the 1940s income tax differentiation became more common and more pronounced. By the 1960s, marginal taxes were around 70 percent and during the late 1970s they reached 90 percent. The speed of this change was partly due to the socialist aspirations of the ruling party but also due to the unintended consequences of inflation, which implied that tax rates originally designed for the very rich suddenly began to affect ordinary income earners. Anecdotally, the marginal tax rates were said to be even higher and the very popular children's book author Astrid Lindgren famously claimed to be paying 102 percent on her royalties. This is likely apocryphal but was highly influential. In the major tax reform of 1990/91, the big issue was the lowering of income taxation (Swedish Green Tax Commission, 1997). There was also major discontent concerning a whole battery of progressive taxes: wealth taxes, inheritance taxes, property taxes, and so on, which were reduced or abolished.

For the average person, the most striking aspect of the reform was the simplification of taxes which started in 1991 and has continued since then. Instead of saving receipts for so-called deductible items and employing accountants and spending long days preparing tax returns, most young people nowadays simply do it with a few clicks on their mobile phone! The taxes were lower, but most exemptions had also been abolished. It seems that this reduced manipulations but also the burden of tax preparation, and on the whole, this was well received.

At the same time there was general agreement on not cutting down too much of the "welfare state" – that is, state expenditure – or revenue. The solution was to broaden tax bases, reduce deductions, simplify, lower direct tax rates and increase indirect taxation (Agell, Englund and Södersten, 1996). In this context, the carbon tax was first not a big issue per se, and second perceived rather as being a part of the solution and not seen as a new problem. A contributing factor to why this could be the case is related to environmental awareness and resource base factors in Sweden.

Sweden also has a fairly peculiar history and resource base. It industrialized late and most people have a strong connection to their rural roots as farmers. There is a big interest in environmental issues. It is also like Canada, a sparsely populated country with ample resources of hydropower and much forestry. There are, however, no fossil-fuel resources. Apart from some peat, Sweden simply does not have any coal deposits, oil or natural gas worth exploiting and thus also does not have any major companies in these industries. This means that there is a notable absence of the anti-climate lobbying that is frequently found in economies with rich fossil endowments. Oil and other fossil fuels have thus always been imported and there are always some traces of mercantilist thinking that make it much easier for politicians to resort to taxing imports than export industries. Sweden has a severely cold climate and we have always had a concern for fuel dependency and fuel security. This has also favored policies for energy efficiency, biomass use, collective solutions for urban (district) heating and public transport – and again taxes. Two other features of the Swedish economy and political system that came to have some importance for the actual implementation of the carbon tax are (1) a relatively low level of corruption and high degree of trust in the political system; and (2) a very skewed distribution of industrial size with a small number of very large firms (ABB, Volvo, IKEA, etc.) and relatively less importance of small or mid-sized firms.

The introduction of CO_2 taxation was, as mentioned, just a small part of the (partial) funding of this reform that overall implied dramatically lower taxes on capital and labor. The political opportunity to introduce this rather unique tax consisted of the confluence of two separate political processes. On the one hand, there was a demand for a drastic reduction in marginal income tax rates, which had reached very high levels. At the same time there was an increasing interest in environmental issues. The CO_2 tax was thus introduced at a moment when there was a need to fill a gap created by reduced taxes on other factors of production (Hammar and Åkerfeldt, 2011). As the propaganda against carbon taxes often revolves around avoiding an increase in general taxation, it may be worth pointing out that the introduction of carbon taxes in Sweden in no way increased overall taxes. On the contrary the "burden" of taxation has decreased by about 10 percentage points of GDP since 1990.

CARBON PRICING IN SWEDEN

As mentioned, the CO_2 tax was introduced in 1991. The tax has grown fast, but changes have been implemented stepwise so that households and companies have had time to adapt. Typically, tax increases for companies and households in the energy and environmental areas have been combined with general tax relief in other areas in Sweden in order to avoid increases in the overall level of taxation, address undesirable distributional consequences and stimulate job growth (Hammar and Åkerfeldt, 2011). Due to its cold climate, Sweden reacted strongly to the "oil crises" of the 1970s and started ambitious programs of renovating the building stock to mitigate and avoid the existence of problems of "energy poverty".

The distributional fairness has thus not been a dominant item in the debate. Analyses show that the different deciles of the income distribution pay roughly the same income share on transport fuels, so in this sense there is no big distributional effect (Berg and Forsfält, 2012). In France, the situation is somewhat similar for road transport but one significant difference between France and Sweden is a larger problem in France with low-income households who struggle to pay their heating bills. In Sweden, the quality of housing and retrofit investments appear to have largely solved this problem. In Sweden, the dominant problem with a carbon tax was perceived risk of losing jobs: an essential aspect when designing the energy taxation system has been to strike a balance between fulfilling environmental objectives and accounting for the risks of carbon leakage (the risk that business moves outside Sweden to countries with laxer environmental regulations and taxes) (Sumner, Bird and Dobos, 2011).

Industry was initially granted an exception and only paid a quarter of the tax (which is still a very high tax by international standards). Given the considerable importance of a handful of big companies it was very important to avoid disruptive effects on competitivity, but now these exceptions have been abolished. In fact, since 1991, the number of exceptions and their level have generally been reduced as the governments have successively chipped away the various tax expenditures. There is today one major exception, and that is that Sweden was obliged to remove the CO_2 tax within the industries that are part of the cap and trade program, the EU Emissions Trading Scheme, since it conflicts with the EU principle against double taxation (Swedish Energy Agency, 2012).

Within the framework of this brief chapter, we cannot establish causality, but we can point to the fact that Sweden has seen big reductions in carbon intensity, particularly in the sectors where the full tax is applied. This is the case, for example, in the district heating sector, where district heating is very common. Instead of using oil, the district heating system mainly uses wood, biomass, heat pumps and waste heat from industry or waste incineration. Houses are well insulated and generally use less energy for heating than what is common in warmer countries in Central or Southern Europe.

When it comes to the transport sector, we can broadly take the whole of the Organisation for Economic Co-operation and Development (OECD) experience as a natural laboratory. In virtually the whole of Europe and Japan, fuel taxes are high, while other countries such as the US have low levels of taxation, and countries such as Australia, Canada and New Zealand are somewhat intermediate (OECD, 2018). Sweden is thus not unique when it comes to fuel taxes – they are high across the continent and the only difference is that they are overtly called CO_2 taxes in Sweden rather than just fuel taxes – but they are assumed to have the same effect. The differences with prices in most European countries are sizeable, being far in excess of twice as high as US prices and consumption per capita less than half (see, for instance, Sterner, 2007 or Andersson, 2019).

CONCLUDING REMARKS

A CO_2 tax assumes that different fossil fuels are taxed strictly according to actual CO_2 emissions. The Swedish experience can be summarized by increased tax levels over time and steps taken towards a more uniform national price on fossil CO_2. Moreover, the CO_2 tax base is only moderately sensitive to price changes (particularly in the short run) when it comes to petrol and diesel, implying quite stable tax revenues but only slow decarbonization. When Sweden today wants to become fossil free in a short period of time it is difficult to rely only on carbon taxation in the transport sector. In particular, since the

EU does not appear to understand or accept the motive for Swedish carbon taxes and therefore does not accept the exception it has for biofuels. Currently, Sweden has now (in the transport sector) resorted to regulation concerning the phase-out of fossil components in transport fuel (a fossil-fuel replacement mandate) instead of relying entirely on the carbon tax. On the other hand, the CO_2 tax seems to have had a major impact on fuels used for heating purposes, where biofuels and other non-fossil energy sources (such as energy from waste and surplus heat from industrial processes) have significantly increased their shares. Ironically, this means that there are now very low tax revenues (in the heating sector) from the carbon tax in Sweden. In fact, Sweden generally has quite a small share of tax revenues from environmental taxes. Sometimes this is misinterpreted as saying that the Swedish carbon (and other environmental) taxes are not efficient or do not apply everywhere. The opposite is true. The tax has been so effective and over such a long time that tax base erosion has set in – we simply don't use any oil for heating anymore!

The Swedish experience thus shows that once a tax is put in place – it works. This is not really surprising. At this level, economics is quite simple: if things are expensive, people economize. The Swedish experience also shows that emission reductions can be combined with economic growth. During the 1990–2010 period, the CO_2 equivalent emissions were reduced by 8 percent, while at the same time economic activity increased by 51 percent. Since then the same pattern has continued. In addition to the above, a further important advantage of a tax (as compared with a cap and trade program) is that the tax works well together with other instruments of climate and energy policy such as green certificates, subsidies to renewables, regulations that have been introduced after (or in some cases before) the tax.

The bigger question of why Sweden was able to introduce a carbon tax when other countries have failed (and implicitly how can it be spread to other countries) is more complex. Sweden does have some obvious starting points: it has no fossil fuels and hence no producer lobbyists. I think this is very important. Furthermore, most Swedish industry is in manufacturing and mechanical engineering; there are relatively few big energy users to form a lobby. Finally, Sweden did have abundant hydro, biomass, other renewables, and also nuclear industries that probably did not object to carbon pricing (see also Criqui, Jaccard and Sterner, 2019 for a discussion of the differences between Canadian, French and Swedish experiences with introducing carbon taxes).

Due to Sweden's particular history and resource base, the Swedish experience may not be exactly transferable to other countries but there are aspects of the design of the tax that can be taken onboard. A further line of analysis emphasizes that the Swedish carbon tax was introduced as part of a total tax reform that was driven by many other goals and ambitions – it was not an isolated carbon tax. The question of "refunding" carbon taxes never arose – the revenues were needed to fund other tax reductions and public goods provision. This has the advantage of respecting the usual budgetary process. Presumably, an important boundary condition is that Swedish governments generally do take some income distribution and legitimacy issues into account. The group of people in society who feel that everything is unfair may have been somewhat smaller than in other countries where attempts at fuel taxation have been resisted more vehemently – but this is speculation.

NOTE

1.   Based on an exchange rate of 10.23 SEK/€ on January 1, 2019.

REFERENCES

Agell, J., Englund, P. and Södersten, J. (1996). "Tax reform of the century – the Swedish experiment". *National Tax Journal*, **49** (4), 643–64.
Andersson, J. (2019). "Carbon taxes and CO_2 emissions: Sweden as a case study". *American Economic Journal: Economic Policy*, **11** (4), 1–30.
Berg, C. and Forsfält, T. (2012). "Samhällsekonomiska effekter av energi- och koldioxidskatteförändringar som beslutades av riksdagen 2009" [Socioeconomic effects of energy and carbon dioxide tax changes decided by the Riksdag in 2009]. *Fördjupnings-PM*, No. 10. Konjunkturinstitutet.
Criqui, P., Jaccard, M. and Sterner, T. (2019). "Carbon taxation: a tale of three countries". *Sustainability*, **11** (22), 6280.
Edenhofer, O., Flachsland, C. and Kalkuhl, M. et al. (2019). "Options for a carbon pricing reform: expertise by MCC and PIK for the German Council of Economic Experts". Mercator Research Institute on Global Commons and Climate Change. Accessed August 10, 2020 at https://www.mcc-berlin.net/fileadmin/data/B2.3 _Publications/Working%20Paper/2019_MCC_Options_for_a_Carbon_Pricing _Reform_ExecSum_final.pdf.
Hammar, H. and Åkerfeldt, S. (2011). "La imposición del CO_2 en Suecia: 20 años de experiencia, mirando hacia el futuro" [CO_2 taxation in Sweden: 20 years of experience and looking ahead]. In Centro de Innovación del Sector Público de la Fundación de PwC e IE Business School, *Fiscalidad Verde en Europa: Objetivo 20/20/20* (pp. 16–25). Accessed August 10, 2020 at https://foes.de/pdf/2012-05-29 _Fiscalidad_verde_ok4.pdf.
Organisation for Economic Co-operation and Development (OECD) (2018). *Effective Carbon Rates 2018: Pricing Carbon Emissions Through Taxes and Emissions Trading*. Paris: OECD Publishing.
Sterner, T. (2007). "Fuel taxes: an important instrument for climate policy". *Energy Policy*, **35** (6), 3194–202.
Sumner, J., Bird, L. and Dobos, H. (2011). "Carbon taxes: a review of experience and policy design considerations". *Climate Policy*, **11** (2), 922–43.
Swedish Energy Agency (2012). *Energy in Sweden 2011*. Ekilstuna.
Swedish Government (1994). *Lag (1994:1776) om skatt på energi* [Law (1994:1776) on Tax on Energy]. Accessed http://www.notisum.se/rnp/Sls/lag/19941776.htm.

Swedish Government (2008). *Regeringens proposition 2008/09:162: En sammanhållen klimat- och energipolitik – Klimat* [Government Bill 2008/09:162: A Coherent Climate and Energy Policy – Climate]. Accessed April 2, 2020 at http://www.sweden.gov.se/sb/d/11547/a/122778.

Swedish Government (2009). *Regeringens proposition 2009/10:41: Vissa punktskattefrågor med anledning av budgetpropositionen för 2010* [Government Bill 2009/10:41: Certain Excise Tax Issues Due to the Budget Bill for 2010]. Accessed April 2, 2020 at http://www.regeringen.se/sb/d/11453/a/134192.

Swedish Green Tax Commission (1997). *Taxation, Environment, and Employment.* Stockholm: Fritzes.

6. Lessons from the Obama White House: how climate policy really gets done

Alice C. Hill

On January 20, 2009, then 47-year-old Barack Obama stood on the steps of the United States Capitol, his wife, Michelle Obama, by his side. He placed his left hand on the Bible held by his wife, raised his right hand, and took the oath of office to become the 44th President of the United States of America. The son of a white mother from Kansas and a black father from Africa, his inauguration was historic for many reasons. Not least among them was the fact that he would be the first president of the United States to develop a plan to tackle multiple aspects of climate change – mitigating greenhouse gas emissions, preparing for the impacts, and leading internationally on climate change policy. Just days before the November 2008 election, Obama vowed that his presidency "would mark a new chapter in America's leadership on climate change that will strengthen our security and create millions of new jobs in the process."[1] It would take two terms in office to accomplish that vision. But, at the end of eight years in the White House, Obama left a legacy of climate policy that set the country on the course of, for the first time ever, tackling the dire threat of global warming. For those efforts, he has earned place in history as the "first climate president."[2]

This chapter examines how President Obama wrote that new chapter on United States climate policy. It looks at how, despite limited success in his first term, the president used his second term to significant advantage in achieving historic progress on climate change. Three factors contributed greatly to that progress. First, Superstorm Sandy struck right before the 2012 presidential election and provided the nation with a graphic illustration of what was at stake with climate change. The president and his team almost immediately put that picture to good use as they advocated for increased climate action. Second, winning his re-election campaign in many ways freed the president from worrying about political opposition to his climate efforts. Re-election allowed him to push climate policies despite strong political headwinds. And, third, once safely re-elected, the president recruited the consummate political insider, John Podesta, to set the framework for accomplishing his climate goals. Podesta was put in charge of making sure the federal bureaucracy did what it was supposed to do and then communicating, communicating, and communicating some more about what the executive branch was doing to fight climate change.

OBAMA'S UNEVEN START

Almost immediately after President Obama first took office in January 2009, he started writing the first lines of the new climate chapter he had promised to the American people. More than three decades earlier, the National Academy of Sciences had warned then President Jimmy Carter that because the climate system had a "built-in time delay," postponing action on climate change until the impacts emerged was in fact the "riskiest strategy."[3] After Carter's defeat in 1980, however, the issue received scant presidential attention.[4] Precious time had been lost and now President Obama had a chance to finally reverse course.

He quickly issued an executive order establishing the White House Office of Energy and Climate Change Policy and appointed a climate czar to run it. Within his first month in office, and with the global economy in freefall, he signed a $787 billion stimulus package that included a host of "green" programs to promote clean energy, battery development, improvements to the electrical grid, and energy efficiency. A Climate Change Adaptation Task Force with representatives from over 20 federal agencies was launched. And in October 2009, Obama issued his first executive order directing federal agencies to set goals for sustainability and begin adaptation planning.

But as early as the summer of 2009, it was reported that the White House had come to view discussions about climate change as a political liability.[5] In subsequent months, momentum began to falter. Just shy of finishing his first year in office, Obama appeared in the final hours of the United Nations Framework Convention on Climate Change Conference of Parties in Copenhagen. His performance, however, proved a major disappointment to attendees when the talks resulted in an agreement that fell far short of original hopes for reductions in emissions.[6] The outcome was so bare bones that even Obama himself conceded that people were "justified in being disappointed."[7] And then the 2010 mid-term elections saw the Republicans gain control of the US House of Representatives, which gave the president, in his own words, a "shellacking."[8]

By the following summer, Obama's signature legislative push to cut greenhouse gas emissions, known as the Waxman-Markey Bill, died in the Senate before it even came to a vote. In 2011, the White House Office of Energy and Climate Change Policy folded after Congress denied funding. Obama's stimulus package, the American Recovery and Reinvestment Act of

2009, contained provisions to increase spending on green energy but received withering partisan criticism for financing a half-billion-dollar loan to a solar manufacturer called Solyndra that subsequently went bankrupt.[9] The administration failed to issue the Clean Power Plan despite a settlement agreement that required the Environmental Protection Agency (EPA) to publish final rules for new and existing power plants' emissions by May 2012.[10] To be sure, there were successes, including an historic agreement with automakers to improve fuel efficiency standards, a measure they had long resisted. Yet, despite some progress, in Obama's January 2012 State of the Union Address, the issue of climate change received nothing more than a glancing mention.[11] During the entire 2012 campaign season, neither he nor his Republican opponent Mitt Romney seemed to have any public appetite for the issue.[12] Neither they, nor the moderators, raised it during the public candidate debates.

Toward the end of President Obama's first term, environmentalists reportedly started marking the number of months that went by between times the president uttered the phrase "climate change."[13] As Daniel Kammen, founding director of the Renewable & Appropriate Energy Laboratory at the University of California, Berkeley, put it, "The first term was essentially lost territory."[14]

A BOOST FROM SUPERSTORM SANDY

Superstorm Sandy struck on October 29, 2012, just days before the 2012 presidential election. It was, no question, a serious crisis for the president and the nation. Sandy impacted 24 states, stretching roughly 1000 miles in diameter.[15] It cut off power to more than 8 million people.[16] The storm caused what was then the second largest blackout in US history, and the third largest overall.[17] Without power, daily life ground to a halt for people as the region's economy and infrastructure sputtered. Schools were closed, hospitals were evacuated, and planes and trains stopped running.[18]

Just days after the storm struck, President Obama was re-elected. He and his team would adhere to the advice his first Chief of Staff, Rahm Emanuel, famously offered shortly before Obama's first election, namely, "You never want a serious crisis to go to waste."[19] Sandy had given the nation a graphic lesson on just how painful the impacts of climate change would be. In its wake, the Obama administration would repeatedly invoke Superstorm Sandy to push for greater climate action by the United States. Indeed, when President Obama issued his Climate Action Plan the summer after Sandy, he again referenced the storm, noting, "We can choose to believe that Superstorm Sandy, and the most severe drought in decades, and the worst wildfires some state have ever seen were all just a freak coincidence. Or we can choose to believe in the overwhelming judgment of science – and act before it's too late."[20]

Throughout Obama's second term, members of his administration continued to reference Sandy, as they sought to push a climate agenda. In 2014, Obama directed the Department of Energy to conduct a quadrennial energy review to look at vulnerabilities from climate change, including the type of fallout from the failure of the energy sector during Sandy.[21] In 2015, building on a recommendation from the Hurricane Sandy Rebuilding Task Force, President Obama issued an executive order requiring all future federal investments in or near the floodplain to be resilient to climate change-exacerbated flooding. In 2015, the president's National Security Advisor, Susan Rice, referenced the storm and its destruction in a policy speech about the need to prepare for the national security risks from climate change.[22] On the third anniversary of the storm, Shaun Donovan, the head of the Office of Management and Budget in the White House, wrote that since Superstorm Sandy, the Obama administration had "led the Federal government in integrating resilience into the fabric of how we build, rebuild, plan, and prepare for the impacts of climate change."[23]

THE NO-HOLDS-BARRED SECOND-TERM AGENDA

When President Obama won his re-election campaign, he was largely set free from the political constraints on climate change that had hampered his first four years. He immediately "put energy and the environment at the top of his second-term agenda."[24] Indeed, in his second inaugural address on January 21, 2013, he pledged that his administration would "respond to the threat of climate change, knowing that the failure to do so would betray our children and future generations."[25] He took a no-holds-barred approach to achieving historic results in the fight to address global warming.

And the accomplishments began to roll. In the summer of 2013, he announced his Climate Action Plan on a sweltering July day in Washington, DC during a speech devoted solely to climate change. Cobbled together in secrecy in the White House, that plan set out his overall vision for climate change – mitigating greenhouse gas emissions, preparing for the impacts, and leading internationally on climate change policy. In the face of Congressional inaction, Obama increasingly focused on what he could accomplish by going it alone. He issued executive order after executive order, created hundreds of climate policies, and went on to reach the historic Paris Agreement in 2015.[26] His climate policies ranged from creating a wildfire building standard for federal buildings to issuing the Clean Power Plan to requiring the national security apparatus to plan for the national security risks posed by climate change. He also put one of the most effective insiders in Washington, John Podesta, in charge of his climate efforts. Podesta had served as President Bill Clinton's Chief of Staff, was an ardent environmentalist, and knew how to navigate Washington's bulging bureaucracy. Podesta offered the necessary leadership to make sure the president's climate agenda was accomplished.

"BEFORE PODESTA AND AFTER PODESTA"

In late 2013, President Obama recruited John Podesta to serve as his counselor. John Podesta had served as White House Chief of Staff to President Bill Clinton and spent years working on Capitol Hill in various positions. He also founded the Center for American Progress, a progressive think tank in Washington.[27] Podesta had a reputation for knowing how to get things done in Washington and Obama wanted him to oversee the implementation of the Climate Action Plan.[28] Podesta's arrival marked a change in the White House's approach to climate work. Or, as one Democratic strategist put it according to the *Atlantic*, "You can divide the Obama administration's environmental policy-making into BP and AP. Before Podesta and After Podesta."[29]

Shortly after his arrival, Podesta gathered White House officials and agency leaders for a Saturday morning meeting to scope out the implementation of the Climate Action Plan in the coming year. The meeting covered everything from creating a sense of urgency in the American public to increasing resilience to issuing EPA rules for lowering emissions. Podesta established a regular meeting schedule for leaders across the federal agencies working on the president's climate agenda.

He put to good use his experience working with Washington's notoriously ponderous bureaucracy. For the newly created "climate team," he made clear that, at least for purposes of his weekly climate meetings, reports of hosting a meeting or making contact with potential collaborators carried little value. Of course Podesta knew that such meetings were necessary. But having a meeting was different from achieving results. Podesta was interested in results. He wanted to hear about policies, initiatives, and partnerships created and acted upon. It did not take long for those assembled to assimilate the lesson he conveyed. They sensed that, under Podesta's leadership, they had a precious opportunity to change the trajectory on climate change.

Podesta supported the use of executive orders to accomplish goals that would otherwise die on Capitol Hill. He conveyed to federal bureaucrats and political appointees alike that now was the time to get climate policy done. He brokered fights between competing agencies, including one over the scope of a federal flood risk management standard to avoid Superstorm Sandy-like flood damage in the future. Podesta's weekly climate meetings began yielding identifiable results. The Obama administration had begun to deliver a startling array of accomplishments, ranging from the release of masses of federal climate data to new pollution standards for power plants to the billion-dollar National Disaster Resilience Competition. According to Todd Stern, the State

Department's climate envoy, Podesta understood "how to make things happen, and how to make things work in an administration and from the perch of the White House."[30]

Podesta also insisted that the White House communications team develop a strategy and schedule to communicate every new climate policy. The team created a rhythm of announcements, making sure that some new project, initiative, or policy hit the news cycle every week. A constant flow of fresh announcements succeeded in creating a public impression that the entire federal government was firing on all cylinders to combat climate change.[31] And that flow lasted up to the very last days of President Obama's second term.

WILL IT BE ENOUGH?

Just as Barack Obama's first inauguration was historic, so was his presidency. He proved himself to be the first climate president. Taking advantage of Sandy's destruction to make the case for further climate action and bringing in a consummate political insider to craft the efforts, Obama pushed forward a climate agenda that remains unprecedented in its scope and range. The effort, of course was warranted. As he observed, "No challenge – no challenge – poses a greater threat to future generations than climate change."[32]

Yet, the election of the 45th President of the United States, Donald J. Trump, has made clear that even an historic effort in a second term may not be able to withstand a change in who occupies the White House. Much of the fine policy work done by President Obama and his team began to unravel almost immediately after the new president placed his hand on the Bible and was sworn into office. President Obama's second-term climate policy accomplishments proved highly vulnerable to undoing by a president who called climate change a "hoax."[33] Undoubtedly, Obama left an historic legacy on climate change. The question that remains, as even Podesta, his trusted counselor, has noted, is whether "50 years from now, is that going to seem like enough?"[34]

NOTES

1. John M. Broder, "Obama affirms climate change goals," *New York Times*, November 18, 2008, accessed August 17, 2020 at https://www.nytimes.com/2008/11/19/us/politics/19climate.html.
2. John Abraham, "Barack Obama is the first climate president," *The Guardian*, November 2, 2016, accessed August 17, 2020 at https://www.theguardian.com/environment/climate-consensus-97-per-cent/2016/nov/02/barack-obama-is-the-first-climate-president.
3. Claude Henry and Laurence Tubiana, *Earth at Risk* (New York: Columbia University Press, 2018), p. 78.
4. Ibid., p. 81.

5.   Suzanne Goldenberg, "Revealed: the day Obama chose a strategy of silence on climate change," *The Guardian*, November 1, 2012, accessed August 17, 2020 at https://www.theguardian.com/environment/2012/nov/01/obama-strategy-silence -climate-change.
6.   Suzanne Goldenberg and Aleggra Stratton, "Barack Obama's speech disappoints and fuels frustration at Copenhagen," *The Guardian*, December 18, 2009, accessed August 17, 2020 at https://www.theguardian.com/environment/2009/ dec/18/obama-speech-copenhagen.
7.   Alister Bull and Tabassum Zakaria, "Obama says disappointment at Copenhagen justified," *Reuters*, December 23, 2009, accessed August 17, 2020 at https:// www.reuters.com/article/us-obama-climate/obama-says-disappointment-at -copenhagen-justified-idUSTRE5BM4DO20091224.
8.   Liz Halloran, "Obama humbled by election 'shellacking'," *NPR*, November 3, 2010, accessed August 17, 2020 at https://www.npr.org/templates/story/story.php ?storyId=131046118.
9.   Joe Stephens and Carol D. Leonnig, "Documents show politics infused Obama 'green' programs," *Washington Post*, December 25, 2011, accessed August 17, 2020 at https://www.washingtonpost.com/solyndra-politics-infused-obama -energy-programs/2011/12/14/gIQA4HllHP_story.html.
10.   Environmental Protection Agency, Notice: "Proposed settlement agreement, Clean Air Act citizen suit," *Federal Register* 75, No. 250 (2010): 82392–3, accessed August 17, 2020 at https://www.federalregister.gov/documents/2010/12/ 30/2010-32935/proposed-settlement-agreement-clean-air-act-citizen-suit.
11.   Barack Obama, "State of the Union Address," January 24, 2012, American Presidency Project, accessed August 17, 2020 at https://www.presidency.ucsb .edu/documents/address-before-joint-session-the-congress-the-state-the-union -15.
12.   John M. Broder, "Both Romney and Obama avoid talk of climate change," *New York Times*, October 25, 2012, accessed August 17, 2020 at https://www.nytimes .com/2012/10/26/us/politics/climate-change-nearly-absent-in-the-campaign.html.
13.   Darren Samuelsohn, "The greening of Barack Obama," *Politico*, November 18, 2014, accessed August 17, 2020 at https://www.politico.com/story/2014/11/ barack-obama-environment-112974.
14.   Marianne Lavelle, "2016: Obama's climate legacy marked by triumphs and lost opportunities," *Inside Climate News*, December 26, 2016, accessed August 17, 2020 at https://insideclimatenews.org/news/23122016/obama-climate-change -legacy-trump-policies.
15.   Federal Emergency Management Agency (FEMA), *Hurricane Sandy FEMA After-Action Report* (Washington, DC: FEMA, 2013), pp. 1–4.
16.   Office of Electricity Delivery and Energy Reliability, *Comparing the Impacts of Northeast Hurricanes on Energy Infrastructure* (Washington, DC: Department of Energy, 2013), p. iv, accessed August 17, 2020 at https://www.energy.gov/sites/ prod/files/2013/04/f0/Northeast%20Storm%20Comparison_FINAL_041513b .pdf.
17.   Peter Marsters and Trevor Houser, "America's biggest blackout," *rhg.com*, October 26, 2017, accessed August 17, 2020 at https://rhg.com/research/americas -biggest-blackout-2/.
18.   Alice C. Hill and William Kakenmaster, "Resilient infrastructure: understanding interconnectedness and long-term risk," in *Optimizing Community Infrastructure:*

Resilience in the Face of Shocks and Stresses, ed. Ryan Cooker (Oxford: Elsevier, 2019).
19. Viveca Novak, "Bum rap for Rahm," *FactCheck.org*, January 13, 2011, accessed August 17, 2020 at https://www.factcheck.org/2011/01/bum-rap-for-rahm/.
20. Barack Obama, "State of the Union Address," February 12, 2013, American Presidency Project, accessed August 17, 2020 at https://www.presidency.ucsb .edu/documents/address-before-joint-session-congress-the-state-the-union-2.
21. Barack Obama, "Presidential memorandum – establishing a quadrennial energy review" (Washington, DC: Office of the White House, 2014).
22. Susan Rice, "Remarks on climate change and national security," speech, October 12, 2015, Stanford University, Palo Alto, California.
23. Shaun Donovan, "In ongoing response to Hurricane Sandy, we must remain focused on climate change's long-term impacts" [White House blog], October 29, 2015, accessed August 17, 2020 at https://obamawhitehouse.archives.gov/blog/ 2015/10/29/ongoing-response-hurricane-sandy-we-must-remain-focused-climate -changes-long-term.
24. John Deutch, "Obama's second-term energy policy is working," *Wall Street Journal*, August 18, 2014, accessed August 17, 2020 at https://www.wsj .com/articles/john-deutch-obamas-second-term-energy-policy-is-working -1408404210.
25. Barack Obama, "Inaugural Address," January 21, 2013, American Presidency Project, accessed August 17, 2020 at https://www.presidency.ucsb.edu/documents/ inaugural-address-15.
26. White House, *The Record: President Obama on Climate and Energy* [video] (Washington, DC: Office of the White House, 2017), accessed August 11, 2020 at https://obamawhitehouse.archives.gov/featured-videos/video/2017/01/09/record -president-obama-climate-and-energy.
27. Podesta later served as chair of the 2016 Hillary Clinton presidential campaign.
28. Juliet Eilperin, "A year in the White House: John Podesta reflects on Obama's environmental record," *Washington Post*, February 23, 2015, accessed August 17, 2020 at https://www.washingtonpost.com/news/energy-environment/wp/2015/ 02/23/a-year-in-the-white-house-john-podesta-reflects-on-obamas-environmental -record/.
29. Ben Geman and National Journal, "The audacity of John Podesta," *The Atlantic*, November 21, 2014, accessed August 17, 2020 at https://www.theatlantic.com/ politics/archive/2014/11/the-audacity-of-john-podesta/446901/.
30. Ibid.
31. Ibid.
32. Barack Obama, "State of the Union Address," January 20, 2015, American Presidency Project, accessed August 17, 2020 at https://www.presidency.ucsb .edu/documents/address-before-joint-session-the-congress-the-state-the-union -20.
33. Donald Trump (@realDonaldTrump), "Ice storm rolls from Texas to Tennessee – I'm in Los Angeles and…" *Twitter*, December 6, 2013, 8:13 AM, accessed August 17, 2020 at https://twitter.com/realDonaldTrump/status/408977616926830592?s= 20.
34. Colleen McCain Nelson and Carol E. Lee, "Former Clinton aide Podesta played key role in developing carbon rule," *Wall Street Journal*, June 3, 2014, accessed August 17, 2020 at https://www.wsj.com/articles/former-clinton-aide-podesta -played-key-role-in-developing-carbon-emmissions-rule-1401839771.

7.   Climate policy in China: an overview

Ye Qi, Xiaofan Zhao and Nicholas Stern

CHINA'S CARBON EMISSIONS AND DECARBONIZATION: A BACKGROUND FOR CLIMATE CHANGE POLICY

Carbon emissions in China have undergone a continuous increase since the 1980s and experienced a particular surge during the 2000s, in large part due to its accession to the World Trade Organization (Figure 7.1). In 2006, for the first time in history, China exceeded the United States to become the world's largest greenhouse gas emitter. In 2018, China's carbon emissions amounted to 9.4 Gt, approximately 28.5 percent of the world's total and exceeding emissions of all member countries of the Organisation for Economic Co-operation and Development (OECD) (BP, 2019). Manufacturing, buildings, and transportation are the three primary sectors responsible for carbon emissions in China, accounting for 64.3 percent, 18.7 percent, and 11.9 percent of total

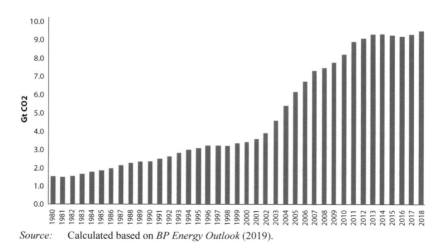

Source: Calculated based on *BP Energy Outlook* (2019).

Figure 7.1   *Carbon emissions in China (1980–2018)*

Table 7.1   *Breakdown of end-use CO_2 emissions in China by sector (2016)*

	Emissions (Mt CO_2)	% in total
Energy industry	286	3.3
Agriculture	159	1.8
Manufacturing	5578	64.3
Transportation	1033	11.9
Buildings	1618	18.7
Total	8674	100.0

Source: Table 11-15 in Liu and Li (2018).

end-use CO_2 emissions in 2016 (Table 7.1). The predominance of man-ufacturing-related emissions shows the urgency and significance of a structural change from the emissions-intensive, manufacturing-based economy toward a high-tech-driven, service-based one. Despite a relatively small share of the national total, the high speed at which transport-related carbon emissions (10.3 percent annual growth rate) have grown in the 2005–18 period is particularly worth noting: transport-related carbon emissions in China more than tripled from 0.40 Gt in 2005 to 1.04 Gt in 2018, its share within the national total carbon emissions increasing from 6.1 percent to 12.1 percent over the same period (Tsinghua University, 2020a). International experiences suggest that transport-related emissions will become an increasingly important driver of emissions in China with the acceleration of urbanization.

As the world's largest energy consumer and carbon emitter, China has increasingly recognized the urgency and necessity of addressing global climate change. It has become a general consensus among Chinese policy-makers that clean growth is the growth story of the twenty-first century. China's Nationally Determined Contribution (NDC) aims to peak carbon emissions around 2030, lower CO_2 emissions per unit of GDP in 2030 by 60 percent to 65 percent from 2005 levels, and increase the share of non-fossil fuels in primary energy consumption to around 20 percent by 2030, among other targets. Fulfilling these pledges is integral to global climate change mitigation in general, and to meeting the Paris Agreement objective of limiting average global temperature increase to below 2°C, while pursuing efforts to limit the temperature increase to 1.5°C above pre-industrial levels. The past decade witnessed China's rapid decarbonization of its energy system. The backbone of this decarbonization trend is the decelerated growth of coal consumption and fast development of renewable energy. The share of coal in China's total energy consumption decreased from 76.2 percent in 1990 to 61.8 percent in 2016, while the share of non-fossil fuels increased from 5.1 percent to 13.0 percent in the same period

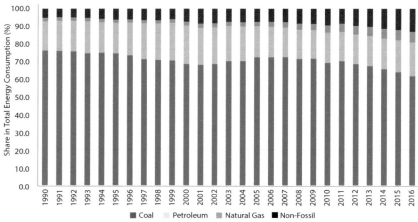

Source: Table 11-1 in Liu and Li (2018).

Figure 7.2   *Change in China's energy structure (1990–2016)*

(Figure 7.2). China's coal use dropped to 2.8 billion tons of coal equivalent (tce), a decrease of 0.77 percent, in 2014, with another 1.48 percent decrease in 2015, and a further 1.69 percent decrease in 2016, all while gross domestic product (GDP) continued to grow (Figure 7.3). Despite the slight reversal of the trend in 2017 and subsequently in 2018 when coal consumption increased by 0.13 percent and 0.86 percent, respectively, China has shown signs of entering the era of post-coal growth. In other words, China's economic growth has started to decouple from coal use (Qi & Lu, 2018; Qi et al., 2016).

Today, China leads the world in renewable energy installation and investment. In 2015, China's investment in renewable energy contributed to more than one-third of the global total (Dong et al., 2018). Although this share slightly decreased in 2016, China continued to lead the world in renewable energy investment in 2017 and even further increased its share in the global market. Domestic investment in renewable energy reached 126.6 billion USD, approximately 45 percent of global total (Qi, 2018). In 2017, renewable energy (excluding large hydro) accounted for 21.9 percent of China's total power installation (Figure 7.4). Of China's new installed capacity in 2017, 58.4 percent was contributed by renewable energy, of which 43 percent was from solar photovoltaic and 13 percent from wind. New installation of photovoltaic systems amounted to 53 GW, more than 50 percent of the global total, and 15 GW of wind capacity was installed, approximately one-quarter of the global

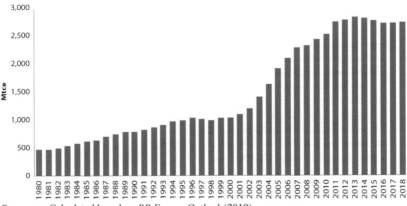

Source: Calculated based on *BP Energy Outlook* (2019).

Figure 7.3   *Coal consumption in China (1980–2018)*

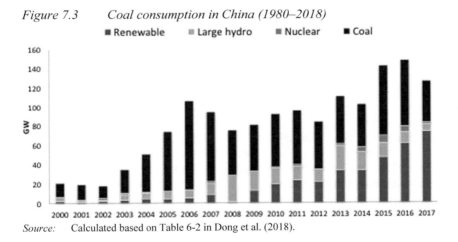

Source: Calculated based on Table 6-2 in Dong et al. (2018).

Figure 7.4   *New installed capacity for electric power generation
(2000–2017) in China*

total. Meanwhile, the share of investment in renewables increased from 13 percent in 2005 to 77 percent in 2017 (Figure 7.5).

This chapter is organized around four themes: an overview of China's climate change policy, climate policy-making, climate policy implementation, and climate policy and its role in global governance. Together the four sections aim to present a comprehensive picture of climate policy in China.

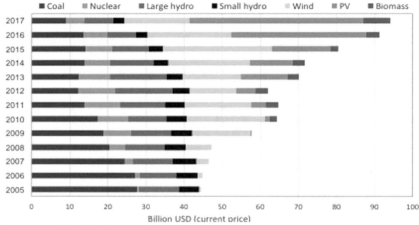

Source: Table 6-3 in Dong et al. (2018).

Figure 7.5   Share of investment in renewable energy in China (2005–17)

AN EVOLVING SYSTEM OF POLICIES FOR CLIMATE CHANGE

Climate policy has been a key component of China's environmental policy and environmental diplomacy since the early 1990s. China was among the first ten parties that signed the primary international agreement on climate change, the United Nations Framework Convention on Climate Change (UNFCCC), at the Earth Summit in Rio de Janeiro in 1992. Six years later, China signed the Kyoto Protocol to the UNFCCC, which was ratified in August 2002 and entered into force on February 16, 2005. During the 15th session of the Conference of the Parties (COP15) in Copenhagen in 2009, the Chinese government put forward an independent emissions reduction target to reduce national carbon intensity by 40–45 percent compared to 2005 levels by 2020; to increase the share of non-fossil energy in China's primary energy mix to 15 percent; and to increase forest stocks by 1.3 billion m^3 compared to 2005 levels. Both the carbon intensity and the forest stocks targets had been overfulfilled by 2018: the carbon intensity was reduced by 45.8 percent, and forest stocks increased by 1.51 billion m^3. China is also on track to reach the non-fossil energy target of 15 percent: the share of non-fossil energy in China's primary energy mix increased from 7.4 percent in 2005 to 14.3 percent in 2018 (Ministry of Ecology and Environment, 2019; Tsinghua University, 2020a). In 2016, China submitted its NDC mitigation pledges under the 2015 Paris Agreement of the

UNFCCC, pledging to reduce CO_2 intensity by 60–65 percent compared to 2005 levels by 2030, to increase the share of non-fossil energy in the national primary energy consumption to 20 percent and to reach peak CO_2 emissions around 2030 or earlier. Fulfilling these pledges is integral to global climate change mitigation in general, and to meeting the Paris Agreement objective of limiting the average global temperature increase to below 2°C, while pursuing efforts to limit the temperature increase to 1.5°C above pre-industrial levels.

Looking back, it is clear that China has pursued an evolving strategy for climate change since the 1990s. Two key features emerge from China's climate change strategy, which are worth particular attention. First, the central government views climate policy as part of its sustainable development policy, especially part of its energy consumption and economic development policy (Qi & Ma, 2007). This means that climate change is not treated as a separate issue by the Chinese government, but as a component of its overall development strategy. Although such a strategy recognizes the linkages between climate change and other developmental issues, which allows for policy coordination and co-governance, it also reveals insufficient recognition of the distinctive significance of climate change. This has in a large part led to the lack of specific climate change mitigation and adaptation policy for a long period of time. The 12th Five-Year-Plan (FYP) dedicated a whole chapter to climate change. Prior to that, it is hard to find any distinctive climate polices. Instead, climate mitigation was only implicitly embedded in China's energy-saving policies, which reduce carbon emissions as a result. The 12th FYP officially included policies specifically targeting climate change such as the mandatory national carbon intensity target, low-carbon city pilot, carbon trading pilots, and the national carbon market.

Second, China insists on the principle of "common but differentiated responsibilities" and actively participates in international activities related to climate change. China treats climate change as a key part of its environmental diplomacy. By complying with international climate agreements, China hopes to play a role in international climate governance as an environmentally responsible country while protecting its national interest. Given that a stable climate is a global public good, the Chinese government emphasizes the importance of international cooperation on climate change. This position shows that China views climate change as an international problem triggered by international pressure initially (e.g., following the release of the Fourth Assessment Report by the Intergovernmental Panel on Climate Change [IPCC] in February 2007, Chinese embassies and consulates worldwide received, for the first time, numerous calls and questions regarding Chinese actions on climate change), and then as a domestic sustainable development problem when climate change impacts become more clear and profound (Qi & Ma, 2007; Qi & Wu, 2013). In recent years, China has realized that low-carbon economic development will contribute to its economic transition towards a green economy. President Xi Jinping made it clear during his meeting with former US Secretary of State John Kerry in 2014, that addressing climate change "is not at others' demand but our own will. We have already taken many measures and will do more in the future."

As of 2020, China has created a relatively comprehensive policy framework for climate change with broad coverage, including administrative mandates, economic incentives (including price policies, carbon cap and trade, and fiscal subsidies), regulatory measures (e.g., laws, regulations, and standards), and low-carbon pilots, in addition to policies closely related to climate policy such as power sector reform and taxation reform, and research and development policy. Climate policies in China can be classified into seven broad categories, as follows.

Adjusting the Industrial Structure to Limit Energy-intensive Industry

China's industrial policy promotes transformation and upgrade of energy-intensive industries towards energy-saving ones. This includes increasing the share of service industry and lowering the share of mining and manufacturing industry. Among the so-called strategic emerging industries,[1] information and communication technology, green manufacturing, and biotechnology are emphasized. While meeting other targets for industrial and economic development, the new and high-tech industries tend to consume less energy, and emit less greenhouse gases for every dollar of production, as compared to the traditional industry. In addition, a key initiative for upgrading traditional industries is the elimination of obsolete production capacity in energy-intensive industries. During the 11th FYP period (2006–10) alone, the Ministry of Finance provided 21.91 billion renminbi (RMB) of subsidies to enterprises in less-developed regions to encourage their phase-out activities (Zhao et al., 2014).

Promoting Energy Saving and Improving Energy Efficiency

Energy saving and energy efficiency has been the bedrock of China's climate mitigation policy. In fact, the energy-saving policy started in the late 1970s to address a severe shortage of energy when China made a deliberate decision to shift the focus of the country from political campaigns to economic growth. The national government makes an explicit target for energy intensity (defined as energy use per unit of economic production) for every five-year plan period. Since the inception of the energy-saving policy, China's energy intensity has been declining at about 5 percent a year on average with the only exception for the 10th FYP (2000–05) when no energy intensity target was made in the

FYP. Since 2005, China has resumed the energy intensity target and created a series of tough measures to promote energy saving, including prominently the Top 1000 Enterprises Program for the 11th FYP period, the Top 10 000 Enterprises Program for the 12th FYP period, and the Top 100–1000–10 000 Enterprises Program for the 13th FYP period. The national government launched the Top 1000 Enterprise Program in 2006 to achieve energy savings of 100 Mtce by 2010. The program originally covered the 1008 most energy-intensive enterprises in nine major energy-consuming industries, each consuming a minimum of 180 000 tce annually. In the 12th FYP period, the national government replaced the Top 1000 Enterprises Program with the Top 10 000 Enterprises Program. The Top 10 000 Enterprises Program aims to achieve an energy-saving target of 250 Mtce for the so-called Top 10 000 Enterprises.[2] There were approximately 16 078 Top 10 000 Enterprises in 2010, altogether accounting for 60 percent of total energy consumption in China. During the 13th FYP period, the Top 10 000 Enterprises Program was again replaced by the Top 100–1000–10 000 Enterprises Program. The Program classifies key energy-consuming entities in the country into three categories: (1) the "Top 100" Enterprises (there are 100 such enterprises, hence Top 100), whose annual energy consumption exceeded 3 Mtce in 2015; (2) Top 1000 Enterprises (there are 1000 such enterprises, hence Top 1000), whose annual energy consumption exceeded 0.5 Mtce in 2015; and (3) all other key energy-consuming entities. In addition to these programs targeting industrial enterprises, the Chinese government launched the Energy-Saving Key Projects, reformed energy-saving standards and labels, promoted energy-saving technologies and products, and refined fiscal policies and market instruments related to energy saving.

Decarbonizing the Energy System by Limiting Total Energy Consumption and Promoting Renewable Energy

China has endeavored to decarbonize the energy system by developing renewable energy and limiting the total energy consumption, particularly its fossil fuel use. As one of the few countries in the world that ever implemented a nationwide energy consumption cap (Qi, 2018), China set a limit on the amount of total coal consumption for ten eastern provinces. In particular, Beijing, Tianjin, Hebei and Shandong were together required to cut their coal consumption by 83 million tons from 2012 to 2017, a reduction greater than the total coal consumption of the UK (Qi et al., 2016).

Substitution of coal by non-fossil fuels has proceeded rapidly in the power-generation sector. In 2007, 83 percent of electricity was generated with coal, but that share fell to 72 percent in 2015. At the same time, there has been a rapid growth of solar, wind, nuclear and hydropower generation (ibid.). The amount of electric power generated from renewable sources has tripled and wind and solar power capacity grew 25 times in the decade from 2008 to 2018. Currently, 30 percent of all electricity comes from non-fossil fuels (United Nations Environment Programme [UNEP], 2019). China has committed significant financial resources to the development of renewable energy, especially through preferential policies and fiscal subsidies for solar photovoltaic and wind equipment manufacturing, power plant construction, and power transmission provided by both central and local governments at all levels. The Chinese government's support to boost renewable energy in terms of land use, taxation, and loan issuance is unparalleled by any other country in the world (Qi, 2018).

Increasing Carbon Sinks

China's carbon sink policy targets forest, cropland, grassland, and wetland. In terms of forest carbon sink, China has implemented the Special Action Plan for Forestry for Addressing Climate Change, which aims to accelerate afforestation on barren hills and promote urban landscape construction as well as continuing to implement forest ecological projects such as the conversion of cropland to forest, rocky desertification treatment, and shelter forest construction. China has continued to implement grassland ecosystem remediation projects such as returning grazing land and cultivated land to grassland. In 2018, the central government allocated a 300 million RMB budget for wetland protection projects and set up a wetland fiscal subsidy of 1.6 billion RMB (Ministry of Ecology and Environment, 2019). In addition to a nature-based solutions to promote carbon sinks, China takes seriously the promotion of carbon capture and sequestration (CCS) technology. The International Energy Agency (IEA) (2015) estimates that to limit global average temperature rise to below 2°C, CCS could contribute to 11 percent of emissions reduction in China. The theoretical geological storage reserve in China is estimated to be on the scale of teratons (Administrative Center for China's Agenda 21, 2019). On August 31, 2018, a CCS demonstration facility in Jilin Province reached a carbon storage capacity of 0.6 Mt. There are a number of other facilities (e.g., Sinopec Qilu Chemical CCS Project, Shaanxi Yanchang Petroleum Shaanbei Coal Chemical CCS Project) with storage capacities of approximately 0.4 Mt. According to data from the Global CCS Institute, by 2020 the existing CCS facilitates in China have a total capture capacity of 4.78 Mt/year, much less than the CCS deployment goal set in Asian Development Bank's (2015) CCS Roadmap, that is, 10 Mt/year. The gap is largely due to the immaturity of the technology and high capital and operation cost (Tsinghua University, 2020b).

Controlling GHG Emissions from Sources Other than Fossil Fuel Combustion

China has addressed the issue of hydrofluorocarbons (HFCs) in the industrial sector. In 2018, the Ministry of Ecology and Environment (MEE) issued the Notice on Launching Relevant Work on the Disposal of Hydrofluorocarbons, arranged for the disposal verification of HFCs, published the auditing results of a total of 11 enterprises in 49 provinces, and provided enterprises that destroyed HFCs with a subsidy amounting to over 200 million RMB (Ministry of Ecology and Environment, 2019). In order to promote the recycling of renewable resources and comprehensive utilization of renewable resources such as scrap iron and steel, the Ministry of Industry and Information Technology published six batches of enterprises that meet the entry require-ments for the scrap iron and steel processing industry.

China has made efforts to control greenhouse gas (GHG) emissions from the agricultural sector with the intention to reduce chemical fertilizer use, which was 328.5 kg/ha for crops in 2015, much greater than global average of 120 kg/ha, 2.6 times its counterpart in the United States, and 2.5 times its counterpart in the European Union (Ministry of Agriculture, 2015). In 2015, the Ministry of Agriculture launched the Action Plan to Achieve Zero Growth of Fertilizer by 2020, mainly through formulated fertilizer use based on soil testing (*cetu peifang shifei*). Demonstration projects for reducing the quantity of and improving the efficiency of chemical fertilizers were launched in 300 counties. Despite the still high per hectare chemical fertilizer use, fertilizer intake has gradually improved. For instance, fertilizer intake of the three major grain crops in China (i.e., rice, corn, and wheat) increased from 35.2 percent in 2015 to 37.8 percent in 2017 (Ministry of Ecology and Environment, 2019). Fertilizer use growth rate declined from 2.8 percent in 2005 to 1.3 percent in 2013 and reached zero growth by 2017, three years in advance of the target (Ministry of Agriculture, 2015; Ministry of Ecology and Environment, 2019). Livestock and poultry excrement resource utilization was promoted in 585 major counties for animal husbandry, and support was given for the construc-tion of facilities for collection, storage, treatment, and utilization of excrement resources. China has also implemented pilot projects for the comprehensive utilization of straw. Since 2018, China has started to control GHG emissions from the waste disposal sector by promoting the classification of waste in residential areas.

Building a National Carbon Market

Market-based instruments for enforcing and incentivizing climate governance have gradually evolved. In October 2011, China launched its pilot carbon

Table 7.2   *Overview of the seven carbon-trading pilots in China*

	Launch Date	Accumulated Transaction Amount, July 31, 2019 (Mt)	Accumulated Transaction Turnover, July 31, 2019 (million RMB)
Guangdong Province	December 2013	112.30	1588.80
Hubei Province	April 2014	322.19	7452.12
Beijing	November 2013	29.69	642.02
Chongqing	June 2014	8.91	32.99
Shanghai	November 2013	36.76	443.21
Shenzhen	June 2013	62.50	1795.60
Tianjin	December 2013	6.83	89.90

Source: UNEP (2019).

market in two provinces, that is, Guangdong and Hubei Provinces, and five cities, namely Beijing, Chongqing, Shanghai, Shenzhen, and Tianjin. These seven pilot regions have been trading on the market since June 2013 (Table 7.2). As of May 2019, trading in these seven pilots had covered more than 20 industries, including power generation, cement, iron and steel, and chemical production. Nearly 3000 key emitting entities participated in trading, with an accumulated turnover of almost 580 million tons of CO_2 or just more than 12 billion RMB (UNEP, 2019).

The carbon trading pilot program has generated co-benefits of enhancing local economic growth, promoting energy conservation and emissions reductions, raising awareness of low-carbon transformation, improving carbon-asset management capacity, and expanding financing channels for research and development in low-carbon technology and low-carbon projects. Meanwhile, the carbon market has incentivized the development of supporting services such as emissions verification, carbon accounting, carbon auditing, carbon-assets management, carbon financing, and carbon trading, all of which have created new employment opportunities.

In December 2017, the National Development Reform Commission (NDRC) issued the Scheme for Building a National Carbon Emissions Trading Market for the Electric Power Industry, which marks the official start of a national carbon cap-and-trade system. The Interim Regulations on the Administration of Carbon Emissions Trading have been drafted to solicit comments in 2019. The national carbon-trading program is expected to reach an estimated trading volume of more than 3 billion tons of CO_2, making China the largest carbon market in the world. The national carbon market takes the fossil fuel-based power generation industry as a starting point and will expand to others, including the chemical, petrochemical, iron and steel, non-ferrous metals, building materials, paper and aviation industries (facilities with an annual energy consumption >10 ktce or emissions 26 ktCO$_2$) step by step. More than 1700 power plants are covered by the national carbon trading program so far, responsible for more than 3 GtCO$_2$, nearly one-third of China's national emissions. The estimated trading volume will account for approximately 45 percent of the country's CO$_2$ emissions in the fossil fuel-based power generation industry.

National Low-carbon Development Pilots

Local pilots are often conducted by the central government as a key approach to policy innovation, to identify good practices that can be dispersed to other municipalities and provinces. Three pilot programs are of particular relevance to addressing climate challenges in China, namely the national pilots for low-carbon development, renewable energy pilots and the sponge city[3] pilots (UNEP, 2019). The low-carbon pilot program was first initiated in 2010 and then augmented in 2012 and 2017. A total of 78 cities of various sizes are included in the three batches of the pilot program. Seventy-two of them declared to peak their CO$_2$ emissions five to ten years earlier than the national commitment under the Paris Agreement. All pilot cities achieved reductions in CO$_2$ emissions between 2010 and 2015.

CLIMATE POLICY-MAKING

An Initial Learning Process for China's Climate Policy-making (1990s–2003)

Climate change did not immediately emerge as a priority issue on the national agenda in China. It was initially treated by the central government as a scientific issue with international significance. In 1990, the National Coordination Group on Climate Change (NCGCC) was established as the first official institution on climate change, deputed under the State Council's Environmental Protection Committee (SCEPC). Then State Councilor Song Jian, the Chairman of SCEPC, was designated to lead the NCGCC, with its secretariat set up in the State Meteorological Administration (now China Meteorological Administration). NCGCC played a key role in developing China's position on the UNFCCC and the Kyoto Protocol. China's early efforts focused on learning and fact-finding, developing a coherent and comprehensive understanding of the processes and the likely consequences of climate change. The personnel behind the efforts were aptly suited to the task: Chairman Song Jian was an experienced scientist, and the State Meteorological Administration boasted a cadre of accomplished climatologists. The learning and fact-finding process was used to support key decisions taken on the UNFCCC and the Kyoto

Protocol. The process also contributed to the realization that climate change was much more than a scientific issue, as it was caused by economic activities, particularly fossil fuel burning. Thus, China's climate change actions have consequently been oriented around economic development. As a result, the scientific issue of climate change has become a strategic issue.

This new understanding of the climate change issue led to an important reorganization of the top institutions, beginning with fundamental reforms at NCGCC in 1998. First, it was renamed the National Coordination Group on Climate Change Strategy (NCGCCS). The newly added word "strategy" highlighted the shift of the group's function from fact-finding to the development of strategies, both domestically and internationally. Second, the secretariat was relocated from the State Meteorological Administration to the State Development Planning Commission (SDPC), which was later further reorganized into the National Development and Reform Commission (NDRC). This was a significant change because SDPC was not only responsible for policy-making, program development, and funding allocation on sustainable development; it was also the most powerful general policy-making agency in the central government. With the State Council's Environmental Protection Committee dissolved in 1998, the newly established NCGCCS was put under the direct leadership of the SDPC Chairman, Mr. Zeng Peiyan, who soon became a vice-premier of the country. This institutional arrangement continued under the new administration of President Hu Jintao and Premier Wen Jiabao, with SDPC reorganized into the current National Development and Reform Commission (NDRC). Mr. Ma Kai, Chairman of NDRC, took the leadership of the NCGCCS in 2003.

From an International Issue to a Priority Policy Agenda (2003–12)

During the Chinese leadership under President Hu Jintao and Premier Wen Jiabao (2003–12), a wave of popular interest and international pressure motivated the central government to formally elevate the priority of climate change in China's domestic policy agenda and in top-level diplomacy. The emphasis on development and the strategic nature of climate change were further highlighted by the central government when NCGCCS was reorganized again and elevated into the National Leading Group on Climate Change (NLGCC), led by Premier Wen Jiabao in June 2007. Members of this group include almost all ministers of the central government, representing 20 ministries. It is useful to note that NLGCC also serves as the State Council Leading Group on Energy Saving and Pollution Reduction, which means the central government officially coupled climate change and energy-saving policies. Specifically, the NGLCC is charged with formulating key national climate change strategies, making arrangements for domestic and international climate change efforts and coordinating key problems in national climate change efforts. Only one month after the creation of the NLGCC, Premier Wen Jiabao presided over the first meeting of the NLGCC. During Wen's six-year term as the head of the NLGCC (2007–13), he convened four meetings of the NLGCC, in 2007, 2009, 2010, and 2011, respectively, which shows the level of priority attached to climate change by China's leadership.

On June 27, 2008, the Politburo, the top policy-making body of the Chinese government, organized the sixth collective learning of the term around the theme of global climate change and capacity building on climate change in China. Two scientists were invited to present their professional views and advice on addressing climate change in China. President Hu Jintao took this opportunity to stress the significance and urgency of climate change and emphasize that China will strengthen climate change capacity building and make continuous efforts in domestic and global sustainable development. In July 2008, the NDRC established the Department of Climate Change to take formal charge of policy formulation, international negotiation, and capacity building, and the creation of the carbon cap-and-trade market. The creation of the Department of Climate Change within the NDRC marked the formal establishment of an implementing agency of climate policy at the national level. Many provinces and municipalities followed the step of the central government by creating agencies in charge of climate change within their respective jurisdictions.

In June 2012, the National Center for Climate Change Strategy and International Cooperation (NCSC) was created as a research institution under the direct supervision of the NDRC. The NCSC was intended to provide strategic research support to climate policy-making at the national level as well as facilitating international cooperation on climate change. The NCSC mainly engages in research in the fields of strategic plans, policies and regulations, international policy, carbon market, and climate information consultation.

Not only did the Hu–Wen administration strengthen the policy-making institutions for climate change by creating the NLGCC and subsequently the Department of Climate Change within the NDRC, the administration also started formal formulation of climate policy during this period. The State Council released China's National Climate Change Program in June 2007, immediately following the creation of the NLGCC. The Program laid out China's efforts in combatting climate change, government understanding of climate change impact on China, the guiding principles the government takes, national objectives and measures, and China's position on international cooperation on climate change. The Program also set out the target of "reducing national average energy consumption per unit of GDP by 20 percent by 2020 compared to 2005 level, and correspondingly mitigating carbon dioxide emissions." This target again shows that climate change is not treated a distinct policy field, but closely intertwined with energy and environmental policies. The National Climate Change Program became the fundamental reference for climate policy-making in China. In addition to the Program, the Chinese government has consecutively released the annual reports entitled *China's Policies and Actions for Addressing Climate Change* since 2008, which introduces China's efforts and strategy for addressing climate change.

China's FYPs show the weights assigned to different issues on the Chinese policy agenda. The 12th FYP is a landmark in China's national policy-making on climate change. It marked the first national legislation on climate in China. Although China released its first policy document on climate change in 2007, that is, the National Climate Change Program, it was not until the adoption of 12th FYP that climate change was made an explicit component of national objectives. A whole chapter was dedicated in the 12th FYP to detailing national plans for concrete action on low-carbon development and set out a specific target of reducing carbon dioxide emissions per unit of GDP by 17 percent. Since FYPs are reviewed, debated, and voted on in the National People's Congress, they are effectively part of the national legislation (Qi & Wu, 2013).

Elevated Leadership for Climate Policy-making (2013–present)

With the advent of the new leadership under President Xi Jinping, China's climate policy-making entered a new era where climate change came under the direct supervision of President Xi Jinping, despite NLGCC's official status as the climate decision-making institution. In 2013, Premier Li Keqiang took over the leadership of the NLGCC, whose member ministries expanded from 20 to 26. In the past six years (2013–19), Premier Li convened two meetings for the NLGCC, in 2015 and in 2019, compared to four meetings convened by Wen Jiabao during his six-year term (2007–13) leading the NLGCC. On the other hand, President Xi took the leadership on both the domestic and international fronts related to climate change policy-making. When the US Secretary of State John Kerry was visiting Beijing early in 2014, it was Xi who met with him and made it clear that climate change is a national priority on China's policy agenda. Later in the year, Xi directly talked with US President Obama, and made the China–US Joint Announcement on Climate Change, which set an important foundation for the Paris Agreement in 2015. The Announcement was later adapted to become the Joint Presidential Statement on Climate Change between Xi and Obama in September 2015. During his state visit in Washington, Xi also announced the establishment of China's national carbon market for eight sectors of the economy, the largest carbon market in the world. In the same week, Xi attended the United Nations Climate Change Summit in New York, the first time the Head of State of China attended an international gathering on climate change. It used to be that the premier, head of the National Leading Group on Climate Change, appeared on such occasions. A few weeks later, Xi once again attended the Paris Conference on Climate Change and stated China's national position on the issue and called for strengthened cooperation among all nations. Xi's visible leadership on climate policy-making in China is also shown in his effort to make the issue an opportunity for China to play a bigger role in global governance in general. This will be discussed in the next section. It is clear that the leadership on climate change policy-making in China shifted from the NLGCC to the head of state during the Xi era.

Elevating the leadership for climate policy-making to the top level has important implications. First, it accelerated international negotiation. In 2014, the climate negotiation between the world's two largest emitters was between two heads of state and the decision was a political one, while five years before that the negotiations remained primarily at a technical level. Even the premier's involvement and position were largely based on recommendations from the technocrats. Second, all levels of government become more serious about climate change policy implementation. Development of the national carbon market has been accelerated since Xi made the announcement. Since 2013, President Xi Jinping has reinforced China's commitment to addressing climate change. For the first time, China issued a series of mid- to long-term strategic plans for climate change, including the National Climate Change Adaptation Strategy (2013–20) and the National Climate Change Plan (2014–20). These strategic plans put forward China's main objectives and key tasks to address climate change mitigation and adaptation before 2020. The 13th FYP dedicates a whole chapter to climate change entitled "Employing a proactive approach to climate change," expanding the number of planning target indicators for natural resources and the environment from seven to ten, including: most prominently, reducing energy consumption per unit of GDP by 15 percent within the FYP period; increasing the share of non-fossil fuels in China's primary energy consumption by 3 percent; and reducing carbon dioxide emissions per unit of GDP by 18 percent. In the 2015 Paris Conference on Climate Change, China submitted its Intended Nationally Determined Contribution (INDC) to the Secretariat of UNFCCC, outlining its objectives including achieving the peaking of carbon dioxide emissions around 2030 and making best efforts to peak early, and proposing policy measures to ensure their implementation.

The elevation of policy-making leadership also helped with the reorganization of the climate change agency. In 2018, the functions of climate change and emissions mitigation within the NDRC were merged into the newly established MEE, which was considered the most significant institutional rearrangement in the history of climate change governance in China. The NLGCC was reorganized shortly after, with the addition of four ministries including the Ministry of Culture, the People's Bank of China, and the newly created Ministry of Justice and China International Development Cooperation Agency. A general consensus is that moving the functions of climate change and emissions mitigation from the NDRC to the MEE is conducive to co-governance of the environment and climate change, since many energy-saving and carbon mitigation actions can generate co-benefits for air pollution control and GHG reduction. However, there are also concerns that this government reorganization may weaken the previously improving status of climate governance on China's policy agenda. After all, climate change governance requires coordination and collaboration among different agencies, particularly those related to economic and industrial policy. As the most powerful general policy-making agency in the central government, the NDRC oversees China's economic policy-making on a macro level and can coordinate the actions of departments that matter for climate change, which can facilitate the making of a unified, coordinated strategy for the transition toward a green, low-carbon economy. On the other hand, the ministry/agency in charge of the environment has been historically weak in terms of de facto power among all ministries at the central level. Most significant of all, due to the stereotype about environmental issues being in tension with economic growth, moving the function of climate governance to MEE might leave a false impression that the ministry would push forward climate initiatives at the cost of growth, which would dampen the existing ambitions around climate action.

CLIMATE POLICY IMPLEMENTATION

Target Responsibility System: Government Hierarchy as the Primary Apparatus for Climate Policy Implementation

The core institutional arrangement for ensuring the fulfillment of China's carbon reduction targets is the Target Responsibility System (TRS), based primarily on the five-level government hierarchy from the central level at the top to the county and township levels at the bottom. Under such a system, the central government makes energy intensity or carbon intensity targets, disaggregates the targets among all provinces, and then each province, in turn, disaggregates its own targets among all municipalities, until all the targets are assigned to all governments. Each government assigns targets to all relevant enterprises within its jurisdiction. The agreed target will then be monitored and verified as part of the key performance indicators to evaluate each government and enterprise. Reward and penalty are given based on the fulfillment of the requirements (Zhao & Wu, 2016). TRS is a typical policy implementation mechanism employed by the Chinese government to ensure policy performance and has been applied to a wide range of policy arenas

Table 7.3   *National ministries in charge of different industries prior to 2000*

Industry	Corresponding Ministry in Charge of the Industry
Iron and steel	Ministry of Metallurgical Industry (1982–98)
Non-ferrous metal	Ministry of Metallurgical Industry (1982–98)
Petroleum and petroleum engineering	Ministry of Petroleum Industry (1982–88)
	Ministry of Energy (1988–93)
Chemical engineering	Ministry of Chemical Industry (1982–98)
Construction materials	National Construction Materials Bureau (1982–2001)
Coal	Ministry of Coal Industry (1982–88; 1993–98)
	Ministry of Energy (1988–93)
Electric power	Ministry of Hydropower and Electric Power (1982–88)
	Ministry of Energy (1988–93)
	Ministry of Electric Power Industry (1993–98)
Papermaking	Ministry of Light Industry (1982–93)
	China Light Industry Association (1993–98)
Textiles	Ministry of Textile Industry (1982–93)
	China Textile Association (1993–98)

Source: Zhao et al. (2014).

including economic growth, family planning, and land use management (Li et al., 2013). TRS was first introduced to the field of energy saving and pollution emissions reduction during the 11th FYP period (2006–10) and subsequently to climate change mitigation, more specifically to enforce the national carbon intensity reduction target.

The key to the TRS is division of responsibilities among different administrative regions, or "blocks" (*kuai* in Chinese), while the previous system relied on responsible ministries and their lower-tiered agencies at various levels, or through "lines" (*tiao* in Chinese) (Qi & Wu, 2013). From 1980 to 1998, when most of the plants and factories were administered through responsible ministries, energy management was also put under ministerial control (Table 7.3). For example, energy saving in the iron and steel industry was administered by the Ministry of Metallurgical Industry, power plants by the Ministry of Electric Power, chemical industry by Ministry of Chemical Industry, and so on. Since 1998, these ministries have been reorganized into state-owned companies or industry associations, with their regulation responsibilities being essentially dissolved. Most of the enterprises previously administered by the ministries were either transformed into share-issuing corporations or into purely privatized companies, regulated by local governments under the principle of localized management. However, during this process of reform, the function of energy-saving regulation was not automatically transferred, leaving a gap in energy-saving governance from 1998 through 2007. As a result, energy intensity reversed its 22-year decreasing trend.

In 2007, TRS was established as the basic energy policy implementation mechanism in China. It reinforced the role of the local government as the main implementer of energy policies, which marked the transition of China's energy-saving governance structure from a line-based system to a block-based one (Qi & Wu, 2013). Under the TRS, the national energy intensity reduction target was to be met using "responsibility contracts," which assigns energy-saving targets to lower levels of government and key energy-consuming enterprises, and then keeps track of and evaluates target performance through the Statistics Indicators, Monitoring, and Examination (SME) system (Li et al., 2013, 2016). The shift from a line-based approach to a block-based approach to energy saving not only changed the ways of implementing the policies but also changed the politics of local and central interactions. This change is expected to have a profound impact on climate change politics in China.

While TRS was only applied to energy-saving targets in the 11th FYP period, starting with the 12th FYP period, the TRS expanded to deliver the carbon intensity target set in the 12th FYP. The carbon mitigation TRS differs from the energy-saving TRS in terms of both the scope of target and the disaggregation paths. While the energy-saving target is both disaggregated to subnational governments and to enterprises, the carbon intensity target so far has only been disaggregated to provincial governments.

The transfer of pressure for saving energy and reducing carbon intensity from higher-level governments to lower-level governments (and key energy-consuming enterprises in the case of energy saving) is the basic characteristic of China's policy implementation system for reducing energy and carbon intensity. Although the TRS has proved effective in bringing down the national energy and carbon intensity, the mandatory targets and the associated performance evaluations have increased the tension and the chances of gaming between central and local governments. Compliance and enforcement were under pressure from the top, and self-enforcement by local governments and self-compliance by enterprises were less proactive, as the benefits are not as obvious as the immediate costs. Local governments and enterprises felt that they were paying to benefit the global environment, even as they struggled to meet their own economic targets. This, of course, is one of the pressing challenges of climate change policy implementation in the hierarchical structure of the Chinese government.

Since county governments and township governments are located at the bottom of the political hierarchy, they are the ultimate bearer of the pressure for saving energy and reducing carbon intensity. However, their ability to carry out energy-saving and carbon mitigation activities, which is a function of human capital, institutional arrangement, financial resources and the authority of policy-making, does not match the amount of pressure that they bear (Li et al., 2013). First, compared to municipal and provincial governments, county and township governments possess much less capital that they can mobilize to support energy-saving and low-carbon activities. Moreover, although local governments are authorized to regulate all energy-consuming enterprises within their jurisdiction, in practice it is very difficult for lower-level governments to regulate large-scale state-owned enterprises, which have higher ranking in the political hierarchy. Last but not least, county and lower levels of government lack the technical capacity needed to meet local enterprises' demand for energy-saving technical services.

The asymmetry between pressure and capacity forces lower levels of government to more heavily rely on administrative measures when meeting their energy-saving targets, which could negatively impact society (Li et al., 2016; Zhao & Qi, 2020; Zhao et al., 2020). As previously mentioned, in the second half of 2010, that is, as the 11th FYP period came to an end, a number of local governments took extreme actions, such as power rationing, to ensure that their 11th FYP energy-saving targets were met. Some of these governments even restricted residential use of electricity. For example, Anping County, Hebei Province implemented county-wide power rationing in three batches, each lasting for 22 hours. During the period of power rationing, power supply was cut off for all households, hospitals as well as traffic lights. Although power rationing to some extent contributed to the goal of saving energy, such savings sometimes came at the expense of the normal functioning of society.

Visible and Invisible Hands for Renewable Energy Development

While energy-saving policy is not self-implementing and has to rely on pressure transfer down the government hierarchy, through the target responsibility system, renewable energy policy creates incentives to attract businesses into the playing field and it results in "win–win" situations between climate mitigation and economic growth. Developing renewable energy helps promote new industries through research and development, equipment manufacturing, deployment, and services. Such incentives may filter down to policy implementers at lower levels of government, presenting a means to improve both climate compliance and real economic growth. Large government assistance funds have helped China establish significant market shares in renewables by exploiting economies of scale. Investments in green power will continue to play an important role in development strategy in coming years, as the central government retains the renewable energy sector as a focal point of industrial policy (e.g., 12th FYP).

The National People's Congress passed the first Renewable Energy Law in 2005. The legislation encouraged the use of renewable sources for power generation, buildings and transportation by providing mandates and financial incentives. According to the legislation, major power generation companies were given quotas for renewable power similar to the Renewable Portfolio Standards (RPS) in the United States. The feed-in tariff to power grids was carefully set to ensure the profitability of power generation. Wind power installation capacity increased by more than 40-fold in the five years from 2005 to 2010, four times the target set by the central government.

Major state-owned banks were the main sources of financing for wind power equipment and installation, accounting for 80 percent of total project cost, and power companies only needed to come up with the remaining 20 percent of equity (Qi & Wu, 2013, Zhu et al., 2019). The financiers had little risk to worry about because most projects were financed against the balance sheets of the power generators companies, which are large, profitable, and state-owned. Local governments were also enthusiastic about wind power deployment in their territories, because the projects tended to bring investment and jobs. More importantly, local governments often required or persuaded the project developers to invest in equipment manufacturing in their regions under the "resource for industry" principle. This, too, made business sense because the long-distance transportation of wind turbines was a major concern in the industry. As a result, China now has not only the largest installed capacity of wind power generation but has also become the largest manufacturer of wind power generators.

The real politics in the wind energy business has been between the state and the state-owned power grid companies. As a mandate, the grids must take all electricity generated from the wind towers. Because of the remote locations and the intermittence problem of wind-generated electricity, grid companies considered this type of power as "garbage electricity" that creates more trouble than profit. Consequently, they tried vigorously to avoid the obligations imposed by the legal mandates. The amendment of the renewable energy law in 2009 required that power grids must take all power generated from wind. This new requirement seems to have taken the fight away from the politicians and moved it into the wider field, where the interests of the power generators and the grid companies need to be better aligned. However, implementation of the new law has been irregular because of the resistance from the grid companies.

Under the resource and policy support of central and local governments, large state-owned wind power developers and major state-owned banks worked together to form the unique wind power developing model in China. The implementation mechanisms for wind power developing can be summarized as: the central government creates policy and an institutional environment that is conducive to market development; the local government willingly cooperates with the central government; and project developers and financial institutions also proactively respond to government policies at all levels. Such a policy implementation model is hence characterized by a positive feedback mechanism and is self-implementing.

While wind power development in China is a central government-led process, solar power development took full advantage of market creation and development. The solar power industry had an unexpected, spectacular opportunity to grow. In 2005 when China passed the renewable energy legislation, the Kyoto Protocol took effect. Under the Protocol, the developed countries were required to cut their greenhouse gas emissions by a few percent by 2008–12, which created a demand for emissions reduction technology. In particular, solar power deployment in Europe created a sizable market worldwide for solar panels. The Chinese businesses seized the opportunity and developed into the largest suppliers of these panels, with the benefit of technology transfer from Europe and other developed countries. The invisible hand was a major pulling force for the renewable energy industry in China.

To the local governments who may not understand the importance of addressing climate change and GHG reduction, solar panel manufacturing is a perfect opportunity for industrial development. It means jobs, growth, and revenue. These local governments are so willing to promote this industry that they compete against each other to offer all possible assistance to solar panel manufacturing businesses, ranging from zero-cost land, to subsidized loans and tax refunds. The visible hand became a huge pushing hand for the industry. Local governments have not only promoted the manufacturing of solar PV panels, but also pushed the central government for preferential policies of deployment. For instance, the province of Jiangsu persuaded the NDRC to develop a high on-grid policy for solar PV generation.

CLIMATE POLICY AND GLOBAL GOVERNANCE

A Contributor and Leader in Global Climate Governance: China's Newfound Role

China has assumed an increasingly active role in global governance in recent years. At the center of President Xi's diplomatic philosophy is the concept of "a community of shared future for mankind" (*renlei mingyun gongtongti*), an idea culturally rooted in the Confucian concept of "*tianxia*," meaning "all under heaven" and emphasizing win–win cooperation rather than confrontation. Through the Belt and Road Initiative and the Asian Infrastructure Investment Bank, China is seeking to reshape global governance and transform the existing international system to address the global challenges. In the process, China attempts to transform its role from a rule-taker that "keeps a low profile" (*taoguang yanghui*) to a rule-maker that "strives for achievement" (*yousuo zuowei*) (Yan, 2014).

The country's growing leadership in global climate governance is illustrative. As President Xi Jinping said in his speech made at the 19th CPC Congress, "taking a driving seat in international cooperation to respond to climate change, China has become an important participant, contributor, and torchbearer in the global endeavor for ecological civilization." In the Joint Presidential Statement between Xi and Obama in 2015, it is stated that climate change is the greatest threat to humanity. Despite divergent national interests, all nations in the world share a common interest in climate change, hence are more willing to cooperate in global climate governance than in other world affairs such as security, trade, arms, and geopolitics. China therefore views joint efforts in global climate change as a key testing field and a demonstration case for the philosophy of building a community of shared future for humankind.

China's climate policy will have a major impact on global climate change governance given its role as the world's largest net exporter of embodied carbon (Liu et al., 2016). The past three decades have witnessed low-cost, emissions-intensive manufacturing moving to developing countries, particularly China, which has been producing emissions-intensive products for consumption in developed countries. The net emissions transfer via international trade from developing to developed countries increased from 0.4Gt CO_2 in 1990 to 1.6 Gt CO_2 in 2008 (Peters et al., 2011). Embodied carbon flow is considered a primary factor behind the slowdown of carbon emissions in developed countries and the rapid growth of emissions in developing countries (Jiang et al., 2019; Long et al., 2018; Weber et al., 2008). In 2007, emissions in China were 7.3 $GtCO_2$ (production-based emissions), of which 1.7 Gt (23 percent) were related to goods exported and ultimately consumed in other countries (Feng et al., 2013; Weber et al., 2008). Since manufacturing in developing countries such as China is more carbon intensive than in developed countries, international trade increases global CO_2 emissions, that is, the carbon leakage problem. China's efforts to improve production technologies and decarbonize the underlying energy systems will, to a great extent, reduce global trade-related emissions.

While China tries to reshape global governance through the Belt and Road Initiative, the potential carbon footprint of this global initiative can hardly be overlooked and may potentially put the Paris Agreement at risk. The infrastructure projects as planned in Belt and Road countries not only require substantial energy consumption, but also create carbon lock-in in the next few decades since a large proportion of the construction infrastructure is energy facilities, particularly fossil fuel-fired power plants (Qi et al., 2019). Extending

China's supply chain by streamlining exports to Belt and Road countries also leads to the growth of China's energy-intensive industries, which further increases global carbon emissions. It is therefore strongly recommended that development financial institutions in China establish or adopt guidelines and specifications for financing green, climate-friendly projects in the Belt and Road Initiative, such as the Green Investment Principles (Green Finance Committee [GFC], 2018).

International Climate Collaboration

China has worked closely with major economies in the world to address global climate change through bilateral and multilateral platforms. In 2015 alone, China made joint announcements on climate change: with the European Union in June, with the United States in September, and with France in November. China also played a critical role in facilitating climate collaborations on multilateral platforms such as the Group of Twenty (G20) Summit, BRICS (an association of five major emerging national economies: Brazil, Russia, India, China and South Africa) Meetings, and the Major Economies Forum on Energy and Climate. Take the G20 Summit as an example. As the host state of the G20 Summit in 2016, China effectively advanced the multilateral process on climate change under the G20 framework. China, along with the US, submitted its ratification document for the Paris Agreement to Ban Ki-moon, then Secretary General of the United Nations, launched a Climate Finance Study Group (CFSG) in addition to the Green Finance Study Group (GFSG), as well as announcing the Presidency Statement on Climate Change at the G20 Sherpa Meeting.

Moreover, China has been a supporter and practitioner of South–South cooperation on climate change, mainly in the forms of a climate fund, material donation, and capacity building. In June 2012, then Premier Wen Jiabao announced at the UN Conference on Sustainable Development (Rio+20) that China would provide 200 million RMB to support South–South cooperation on climate change in the next three years. In September 2014, Vice-Premier Zhang Gaoli, who was also President Xi Jinping's special representative, announced during the UN Climate Summit that China would increase its support to and create a fund for South–South cooperation. In September 2015, the China–US Joint Announcement on Climate Change specified the size of the climate fund: 20 billion RMB. In December 2015, President Xi Jinping announced the "Ten-Hundred-Thousand" program: launching ten low-carbon demonstration zones and 100 mitigation and adaptation projects in developing countries and training 1000 officials for climate change. As of October 2019, China has signed material donation memoranda with more than 20 countries and regions, deploying designated funds worth over 720 million RMB, donating large amounts of energy-saving products to developing countries, and providing them with over 4000 training opportunities.

To summarize, China has developed a system of climate policy over a course of three decades. The policy-making and implementation system has gone through several stages of evolution. It started by treating the issue of climate change as a natural phenomenon to be addressed by scientists, and then as an international issue handled by diplomats, and finally as a strategic issue related to economic development and global governance and thus to be led by the top leadership. Increasingly climate policy-making has moved up to become a national priority on the policy agenda and take a unique place in China's strategic planning and the FYPs. Climate policy implementation initially relied primarily on the government hierarchy and the government's dominating influence on businesses. Gradually, economic incentives are added to the mechanisms of implementation. Currently, the carbon market is given high hopes and expectations as a major instrument for climate policy implementation in China. It is worth noting that China's national low-carbon development pilot program spanning the whole decade since 2010 has played a significant role in policy learning, design and diffusion. Under the current administration, climate policy-making has not only moved up to the top leadership, but also been given unprecedented significance as China's opportunity to help reshape global governance. With concerted international efforts, this may also develop into a real opportunity for the world.

NOTES

1. China's nine strategic emerging industries include next-generation information technology (IT), high-end equipment manufacturing, new materials, biotechnology, new-energy vehicles (NEVs), new-energy, energy-efficient and environmental technologies, digital innovation, and related services.
2. The legal term for the Top 10 000 Enterprises, as defined in the 2008 China Energy Conservation Law, is key energy-consuming entities (*zhongdian yongneng danwei*), which refers to two categories of energy-consuming entities: (1) organizations whose annual energy consumption exceeds 10 000 tce; and (2) organizations whose annual energy consumption ranges between 5000 tce and 10 000 tce but are designated by the relevant national agencies of the State Council or provincial-level government agencies in charge of energy saving to be key energy-consuming entities.
3. "Sponge cites are designed to absorb large quantities of water and disperse it back into the environment in a slow manner...[utilizing][p]ermeable roads and sidewalks, green roofs, wetlands and natural vegetation absorb, infiltrate, store, purify, drain and manage rainwater" (Fuldauer, 2019).

REFERENCES

Administrative Center for China's Agenda 21 (2019). *China Carbon Capture and Storage Technological Development Roadmap*. Beijing.

Asian Development Bank (ADB) (2015). *Road Map for Carbon Capture and Storage Demonstration and Deployment*. Manila: ADB.

BP (2019). *BP Energy Outlook: 2019 Edition*.

Dong, W., Gao, J., Liu, X., & Zhang, Z. (2018). China's renewable energy investment under the background of green finance. In Y. Qi & X. Zhang (Eds.), *Annual Review of Low-Carbon Development in China (2018)* (1st ed., pp. 121–35). Beijing: Social Sciences Academic Press.

Feng, K., Davis, S.J., & Sun, L. et al. (2013). Outsourcing CO_2 within China. *Proceedings of the National Academy of Sciences, 110*(28), 11654–9.

Fuldauer, E. (2019). China's sponge cities are turning concrete green to combat flooding. *Tomorrow Mag*. Accessed August 11, 2020 at https://www.smartcitylab.com/blog/urban-environment/chinas-sponge-cities-are-turning-concrete-green-to-combat-flooding/.

Green Finance Committee (GFC) of China Society for Finance and Banking and the Green Finance Initiative (GFI) (2018). "Green investment principles for the Belt and Road. Accessed August 15, 2020 at http://www.gflp.org.cn/public/ueditor/php/upload/file/20181201/1543598660333978.pdf.

International Energy Agency (IEA) (2015). *Energy Technology Perspectives 2015: Mobilising Innovation to Accelerate Climate Action*. Accessed August 11, 2020 at https://elering.ee/sites/default/files/public/tarkvork-konv/2015.10.15_SG_Conference_-_Jean-Francois_Gagne.pdf.

Jiang, M., An, H., & Gao et al. (2019). Factors driving global carbon emissions: a complex network perspective. *Resources, Conservation and Recycling, 146*, 431–40.

Li, H., Zhao, X., Ma, L., & Qi, Y. (2013). Policy implementation: energy conservation target responsibility system. In Y. Qi (Ed.), *Annual Review of Low-Carbon Development in China (2013)*. Beijing: Social Sciences Academic Press.

Li, H., Zhao, X., & Yu, Y. et al. (2016). China's numerical management system for reducing national energy intensity. *Energy Policy, 94*, 64–76.

Liu, Z., Davis, S.J., & Feng et al. (2016). Targeted opportunities to address the climate–trade dilemma in China. *Nature Climate Change, 6*, 201–6.

Liu, T., & Li, H. (2018). Low carbon indicators. In Y. Qi & X. Zhang (Eds.), *Annual Review of Low-Carbon Development in China (2018)* (1st ed., pp. 225–49). Beijing: Social Sciences Academic Press.

Long, R., Li, J., & Chen, H. et al. (2018). Embodied carbon dioxide flow in international trade: a comparative analysis based on China and Japan. *Journal of Environmental Management, 209*, 371–81.

Ministry of Agriculture (2015). *Action Plan to Achieve Zero Growth of Fertilizer by 2020*. Beijing.

Ministry of Ecology and Environment (2018). *China's Policies and Actions for Addressing Climate Change (2018)*. Beijing.

Ministry of Ecology and Environment (2019). *China's Policies and Actions for Addressing Climate Change (2019)*. Beijing.

Peters, G.P., Minx, J.C., Weber, C.L., & Edenhofer, O. (2011). Growth in emission transfers via international trade from 1990 to 2008. *Proceedings of the National Academy of Sciences of the United States of America, 108*, 8903–8.

Qi, Y. (2018). Foreword: accelerated decarbonization of all countries in the context of energy revolution. In Y. Qi & X. Zhang (Eds.), *Annual Review of Low-Carbon Development in China (2018)* (1st ed., pp. 1–6). Beijing: Social Sciences Academic Press.

Qi, Y., Dong, W., & Guo, Y. et al. (2019). Research on green investment and financing standards for policy banks in the Belt and Road Initiative. National Resources Defense Council. Accessed August 15, 2020 at http://coalcap.nrdc.cn/datum/info?id=99&type=1.

Qi, Y., & Lu, J. (2018). China's coal consumption has peaked. *China Daily Africa Weekly*, January 19, p. 10. Accessed August 15, 2020 at http://africa.chinadaily.com.cn/weekly/2018-01/19/content_35538975.htm.

Qi, Y., & Ma, L. (2007). Towards proactive climate change policy. *China Population, Resources and Environment, 17*(2), 8–12.

Qi, Y., Stern, N., & Wu, T. et al. (2016). China's post-coal growth. *Nature Geoscience, 9*, 564–6.

Qi, Y., & Wu, T. (2013). The politics of climate change in China. *Wiley Interdisciplinary Reviews: Climate Change, 4*(4), 301–13.

Tsinghua University (2020a). *Strategy and Pathway for China's Low-Carbon Development Transition*. Tsinghua University China's Low-Carbon Development Transition Strategy and Pathway Project. Beijing.

Tsinghua University (2020b). *Emission Reduction Technologies in China in Medium-to-Long Term: Cost–Benefit Analysis, Assessment and Roadmap*. Tsinghua University China's Low-Carbon Development Transition Strategy and Pathway Project. Beijing.

United Nations Environment Programme (UNEP) (2019). *Synergizing Action on the Environment and Climate: Good Practice in China and Around the Globe*. Accessed August 15, 2020 at https://ccacoalition.org/en/resources/synergizing-action-environment-and-climate-good-practice-china-and-around-globe.

Weber, C.L., Peters, G.P., Guan, D., & Hubacek, K. (2008). The contribution of Chinese exports to climate change. *Energy Policy, 36*, 3572–7.

Yan, X. (2014). From keeping a low profile to striving for achievement. *The Chinese Journal of International Politics, 7*(2), 153–84.

Zhao, X., Li, H., Wu, L., & Qi, Y. (2014). Implementation of energy-saving policies in China: how local governments assisted industrial enterprises in achieving energy-saving targets. *Energy Policy, 66*, 170–84.

Zhao, X., & Qi, Y. (2020). Why do firms obey? The state of regulatory compliance research in China. *Journal of Chinese Political Science, 25*, 339–52.

Zhao, X., & Wu, L. (2016). Interpreting the evolution of the energy-saving target allocation system in China (2006–13): a view of policy learning. *World Development, 82*, 83–94.

Zhao, X., Young, O.R., Qi, Y., & Guttman, D. (2020). Back to the future: can Chinese doubling down and American muddling through fulfill 21st century needs for environmental governance? *Environmental Policy and Governance, 30*(2), 59–70.

Zhu, M., Qi, Y., & Belis, D. et al. (2019). The China wind paradox: the role of state-owned enterprises in wind power investment versus wind curtailment. *Energy Policy, 127*, 200–212.

8. The Paris Agreement on climate change: what legacy?

Laurence Tubiana and Emmanuel Guérin

The Paris Agreement on climate change was adopted in 2015 and entered into force in 2016 with the explicit intent of addressing the shortcomings of previous Multilateral Environmental Agreements (MEAs), building on the lessons learned from previous errors in crafting a truly global and effective climate agreement. It was also designed with a view to providing a durable but dynamic framework for reducing global greenhouse gas (GHG) emissions, building resilience to the effects of climate change, and reorienting financial flows and technological investments towards the objectives of climate change mitigation and adaptation.

Today, nationalism is on the rise and multilateralism is increasingly challenged as an approach to addressing global issues (trade, security, immigration, climate change, biodiversity losses) through international cooperation. At the same time, the need to increase the level of ambition of climate actions is also becoming even more pressing and urgent, to keep the objectives set by the Paris Agreement within reach and deliver on the promise for sustainable development more broadly (UN Environment, 2018). It is therefore more important than ever to better explain what the Paris Agreement really is, how it came to be, and how it can provide the basis for the necessary acceleration of climate actions.

Both of us actively took part in the negotiations of the Paris Agreement.[1] Many people, from many different countries and backgrounds (representing countries, local authorities, civil society organizations, the business sector, workers and trade unions, the science and technological community, faith groups, indigenous peoples, the youth movement and many other individuals) can claim credit for the success of COP21 (Profiles of Paris, n.d.). Through this chapter, we would like to share our own perspective on the negotiations of this agreement, lay out the key concepts from international relations and global governance theories it builds onto, and briefly discuss some of the necessary next steps in light of the latest trends in global politics and climate science.

THEORETICAL FOUNDATIONS OF THE PARIS AGREEMENT

Sovereign Choices: Nationally Determined Contributions (NDCs)

The theory of international agreements often distinguishes two broadly differ-ent types of agreements: bottom-up and top-down (Michaelowa, 2015). These two categories in fact contain several overlapping dimensions, including: "only" domestically legally binding commitments vs internationally legally binding ones (with sanctions in the case of non-compliance); and voluntary commitments (i.e., self-determined contributions) vs commitments based on an explicit formula for sharing the global costs (or "burden") and benefits.

Reality is, as always, more subtle and more complex. The Paris Agreement could be described as a hybrid between a top-down and a bottom-up approach, even if it leans more towards a bottom-up approach. But the distinction between top-down and bottom-up agreements is nonetheless useful, even in practice, because it captures the trade-off negotiators inevitably face between: participation (the main concern of those in favour of bottom-up approaches); and effectiveness (the key objective of those arguing for top-down approaches) (Raustiala, 2005).

At the centre of the Paris Agreement lies the concept of NDCs. NDCs are the vehicle for all countries to attach to the agreement itself their contributions in terms of climate change mitigation and adaptation; and, in the case of devel-oped countries, their contributions to the needs of developing countries for climate finance, technology and capacity building.

From the start, it was made very clear that the agreement itself (which includes the collective long-term goals for climate actions, the rules and princi-ples for individual contributions, the transparency system and the cooperation mechanisms) and the NDCs were both part of the Paris Agreement "package", but also clearly separate: because they have a different legal status (the frame-work agreement being internationally legally binding – even if it does not include sanctions in the case of non-compliance, while the NDCs are "only" domestically legally binding), but also because they have a different timeframe (the framework agreement being open ended and not time bound, while the NDCs are to 2025 or 2030 and need to be periodically revised and enhanced).

Several considerations prevailed to make a clear distinction between the framework agreement and the NDCs. Chief among them was the willingness, shared by all parties, to design an agreement that would make it possible for the US to join without requiring a two-thirds majority vote from its Senate. Hence the clear distinction between the obligation for the US (and every other country) to submit an NDC as part of the Paris Agreement; and the voluntary commitment to reach a particular target for reducing its GHG emissions (and provide a specific amount of finance to developing countries) (Roberts & Arellano, 2017).

But the distinction between the legal status of the framework agreement and the NDCs was not just a way of taking into consideration the particular circumstances of the US. In fact, it is a concern that was also shared by most emerging countries, including China and India (unlike the European Union, the Least Developed Countries [LDCs] and the Small Island and Developing States [SIDS], which did not have an issue with taking an internationally legally binding commitment to reduce their GHG emissions).

In fact, the major concern for most developing countries participating in a multilateral system, whose design they had often played no part in, was and still is the protection of their national sovereignty. Negotiations in Copenhagen at COP15 demonstrated how anxious developing countries' governments and non-governmental organizations (NGOs) were about the external imposition of norms on their own policy and development space. The assumption at that time was that the distribution of the remaining carbon budget limited *by definition* their capacity to grow on the same development path. Protection of sovereignty was even mentioned in the final Copenhagen text drafted in December 2009 between a number of emerging countries and the US as a desperate attempt to find a common ground.

Any global policy instrument, and in particular the idea of a global carbon market, was perceived as a breach of that protective fence, as was the notion of a global agreement constraining emissions. The Paris framework had to respond to that fundamental anxiety to ensure a broad participation, building on the assumption that perception of interests will evolve over time as the risk of climate change will become more evident to all and that responses to it look increasingly workable and beneficial. The Paris Agreement was conceived from the start as a learning process betting on the power of ideas diffusion and narrative performance.

The need to make it crystal clear to countries, in particular those especially wary of their sovereignty, that they would not face international sanctions if they did not meet their domestic commitment to reduce their GHG emissions, was not the only reason for treating the framework agreement and the NDCs differently. Another reason was to make it plainly obvious that they had different timeframes: the framework agreement was here to stay, while the NDCs were to be periodically revised and enhanced (as we will discuss in further detail below).

Before the adoption of the Paris Agreement, the efforts of the international climate community were indeed almost entirely consumed in the endless negotiation and renegotiation of international agreements (the United Nations Framework Convention on Climate Change [UNFCCC] was adopted as early as 1992; the Kyoto Protocol, which the US never ratified, was then signed in 1997; the climate negotiation process derailed in Copenhagen in 2009, when it failed to reach a global deal; it was rescued one year later in Cancun; etc.) (Center for Climate and Energy Solutions, n.d.). The objective at COP21 was to make sure that the process would deliver a durable framework (i.e., one that does not have to be renegotiated all the time and is therefore flexible enough) to make it possible to concentrate efforts after that on the much more important objectives of actually reducing GHG emissions, adapting to climate change, and reorienting financial flows and technological investment towards these goals.

A Clear Long-term Goal: Zero GHG Emissions

Bottom-up contributions by nation-states are, by definition, insufficient to address a global issue. And the Paris Agreement would be of limited use, if any, if it did not do more than simply capture self-determined contributions by countries. The value of international cooperation is precisely to unlock collective action that amounts to more than the sum of its parts. One of the most important contributions of the Paris Agreement is in fact, for the first time, to lay out a clear collective long-term goal for reducing global GHG emissions and addressing climate change more broadly (Carbon Brief, 2015).

The ways in which the international community has expressed this long-term goal has evolved over time (Gao, Gao & Zhang, 2017). This evolution reflects both the tension between politics and science, and the difficulty for countries (but also simply for people) to face the individual consequences of what they are ready to accept as a necessary (and mutually beneficial) collective objective, but also the evolution of climate science itself (the functioning of the climate system, the nature and magnitude of climate impacts in different scenarios of GHG emission concentrations, and the costs and benefits of the different mitigation options).

Before the Paris Agreement, the agreed long-term goal for reducing global GHG emissions (as included in the Cancun Agreement, 2010) was to reduce them at a level consistent with an increase in average temperatures maintained below 2°C compared to pre-industrial levels. The Paris Agreement made an important contribution to both the level of ambition and degree of precision of this goal.

First, the Paris Agreement states that the objective is to limit the average increase in temperatures compared to pre-industrial levels "to well below 2°C, aiming for 1.5°C". The explicit mention of 1.5°C as an aspirational objective is an important step forward, in particular for the LDCs and SIDS (i.e., those contributing the least and suffering the most from climate change) who have long demanded that this is the stated goal of climate actions. The Intergovernmental

Panel on Climate Change (IPCC) Special Report (SR) on 1.5°C (IPCC, 2018), mandated by Paris decisions, provided much detail as to the great differences of impacts between the 1.5°C and 2°C average temperature increase scenarios, as well as the global GHG emission reduction pathways consistent with the 1.5°C objective.

Second, the Paris Agreement also spells out clearly, for the first time, the global GHG emission reduction pathways consistent with these average temperature increase limits. In particular, it clearly states that the objective is to achieve "the balance between GHG emission sources and sinks" (i.e., net-zero GHG emissions) during the second half of the century. Since then, the IPCC 1.5°C SR clarified that: in order to limit the average temperature increase to below 2°C, global GHG emissions need to reach net zero by 2085 (global CO_2 energy- and industry-related emissions by 2070); and to limit the average temperature increase to 1.5°C, global GHG emissions need to reach net zero by 2070 (global CO_2 energy- and industry-related emissions by 2050).

Being clear about the fact that global GHG emissions need to reach net zero (before they have to turn net negative) to stick to the objectives of the Paris Agreement (in fact, to any given average temperature increase objective) dramatically changed the debate (if not yet the actions) on climate mitigation. The fact that, given that human-induced climate change is correlated to the stock of global GHG emissions (and not their flow), global GHG emissions have to stay within a given global carbon budget in order not to exceed a certain level of average temperature increase, is something that was well known for a long time by climate scientists. But the fact that the objective of climate change mitigation is now framed in the public discourse as "zero emissions" has profound impacts on how to approach GHG emission reduction strategies.

Before that, every country (or every sector within a country) entered into the debate by arguing why others should do more (because they had contributed more historically; because they had higher per-capita or per-GDP GHG emissions; because it was more cost effective to reduce GHG emissions in other sectors, etc.). Now, even if the timing of reaching net-zero GHG emissions arguably has to be different for different countries and sectors, this has become the ultimate objective for all. Moving away from an incremental deviation from business-as-usual and burden-sharing approaches towards a shared vision for a net-zero economy and society is probably the most important contribution from the Paris Agreement to the narrative of climate action. From there every action or policy will have to be evaluated against this benchmark. As so often happens, this key result was not at the core of the trade-offs on which negotiators were debating: more time was dedicated to arguing on the level of responsibility of nations or X than on the global goal of the regime.

A Periodic Assessment and Increase of Short-term Actions

Although the Paris Agreement clearly spells out the global GHG emission reduction pathways consistent with the objective of limiting the average temperature increase well below 2°C, aiming for 1.5°C, the NDCs made by countries at COP21 and attached to the agreement are inconsistent with these pathways. And the difference between the projected level of global GHG emissions in 2030 (provided NDCs are fully implemented) and the level consistent with a well below 2°C or 1.5°C emission reduction pathway is not small: the gap is between 13 and 15 Gt of CO_2 equivalent for a well below 2°C scenario; and between 29 and 32 Gt of CO_2 equivalent for a 1.5°C scenario. As a reference, the level of GHG emission today is slightly higher than 50 Gt of CO_2 equivalent (UNEP, 2018).

By and large, what is needed is therefore an increase by a factor of three or so of the level of ambition of the current NDCs to 2030. The NDCs pledged at COP21 do not even achieve a peaking of global GHG emissions in 2030, when they need to peak by around 2020 to keep the option open of achieving the goals set by the Paris Agreement.

There are two ways to look at the discrepancy between the sum of NDCs and the global GHG emission reduction pathways consistent with the objective of limiting the average temperature increase well below 2°C, aiming for 1.5°C. The first is to consider that the Paris Agreement is intrinsically flawed because of this gap (Lowe, 2018); that countries are fundamentally incapable of facing the individual consequences of their collective choices; and that the Paris Agreement is insufficient at best, maybe useless altogether, to address effectively the issue of climate change (Cass, 2015).

The dissonance between the ambition of the collective long-term goal and the modesty of short-term individual actions, as well as the rhetoric between self-proclaimed climate leadership by some and the reality of their climate actions, is indeed profoundly worrying and should be challenged. We are running out of time to address climate change, which would come at great costs not just for the environment or the economy but also simply for people's lives; and the window of opportunity to keep open the option of delivering on the objectives set at COP21 is closing fast. But this is precisely why the Paris Agreement includes a mechanism for the periodic review and assessment of the adequacy of NDCs compared to the long-term goal, every five years. And the first of these moments, when NDCs need to be revised and enhanced, comes up in 2020.

The first – unexpected – test for the Paris Agreement was the US decision to withdraw. The fact that no other countries, including China, withdrew following the US decision, proved the resilience of the Paris Agreement, as well as the failed attempts at G20 and G7 to erase the reference to the Paris

Agreement. But the resilience of the Paris Agreement to such a big shock, although it is a necessary condition for its durability and therefore its effectiveness in the long run, is certainly not a guarantee of its ability to deliver the necessary global GHG emission reductions in the short term. And the real test for the effectiveness of the Paris Agreement in addressing climate change will be its ability to deliver a significant increase in the level of ambition of the current NDCs in 2020.

2050 Decarbonization Strategies: The Link Between Bottom-up and Top-down Approaches

To progressively close this gap, the NDC increase in 2020 needs to be guided by the ultimate objective of reaching net-zero GHG emissions. The Paris Agreement contains an important – although sometimes overlooked – provision, inviting countries to submit a 2050 decarbonization strategy (2050 Pathways Platform, n.d.) ("long-term low-GHG development strategy") before 2020.

Not much attention was paid in the run-up to COP21 to the issue of 2050 decarbonization strategies. It was mainly an issue for the scientific community (Deep Decarbonization Pathways Project, n.d.), while the negotiations by countries and the pressure from civil society concentrated on the issues of NDCs and the long-term goal. The reason why we insisted so much to include this provision in the agreement is because we knew these 2050 decarbonization strategies would provide the missing link between: the fundamentally bottom-up nature of an agreement based on self-determined contributions and the necessary top-down nature of an agreement aimed at keeping GHG emissions within a global carbon budget.

For a long time, climate negotiations stumbled over the obstacle of agreeing on a "burden-sharing" formula (i.e., a recipe that would establish by how much countries need to reduce their GHG emissions by when, so that each country would do its fair share of the global effort). No negotiation was able to find the magic number that could satisfy justice criteria, in particular taking into account the enormous quantity of CO_2 stock in the atmosphere due to the emissions of industrialized countries over two centuries, and could be safe from the point of view of the carbon budget left.

In addition, climate actions were framed as a cost and the purpose of the international negotiations was to share this cost equally across countries. This approach reached an impasse, not only because of the lack of incentives for countries to engage in cooperation to share a cost, but also because of their inescapably conflicting views over the criteria to be chosen for the equitable sharing of the global carbon budget (historical emissions; current or projected emissions; per-capita or per-GDP emissions; least-cost options, etc.) (Cameron, 2012).

NDCs provided a response to the impossibility of agreeing on a burden-sharing formula. But of course, they do not provide a solution to the fact that they need to add up to a certain level of global GHG emissions reduction. 2050 decarbonization strategies provide a possible way out (Hare et al., n.d.). Not a perfect one, at least from the point of view of making sure that they add up to the necessary level of global GHG emissions reduction, which would require agreeing on a burden-sharing formula as well (an elusive task from a political perspective), but certainly a second best in the suboptimal world of global politics and definitely an improvement to the pure bottom-up world of NDCs.

Indeed, if reducing GHG emissions entails short-term costs,[2] it yields benefits in the long run. Looking at 2050 as the horizon for decarbonization strategies – as opposed to 2025 or 2030 only – therefore shifts the terms of the debate from short-term opportunity costs to long-term development opportunities. It also makes the co-benefits (or rather, the primary benefits) of climate actions (energy security, food security, jobs, air quality, technological innovation, etc.) much more visible (The New Climate Economy, n.d.).

There is no easy answer to the question of what countries' 2050 target for reducing their GHG emissions should be. But the fact that, collectively, all countries have to reach net-zero GHG emissions during the second half of the century makes it possible to define a simple rule of thumb: high-income countries should reach net-zero GHG around 2050; middle-income countries around 2060; and low-income countries around 2070. This simple rule should not be interpreted as a straightjacket, and the fact that countries embark on an exercise to design their long-term development strategies (in the sectors of energy, industry, buildings, transport, agriculture, etc.), guided by the objective of reaching net-zero GHG emissions at some point during the second half of the century[3] is more important – at least at first – than insisting on a particular date. It means clearly that every country has to design a low- and then zero-carbon path, and that the carbon market (i.e., buying emissions reductions where they are less costly) is not a long-term solution.

Beyond Nation-states: The Role of Non-state Actors (NSAs)

As sovereignty protection is a red line for many countries in a world where no clear hegemon can operate, enforcement mechanisms are a major challenge in any international agreement. This was a very strong argument for involving NSAs actors in the preparation process and to consider them as powerful levers of implementation. The Paris Agreement can be considered as an innovation in terms of global governance is because of the central role played by NSAs.

Associating NSAs as observers to the design of an international agreement – or even in some cases as implementers – is not an innovation as such. Since the first UN Environment and Development Conference in 1992, known as the Earth Summit, nine Major Groups and other Stakeholders (MGoS) participate, in different ways, to the UN processes on sustainable development (Sustainable Development Knowledge Platform, n.d.): women, children and youth, indigenous people, NGOs, local authorities, workers and trade unions, business and industry, scientific and technological community, farmers. But in the case of the Paris Agreement, they played a much more active and central role than in many other international processes (Hale, 2018). Local authorities (cities, regions and states) and businesses (including investors) were particularly key, not just to encourage countries to adopt a global climate deal or make sure their concerns were addressed (direct access to finance, competitiveness, etc.) the way they traditionally do, but because they also took commitments of their own to reduce their GHG emissions, improve resilience to climate change, mobilize climate finance and divest from high-carbon assets, and invest in low-carbon technology deployment and innovation.

The contribution to the Paris Agreement "package" was explicitly recognized, encouraged and organized within the Climate Action Agenda (UNFCCC, n.d.). The objective was twofold:

Catastrophism vs agency
First, to create a positive narrative around climate action and to demonstrate, through concrete actions and commitments on the ground by local authorities, to businesses and investors that climate actions could be an opportunity and yield benefits, that they were not just a constraint or a cost. The importance attached to narratives, and of the role to be played by NSAs to create a positive narrative came from the realization of the limitations of catastrophism as a trigger for action. It is well established by now by social psychology that, even if the risks are well understood and the threats perceived as great and imminent, people need agency to act. The Climate Action Agenda was designed with this purpose in mind, and not just as a framework to encourage individual commitments from NSAs, but also to communicate around them as a whole.

Rational expectations and self-fulfilling prophecies
Beyond the need to create a positive narrative and to provide agency to NSA willing to take actions and make commitments, the Climate Action Agenda was therefore conceived as a way to shape expectations that the transition to a zero-GHG and climate-resilient future was not only necessary (a point well established by the scientific community a long time ago), not just beneficial (a point consistently stressed by NGOs for a long time also), but also inevi-

table, already well underway, and poised to accelerate; and therefore, that the early movers would reap its benefits while the laggards would bear the costs (We Mean Business Coalition, 2015).

The Climate Regime: A Regime Complex

The Paris Agreement is therefore very different from the traditional type of international agreement among nation-states. And beyond the fact that the agreement is largely bottom-up in nature, because it is based on self-determined contributions, the fact that it involved so many different stakeholders in its design, who now have a stake in its continuation and implementation, surely explains why it proved resilient to the US withdrawal. The We Are Still In movement (We Are Still In, n.d.) in the US, which gathers the US states, cities, businesses and investors committed to the implementation of the Paris Agreement and climate action more broadly (and will hopefully provide the political basis for the US to re-enter the Paris Agreement after the end of Trump's mandate) is a direct application at the federal level of the method that was applied globally with success at COP21.

In the language of international relations theory, the global climate regime would therefore be called a regime complex (Keohane & Victor, 2010). The idea is that there is not a single institution, or even a single process, governing the global response to climate change. The Paris Agreement is, arguably, the centre of this regime complex. But the Montreal Protocol plays a vital role in progressively phasing out a specific GHG: hydrofluorocarbon. GHG emissions from international aviation and shipping, because they are global in nature, require a special treatment within the context of their respective organizations (International Civil Aviation Authority and International Maritime Organization). It has started, even if far too slowly, but already major shipping companies are committing to net-zero emissions by 2050.

The Major Economies Forum (MEF), initiated by George W. Bush as a substitute to UN negotiations, ended up playing a very useful complementary role to the UN process under the Obama administration. But precisely, these other approaches – and probably others to be designed – are a complement, not a substitute, to the Paris Agreement as a global framework agreement.

THE LEGACY OF THE PARIS AGREEMENT: A PLATFORM FOR THE ACCELERATION OF CLIMATE ACTIONS

No text can deliver action per se. But a text, with clear goals and milestones, approved by so many countries, supported by so many constituencies from businesses to cities, NGOs, labour unions, financial institutions and even climate activists, is a platform that can act as a reference and accelerate action. Activists already use it to sue governments, by shareholders to question management strategies of companies' boards and, to vote, and increasingly by financial actors to measure the risks of their portfolios.

In 2020, the first year of implementation of Paris Agreement, all governments have to present improved climate plans for 2030 and long-term strategies for 2050. Diplomatic pressure, mobilization of actors inside countries, international financial institutions, will help force the major emitters to be consistent with their commitments.

Already the Paris goals, that is, going to net-zero emissions by 2050 or soon after, are spreading beyond governments' plans. Not only have a number of countries (as of today 114) committed to be carbon neutral or even climate neutral by 2050, but local authorities, cities and subnational entities, businesses and financial actors are doing it as well. A reality check is needed to test how serious these commitments are. A way to ensure credibility, a condition to change beliefs and mindsets, is to engage around clear plans and roadmaps as much as short-term decisions consistent with Paris goals.

The legacy of Paris relies on the capacity of its logic and goals to be transmittable to all sectors of activity. This "contamination" is proving effective as even actors that are by definition not bound by any intergovernmental treaty are internalizing the Paris Agreement in their strategies and objectives. Progressively, the Paris norms are seen as undeniable.

This normalization process is crucial as a founding block of peer pressure, the only enforcement mechanism of the Paris Agreement. Peer pressure is clearly a very weak mechanism but it is the only mechanism we have in international law. But this weakness can be transformed into a much stronger force if the pressure comes from all fronts, inside countries and outside, outside businesses and inside, and so on.

Then, of course, these norms have to be transmitted into the realm of policies in countries, across sectors, investment, tax, industry, innovation, labour, trade, fiscal, agriculture, and so forth. The transformation of the regulatory framework will operate the real implementation of Paris Agreement. Because of this normalization, some countries have already started the process, in Europe and elsewhere.

But the implementation of the Paris agreement has to go beyond governments and organized constituencies and interests. The scope and breath of the transformation required to eliminate fossil fuels needs the buy-in of a broad range of actors in the societies. The legacy of the Paris Agreement will be secured if citizens consider a zero-carbon future as a positive endeavour, a development prospect that responds to their concerns. It means that the Paris goals have to be embedded in a broad social compact where the relations between human societies and nature are rebalanced. The Paris Agreement cannot be implemented from the top only. Forcing societies to shift through imposition of policies from governments without consultation and participation of citizens in the decision-making will create insuperable oppositions. Social justice has to go hand in hand with deep climate action. This is the real test for the Paris Agreement.

NOTES

1. To the extent that countries, in particular low emitters, are happy to join an agreement where large emitters self-determine their contribution to the global effort.
2. Investment costs, or transition costs.
3. And revise their GHG emission reduction target for 2025 or 2030 based on this strategy.

REFERENCES

Cameron, E. (2012). What is equity in the context of climate negotiations? *WRI.org*, 14 December. Accessed 6 April 2020 at https://www.wri.org/blog/2012/12/what-equity -context-climate-negotiations.

Carbon Brief (2015). Explainer: The long-term goal of the Paris climate deal. Accessed 6 April 2020 at https://www.carbonbrief.org/explainer-the-long-term-goal-of-the -paris-climate-deal.

Cass, O. (2015). Why the Paris climate deal is meaningless. *Politico.eu*, 29 November. Accessed 6 April 2020 at https://www.politico.eu/article/paris-climate-deal-is -meaningless-cop21-emissions-china-obama/.

Center for Climate and Energy Solutions (n.d.). History of UN climate talks. Accessed 6 April 2020 at https://www.c2es.org/content/history-of-un-climate-talks/.

Deep Decarbonization Pathways Project (DDPP) (n.d.) [website]. Accessed 6 April 2020 at http://deepdecarbonization.org/.

Gao, Y., Gao, X., & Zhang, X. (2017). The 2°C global temperature target and the evolution of the long-term goal of addressing climate change – from the United Nations Framework Convention on Climate Change to the Paris Agreement. *Engineering*, 3(2), 272–8.

Hale, T. (2018). *The Role of Sub-state and Non-state Actors in International Climate Processes*. London: Energy, Environment and Resources Department, Royal Institute of International Affairs.

Hare, B., Ancygier, A., De Marez, L., & Yanguas Parra, P. (n.d.). Facilitating global transition: the role of nationally determined contributions in meeting the long-term temperature goal of the Paris Agreement. Accessed 6 April 2020 at http://ndcpartnership.org/facilitating-global-transition-role-nationally-determined -contributions-meeting-long-term.

Intergovernmental Panel on Climate Change (IPCC) (2018). *Global Warming of 1.5°C: An IPCC Special Report.* Accessed 6 April 2020 at https://www.ipcc.ch/sr15/.

Keohane, R.O., & Victor, D.G. (2010). The regime complex for climate change. *Harvard Discussion Papers*, No. 10-33. The Harvard Project on International Climate Agreements.

Lowe, T. (2018). The Paris Climate Accords are even more useless than you thought. *Washington Examiner*, 15 December. Accessed 6 April 2020 at https://

www.washingtonexaminer.com/opinion/the-paris-climate-accords-are-even-more
-useless-than-you-thought.

Michaelowa, A. (2015). Overview and assessment of international climate policy
architectures and scenarios. *Climatepolicyinfohub.eu*, 18 February. Accessed 6 April
2020 at https://climatepolicyinfohub.eu/international-climate-policy-architectures-
%E2%80%93-top-down-and-bottom.

Profiles of Paris. (n.d.). Profiles. Accessed 6 April 2020 at https://profilesofparis.com/
profiles/.

Raustiala, K. (2005). Form and substance in international agreements. *American
Journal of International Law*, *99*, 581–614.

Roberts, T., & Arellano, A. (2017). Is the Paris climate deal legally binding or not?
Climatechangenews.com. Accessed 6 April 2020 at https://www.climatechangenews
.com/2017/11/02/paris-climate-deal-legally-binding-not/.

Sustainable Development Knowledge Platform (n.d.). About Major Groups and other
Stakeholders. Accessed 6 April 2020 at https://sustainabledevelopment.un.org/
aboutmajorgroups.html.

The New Climate Economy (n.d.). The Global Commission on the Economy and
Climate [website]. Accessed 6 April 2020 at https://newclimateeconomy.net/.

2050 Pathways Platform (n.d.) [website]. Accessed 6 April 2020 at https://www
.2050pathways.org/.

UN Environment (2018). *Emissions Gap Report 2018*. Accessed 6 April 2020 at http://
www.unenvironment.org/resources/emissions-gap-report-2018.

United Nations Framework Convention on Climate Change (UNFCCC) (n.d.). Global
Climate Action [website]. Accessed 6 April 2020 at https://climateaction.unfccc.int.

We Are Still In (n.d.) [website]. Accessed 6 April 2020 at https://www.wearestillin
.com/.

We Mean Business Coalition (2015). Business leaders: Paris Agreement will accelerate
shift to thriving, clean global economy [blog]. Accessed 6 April 2020 at https://
www.wemeanbusinesscoalition.org/blog/business-leaders-paris-agreement-will
-accelerate-shift-to-thriving-clean-global-economy/.

PART II

Defenders

9. Introduction to Part II

Jonathan Watts

LAST STAND FOR NATURE

In any conflict, the last thing a dominant power wants is for the outside world to know the cost of victory. They criminalize and dehumanize their opposition, downplay the importance of the struggle, obscure the number of victims and undermine media coverage.

This is particularly true of the battle for the global environment, which goes underreported because it often takes place in remote regions that are expensive or dangerous to reach. If disputes are covered at all, they are usually portrayed as disparate, distant, low-intensity challenges to "development" and the establishment.

But gather those cases together – as we have done in this part of the book – and a pattern starts to emerge of a war against nature on many fronts. Tally the deaths and it becomes clear the toll is higher than many conflict zones. Then add names, portraits, profiles and family stories and there is no avoiding a discomforting connection with those on the front lines of ecological crisis.

That was what I learned from *The Guardian*'s year-long Defenders project, which I helped to oversee and report on during my first year as the paper's global environment editor. The experience also convinced me of the need to make global stories personal, to collaborate more widely, to disrupt business-as-usual journalism, and to look for creative ways to break out of the "environment media ghetto". Some of these approaches might apply to wider battles over the climate and other issues of global importance.

I admit my feelings were mixed when I first took over Defenders coverage for *The Guardian*. That was July 2017. A long-time foreign correspondent in Asia and Latin America, I had just moved back to London for the first time in 22 years to take my current post. My overriding priority was the climate crisis and the collapse of biodiversity, so when I was told that my duties included a series on the killings of people who were defending their land and environment, I was sympathetic but wary. Back then, it seemed a remote concern. I realized later how wrong that was.

But I was also pleased to focus on a topic that would show that courage, fear, desperation, anger, love and other human feelings are part of the environment story. The primary challenge for a journalist is to make a subject feel personal. Without that, the science becomes abstract, global issues seem too huge to grasp, and it becomes difficult to relate to far-off places and other species. Without that, the "environment" slips too easily into an elite pigeonhole for academics, policymakers and predominantly middle-class white people, when it should be recognized as the main driver of inequality, conflict and injustice. Without that, most people don't realize this underlies politics and economics. This is not just another subject; it is a prism through which to see everything else.

It is also a way to explain much of the world's violence – against people as well as against nature. During the year of the project, I talked to the families and friends of dozens of victims: Aysin and Ali Büyüknohutçu, the Turkish beekeepers and environmental defenders who were murdered for challenging marble quarries; Efigenia Vásquez, a radio and video journalist of the indigenous Kokonuko people in Colombia, who was fatally shot as she attempted to cover her community's attempt to regain land lost to a farm owned by a former general; Samuel Loware, a Ugandan ranger who narrowly survived an attack by poachers; Maria do Socorro Costa Silva, a descendant of rebel slaves now suffering death threats as she battles one of the world's biggest alumina refineries in the Amazon; Nonhle Mbuthuma, the Amadiba activist who overcame the death of a fellow campaigner to win a high court battle against a titanium mine on South Africa's Wild Coast; Fatima Babu, the Indian anti-pollution activist who helped to close down a giant copper smelter after the massacre of more than a dozen protesters in Tamil Nadu; Isela González, the former nurse who devotes herself to indigenous land rights in Mexico; and Ramón Bedoya, a 19-year-old Colombian *campesino* (rural farmer) who wants to create a biodiversity zone on the edge of a palm oil plantation – a project that led to the assassination of his father. These and many others are risking their lives for their land and our Earth, defending forests, rivers, coastlines and wildlife as far afield as the Coral Triangle, Sierra Madre, Pondoland, Anatolia, Mindanao, Tamil Nadu, the Brazilian Amazon and the Ugandan savanna.

In 2017, more than 200 Earth defenders were murdered while trying to protect their land and environment, according to non-governmental organization (NGO) Global Witness, which partnered *The Guardian* on the project. Last year (2019), the number was 212 – a record. A longer-term study by the University of Queensland found that killings of environmental and land defenders have doubled over the past 15 years to reach levels usually associated with war zones. The paper, published in *Nature Sustainability*, found that 1558 people in 50 nations were killed between 2002 and 2017. Almost all the killings occurred in the countries that scored lowest for corruption, fundamental rights, government powers, transparency and legal oversight. These are also areas of great natural abundance. Most of the deaths were related to agriculture or mining in tropical and subtropical countries, particularly in Central and South America.

Brazil, the biggest Amazon forest nation has been the most murderous for defenders almost every year since the tallies began, though it was surpassed in 2018 by the Philippines. Other hotspots are Colombia (another Amazonian nation), the Democratic Republic of Congo (home to Africa's biggest tropical forest) and Mexico, where the government's approval for mining and farming concessions in indigenous territory has dramatically increased the death toll in recent years.

Most victims are compelled to fight by circumstance rather than conviction. Their struggle is existential. They need land for food, water to drink, air to breathe, animals to hunt, forests to tap for medicine. Only occasionally – usually when there is a chance of NGO support or media coverage – do they talk about their contribution to the climate or biodiversity. For them, the problems are personal, at least to begin with.

Although the campaigns often start locally and accidentally, several defenders saw themselves caught up in a bigger fight for the natural world: "We didn't realize this at first, but it's global", says Turkish forest defender Tuğba Günal. "If you want to protect the environment, you are treated as a terrorist. It's everywhere now". There is a similar refrain from Fatima Babu in India who recently saw her 24-year campaign against a copper smelter explode into violence with the police slaughter of 13 protesters – one of an increasing number of environment-related massacres. "Something is happening in the world. Activists are being branded as terrorists", she says. "This phenomenon of destroying people and the planet for profit is not just happening in India. It's across the globe. We need to come together for future generations. We need to be strong and courageous and hold on to our values".

The majority of the defenders are from indigenous groups and poor black communities, who have been pushed over decades or centuries to the fringes of society. Not coincidentally, that is where nature is most abundant, where resources remain untapped, where the law often serves as a tool for exploitation rather than social stability.

Once isolated communities now find themselves on the front line. Like many endangered species, indigenous communities have been pushed from coastlines and fertile plains to remote mountain slopes and deep forests. Now even these areas are threatened by plantations, loggers and mining companies, who are granted concessions by governments that put business ahead of people. With nowhere left to flee, the local communities are forced to fight. They usually do this in the courts or the media. Defenders tend to be poor, outnumbered and outgunned, so armed struggle is rarely an option.

Yet, they are often criminalized, labelled terrorists or portrayed by their enemies as anti-development. Many of the killings are linked to government security forces, particularly in the Philippines, which is the most dangerous country in Asia for activists. In Latin America, gangs or hired assassins are a bigger threat.

Impunity is a major problem. Defenders are often cheated of land rights by corrupt lawmakers and local politicians. When they resist, they are criminalized. When they are killed, nobody gets punished. The *Nature Sustainability* study found that only 10 per cent of defender murders result in a conviction, which is very low compared to the 43 per cent average for all global homicides. Many murders are not even investigated.

This is a challenge for capacity and governance that the United Nations Environment Programme has tried to address, but there is little it can do without the support of state governments – many of which are moving away from global cooperation and pushing populist, nationalist agendas that favour extractive industries.

A new generation of political "strongmen" – Rodrigo Duterte in the Philippines, Recep Tayyip Erdoğan in Turkey, Narendra Modi in India, Donald Trump in the United States, Jair Bolsonaro in Brazil and several others – are committed to eroding the legal protections that environmental campaigners and indigenous groups are able to use to hold back mines, farms, factories and major infrastructure projects such as hydroelectric dams and roads. In many cases they have accused activists of colluding with foreign interests to slow economic development.

Such extreme nationalist leaders should not be blithely dismissed as populists. They are the hired guns of the industries working against the Paris Accord and other international agreements that aim to prevent further environmental catastrophes, which hit the poorest hardest. Their "anti-globalism" is first and foremost anti-nature and anti-future. An extraction-first approach may bring economic benefits in the short term, as campaign donors clear more forests, open up plantations and dig more mines – but the profits are concentrated and short-lived while the environmental stress is shared and long-lasting.

The great fear climate scientists have is that a warming planet could create feedback loops that will make everything much worse. But there has not been enough study of economic and political feedback loops: how drought in China puts pressure on the Amazon to produce more food and clear more forest. Or how powerful business interests will choose a dictator over a democrat if it means easing environmental controls that threaten their ability to meet quarterly growth targets.

As the chapters in this part of the book show, defenders are in the middle of a widening gulf between politicians and scientists. While the latter urge more ambitious climate and biodiversity protection, the former know they will receive more campaign funds (and, often, bribes) if they oppose emissions cuts, support extractive industries and weaken pollution regulations. It is not just dictatorships. Britain is pushing ahead with coal mining and Norway with oil exploration.

At some point, people will realize – as many defenders already do – that ecological stress is at the core of the world's current woes. The aha! moment may be when water grows prohibitively expensive, or crops fail owing to successive heatwaves, or the refugee crisis sparks war, or a virus shuts down the global economy, but at some point the weakness of the strongmen will be apparent, and people will seek change.

Defenders are often not well educated, but they have much to teach us. They know this is a battle for survival. They are fighting both for and against "us". On one hand, most are resisting the extractive businesses that provide wealthy far-away consumers with coffee, palm oil, fish and the titanium, aluminium and copper in our laptops, mobile phones, cars and bicycles. On the other, they are protecting the forests, oceans, climate and other natural life support systems on which we all depend on a far more existential level.

Some defenders have support from international NGOs, lawyers' groups, academics and the United Nations. In UN conferences and academic papers, there is a growing recognition that the cheapest and most effective way to reduce carbon emissions and protect biodiversity is by granting land rights to forest communities. As Amazon resident, Maria do Socorro Costa Silva writes in this part of the book, "The people who live here sustain the forest…Without us, there is no river, there are no animals, there's nothing. If you want to normalize the planet's temperature, you have to take care of us. Because without us there is no future generation".

No defender sets out to be an activist, let alone a pin-up for the environment. Some – such as the eco-vigilante Bobby Chan – are motivated by idealism or religious faith. Others see the struggle in gender terms. A high proportion, perhaps the majority, are women. But most are compelled to fight by circumstance rather than conviction. Several inherited their struggles or became caught up in disputes when outsiders threatened their homes. As they realize the global pressures behind their local conflicts, they want their stories to be told more widely so others can learn, follow and help. They have lessons for all of us.

Defenders are not always easy to interview as I and the project's photographer, Thom Pierce discovered. Chan rarely dares to leave his organization's headquarters in Palawan because of the dangers of assassination. Bedoya is at such high risk that he has been assigned two armed bodyguards and a bulletproof car by the Colombian authorities. González was unable to visit the communities she represents because of the threats to her life. Babu was reluctant to be photographed near the smelter because police might recognize and harass her. For journalists, such anxiety is a temporary inconvenience. For the subjects, it is a fact of everyday life. As Mbuthuma said: "I thank God each morning that I am still alive".

The stories could be both horrifying and inspiring. Even before I knew who she was or what she had suffered, there was clearly something special about Marivic Danyan. The young T'boli woman was standing silently in a noisy crowd when we reached the village of Datal Bonglangon, deep within the conflict-riven island of Mindanao, in the Philippines. The 28-year-old was so diminutive that I thought at first she was a teenager, but there was an intensity in her gaze and a strength in her handshake that suggested she had something extraordinary to relate. It was not until two days later, when she felt fully able to trust us, that she revealed how her husband, father and two brothers had been killed in a single attack by the Philippine army. Talking quietly at night over a chorus of insects and frogs, she described how she narrowly escaped death, and then had to piece together her loved ones' bodies so she could bury them. She is now looked up to as a leader – a first for a woman in her community – and is determined to continue her father's campaign to regain ancestral land from a coffee plantation linked to one of the country's richest families. Her story was a reminder that environmental crime is the ultimate theft from the poor. The destruction of the global commons – clean rivers, unpolluted air, fertile soil – worsens inequality and injustice, and usually goes hand in hand with corruption.

But the stories are rarely black and white. Although defenders are generally portrayed as plucky individuals against giant corporations, the battle lines can be murky. Many villages are violently divided over new mines, dams and plantations that bring jobs as well as environmental and cultural degradation. Defenders suffer and their friends are killed so managers can earn bonuses, politicians can secure bribes, companies can turn a hefty profit and people in richer nations can pay a low price for coffee, palm oil, plastic, fish, aluminium and energy. But that is not the only reason. They also sometimes suffer because neighbours want jobs, roads and better schools. Many individuals cross sides.

In very few of these cases are major corporations directly accused of killings, beatings and intimidation. But they often bear indirect ethical responsibility for creating the social and environmental conditions that led to violence. Culpability is legally and morally diffused by layers of intermediaries, gangs and corrupt politicians. Those who carry out assassinations and beatings are often as poor as the victims. They are usually paid by local businesspeople or city mayors who stand to benefit from agricultural or industrial projects that supply world markets with food and minerals.

Few of the defenders I met were against economic development, but they all want more choice in how it takes place. Some urged consumers to shop carefully, to consider supply chains and boycott firms and products linked with violence or environmental crimes. Most, though, said they needed broader political change – a greater global push for land rights, stronger civil society guarantees, transparency, tighter regulations on companies and more efforts to punish the officials and gang bosses who are often behind the killings.

Having reported on many of these cases, I believe a wider challenge is to close the gulf between them and us, the local and the global, between the points of production and consumption, between the environmental periphery and the economic centre. On a psychological and philosophical level this means narrowing the gap between the subjective self and the objective other.

This requires a change not just in global governance, trade rules and international law, but in our feelings about nature, our valuation of the commons, and our responsibility to other species and future generations. Chemistry, biology and physics are essential to prove how we rely on declining life support systems, but datasets are not enough. Truth must resonate on an emotional level. A good place to start would be to champion abundance over income, collective well-being over individual consumption, and to change the language we use to describe our place in the world.

I have never been entirely comfortable using the term "environmental defenders". This was partly because many campaigners are fighting for territory – their land and our Earth. But the problem is mainly with the word "environment", which always seems to widen rather than close the distance between subject and object. In English, this term is uneasy on the ear and stiffly at odds with the vibrant orgy of life it represents. This reflects the word's hodgepodge Victorian origins. The first use of "environment" in its modern sense was in 1828 by the Scottish thinker Thomas Carlyle, who borrowed the French *"environ"* (surrounding) to express the German term *"Umgebung"* (which conveys more of a sense of encompassing) in a controversial translation of Goethe. In that era, the word denoted – as now – a flux of landscape, spirit and culture that shaped humanity more naturally than the mechanistic drives of the Industrial Revolution. But it was also wrapped up inside a Western Enlightenment duality of self and "other". The environment became something to exploit, rather than something that humanity was part of. As Albert Einstein later put it: "The environment is everything that isn't me". This was a brilliantly simple way of describing how every individual feels themselves to be the centre of their own universe, but it also suggested that nature is something separate that we can affect without being affected: that we can run down without paying a price.

Carlyle and Einstein would probably be horrified at how far this duality has gone. Tension between the natural environment and the human economy has been building for over two centuries. Starting in Britain, the carbon-capital industrial model has long been extracting minerals and organic resources, and discharging the waste into the air, sea and land. As more nations developed, they exported their environmental stress to the next country rising up the economic ladder. Now that the world's most populous countries, China and India, are replicating this paradigm, there are very few places left to absorb the impact. Competition for what is left is growing.

Today, the natural environment and the human economy are treated as antonyms. The greater the gap between them, the more peripheral and frightening nature seems. No wonder those who defend it suffer such persecution.

Closing distance is one role of a journalist. After all, the word "media" essentially means go-between. International institutions, NGOs and companies can also play a part. Showing how defenders fight not just for themselves, but for us is a step in the right direction. Supporting them with laws, lobbying and financial backing for civil society would go much further. Their struggle is linked to that of Greta Thunberg, the school climate strikers, Extinction Rebellion, the Sunrise Movement and those who do their fighting in parliaments, conference halls and executive boardrooms. There are many battles, but one war. In a world pushed beyond ecological limits, there are no margins left. The periphery is the centre. In this last stand for nature, defenders are on the front line, fighting for all of us.

10. To protect the Amazon, defend the people of the forest

Maria do Socorro Costa Silva

I am a defender of the rivers and forest of the Amazon, representing about 20 000 people in my organization, Cainquiama. They chose me as president because I am one of them, because the struggle is in my blood.

I am a quilombola – a descendant of African slaves who escaped captivity and made a home deep in the Amazon rainforest in the late nineteenth century. I am also partly indigenous. One of my grandfathers was from a tribe here in the northern state of Pará. For many years, my community was hidden. The first record of my people was recorded by a group of Jesuit missionaries who came to Murucupi, the headwater of the Pará River, more than 100 years ago. They counted 157 residents in our settlement in what is now Barcarena. Among them was my great-grandmother, Januária. At that time, this was a land of great abundance. Ample fresh water, good land and lots of fish. That has changed in my lifetime.

I was born in 1965. Around the age of five, I started to notice how "progress" was encroaching on our village. First came a ferry service that connected our island to other towns. My parents were happy about that. I was not too pleased. The port took the land where we used to bathe. And the ferry brought handsome men in beautiful clothes who studied our land and left with notes and surveys. Back then, the military dictatorship that ruled Brazil described the Amazon as a "land without men for men without land". Human beings like us did not exist for the white elites, except to be ravaged like the forest. My parents were uneasy, but they didn't know what to say. Then came the road, ripping through the forest and covering over the streams. In 1973, an accommodation block was built on top of the ancient woods where I used to collect Brazil nuts, which staved off hunger. More and more construction work opened up the region.

My uncle and aunt were hired to help with the projects. Their bosses took a shine to me. I was only 14, but very pretty. My uncle and aunt encouraged me to start consorting with a director of the company. It was the same for many of the girls in my community. Many of us were raped. Many of us were forced to have abortions. I do not cry about this because I am tough. I am an activist.

But I have to mention these crimes so they don't happen again. They are crimes against women and children and they are crimes against the forest and the river. As I was being sexually abused, more outsiders moved in and forced out existing families. They expropriated land and opened up a wide area for an orange grove. It was so small-minded and destructive. They had no care for the giant Brazil nut tree that had been growing for more than generations. That was the real wealth of our people. It was part of our identity. My grandparents felt helpless, but I knew something was wrong.

In 1984, our community took another step towards "progress". Barcarena became a municipality and we got our first mayor, council and notary office. This did not mean more rights; it meant more laws and rules were imposed on us. It provided legal justification for the expulsion of forest dwellers. This was around the time I decided I had to fight back.

Our houses were made of clay, straw and sticks. For me, this was home. I wanted to remain where I had grown up. I wanted to stay until my dying day. But the regulations demanded we leave. The regulations demanded the community school be demolished. I was pressured to have sex with a foreign man. There was no wedding. I conceived and miscarried. My parents and grandparents were ordered to find new homes. They gave in. Our old homes were destroyed. No one gave us a choice. The government's priority was to ensure huge new mines could be opened up in our area. It was perfect for mineral companies because they need water and we had lots of that.

Now, nobody lives where we once had our homes. Instead, we have one of the world's biggest bauxite pits and aluminium factories. The Norwegian firm Hydro Alunorte (Norsk Hydro in its own country) buys ore from the mining firm Paragominas and then processes it here in Barcarena using water from the river. The effluent goes back into the river – millions and millions of litres of caustic soda, uranium, alumina, lead and nickel. They say it is treated, but these metals corrode. Our rivers and our forest have been poisoned. Every day we drink this water and die a little. I believe I am living proof of that. I have cancer. For me, there is no doubt that this came from heavy metals. I drank from the contaminated river, I bathed in it, I cooked my food with water I took from it. It is not just me. Eight members of my family have cancer, including my grandson. The future generation is born and dies. The company denies irregularities, but this is not just my imagination. In March 2018, the Evandro Chagas Institute, part of the Brazilian Health Ministry, detected high levels of aluminium, iron, copper, arsenic, mercury, and lead in the Murucupi River. Brazilian courts temporarily halted part of production at Alunorte, but it is back up and running. Once again, we are suffering for the world's non-stick pots and pans, beer barrels, and plane parts.

"So what?" you might ask. Why shouldn't industry and progress come before the health of forest dwellers like me? Well, you need to think about what you want. If you want to stabilize the climate, or protect wildlife, then we are important. If you want to care for the forest, you need to take care of us because nobody looks after the forest better than those who have lived in it for generations. We don't have huge destructive mines or plantations. Whatever we plant, we harvest 70 per cent and leave 30 per cent to feed animals.

What is this progress we are promised? The words are always very beautiful – fine houses, more gold, welfare, environmental protection. It is all a lie. They have destroyed our land and water, and with it they have taken my past and my present. We cannot eat aluminium. All the benefits go overseas to the shareholders in different countries, to people who buy things we cannot afford.

That is my message, but a message is not enough. We need to be brave. We need to fight. I live in the most murderous state in the most murderous country in the world for environmental defenders. My home is just 700 metres from the factory. My colleagues have been murdered for this fight. I have had a pistol pressed against my face. Yet I have filed more than 40 lawsuits against the world's biggest aluminium company. And I will file more if necessary. And I will resist the local government and the courts, who are in the pocket of big business. And I will oppose the president of Brazil, who attacks quilombolas and indigenous people. I am not afraid. Until I am killed, I will speak out. This forest sustains the world. The people who live here sustain the forest. Without us, Brazil will suffer irreparable loss. Without us, there is no river, there are no animals, there is nothing. If you want to normalize the planet's temperature, you have to take care of us. Because without us there is no future generation.

Forest people need to unite. We need to be more political. I am not naive or backward or perfect. I want gold, I want a plasma TV, I want Nike brand products, I want good things. But I want health and a home most of all. I don't know if future generations will continue our fight. But we need to clean up the rivers. We want to take back control. What we really need is a forest people's republic and a forest people's president. Let us start in each city and spread this movement across the world. If you want to protect the Amazon, defend the people who traditionally live here.

11. Of chainsaws and grace: direct action by eco-vigilantes in the Philippines

Bobby Chan

I confiscated my first chainsaw in 1998. Previous to that, I was a fresh law intern from Ateneo de Manila University trying to change the world with Pentel pens and brown manila paper, idealistically educating tribal communities on environmental laws in Palawan, the Philippines' last frontier. That did not work very well. Either people were too poor or corruption was too ingrained. And it felt really hypocritical of me to spend non-governmental organization (NGO) funds on training sessions and workshops, while a stone's throw away, I could hear the hum of a chainsaw and the blasts of dynamite fishing. So, in 1998, I decided to ditch my teaching tools and go after the bumble bees of the forests.

Environmental law enforcement in Palawan, and in the rest of the Philippines for that matter, is archaic. Authorities are either inadequate, inefficient, and more often than not, in cahoots. Statistics from the Department of Environment and Natural Resources reveal that there is one ranger for every 4000 hectares of forest in the nation. In Palawan, the ratio rises to one in 10 000. The Palawan Council for Sustainable Development and the provincial government still believe in guarding the forests via checkpoints where the trees are already dead. And in my neophyte years, I turned over a ton of confiscated items and conveyances to the authorities, only to learn later that they were returned to the violators. Never again, I said to myself.

Any solution should not just be out of the box; it should be radical. I am a Christian who follows the teachings of Christ. And Christ is radical. Jesus whipped the money changers, proclaimed 'blessed are the poor', and resurrected himself to give his disciples burning hearts. I asked myself, how I can be more like Christ?

First, I needed a commandment. A law saying I can do things directly, without going through a corrupted structure. If there is one thing salvific that we got out of copying our laws from the Americans, it's the statute on citizen's arrest. Thanks to this, we were able to conduct community-led confiscations. Naively, we started confiscating illicit timber. But these being both hardwood and huge, it became too taxing both physically and financially. So, we set our sights on the chainsaws. And what a glorious result – 50 in the first year.

But like Christ, our efforts were belittled. Some people said we only confronted small carabao-logging[1] crimes. So, in 2010 and 2011, we seized two large vessels, one loaded with logs destined for Malaysia and another for cyanide fishing destined for China. We also impounded logging trucks, jeepneys,[2] and tricycles, as well as dynamite-fishing boats and commercial fishing nets infringing on waters earmarked for small fishers. Yet, it is true that no prophet is welcome in his hometown as our critics remain unconvinced. So, in 2013, we thought, maybe if we help them with their fight against mining, they would love us. This we did, hauling two diamond hydraulic drills from the gold mining operations of one of the richest men in the country, in no less than a protected area in the south. Still, we were not accepted.

This revolution did not come without a cost. Twelve dead. Some in the most gruesome ways unimaginable. Roger Majim, prostate cut off and shoved in his mouth, tongue cut off, stabbed several times and full of cigarette burns. 'Tay Albet, shot-gunned at close range on his way to their watershed guard house. Nestor Lubas and Tinde Salamat, ambushed on their motorbike and shot between their eyes to make sure they were dead. Loggers and illegal fishers are armed. And among our confiscated items are an array of long and short firearms with piles of machetes and bolos.[3] While these deaths should necessarily scare my team, it puzzles me how they turn it into a desire to plan the next operation.

Then there are the harassment lawsuits to contend with. Charges range from robbery, coercion, usurpation of authority and, my favorite, extortion in exchange for non-filing of cases. Two of these cases reached the Supreme Court. Both upheld me and my para-enforcers. Each is its own agony in the garden and a crown of thorns because you do not sleep too well with these lingering at the back of your head. Then after carrying your cross, there is the resurrection. No cases against us have prospered and we have never been incarcerated.

Which brings me to our secret weapon that explains how so much has been achieved by a bunch of farmers, fisherfolk, and tribal people turned para-enforcers. Prayer. And Grace. I was not always a religious person. In fact, my closest epiphany was going to mass to look at girls and joining a Catholic organization to pursue a lady who would soon become my wife. But slowly you learn to listen to a voice inside that tells you what to do; gives you direction; and a peace that surpasses all understanding, because it is rooted in pain and suffering yet results in joy. Does that make sense? Maybe it should not because as I try to define it, it loses its mystery and its weight. The closest I can get is to a Jesuit priest's decoding of being in a state of 'having singularity of purpose', where all fear, all doubt, all worry is subsumed, not erased, and everything is in place. Grace.

What we in the environmental movement need to realize is that our affairs should mostly be governed not by doing what is right, but by grace. True power is knowing you can wield it and yet you yield. Compassion. Administer cases so as not to imprison the poor logging helper but to exact a toll on the financier who loses his equipment and conveyance. Grace in controlling situations beyond your control, the weather, your team's health, your adversaries' thoughts and emotions, the influx of funds, and multiplication of bread. All is grace. And everything can be Eucharist.

Whilst my writing might suggest no concrete strategy other than divine intervention, allow me to reconcile it with a more logical mind to promote a change in our way of thinking. Most environmentalists seek recognition. Jesus took a child and set him in their midst. Humility. So, I suggest the following strategies: (1) meet the need for a lawyer for communities; (2) allow civil society more executive powers – for example, to impound equipment; (3) focus on a cultural trait that brings people together for something other than for money or payment, in this case religion; and (4) shift funding from education and research to enforcement and direct action.

I have come to believe the problem that plagues us is not poverty, but pride. Our leaders, and more so, fellow advocates, just have too much pride, and this prevents resources and funds, which are needed to combat environmental violations, from going where they should go or where they are most effective, simply because it will not be them who will be recognized, or it is not their idea. They tend to be Messianic, as though they are the only ones who can save the forests or corals. And in the process end up trying to stop a logger or dynamite fishers by holding a heavily funded environmental education workshop or seminar, while programs like ours beg for gas money and are often put down, ignored or downplayed. We need open-minded policymakers and funding agencies that will support Third World solutions to Third World problems, and not First World remedies that are intellectually stimulating and really look good on paper but have no real effect in the area.

Over two decades and 700 chainsaws later, I'm still here.

NOTES

1. Carabao-logging is logging in Philippine forests that are inaccessible to trucks and bulldozers due to steep terrain, so the timber has to be ferried out by carabaos into flat or level areas where they can be loaded into trucks.
2. Sometimes called jeeps, jeepneys are buses and the most popular means of public transportation in the Philippines. They are known for their crowded seating and colorful decoration.
3. A bolo is a long knife or machete.

12. Social justice goes hand in hand with environmental campaigns – and not just in Africa

Phyllis Omido

My experience shows that climate and environmental campaigns are more effective if they are linked to issues of social justice. Without that, many communities feel the issues are too distant.

I used to work in a battery recycling smelter that poisoned the neighbouring community. I didn't realize at first. I was working in the company office. I started to grow concerned in 2010 when my baby son fell ill. Blood tests showed the amount of lead in his blood was 35 times above the World Health Organization's level of concern. I suspected I had passed this on to him through my breast milk, which meant that I was contaminated and so, probably, were others who worked at the smelter or lived nearby. I arranged for three more children to be tested, all of whom proved to have tainted blood. When I talked to local people, they told me about unusually high numbers of miscarriages and respiratory disease. This started a campaign that rallied thousands of people and led to death threats against me, but it is proving effective and there are lessons for others.

Strategies to combat climate change and protect the environment vary from place to place depending on ecosystems and the ways of life of the indigenous communities in each area. In my hometown of Mombasa, we began by mobilizing the local community through demonstrations and public picketing in order to get the state to act. I wrote letters to the National Environment Management Authority and the public health authorities. The aim was to remove the source of lead exposure for the 3000 Owino Uhuru community members. This meant either relocating or shutting down the smelter that was the source of water and air contamination.

Our strategy was permissible by law but very dangerous. Between 2016 and 2018 I received numerous threats both at gunpoint and via text messages. Several times I had to go into hiding. The powerful interests behind the smelter also got the police on their side. This led to my arrest alongside 16 community members. I was charged with inciting violence and illegal gathering. The one-year trial appeared designed to silence us. We had to devote so much energy to secure our freedom. We were worried about the legal costs and the possibility of prison terms of up to 15 years. All manner of dirty tricks were used against us. At one stage, our lawyers were contracted by the smelter and they left us in court without legal representation. Luckily, we had contacts in Lawyers Without Borders, which was working with the East Africa Law Society. They provided a pro bono lawyer who secured our acquittal in November 2018. Meanwhile the smelting corporation – which was free from our interference during this period – continued to spew hazardous waste into the community.

I had already decided to rethink our strategy. We went on the counterattack with media advocacy and litigation coupled with civil society activism to challenge violations of environmental management by the company and the state. We fought on the basis that indigenous and marginalized groups in Kenya should have as much right to a clean environment as anybody else. Foreign non-governmental organizations (NGOs), including Front Line Defenders and Human Rights Watch, provided advice and media support. Our work gained international recognition when I was awarded the Goldman Environmental Prize (a co-winner in 2015 with Honduran environmental activist Berta Cáceres, who was later murdered for her activism).

Initially, the Kenyan authorities refused to close the plant. I went over their heads by appealing to the East Africa Community. This regional body banned lead recycling in Kenya, forcing the closure of more than a dozen smelters, including the one at Owino Uhuru.

We tried to use the media as a tool for environmental justice by reaching out to journalists and providing them with information to understand what was happening. This was very important to counter the negative publicity put out by bloggers who were paid to mislead the public. This strategy proved effective in pushing our local campaign to a national and international level. The community received visits by the Senate and Congress. We followed up with petitions to Parliament that led to two key reports by committees in the Upper and Lower Houses. Those studies made people more willing to take our concerns seriously. A detailed medical investigation was carried out under the auspices of the Ministry of Health, which shows the myriad of negative health and environmental impacts in the community that were linked to the smelter.

These reports were an excellent basis from which to prove our case in a class action litigation suit. The combination of media and legal outreach helped us to win in the court of public opinion and prompted state actors to engage with our situation, which had previously been ignored. As a result, we have forced the closure of the plant and are now campaigning for compensation for the victims and a clean-up of the community.

We want to go further still. We have launched a major constitutional case on the right to a clean healthy sustainable environment, which also has a strong human rights focus. This project has led to collaborations with wider civil society groups to promote environmental rights in Kenya. Our campaigns have also enabled us to penetrate the related processes and systems of government. Our goal is to hold the authorities accountable so that all citizens are guaranteed a healthy environment.

For us, the environment and human rights go hand in hand. We mobilize resources (funds and action) on both. Until now, very few campaigns have been focused on environmental impunity. Too many people think the environment is just about conservation of wildlife or natural parks, but it should be about helping communities to achieve justice. Environmental destruction takes place when powerful people feel they can benefit from impunity. To address this, we need access to information, public participation and to justice.

It is not enough to argue the case for the environment or the climate on the grounds of conservation or science alone. In many communities, that is too vague. Far more effective and important is to demonstrate that it is a matter of justice and equality.

13. Living our values: using art and technology to campaign for nature in Turkey

Birhan Erkutlu and Tuğba Günal

We never planned to become forest guardians. It just happened. We have known each other since our teens. We grew up in middle-class neighbourhoods of Istanbul. We were artists, city dwellers, cogs in a capitalist culture, living a life that the system wanted us to live. The key moment was when we realized this life is destroying the natural world we love. Although we tried to be sensitive, careful consumers, there came a point when it felt unbearable to be part of this crime.

So, in 2004, we moved into the wild to try to experience living simply and in harmony with nature. We made an earthen house in Alakır Valley from the natural materials that we found around the land. It was near a natural spring and we made a garden for food. Everything was going well for us. While observing and learning we fell in love with the wild and became like a family with all the living beings around. A few years later, a handful of companies came to destroy the valley we live in. They planned to build a hydroelectric power plant on the beautiful and pristine Alakır River. This would have destroyed the unique biodiversity of the valley.

We decided to resist. Until this moment, we had not been using electricity, technology or the internet. We did not need to. But to spread the word about the threat to the area, we started using mobile phones, cameras and social media. All powered by a small solar panel. We used them to raise awareness and show people how destruction in the wild was directly related to consumption. At the same time, we shared our experiences living off-grid. That attracted the attention of many people and some big media organizations. We took the company to court to fight for the river and nature, made peaceful demonstrations and organized meetings and art festivals to raise awareness of the ecological breakdown. We made four music albums to raise the funds needed to pay our court costs. Using art was a bridge for us to tell people about the destruction of the wild, which is normally far from their eyes. We reached out to universities, scientists and environmental groups. Within two years, various scientific field trips to the valley discovered three new plant species.

When we started our struggle to protect nature in the valley, we defined three key strategies that we saw as the legs of a tripod: law, science and action. While opening up cases in the courts to protect the valley, biodiversity research showed what we were trying to protect and the peaceful demonstrations, meetings and art festivals drew more attention to the issue. On the internet, we connected with others in our region and around the world, all people on the front line of the fight to save nature. Sharing our experiences and realizing that we were not alone helped us a lot psychologically and technically. We used social media effectively from the accounts we opened up specifically for this issue. We called this togetherness 'Alakır Nehri Kardeşliği' (Friendship of Alakır River).

After eight years of our campaign, the authorities cancelled two hydroelectric power plant projects and designated the area a strictly protected site. However, our struggle continues as we try to protect the biodiversity of the valley against deforestation and hunting, which are other elements in the climate crisis and ecological breakdown.

This experience showed us how much can be achieved by even just a couple of people living in harmony with nature and an awareness of what is going on around them. By peacefully struggling against dirty projects that are harming nature, and taking support from the cities, millions of lives can be saved.

Turkey is like much of the rest of the world in madly pumping the consumer lifestyle and attacking nature to try to satisfy its endless desires. But now many people have started to live in nature and defend the areas where they live. More recently, this is evident in the İda Mountains in the Northern Aegean part of Anatolia. The people who moved into that area are now strongly campaigning against the planned gold mines there. They are also receiving strong support from sympathetic outsiders. We went there to show solidarity and to share our experiences. Now the defenders there are building a winter camp near a gold mining operation that will poison the spring water and has already started cutting down thousands of trees.

All these experiences show us that first, we humans have to be honest with ourselves. If we do not change anything in our consumption levels and still talk about protecting nature, we become as hypocritical as the system we are trying to change. And secondly to act… We must all do whatever we can do without thinking if it is big or small. Civil disobedience will be the key. Everyone who truly cares about the environment and the future must create or get involved in the nearest non-violent groups. We all have to push the decision-makers and politicians for environmental justice for all the living beings on the Earth. The time is now. And everyone is needed.

PART III

Litigants

14. Introduction to Part III

Marie Toussaint and Claude Henry

The current situation of climate emergency is unprecedented. There is a huge gap between those whose rights are violated due to a human-induced environmental crisis and the indisputable impunity of those who contribute the most to the collapse of the balance of nature. Their commitment to engage in harmful conducts is no longer in dispute: a small number of private and public entities are still deliberately acting against the general interest, neglecting the disruption of human lives and the annihilation of the living world. Nonetheless, so far, the law has failed to prevent such acts.

The authors of the chapters in this part of the book are all committed to strengthening the climate crisis victims' voice. They all claim judicial standing, either directly by alleging violation of their right to life and/or to a sustainable future, or indirectly by emphasizing that the general interest resides where the interest of the planet dwells. Nevertheless, their access to justice is constantly denied, and their voices barely heard by legislators and policymakers.

To fight for their rights, the plaintiffs therefore had to give up their right to privacy and expose themselves to public scrutiny. In order to secure access to courts and voice their concerns, the suffering of their communities and the degradation of the planet, they are championing a climate-oriented interpretation of existing human rights frameworks, notably through the right to life, the right to intergenerational equity and the rights of Indigenous peoples. Finally, they had to rely on the scientific expertise of numerous specialists and professionals, capable of proving causation between human actions, the impacts on nature and the damage they suffer. However, how many victims of the climate crisis still lack access to these precious resources and are barred from bringing their claims before the judicial branch?

The imagination, inventiveness and creativity shown by those who engage in climate justice actions are striking, and the means on which they rely to fight the righteous fight of our time are extremely promising. Take the example of the Maori Council claim in New Zealand. They pursued a groundbreaking climate action by invoking their right to active protection by the New Zealand authorities. It is because they want to preserve their sovereignty, which can only be guaranteed if surrounding ecosystems are protected, that they took legal action. It is because they see themselves as the allies and guardians of nature that they understand how their lives will only be valuable and safe-guarded if the whole of life is preserved. This is a major philosophical break with the current anthropocentric paradigm.

Climate litigation strategies are neither traditional legal proceedings, nor political stances pleaded through the language of the law: by taking action, the victims of global warming can proactively engage humanity in a new era – an era of recognition and respect for the living. Here too young people are on the front line.

In India, Ridhima Pandey, then nine years old, filed a petition with the National Green Tribunal in Delhi – asking the Tribunal to order the federal government "to protect the vital natural resources, on which today children and future generations depend on for survival". Ridhima is living in the state of Uttarakhand, which nowadays is routinely hit by devastating floods and landslides linked to changing conditions in the Himalayan mountains under climate change. She has acted on behalf of fellow students, and more generally of all children who will suffer in the future.

In the US, 21 citizens aged 11 to 22, from ten different states, are suing the federal government over the immediate and future damage due to climate change denial or negligence. The government asked for the case to be dis-missed, but on August 2, 2018, the Supreme Court unanimously acknowledged that "the breadth of the claims is striking" and ruled that the case should be heard as planned in the Oregon Federal Court. Eventually the Supreme Court itself will hear the case and decide whether the government has indeed failed the younger generations.

The action against the French state known as L'Affaire du Siècle pursues similar objectives, but it is still at an early stage. It was launched with fanfare in December 2018 with more than 2 million people signing a supportive petition.

The last three cases considered in this part of the book have run their course. The outcomes are contrasted. The People's Climate Case is an action against the European Parliament and the European Council over their lack of proper initiatives to tackle the climate crisis and its effects on the plaintiffs' lives. The European Court in charge dismissed the case on spurious legalistic grounds; one would have expected a more open-minded approach from a relatively young institution not burdened by rigid traditions.

In 2017, a group of 25 children and young people from 17 cities in Colombia filed a lawsuit against the state for failing to stop deforestation in the Amazon region. The plaintiffs claim that high deforestation rates are accelerating climate change, threatening their health, their access to water and food, hence violating fundamental human rights. In April 2017, the Supreme Court ruled in their favor and ordered the government to take the necessary measures for eliminating deforestation. The rule resonated in public opinion and in the media. For the time being, however, while the deforestation upward trend has been halted, it proves very difficult to obtain full implementation of the Supreme Court's rule.

In the Netherlands, the Urgenda case sails to a happier end. The central claim of the Urgenda Foundation and its 886 co-plaintiffs before the District Court of The Hague is that the state has failed to adopt a necessary and proportionate level of ambition in its climate policy, thereby threatening the well-being of the citizens. The District Court basically agreed in June 2015 and, three years later, the Appeal Court affirmed the order that the state take appropriate measures in order to reduce the quantities of CO_2 emitted in the Netherlands by 25 percent before December 2020. It appears that the country is now on course to achieving this objective.

15. The Urgenda case in the Netherlands: creating a revolution through the courts

Marjan Minnesma

PROMISES, PROMISES, PROMISES

Large parts of the Netherlands are situated below sea level.[1] Rising sea levels may thus become an existential threat to this country fronting the North Sea. And this threat may develop much more rapidly and with much greater severity than for other European countries. The Netherlands was a front runner on environmental policies in the 1980s and early 1990s when it belonged to the small group of countries that pushed for an international Climate Change Convention. However, somehow, the Netherlands changed from being a leader and a front runner into a laggard.

Although you could argue that countries like the Netherlands have a special responsibility to lead by example in light of their wealth, historic contribution, and per capita emissions, most such countries have dragged their feet and delayed significant action for years. The Netherlands has time and again adopted 'ambitious' future targets, only to abandon or neglect those targets a couple of years later. The result has been that, in 2018, just 7.4 percent of all energy in the Netherlands was generated by renewable sources (of which 4.5 percent was from biomass, which is not as sustainable as we once thought).[2] In 2018, the Dutch CO_2 emissions were nearly at the same level as they were in 1990, and there was only a slight reduction in other greenhouse gases (GHGs).[3] Action to reduce emissions keeps getting pushed into the future. But as climate science shows, the lingering effects of carbon in the atmosphere demand emissions reductions as quickly as possible. Acknowledging the urgency of the problem is not enough: effective actions are necessary.

The Urgenda Foundation is a not-for-profit organization for innovation and sustainability. It started at the Dutch Research Institute for Transitions (Drift) at the Erasmus University Rotterdam. It aims, based on science, at a fast transition towards a sustainable society, along with entrepreneurs, civil society organizations, local governments and companies who have understood the need for a rapid transformation. Urgenda helps front runners with scaling up and opens up and stimulates new markets. In 2008, it imported the first electric vehicles that were made in series in Norway and sold them to Amsterdam and other cities. That stimulated the cities to start a network of charging stations and in this way kickstarted the market for electric vehicles. In 2010, Urgenda organized the first collective buying initiative for solar panels and imported 50 000 solar panels (PV) for thousands of citizens, which reduced the Dutch market price by 30 percent. Others followed with numerous collective buying initiatives.

Thus, Urgenda looks for innovative ways to make the necessary changes in the system. The climate case that Urgenda started in 2012 can also be seen as an innovative way of working within the legal system, to force a government and its politicians to do what their duty of care demands from them. This means to finally implement their own norms and plans, based on science, and live up to the promises that they have made year after year to reduce GHGs.

The goal of reducing GHG emissions was discussed amongst almost all countries in the world within the United Nations Framework Convention on Climate Change (UNFCCC) and its related agreements. In 2010, at the climate summit in Cancún, it was decided that so-called Annex 1 countries (the 'old' developed countries) should reduce their GHG emissions by 25–40 percent against 1990 levels by 2020 in order to keep the temperature increase below 2°C compared to pre-industrial times. This emission reduction range was based on broad scientific agreement. Based on that broad scientific agreement, the Netherlands in 2007 had set its own goal of 30 percent reduction by 2020. However, there was no concrete action and, three years later, a newly elected Dutch government abandoned this target out of political convenience without any scientific justification.

It was the lack of concrete action and the lack of ambition by the Dutch government in the face of dangerous climate change that convinced Urgenda of the need to find new tools to tackle the crisis. The climate crisis can no longer be solved by consumer and business action alone. It will need the full force of government action as well, as we have waited too long to take action and time is running out. According to both science and the countries' negotiation in the context of the UNFCCC, a reduction in GHG emissions of 25 percent by 2020 was the absolute minimum necessary to stay below 2°C. And yet, according to Urgenda, such reduction was not even enough to avoid dangerous climate change, and the Netherlands would be highly unlikely to meet this target without substantial extra efforts. It was against this background that, in 2012, the Urgenda Foundation demanded greater action from the Dutch government by suing it for failing to implement effective climate policies to live up to its own acknowledged goal of 25–40 percent reduction by 2020.[4]

886 CO-PLAINTIFFS

In the Netherlands, a non-governmental organization (NGO) like Urgenda is allowed to represent so-called 'public interests' in court, such as the interest in a sustainable future. Urgenda, however, did not want to run the case by itself. Climate change affects each and every person from all parts of society, so Urgenda decided to create the opportunity for normal citizens to join the case as co-plaintiffs. We also introduced a new word, not crowd *funding*, but crowd *pleading*: Urgenda invited people to help with the court case and send Urgenda any useful arguments or court case material or legal papers that could be of any help. Within a few weeks, more than 1000 Dutch people indicated that they wanted to support the case. In the end, 886 people became formal co-plaintiffs, including about ten children. Our co-plaintiffs would join us at all the court hearings and become active advocates of the case in the media, social platforms and in their own communities. Through our co-plaintiffs, we were able to explain to the broader public that our case was not 'just' an environmental case, but that our case was fundamentally about people and the future in which they would grow up.

At that time, this was the biggest climate lawsuit that had ever been filed. Because our case was a world first, many dismissed it as a publicity stunt. It clearly wasn't. We were dead serious in our demands and our conviction that our government was breaking the law by knowingly contributing to a climate catastrophe and not taking action to help avoid it. At that time, most people thought we could not win. There was little media attention, but the co-plaintiffs were very supportive right from the beginning.

START: A LETTER TO THE GOVERNMENT (2012)

The case was launched in 2012, with an event in The Hague close to the Parliament, where several well-known scientists, including James Hansen, highlighted the urgency of taking action and reducing GHG emissions. We subsequently wrote a letter to the government in which we outlined our demand that the government reduce its GHG emissions by 25–40 percent by 2020, and, preferably, reduce them by 40 percent. We also informed the government that we intended to start litigation if it did not increase its climate ambition and act upon it. What we demanded, in essence, was that the government would reduce emissions to the level that it had recognized itself was necessary to avert dangerous climate change. For years, the Dutch government had recognized that average global temperatures should not increase by more than 2°C above pre-industrial levels and that, in order to do so, countries such as the Netherlands would need to reduce their emissions by at least 25–40 percent by 2020.

The response of the government to our letter was predictable yet emblematic of the attitude of so many governments around the world. The Dutch government recognized the severity of the climate crisis and the need to take more action. But it was only prepared to act if other countries acted as well: 'if others don't act, we don't act'. The Netherlands, at that time already a laggard in Europe, wrote to us: 'we do not want to be a front runner, because that is not good for our economy'. After this refusal of the government to take the necessary action, Urgenda commenced the preparation to file the lawsuit.

THE URGENDA CASE FOR CLIMATE ACTION

The central claim of Urgenda and its 886 co-plaintiffs before the District Court of The Hague was that the state had acted negligently in failing to adopt a necessary and proportionate level of ambition in its climate policy, thereby threatening the well-being of its citizens, and that this behavior was contrary to the state's duty of care towards Urgenda, the people it represents, and broader Dutch society. By acknowledging the nature, seriousness, and timing of climate change and continuing to contribute to the problem, Urgenda and its co-plaintiffs also claimed that the state was violating their rights to life, health, private life, and family under the European Convention on Human Rights (ECHR).

In essence, Urgenda claimed that delaying emissions reductions into the future would result in higher total emissions, increasing the chance of exceeding the remaining carbon budget. Relatedly, implementing emissions reductions at a later point in time is less cost effective than reducing emissions now. By kicking the can down the road, the Dutch state is only increasing the risks and the costs of climate change. Urgenda therefore requested an order that the state limit its emissions by 25–40 percent by the end of 2020 (compared to 1990 levels) because this is what science had determined as the minimum reduction for countries such as the Netherlands in order to avoid dangerous climate change, a necessity that had been frequently formally recognized by the state, so it was not invented by Urgenda or the judges. Urgenda simply demanded that the Dutch state live up to its own norms.

While the state acknowledged the severity of the climate crisis and the need to limit global temperature rises, it claimed that its current climate policies were sufficient to achieve this objective and that different reduction paths were available. In addition, the state dismissed the role of the courts in enforcing obligations in the context of climate change by arguing that the judiciary has no role to play in adjudicating 'political' disputes. Furthermore, the state argued that there is no legally binding obligation arising from national or international law to take measures to achieve a 25 percent emissions reduction target and, therefore, that it cannot be forced to adhere to such a target. The government shirked its responsibility by arguing that stronger ambition would have very little effect on global mitigation efforts because of the small contribution of the Netherlands to global emissions.

In summary, the dispute between the parties did not concern the need for mitigation, but rather the level at which the state needs to reduce GHG emissions, and whether the state could be forced by judges to act.

DEFINING THE DUTY OF CARE AND THE 'REFLEX EFFECT'

In its judgment of 24 June 2015, the District Court found that Urgenda, as a foundation, had standing under Dutch law.

The heart of judgment of the District Court was based in civil law/tort law. Thus, the judgment was not based *directly* on environmental law, public law, international law or human rights law, as many people incorrectly wrote. Furthermore, Urgenda did not fight a decision or an act of the state. Urgenda's basic claim was that the state, in *not* doing what was necessary to avoid dangerous climate change, breached its duty of care towards Urgenda and the citizens. The District Court concluded that there is no directly legally binding obligation on the state based on Article 21 of the Constitution, nor one based on the 'no harm' principle or the UNFCCC (climate treaty) and its protocols, nor directly based on European Union (EU) law. However, as Urgenda had submitted, the Court acknowledged that the duty of care under Dutch tort law is a so-called 'open norm' and that this norm could be 'colored' or filled in by acknowledged norms in international law. Thus, international law, including the ECHR, can be a source of interpretation of open private-law standards, like the 'standard of care of responsible conduct' to which the state must abide. These international norms and standards of what the state *ought to do*, have a 'reflex effect' in national law and can be used by the courts to establish and set the standard of care and proper conduct of what the state *must do* according to national law. This 'reflection effect' is an acknowledged rule in the Dutch legal system and is comparable to the concept of 'consistent interpretation'. This means that the Court found that decisions and standards that were developed under the UNFCCC and European Union treaties should be considered and provide guidance in determining the scope of policymaking and the state's duty of care. Similarly, the Court listed several guiding principles at play, including the equity principle, the precautionary principle, and the sustainability principle. In addition to determining the minimum degree of care, the indirect use of international and constitutional rules was also used to determine what degree of discretionary power the state is entitled to exercise.

UNLAWFUL HAZARDOUS NEGLIGENCE?

The legal question to be answered was: is there a breach of the duty of care for taking insufficient measures to prevent dangerous climate change (unlawful hazardous negligence)? The District Court was very clear: yes.

The Court found that in order to prevent irreversible climate change, world-wide GHG emissions reductions are necessary. Citing the scientific consensus on the need to reduce emissions, the Court reiterated that industrialized nations such as the Netherlands must reduce their emissions by 25–40 percent by 2020 to prevent dangerous climate change. However, based on the state's climate policy as at 2015, the Netherlands would only achieve a 14–17 percent reduction in emissions by 2020. Thus, the Court found that the Netherlands' reduction target was below the standard deemed necessary based on climate science and international climate policy to prevent a global increase in temperature beyond 2°C.

The Court stated very clearly that current global emissions and the reduction targets of signatories to the UNFCCC were insufficient to realize the 2°C target and that the chance that dangerous climate change would occur was very high. It stated further that mitigation measures should be taken expeditiously, as 'the faster the reductions can be initiated the more chance danger will subside'. Taking into account that the state had known about this danger since at least 1992, and given the high risk of hazardous climate change, the Court held that 'the state has a serious duty of care to take measures to prevent it'. Furthermore, the Court made clear that the state plays a crucial role in, and should take a high level of care for, the statutory and instrumental framework. The Court also found that taking action would *not* be too 'onerous': the Dutch state can afford the measures, and immediate action is more cost-effective than postponing action. There is no cost obstacle to adhere to a stricter target of 25–40 percent (indeed, in 2010 the Netherlands had a goal of 30 percent reduction by 2020).

The Court explained that mitigation is the only effective tool and that 'the state has a duty of care to mitigate as quickly and as much as possible'.

DISCRETIONARY POWER

The Dutch government's main line of reasoning both in and outside the Court was that this was a political question and not up to the courts to decide. The judges admitted that a government has significant discretionary power, but that its discretion in deciding upon its policies is not unlimited and therefore not completely exempted from any judicial scrutiny. In other words, if there is a high risk of dangerous climate change with severe and life-threatening consequences for humans and the environment, the state has an obligation to protect them. The Court added that the only effective remedy is to reduce emissions of greenhouse gases, and that, therefore, the state has limited options: 'mitigation is vital for preventing dangerous climate change'.

The Court did *not* agree with the state's submissions that this case was an interference with the distribution of powers. In the Netherlands, there is not a full separation of powers, but there is a balance between state powers. The judiciary has its own task and responsibility based on the law (thus, a democratic function with democratic legitimization) that requires that the courts *must* provide legal protection to citizens who demand to be protected from a government that fails its responsibilities and duties – here, refusing to prevent dangerous climate change. The state did not bring forward any compelling other social interests that could demand another outcome. In words of the Court:

> [T]he possibility of damages for those whose interests Urgenda represents, including current and future generations of Dutch nationals, is so great and concrete that given its duty of care, the state must make an adequate contribution, greater than its current contribution, to prevent hazardous climate change.

The Court found that the Netherlands' relatively small share of global emissions did *not* interfere with the country's responsibility to meet its prior commitment of a 25–40 percent reduction target by the end of 2020. The Netherlands cannot solve the climate change problem, but it must do its fair share, just like all other countries, as no country can solve the problem on its own.

All the arguments of the state failed, and Urgenda won the case on all arguments. The landmark verdict was delivered on 24 June 2015. It was written by three judges who must have spent hundreds of hours on the case and deeply understood the urgency and the need for the judiciary to step in and fulfill its role to protect citizens against a government that is failing to act in an emergency situation.

THE DUTCH STATE APPEALED

Tens of thousands of people from all over the world asked the Dutch government 'Do Not Appeal', from famous actors to scientists, from citizens to companies, and all the co-plaintiffs. But the Dutch government still appealed the decision in September 2015. Its main argument in the press was that 'the judges were sitting on their chairs'. In reality, the government fought the judgment with every argument that it could find. It had 29 grounds of appeal.

Although Urgenda was very happy that it had won its case based on 'hazardous negligence' and breach of the duty of care in tort law, it considered that there was one thing in the verdict that was not correct and that it was worth filing a cross-appeal given that the state was appealing.

In its judgment, the District Court had not ruled on the question of whether the state's inaction on climate change also constituted a *direct* violation of the ECHR. The District Court found that Urgenda itself, being a legal body and not a human being, could not be designated as a direct or indirect victim of climate change and that therefore it could not claim a violation of human rights, specifically in relation to Articles 2 (right to life) and 8 (right to private life and family) of the ECHR. Thus, although the District Court found that these Articles could serve as a source of interpretation for the scope of the duty of care of the state under civil law/tort law, Urgenda as an NGO could not invoke these articles directly.

In contrast to the District Court, Urgenda was of the opinion that although it could not be seen as a direct victim of climate change, it could still be allowed under Dutch law to represent the interests that are protected by Articles 2 and 8 of the ECHR and that therefore Urgenda should also be allowed to directly rely on these provisions during the proceedings. It was on this question – the ability of an NGO under Dutch law to rely on the provisions of the ECHR – that Urgenda filed a cross-appeal.

THE HUMAN RIGHTS DIMENSION OF CLIMATE MITIGATION

All the 29 arguments of the state were dismissed, one by one by the Court of Appeal. But our one argument in the cross-appeal was accepted! The Court of Appeal agreed with Urgenda and found that the District Court erred in concluding that Urgenda could not invoke Articles 2 and 8 under the ECHR. On 9 October 2018, the Hague Court of Appeal upheld the decision of the District Court, ordering the state to achieve a reduction of at least 25 percent by the end of 2020.

The Court stated that the state owed a duty of care under the ECHR, which is European Law, and which is of a higher order than national law. Thus, now the Urgenda case was walking on two legs that led to a duty of care to reduce the emissions by at least 25 percent, one from tort law and one from international human rights law.

The Court of Appeal, agreeing with the District Court, ruled that the requested order did not undermine the separation of powers. When the state violates its duty of care, the Court must exert its review power over the unlawful actions, while still giving the state sufficient room to decide how to comply with the order. On this point, the Court reiterated that Urgenda's claim is not intended to create legislation or to determine exactly how the state should reduce emissions. The state retains complete freedom to determine which measures it will implement to comply with the order. The Court held that, while a reduction of GHG emissions by 40 percent might be necessary, it is within the discretionary power of the state to determine the upper limit of required actions, but the minimum threshold of a reduction of GHG emissions by 25 percent must be met. At that point, the political discretion reaches its outer limits and it is the role of the judiciary as a co-equal branch of government, to guarantee that these limits are observed by the political branches of government.

In sum, the Court of Appeal found that the state had done too little to prevent dangerous climate change, failing to fulfill its duty of care. To remedy the situation, the Court affirmed the order to reduce emissions by at least 25 percent by the end of 2020.

On 8 January 2019, the state moved to appeal to the Supreme Court. On 24 May 2019, the case was heard before the Supreme Court, with both parties submitting written replies the following month. The independent advice of the Advocate General and the deputy Procurator General was issued in September 2019 to the Supreme Court. These two independent advisors stated in the extremely long and outstanding advice that the decision of the lower courts should be upheld. This was exactly what the Supreme Court did on 20 December. We finally won!

ASSESSING THE IMPACT OF THE URGENDA CASE IN THE NETHERLANDS AND BEYOND

The court decision mandating the state to meet a 25 percent reduction by 2020 has transformed climate change policy in the Netherlands. Despite the decision to appeal both judgments, the state announced it would uphold its commitment to implement the order to reduce emissions. Although the government still has to close part of the gap towards the 25 percent reduction by 2020, it has adopted a range of additional policy measures, ranging from energy efficiency measures for consumers and industry, stimulating more renewable energy production and the closure of at least one coal-fired power plant. A larger implementation plan was presented to the Dutch Parliament in April 2020, including a large reduction of the capacity of coal fired ower plants (roughly with 75%), and the implementation of 30 measures that Urgenda had proposed in its '54 climate solutions plan'.

After the judgment, climate change has also dominated the agenda of the new coalition government. Both favorable decisions have allowed public officials supporting climate ambition to anchor their legislative proposals in the need to implement the court's order. Together with the Paris Agreement, the case inevitably transformed the political discourse, allowing politicians to leverage the space to push for more climate ambition in the legislative sphere and request periodic updates on the implementation of climate targets. In the aftermath of the judgment, the government passed legislation to phase out all coal power plants by 2030 and passed the Climate Act, which calls for a 49 percent emissions reduction by 2030 and a 95 percent reduction by 2050. In essence, the Urgenda case has helped to build broad consensus around the fact that the Dutch state is not doing enough on climate change, creating significant momentum for action in the short term.

The Urgenda case has raised the visibility of climate change in the Netherlands, placing it as a major issue on the political and social agenda. Climate change went from being a non-issue to one of the most important issues in public discourse, with extensive coverage in national and international media. The case also helped build a stronger narrative for climate action, by framing the problem as an issue affecting current and future generations in the Netherlands. Perhaps most importantly, the case elevated the responsibility of the government in tackling climate change, particularly when the Dutch state acknowledges the problem and has committed year after year to take action. In March 2019, the country witnessed one of the greatest social mobilizations in its history, when over 40 000 people marched to demand stronger action by the government.

The Urgenda case, and particularly the decision of the Supreme Court, represented what many scholars have referred to as a 'rights turn' in climate change litigation. The judgment has signaled the role of grounding legal arguments in human rights law and the increasing receptivity of courts towards these types of claims.

Climate litigation has the potential to shake the status quo by demanding real action from national governments. Lawsuits build on the national and international obligations of states to prevent and limit catastrophic climate change. They do not create new obligations; they simply ask governments to honor their existing commitments. While climate litigation by itself will not solve the problem, it is an additional strategy in a broader toolkit to demand that governments respect, promote and fulfill their human rights obligations in the context of climate change.

Since 2015, dozens of cases that were inspired by the Urgenda judgment have been filed around the world, many of which raise similar legal arguments regarding the obligation of states to prevent dangerous climate change. While each context is unique, all governments must fulfill their legal obligations as they relate to the threat of dangerous climate change. The case has pushed the boundaries of legal thinking and inspired further innovation in the field. The case has set an important precedent and has given advocates hope at a moment when many have lost faith in the political process. Ultimately, it has given people around the world a new tool with which to claim protection of their fundamental rights.

NOTES

1. Planbureau voor de Leefomgeving, 2010. 'Correctie formulering over overstromingsrisico Nederland in IPCC rapport', accessed 26 August 2020 at https://www.pbl.nl/correctie-formulering-over-overstromingsrisico.
2. CBS (2019), 'Aandeel hernieuwbare energie naar 7.4 procent', 25 May, accessed March 2020 at https://www.cbs.nl/nl-nl/nieuws/2019/22/aandeel-hernieuwbare-energie-naar-7-4-procent.
3. Planbureau voor de Leefomgeving (2018), '2020 doesteling niet-emissiehandelssectoren ruim haalbaar', accessed March 2020 at https://themasites.pbl.nl/balansvandeleefomgeving/jaargang-2018/themas/energie-klimaat-lucht/emissies-broeikasgassen.
4. Urgenda (n.d.), 'The Urgenda climate case against the Dutch government', accessed March 2020 at https://www.urgenda.nl/en/themas/climate-case/.

16. *Juliana* v. *United States* and the global youth-led legal campaign for a safe climate

Patti Moore, Danny Noonan and Erik Woodward

I have no doubt that the right to a climate system capable of sustaining human life is fundamental to a free and ordered society. (U.S. District Court Judge Ann Aiken, *Juliana* v. *United States*, 217 F. Supp. 3d 1224, 1250 (D. Or., 2016))

INTRODUCTION

The year 2018 heralded two pivotal moments in the climate crisis. On August 20, Greta Thunberg held the first of her school strikes that would quickly ignite a global movement. Less than two months later, on October 8, the Intergovernmental Panel on Climate Change (IPCC) released its Special Report on global warming of 1.5°C above pre-industrial levels, giving rise to the "12 years" (now ten) narrative and crystallizing the scale and urgency of the climate crisis for the general public.

There was almost a third moment. On October 29, the constitutional climate change lawsuit *Juliana* v. *United States*, filed in the U.S. federal courts in 2015 by 21 young Americans against the executive branch of the U.S. government, was supposed to begin trial. But ten days prior to trial, the U.S. Supreme Court intervened and issued a temporary stay, leading to a delay and appellate process that is ongoing at the time of print.[1] More importantly, preventing trial has prevented the U.S. government's culpability for the climate crisis from being scrutinized in a court of law.

While the *Juliana* plaintiffs await their day in court, the movement their lawsuit anticipated continues to grow. New lawsuits inspired by the *Juliana* case continue to be filed in the United States and globally,[2] and youth are taking to the streets in ever-increasing numbers to protect their right to a livable climate.[3] This chapter provides an overview of the legal and factual bases for the *Juliana* lawsuit, and its connections to other lawsuits and the burgeoning youth-led response to the climate crisis.

JULIANA V. *UNITED STATES*

On August 12, 2015, 21 youth plaintiffs filed a suit against the United States and several of its agencies. Also named as plaintiffs are future generations, with climate scientist James Hansen as guardian, and the non-profit organization Earth Guardians. The suit alleges that the U.S. government has known since the 1960s that fossil fuels are causing global warming, and that unless emissions are drastically reduced, the consequences will be catastrophic. Despite this knowledge, the government has continued to subsidize, promote, and authorize consumption of fossil fuels. The litany of dangers this has created to the natural systems on which its citizens depend is immense and has resulted in specific, present-day injuries to each of the individual *Juliana* plaintiffs.

The legal claims in *Juliana* can be said to fall into four broad categories.

First, the fact that climate change is substantially caused by the actions of the U.S. government, and is presently causing harms to the youth plaintiffs' recognized constitutional rights to life, liberty, property, personal security, bodily integrity, and family autonomy, means that the actions of the U.S. government should be subject to "strict scrutiny" by the courts. The *Juliana* plaintiffs further argue that a climate system capable of sustaining human life underpins each of the previously recognized constitutional rights, and therefore itself should be recognized as a constitutional right.[4]

Second, the *Juliana* plaintiffs allege that the U.S. government has assumed control over fossil fuel regulation, the atmosphere, and the climate system, taking the ability to meaningfully affect these systems out of the hands of its citizens and contributing to dangerous levels of greenhouse gases in the climate. Because it has assumed this responsibility, and because its actions render its citizens more vulnerable to dangerous climate change, it has a constitutional duty to act to minimize those dangers. It has repeatedly and systematically failed to do, despite knowing the likely effects of its actions to continue to support systems that will harm its citizens.

Third, because the harms of climate change fall disproportionately upon young people and future generations, the lives and quality of life of these citizens are being subordinated for the advantage of past and present adults. Thus, children as a group are being discriminated against with respect to their fundamental rights and are therefore not receiving equal protection under the law as guaranteed in the U.S. Constitution. And fourth, the *Juliana* plaintiffs argue that the "public trust doctrine" – an ancient legal doctrine that can be traced through the common law to Roman law – requires the U.S. government to prevent substantial impairment to the atmosphere and other commonly held natural resources that depend on a healthy atmosphere, including coastlines and territorial waters.

The *Juliana* plaintiffs do not seek monetary compensation; instead, they request a national remedial plan to phase out fossil fuel emissions and draw down excess atmospheric carbon. The good news is that this remedy is achievable with the coordinated efforts of multiple government agencies mobilizing different sectors of society. Government is the only force that can compel that level of effort in the remaining, rapidly narrowing window of opportunity to avoid surpassing climatic tipping points. Because the political branches have failed to do so, instead doubling down on fossil fuels, the *Juliana* plaintiffs seek an injunction from the courts that will order the legislative and executive branches of the government to cease the actions that have brought our climate to the brink of disaster, and to implement a plan commensurate with returning atmospheric concentrations of greenhouse gases to safe levels.

THE SCIENCE SUPPORTING *JULIANA*

Much of the media coverage around the IPCC's 1.5°C Special Report focused on the 12-year window in which global temperatures can be kept below the 1.5°C threshold, along with the apocalyptic consequences of warming beyond that threshold. Largely overlooked in this coverage was the report's statement that "Warming of 1.5°C is not considered 'safe' for most nations, communities, ecosystems and sectors and poses significant risks to natural and human systems as compared to the current warming of 1°C (*high confidence*)."[5] Therefore, 1.5°C of global warming is no safe haven for humanity, or for human rights. Greater ambition is needed than even that implied by the "12 years" narrative.

These latter findings were no surprise to the plaintiffs, lawyers, and expert witnesses behind *Juliana* v. *United States*. Over 20 experts support *Juliana* and have helped to develop the evidence and scientific arguments that link the government's actions to present and imminent harms. These experts are in consensus that the politically motivated Paris Agreement targets, 1.5°C and "well below" 2°C, are dangerously high, and that returning atmospheric CO_2 concentrations to under 350 ppm – consistent with returning global temperatures to 1°C above pre-industrial levels by 2100 – is necessary to preserve a safe climate.

THE FIERCE URGENCY OF NOW MEETS THE LONG ARC TOWARDS JUSTICE

Clearly the stakes in *Juliana* are high. Major impacts are already being felt by the *Juliana* plaintiffs, communities through the U.S. and around the world, including drought, massive storms, forest fires, crop failures, and deadly heatwaves. And time is running out to mitigate these impacts and prevent catastrophe. For children, the dissonance between this sense of urgency and the Trump administration's seemingly headlong rush towards disaster, fueled by its full-throated support of fossil fuels, is especially alarming.

Compounding this frustration is the fact that, although the *Juliana* plaintiffs filed their claim in 2015, and although the plaintiffs had fought off a myriad of government challenges, the case did not reach trial. Instead, over the past four years, the government defendants have filed a nearly unprecedented onslaught of dilatory motions and petitions.[6] The case has gone before the Ninth Circuit five times and the Supreme Court twice. Following the temporary stay issued by the Supreme Court in October 2018 and a subsequent temporary stay issued by the Ninth Circuit in December 2018, the district court certified an interlocutory appeal of its earlier decisions, placing the immediate fate of the case in the hands of the appellate courts. On June 4, 2019, a three-judge panel of the Ninth Circuit Court of Appeals heard oral arguments for this appeal. On January 17, 2020, the Court ruled to dismiss the case in a two-to-one decision, finding that it was beyond the power of the courts to "order, design, supervise, or implement the plaintiffs' requested remedial plan."[7] The dissenting judgment was scathing of this reasoning, stating:

> My colleagues throw up their hands, concluding that this case presents nothing fit for the Judiciary… But a federal court need not manage all of the delicate foreign relations and regulatory minutiae implicated by climate change to offer real relief, and the mere fact that this suit cannot alone halt climate change does not mean that it presents no claim suitable for judicial resolution.[8]

The plaintiffs have now filed an "*en banc*" petition, seeking further review from the Ninth Circuit.[9] Should the plaintiffs not succeed there, their final recourse is the Supreme Court.

The unprecedented extent to which the current administration has gone to obstruct litigation and delay judicial accountability attests to both the lawsuit's enormous stakes, and the threat it poses to existing structures of political and economic power. These extraordinary delay tactics are but a further example of the U.S. government's long-term abdication, in the name of short-term political expediency, of its duties to ensure the survival of its citizenry. The gravity of the youths' allegations compels that they have their day in court. If they succeed, the government will finally have to undo the damage it has been knowingly causing to the climate system for over 50 years.

GLOBAL YOUTH IN THE COURTS AND IN THE STREETS

The odds are so stacked against the *Juliana* plaintiffs, as well as other young people fighting for a stable climate, that they could be forgiven for crumbling under the weight of it all. But today's youth have a different idea. In the words of *Juliana* plaintiff Vic Barrett, "We are learning every day that we are the ones who must secure our future. We must do the work. We must take to the streets. Being young is being an activist today."[10]

Juliana not only presaged the global youth-led climate movement, it continues to be a major part of it. Particularly in recent years, young people have formed the vanguard of a movement demanding that governments take decisive, science-based action to mitigate both the causes and impacts of climate change and to ensure that a hospitable climate system can be enjoyed by future generations. That movement is growing – on March 15, 2019, an estimated 1 million people in 125 countries and spanning all seven continents participated in the Global Climate Strike for the Future[11] – and it's working, having been recognized by the Secretary General of the Organization of Petroleum Exporting Countries as the "greatest threat" to the survival of the fossil fuel industry.[12]

Where activism alone has been unable to yield the urgent action demanded by climate change, youth across the globe have drawn inspiration from the *Juliana* plaintiffs and taken their governments to court. Youth plaintiffs have initiated litigation against their governments in at least ten countries to compel science-based government action on climate change.[13] These young plaintiffs have already set groundbreaking legal precedent and advanced critical legal victories. For example, in 2018 the Supreme Court of Colombia held that the constitution protects the right to a healthy environment and climate, and ordered the Colombian government to prepare a plan to prevent deforestation in the Colombian Amazon.[14] Similar youth-led lawsuits to the *Juliana* case are in progress in Canada, Pakistan, Uganda and India, and several more are in the works.

CONCLUSION

In the fight for climate stability, the stakes could not be higher nor the timeline more urgent. When the political branches of government fail to act, the courts can intervene to compel that action. It is the most basic duty of any government to ensure that its people have the opportunity to live productive, dignified lives. The science is clear that the fundamental right to a safe climate is not a right that can be left to future generations to realize; it must be secured now or not at all. Never before has it been so imperative that the courts hear the evidence and enjoin the governments of the world to take the action they have so far refused to take.

While others are suing the courts, public support for their efforts and for the activism occurring around the world is essential. Only when the voices and votes of the public speak louder than the money of fossil fuel interests will meaningful change happen. And the time for meaningful change was yesterday. While youth advocate in the courts for the protections we deserve, we also must be advocating in the streets, in the voting booths, in the media and wherever we have a chance. Too much is at stake.

NOTES

1. John Schwartz, "Judges give both sides a grilling in youth climate case against the government," *New York Times* (June 4, 2019), accessed March 22, 2020 at http://www.nytimes.com/2019/06/04/climate/climate-lawsuit-juliana.htm.
2. Sabin Center for Climate Change Law (2020), "Climate Change Litigation Databases," accessed March 22, 2020 at http://www.climatecasechart.com.
3. Alejandra Borunda, "These young activists are striking to save their planet from climate change," *National Geographic* (March 13, 2019), accessed March 22, 2020 at http://www.nationalgeographic.com/environment/2019/03/youth-climate -strike-kids-save-the-world/.
4. *Juliana* v. *United States*, 217 F. Supp. 3d 1224, 1249–50 (D. Or. 2016).
5. Roy, Joyashree, Petra Tschakert and Henri Waisman et al. "Sustainable development, poverty eradication and reducing inequalities." In Intergovernmental Panel on Climate Change (IPCC), *Global Warming of 1.5°C. An IPCC Special Report on the impacts of global warming of 1.5°C above pre-industrial levels and related global greenhouse gas emission pathways, in the context of strengthening the global response to the threat of climate change, sustainable development, and efforts to eradicate poverty* (2018, p. 455).
6. Stephen Vladeck, "Comment: the Solicitor General and the shadow docket," 133 *Harvard Law Review* 123 (2019), 144–6.
7. *Juliana* v. *United States*, No. 178-36082, 2020 WL 254149 (9th Cir. January 17, 2020), App. 25.
8. Ibid., p. 33.
9. An *en banc* (lit. in bench) review is a session in which a case is heard before all the judges of a court rather than by one judge or a panel of judges. It is often used for unusually complex cases. See Jonathan Adler, "Kids climate plaintiffs to seek rehearing en banc," *Reason* (January 20, 2020), accessed March 22, 2020 at https://reason.com/2020/01/20/kids-climate-plaintiffs-to-seek-rehearing-en-banc.
10. *No Ordinary Lawsuit: Mini Episode: The Plaintiffs Rally in Portland* (July 22, 2019) [podcast], accessed March 22, 2020 at https://www.podbean.com/ew/dir -b2x7m-687e6d5.
11. Jessica Glenza, Alan Evans, Hannah Ellis-Petersen and Naaman Zhou, "Climate strikes held around the world – as it happened," *The Guardian* (March 15, 2019), accessed March 22, 2020 at http://www.theguardian.com/environment/live/2019/ mar/15/climate-strikes-2019-live-latest-climate-change-global-warming.

12. Greta Thunberg, "Greta Thunberg: 'They see us as a threat because we're having an impact'," *The Guardian* (July 21, 2019), accessed March 22, 2020 at https://www.theguardian.com/culture/2019/jul/21/great-thunberg-you-ask-the-questions-see-us-as-a-threat.
13. Globally, youth-led climate lawsuits have been brought in the United States, Canada, India, Korea, Mexico, Pakistan, Peru, Uganda, the Ukraine, Sweden, Norway, Colombia, Canada and New Zealand. In the United States alone, at least four separate lawsuits are currently pending at the state (i.e., subnational) level.
14. DeJusticia, "Climate change and future generations lawsuit in Colombia: key excerpts from the Supreme Court's decision" (April 13, 2018), accessed March 22, 2020 at https://www.dejusticia.org/en/climate-change-and-future-generations-lawsuit-in-colombia-key-excerpts-from-the-supreme-courts-decision/.

17. How policymakers imperil coming generations' future and what to do about it

Ridhima Pandey

Ridhima Pandey, a 12-year-old girl, hails from Haridwar town, in the Himalayan State of Uttarakhand in India; she is a student in lower secondary education. Her father, Dinesh Pandey is an environmental activist and her mother works in Uttarakhand Forest Department. From a very young age, Ridhima has been visiting forests and learning about nature and the environment from her parents. Her first encounter with an extreme weather event was the 2013 Uttarakhand floods that resulted in much devastation and loss of lives as well as damage to the Himalayan ecosystem. She witnessed the heart-breaking accounts of loss on the television and read about them in the newspapers. That was when her parents told her that it was all due to climate change. Her parents and teachers also told her lot of things about climate change and guided her on conservation of nature. This disaster affected her deeply and she asked her father, "You work to protect environment and wildlife than why don't you approach the government to save the climate?" Thus, her father decided to file a Public Interest Litigation in her name.

India is one of the countries most vulnerable to the adverse impacts of climate change and it has already experienced several impacts in the form of flash floods, receding glaciers, rising sea levels and other calamities. India is ranked third in the world among the largest emitters of CO_2 emissions. Therefore, India has a particularly important role to play in addressing these issues. However, there is no law in existence to deal with climate change issues in India. There are several laws in existence with respect to environmental pollution and to regulation of forest diversion, but they are not framed in a manner to regulate and mitigate the impacts of climate change. Despite signing and ratifying the Paris Agreement, the Government of India has not yet passed any national legislation that the country would need to follow in order to reduce its carbon emissions as well as ensure minimal adverse impacts of climate change on the ground.

Ridhima approached the National Green Tribunal (NGT) in 2017, raising serious concerns regarding the actions and inaction of the government on the issues of climate change. She is directly affected by the adverse impacts of climate change and rising global temperatures. Children of today and the future will disproportionately suffer from the dangers and catastrophic impacts of climate change. Ridhima pointed to the failure of the Government of India to address the adverse impacts of climate change under the existing framework of environmental law.

VOLUNTARY COMMITMENTS MADE BY INDIA UNDER THE PARIS AGREEMENT

India has ratified the UN Framework Convention on Climate Change (UNFCCC), which was adopted in 1992 at the UN Conference on Environment and Development in Rio de Janeiro. Under the regime of the UNFCCC, the parties have to submit their Intended Nationally Determined Contributions, which are essentially communications on behalf of the state parties as to how they plan to contribute to the enforcement of the goals of the Paris Agreement, by taking domestic actions in the context of their national priorities, circumstances and capabilities. In December 2015, the Paris Agreement was adopted under the aegis of the UNFCCC, the nations around the world agreeing to "holding the increase in the global average temperature to well below 2°C above pre-industrial levels and pursuing efforts to limit the temperature increase to 1.5°C above pre-industrial levels". The Paris Agreement was ratified by India in October 2016, whereby India committed to follow a "low-carbon path to progress". However, Ridhima highlighted that this commitment is not reflected in the domestic actions of the government, which has approved several carbon-intensive projects since the Paris Agreement, in complete contravention to the government's own targets and commitments under the said Agreement. In fact, several coal mining projects and coal-fired thermal power plant projects have been considered and recommended for environmental clearance and forest clearance under the provisions of the Environment (Protection) Act, 1986, and Forest (Conservation) Act, 1980, without there being any discussion or any impact assessment on climate-related issues. Evidence was provided to the NGT that the government had failed to take effective measures to address the adverse impacts of climate change, in violation of the existing framework of environmental legislations in the country.

INADEQUATE PLAN FOR TACKLING CLIMATE CHANGE

Ridhima's petition before the NGT also highlighted the government's inaction on specific issues of climate change. One of these issues is that the Government's National Action Plan on Climate Change (NAPCC) is not target oriented. This Plan, published in 2008, is merely a list of proposed activities; it doesn't set any time-bound goals with regard to emissions reduction. In fact, it is not even based on an investigation of what are the major sources of emissions in India.

It was also highlighted that the Prime Minister's Council met thrice, in 2009, 2010 and 2011. The Council was reconstituted in 2014, and only one meeting has taken place since then (in January 2015). Hence the NAPCC has not been updated since it was first published in 2008, despite numerous critical developments in matters of climate change in the international as well as domestic arena, including the release of two reports by the Intergovernmental Panel on Climate Change (IPCC) and the adoption, ratification and entry into force of the Paris Agreement.

DEPLETING CARBON SINKS

The Petition also highlighted that while India was giving several statements before the world community that the country is well on the path to achieving its targets under the Paris Agreement, in the last one year, the government allowed about 10 000 ha of forests to be diverted. Deforestation is the second-largest source of anthropogenic carbon emissions after fossil fuels.

Forestland captures carbon that would otherwise be released into the atmosphere. Thus, when trees are cut down or destroyed, more carbon is emitted into the atmosphere. It was submitted before the NGT by Ridhima that even after having all the data available and threats made visible, no concrete step has been taken by the government that could reduce India's contribution to climate change, especially with regard to the increasing trend in forest diversion and consequent loss of carbon sinks.

RELIEF SOUGHT FROM THE NATIONAL GREEN TRIBUNAL

Thus, the Petition sought specific directions from the NGT to the government for including mandatory Environmental Impact Assessments (EIAs) of the projects, which require environment clearance under the environmental law regime (EIA Notification, 2006) and also when diverting forest for non-forest use under the Forest (Conservation) Act, 1980. The Petition also sought for a realization of an inventory of each and every substantial source of greenhouse gas (GHG) emissions in India. Without such inventories it is not possible to achieve any agreed target. Most importantly, the Petition sought for a time-bound national climate recovery plan within the existing legal framework that includes successive CO_2 reduction targets and mitigation actions.

PROCEEDINGS BEFORE THE NATIONAL GREEN TRIBUNAL

The government, in response to the Petition, asked for the dismissal of the case on frivolous grounds. Its main argument was that the issue of climate change is global in nature and is a policy issue with which the NGT ought not to interfere. The government also stressed that the NAPCC was sufficient to deal with the issue of climate change and there was no need for any further steps to be taken in this regard.

In reality, most of the steps that the government has claimed to have taken are only on paper and in the form of policy frameworks that cannot be enforced or implemented. The government has even diverted money away from the National Clean Energy fund for other purposes. It has granted permission for new thermal power plants in contradiction to statements made by the Ministry of Power. There is no programme in place aiming at sufficiently reducing the use of fossil fuels to achieve the required target of GHG emissions reduction. Burning fossil fuels already causes increased asthma, cancer, cardiovascular disease, heat-related morbidity and mortality, food-borne diseases, and neurological diseases and disorders.

In January 2019, the NGT closed Ridhima's Petition by observing that there is no reason to presume that the Paris Agreement and other international protocols are not reflected in the policies of the Government of India, or are not taken into consideration in granting environment clearances; therefore, there was no need for the NGT to pass any further directions on this issue. What is slightly disappointing is that despite presenting several arguments as well as evidence on the lack of a EIAs while appraising projects, the NGT closed the case on a clearly erroneous presumption. Ridhima has filed an appeal before the Supreme Court of India. She is also strategizing on leading the discussion on climate change into fruitful and effective action on the ground. Ridhima is positive that her efforts as well as the efforts of all the children around the world who are fighting for effective measures to tackle adverse impacts of climate change will definitely bring about a change in the way governments are dealing with the issue.

Acronyms and abbreviations

EIA	Environment Impact Assessment
GHG	Greenhouse gas
IPCC	Intergovernmental Panel on Climate Change
NAPCC	National Action Plan on Climate Change
NGT	National Green Tribunal
UNFCCC	UN Framework Convention on Climate Change

18. Protecting the rights of future generations through climate litigation: lessons from the struggle against deforestation in the Colombian Amazon

Camila Bustos, Valentina Rozo-Ángel and Gabriela Eslava-Bejarano

In 2017, a group of 25 children and young people from 17 cities in Colombia filed a lawsuit against the state for failing to stop deforestation in the Amazon region. The plaintiffs come from some of the cities and towns most vulnerable to climate change in the country, ranging from coastal areas to high altitudes. They all rely on their environment for their daily activities and have seen a range of their human rights threatened by increasing deforestation in the Amazon region. With the support of the Center for the Study of Law, Justice, and Society (Dejusticia), the plaintiffs came together to file a *tutela* action, a special kind of legal mechanism to protect fundamental rights. They claimed that the high deforestation rate in the country and its connection with climate change was threatening their right to life, health, water, and food and violating their right to a healthy environment. In doing so, they joined a global movement demanding action on climate change from national governments.

According to the Institute of Hydrology, Meteorology and Environmental Studies (IDEAM), the state agency tasked with producing environmental data in the country, the main source of greenhouse gas (GHG) emissions in Colombia is deforestation. The most recent national inventory indicates that 36 percent of emissions come from deforestation alone.[1] At the time of filing, deforestation rates had increased 44 percent between 2016 and 2017,[2] with over 40 percent of early deforestation warnings located in the Amazon region.[3]

While climate change impacts are already being felt throughout the country, future generations of Colombians will disproportionately face the burden of climate impacts as a result of emissions today. During the period 2041–70, Colombia will experience a 1.6°C increase in average temperatures and a range of impacts including changes in rainfall patterns, droughts, and severe flooding. In addition, plaintiffs living on the Atlantic and Pacific coasts are likely to face an increase in sea level rise, while plaintiffs located in the capital city of Bogotá may see their main source of potable water – a high-elevation ecosystem known as *paramo* – threatened by water shortages resulting from deforestation.[4] Based on these climate change scenarios, the lawsuit defines "future generations" as those who will be adults during this period, but who currently are not old enough to occupy a high rank in government or to be taken seriously in the decision-making process. In light of this fact, the lawsuit centers intergenerational equity in the plaintiffs' demands.

THE LEGAL OBLIGATION TO STOP DEFORESTATION

According to the National Development Plan (2014–18),[5] the Colombian government had set the goal of limiting deforestation to 90 000 hectares by the end of 2018. Nevertheless, by 2017, deforestation was already twice this amount (178 000 hectares). Furthermore, Colombia committed to reduce its emissions by 20 percent by 2030 based on a business-as-usual scenario as part of its Nationally Determined Contribution (NDC) in the context of the Paris Agreement. Prior to this, the state also signed a cooperation agreement with Germany, Norway, and the United Kingdom to reduce deforestation in the Amazon to net zero by 2020. Despite all these national and international commitments, deforestation rates had continued to increase by the time the plaintiffs filed the lawsuit; approximately 66.2 percent of deforestation was concentrated in the Amazon region. In addition to these commitments, the Colombian government is bound by the national Constitution, which includes a provision on the right to enjoy a healthy environment and to participate in the environmental decision-making process. The Constitution also protects the fundamental right to life, health, food, and water.

The plaintiffs alleged that these fundamental rights were threatened by increasing deforestation. Deforestation contributes GHG emissions because the forest acts as a carbon sink. It also disrupts key ecosystem services like water cycle regulation that affect people across the country. In this sense, government inaction contributes to the climate crisis. All the towns and munic-ipalities where the plaintiffs come from are vulnerable to climate impacts and each individual plaintiff faces concrete threats to their rights, depending on their location and lifestyle. Despite the fact the climate change is a multi-causal problem, deforestation is the main contributor to GHG emissions in Colombia.

The lawsuit also invoked five legal principles enshrined in the Constitution or in international environmental treaties that have been ratified by Colombia. The precautionary principle was applicable insofar as plaintiffs sought to prevent the realization of an irreversible harm. The rise of GHG emissions resulting from deforestation and the link between an increase in the frequency and intensity of natural disasters and the deforestation rate in the Colombian Amazon served as evidence of the imminent threat posed by the climate crisis. In addition, the principle of intergenerational equity within the framework of sustainable development sets the ground for the plaintiffs' claims, who will suffer the consequences of the decisions made today if current generations fail to act on deforestation and climate change. Similarly, the principle of the priority of children's' interests and well-being ought to serve as a key consideration when making decisions that will directly impact the rights of children, while the principle of public participation gives voice to young people in decision-making processes that will directly affect their future. Finally, the solidarity principle enshrined in Colombian and international law requires that the government and citizens consider and incorporate the public interest and how actions will have a beneficial or detrimental impact on others into their decision-making process. Together, the lawsuit asked the Court to interpret and apply these principles when reaching a decision.

THE SUPREME COURT RULES ON THE SIDE OF FUTURE GENERATIONS

In March 2017, the Superior Tribunal of Bogotá ruled against the plaintiffs, arguing that the *tutela* mechanism was not the appropriate vehicle for their claims since the right to healthy environment is not a fundamental right, but a collective one.[6] After losing in the Court of First Instance, the plaintiffs appealed the decision. On April 5, the Supreme Court ruled in favor of the plaintiffs, holding that the Colombian government was in fact threatening their constitutionally protected rights.

In the ruling, the Court found that the omissions of the Presidency of the Republic, the Ministry of Environment and Sustainable Development, and the Ministry of Agriculture and Rural Development, as well as the mayors of the Amazon region and environmental authorities, constituted a breach of their legal duties. By allowing deforestation in the Amazon, one of the most biodiverse ecosystems in the world, government agencies were violating the right of youth to a healthy environment. Since deforestation increases emissions, and in turn contributes to an increase in global temperature, the government has an obligation to address the problem. Likewise, the Court acknowledged that the omissions of the state to fulfill its already existing commitments threaten the fundamental rights to life, water, health, and food of the plaintiffs, all of whom are likely to be alive during the first scenario of climate change predicted by the IDEAM.

First, the Court ordered the state to create a short-, medium-, and long-term action plan to stop deforestation in the Amazon region. Second, the Supreme Court granted the plaintiffs' petition and ordered the Presidency and the

Ministries of Environment and Agriculture to create an "intergenerational pact for the life of the Colombian Amazon," with the participation of the plaintiffs, affected communities, and research and scientific organizations. The plan must aim to reduce deforestation to zero and mitigate GHG emissions. Third, the Supreme Court ordered the municipalities of the Amazon to update their Land Management Plans within a five-month period, and to develop an action plan to reduce deforestation to zero. Fourth, the Court ordered the Regional Autonomous Corporations in the Amazon (*Corporaciones Autónomas Regionales*), the environmental authorities in the region, to issue an action plan to reduce regional deforestation.

In order to protect this vital ecosystem, the Supreme Court also recognized the Colombian Amazon as an "entity subject of rights". This was the second time in the country's history that a court granted nature this type of legal status, after the Constitutional Court designated the Atrato River subject of rights in 2017. This means that the Amazon has the right to be protected, conserved, maintained, and restored. In addition, the Court extended the right to a healthy environment to future generations based on the principle of solidarity and intrinsic value of nature.

THE IMPLEMENTATION OF THE RULING: LESSONS FOR CLIMATE CHANGE LITIGATION AND ADVOCACY[7]

Traditionally, human rights studies and practice have been more occupied with litigation than on monitoring the implementation of a judicial decision. The same has happened around the world in the emerging field of climate change litigation. To counteract this trend, the plaintiffs and stakeholders in the Colombian case have pushed for compliance with the court ruling. What lessons can be learned for future climate change litigation based on what has happened in Colombia since the Supreme Court issued a favorable decision?

The first lesson is that lawsuits have become an increasingly frequent route for citizens' claims to urgent action on climate change. Since the decision of the Supreme Court, similar decisions have followed. Courts in Australia and the United States have held that the negative impacts of climate change can be the basis for denying licenses to carbon-intensive and oil projects. Dutch courts issued a pioneer ruling in the Urgenda case (see Chapter 15), which obliged the government to commit to a more ambitious and urgent mitigation target. New cases continue to be filed, joining more than 800 cases against both governments that have failed to act in the context of the climate crisis, and fossil fuel companies that have prospered at the expense of global warming.[8] The evolution of climate litigation has closely followed advances in scientific knowledge. The claim in the Colombian case – like others, such as the case of

Juliana v. *United States* (see Chapter 16) – has cited recent climate science, which can now attribute more accurately the link between climate change and extreme weather events, such as floods and heatwaves.[9]

The second lesson is that understanding the impact of this kind of litigation requires taking into account its effects on both public policies and the public sphere. The court ruling in the Colombian Amazon case has until now had more effects on the public sphere than on government action against deforestation and climate change. Together with the efforts of many human rights, indigenous and environmental organizations, our claim and follow-up to the decision contributed by bringing the deforestation of the Amazon to the forefront of public debate. The media continuously monitors the issue and Colombian President Iván Duque declared it one of his priorities in his inauguration speech in 2018. However, promises have not been followed by the difficult decisions required to drastically reduce deforestation, such as the regulation or prosecution of illegal and legal actors who are promoting the colonization of the Amazon for mining and livestock. The good news is that, in 2018, deforestation went down from 219 973 to 197 159 hectares.[10] The bad news is that this level is still well beyond what would be needed for Colombia to bring down deforestation to net zero any time soon.

The third lesson is that litigators need to pay close attention to the implementation phase of their efforts, in order to keep the pressure on relevant public officials to comply with courts' orders and prevent governments' opportunistic use of such orders to pursue policies that run against the spirit and orders of judicial decisions. As for the results of implementation efforts in the Colombian case, the balance thus far is mixed. On the one hand, the convergence of various efforts and factors (including the Court's ruling) has contributed to halt deforestation's upward trend, at least temporarily. On the other hand, the government has been hesitant and slow in implementing the Court's orders. Although it published a document called "Action Plan for Reducing Deforestation and Tackling the Effects of Climate Change in the Colombian Amazon – STC 4360 from 2018", compliance with the Court's orders remains challenging. The document was not developed in a participatory way despite the imperative of including the plaintiffs and other stakeholders in the process. Furthermore, the document was based on an existing governmental policy known as the "Integral Strategy for Controlling Deforestation and Managing the Rainforests". The strategy was developed during the eight years prior to the lawsuit and the judgment, with no input from younger generations or the plaintiffs.

As part of the implementation process, the Ministry of Environment also organized seven different workshops at the national and regional level. Although the government claimed that there had been active plaintiff participation, only four plaintiffs were able to attend each of the workshops. Overall, the voices of young people were absent from the process in addition to the failure to include other key stakeholders such as small farmers, Afro-Colombians, and indigenous communities. The limited involvement of a range of societal actors has undermined the inclusivity and potential impact of the process.

With regard to the order to develop an intergenerational pact, the Ministry of Environment sent a letter to the Court explaining the progress thus far on the second order. The Ministry submitted the document "Developing Agreements to Guarantee the Life of the Colombian Amazon – Progress in the Development of the Pact" and requested ten extra months for fulfilling the order. A review of the record in April 2019 indicated no evidence of any further advances.

Perhaps in response to the limited participation of young people and local communities in the development of the intergenerational pact, the Ministry of Agriculture launched an online platform for people all over the country to contribute ideas for the development of the document. Nevertheless, the plaintiffs explained that an online tool does not take into account that more than half the poorest households in Colombia do not have internet access.[11] This severely limits the participation of the people most affected by deforestation, both in the Amazon region and across the country.

The government submitted a draft of the pact that was originally developed by the plaintiffs as a working paper. The document was meant as a starting point and thus was not developed in collaboration with government officials, communities, or scientists, as ordered by the Supreme Court. The plaintiffs had submitted the draft to the Ministry of Environment hoping to receive feedback. Yet, the document was modified without the plaintiffs' permission and submitted to the Court as evidence of compliance with the order.

As for the potential for backlash and the opportunistic use of court orders by recalcitrant governments, the Colombian litigation also offers useful lessons about the need to anticipate risks and blind spots. On several occasions, the Colombian government and the Attorney General's Office have invoked the ruling in order to crack down on small peasants, as opposed to large landowners, cattle ranchers, large-scale loggers and the other powerful actors who are the main drivers of deforestation. Although the government has failed to meaningfully engage with plaintiffs, it has neglected even more local communities in the Amazon region, including indigenous peoples' communities and organizations, who bear the direct impact of deforestation. This is a particularly salient omission in a country that is undergoing a challenging post-conflict process that, albeit putting an end to a five-decade-old armed conflict, has also created new vulnerabilities for the Amazon's inhabitants and ecosystems, as has happened in other countries and regions in the aftermath of civil wars.[12]

Since the will of governments is not enough, the impact of litigation depends on the engagement and mobilization of local communities and citizens. This is the fourth lesson from the case. In the past year, 16-year-old Swedish activist,

Greta Thunberg started a wave of climate protests. Hundreds of thousands of students and young people, including the plaintiffs of the Colombian lawsuit, have joined her. Litigation led by adults may help, but a more lasting and decisive impact will most likely come from action by youth, who may suffer the most severe effects of an uninhabitable planet.

Litigation and mobilization steered by youth may be the nudge needed to draw the urgent attention that the climate crisis has lacked. After all, as asserted by scientific expert James Hansen in his statement before the Colombian Supreme Court in support of the case, this is a crisis that "may be an unbearable burden to the youth and coming generations".

NOTES

1. Institute of Hydrology, Meteorology and Environmental Studies (IDEAM) and United Nations Development Programme (UNDP) (2016). *National and Departmental Greenhouse Gas Inventory – Colombia: Third National Communication to the United Nations Convention on Climate Change (UNFCCC)*. Available in Spanish at https://www.undp.org/content/dam/colombia/docs/cop22/ IDEAM_TCNCC_INGEI_WEB.pdf. Accessed August 3, 2019.
2. Institute of Hydrology, Meteorology and Environmental Studies (IDEAM) and United Nations Development Programme (UNDP) (2017). *National and Departmental Greenhouse Gas Inventory – Colombia: Third National Communication to the United Nations Convention on Climate Change (UNFCCC): Executive Summary*. Available in Spanish at http://documentacion.ideam.gov.co/ openbiblio/bvirtual/023732/RESUMEN_EJECUTIVO_TCNCC_COLOMBIA .pdf. Accessed August 3, 2019.
3. The IDEAM produces early warnings on deforestation every three months, identifying regional deforestation hotspots. See *Boletíns de alertas tempranas de deforestación* [Deforestation early warning bulletins], Nos. 10, 11 and 12 at http:// www.ideam.gov.co.
4. This type of ecosystem is replenished by rainfall coming from the Amazon. As more forest is cut down, the water cycle is likely to be disrupted.
5. The National Development Plan 2014–18 was codified into law through Ley 1753 of 2015.
6. Under Colombian law, plaintiffs may file a class action known as *acción popular* to demand the protection of collective rights such as the right to a healthy environment.
7. This section is partially taken from César Rodríguez-Garavito (2019). "Climate change and human rights: lessons from litigation for the Amazon". *Openglobalrights.org*, April 25. Accessed July 30, 2019, at https://www .openglobalrights.org/climate-change-and-human-rights-lessons-from-litigation -for-the-amazon/.
8. See UN Environment and Sabin Center for Climate Change (2017). *The Status of Climate Change Litigation: A Global Review*. Accessed August 13, 2020 at https://wedocs.unep.org/bitstream/handle/20.500.11822/20767/climate-change -litigation.pdf?sequence=1&isAllowed=y.

9. Sophie Marjanac and Lindene Patton (2018). "Extreme weather event attribution science and climate change litigation: an essential step in the causal chain?" *Journal of Energy & Natural Resources Law*, **36** (3), 265–98.
10. *El Espectador* (2019). "En 2018, Colombia deforestó 197.159 hectáreas de bosque" [In 2018, Colombia deforested 197 159 hectares of forest]. Accessed July 30, 2019 at https://www.elespectador.com/noticias/medio-ambiente/se-redujo-la -tasa-de-deforestacion-en-colombia-articulo-870196.
11. Presidencia de la República (2019). *Bases del Plan Nacional de Desarrollo 2018–2022* [Bases of the National Development Plan 2018–2022], p. 647. Accessed August 13, 2020 at https://colaboracion.dnp.gov.co/CDT/Prensa/ BasesPND2018-2022n.pdf.
12. César Rodríguez-Garavito, Diana Rodríguez-Franco and Helena Durán (2017). *Environmental Peace: Challenges and Proposals after the Peace Accord*. Bogotá: Dejusticia. Available in Spanish at https://www.dejusticia.org/publication/la-paz -ambiental-retos-y-propuestas-para-el-posacuerdo-2/. Accessed July 30, 2019.

19. People's Climate Case – families and youth take the EU to court over its failure to address the climate crisis

Gökşen Şahin

We wouldn't take the European Union to court if our families, friends, homes, traditions and the future of our children weren't at stake. For us, climate change is no longer about high-level diplomacy or negotiations. It is happening to us. (From a joint letter of plaintiffs of the People's Climate Case to the European Environment Ministers)

They are farmer, forester, hotel owner and animal herder families from Portugal, Italy, France, Germany, Romania, Kenya and Fiji, and a youth association representing the indigenous Saami youth in Sweden. In 2018, they sued the European Parliament and the European Council over the inadequacy of the European Union's (EU) 2030 climate target to tackle the climate crisis and to protect their lives, livelihoods and fundamental rights.

How did they come together? What does a Fijian family with three kids have in common with young Saami reindeer herders in Sweden? And a Kenyan farmer with a German islander? The answer is clear. They all demand climate justice. They are not the ones who caused the climate breakdown but the ones suffering from it. Devastating impacts of the climate crisis are progressing even faster than the scientists have predicted. For these families and millions of other people hit by climate change, every day brings a new fight for survival. And yet the governments, even the EU who pretends to be a global climate champion, are failing to protect them.

These families are not alone. They are a part of global climate litigation movement. Today, citizens across the world are holding their governments accountable for their inadequate climate policies and challenging fossil fuel companies for deepening the climate crisis. Climate change litigation is becoming an important tool to tackle climate change and the violation of human rights at the same time.

In the landmark People's Climate Case, the plaintiffs argue that climate protection is a duty of care that is not determined by political discretion but an objective one. Therefore, the EU has a legal obligation to simply do what it can to protect citizens and their rights, while also avoiding further harm.

This legal obligation is not only coming from the European treaties and laws but also an international one. By adopting the Paris Agreement in 2015, the world, including EU countries, decided to pursue efforts to limit temperature rise to 1.5°C. As a consequence, they also accept to take pledges that "reflect the highest possible ambition". However, the EU's climate target, which was set in 2014 to reduce emissions by at least 40 per cent by 2030, has not been amended since the Paris Agreement. It is contributing to a 3°C temperature increase by the end of the century and definitely far from being the most ambitious climate target that the EU can take.

These families, as well as the Saami youth, whose lives depend on nature, are already severely suffering from the consequences of climate change. Some of them tried to realize adaptation projects to save their lands but the impacts got worse much faster than expected. Today, they have reached a point where their health situation and their lands cannot adapt to the climate crisis anymore. They need URGENT climate action.

The anger, fear and disappointment that they feel due to governments' failure to tackle the climate crisis have transformed them from being ordinary peasants, hotel owners and herders into activists of all ages who stand up and fight for their rights. Today, in court, they are not asking financial compensation for their losses. They ask courts to order the European decision-makers to make better climate legislation to protect citizens, their fundamental rights, and future generations. Outside of court, they join the youth and citizens to demand climate justice.

As one of the plaintiffs, 73-year-old French lavender farmer Maurice Feschet said: "We have lived on this land for six generations. My son Renaud is the first generation to start other businesses, as the lavender farming can no longer guarantee sufficient income for the whole family. At my age, besides joining climate marches with young people, this legal case is the only thing that I can do to protect my children and grandchildren. As a citizen, I will keep turning to the courts as politicians fail to deliver the needed climate action".

These families and youth are asking the courts to protect their human rights when the governments fail to do so. They are vanguards in the fight for a safe future, just like millions of other people advocating, mobilizing, boycotting, and striking for climate. They are among millions who lead on climate action. They prove to us that US social activist Grace Lee Boggs was right when she said, "we are the leaders we've been looking for".

Now, with more and more climate cases in courts, millions of young people taking to the streets, businesses and cities taking action to reduce emissions, we see that a change is coming in Europe – a change led by youth and people who are moving from front line of climate change to the forefront of climate action.

Thanks to their efforts and pressure, the European Parliament has declared the Climate Emergency in 2019 and currently calls on the EU to increase its 2030 climate target to 60%. EU Member States are discussing to enhance the climate target before the end of 2020. This is the story of families and the indigenous youth who contributed to the momentum for a change in Europe.

FROM THE FRONT LINE OF CLIMATE CHANGE TO THE FOREFRONT OF CLIMATE ACTION

Sanna Vannar is a 23-year-old Saami reindeer herder from Jokkmokk, Sweden. She represents the Saami Youth Association in the People's Climate Case. For the Saami people, who live in the harsh Arctic environment, their entire way of life is strongly connected to nature. For centuries, they have adapted, persevered and survived. Now, they feel endangered because of climate change.

Everything that surrounds Sanna and the Sami people is changing: wildfires hitting the Saami grazelands, reindeer dying due to a lack of food, and emotional stress caused by the uncertainty of climate conditions are becoming unbearable for the Sami youth. Sanna explains: "Already hundreds of Saami words describing different types of snow are no longer used. Our language is changing, but so is all the traditional knowledge. We cannot predict where to find fish, which signs to read in nature anymore. We are even losing the traditional knowledge of our elders, like knowing how the weather will change by reading the signs. Because nobody can read the signs of nature anymore".

Today, the indigenous Saami people are living the consequences of governments' lack of climate action. They deserve to be heard in court but also in decision-making processes, as their indigenous knowledge on land and nature provides invaluable solutions to the climate crisis.

In the People's Climate Case, the Saami youth are accompanied by many other families from Europe who are affected in many different and peculiar ways. Portuguese Armando Carvalho and his son have dedicated their lives to showcasing sustainable forest management practices by replacing pine and eucalyptus trees with local species such as oak and chestnut. For 20 years, they have invested in their forested land in the centre of Portugal. In 2017, Portuguese wildfires, which are scientifically associated with climate change-induced heatwaves and droughts, hit all their forested land. The family home was also surrounded by flames, and his agricultural machinery and garage were damaged by the fire. Armando and his son were lucky to survive the forest fire, but they have never forgotten it. They are now investing in rehabilitation of their forested land, but it is nevertheless impossible to estimate if and when they will again have a mature forest, given the risk scenarios of climate change in Portugal. Having once lived this disaster, they are now trying to avoid the worst for others.

The Sendim family have owned a family farm in Portugal for more than 100 years. Alfredo Sendim, a farmer for 30 years, created a farmers' cooperative on his land and today more than 35 families work and depend on this land. For a decade, the impacts of climate change have been getting worse in the region, and land use and working conditions are becoming increasingly difficult due to rising temperatures and lack of water. Every year, they are investing more to continue farming activities, while their income from the land continues to decrease. All families who depend on this land are asking themselves the same questions: "When to leave our land?" "Where to go?" Therefore, Alfredo Sendim and the Caixeiro family who are members of the farmers' cooperative joined this climate case to alert the EU courts to the fact that climate protection is no longer a political or purely diplomatic issue. It is about protecting citizens lives, livelihoods and rights in Europe.

Maike and Michael Recktenwald have built their family, hotel and restaurant business from scratch in 20 years on Langeoog island in Germany. Today, their livelihood is at risk of disappearing due to the increasing risk of the North Sea breaking through sand dunes into their freshwater reservoir. Scientific studies already show that short-term emission reduction is critical, especially with regard to sea level rise. When it comes to reducing emissions to protect their island, every minute counts. They believe that activating jurisdiction is the only way to hold governments accountable for their inaction and provide a better future for their son.

In the Italian Alps, Giorgio Elter owns a small bed & breakfast hotel, which is fully dependent on the famous ice-climbing opportunities in the region. The changes in temperature are making the ice climbing dangerous, which severely affects the Elters' family business, as well as many others in the region. He explains: "Today, I can hardly take care of my family and can't guarantee a safe future for my daughters. We are not responsible for the climate breakdown but we are the ones who suffer. Just like any parent, I am trying to protect the future of my children".

The European plaintiffs of the People's Climate Case have also joined forces with the Guyo family from Kenya and the Qaloibau family from Fiji to demonstrate that the EU's climate inaction has devastating consequences in the Global South. Just like the climate crisis, this growing climate litigation movement knows no borders.

GLOBAL SOUTH JOINS EUROPEANS TO SEEK STRONGER CLIMATE MEASURES

The People's Climate Case is the first climate case to claim that the EU's failure to address the climate crisis has effects beyond its borders, and people living outside Europe are also entitled to the EU fundamental rights to health, occupation, property and equal treatment. Two families from the Global South challenge the EU for the equal protection of their human rights.

The Qaloibau family, with their three children, live in a village on the island of Vanua Levu in the Republic of Fiji. Like most of Fiji's rural communities, the family relies on marine resources and subsistence farming. Petero Qaloibau explains: "In 2002, houses are blown away in my village due to hurricanes. My small shop is destroyed during Cyclone Thomas in 2010. Tropical Cyclone Winston hit Fiji with a wind speeds of more than 230 km/hour in 2016 and our farm was inundated with sea water almost 200 m inland. Today, my mind is set: I'm affected by climate change. Science confirms it and the EU who is supposed to be a climate leader is failing us".

Petero Qaloibau is not the only Pacific Islander who asks the EU to ramp up climate action. In 2019, the president of Marshall Islands, Hilda Heine, and Prime Minister of Fiji, Frank Bainimarama, wrote a joint letter to the EU leaders. They said: "Every day our people, the people of island states, are confronted with the harsh realities of climate change. We are reaching a critical juncture in the fight against this change and the European Union should help us by raising its own climate ambition".[1]

The landmark report of Intergovernmental Panel on Climate Change (IPCC), *Global Warming of 1.5°C*, made it crystal clear that we have far less time available than we thought to turn the tide. Only short-term action can effectively preserve life on small island states. And EU leaders must take the responsibility and do their part to step up short-term climate action.

The Guyo family, with their five children, live in a village in Marsabit County, Northern Kenya, close to the Ethiopian border. All members of the family are suffering from extreme heatwaves, longer and more severe droughts and lack of water. Children are particularly vulnerable as they need to walk a 1.5 km distance to school every day. During heatwaves when the temperature is above 40–45°C, kids suffer from headaches, disturbed sleep and other heat-related health problems. On top of this, their right to education is also violated as they cannot attend school due to there being no shade on their route to school.

Roba Guyo explains the complexity of the climate crisis: "We have seen all kind of sufferings related to climate change. We used to harvest all season round. Our granary was always full and we were able to feed our animals with what we produce from our farm. We are not used to this drought where our animals die and our farmland dries up. These days, there are a lot of people and livestock who are fleeing from droughts".

Dima Guyo, mother of five children adds: "Climate change is mostly women's problem. In Africa, women take care of families, livestock and kids. When I need to walk further to get water for my kids, I don't have time to cook or even eat something. If I walk that distance under extreme temperatures,

I need to deal with a lot of health problems. Given the severity of these consecutive droughts, I don't know if I will survive from the one that will hit us next, or the year later. I don't know in which conditions my kids will live. I just want to go to court, to look in the eyes of those decision-makers, and ask: why are you doing this to my children?"

Devastating impacts of climate change are borne disproportionately by the most vulnerable, including the rural poor, women and indigenous populations. Both in Europe and the Global South, farming communities who depend on nature, indigenous people, women and children are more exposed to the consequences of climate change. The report published in June 2019 by Philip Alston, the UN Special Rapporteur on extreme poverty and human rights, clearly explains the human rights impacts of the climate crisis: "Climate change threatens the future of human rights and risks undoing the last fifty years of progress in development, global health, and poverty reduction". It is not surprising to see all different communities from Europe and the Global South coming together in the People's Climate Case to seek to force governments to adopt more stringent climate regulation to protect our common future.

OPENING COURT DOORS TO THE PEOPLE AFFECTED BY CLIMATE CHANGE

The People's Climate Case is novel on many different levels, even though a legal victory is by no means certain. This case is not only putting the EU's failure to provide necessary climate protection in the spotlight but also its blockage to access to justice for citizens and non-governmental organizations (NGOs) on environmental issues.

According to the European Courts' interpretation of the Treaty of Functioning of the EU since the 1960s, a citizen is only regarded "individually concerned" and allowed to go to court, if he or she is affected like an addressee, thus in an "exclusive/unique/peculiar" way by a piece of EU law. Therefore, a year after the People's Climate Case is filed, on 8 May 2019, the European General Court – the Court of First Instance – dismissed the People's Climate Case by recognizing that plaintiffs are affected by climate change but they are not sufficiently unique to challenge the EU legislation. Even though the plaintiff families and the Saami youth had set out their individual concerns in detail, with regard to their property, farms and other businesses, as well as to their health and educational rights, these are not seen as "unique" enough by the European General Court.

As it stands, the Court's decision means that the more people are affected and the more serious the damage, the less they can have access to justice in the European Courts. This represents a major barrier to access to justice for individuals who are trying to challenge EU legislation on environmental grounds.

This decision also disrespects the very rationale of fundamental rights, which is to grant protection to every single person, and disregards the seriousness and magnitude of the climate crisis addressed by plaintiffs. By the time this book is published (or sent to print), the plaintiffs are still seeking justice in the higher instance court, the European Court of Justice, by explaining why people affected by the climate crisis should be protected through the EU legal system.

Even though it is already shameful that families and indigenous youth from Europe and the Global South need to go court to urge the EU to step up climate action, all the time lost in the procedural battles to get their rights recognized – to simply enter courtrooms – proves that our legal systems should also be adapted to the magnitude of the ongoing climate crisis. We definitely need reinterpretation of existing laws to the context of climate change but, more urgently and importantly, we need the EU to step up climate action in an unprecedented way so that citizens would not need to go to courts to search for climate justice.

Time is pressing. Every day more and more people are hit by climate change-induced disasters. In summer 2019, heatwaves, droughts and forest fires were wreaking havoc once again in Europe. The European Union's Earth Observation Programme, Copernicus, announced that the entire Earth had experienced its warmest June on record in 2019. This announcement was followed by World Weather Attribution group, who stated that record-breaking temperatures that hit Europe were at least five times more likely to happen in the future due to climate change.

The EU must understand that all these climate disasters are not simply about numbers or scientific projections. Today, they are citizens' top concern. And people will keep mobilizing every possible way to protect their lives, livelihoods and human rights. They will not allow politicians to keep arguing for the status quo and failing to take unprecedented climate action.

As Martin Luther King said: "Our lives begin to end the day we become silent about things that matter".

PEOPLE'S CLIMATE CASE LINKS

Legal documents of the People's Climate Case may be found at https://peoplesclimatecase .caneurope.org/documents/. Accessed 26 August 2020.
More information about the plaintiffs may be found at https://peoplesclimatecase .caneurope.org/who-we-are/. Accessed 26 August 2020.
The full text of the Paris Agreement may be found at https://unfccc.int/files/essential _background/convention/application/pdf/english_paris_agreement.pdf.   Accessed 26 August 2020.

NOTE

1. https://www.euractiv.com/section/climate-environment/opinion/a-question-of
-legacy-eu-must-step-up-and-lead-on-climate/.

20. Climate change claim on behalf of New Zealand's indigenous Māori peoples

Michael Sharp, Nicole Smith and Tania Te Whenua

In May 2016, a claim was filed in New Zealand's Waitangi Tribunal by representatives of the Mataatua District Māori Council, claiming that the New Zealand government had failed to implement adequate policies to address the threats posed by global climate change to the Māori indigenous peoples of New Zealand.

THE LITIGANTS

Mataatua District Māori Council is one of a number of statutory representative bodies established[1] to promote the interests of the indigenous Māori people in New Zealand. Mataatua District Māori Council has responsibility for an area in the eastern part of the North Island of New Zealand. The Waitangi Tribunal claim was brought on behalf of the Council by Maanu Paul, David Potter and Andre Paterson. Andre Paterson has passed away since the claim was filed. Maanu Paul is a well-known Māori activist, who has been involved with numerous campaigns on behalf of Māori over the decades. For example, he was an original claimant and continues to be involved with claims in establishing Māori interests in fresh water.[2] Maanu Paul was a former chairperson of the New Zealand Māori Council, and was recently made an Officer of the New Zealand Order of Merit (ONZM).

THE LITIGATION

The claim was brought in the Waitangi Tribunal, which is a tribunal established in New Zealand for Māori to bring claims that the government is acting in breach of its obligations under the Treaty of Waitangi towards Māori.[3] The Treaty of Waitangi is a treaty signed in 1840 between the British Crown and Māori chiefs under which the British Crown accepted certain obligations towards Māori people. This included what has been subsequently interpreted by the courts in New Zealand as an obligation of 'active protection', to actively protect Māori interests over their land and resources.[4]

In hearing claims before it, the Waitangi Tribunal acts as a commission of inquiry. Although the tribunal can make recommendations to the government to address found treaty breaches, the findings are not binding, and are generally used by the New Zealand government to negotiate settlements of claims with Māori.

The statement of claim filed[5] on behalf of the Mataatua District Māori Council alleged that the New Zealand government had breached its obligations of active protection towards all Māori by not adequately responding to the global threat of climate change. In this regard, particular emphasis was placed upon the traditional role of Māori as guardians of the natural environment upon which Māori rely.

In Māori terminology this guardianship role is encompassed within the principle of '*kaitiakitanga*', which has been described as 'the ethos of sustainable resource management [and] guardianship'.[6] *Kaitiakitanga* involves living in balance, as part of one ecosystem where all things have the potential to endure, and where possible to thrive. This is often described as the Māori holistic world view, a view that is particularly pertinent with respect to climate change as it has the potential to affect the ecosystem as a whole.

The claim alleged that the New Zealand government had breached its obligations to protect Māori in this guardianship role by failing to ensure that New Zealand bears its fair share as a developed nation in reducing greenhouse gas emissions so as to keep global temperature rises below dangerous levels that would affect Māori in the use of their land and resources.[7] In this regard, reference was made to: degradation of the natural ecosystem caused by global warming and rising seas, resulting in shortage of water resources for Māori communities, impact on Māori commercial interests, such as in forestry and agriculture, impact on Māori fishing rights and interests, the threat posed to Māori coastal communities by rising sea, and general impacts on Māori health and well-being.

Claims before the Waitangi Tribunal typically take some years before they get to a hearing. Given the perceived urgency in having the claim heard, the claimants filed an application to the Waitangi Tribunal to have its claim heard urgently. On 17 October 2017, the Waitangi Tribunal declined the application for an urgent hearing on the basis that, although the claim raised important issues, the government was still developing its domestic policies surrounding the implementation of the United Nations Paris Agreement, and there remains an opportunity for Māori to participate in that process.[8]

At present, the claimants are continuing in their efforts to have their claim heard and will shortly make a further application to the Waitangi Tribunal to allocate the claim a priority hearing.

POTENTIAL FOR SUCCESSFUL CLIMATE CHANGE CLAIM THROUGH NEW ZEALAND'S WAITANGI TRIBUNAL

Compared with other litigation options, the claim through the Waitangi Tribunal offers perhaps the best option for successfully bringing a climate change claim in New Zealand. An alternative litigation route would be to bring an application for judicial review of government policy through the New Zealand High Court. However, historically, the High Court in dealing with judicial review applications of government policy has been reluctant to interfere with government decision-making.[9]

This is illustrated by recent judicial review proceedings brought by an individual against aspects of the New Zealand government's climate changes policies, resulting in the decision *Thomson* v. *Minister for Climate Change Issue* [10] While the Court accepted that the Minister for Climate Change should have had regard to the most recent United Nations Intergovernmental Panel on Climate Change (IPCC) AR5 report in reviewing New Zealand's 2050 emission targets, the judge was not convinced that this would have made any difference to the outcome, given the contents of the AR5 report, and the fact that a new government had recently been elected The judge also rejected the argument that New Zealand's pledged Nationally Determined Contribution (NDC) under the United Nations Paris Agreement of reducing emissions by 2030 by 11 per cent from 1990 levels was unreasonable given that it was not in line with the 2050 target and contributions committed to by other comparable countries. The judge considered that the NDC was not inconsistent with New Zealand's international obligations and could be reviewed at a later date, including by the incoming new government.[11] On this basis, the application for judicial review was dismissed.

By contrast with this outcome, there will be a much wider scope for the Waitangi Tribunal to make findings in regard to government efforts to address climate change. The Tribunal has wide jurisdiction to hear any claim by or on behalf of Māori that they are being prejudiced by any legislation, government policy or action.[12] In investigating such claims, it has all the powers and scope of a commission of inquiry in calling and considering evidence. In considering a claim, it can go beyond the restricted jurisdiction of the High Court judicial review to only consider whether government action is illegal and look to the government's broader obligations under the Treaty of Waitangi.

As such, if and when the Mataatua District Māori Council claimants finally have their claim heard there will be no jurisdictional barriers limiting the Waitangi Tribunal in considering the claim that government policy in regard to climate change has been in breach of obligations of active protection towards Māori.

POTENTIAL FOR THE DEVELOPMENT OF INDIGENOUS-BASED PUBLIC TRUST PRINCIPLES

The Mataatua District Māori Council claim also illustrates the potential for indigenous groups globally to bring environmental claims in their capacity as traditional guardians of the natural environment. In this regard, the claimed breach of the duty of active protection towards Māori in their role as guardians of the natural environment has parallels with the 'public trust doctrine' argued in climate change cases in the United States of America. In *Juliana* v. *United States of America* (see Chapter 16),[13] where the claimants were successful in invoking the public trust doctrine in arguing that inadequate government climate change policies breached the state's fiduciary obligations to protect the environment that is common property of all citizens,[14] the court found that inadequate climate change policies had such a profound effect on the environment and the community that the government can be considered as being in serious breach of its fiduciary obligation in failing to take adequate steps.[15]

In the Mataatua District Māori Council claim, it has been submitted that the approach adopted in the *Juliana* case of applying the public trust doctrine should be followed by the Waitangi Tribunal to find that the New Zealand government has breached its Treaty of Waitangi-based fiduciary obligations towards Māori in failing to put in place adequate policies to deal with the threat of climate change. In further support of this submission, reference has been made to past decisions of the New Zealand Court of Appeal that the Crown's Treaty of Waitangi obligation of active protection towards Māori 'creates responsibilities analogous to fiduciary duties' to Māori people in the use of their lands and resources.[16]

This approach of indigenous peoples basing claims upon their traditional roles as caretakers of the environment may well provide indigenous groups around the world with unique standing to bring litigation against governments for failing to adequately protect the environment. For example, Torres Strait Islanders have brought a claim before the UN Human Rights Commission against the Australian government for its failure to take action on climate change issues. Torres Strait Islands are geographically separate from, but legally part of, Australia, and its residents are recognized as indigenous Australians. The Torres Strait Islanders argue that the Australian federal government has failed to uphold human rights obligations and violated their rights to culture, family and life.[17]

In New Zealand itself, it has been recently announced by a representative of the Iwi Leaders Group – an organization of leaders of Māori tribes – that they had filed in the High Court judicial review proceedings claiming that the current Labour Party-led government had failed to take adequate steps to address climate change issues.[18] It remains to be seen if the High Court will give this claim any broader consideration then it did in *Thomson* v. *Minister for Climate Change*, given that the new claim has been brought on behalf of Māori. There is at least the potential that the court could develop New Zealand common law to accommodate the type of indigenous-based public trust principles that have been argued for in the Mataatua District Māori Council claim before the Waitangi Tribunal.

Environmental claims by indigenous peoples based on their traditional guardianship roles can in turn lead to these roles being legally recognized. For instance, past settlements of Treaty of Waitangi claims in New Zealand have led to Māori being given a legally recognized guardianship role in caring for the natural environment. Legislation has been enacted granting a separate legal personality to a river and a geographically significant area, and establishing a board including Māori representatives to make decisions for the protection and promotion of these environmental features.[19] Similarly, in India, the Ganges and Yamuna Rivers have been declared to be legal persons based on the sacred nature of these rivers, with state representatives appointed to protect them.[20]

POTENTIAL FOR INDIGENOUS GROUPS TO DRIVE COMMUNITY-BASED ENVIRONMENTAL CLAIMS

The Mataatua District Māori Council Waitangi Tribunal claim also illustrates the potential for indigenous groups to drive environmental claims in the interests of local communities in general. Although the claim is ostensibly brought on behalf of the indigenous Māori people in New Zealand, it is based on the premise that Māori are guardians of the natural environment that all in New Zealand rely upon.

Indigenous-led claims could be particularly effective when it comes to climate change issues. This is against the background that the challenge of addressing climate change is considered to be too long term and complex for democratically elected governments to take the initiative in providing effective solutions.[21] Given this, there will not be any real progress on climate change policy until there is such a broad shift in the view of the public, that such measures are absolutely required for the future of the community, that governments will be forced to act. One way in which such a shift in social norms can evidence itself and put pressure on governments is by climate change claims through the courts, where the judiciary – the third arm of government – recognize broad community support for more effective government action on climate change.[22] Indigenous groups, given their traditional environmental guardianship roles, are ideally placed to bring such claims.

CONCLUDING COMMENTS

In New Zealand there remains a real and immediate need for the Mataatua District Māori Council claimants to obtain a hearing for their claim as soon as possible. Leading up to the 2017 general elections, the Labour Party leader Jacinda Ardern declared that climate change was her generation's 'nuclear-free moment' that a Labour-led government would "tackle head on".[23] However, subsequent to the Labour Party-led government being formed, its climate change polices to date have failed to live up to earlier aspirational rhetoric of the current prime minister. Although the government enacted legislation that essentially duplicates the UK approach of establishing a climate change commission and emissions budgets,[24] there is little progress in formulating policies that will drive down future emissions. In the meantime, amongst developed nations, New Zealand continues to have among the highest levels of emissions per capita and is one of the few whose greenhouse gas emissions are still increasing.[25] The climate change monitoring organization Germanwatch, in its 2020 report, ranked New Zealand's climate change policies as 30th out of 61 developed nations.[26]

New Zealand's Paris Agreement NDC of reducing net greenhouse gas emissions in 2030 by 11 per cent from 1990 gross emission levels[27] has been assessed by the climate change policy monitoring organization Climate Action Tracker as insufficient compared with what will be necessary meet the Paris Agreement objectives of keeping global temperature increases within 1.5°C, and New Zealand's current climate change policies as being 'insufficient' to meet the NDC in any case.[28]

It is against this background that claimants in the Mataatua District Māori Council Waitangi claim are continuing their attempts to have their claim heard within the next year or so to obtain recommendations from the Waitangi Tribunal that the government enhance New Zealand's final NDC before it comes into effect in 2021.

NOTES

1.   Maori Community Development Act 1962.
2.   National Fresh Water and Geothermal Resources Inquiry Wai 2358.
3.   Treaty of Waitangi Act 1975.

4. *New Zealand Maori Council* v. *Attorney-General* [1987] 1 NZLR 641.
5. Wai 2607 #1.1.1. This and other claim documents can be found through the Waitangi Tribunal website, www.waitangitribunal.govt.nz, and by searching under inquiry documents with the claim reference WAI2607.
6. G.R. Harmsworth and S. Awatere (2013), in J.R. Dymond (ed.), *Indigenous Māori Knowledge and Perspectives of Ecosystems*, Lincoln, NZ: Manaaki Whenua Press, p. 284.
7. Statement of Claim dated 30 May 2016, WAI2607 #1.1.1, paragraphs 52–53.
8. Decision on application for an urgent hearing, WAI2607 #2.5.4.
9. Palmer, G. (2018), 'Can judges make a difference? The scope for judicial decisions on climate change in domestic New Zealand law', paper presented at Pacific Oceans, Pacific Climate Conference, Wellington, 21–23 February 2018.
10. *Thomson* v. *Minister for Climate Change Issues* [2018] 2 NZLR 160.
11. Ibid., paragraph 176.
12. Section 6, Treaty of Waitangi Act 1975
13. *Juliana* v. *United States of America*, Case 6:16-CV-01517-TC Opinion and Order 10 November 2016 in the United States District Court for the District of Oregon, Eugene Division.
14. Ibid., p. 38.
15. Ibid., pp. 51–2.
16. *New Zealand Maori Council* v. *Attorney-General*, p. 38.
17. Client Earth (2019), 'Human rights and climate change: world-first case to protect indigenous Australians', 12 May, accessed 8 June 2020 at https://www.clientearth.org/human-rights-and-climate-change-world-first-case-to-protect-indigenous-australians/.
18. Neilson, M. (2019), 'Iwi leader suing government over "failure" to protect Maori from climate change', *New Zealand Herald*, 16 July.
19. Te Awa Tupua (Whanganui River Claims Settlement) Act 2017 in regard to the Whanganui River; Tūhoe Claims Settlement Act 2004 with regard to Te Urewera Area.
20. Safi, M. and agencies (2017), 'Ganges and Yamuna rivers granted same rights as human beings', *The Guardian*, 21 March, accessed 8 June 2020 at https://www.theguardian.com/world/2017/mar/21/ganges-and-yamuna-rivers-granted-same-legal-rights-as-human-beings.
21. R.H.J. Cox (2012), *Revolution Justified: Why Only the Law Can Save Us Now*, Maastricht: Planet Prosperity Foundation.
22. Ibid.
23. Claire Trevett (2017), 'Jacinda Ardern's rallying cry: climate change the nuclear free moment of her generation', *New Zealand Herald*, 20 August.
24. Climate Change Response (Zero Carbon) Amendment Act 2019.
25. Ministry for Environment (2019), *New Zealand Green House Gas Inventory 1990–2017*, New Zealand Government.
26. Germanwatch (2020), 'Climate Change Performance Index, results 2020', Germanwatch, Climate Action Network and New Climate Institute, p. 17.
27. Which the Labour-led government confirmed as an 'ambitious target' at COP24 at Krakow in 2018.
28. Climate Action Tracker (2019), *Warming Projections Global Update*, December, p. 11.

21. France: *L'Affaire du Siècle*: the story of a mass mobilization for climate

Marie Toussaint

On December 18, 2018, France faces an earth-shaking momentum: the launch of a climate litigation action gathers the support of hundreds of thousands of citizens. For the first time, France wakes up with a massive and unprecedented mobilization for climate, and against the decadal inaction of the successive governments. Within 36 hours, the petition 'L'Affaire du Siècle' is already strong with than 1 million signatures. In less than three weeks, at Christmas time, this 1 million has become more than 2 million.[1]

In a neighboring country, Sweden, a young woman had already been shaking the status quo: Greta Thunberg was now calling for a global youth mobilization on March 15, 2019. The very same day when the four organizations who denounced France's failure to tackle the climate crisis planned to submit their final arguments in court and were already mobilizing the youth movements to push the request together. The spontaneous convergence of dates is striking: was the beginning of 2019 a turning point in the story of humanity? Will the masses finally manage to get environmental and climate action from the policy-makers? Will we be able to create a brand new social movement calling for the overthrow of the growth ideology and open up a new era for harmony with the living?

Economic and political forces tremble. Suddenly, the entire world is getting angry and taking action for change. A change against climate change. A change to save the Earth.

HOW WE GOT INVOLVED IN CLIMATE LITIGATION

Climate change is not new. We find traces of denunciation of environmental damages in the literature of the eighteenth century.[2] The US, Exxon, and scientists already knew about it in the 1970s.[3] The global community expressed its concerns in 1972 and then again in 1992 and every year since then. Scientific reports are multiplying. The book *Silent Spring*, by Rachel Carson, dates from 1962; *The Limits to Growth* report, by Meadows and others, dates from 1972; *Our Common Future*, by Brundtland and the United Nations, dates from 1987, and so on. The Intergovernmental Panel for Climate Change (IPCC) was created in 1988 and ever since, the scientists have not stopped raising the alarm about the state of the world, and, in report after report, the international community of scientists has become increasingly concerned about the impacts of climate change and environmental degradation. At last, in 2009, the Stockholm Resilience Centre devised tools to measure the 'nine planetary boundaries within which humanity can continue to develop and thrive for generations to come'[4]. And, no surprise, we have crossed more than half these boundaries.

For years, we, the citizens of the world, have been acting. Acting against predation on resources. Acting in our everyday lives, changing our habits. The consumption of organic products exploded: nine out of ten French people declare they consume organic food regularly. And this is a global tendency – acting collectively, supporting non-governmental organizations (NGOs) and their lobbying, signing petitions, demonstrating, pushing forward alternative economic models.

On September 8, 2018, more than 50 000 people gathered in Paris to call for environmental action, the biggest climate march organized yet in France. On September 28, 2019, more than 7 million people demonstrated throughout the planet to save the Earth. The movement is growing, and will not stop, despite and since no government is concretely reacting to these massive mobilizations. The defenders of the environment are increasingly in danger. Over the last few years, about 200 activists annually have lost their lives to protect the environment, throughout the world and especially in Latin America and Southeast Asia, but also in the European Union with the recent death of two forestry officers in Romania. News of killings of environmental defenders is reaching us each week, mostly Indigenous peoples or forestry officers and rangers in Sub-Saharan Africa fighting against illegal exploitation of resources.[5] In 2018, according to the United Nations Environment Programme (UNEP) and Interpol, environmental criminality was the third most lucrative criminal transnational activity and the most important source of finances of the current conflicts. The illegal financing of armed groups involved in those conflicts represents 38–64 percent of their revenues.[6] In 2015 and 2016, illegal exploitation of natural resources was the first source of financing for Islamic State.[7]

But neither the facts nor the civil mobilizations have managed to push for climate action. The forces we oppose are strongly attached to their ways and as the firms spend billions in lobbying for their polluting products, the states do not react with ambition and daring.

Despite the international conferences and commitments, we are walking straight towards a global warming of +5°C. According to the United Nations Environment Programme and the World Resources Institute, 150–200 living species (plant, insect, bird and mammal) become extinct each day and the rate is worsening.[8] Everyone now knows and feels it, even in our quite protected countries, that pollution is everywhere, allergies and sicknesses multiply, working conditions are getting harder and harder with the heat, agriculture and fish farming are declining, houses are disappearing in the waters, and so on. It is the Anthropocene – we are killing the Earth and the living. We are no longer heading for a disaster – we are living the disaster. And no reaction is forthcoming.

FRANCE HAS NEVER BEEN A CLIMATE LEADER

France has pretended to be the leader of climate action throughout the world. Our country adopted pioneer legislation, organized the conference that produced the Paris Agreement, called the world to be 'green and great again'. However, our laws are still leading us to a warming of 2.6°C and they are not even respected.

Let us have a broader look: the French firms – such as the carbon major Total and other energy firms, our banks, but also our food system – are still not on the road to respecting the Paris Agreement. France is the biggest EU importer of soya from Argentina and Brazil; the way we feed our cattle is a major cause of deforestation. By doing so, those firms are committing ecocide. Nevertheless, the law does not yet recognize ecocide.

Many reports show that we are not acting on the actions of the private sector, despite the fact that it is the main contributor to greenhouse gas emissions. The Carbon Disclosure Project shows that 25 private and public firms were responsible for 51 percent of global emissions between 1988 and 2015, and their pollution is accelerating.[9] Investigations from NGOs showed that 250 million euros were spent between 2010 and 2018 on lobbying European institutions by five fossil fuel firms: Shell, ExxonMobil, Total, Chevron and BP.[10] France pretends to give absolutely no money to this fossil fuel industry. However, we know that 11 billion euros are still given each year to fossil fuels, mainly through exoneration from taxes.[11] But France seems to be neither fully transparent about all existing subsidies to fossil fuel activities, nor about the hidden ones.

Finally, regarding our national public commitments, we are still not there. Even the weak goals settled in law for our internal emissions are not reached. France is late on every single trajectory planned and adopted within the law: emissions in the housing sector are more than 20 percent above the limits, and in transport more than 10 percent. The Haut Conseil pour le Climat (High Council for Climate), put in place by the government in 2019, confirmed the delay and denounced the huge rise of imported emissions: in 2011, the emissions of CO_2 were assessed to reach 9 tons per person, and up to 11 tons per person in 2018.[12]

IN THE NAME OF ALL, OUR COMMON MATTER

The year 2019 was not only a turning point for climate litigation, it was also an ideological turnaround: everywhere, environmental mass destruction, social inequalities and human rights are linked. It is also quite clear that our law, built within a philosophy that considers humans as superior to nature, is neither able to prevent nor stop the catastrophe.

In June 2019, the UN Special Rapporteur on extreme poverty and human rights, Philip Aston, denounced a 'climate apartheid': 'We risk a "climate apartheid" scenario where the wealthy pay to escape overheating, hunger, and conflict while the rest of the world is left to suffer', while climate change could push 120 million people to poverty by 2030.[13] Climate change indeed has a lot in common with slavery, colonialism and apartheid. It is a fight for resources when 1 percent of the global population owns 50 percent of the global wealth, the top 10 percent of emitters contribute 45 percent of global emissions, while the bottom 50 percent of emitters contribute 13 percent of global emissions.[14] It is a fight for land, as the poorest countries are the first to suffer from desertification or disappear under the seas. It is a fight for freedom and equal dignity.

At the global level, at the European level, but also at the national level, according to the NGO Germanwatch, France is the European country most impacted by weather-related events,[15] and life conditions are worsening for a growing number of people, especially those who are at the bottom of the social scale. This is why we launched the Notre Affaire à Tous organization, Our Common Matter. We had the urgent feeling that rights for nature had to be recognized and defended, to allow survival for all and not only for the wealthiest. We had the urgent feeling that it would only be achieved through a new universal set of rights, which could be built either through lobbying states or through a new jurisprudence. We had the urgent feeling that pushing lawyers to join forces with us was essential. We thought that an organization that could gather climate lobbyists, lawyers from all sectors, more traditional social movements and all the different kinds of victims would be a key.

And we did not stop there. In France, as everywhere, litigation has always accompanied the battles for rights. In the nineteenth century, workers fought for their rights against the leaders of the industrial world. They did so by walking in the streets, by organizing strikes, and through litigation. After an entire century of mobilization and debates, they obtained a new right: the right to be covered for any industrial accident or incident. This is the same kind of war that we must wage today, except that it is even more vital.

Acting through climate litigation was not a fad. It was a strategical opportunity. A collective necessity. In some ways, a last attempt to finally get a peaceful answer before the world falls into chaos. At a time when movements such as Youth for Climate/Fridays for Future, We Rise Up, Extinction Rebellion or Alternatiba are taking civil disobedience action, we support them in front of the tribunals defending a 'state of necessity'. The state of necessity means that the use of illegal actions can actually be considered legal when citizens are facing an imminent and grave threat.

At a time when fossil fuel companies keep on increasing their production capacities, we ask them to respect the Paris Agreement and contribute to the climate change battle, as any citizen of the world should do. We gathered 14 collectivities and three other NGOs to launch 'Vigilance TOTALe', a climate litigation action echoing the complaints of many collectivities in North America and of the Peruvian farmer Saúl Luciano Lliuya against the carbon majors. This action is based on the recent French 'duty of vigilance' law, requiring multinationals to protect human rights and the environment throughout their supply chains and activities.

But our main aim was to hold our government responsible, to oblige it to act. L'Affaire du Siècle is an application against France for failure of action regarding its climate policy. We asked first the French state, then the Administrative Court of Paris, to act in a way that could remedy the delays marring all sectors of climate policy. We claimed that the international commitments on human rights issues as well as on climate and environmental matters, that the European commitments regarding human rights and climate goals, and our national commitments through the law were being denied and violated. We asked the judges to recognize as a general principle of law an obligation to act, and to take all necessary measures to reach the goals written in the law. The Court now must answer our claims and requests.

L'AFFAIRE DU SIÈCLE

L'Affaire du Siècle was not aimed to be our private contribution to the battle. We wanted it to be a collective, a general action. But, as we feared our action would be rejected by the Court on individual grounds – just like the Dutch Court rejected the application of the 886 citizens in the Urgenda case (see Chapter 15) but accepted the complaint from the association Urgenda – we chose for this action to be led by NGOs. We chose to gather the three environmental organizations Greenpeace France, La Fondation pour la Nature et l'Homme and the solidarity NGO Oxfam France, in order to illustrate our environmental and social concerns.

To awaken citizens' conscience, we wanted to gather personal testimonies about how climate change is upsetting our lives, and we put victims on the front line of the battle. We worked very hard to launch the case with many and diverse allies, such as Cyril Dion, Marion Cotillard and Juliette Binoche from the movie industry; Abd al Malik and L.E.J. from the music industry; comedian Élie Seimoun; Pablo Servigne, Aurélien Barrau and other ecologists; and web influencers.

We asked many other organizations to gather forces and look for the broadest support ever brought together from civil society. With success. L'Affaire du Siècle is the largest petition in the history of France, gathering more than 2 million signatures in two weeks. A way to tell the courts that we care, a way to put pressure on the French state so that it would at last act.

Our success is relative. The Minister of Ecology first tried to pit us against the yellow vest movement so that he could justify his inaction by a supposed and politically constructed 'equilibrium of social forces'. To our request, the government just answered that it was already doing everything in its power, and that companies and citizens were preventing climate action and the curb of emissions. No explanations on the huge delay on transportation or housing were given, although these sectors depend entirely on public policies. No decisions on aviation, maritime transportation, agriculture or on socially fair environmental taxation were taken. No upgrade of French proposals for the European Union or the world were made.

In December 2019, almost no sign of policy change could be perceived, but we will keep trying and trying, until the tribunals prove us right.

IN THE NAME OF THE EARTH

By its numerical strength, our action is unique. But we belong to a more global movement. We act for all and we act for the planet, using the law, and we are becoming increasingly numerous all over the world. Notre Affaire à Tous was helped by our US counterpart Our Children's Trust, our Dutch victorious counterpart Urgenda, our European partners CAN Europe and climate change lawyer, author and climate change activist Roda Verheyen. It's our turn to help: the Italians, the Slovenians and all the others who would like to launch massive climate litigation actions in their countries, to push their governments and/or their economic sector to act. Acting alongside throughout the world is an obligation. It is also a testimony of the world we want to build – a world of solidarity.

We have hope. The victories of Urgenda in the Netherlands, of DeJusticia in Columbia, of farmer Ashgar Leghari in Pakistan, of the Amadiba Crisis Committee in South Africa, show that we can win. The victories of some American citizens and families, or French farmer Paul François against Monsanto, also prove that we can beat the polluters. We managed to gather 15 cities to file a lawsuit against Total. Thousands of complaints are being filed against the polluters and their banks. We have lost a lot. But it does not always have to be that way.

We also rely on the victories of nature. In the US, in New Zealand, in India, in Columbia and in a growing number of countries, the legal rights of natural entities and ecosystems are being finally recognized. They earn it through the law but especially through litigation. France is still not open to that. But we know that time will come soon. This time, by establishing new massive solidarity between humans and with all the living, we will win.

NOTES

1.   L'Affaire du Siècle (n.d.) [website], accessed August 26, 2020 at https://laffairedusiecle.net/.
2.   Buffon, G.-L. (1778), 'Époques de la nature', *Supplément à l'Histoire naturelle*, vol. V, pp. 243–4, among others.
3.   See Nathaniel Rich, 'Losing Earth: the decade we almost stopped climate change', *New York Times Magazine*, August 2018.
4.   Stockholm Resilience Centre (n.d.), 'Planetary boundaries research', accessed August 26, 2020 at https://stockholmresilience.org/research/planetary-boundaries.html.
5.   Global Witness (2019), *Enemies of the State: How Governments and Business Silence Land and Environmental Defenders*, July.
6.   Interpol, Rhipto [a Norwegian UN collaborating center] and The Global Initiative (2018), World Atlas of Illicit Flows, accessed August 26, 2020 at https://globalinitiative.net/wp-content/uploads/2018/09/Atlas-Illicit-Flows-Second-Edition-EN-WEB.pdf; see also: UNEP and Interpol (2016), *The Rise of Environmental Crime – A Growing Threat to Natural Resources, Peace, Development and Security*, accessed August 26, 2020 at https://wedocs.unep.org/bitstream/handle/20.500.11822/7662/-The_rise_of_environmental_crime_A_growing_threat_to_natural_resources_peace,_development_and_security-2016environmental_crimes.pdf.pdf?sequence=3&amp%3BisAllowed.
7.   A report published in 2014 by Jean-Charles Brisard and Damien Martinez for Thomson Reuters shows that up to 60 percent of the revenues of the Islamic States are originated in the exploitation of natural resources. See http://www.gdr-elsj.eu/wp-content/uploads/2015/11/Islamic-State.pdf, accessed August 26, 2020.
8.   Intergovernmental Science-Policy Platform on Biodiversity and Ecosystem Services (IPBES), *Global Assessment Report on Biodiversity and Ecosystem Services*, 2019.
9.   Carbon Disclosure Project, *The Carbon Majors Database: CDP Carbon Majors Report 2017*.
10. Corporate Europe Observatory, 'Big Oil and Gas buying influence, October 2019', accessed August 26, 2020 at https://corporateeurope.org/en/2019/10/big-oil-and-gas-buying-influence-brussels.
11. Reseau Action Climat France, 'En 2019, la France offre 11 milliards d'Euros de subventions pour les énergies fossiles', March 28, 2019, accessed August 26, 2020 https://reseauactionclimat.org/stop-subventions-fossiles-2019/.
12. Haut Conseil pour le Climat, *Agir en cohérence avec ses ambitions: rapport annuel Neutralité Carbone*, June 2019.
13. *Report of the Special Rapporteur on extreme poverty and human rights*, Philip Alston, 25 June 2019, accessed 26 August 2020 at https://

srpovertyorg.files.wordpress.com/2019/06/unsr-poverty-climate-change-a
_hrc_41_39.pdf?fbclid=IwAR0NcZEQklx4_ubtcJwsBOkk6_mGKF_nbreLZ2Sy
-jhX0boKW9QM8gftdYI.

14. Lucas Chancel and Thomas Piketty (2015), *Carbon and Inequality: From Kyoto to Paris*, accessed August 15, 2020 at http://piketty.pse.ens.fr/files/ ChancelPiketty2015.pdf.

15. David Eckstein, Marie-Lena Hutfils and Maik Winges (2019), 'Global Climate Risk Index, 2019: who suffers most from extreme weather events?', *Germanwatch. org*, accessed August 15, 2020 at https://germanwatch.org/sites/germanwatch.org/ files/Global%20Climate%20Risk%20Index%202019_2.pdf.

PART IV

Coming generations on the front line

22. Introduction to Part IV

Claude Henry

In Chapters 23, 24, and 25 of this part of the book, Anuna De Wever Van der Heyden, Luisa Neubauer, Hilda Nakabuye, Sadrach Nirere, Adenike Titilope Oladosu, Sophie Handford, Raven Maeder, leaders of the movement Fridays For Future (FFF) in Belgium, Germany, Uganda, Nigeria and New Zealand, respectively, make several references to two tenets of the movement, formulated initially by their friend Greta Thunberg: (1) "Why should I study for a future, that soon will be no more? Ask yourself this: wouldn't you go on strike too, if you thought doing so could help protect your own future?"; (2) "Why do you want me to study sciences if you do not listen to what scientists have to say? The scientists have been very clear about what we need to do to tackle climate change. We are uniting behind the scientists. We are only asking that our leaders do the same".[1]

It is obvious that various applications of science are at the root of various critical situations – the climate crisis in particular – in which humankind is trapped. It is no less obvious, notwithstanding vociferous denials, that scientific knowledge is crucial for understanding the problems and for opening up paths to overcome them. The FFF activists have a perfectly clear view on that and equally clear and effective ways of promoting it. They have been able to find inspiration and support from a remarkable organization, 350.org, the founder of which, William "Bill" McKibben, is the author of Chapter 26.

In a rather different context, that of an "elite scientific university", students at the French École Polytechnique, Antoine Bizien, Elsa Deville and Lucas Dubois in Chapter 27, happen to share the FFF view on science. Moreover, they criticize their institution for not providing them with appropriate scientific tools, that is, tools useful and necessary to navigate the critical situations that they expect they will face. Alessia Lefébure shows in Chapter 28 that such failure is not specific to the Polytechnique, it is common among higher education institutions.

Between coming generations and older ones, the chasm is not only about different appreciations of the role of science. Students at École Polytechnique, and other "elite" schools and universities in Europe, to whom the "best" jobs are offered after they graduate, refuse – in ever-greater numbers – offers that don't open up ways towards transitioning to a sustainable society and economy. There are employers who seem unable to redefine the jobs in ways that would attract ecologically conscious graduates, like the oil major Total (the CEO of which and seven out of eight of his immediate predecessors graduated from the Polytechnique). Others simply dismiss students' concerns as mere transient youth idealism. For the students, escape is often found in small, recently established organizations. As Alessia Lefébure shows, based on an analysis of the values, beliefs and aspirations of the current young generation, these tensions are not restricted to the Polytechnique, but magnified.

Between FFF activists and older generations, confrontation takes more muscular forms: we've relied on adults to make the right decisions to ensure that there is a future for the next generation. If those in power today don't act, it will be our generation who will live through their failure. Those who are under 20 now could be around to see 2080, and face the prospect of a world that has warmed by up to 4°C. The effects of such warming would be utterly devastating.

Then: *Au Revoir les Enfants?*[2] The chapters here all shout No! as we are determined to build our future, and as we don't yet despair of our parents. Either as actors or authors, or both, women are leading in the initiatives discussed here. Until now men have dominated history on our planet. They have mostly failed. It's time to pass the baton.

NOTES

1. The quotations are either from chapters in this part of the book or from a guest editorial in *The Guardian* by Greta Thunberg, Anna Taylor and others, 'Think we should be at school? Today's climate strike is the biggest lesson of all', 15 March 2019.
2. A film directed by Louis Malle. On a cold morning in January 1944, in a Carmelite boarding school near Paris, students say farewell to three Jewish classmates and to Père Jean, headmaster, arrested on the spot by the Gestapo.

23. Fridays For Future – FFF Europe and beyond

Anuna De Wever Van der Heyden, Luisa Neubauer and Katrien van der Heyden

KICK-OFF BY GRETA THUNBERG

The Fridays For Future movement (FFF) was started in August 2018 by Greta Thunberg, the (then) 15-year-old high school student from Sweden who decided on a message and an action that was so ingenious and, at the same time, simple, that it spread around the world and brought together many climate organizations on all continents.

The message Greta started spreading was intriguing: 'Why should I study for a future, that soon will be no more?' The subsequent demand was just as straightforward – all governments should be in line with the Paris Agreement on climate change (halve global CO_2 emissions by 2030 and to just below zero by 2050). It is the one central demand of the movement.

The main target groups Greta wanted to convey her message to were twofold. On the one side, she addresses policy-makers and politicians, whom she urges to act. On the other side, she asks all other individuals and economic leaders in society to join her protest. Greta realized that the message about rising CO_2 levels had been spread for decades, but that apparently no one was listening. She realized this had to be repeated, but differently. So, Greta chose to challenge leaders everywhere by confronting them with the following two paradoxes: (1) 'Why do you want me to go to school if scientists are clear that we won't have a future due to climate change disasters that will lead to the collapse of our societies?'; (2) 'Why do you want me to study sciences if you do not listen to what scientists have to say?' Indeed, this is a reformulation of the matter from the perspective of young people who have their future ahead of them and it brilliantly exposes the 'Catch-22' situation these young people are in. It literally throws back the challenge they face at the feet of the generations that caused it.

Greta decided to bring this message to the policy-makers by sitting in front of the Swedish Parliament one day a week – every Friday (hence Fridays For

197

Future) – until her country was in line with the Paris Agreement. She started doing this in September 2018 and she has continued her protest in the same way ever since.

Parliaments tend to be 'neutral' places where no demonstrations are allowed. For Greta this meant a bit of a challenge before her occupation of her corner close to the Parliament every Friday was accepted. She has a guest book to accommodate the many visitors passing by, but never hoped that it would amount to much more than that. At first she did not endeavour to call on other young people to join her; that was a step taken by her followers in other European countries, most notably Germany, Belgium and the UK, but later on also France, Italy, the Netherlands and Eastern European countries. A common feature embedded into most of the youth climate activists' vision is that they are not thinking about the consequences of failure – they just start. They are willing to do 'the walk of shame' should their actions amount to nothing.

It did not take very long before the 'Greta story' started to spread on social media and soon it was picked up by other students around the globe. There had been some actions in Australia, and in Germany Luisa Neubauer started to organize the Fridays For Future demonstrations. Then other countries followed and one of the most amazing cases with regard to scale and amplitude was Belgium.

THE BELGIAN CASE OF FRIDAYS FOR FUTURE – YOUTH FOR CLIMATE

To illustrate the depth and breadth of the students' actions, we will now turn to the case study of Belgium.

Interestingly, despite the FFF movement becoming very popular all over the world, sharing the one common demand – to be in line with the Paris Agreement – the start of the action in each specific country seems also to be influenced by the local politics of the country where it takes shape. In the case of Belgium, there was a huge climate demonstration mid-December 2018 to pressure the Belgian government before it attended the COP (Conference of the Parties) climate meeting in Katowice, Poland. Estimates of participants in this demonstration ranged between 65 000 and 75 000. This is huge, given the fact that the Belgian population is only around 11 million.

Then, one week later, the Belgian political delegation came back empty-handed. Belgium was one of the few countries in Europe not to sign the agreement and the delegation even left before the COP was finished. This context is important, as the students starting the school strikes in Belgium (Anuna De Wever Van der Heyden and Kyra Gantois), began their actions because they were offended by the lack of democratic consciousness the politicians showed as they completely ignored the voices of so many people by not signing the COP agreement. The political arrogance that was demonstrated – one minister even flew there in a private jet, one of the most environmentally unfriendly ways of travelling – by ignoring the demonstration was the trigger to get the Belgian school strike movement going.

The origin of the school strikes in Belgium is not just the fear of students about the warming climate, as much as the worries about a failing government. The urgently felt need for people to step in and save democratic values motivated them as much as anything else to take to the streets. There is discrepancy in the Belgian case on climate policy. This country has the highest number of climate change measures of all European countries (around 150) but ranks almost lowest on results. This discrepancy can only be understood by taking a closer look at the Belgian political system.

Indeed, the Belgian governmental system had been in deadlock for decades with a complicated system of regional, federal and community governments, all producing an energy, environment and a transport minister, which had resulted in a 'Kafkaesque' battle and a bureaucratic nightmare where in the end nobody was satisfied with the climate policy. A political proverb in Belgium says: 'In Belgium every minister claims the competence, but none are responsible'.

The joint group of environment, energy and transport ministers were supposed to construct one comprehensive climate action plan, but even that task had not been accomplished by the end of the legislature in December 2018. This lack of political response on the matter led to the shameful fact that Belgium – among the top European countries in economic terms – was on the last but one spot in the European ranking on climate change results.

It is precisely this discrepancy between the worrying scientific information young people like Greta and Anuna get in schools on the one hand and the utter ignorance they witness among their governments in dealing with this, that motivates them to take a *fearless* stance. The word *fearless* is used very consciously here, meaning a non-aggressive way of challenging the powers that be by exposing their charade rather than attacking them violently. The tale of the Emperor's clothes has been mentioned in this context as well. It is not uncommon for a younger generation to step up and challenge the order of things. However, what makes the climate actions a unique case is the very young age of its leaders and their sex and gender.

Obviously, we've had female leaders before in many movements, but that would typically only be in women's movements. Even in labour movements, where we have wonderful examples of women taking prominent roles, quite often it was in a broader movement where men had the final say. Not here. Young girls build context, construct vision, theories and strategies, mobilize for actions and are the frontline figures.

In a conversation,[1] Greta Thunberg expressed it as follows: 'Boys run ever forward in a worldwide rat race, competing with each other. Girls will never win that race; we don't even want to be part of it. Girls have the ability to take a step back and contemplate about where they want to go. This wider vision is needed to see the broad picture of what is really going on in the world'. As such, this is also a shift in the definition of what it means to be a leader. In a world where leadership positions are typically shaped by hyper-masculine stereotypes, these young female leaders redefine the concept of power. They turn it around from being dominant into being serving and caring.

There is another innovative trend to be watched in this movement: their young age. Anuna – the leading figure in the Belgian case – took to the streets the moment she realized that the next elections were in May 2019, where she would not have the right to vote yet because she only turned 18 in June 2019. She would not have a chance to weigh in on the next legislation, which will be the last legislation that can possibly make a shift in time to curb climate change. This feeling of utter injustice – that the fate of the future generations is decided by the older generations alone – has been a huge motivator for high school students to take to the streets.

It is also interesting to see how they feel inspired by other civil movements, most of all the black liberation rights movement in the US. Anuna regularly cites examples of public disobedience actions like Rosa Parks refusing to give up her seat on the bus. The school strikes want to bring home the same message of doing something inspiring and non-violent that challenges the system by being disobedient in a provocative, publicly visible way.

Indeed, the Belgian school system was at a loss when three weeks into the school strikes, 35 000 high school students left their classes and took a train to Brussels to protest. Even after six months, the educational policy-makers had not come up with a comprehensive plan on how to respond. Each school board had to decide individually on how to respond. On average, private Catholic schools were a lot harsher in their sanctions than public schools – for example, some pupils receiving 0 on every test missed on a school strike day and teachers deliberately planning as many tests as possible during such days. In other schools, students were allowed to catch up on missed tests on other days. Other schools even supported the strikes and sometimes even teachers went along with their pupils to Brussels.

It was not only schools that had a hard time dealing with the striking students. There was a huge evolution in how the politicians responded too. At first it was deemed 'cute'. A word often heard during the first weeks, but one that has a double-bind message: 'Yes, it is nice that young people want to do something for the climate but let's not take this too seriously'.

This radically changed in Belgium when – around six weeks into the strikes – the Flemish environment minister, Joke Schauwvliege, had to resign. It was clear that after the 'cute' phase, she had started to feel increasingly uncomfortable about the movement, which voiced outright criticism of all policy measures she took. She had made the tactical mistake of claiming in the beginning that she felt that the students supported her policies and measures, only to be answered on the next strike by hundreds of slogans that ridiculed her. Next she made an even bigger mistake by claiming in a speech that the school strike movement was actually a conspiracy against her, supposedly confirmed by the state security agency. This announcement immediately made the headlines. No wonder, as this was a very serious allegation against minors. When the state security agency announced there was no such investigation or conspiracy and that there had never been a communication about this with the minister, she had to resign within 24 hours.

This also marked the moment when politicians started to take the students seriously. The tone in their communication turned from 'cute' and 'heroes' to 'fearmongers' or 'neurotics'. Indeed, that is the moment the political parties took sides, with the political left proclaiming the school striking youth were heroes, and the right political spectrum describing them as blind radicals, kids with neurotic panic attacks or doomsday preachers. One of the most frustrating and unfortunate outcomes of the school strike movement was this political split. All over Europe we see the old left and right dichotomy tearing communities and families apart over issues like migrants and refugees, women's rights and economic systems. The Belgian youth that started the movement were well aware of this trap. Once caught in the left or right hegemonic block, the same old mechanisms of political power struggles would capture the energy and divert it towards fighting the other block, instead of connecting people across generations, political opinions, race, gender, to fight for a common goal to save humanity.

Anuna De Wever Van der Heyden – the Belgian spokesperson of the movement – kept on repeating in each interview that she wanted to unite rather than divide. Climate should not have a political colour because it concerns every single person and humanity as a whole. It is clear by now that such a message is countering any institutional logic built into political systems of countries dominated by a 'particracy' instead of a 'democracy'. This is but an illustration of a point made earlier that the youth were as much aware of the institutional and political crisis in our democracy as they are aware of the climate crisis. Nevertheless, despite chronic attempts to the contrary, the political level continued to push the movement into the left side of the playing field.

THE GERMAN CASE FOR FRIDAYS FOR FUTURE

In Germany, the publicly most well-known figure in Fridays For Future is Luisa Neubauer. Luisa had been a climate activist for quite some time and had, rather coincidentally, met Greta Thunberg in Katowice in December 2018. Impressed by Greta's message and her way of conveying it, she decided to start the same type of action in Germany to enlarge the impact of the school strikes. So, upon returning to Germany after the climate conference in Katowice, Luisa – back then a university student – started climate school and university strikes in front of the Bundestag in Berlin.

Similar to the Belgium case, in Germany too the momentum was decisive. There was a 'vibe' already in Germany about the climate. Not only had the European heatwave in the summer of 2018 had an unprecedented impact on German agriculture and industry (for several weeks, ships weren't able to carry goods on the Rhine as the water level was historically low), but also, Germany was in the middle of a debate over a so-called coal exit while the government had just announced it would miss its 2020 emission targets. Not surprisingly, Luisa was not the only one who felt irritated by the lack of drastically needed political climate action. Hence, she quickly got in touch with others who had the same idea. They reinforced each other to get the strikes going in other cities as well. On the first Germany-wide #FridaysForFuture climate strike on 14 December 2018, there were strikes going on in 14 different cities.

After this first day of strikes, the movement grew exponentially. The key mobilization and organization of the climate strikes happened online, via WhatsApp. Links to the WhatsApp group were shared widely and uploaded on a website to make it as easy as possible for people to join and to stay in the loop. As such it was very organic in its origin, not specifically planned, but catching up on the vibe that was already there.

Deriving from the first handful of people who coordinated similar strike actions on the same Friday in a different city, a decentralized movement structure was established. The first person from a specific city or town that wanted to start striking would open up a local Fridays For Future chapter by simply creating a WhatsApp group and spreading the link to the group. Almost organically, a democratic structure was established: each chapter would send one delegate to the weekly telephone conference where decisions were made democratically, with each chapter having one vote in a majority vote.

This is different from the Belgian case where in the first six months the core team took all decisions. The German model was more democratic. Easy online access to the movement, low participation barriers and the possibility to have a say on all decisions attracted an enormous number of organizers. One month after the first strike in December, the number of cities where a strike was organized grew from 14 to 55. More than four months later the organizers met for the first time in real life.

There were notable spillover effects from other countries that shaped the German Fridays For Future movement. In Germany, FFF was inspired, for example, by the initiatives that the Belgians took to call on the scientists to write up a climate plan. So, in Germany, Luisa and others reached out to scientists to support FFF – only to find out that hundreds of scientists had already started to get together as 'ScientistsForFuture'. In March 2019, more than 20 000 scientists had signed a support paper for Fridays For Future.

The strikes happened primarily in political spaces – near town halls, ministries and parliaments. Throughout the year 2019, however, protests were also organized in front of coal plants (in the Rhine area) and in front of the European Commission building (Brussels) in the week before the elections of the European Parliament. The German FFF activists later also travelled to Romania by bus to meet the European heads of state who had gathered there for a meeting to determine the agenda for the next EU legislation. During the summer of 2019, they attended the European climate youth conference in Lausanne and organized an international strike in Aachen where youth from more than ten countries were invited to unite.

The main challenge was to keep people motivated for a cause that seems hopeless as the reaction of the politicians was not what they had hoped for. Yes indeed, most politicians in Germany wanted to talk but claimed at the same time that a lot had already been done to avert climate change. Three common answers given when strikers challenged decision makers where that:

- a lot had been done in the past;
- more ambitious climate action was not politically feasible as jobs and economic growth had to be secured while Germany was also the only country in the world that had plans to phase out both nuclear and coal energy;
- that it was up to China, the US and India to act, as German emissions in 2019 would only add up to 2 per cent of global emissions.

However, as the climate targets in Germany had been missed in the past, and those for the future were not even in line with the Paris Agreement and the concerns for equity, the gap between the expectations of the young people and the political will to take further steps remained wide open.

The support the climate striking youth received from the general public was rather positive about the initiatives at first and remained strong among certain people, while others dropped out. The young people were praised initially for their engagement in trying to solve the crisis. However, as time went on and nothing was really achieved on a political level, a climate-tiredness settled in and the emotional support towards the movement became rather ambivalent. It is now clear that the current environment is much more polarized (both in Germany and Belgium) and people are now all fervently for or against, with hardly any middle ground left. The strategy to deal with this polarized environment is straightforward: stick to the key messages, try as hard as possible to not get lost in the nitty-gritty of climate politics, and bear in mind that science is behind the movement.

The strength of the German network is, first, ownership. People can join in the decisions, they feel involved, so even if people don't have much time, they feel part of the movement and join every Friday. The second notable strength is the size of the movement. From a certain point onwards, the 'climate kids' were so many, they have started framing the perception of an entire generation. They are widely considered the 'cool kids' – attracting more and more young and, increasingly, older people to join the club.

COMMON THREATS AND CHALLENGES OF THE CLIMATE SCHOOL STRIKE MOVEMENT

Online Threats and Hate

There is a paradoxical situation that the school strike movement would never have grown this big in such a short time span without the use of social media. It is a well-known fact that it can 'make or break' people and movements. So, just as the political spectrum has been split with an ever-widening gap in the middle, the same holds true of any social media platform.

Right from the very start (organized) campaigns started to troll the frontline persons of the movement. Greta herself has been painfully and chronically hit by trolls, not even shying away from ridiculing her autism spectrum disorder, but also the spokespersons in each European country (Anuna in Belgium, Luisa Neubauer in Germany, etc.) have been trolled relentlessly by any means possible. Anuna, for example, received hate messages and threats via Facebook, on websites, through e-mail and posted letters, Instagram, WhatsApp, Messenger, and so on.

However, despite the diversity in the means of communication used by the trolls, the content of the trolling messages is surprisingly homogeneous. Interestingly enough, hardly any troll message contains opinions about climate change. It is the elephant in the room, trolls do not want to get into it (since obviously with all the scientific back-up, it would be an argument hard to win). Instead, there is a huge amount of gender-based harassment going on. In the case of Anuna (who is an outspoken member of the LGTBQI[2] community as well, being gender-fluid and having a lesbian relationship) she received a worrying number of messages from men who wanted to rape her to 'cure' her homosexuality. In an all-time low attempt at intimidating her, she received the following message: 'Just wait until she gets a Nigger Dick into her pussy, then she'll know she's a woman'. 'CO_2 prostitute' was another favourite name to call her. When trolls found out that Anuna had an identical twin sister they proclaimed: 'So, now we need to get a double-barrelled gun'. Others called for a 'Flemish Breivik' to get rid of the nuisance called Anuna.

The sexual content is omnipresent in most messages and is in line with the age-old patriarchal way of intimidating women, by imposing masculine sexual violence upon them. Indeed, looking at sexuality as a means to submit women to masculine power has been an ever-popular identity marker used by most (extreme) right-wing movements. Increasing your show of disdain for women can get you up the ladder of the pecking order in toxic masculine environments and as such this shows how it is more about themselves establishing their male power pyramid than about entering into a real dialogue with the school strike students. Apparently, in some right-wing movements you can score by sexually bashing minor girls, all the more so if they are celebrities of the climate movement.

Systemic Errors on a Macro Level

Another challenge the school strike movement had was the organizational inexperience the youth showed at structuring their movement. This was a threat coming from within. Right from the start, is was clear that climate change requires a system change. Indeed, the systemic errors like the democracy crisis, the hyper-masculine stereotypes dominating leadership positions and the economic mechanisms that have slowly turned from creating welfare to pillaging the last resources we have, were all profoundly questioned by the youth taking to the streets.

As with all movements, it is not always easy to translate this new vision into the nitty-gritty of daily lives and the functioning of a grassroots movement. A first symptom of the rather chaotic way everything was organized, is the high diversity in concepts and names used. For example, while it is Greta Thunberg who coined the 'Fridays For Future (FFF)' actions, Anuna in Belgium was not yet aware of that name (FFF) when she started her school strikes, so she called them the 'Youth for Climate' actions.

Also, when it comes to the aspirations of changing the world economic system, lots of different concepts are used. 'Transition economy', 'circular economy' and 'new green deal', are used synonymously as they refer to the idea that things need to move away from a fossil fuel economy into a more ecologically sustainable model.

Another potential confusion among the school strikers was the demands of the movement. Greta Thunberg had been very clear right from the start to continuously repeat the one demand: 'be in line with the Paris Agreement'. This demand was difficult to maintain for months on end, since journalists kept on asking the students what measures needed to be taken to be in line with the Paris Agreement. Obviously, this is a potential media trap, since we cannot expect high school children to provide the world with expertise on climate change and scientifically tested and approved solutions. In one interview, Anuna proclaimed that as far as she was concerned, banks should print additional money to cover the climate costs. This view was ridiculed for the weeks to follow, until some expert economists actually took her side and came up with historic examples where printing money had indeed pushed societies out of a deep crisis.

To circumnavigate this media trap in her future interviews with the media Anuna and her movement then decided to call on Belgian climate scientists to organize a panel and write up an action plan of what Belgium should do to be in line with the Paris Agreement. This call was met by hundreds of scientists from all sorts of scientific fields who then spent the next months voluntarily writing this action plan, which was presented two weeks before the May elections. A unique feat in Belgian history.

In Germany, the demands evolved into a different direction, as the biggest challenge there is the closure of the remaining (brown-) coal plants. Luisa Neubauer and her movement oriented their demands to focus on the elimination of coal.

In the UK, the situation was more complex because the political crisis was even more omnipresent than elsewhere by being in gridlock over Brexit. Putting any other item on the political agenda was almost a mission impossible, but somehow the climate message also gave a feeling of relief to quite a number of people, that maybe, this might finally be an issue that can unify rather than divide the country.

Systemic Errors on a Micro Level

There were also systemic errors within the movement itself. As has been said, by the time the 'Fridays For Future' name was widely communicated, some local movements had already started with other names. This is why 'school strike movement' might be a better name for the young students' movement following in the footsteps of Greta Thunberg. But, what's in a name? Surely that has not really tempered any enthusiasm among the followers? However, the way in which their organizations – whatever the name – would and should be structured, posed a much bigger problem.

In Belgium, Anuna's team chose a more centralized approach, having a core team with members who each had a clearly defined responsibility (e.g., local strikes, communication and media, climate action plan, etc.). The core team members were in no way democratically chosen, but rather formed organically through the involvement of various young people in the movement. It seems that the most important criteria to get in the team was to be very involved and to get to know other team members. Obviously, this is not an ideal situation and resulted in tension between the in- and out-group.

In Germany, the approach was quite the opposite of being centrally directed. Luisa was faced with numerous local groups and teams who all wanted to have a word in the final decision. This grassroots democracy proved quite difficult when responding to political steps that needed a quick reaction in the media.

In the UK, the school strike movement went one step further and did not even want to have an official 'face' of the movement or spokesperson. While in Sweden, Belgium and Germany it was very clear that the media should turn to Greta, Anuna and Luisa respectively, this was not the case in the UK, where the endeavour to be borderline anarchistic, resulted in much confusion.

Despite none of these countries solving the institutional paradigm in a satisfactory manner, it remains an incredible feat how many young people they managed to mobilize and take to the streets. As with any organization, there is a steep learning curve and in each country the teams showed creative and innovative solutions to deal with the problems at hand in a much more pragmatic and flexible way than any adults do.

POSITIONING THEMSELVES IN A WIDER SOCIAL LANDSCAPE

Not long after Greta Thunberg started her strikes, President Macron decided to raise taxes on fuel. This led to an immediate revolt generated in some poor rural areas in France where people depend on cars as the main means of transport and face genuine poverty. They felt the environmentally friendly measure would make the poor pay for a problem they didn't create.

As such, this context provided an argument for the press to position the *gilets jaunes* (yellow vests) movement at loggerheads with the climate change movement. This argument only holds when looking at the superficial triggers of the movement, not when looking at the deeper-lying causes of these people taking to the streets.

The common denominator in both movements is the call for a systemic change. None of the yellow vests would mind a change towards an ecologically healthy world, as long as this does not push them even further into poverty. The same holds true for the youth of the school strike movement, who all agree that in the climate shift there needs to be social justice, hence 'climate justice'.

Despite these profound common touchpoints, the relationship between the two movements remained awkward. Mostly this might have been due to the entirely different profile of protesters (age, social class, sex, etc.), but definitely because of the different tactics chosen. The yellow vest movement was clearly aggressive and caused some damage and violence in both Paris and Brussels. In one difficult instance in Belgium, both protests were merged and the climate youth ended up being pushed and challenged by the yellow vests to go on a rampage through the streets. Instead, the climate youth signalled to each other to remain calm and sit down, where they stayed put – 10 000 of them – to give the police time to sort things out. They started to sing and, for many, these were the most powerful moments in all the demonstrations.

Never again did the school strike movement in Belgium protest together with the yellow vests. It remains to be seen how they can find a common ground in the future.

EUROPE AND BEYOND

A common argument that constantly needed answers was the reasoning that this is a worldwide problem and a small country cannot change climate change – as if this was enough reason to give up. It is an argument typically used by climate delayers. Indeed, climate change is a worldwide problem, but this does not mean that small countries cannot make a difference. The definition of small itself is problematic since it refers to the size of the territory or population, but no link is made to the actual CO_2 output per head in the population. According to that last measure, some small countries become big and vice versa.

Another paradoxical fact in climate change is that, on average, the countries suffering most from the consequences (where desertification or floods take place and sea levels rise), are the ones where less CO_2 is emitted. This poses the challenge of creating global solidarity at a time when even solidarity and care within one country are under enormous pressure and are being stripped down by austerity measures.

Despite this unfavourable context, social media do not know borders and the call to action from Greta Thunberg was heard on a worldwide scale. In countries all over the world, teenagers were stepping up and starting school strikes, even in countries like Russia where any opposition to the government puts anybody in real danger. By March 2019, the movement had moved well beyond the European borders. And by 15 March, a global strike was organized. More than 1.5 million young people in 2083 cities of 125 countries across the world participated. All continents were present, even Antarctica, where a team of researchers raised a global strike banner.

Another global strike was held one week before the European elections and, in the week of 20 September 2019, the next one was planned to kick off the new schoolyear and further climate actions were planned as well as a climate school strike every month throughout 2020. It is clear that young people everywhere have woken up and are not ready to go back to sleep before the issue is resolved.

In the late summer of 2019, Greta Thunberg got on a racing sailboat to cross the Atlantic to attend a UN climate meeting in New York, where she was invited by António Guterres, the UN Secretary-General. In the autumn of 2019, several climate youth from different European countries (amongst others, Anuna and two other members of her Belgian team) followed Greta's example by taking a sailboat across the Atlantic to attend the COP25 climate conference scheduled to take place in Santiago de Chile. However, when more than halfway through their six-week sailing journey, social riots and protests started in Chile. In these circumstances the Chilean president deemed it unsafe to host the COP25, so cancelled the event. Some days later, the event was moved to Madrid in Spain but the same dates were kept, making it impossible for Anuna to sail back in time to Madrid. Another huge disappointment for the delegation. However, Anuna and her delegation were invited to take part in an Alternative COP conveyed inside the Amazon forest, so at least that gave the satisfaction of creating a goal to the Atlantic crossing. Meanwhile, Greta had travelled through the USA and Canada giving speeches and participating at rallies all along the way. Greta did catch a racing sailboat and arrived just in time. Also, Luisa Neubauer, who was not expected to attend the COP25 in Chile because travel by sailboat would take too long, ended up taking the train from Germany to Madrid and could attend the meeting after all.

In fact, hundreds of youth climate activists from various movements ended up attending the COP25 and took several actions in and outside the event to raise awareness about the urgency to get to a good deal. However, COP25 ended without the hoped breakthrough, pushing the most important issues at stake to the COP26 meeting in Glasgow in 2021. That will be the last meeting to finalize the Paris Agreement. At the same time, during COP25, the newly appointed president of the EU, Ursula von der Leyen, together with her environment commissioner, Frans Timmermans, announced a European Green Deal. They both specifically stated in their speeches that this happened because of the youth's engagement in climate.

CONCLUSIONS AND RESULTS

It is clear that Greta Thunberg gave voice to a silent scream carried in the hearts of an entire generation of young people who saw their future being sold out to greed and short-sighted profits while neglecting the really important things in life. She struck a match that was then ignited even further by various youth all over Europe and elsewhere, like Australia, New Zealand, Kenya, Nigeria, South Africa, Uganda, and so on, who started to organize massive protests.

The informal way of communication via social media, the chaotic diversity in organizations, structures and even demands, have not posed any threat to the growth and enthusiasm this movement has generated. On the contrary, it is precisely the freedom to join and the emphasis on what connects us rather than what divides us, that makes the movement grow further in a more flexible and creative way.

The movement has an incredible list of results so far. Internationally, they have been able to create the biggest awareness of the climate urgency among diverse societies ever. There is literally no society where climate has not been discussed in one way or another in this past year. Also, they brought the topic home, deep into people's everyday lives. By choosing the tactic of school strike actions, they challenged school children to discuss with their teachers and parents about their motivation to participate. This created an instant inter-generational dialogue that created ownership on the topic across all ages. It is impossible to count the number of initiatives that spontaneously grew out of this awareness, and that stretched far beyond mere CO_2 reduction, like local groups cleaning beaches, parks, and so on.

This heightened consciousness about the environment had a positive spill-over effect on many companies. They decided to change their products and/or production processes to cut down CO_2 emissions or reduce the use of plastics. This in turn stimulated start-up enterprises who took bold steps in developing environmentally friendly alternatives (like bamboo cups or cutlery).

At a political level, the movement had Greta Thunberg touring Europe (and in the autumn of 2019, USA and Canada) and giving her inspirational speeches everywhere. Greta Thunberg, Anuna De Wever Van der Heyden, Luisa Neubauer and some other youth leaders met privately with President Macron in Paris and met him again briefly, together with nine other heads of state, during an informal EU meeting in Romania in May. Again, firmly putting climate change on the top of the political agenda.

In the European elections of May, the green parties doubled their seats and together with other socialist political fractions they seem to be setting the stage to take huge steps forward in the next legislation. Obviously, this also meant that the topic of climate change was high on all political agendas worldwide. Raising it to the top of political priorities has also resulted in all parties formu-lating an opinion on the topic and taking a stand, generating a much belated but still highly needed public debate.

Locally, in each country we can also see huge wins that were generated by the school strike movement. For example, the panel of scientists that volun-teered to write a climate action plan in Belgium. In some cities or countries, a climate emergency was declared as a direct result of the actions by the young people in collaboration with other climate organizations.

In short, it is impossible to overestimate the impact Greta Thunberg had when she decided to skip school on a Friday in September 2018, thereby showing the truth in cultural anthropologist Margaret Meads' saying: 'Never doubt that a small group of thoughtful, committed citizens can change the world; indeed, it's the only thing that ever has'.

NOTES

1.   This was said during a conversation with the authors in Rome, April 2019.
2.   Lesbian, Gay, Transgender, Bisexual, Queer (or Questioning), Intersex.

24. The Fridays For Future Movement in Uganda and Nigeria

Hilda Flavia Nakabuye, Sadrach Nirere and Adenike Titilope Oladosu

BACKGROUND

Fridays For Future in Uganda and Nigeria is a student- and youth-led platform that was launched in February 2019 following the call from Greta Thunberg to school strike. The Fridays For Future movement is gaining track in Africa and is registering success in demanding action. The movement in Uganda began after a dialogue by university students on the climate strikes. During this dialogue we highlighted Greta's courageous act of striking outside the Swedish Parliament, this motivated us to start the strikes in Uganda. We realized that this will help us increase attention to our demands for urgent climate action from our leaders. The discussion focused on the nature of the activity and how to incorporate it in our work. After several discussions, the movement was later started by Hilda Flavia Nakabuye, who was joined by other climate activists like Leah, Bob, Joy and Sadrach after a couple of weeks. From February 2019 to date, over 20 000 students have added their voices to demand urgent climate action and joint efforts to combat this climate breakdown.

Inspired by Greta Thunberg, Fridays For Future Uganda is leading the way towards the growth of a strong youth space through influencing policy, increasing climate action, activism and awareness. On 15 March the movement's first significant strike in Kampala, Uganda took place as part of the global school strike for climate. University students were joined by high school students for the strike that gathered over 150 young people. It is from this strike that the movement decided to write a joint students' demand paper, "The Uganda Students and Youth's Climate Action Demands". This document summarizes the reasons for climate strikes and demands, ranging from calls to leaders to act fast to calling for unprecedented global action towards the climate crisis/ecological breakdown.

On 24 May, Fridays For Future organized the second global school strike for climate. On this day, a group of Fridays For Future Uganda representatives presented the document to the Government of Uganda through the Office of the Speaker. The speaker of parliament is elected by the members of parliament. A discussion between the movement's representatives and Honourable Rebecca Kadaga, the speaker of parliament, was held on the document and the speaker responded positively while noting that the Ugandan government has created policies and action plans to combat climate change. She appreciated the Fridays For Future movement in Uganda for championing the move for urgent climate action.

On 12 July, a massive mobilization strike in preparation for the 20 September global climate strike was held with hundreds of students in Kiboga District to reaffirm the demands made in the document that was presented to the speaker of parliament. Many mobilization strikes are taking place in Uganda in places such as schools, universities, public places, workplaces along with activities such as tree planting, climate awareness, plastic pick-ups, among others. The Fridays For Future movement in Africa realized a turnout of over 1400 people for the global climate strike day on 20 September and over 2000 people for the entire global strike week of 20–27 September 2019.

The mass global climate strike week was open to youth, students, elders and everyone to raise the momentum on pushing for urgent climate action. Nigeria and Uganda are two of the African countries that participated in this global strike. The strikes in Uganda took place in different parts of the country. For instance, the major strike took place in Wakiso District and in other towns, In Kampala, Uganda Christian University, Jinja also held strikes. This was to enable everyone to be part of the strikes and for those people who were not able to join the major strike in Mukono. The strike in Uganda included primary and secondary students from different schools, university students, farmers' associations, teachers, local chairpersons, environmentalists and the general public. The global climate strike was held alongside the United Nations Climate Action Summit, hosted by the United Nations Secretary General António Guterres, which took place in New York, and aimed to boost ambition and accelerate actions to implement the Paris Agreement on climate change. A youth climate summit also took place as part of the weekend events. This was the first ever UN climate summit for young people and it provided a platform for young leaders to showcase their solutions and also meaningfully engage with decision-makers.

Therefore, from February 2019 until now, every Friday, students have held both group and individual strikes. The strikers have held talks in several universities, schools and communities to mobilize others to join the action as well as the Fridays For Future movement. The strikes are held on high-traffic roadsides and in public places, among others.

The growth of the movement in Uganda has inspired similar action in Nigeria, South Africa, and other countries. In South Africa, campaigners are demanding emissions reduction and driving youth participation in communities and schools in several South African cities. Nigeria too has participated in the Fridays For Future movement to bring together young people in the fight to demand government action.

THE MOVEMENT IN NIGERIA

The movement is getting stronger here and awareness on climate change is rising, as everyone is taking one climate action or another to demand for climate justice. At first, Adenike Titilope Oladosu started alone. Yet, she was optimistic that it would spread to all the states in Nigeria. Then, before the first global climate strike, other youths saw it as an avenue to demand environmental and climate justice, and they joined. At the first global climate strike, hundreds turned out in Abuja, Lagos and Kaduna. In Abuja, the climate strike was led by Adenike Titilope Oladosu (now the country director for Fridays For Future in Nigeria), Michael Fagbemi led the Lagos climate strike, Ibrahim Muhammad Shamsuddin and Sakeenat Bello led that of Kaduna. People who saw it were then awakened by leaders' inaction over the years even though Nigeria is one of the countries that signed the Paris Agreement. During the second global climate strike, the influence of the previous strikes engineered an increase in the number of people participating as many states joined the strike in the demand for climate justice. Climate change is real and the vulnerability is greater in African countries. Though we have not yet moved tens of thousands in the streets because of security challenges, our message is audible. Then, at the third global climate strike on 20 and 27 September, the dream was realized as it has spread into the corners of Nigeria: we witnessed a massive turnout in almost all the states in Nigeria as students, workers, adults, the physically challenged, children and other groups participated. As at the first global climate strike, there was no media attention, but as time passed we began to gain media attention from newspapers and organizations as they began to take interest in the action. One of the challenges we are yet to overcome is the sponsorship of our climate strikes.

The specifics of Nigeria are unique, hence the uniqueness of our approach in driving the Fridays For Future/climate strike movement in Nigeria. What we consider remarkable is the consistency with which we have driven the movement despite political and social barriers. While we may not freely take to the streets in places like Abuja, we must focus our energy and resources on educating students in schools, groups and gatherings. Regardless of the audience, our message is the same: to communicate on the climate crisis in Nigeria, to demand improved commitment and environment-focused policies from the government of Nigeria, to increase public drive towards climate action. For over 46 weeks, our group has been moving from schools to religious organizations, to social events and across various media platforms to make public the climate crisis Nigeria is facing and stress the need for well-targeted and cohesive efforts toward building climate resilience. We understand the peculiarities in Nigeria; hence, we understand that we may not be able to mobilize 100 000 young people to boycott school. Nonetheless, from the country's capital Abuja, to the country's most populous city Lagos, to marginalized communities in Benue State, and in rural areas of Kaduna State, we have decentralized ourselves to share the same message among different communities. We are still struggling with getting the needed media support to cover our activities and improve our storytelling skills required to convince more people to join us and show the government the urgency of our message.

Nigeria is one of the countries experiencing the severe impacts of climate change, which is leading to conflict, especially among herders and farmers. The Boko Haram saga is also fuelled by the impacts of climate change, including issues in the Niger Delta. The effect is felt greatly as it leads to migration of people from their community to others, resulting in atrocities due to limited resources. This has been affecting livelihoods, as most of these zones depend on agriculture as their primary means of occupation. As such, climate change has been a threat to our food security. Flooding is also another threat to our environment. This has created many internally displaced people camps, in unsafe places that can be dangerous for women; and most times such people are affected by diseases and infections of all kinds. Deforestation is on a rise as people depend on it for cooking materials since there is no clean, subsidized alternative. This has led to intense heatwaves that we witness during the dry season.

Other African countries like Kenya, Ghana and South Sudan are also taking an interest in the school strikes for climate but are yet to join the movement that will form a platform for youth to participate in the action in their respective countries. Many of the most troublesome aspects of environmental change are direct consequences of human behaviour, so it is appropriate that changing that behaviour should be high on the list of goals for any programme of environmental preservation.

While the strikes started within just three locations in Nigeria, from our reports of the third global climate strike held on 20 and 27 September it appears that about 36 locations around the country were involved. That shows the significant progress the movement is making in Nigeria, even though we believe we need to do more and keep pushing harder for climate action.

The federal government also, through the Federal Ministry of Environment, has been playing a significant role towards mitigation and adaptation, by involving Nigerian youth from all over the country in roundtable meetings and seminars aimed at harnessing their climate-smart ideas and actualizing them towards achieving Nigeria's Nationally Determined Contribution (NDC) commitment to the Paris Agreement of a 20–45 per cent reduction in emissions by 2030.

CHALLENGES TO THE FRIDAYS FOR FUTURE MOVEMENT AND THE REASONS WE STRIKE

Challenges faced by the movement include empty promises and inaction from politicians. Uganda signed the Paris Agreement in 2015 but very little or nothing has been done yet to combat the effects of climate change; we are running out of time. Promises have been made to us about taking climate action but haven't been put in play. For instance, the speaker of parliament of Uganda promised to organize a climate debate with fellow members of parliament, but all in vain. The movement has been criticized in Uganda as political. Indeed, one of the candidates for the 2021 presidential election, Honourable Robert Kyagulanyi (known as Bobi Wine) was mistakenly identified as a founder of our movement. This candidate has built his own movement, "People Power", which promotes political and social change.

There is no teaching about climate change in schools. This makes it hard for people to understand climate change the first time they hear about it during our climate awareness and public engagement sessions. However, despite the ignorance, everyone is familiar with effects of climate change because they affect each and every one of us in various ways.

Sometimes the community does not support us in our strikes because we disagree with some of the activities in some areas, such as cutting trees for timber to earn a living, environmentally unfriendly farming and fishing methods, sand mining in lakes, disposal of waste in lakes and rivers, unnecessary driving that contributes to air pollution and CO_2 emissions, and so on.

Inaction at large is putting everything at risk. For instance, the numbers of climate refugees within our countries are increasing at an unacceptable pace. Diseases like malaria and cholera, among others, are on the rise due to increasing temperatures. The health and the welfare of our people are at risk if we marginalize climate change as only one among various environmental issues:

- The fact that the Fridays For Future movement is growing globally in different countries around the world, such as Germany, Belgium, African and Latin American countries among others, proceeds from the need to have unprecedented global responses for fighting the climate change crisis. Such global action is portrayed in the ways youth in different countries are standing up for action and creating initiatives such as Zero Hour, Earth Uprising, climate marches, youth climate strikes, youth climate councils, lake-shore clean-ups, plastic pick-ups, tree planting, and so on. These actions include powerful speeches by climate activists directed at policy-makers and politicians.

- We are the first generation to know what is happening to our Earth and this puts us in a position to find solutions to stop it.
- Africa in particular is headed for trouble if countries do not adopt sustainable development. With the increasing global heat, agro-based societies in the Sub-Saharan region will not survive because agriculture is essential to all livelihoods – it's far more than energy, technology, business, health or science. Agriculture is the lead employer and source of income for African economies. A weak agricultural sector will lead to food insecurity, malnutrition, extreme poverty and unhealthy conditions. The increasing global heat will lead to water scarcity, evolving human, plant and animal diseases, soil erosion and lack of reliable energy sources.
- With increasing droughts, cyclones, floods, failing crops and decreasing water levels, many countries like Uganda, Mozambique, Zimbabwe, Kenya, Ethiopia, South Africa and South Sudan will be among the first to be severely broken down. Today, Mozambique's economy is being crippled by the deadliest tropical Cyclones, Idai, which killed over 1300 people in 2019, and Kenneth, sweeping over several coastal locations.
- In Uganda and other countries, despite the ban on plastics, there is an ever-increasing rate of littered plastic. The East African region harbours the African Great Lakes and this plastic is an increasing threat for the survival of many livelihoods. Lake Victoria is home to over 40 million people on its shores, generating tonnes of plastic every day. As a way of mitigating this plastic problem, increasing momentum on the demand to ban plastics, the Fridays For Future movement in Uganda started a petition to enforce the ban on plastic bags, as well as a lake-shore clean-up activity carried out every week on water bodies to beat plastic pollution and preserve our water resources.
- The rate at which our forests are being cleared and trees cut down for timber and charcoal is accelerating. The bare land is then used for industrialization or sugarcane plantations by investors and businesspeople. An example is the Mabira Forest in Uganda. The same applies to wetlands, which are being cleared for industrialization, settlement and rice plantations. Their protection is yet another demand of the movement.
- Therefore, young people with more life ahead of them, have the most to lose from an unsafe future and Fridays For Future emphasizes this. Today, more than 60 percent of the population in Sub-Saharan Africa is under the age of 25 years; moreover, the African youth population is expected to double by 2050.

Mobilization to rally more students to participate in the movement's activities continues. Today, over 20 000 students in Uganda and 100 000 in Nigeria have been enrolled. Mobilization is done through educating and sharing information and action about climate change and other pressing environmental issues like deforestation, plastic accumulation and water pollution. This gives us opportunities to call fellow students and other people to participate in the strikes.

In conclusion, the Fridays For Future movement faces social and political barriers, especially in Africa, but with consistency, hope, desire, unity and hard work we will keep pushing to realize our objectives and goals, which are in line with the Paris Agreement.

25. The origins of School Strike 4 Climate NZ

Sophie Handford and Raven Maeder

School Strike 4 Climate NZ (SS4CNZ) is a student-led, student-powered movement made up of young Aotearoa New Zealanders from every corner of the country, who are mobilizing to put pressure on their government to take immediate, transformative action on the climate crisis. These students, ranging from ages 8–22, are united by their shared concern for their futures, and their belief that achieving climate justice is and must be possible. In line with the international School Strike 4 Climate (SS4C) and Fridays For Future (FFF) movements, their overarching demand is simple: our leaders must take urgent action on the climate crisis and protect our generation, and all coming generations' right to a safe future on this planet.

The international FFF movement was sparked by the courageous actions of Greta Thunberg, a 15-year-old Swedish teenager, in August 2018. After years of anxiety, frustration and fear about her government's inaction on the climate crisis, Greta decided to stage a solo strike, and sit outside the Swedish Parliament every Friday rather than attending school. Her message to her leaders, and those around the globe, was "why should we study for this future, if no one is doing anything to protect that future?".

This message was one that resonated with young people around the world, and though Greta may not have realized it at the time, was the beginning of an international movement of millions, FFF. Soon students in over 40 countries began striking from school weekly for the climate, each with demands for their governments and elected leaders specific to their local context. Out of FFF, grew SS4C, which is rooted in Australia. Although the movements are very similar in their demands for climate action, SS4C uses the tactic of organizing less frequent strikes, with more effort to mobilize a larger portion of the population.

At the end of 2018, Sophie Handford, an 18-year-old recent high school graduate from Kāpiti, Aotearoa New Zealand, was scrolling through her Instagram when she came across photos of the first nationwide strike the Australian School Strikers had led. The messages on the placards, emotions on faces and chants of thousands of voices resonated deeply with Sophie and the fear she had been feeling around the future her generation would inherit if we failed to treat climate change like the crisis that it is and act, now. Only several days after this moment, an Aotearoa New Zealand branch of SS4C was born. Having recently graduated, Sophie luckily still had a network at her high school, Kāpiti College, namely their Eco Action Group, who were all extremely excited to be involved in the early stages of bringing this movement to Aotearoa New Zealand. Sophie had also been added to a Facebook group of young environmental activists from across Aotearoa New Zealand in the middle of 2018 and used this group as an avenue to reach out to more people to get the movement off the ground. Within three days, the team, mainly from Kāpiti College, had a social media presence and a website. They also had two video calls to plan for the coming weeks and months.

Throughout the early stages, Sophie was also being introduced to the international movement and was quick to find out that there was an international strike on 15 March 2019. The SS4CNZ national team at the time worked alongside scientists, older activists and other existing climate groups to develop a clear set of demands for their elected leaders.[1] They also began signing up people from around the country to join this team through their website. Importantly, Sophie decided to have a phone conversation with each new person that signed up from a new town and asked them if they would be a regional coordinator for their community. And so the SS4CNZ movement began to grow.

A BRIEF NOTE ON THE WIDER CLIMATE MOVEMENT IN AOTEAROA NEW ZEALAND

It is important to note here that SS4CNZ is a very young organization situated within a diverse and well-established wider climate movement in Aotearoa New Zealand, which has been built by many different groups and communities' over many years. SS4CNZ recognize that their work exists on the back of decades of resistance to fossil fuel development and activism by many different communities to protect the natural environment on which we depend, and which is a *taonga* (treasure) for our nation. SS4CNZ takes inspiration and guidance from those who have fought for climate justice before them, standing on their shoulders to play their part in mobilizing the next generation of climate activists in this eleventh hour of the fight to save our futures and our collective home.

A significant stream of the wider climate movement that exists in Aotearoa New Zealand has been the movement to end oil and gas exploration and extraction in our lands and waters. After decades of grassroots campaigning by communities, local oil-free groups, non-government organizations such as Greenpeace Aotearoa New Zealand, and Iwi and Hapu (Indigenous Māori tribes and sub-tribes), the newly elected coalition government announced in 2017 that they would end new offshore oil and gas exploration in Aotearoa New Zealand.[2]

This was a monumental win for the Aotearoa New Zealand climate movement, and a testament to the power of grassroots, people-powered movements. The newly elected Prime Minister, Jacinda Ardern, said many times on the election campaign trail that climate change was her generation's "nuclear free moment", and this politically brave step was seen by many as a strong example of this sentiment being backed by action. This win was a fresh gust of air beneath the wings of the Aotearoa New Zealand climate movement; an indication that we could win if we all came together. However, despite this step being world leading, there was still so much work to be done.

Although this announcement promised an end to new offshore oil and gas development, 57 oil and coal exploration permits remained unaffected, many of which will last for decades. Further, the government has continued to open up land onshore for fossil fuel exploration; in 2018, they opened up 2200 square kilometres of land for potential oil and gas drilling, a move that was heavily criticized by School Strikers, environmental groups and local Iwi.[3] This shows that fossil fuel development is far from over in Aotearoa.

SS4C has taken on the mantle of holding the government to account on the need for bold, transformative action on a systemic level to address the climate crisis. We stand firm in the belief that no political party is currently doing enough to address this crisis. However, while many have hailed SS4C as being the "re-awakening" of youth political consciousness, we are by no means the only young people who are mobilizing on a national level in this space. Other youth activist groups, particularly Indigenous youth groups, have been actively mobilizing their communities on this issue for many years.

Two such groups are the Pacific Climate Warriors, a group of Pasifika youth who have been active in Aotearoa New Zealand for the last few years, and in the wider Pacific region for over a decade[4] and Te Ara Whatu, a group of Māori and Indigenous Pacific young people from Aotearoa who have sent Indigenous Youth Delegations to the International UN Climate Conference for the past three years.[5] They are the first all-Indigenous Youth Delegation to attend these negotiations from Aotearoa. Both the Pacific Climate Warriors and Te Ara Whatu work tirelessly to bring Indigenous knowledge and understanding to spaces that are often otherwise dominated by Western scientific frameworks and worldviews. They also fight on the front lines for their communities here in Aotearoa New Zealand and the Pacific, who are not only disproportionately affected by the impacts of the climate crisis, but in their Indigenous knowledge and understanding, also hold the solutions that our world so desperately needs. For these reasons, it is fundamental that these voices are at the centre of conversations about the climate crisis and achieving climate justice.

Drawing attention to these, and the many other environmental groups, is important in explaining the story of SS4C in Aotearoa New Zealand, because it highlights the context in which we have come to exist, and the niche we currently occupy as a movement for young Aotearoa New Zealand students to organize, mobilize and be a part of the conversation about our futures. While SS4CNZ brings a new element to the climate movement in Aotearoa New Zealand, it is important to acknowledge our allies who are in this fight alongside us.

REFLECTING ON SS4CNZ'S FIRST YEAR

On 15 February 2018, Sophie Handford was invited to speak on the TV New Zealand Breakfast Show, launching the SS4CNZ movement in national news and serving a notice to the nation that students across the country would be striking from schools, kindergartens and universities alongside the global School Strike movement on 15 March.[6] Sophie was invited to bring along someone else who was involved in the movement and based in Wellington, so she invited Raven Maeder, a student at Victoria University of Wellington who had been heavily involved in getting SS4CNZ off the ground, and had been involved in mobilizing young people in the wider Aotearoa New Zealand climate movement for a number of years.

This interview propelled the movement into the national consciousness and soon more and more youth from every corner of the country were getting in contact wanting to host a strike in their town or city. By 24 February, over 15 community actions had been confirmed, with strikes in major cities such as Christchurch, Wellington, Auckland and Dunedin, some being organized by students as young as 12 years old.[7] This would only increase in the following weeks.

At this time, the national response from parents, schools, media commentators, politicians and the general public was very mixed. While there was an overflowing of support from many parents, teachers and community groups who said they were inspired by young people rising up for their right to a future, and wanting to support this mobilization, there was also significant criticism and resistance. Much of the discourse in the media became centred around criticisms of the strikes taking place during school hours, rather than on the weekend. Many schools threatened to mark students as truants if they took part in the strike, with some principals saying it was just an excuse for students to skip school and their impact on climate change would be "probably zero".[8]

The initial response from Members of Parliament was also very mixed. Many National Party MPs criticized the strike publicly. National MP Judith Collins was particularly dismissive, saying "Their little protest is not going to help the world one bit", and the National Party leader, Simon Bridges, accused the strike of being just "a couple of chants as they march along and maybe McDonald's afterwards".[9] The Prime Minister, Jacinda Ardern, also had a rather unenthusiastic initial response to SS4CNZ's announcement of the first strike, telling the media: "What I'd like to think is in New Zealand there is less cause for protest. We are certainly trying to do our bit".[10] However, the Minister for Climate Change and Green Party co-leader, James Shaw, came out publicly in support of SS4CNZ, saying "they have every right to fight for their future".[11]

While the media storm that unfolded in the lead-up to the first strike was largely dominated by argument over whether or not school students should be allowed to strike from school, or whether the protest would achieve anything, rather than the demands of the movement and the issue of the climate crisis, there was also significant support and coverage of the positive effects that the movement was already having. Further, the media attention being generated by the rigorous debate on the subject certainly fell in favour of SS4CNZ's hope to get the message about the strike out to the nation. In fact, one opinion piece argued that the school strike had been a success before it had even begun:

> Arguably, it has done more to engage the community about climate change, species destruction and rising sea levels than anything else has managed to do over the past few years. Nationwide, it is igniting conversations around the dinner table about climate change – its causes and its effects – in hundreds of thousands of New Zealand homes.[12]

A significant success came when more than 1000 academics, teachers and researchers made the rare decision to publicly throw their support behind SS4CNZ in an open letter.[13] The open letter thanked the striking students for their "leadership, and commitment to building a different world based on climate justice".[14] It also spoke of the important educational opportunity that it offered for the striking students to learn "practical lessons about an issue that will confront them throughout their lifetimes, as citizens, as future scientists, and as members of the global community".[15] As momentum built in the lead-up to 15 March, the discourse around the strike began to shift slightly. People began realizing that the students were serious, and they weren't going anywhere. Five days before the much-awaited date of the first strike, Raven Maeder got a text from a phone number she did not recognize while sitting on the floor of her bedroom. It was from a staffer in the Prime Minister's Office – the Prime Minister wanted to meet the strikers.

On 13 March, Prime Minister, Jacinda Ardern, and Minister for Climate Change, James Shaw, met with SS4CNZ Wellington organizers at a local high school in a "town hall"-style panel discussion attended by 130 local high school students and staff. The meeting was also live broadcast via social media, with questions coming from SS4CNZ organizers, the live audience and online.[16] While the positive steps made by the government were acknowledged, and the Prime Minister was thanked for meeting with the strikers and recognizing the importance of listening to their concerns, the SS4CNZ representatives also grilled the Prime Minister and James Shaw, focusing squarely on the government's continuation of fossil fuel development and lack of action on emissions from the agriculture sector – which accounts for roughly 50 per cent of New Zealand's emissions profile. Sophie Handford, as one of the SS4CNZ representatives, was firm that "no political party is currently doing enough on climate change". When asked about what impact the student climate strike would have, the Prime Minister told the strikers "don't underestimate the power of your voice… I think too often we make this assessment that in order to have an impact you have to be of voting age. That is just not the case".[17] She also spoke about the importance of movements like this one building more public consensus and pressure for bold action, to give government the social licence to do more.

With this wind beneath their wings, SS4CNZ organizers across the country geared up for their first strike. Sophie and Raven were invited again to speak on the TV New Zealand Breakfast Show on 15 March, the day of the first strike.[18] During this interview, the pair signalled the expected turnout was anywhere between 500 and 1000. However, on 15 March, this prediction was dwarfed by an estimated 20 000 people marching in the streets of their home towns and cities.[19] This turnout far exceeded what organizers up and down the country had hoped for – it was incredible and one of the largest mobilizations the country had seen in years. The mood in the crowds on the day was full of hope that the collective frustration over inaction might finally trigger real political change. The nation's youth were rising up for their futures.

Tragically, on 15 March, there was also a horrific terrorist attack targeted at two separate mosques in Christchurch, claiming the lives of 51 people in their place of worship. This date will now be remembered as one of the country's darkest days.[20] SS4CNZ organizers shared in the national grief and pain of these attacks, meaning that celebration of the first strike felt not only inappropriate but impossible. Many who attended strikes across the country spoke of the sense that 15 March showed the best and worst sides of humanity, a shocking clash of opposing ideologies. In an article published in *The Guardian*, Rebecca Solnit wrote that climate action is the antithesis of white supremacy: "behind the urgency of climate action is the understanding that everything is connected; behind white supremacy is an ideology of separation".[21]

When the international FFF and SS4C movements decided for the next international strike date to be set for 24 May, SS4CNZ organizers knew they needed to mobilize again. A statement was released saying that the 15 March terror attack showed the worst side of human nature, but on 24 May students and the wider community would come together and share hope. As the national security threat level was still relatively high in the aftermath of 15 March, and many communities were still grieving and in pain, the decision of what kind of actions would take place on 24 May was left up to individual communities to decide locally. While some centres chose to strike and march in the streets, others organized beach clean-ups, community gatherings and tree plantings. On 24 May, the turnout was as phenomenal as the 15 March climate strike. However, the third strike, on 27 September, is the one that was truly exceptional, as a historic 170 000 people went on strike for the climate.

The date of 27 September 2019 will be written into the NZ history books, with 3.5 per cent of the population uniting behind collective demands for climate justice.[22] This percentage of population turnout was the second highest per capita turnout internationally for the September school strikes, behind Tuvalu in the South Pacific, which mobilized 20 per cent of its citizens. On this day, the Pacific was leading the world on climate action! In the capital city, Wellington, school strikers and a crowd of 40 000 people delivered an open letter to politicians from each major party on the steps of Parliament calling on elected leaders to do everything in their power to limit warming to 1.5°C and meet the five specific national demands of the movement,[23] the fifth of which had been co-written by SS4CNZ and the Pacific Climate Warriors.[24]

Significantly, the 27 September strikes were a success because of the partnership between a range of youth climate action groups, and saw an important step towards ensuring that the voices of Indigenous youth and their communities were at the centre of the conversation around climate change. In Wellington, the strike was co-hosted by the Pacific Climate Warriors, who mobilized their communities to attend and lead the march to Parliament with traditional song and dance. In Auckland, the strike was co-hosted by SS4C Auckland, 4 Thaa Kulture – a South Auckland-based Indigenous environmentalist group of high school students – and the Pacific Climate Warriors.[25] Members of Te Ara Whatu and other Indigenous youth movements were also actively involved on the day, including speeches from incredible young Indigenous leaders such as Pania Newton, the inspirational young leader who successfully led the struggle by her community to have their ancestral land, Ihumātao, returned to them in 2019, and Brianna Freuan from the Pacific Climate Warriors, who has been leading the way on climate action since she helped found 350 Sāmoa at age 11.[26] Having these marches led by the communities who are on the front lines of the climate crisis was significant because it recognized that leadership needed to come from the communities who would not only be most affected by climate change, but also whose experience and knowledge is crucial in addressing the crisis. It was also fundamental to the massive turnouts, particularly in Wellington and Auckland, where the leadership of these groups meant the mass mobilization of their communities. Overall, this day saw the largest mass mobilization in the country's history, and in the words of the coordinator of the Wellington Pacific Climate Warriors, Mary Moeono-Kolio, it was an "intergenerational march…fighting for our Pacific people – that's what's made it for all these people to stand as one. Standing in solidarity no matter what island we come from, what we speak, just coming together".[27]

In November, the Zero Carbon Bill was passed into law in Aotearoa New Zealand with near-unanimous support in Parliament.[28] This was a historic moment for the nation, and the world, as the target to keep global warming within 1.5°C by 2050 was enshrined in law. Significantly, the blueprint of this bill, before it became adopted by the government, was written and championed by young Kiwi climate activists. The nationwide, youth-led climate organiza- tion Generation Zero began developing the Zero Carbon Bill in 2016 when they realized that if they wanted a law to put Aotearoa New Zealand on track to zero carbon by 2050, they would have to write it themselves. And so they did.[29] Together with many other climate groups, business and industry allies, the scientific community and political youth wings, they campaigned for years to get the bill through Parliament with cross-partisan support. Their success truly shows the power that young people can have in affecting change at all levels.

The passing of the Zero Carbon Bill was also a significant win for SS4CNZ, as it was one of the movement's key demands of Parliament,[30] and the strikes and mobilization were instrumental in building the political consensus for it to pass with cross-party support. The historic intergenerational climate strike on 27 September showed that the Aotearoa New Zealand public would not settle for inaction and were united behind the demand for an ambitious Zero Carbon Bill. However, while the bill passed was a huge success for the climate movement and heralded as "world leading", it fell short of the ambition called for by SS4CNZ, who had been pushing for the target to be pushed forward to at least 2040 to reflect Aotearoa New Zealand's ability and responsibility to lead the world in climate action and ambition. Despite pressure being applied by SS4CNZ and many other climate action groups for the government to move faster and be more ambitious, the target set out in the newly passed bill is 2050. There were also other changes to the bill being called for by SS4CNZ, such as stronger targets for greenhouse gas emissions and for legal enforceability measures to be put in place for the targets; however, these were not included in the final bill. However, overall, the passing of this bill is world leading and a great win for the climate movement in Aotearoa and the world. It sends a strong signal to all societal and economic sectors in New Zealand of the direction in which we are heading as a nation, and that everyone must play their role in moving towards a zero-carbon future.

Reflecting on SS4CNZ's first year, there are many other wins to recount. A significant one has been the increasing support from the government for the strikes, reflected clearly in the Ministry of Education's change of tone towards the strikes[31] and the government's recent announcement that a new climate change education resource will be in schools in 2020.[32] Further, the widespread support from all sectors of Aotearoa New Zealand society has been immense. Over 290 businesses and their staff signed up to support and mobilize during the strike on 27 September[33] and all but one of the major Aotearoa New Zealand universities and tertiary institutions endorsed and took part in 27 September.[34] Unions also supported the September strike, not only through spreading the word through their membership bases, but also financially and logistically. Further, only several months ago, SS4CNZ was named as one of the most powerful groups fighting for climate justice in Aotearoa New Zealand.[35] Members of the movement have been recognized for their work and contributions through a range of national and local awards, including the NZ Youth Award, an Impact Award, a Girlboss NZ Award and Wellingtonian of the Year. Most significantly, the major success of the movement in its first year has been the partnerships that it has formed with groups such as the Pacific Climate Warriors, Te Ara Whatu and 4 Thaa Kulture, without whom these many successes would not have been achieved.

There has also been significant learning, and there is much more work to do to ensure that this movement is successful, and upholds the values, stories and understandings that are needed to fix this crisis. The importance of having full inclusion of Māori and Pasifika *rangatahi* (youth), as well as ensuring the voices of marginalized youth are meaningfully included and empowered in the conversation, has become incredibly clear. With the movement having grown so rapidly, time was of the essence and group structure was lacking. This has meant that issues such as structural racism and negative power dynamics that exist in our society have not successfully been addressed within the movement, meaning that it is currently not a space in which all young Aotearoa New Zealanders feel able to participate and be fully included. Ensuring this is addressed is key to the movement's success and there is still much more work to be done.

Moving forward, SS4CNZ organizers say they have much to learn from older activists, and other youth climate groups who have created structures for movements before and will be continuing to learn to take leadership from decades of resistance that have gone before them. There is a real need for intergenerational solidarity for exchange of learnings, ideas and perspectives and because we are stronger and more resilient together. Further, it is clear that creating space for and upholding Indigenous leadership is key to ensuring that the root causes of the climate crisis are addressed, and that we collectively work towards a future that upholds justice for people and planet, rather than perpetuate existing injustices and the systems that have brought us to the point of ecological and social crisis.

The movement is continuing to grow in Aotearoa New Zealand, with support from older generations, and a political awakening in young people is rippling across the nation. Young people are realizing the importance of having their voice heard at this moment in history to protect and safeguard this planet for generations to come and advocate for the planet that has no voice of its own. This is becoming a catalyst for the creation of a social climate where young people are infiltrating positions of power. In the most recent local council elections, where around 70 youth under the age of 30 ran for a seat at the council table,[36] a number of young candidates, including SS4CNZ's own Sophie Handford, were elected to represent their communities in local government.[37] Running to be an elected member is only one way in which youth from Aotearoa New Zealand have been making their voice heard. There are so many young people taking action in a variety of different ways such as through art, song writing, non-violent direct action, speech and storytelling. Each month, more and more young people are joining the movement, bringing new skills, perspectives and ideas to the team.

The year 2019 was only the beginning of the SS4C movement in Aotearoa New Zealand and the mobilization we have achieved is showing no signs of slowing down. We will not stop until all our demands of our government are met, and leaders internationally act now to address climate change as the crisis that it is. We will continue to stand for our right to a safe, liveable future on this one planet we all call home. This is only the beginning.

NOTES

1. SS4CNZ (n.d.), "The School Strike 4 Climate NZ demands", accessed 13 November 2019 at https://docs.google.com/document/d/1Vb4voJUHwmPv ul75AHlBw7QoIo6oaviCI8U9 HTYIzhs/edit.
2. Hannah Rutherford and Laura Waters (2018), "Government aims to strike balance ending offshore oil exploration: PM", *Stuff.co.nz*, 12 April, 13 November 2019 at https://www.stuff.co.nz/business/103031705/ardern-to-end-to-offshore-oil -exploration-with-shortreprieve-for-taranaki?rm=m.
3. *New Zealand Herald* (2019), "Government offers Taranaki land to oil explorers in block offer but with tight new restrictions, including near top surf breaks", 30 April, 21 November 2019 at https://www.nzherald.co.nz/business/news/article .cfm?c_id=3&objectid=12226614.
4. 350 Pacific (n.d.), "Pacific Climate Warriors", 21 November 2019 at https:// 350pacific.org/pacific-climate-warriors/.
5. Te Ara Whatu (n.d.), [website] 21 November 2019 at https://tearawhatu.org/.
6. Facebook.com (2019), "New Zealand has just been served notice", 15 February, 1 December 2019 at https://www.facebook.com/watch/?v=318382278670482.
7. SS4CNZ (2019), "Everyday, new towns are getting on board and choosing to strike for urgent climate action on March 15th! Send us a message if you're organising something in your community", *Facebook.com*, 24 February, 1 December 2019 at

https://www.facebook.com/schoolstrike4climatenz/photos/a.287831771883948/291224078211384/?type=3&theater.

8. Amber-Leigh Woolf and Adele Redmond (2019), "Students who strike for climate change will be marked as truants, principals say", *Stuff.co.nz*, 7 March, accessed 11 January 2020 at https://www.stuff.co.nz/environment/climate-news/111013724/students-who-strike-for-climate-change-will-be-marked-as-truants-principals-say.

9. Dan Satherley (2019), "Simon Bridges questions whether ends justify the means in climate protest", *Newshub.co.nz*, 11 March, accessed 11 January 2020 at https://www.newshub.co.nz/home/politics/2019/03/simon-bridges-questions-whether-ends-justify-the-means-in-climate-protest.html.

10. Ibid.

11. 1 News (2019), "Minister supports student strike against climate change inaction during school time", 4 March, accessed 11 January 2020 at https://www.tvnz.co.nz/one-news/new-zealand/minister-supports-student-strike-against-climate-change-inaction-during-school-time.

12. Gordon Campbell (2019), "Gordon Campbell on the school climate strike", *Scoop.co.nz*, 14 March, accessed 11 January 2020 at https://www.scoop.co.nz/stories/HL1903/S00081/gordon-campbell-on-the-school-climatestrike.htm.

13. RNZ (2019), "Academics, teachers back students' climate strike", 9 March, accessed 11 January 2020 at https://www.rnz.co.nz/news/national/384350/academics-teachers-back-students-climate-strike.

14. Ibid.

15. Ibid.

16. Lee Kenny (2019), "Prime Minister Jacinda Ardern met with student climate change protesters in Wellington", *Stuff.co.nz*, 13 March, accessed 20 January 2020 at https://www.stuff.co.nz/environment/climate-news/111237038/prime-minister-jacinda-ardern-meets-student-climate-change-protesters-in-wellington.

17. Zane Small (2019), "Student asks Jacinda Ardern what difference School Strike 4 Climate will make", *Newshub.co.nz*, 13 March, accessed 20 January 2020 at https://www.newshub.co.nz/home/politics/2019/03/student-asks-jacinda-ardern-what-difference-school-strike-4-climate-will-make.html.

18. 1 News (2019), "'It is the nuclear-free issue of our generation' – student protest organisers discuss striking for climate change", 15 March, accessed 20 January 2020 at https://www.tvnz.co.nz/one-news/new-zealand/-nuclear-free-issue-our-generation-student-protest-organisers-discuss-striking-climate-change.

19. Ibid.

20. Kate Newton et al. (2019), "New Zealand's darkest day", *RNZ.co.nz*, 15 March, accessed 26 January 2020 at https://shorthand.radionz.co.nz/NZ-DARKEST-DAY/index.html.

21. Rebecca Solnit (2019), "Why climate action is the antithesis of white supremacy", *The Guardian*, 19 March accessed 26 January 2020 at https://www.theguardian.com/commentisfree/2019/mar/19/why-youll-never-meet-a-white-supremacist-who-cares-about-climate-change.

22. RNZ (2019), "Thousands – young and old – demand government action on climate change", 27 September, accessed 26 January 2020 at https://www.rnz.co.nz/news/national/399778/thousands-young-and-old-demand-government-action-on-climate-change.

23. Eleanor Ainge Roy (2019), "'Nothing else matters': school climate strikes sweep New Zealand", *The Guardian*, 27 September, accessed 28 January 2020 at https://

www.theguardian.com/environment/2019/sep/27/nothing-else-matters-school
-climate-strikes-sweep-new-zealand.

24. Georgia Forrester (2019), "Student climate change stroke: why young Kiwis are
    demanding more action", *Stuff.co.nz*, 27 September, accessed 28 January 2020
    at https://www.stuff.co.nz/environment/climate-news/115713822/student-climate
    -change-strike-why-young-kiwis-are-demanding-more-action.
25. Jamie Tahana (2019), "'We're not drowning, we're fighting': Pacific youth lead
    climate march", *RNZ.co.nz*, 27 September, accessed 28 January 2020 at https://
    www.rnz.co.nz/international/pacific-news/399785/we-re-not-drowning-we-re
    -fighting-pacific-youth-lead-climate-march.
26. Josephine Franks (2019), "Climate change strike: up to 80 000 protesters form
    human chain in Auckland", *Stuff.co.nz*, 27 September, accessed 28 January 2020
    at https://www.stuff.co.nz/environment/climate-news/116143489/climate-change
    -strike-up- to-80000-protesters-form-human-chain-in-auckland.
27. Jamie Tahana (2019), in note 25.
28. Henry Cooke (2019), "Zero Carbon Bill passes with near-unanimous support,
    setting climate change targets into law", *Stuff.co.nz*, 7 November, accessed
    28 January 2020 at https://www.stuff.co.nz/national/politics/117244331/national
    -will-support-climate-change-zero-carbon-bill.
29. Generation Zero (2020), "Our story", accessed 26 August 2020 at https://www
    .generationzero.org/our_story.
30. SS4CNZ (n.d.), "The School Strike 4 Climate NZ demands", in note 1.
31. Ministry of Education (2019), "Attendance and the School Strike 4 Climate",
    accessed 28 January 2020 at https://www.education.govt.nz/news/attendance-and
    -the-school-strike-4-climate-change.
32. Stuff (2020), "Climate change education resource to be in schools in 2020", 12
    January, accessed 28 January 2020 at https://www.stuff.co.nz/environment/climate
    -news/118703882/climate-change-education-resour ce-to-be-in-schools-in-2020.
33. Debrin Foxcroft (2019), "New Zealand companies join students in support for the
    global climate strike", *Stuff.co.nz*, accessed 31 January 2020 at https://www.stuff
    .co.nz/business/116139687/new-zealand-companies-join-students-in-support-for
    -the-global-climate-strike; Spreaker (2020), "Lucy Kebbell: businesses join chil-
    dren to march against climate change" [podcast], 31 January 2020 at https://www
    .spreaker.com/user/nzme/lucy-kebbell-businesses-join-children-to; Not Business
    as Usual (n.d.), "This is not business as usual", 31 January 2020 at https://www
    .notbusinessasusual.co/.
34. Josephine Franks (2019), "Climate change strike: Auckland Uni the only NZ uni-
    versity not to back action", *Stuff.co.nz*, 18 September, 31 January 2020 at https://
    www.stuff.co.nz/environment/climate-news/115871974/climate-change-strike
    -auckland-uni-the-only-nz-university-not-to-back-action.
35. Andrea Vance, Charlie Mitchell and Henry Cooke (2019), "New Zealand's
    climate change power list", *Stuff.co.nz*, 16 September, accessed 5 February 2020
    at   https://www.stuff.co.nz/environment/climate-news/115727267/new-zealands
    -climate-change-power-list.
36. Peter MacKenzie (2019), "Echoing Chloe Swarbrick, a 'youthquake' rumbles
    through Wellington's political scene", *The Spinoff*, 7 June, accessed 5 February
    2020 at https://thespinoff.co.nz/politics/07-06-2019/echoing-chloe-swarbrick-a
    -youthquake-rumbles-thro ugh-wellingtons-political-scene/.
37. Charlotte Graham-McLay (2010), "'Youthquake': the young New Zealanders
    voted into office – in between McDonald's shifts", *The Guardian*, 17 October,

accessed 5 February 2020 at https://www.theguardian.com/world/2019/oct/17/ youthquake-the-young-new-zealanders-voted-i   nto-office-in-between-mcdonald s-shifts.

26. 350.org

William "Bill" McKibben

350.org began a decade ago, as a self-conscious attempt to build a global, grassroots movement demanding action on climate change. Such a thing did not exist in 2008, but we felt it needed to: it had become clear that the fossil fuel industry was dominating the politics of global warming. It had lost the argument over the science, but it was winning the argument overall, because the argument was (as most are) about money and power. We knew that we could not match the Exxons and the Shells in money, so we needed to find other sources of power, and we turned to the history of broad-based social movements.

The "we" at the beginning was me and seven undergraduates at Middlebury College, a small college in rural New England in the United States. We had no experience and little in the way of resources; there were seven continents, so each of the students took one and set to work (the young man who took the Antarctic was also responsible for the internet). We started reaching out around the globe and found lots of people eager to go to work. There wasn't, everywhere, someone who thought of themselves as an environmentalist, but everywhere there were people who worried about war and peace, hunger, women's rights, public health – the things at risk in a degrading environment. They rallied for the first global day of climate action in October of 2009 – 5200 demonstrations in 181 countries, what CNN called "the most widespread day of political activity in the planet's history."

Those demonstrations proved that one long-standing shibboleth about the environmental movement was wrong: far from being a project of wealthy white people, it turned out that most of the leadership was coming from the front lines. Those who were working on this cause were mostly poor, black, brown, Asian, young. And so, as 350.org began to grow, that's where its growth began to come from. Many of its early leaders came from the South Pacific, where the Pacific Climate Warriors began to organize on low-lying island nations like Tuvalu, Vanuatu, the Marshalls, Micronesia and the Solomons; from Africa, where rapidly spreading drought was causing concern to rise; from Central and South America where melting glaciers and disappearing rainforests made the problems plain.

From the beginning, 350.org was convinced that the role of the fossil fuel industry was doing much to keep us from solving the climate problem. Thus, we began attacking the power of that industry as best we could. An early salvo came in the U.S., where indigenous groups and Midwestern farmers had been opposing a little-known pipeline project called Keystone XL, designed to carry tarsands oil from Alberta in Canada down to the Gulf of Mexico. 350.org joined forces with those opponents in an effort to make it a test case of the emerging power of the climate movement. In 2011, we organized civil disobedience actions outside the White House that led, over two weeks, to the arrest of more than 1200 people, the greatest number of such nonviolent actions about anything in the U.S. in some years. Even so, no one thought there was much chance of blocking the project: the *National Journal* published a poll of its 300 "energy insiders" on Capitol Hill predicting a permit would be granted for the project within a few months. That did not happen; instead, the opposition swelled, becoming the most important environmental fight in the United States. It has not only stalled the pipeline for almost a decade, but also led to opponents fighting every kind of fossil fuel project around the world. Many of these fights are successful, but even when they're not, they slow down the fossil fuel industry – a worthwhile endeavor since each month of delay lets the engineers drop the price of solar panels and wind turbines another percentage point or two.

We also attempted to cut off some of the money supply to the fossil fuel industry, launching in 2012 a divestment campaign designed to get institutions to sell their stock in coal, oil and gas companies. It was modelled on the anti-apartheid divestment campaigns of a previous generation, and indeed South African Anglican archbishop Desmond Tutu was an early advocate, describing climate change as "the apartheid of our time." Beginning in North America, Australia and Europe, it has spread quickly around the world and become the largest anti-corporate campaign of its kind in history – by 2019, endowments and portfolios worth more than $11 trillion had committed to divest, including the New York City pension fund, the University of California system, half the colleges and universities in the UK, and Norway's sovereign wealth fund, which is the largest pool of investment capital in the world. In 2019, Shell Oil paid the campaign a large backhanded compliment, saying divestment had become a material risk to its business.

350.org has run many groundbreaking campaigns and collaborated with a wide variety of other groups and individuals. In Europe it has helped with the Ende Gelände anti-coal campaigns, and held a variety of financial institutions responsible for their investments; in Africa the #AfricaVuka campaign has been standing up to new fossil fuel plants across the continent; in Brazil it has worked with indigenous groups to pass sweeping bans on fracking across wide swaths of the country; in North America it has worked hard on environmental justice fights from Standing Rock to the Trans Mountain pipeline. In several countries it has affiliated organizations that vet and endorse political candidates. Sometimes 350.org helps catalyze actions – Rise for Climate Action in 2018 was an example of it taking a lead role. Other times it serves as an experienced collaborator helping provide the services that make the actions of others really sing: in 2019, for instance, it helped provide logistical backbone for September's massive youth-led climate strikes across the planet.

For 350.org, the greatest thrill has been watching a large movement grow all over the planet – that was, after all, its founding hope. There are hundreds of independent 350 chapters scattered around the planet, and many of the young people who began their activist careers working for fossil fuel divestment in college went on to found the Sunrise Movement that inspired the Green New Deal, a congressional resolution that lays out a grand plan for tackling climate change. That optimism is tempered, of course, by the other darker development of its first decade: the planet has gotten ever farther from 350 parts per million CO_2.

As it faces its second decade, 350.org remains the largest organization on Earth whose only task is fighting climate change. That sounds more impressive than it is: it means a staff of 160 people spread around the world, or on average about 25 per continent. Those numbers sound small, and they are – but the number of paid staff is amplified by large groups of volunteers, and of course by a philosophy of collaboration with many other groups. It's not clear that it's a big enough movement to win this fight – but at least it's clear there will *be* a fight, which wasn't obvious when 350.org was born.

27. How to become an engineer in the ecological crisis?

Antoine Bizien, Elsa Deville and Lucas Dubois

We live in critical times. The new generation, more than any other, has understood the necessity of seizing its last chance before dramatic consequences ensue. Indeed, the student community has been a driving force in recent years with high-profile media actions, such as Fridays For Future, calling for immediate action by economic and political leaders. Yet, we are struggling to take advantage of this closing window of opportunity. We are realizing that the principles of our world clash with the changes that are necessary and that no profound transformation has begun. As individuals, we struggle with the question "How can I make a difference?" As a group we try to organize ourselves to make our voices heard.

When we arrived at the École Polytechnique, Paris, like many of our fellow students, we wanted to get involved in the Sustainable Development Association, in order to reflect on this individual and collective possibility of making a difference. This interest in environmental issues at school demonstrates the attachment that young people have to thinking about tomorrow and to thinking about their own integration, particularly in the workplace.

It seems obvious to many of us that our values and aspirations must be taken into account in our future jobs. How can we fit into the eroding edifice of our society without contributing to its collapse? How can we work in a world of finite resources? It is indeed essential to know the impact of one's work in one's company but also to be aware of the underlying model. We cannot accept working for a so-called "green company" while continuing to benefit from a system that we should be extricating ourselves from.

Nevertheless, we cannot fail to note a large gap between our questioning and what the professional world can offer us. The themes of sufficiency and degrowth are obviously absent from today's big firm models. But beyond that, the willingness of companies to change is extremely dependent on opinion and returns on investment. This leads students to mistrust big companies that are blamed for having a negative impact on the environment and of not showing much willingness to make amends.

Some students are diverting from the traditional routes. At the École des Mines ParisTech,[1] students have chosen to turn away from traditional careers, with the number of graduates joining big companies dropping from 58 per cent to 36 per cent between 2012 and 2018 (though this could also be due to a rising interest in start-ups).[2] Companies are beginning to notice this change among students and are modifying their discourse accordingly. They voluntarily choose to emphasize their environmental engagement, which does not go unnoticed.

At the École Polytechnique, for example, we have sponsors for each year group; these sponsors are companies that finance part of our associative life in exchange for a privileged access to the students. The last two sponsors, the aircraft builder Airbus and the oil company Total, belong to the most criticized sectors. While it is not always easy to discern the borderline between greenwashing and real change, it is interesting to note that Airbus chose the theme of the electric plane to introduce itself to us in a presentation in front of the whole school. The company Total (independently of its role as a sponsor), wants to set up an R&D centre working on the issues of decarbonated energies and artificial intelligence inside the heart of the École Polytechnique campus. One of the acknowledged objectives of this approach is to develop a special relationship with students.

While it is not yet up to the challenge and does not question the reasons for the ecological crisis, this shift in discourse is too obvious to go unnoticed. It has raised mixed reactions from students. Whatever we think of it, we, students, have played a role in this change of discourse: as a recruitment pool, our opinion matters to companies. For example, seven of the ten former CEOs of Total are from the École Polytechnique, as is the current CEO, Patrick Pouyanné, and the opinion of current promotions is therefore worth listening to. This is the idea behind the "Student Manifesto for an Ecological Awakening", which has gathered more than 30 000 signatures in France.[3] Signatories are committed to working for a company that places ecological transition at the heart of its activities. The Student Manifesto is not only pressure on companies, but also plays on the rope of sensitivity, saying to employers: "You could have been me, a student today, so understand my fears and desires, and you who are in charge today, do what you can".

Beyond this pressure on companies, the Manifesto also highlights the gap felt by students between the courses they receive and what they know about the dangers of tomorrow. Changing the world of business, whether from within or without, requires tools for implementing the positive impact we seek. By definition, it is the education system that is supposed to provide these tools. But the education system is in resonance with the professional world, to provide it with workers capable of responding to its problems. Whatever the job, the upcoming environmental transition is so important that any engineer must be trained to at least know what is at stake.

The current assessment of the education we are receiving is that we are not ready to respond effectively to environmental and social issues. What we feel as students in engineering school is that we are being taught "science as usual", without it being put into the context of today's society. Too many students can become specialists in chemistry, molecular biology, computer science, mechanics without having been made aware of the ongoing collapse of bio-diversity, climate crisis, the depletion of water and soils, in twentieth-century fashion. We are not taught the consequences of what we study, which is a fundamental ethical responsibility of an engineer of our time. The teaching of environmental issues should not be decoupled from the rest of the subjects, but, rather, truly integrated into a thought process.

It should be noted, however, that there is an effort on the part of universities to try to meet the demands of students and the needs of companies for training in the concepts of transitions. At the École Polytechnique, for example, under pressure from students, a two-day seminar was set up to raise awareness on sustainable development among all students.

We immediately need a kind of philosophy of education in ecology that would not only allow training but would also integrate a deeper reflection on the stakes of our studies. For example, will the optimization advocated by our engineering studies be sufficient for the challenges of tomorrow? These are questions that we must ask ourselves and that deserve a thoughtful answer. It would certainly help to have addressed these issues earlier. In the same way that we were taught how to recycle in primary school, we should be introduced to environmental issues throughout our education.

At the École Polytechnique, our association tries to reach as many people as possible. In this context, it is not just a question of being the noisy minority, but rather of trying to be the minority that is listened to and that transmits its questions. On the one hand, we try to change behaviours and major events already existing in campus life in order to make people responsible by including them in the reflection. We also try to make people understand the seriousness of the change that is happening by relying on what is the basis of our education: science. We hope that in the future our association will no longer be necessary because newcomers will already have been trained to understand and reflect on these issues. The principle of an external body whose role would only be to deal with ecology would then no longer make sense, and that is to be hoped for.

In the meantime, it is likely that students will increasingly perceive this mismatch between what we know and feel and what is being proposed to us. Students are questioning their situation and this future that is so personal and collective at the same time. Still, crises as decisive moments should not only be seen through the prism of risk, but also understood by their potential as a catalyst. While we are still struggling to grasp the risk of this ecological crisis, we must also, and most urgently, take that radical turn that seems to be the great omission in current discourse.

NOTES

1. In France, higher education is slightly peculiar: in addition to the university system, there's a Grandes Écoles system, accessible through a nationwide entrance test after two years of intensive preparation classes. The Grandes Écoles system is considered a more prestigious route, because it is more difficult to access. École des Mines ParisTech is one of the top Grandes Écoles.
2. Guillaume Lecompte-Boinet (2018), "Les jeunes ingénieurs des Mines se détournent des grandes entreprises", L'Usine nouvelle, 21 April, accessed 1 April 2020 at https://www.usinenouvelle.com/article/les-jeunes-ingenieurs-des-mines -se-detournent-des-grands-entreprises.N683339.
3. Ecological Awakening (2018), "Wake up call on the environment: a student Manifesto", accessed 1 April 2020 at https://manifeste.pour-un-reveil-ecologique .org/en.

28. Ecological aspirations of youth: how higher education could fall between two stools

Alessia Lefébure

Young people believe they have a responsibility to make a better world but do not feel adequately prepared to do so. This is a serious challenge for higher education institutions who want to meet these expectations and keep recruiting – as they often say – the best and the brightest. The ambitions and aspirations of young people are increasingly converging throughout the planet. Surveys and polls have never been as consistent as in 2019. Over the past 18 months, they have been revealing growing concerns for societal issues at large, but most importantly, for the ecological transition, which higher education institutions cannot ignore.

Released in January 2020, an international barometer measured the perceptions of young people about their future and about how prepared and confident they are. Conducted in 20 countries worldwide, the study analyzes the responses of more than 9000 young people aged between 16 and 25. More than 87 percent of the students surveyed believe their generation is responsible for improving the world and 85 percent express worries about the state of the planet. These students clearly say they are worried about the future, climate change and the environment being the major concern for 82 percent of them. Interestingly, climate change has become the second main source of preoccupation, almost as much as poverty and social inequality (84 percent).[1]

In the same year, Amnesty International and Ipsos asked 10 000 people between the ages of 18 and 25 in 22 countries to choose up to five concerns. Climate change was one of the most important issues facing the world for 41 percent of the respondents, becoming the most commonly cited globally, ahead of pollution (36 percent) and terrorism (31 percent).[2]

The ecological concern has a direct impact on the expectations of the graduates towards their future employer. More and more young people are wary of employers and corporates that are not actively involved in the common fight for the ecological and economic transition. Another 2019 survey, conducted a few months earlier among a smaller group of young people in five European countries (2500 individuals, aged 16–25, in France, Germany, Spain, the United Kingdom and Belgium), reveals a number of unusual criteria when choosing the first job. The level of salary, unsurprisingly, is still the main criterion, ahead of work–life balance, equal career progression and a purpose-driven job. Nevertheless, the corporate social responsibility (CSR) of the employer pops up among the five most cited criteria, counting for 11 percent and 12 percent of the young people's responses. In other words, even if not the majority, a growing share of the young European graduates evaluates – today more than yesterday – the CSR commitment of the company before applying for a job.[3]

Country-based enquiries show similar results. According to the latest Boston Consulting Group (BCG)/Conference des Grandes Écoles (CGE)/Ipsos barometer, released in January 2020,[4] students and graduates of French engineering and management schools express a massive disappointment towards the CSR commitment of large companies. Out of 6200 students and alumni of 187 elite schools in France, 62 percent accuse the corporate world of greenwashing. Even though they acknowledge that companies engage more today than ten years ago in CSR, they still consider such engagements motivated by the need to improve their image, not by conviction. This does not prevent them yet from wanting to join these companies for their career, particularly in the two most wanted areas for their first job: environment (76 percent) and energy (62 percent).

Commenting on these results, Anne-Lucie Wack, the president of the CGE, highlights a change in the relation between the young graduates and their future employers. Today's students intend to give meaning to their professional life and make it widely known. "They will not be hired by a company, they will be hired for a company!" she says. In other words, they want – more than their predecessors did – their aspirations to match the values of the company they join. Instead of making them sweet dreamers, their strong concern for the planet makes them more demanding.

What lessons should we learn from these recent surveys? Each of these figures might not seem striking but the convergence of the aspirations and the trends are noteworthy. A whole cohort of talented and well-trained young professionals starts questioning the values and the commitment of their future employer. Moreover, once in the company, the youngest are determined to contribute to a broader goal. In a global context where one student out of four makes the causes they support their main criteria when choosing a job,[5] not only are the employers under increasing scrutiny, they should also align position and reputation with the social and ecological aspirations of the newcomers on the job market.

The alignment between the young graduates and their employers is not always easy when it comes to the environment. The younger generations have clear professional aspirations and values but do not feel prepared to embrace them in terms of the required skills. In some cases, this feeling of unpreparedness builds on what several psychologists define as "eco-anxiety" or "climate anxiety", a recent mental distress that many adolescents and students develop as they become more aware of the state of the environment.[6] Future employers would like to offer jobs matching these aspirations and values but cannot always do so, because – they say – the young graduates are not sufficiently prepared either. The mismatch might lie with the higher education system.

Young people traditionally enroll in higher education for three main reasons: to increase their knowledge, to be prepared for the future, and find a job. The 2020 WISE Global Education Barometer[7] shows that, while young people are globally satisfied with their education (80 percent of the responses), they would like to see improvements in the way they learn the twenty-first-century skills that will make them ready to face their future and the global challenges ahead. Only 43 percent of the surveyed students worldwide feel ready to understand big societal issues and take action in finding solutions.

If the new generation is expecting action and commitment from their future employers, they are also questioning the higher education system in its capacity to prepare them for the challenges of the ecological transition. Youth will have to act and work in a complex and demanding world; they feel unprepared to do so and are now asking both the employers and the higher education institutions to take their share of responsibility and liability.

Confronted with fierce competition for students and declining enrolment (e.g., in the US), the world of higher education faces a multiple and often contradicting challenge: meeting the expectations of the future students and maintaining the trust of the job market concerning its capacity to prepare and equip youth with the skills and competencies of tomorrow, while providing the foundations for critical thinking and for effective citizenship. Several large corporates already offer their own in-house training programs and apprenticeships, expressing at the same time the capacity to complement traditional education and perhaps a kind of mistrust with regard to the capacity of the higher education system to teach the actual skills that they will need in order to contribute to solutions.

The well-documented growing concern of the new generations for climate change and the environment starts to have an impact on the marketing and recruitment campaigns of universities, to the point that the United Nations Environment Programme (UNEP) proposes on its website a toolkit called "Greening Universities".[8] Thanks to this initiative, university managers can find inspiration and resources in order to "develop and implement their own transformative strategies for establishing green, resource-efficient and low carbon campuses".[9]

The leaders of universities have clearly understood the magnitude of the task. Many have taken action to send signals to their two constituents – students and employers – in order to retain the former and to prove their relevance to the latter. Thus far, these actions are mainly public declarations, manifestos, op-eds and charts. The president, usually joined by a few members of the faculty, often personally embodies the commitment of the institution.

As an illustration of this kind of institutional commitment, in the aftermath of the Paris COP21, under the leadership of Columbia University Mailman School of Public Health, 115 schools of public health and schools of medicine from all continents decided to launch a common initiative, aiming at educating tomorrow's health and public health professionals on the health impacts of climate change. In 2017, they officially joined a Global Consortium on Climate and Health Education (GCCHE), sharing the same "imperative for quick action on many fronts: to recognize and respond to climate-health threats; prevent climate change at its source by reducing heat-trapping greenhouse gas emissions; support 'greener' systems throughout the economy, including healthcare; understand the health co-benefits of adaptation and mitigation; and communicate effectively about these issues".[10] The presidents of these health profession schools acknowledge that climate and health as a topic is underrepresented in the curricula. They agree on the need for further development of the knowledge and the skills of all the future professionals in this area throughout the world, so that they can act, prevent, reduce and respond to the health impacts of climate change. The consortium operates as a resource provider, a space for exchange of practices and information, a facilitator for partnerships, an advocate for spreading the commitment out to other schools. In the absence of any outcome report and data, it is difficult to evaluate its real capacity to produce any significant change in terms of course development and increase in the quality and quantity of teaching devoted to the ecological transition in the health professionals' core curriculum.

Similar initiatives have been flourishing in different regions of the world over the past months, suggesting at least a growing awareness among the university leaders. In the UK, for example, the 24 leading universities composing the Russell Group publicly declared in December 2019 their commitment to "tackling climate change through research, teaching and more sustainable practices". In their joint statement, these universities clearly position themselves as major players in the search for solutions to the common energy and climate challenges, thus fully endorsing their responsibility. Following Columbia Mailman's path, the Russell Group universities created an Environmental Sustainability Network in order to "learn from each other, boost efforts to cut waste, increase recycling", and reduce CO_2 emissions on campus. Their declaration speaks directly to students and openly addresses the questions of the aspirations of the future generations: "Though we do not yet have all the answers, we are striving to empower existing and future generations with the knowledge and confidence to protect our planet, as we each work towards reducing our own impact on the world around us". Each of the statement's words seems to be a direct answer to the questioning that all the barometers are highlighting: "As educators responsible…we aspire to give every student the opportunity to become environmentally literate… We provide all our undergraduates and postgraduates with the opportunity to build environmental sustainability into their wider student experience".[11] Surprisingly enough, the declaration does not push the ambition further, as it does not mention the need to build environmental sustainability into students' *future professional life.* Nevertheless, throughout the statement, the message of these universities to the various stakeholders is clear, and it is about the commitment to take action, to contribute to the transition through research, education and through an ecological behavior.

In France too, higher education leaders are becoming vocal about their determination to introduce more teaching related to climate and environment. In September 2019, the press released declarations signed by presidents of universities and elite schools of the country, joined by thousands of faculty members, scholars and ordinary citizens.[12] They call to be able to train all higher education students in climate and ecological issues and they ask the government to devote additional financial resources to this goal. The vast majority of presidents and deans of French higher education institutions – including the deans of several civil service schools, in charge of the training of the French high civil servants – seem to be willing to "position the climate as the primary emergency" and to engage their communities in a massive, rapid and efficient transformation. They mention three levels of action: support the students with the necessary encouragements, knowledge and skills so that they can be massively involved in ecological, economic and societal transforma-tions; train all the staff; and introduce responsible practices into the operation of the campus and student life.[13]

As in the previous initiatives, it is hard to evaluate the effectiveness of these claims and their capacity to produce concrete changes in the curriculum and in the teaching practice of the French higher education institutions. Yet, the introduction of climate- and energy-related courses in the fundamental core curriculum of all the students, no matter the field of specialization, is a crucial issue. Indeed, the current top management and leadership – private and public sector alike – is not sufficiently aware of the nature and the extent of the climate and energy challenges to take the right decisions. Responding to the climate challenge requires new training for all managers and public officials, and the introduction of climate and ecological concern in all public policies and corporate strategies.[14]

Actually, in spite of the massive engagement of their presidents, higher education institutions are slow in responding to the needs of the ecological transition, often decoupling their narrative and their practice. Given the complexity of the nature of the challenges, the amplitude of the shift, the degree of uncertainty and the planetary scale of interconnection, universities must undertake a profound rethinking of the current curricula and teaching methods. Preparing the future generation to understand the situation, to evaluate the impact of their decision, to act in a timely way, and to find solutions, is an ambitious goal. Universities and schools are unprepared for this difficult task and their traditional research organization, based on departments and disciplines, is obsolete and ineffective in the new context.

A 2019 survey conducted by the International Association of Universities (IAU) gives a state-of-the-art overview of the current engagement of the higher education community around the world on the Sustainable Development Goals (SDGs). In comparison with the results of the first survey of 2016, the universities' commitment is growing and often leads to including sustainable development in their strategic plans. More than half of them declare they allocate a specific budget to sustainable initiatives and projects. Nonetheless, the survey points out a number of difficulties that prevent deeper transformation and the incorporation of sustainable development into every activity: the lack of funding, the lack of staff, and the lack of training opportunities. If the majority of universities (65 percent) offer a growing number of sustainability-focused courses, these courses are usually specialized – belonging to STEM (science, technology, engineering, and mathematics) – and not widely known on campus. Trans- and inter-disciplinary approaches are rare and holistic perspectives seem challenging to implement. Several respondents explicitly mentioned "the lack of reward or gratification mechanisms for transdisciplinary courses" among the difficulties.[15]

In France, the situation is no better than elsewhere. As three students of the École Polytechnique point out, their school, like many others, "mainly trains specialists who know nothing about sustainable development, or environmental specialists who know nothing of other sectors. These typical profiles are not up to the challenge. And those who have chosen the right optional courses are far too few".[16] At the country level, only very few teaching programs (11 percent) offer mandatory courses related to the energy and climate challenges, according to a report published in March 2019 on higher education and climate.[17] Based on an extensive analysis of a sample of 34 higher education institutions in France and 140 interviews, the authors' findings reveal three kinds of inequalities in terms of access to a thorough education on climate issues. Engineering schools offer more courses than business schools and, even in universities, students enrolled in engineering and STEM programs have more climate-related courses than those in other fields. Finally, these courses are usually offered at the graduate and postgraduate level, almost never at the undergraduate level.

The multidisciplinary dimension of the ecological transition – mobilizing knowledge from geography to biology, from philosophy to economics through earth sciences – adds an extra obstacle to the necessary adaptation of higher education and generates various forms of resistance at all levels. As the French intellectual Edgar Morin would say, "Our cognitive structure which, within our civilization, separates the human (individual and society) from the natural biological and physical, is a major hurdle for ecological awareness".[18] Indeed, a core curriculum course, common to all teaching programs and across disciplines, is much more difficult to achieve than any specialized teaching program within the department of earth and environmental sciences. Yet, what is expected from higher education institutions is the capacity and the promise to train all students and all future professionals, not only those who will work in the energy and environment field, to be able to navigate the complexity. Only a strong demand from future students will accelerate these curricula changes, as long as these students are consistent to their values once in the job and know how to respond to the contradictions they will face in their professional life.

NOTES

1. Ipsos (2020), "The WISE Global Education Barometer 2020: youth perceptions on their education and their future", 30 January, accessed 26 August 2020 at https://www.ipsos.com/en/wise-global-education-barometer-2020.
2. Amnesty International (2019), "Climate change ranks highest as vital issue of our time – Generation Z survey", 10 December, accessed 26 August 2020 at https://www.amnesty.org/en/latest/news/2019/12/climate-change-ranks-highest-as-vital-issue-of-our-time/.
3. WISE, Ipsos and JobTeaser (2019), "Preparing the new generation for the future of work: a survey of European youth, employers and education actors", February, accessed 26 August 2020 at https://www.ipsos.com/sites/default/files/ct/news/documents/2019-02/wiseparis_etude_en_web_v2.pdf.
4. BCG, CGE and Ipsos (2020), *Baromètre "Talents: ce qu'ils attendent de leur employ"*, accessed 26 August 2020 at https://image-src.bcg.com/Images/Etude-BCG-CGE-IPSOS_tcm9-237878.pdf.
5. WISE, Ipsos and JobTeaser (2019), in note 3.
6. Anna Kelly (2017), "Eco-anxiety at university: student experiences and academic perspectives on cultivating healthy emotional responses to the climate crisis", *Independent Study Project (ISP) Collection*, No. 2642, accessed 26 August 2020 at https://digitalcollections.sit.edu/isp_collection/2642.
7. WISE (2020), "WISE Global Education Barometer – youth perceptions on their education and their future", accessed 26 August 2020 at https://www.wise-qatar.org/wise-global-education-barometer-2020/.
8. UNEP (2013), *Greening Universities Toolkit: Transforming Universities into Green and Sustainable Campuses: A Toolkit for Implementers*, accessed 26 August

2020 at https://www.unenvironment.org/resources/report/greening-universities
-toolkit-transforming-universities-green-and-sustainable.

9. Ibid.

10. The Earth Institute, Columbia University (2017–18), "Global Consortium on
    Climate and Health Education", Earth Institute Research Projects, accessed 26
    August 2020 at https://www.earth.columbia.edu/projects/view/863.

11. Russell Group (2019), "Joint statement on environmental sustainability", 9
    December, accessed 26 August 2020 at https://russellgroup.ac.uk/news/russell
    -group-publishes-joint-statement-on-environmental-sustainability/.

12. *Le Journal du Dimanche* (2019), "'Formons tous les étudiants aux enjeux clima-
    tiques': l'appel de 80 dirigeants d'établissements", 14 September, accessed 26
    August 2020 at https://www.lejdd.fr/Societe/exclusif-formons-tous-les-etudiants
    -aux-enjeux-climatiques-lappel-de-80-dirigeants-detablissements-3919612.

13. *Le Monde* (2019), "Les universités et grandes écoles doivent intégrer l'urgence
    climatique dans leur stratégie", 19 September, accessed 26 August 2020 at http://
    www.cpu.fr/actualite/les-universites-et-grandes-ecoles-doivent-integrer-lurgence
    -climatique-dans-leur-strategie/.

14. *Le Monde* (2019), "Répondre au défi climatique nécessite de former l'en-
    semble des agents publics", 4 December, accessed 26 August 2020 at https://
    www.lemonde.fr/idees/article/2019/12/03/repondre-au-defi-climatique-necessite
    -de-former-l-ensemble-des-agents-publics_6021502_3232.html?utm_medium=
    Social&utm_source=Twitter#Echobox=1575402722.

15. Stefanie Mallow, Isabel Toman and Hilligje van't Land (2020), *Higher Education
    and the 2030 Agenda: Moving into the "Decade of Action and Delivery for the
    SDGs": IAU 2nd Global Survey Report on Higher Education and Research for
    Sustainable Development*, accessed 26 August 2020 at https://www.iau-aiu.net/
    IMG/pdf/iau_hesd_survey_report_final_jan2020.pdf.

16. La Jaune & La Rouge (2020), "Les élèves de l'école interpellent le système",
    Magazine, No. 751, January, accessed 26 August 2020 at https://www
    .lajauneetlarouge.com/les-eleves-de-lecole-interpellent-le-systeme/.

17. The Shift Project (2019), *Mobiliser l'Enseignement Supérieur pour le Climat*,
    March, accessed 26 August 2020 at https://theshiftproject.org/wp-content/uploads/
    2019/04/Rapport_ClimatSup_TheShiftProject-2019.pdf.

18. Edgar Morin (2020), "En finir avec les malheurs de l'écologie", *Libération*, 2
    February, accessed 26 August 2020 at https://www.liberation.fr/debats/2020/02/
    02/en-finir-avec-les-malheurs-de-l-ecologie_1776814.

PART V

Entrepreneurs

29. Introduction to Part V

Nicholas Stern and Charlotte Taylor

Our lives and livelihoods face profound threats from unmanaged or badly managed climate change; for many they are existential. The science is clear that the potential magnitude of the risks we face is immense and that we must act with great urgency and across the whole economy. The next two decades will be decisive for climate change. If we delay, the consequences could be devastating and many of the changes will be irreversible.

Our current paths of growth and development are unsustainable. Yet we also have in our hands an immense opportunity: we can now see how to embark on a path of strong, sustainable, resilient and inclusive growth that could both drive and be driven by the transition to the zero-carbon economy.

There is real momentum as countries, sectors and technologies change, but we are not moving anywhere near fast enough. Essential to the acceleration we need is the power of ideas and the forces of entrepreneurship. Private individuals and enterprises are a crucial source of initiative and creativity. They generate new ideas, show what is possible and can inspire. The policies and institutions within which they work are vital to their incentives and their ability to achieve.

This part of the book brings these dynamics to life. Their coming together also provides us with an opportunity to identify the common threads, both in terms of the underpinnings of success and the barriers hindering progress, that can help us understand how their potential contributions can be fostered. Their differences too help us understand how creativity can bloom or be discouraged. The examples cover an extraordinary range and all are in areas of activity of particular relevance to the major challenges of managing climate change and other fundamental environmental issues. They range from rural electricity to urban transport, from drip irrigation to mangroves, from managing migration to managing a transition from mining, and from changing an oil and natural gas company to a wind company, to changing a company from chemicals to biodegradable plastics. They demonstrate in an inspiring way what can be achieved. In this short introduction, we highlight just a few of the cases to illustrate their range and creativity.

Responding to the climate and biodiversity crises in a manner commensurate to the challenges will entail many large-scale changes: our future must be very different from our past. Steering, encouraging and managing the necessary transitions will require strong leadership – the kind of leadership exhibited by Mayor Jean François Caron in transforming Loos-en-Gohelle from a mining town into a model of sustainability; or that displayed by chemical scientist Catia Bastioli in growing the company Novamont into a leader in the new market of biodegradable bioplastics.

The examples of effective entrepreneurship with real impact conveyed in this chapter also demonstrate the multiple levels at which strong leadership will be necessary – from grassroots actors, like the trailblazing Iranian farmer who was an early adopter of water-saving drip irrigation, through to multinational companies, like wind power developer Oersted. In stark contrast to his neighbouring farmers and the dam-building engineering firms across Iran, whose disregard for the country's continuing drought has served only to accelerate the encroachment of actual desertification, the lone Iranian farmer is now the only one of his peers who can survive on today's meagre water supplies. He is reaping the rewards of the far-sighted investment he made in a relatively expensive drip irrigation system years ago. This farmer epitomizes important characteristics required from all leaders at the heart of the zero-carbon transition: enlightened vision, strength of conviction, purposeful action. At the other end of the scale, Oersted serves customers in Denmark, Germany, the Netherlands, the UK, Taiwan and the US East Coast, with its 7.5 GW offshore wind power capacity, which equates to around one-quarter of the world's total. But it is not long ago that Oersted existed as Denmark's government-owned oil and gas company, DONG. The company's transformation depended on a decisive push made in 2008 by then CEO (2001–12) Anders Eldrup, in what was, again, an act of strong leadership.

Innovative ideas and actors can arise in response to the specificities of local conditions and local problems. A clear example is Husk Power Systems, where local resources – an abundance of underutilized rice husks and untapped human potential – are being combined to tackle a local problem: very low access to electricity. Similarly, Mangroves for the Future (MFF), an organization that now has projects across South and Southeast Asia, arose from the observations and analyses made by Amat Samsuri in his local district of Probolinggo, East Java. Having spent his childhood in a coastal village, Samsuri's personal experiences led him to recognize the many services provided by mangroves. These include locations for fish breeding, protection from storm surges, and the flourishing of wildlife and biodiversity, in some cases with tourism potential, as well as carbon capture. What began as small-scale experimentation with mangrove cultivation expanded into a venture supported by MFF, which now has around 400 coastal ecosystem projects aimed at mangrove forests, restoration and resilience building.

Collaboration emerges as an important means to facilitate and accelerate the proliferation of new ideas. This is being leveraged by Slow Food, in their development of the Terra Madre network. The international reach of Slow Food's network, alongside its ability to attract media and political attention, underpins the very purpose of the Terra Madre network. The idea is to gather and share knowledge, ideas and experiences so as to promote a system of good, clean and fair food. Collaboration is also the foundational principle bringing together a coalition of companies aiming to drive change in the business models of the agrifood industry. The coalition will begin by meeting at the 2021 UN Convention on Biological Diversity to devise a set of performance indicators, which they expect will aid efforts to rediversify product portfolios, as well as the raw materials they source from.

However, regardless of their ingenuity, even the very best ideas will have to overcome barriers to implementation. These studies highlight a range of such obstructions, from psychological barriers to individual action, to political barriers in agroecological innovation. In some cases, solutions already prevail – the innovative electric urban transport services that are changing the habits and preferences of millions of people in Southeast Asian cities, for example. While in other cases, recognizing the obstacle to be overcome, like the market forces working in opposition to the deployment of carbon capture and storage (CCS) technologies, or identifying advances that need to be made, like increasing the energy storage capacity of supercapacitors to allow for them to replace batteries in electric vehicles, is a valuable first step.

We also see that the social and political context matters greatly. Embedding the introduction of solar cookstoves within a wider 'sociosystem' is recognized as a critical component of successful programmes across the world. In the refugee camps of Chad, Uganda and Nepal, a well-considered strategy for solar cookstove introduction has allowed for the full potential of this transformative technology to be realized, whereas the same cannot be said for refugee camps in Burkina Faso and India. The circular nature of the relationship between cooking technologies and social issues, including education and livelihoods, means that the appropriateness of a given technology is strongly influenced by the social and cultural context. It follows that the success of any programme to introduce a new technology hinges critically on the tailoring of its approach to these aspects of the receiving community. At the other end of the market, Elon Musk's Tesla is pursuing an innovative business strategy that exploits a social aspect of the wider context. The first Tesla models – the Tesla Roadster and the Tesla Model S – were targeted at buyers for whom the novelty and environmental friendliness of an electric vehicle exerts more influence than does price sensitivity. The proceeds of these ventures can then be used to fund mass-market vehicles, such as the Model 3 and Model Y.

Nevertheless, even proven solutions can fall foul to political opposition, as exemplified by the collapse of the Riace experiment under the anti-immigration legislation imposed by the Salvini-dominated Italian government. Riace, in Southern Italy, had been left in a state of abandonment and disrepair following an outflow of people in the mid-twentieth century. That was, until Mayor Mimmo Lucano began to actively support the settlement of migrants and refugees in the small municipality, reviving the local culture through cross-fertilization. However, Lucano met strong opposition, in particular from a Salvini-dominated government, which was anti-immigration to the extent that it introduced legislation making the favouring of illegal immigration a criminal offence. Eventually, the government's removal of financial provisions to Riace created conditions that forced many resettled migrants to leave for other destinations. Managing migration will be an important element in managing climate change and this experience carries both positive and negative lessons.

The entrepreneurship shown in these examples provides a case for optimism. It demonstrates that individuals and communities can recognize the dangers we face and the destruction we can cause if incentives are distorted, perspectives are narrow, and horizons are short. And individuals and teams can act as creative entrepreneurs in finding different ways of doing things, which are cleaner, more productive and more far-sighted. They show that change really is possible and the future that it can foster would be profoundly attractive. Yet, the examples are also frustrating in that, notwithstanding the extraordinary creativity they demonstrate, we have not yet as a world been able to unleash a response on the scale and urgency we need. However, a precondition to successful action is to recognize the problem and to demonstrate that there really are effective responses. In that, the entrepreneurs have been outstanding leaders.

30. Catching mighty North Sea winds

Claude Henry

DONG is the acronym for Danish Oil and Natural Gas, a company created in 1972 for managing oil and gas resources from the North Sea Danish sector, and for producing and distributing electricity as a utility owned by the Danish government. Incidentally, it developed and constructed in 1991 the first offshore wind farm in the world, near Vindeby, off the coast of Lolland Island, South Denmark. The turbines were devised and produced by Siemens (Germany). They were a major innovation at the time. Today, they look like dwarfs compared to the Siemens 10.0-193 turbines developed for the Hornsea Project (UK), planned for completion in 2022 off the Yorkshire coast: rotor diameter: 193 m vs 35 m; power capacity: 10 MW vs 0.45 MW. As recently as 2014, the UK government guaranteed £150 per MWh to get three more wind farms built off the British coast; at Hornsea, the cost per MWh of energy will be of the order of €70, and less for later stages of the project.

The march from Vindeby to Hornsea took a major turn in 2008, when Anders Eldrup (DONG CEO 2001–12) made a decisive push towards transforming DONG into the world leader in offshore wind farms. The metamorphosis was completed in 2017 with the sale of DONG's oil and gas business to INEOS, a UK chemical company. DONG was renamed Oersted, after the Danish scientist Hans Christian Oersted, who in 1820 discovered that an electric current through a wire could move a nearby magnet. In this way he started a new branch of physics, electromagnetism, which plays a crucial role in the functioning of wind turbines. The Danish government is no longer the sole owner of the company; however, it still owns 50.1 percent of the capital. In 2020, Oersted has a total power capacity of 7.5 GW (about a quarter of the world total), serving customers in Denmark, Germany, the Netherlands, the UK, Taiwan and on the US East Coast.

Oersted has actively contributed to spurring the technological advances that led to spectacular reductions in the costs of producing electricity from offshore wind farms, mainly by placing massive orders (up to 500 turbines at a time) with their two main providers, Siemens and Vestas (Denmark), sometimes in anticipation of their needs. Such policy strongly motivated Siemens and Vestas to massively invest in R&D, resulting in size and power increases, and also in improved reliability, as exemplified by Siemens "High Wind Ride Through" system that precludes a sudden shutdown of a turbine when the speed of the wind passes a 25 m/s threshold, above which the integrity of the machine is under threat without this system. Oersted has also enhanced its own operations, in particular with regard to the ways the foundations of the turbines are laid out in the sea (even floating turbines are now seriously considered), and as regards management routines.

Although increasingly burning wood pellets and household refuse in its thermal power plants, Oersted will not completely phase out coal before 2023. Nevertheless, according to Harries and Annex (2018), from Bloomberg NEF: "Not only has Oersted gone green, it has also seen increased earnings".

The University of Southern California (USC), in Los Angeles, is not next door to the headquarters Oersted has inherited from DONG in Fredericia, Denmark. However, a similar big idea is floating within both places. The late George Olah, founder of USC Loker Hydrocarbon Research Institute and one of the most famous twentieth-century chemists, along with two colleagues:

> proposed and developed a feasible anthropogenic chemical recycling of carbon dioxide [that can] be converted by feasible chemical transformations into liquid fuels such as methanol, dimethyl ether… This concept of broad scope and framework is the basis of what we call the Methanol Economy. The required energy for the synthetic carbon cycle can come from any alternative energy source such as solar, wind, geothermal, and even hopefully safe nuclear energy. (Olah, Surya Prakash and Goeppert, 2011)

This way of storing CO_2 would not reduce the amount in the atmosphere, but it would at least close the open carbon cycle associated with the burning of gasoline made from fossil oil. Anders Eldrup had not heard of Olah et al. However, he came to concur with them. During winter 2009–10, the Danish wind farms produced such an excess of electricity, which had to be evacuated through the interconnectors to Norway and Sweden, that the price became negative. With the multiplication of offshore wind farms in Danish waters and elsewhere, it is anticipated that imbalances between production and consumption of electricity might result in negative prices for an increasing number of hours/year. Anders Eldrup came to the view that, rather than incur losses on excess electricity, it should be used to produce hydrogen. Similar conditions will prevail in the USA, in Texas and Midwestern states, as wind farms are multiplied. Then, with hydrogen and CO_2 at hand, it is not difficult to produce methanol, which would in this way also prove a means of recovering electricity in excess, hence dealing with the intermittency and volatility of renewables.

On October 19, 2019, in Copenhagen, Fatih Birol, International Energy Agency (IEA) Executive Director, launched an IEA special report on offshore wind (IEA, 2019a). While praising Denmark, and more generally Europe, for pioneering the technology's development, he also stressed the major role that

China and the US are "set to play in offshore wind's long-term growth". He concluded: "In the past decade, two major areas of technological innovation have been game-changers in the energy system by substantially driving down costs: the shale revolution and the rise of solar PV. And offshore wind has the potential to join their ranks in terms of steep cost reduction" (IEA, 2019b).

REFERENCES

Harries, T. and M. Annex (2018), "Oersted's profitable transformation from oil, gas and coal to renewables", *Bloomberg NEF*, December 12.

International Energy Agency (IEA) (2019a), *Offshore Wind Outlook 2019: World Energy Outlook Special Report*, October 25.

International Energy Agency (IEA) (2019b), "Offshore wind to become a $1 trillion industry", October 25 [press release], accessed August 17, 2020 at https://www.iea.org/news/offshore-wind-to-become-a-1-trillion-industry.

Olah, G.A., G.K. Surya Prakash and A. Goeppert (2011), "Anthropogenic chemical carbon cycle for a sustainable future", *Journal of the American Chemical Society*, **133** (33), 12881–98.

31. Providing electricity from rice husk in rural India

Claude Henry

In 2007, an Indian engineer, Gyanesh Pandey, who had graduated in electrical engineering from Rensselaer Polytechnic Institute (Troy, NY), and who at the time had a good job in Los Angeles, decided to head back to his native Bihar. Bihar is mostly rural and is one of the poorest states in the Indian Federation. More than 80 percent of households there are deprived of access to electricity, a proportion that both reveals and breeds poverty. Those who can afford them use inconvenient and costly kerosene lamps that generate indoor pollution; diesel generators, also polluting and costly, are used to pump water for irrigation and sustain artisanal and commercial activities.

Pandey himself doesn't come from a well-off family, and as a child he suffered from a lack of proper lighting. By 2007, he was determined to try to muster his technical skills to remedy the situation in his home state. After a few unconvincing attempts with solar cells and biofuels, he came upon the idea of using rice husk to generate electricity. He teamed up with a local entrepreneur and with two Indian graduates from Virginia University's Darden School of Business, one of them the current CEO, Manoj Sinha, and Husk Power Systems was started in 2009.

In Bihar, rice is the dominant crop; husk, that is, the envelope of the rice grains, is thus abundant. It is good neither for burning in stoves (because of its very high silica content) nor for returning nutrients to the soil (because of its low nutrient content). However, it can be decomposed by fermentation in a gasifier. Because it had very few uses, 75–80 percent of the 2 million tons obtained each year, as a by-product of the rice crop, was rotting in landfills. The resource is thus plentiful, and its use as a precursor of fuel doesn't harm any other activity.

At Husk Power Systems, small, simple gasifiers are fed with husk. The gas is then burnt to drive a turbine, from which electricity is produced in a standard way. Typically, a 30–40 kW plant consumes 50 kg of husk per hour. The components, from which these mini power plants are made, are not tailor-made; they are bought in such conditions that costs are minimized; however, their arrangement into specific equipment is innovative, with its quest for simplicity and efficiency in using an unusual fuel.

Typically, the investment cost is about $1300 per kW, partially paid for by consumers and partially by modest grants from the Indian federal government, the International Finance Corporation and foundations like the Shell Foundation and the Alstom Foundation. The variable cost is about $0.15 per kWh and is covered by consumers in return for the delivery of enough electricity for one or two low-consumption bulbs and mobile phone recharges; what consumers pay is about half the cost of running a kerosene lamp. Electricity is distributed through local mini networks, that is, simple wiring of a few villages up to 300–500 households in total. For them, it becomes possible to extend home activities, in particular student work, beyond daylight hours. For artisanal and commercial activities, it represents a less polluting, more convenient and cheaper source of energy, making them more productive. Each local network enables a saving of about 40.000 L of kerosene and 18.000 L of diesel per year.

At the "Husk Power University" (more accurately, a "Technical School"), most students are recruited locally. They are trained either as "plant's junior mechanic" – with the perspective of being put in charge of operation and maintenance of a single plant (an eight-week course) – or "senior mechanic" and middle manager for a number of plants, with the ability to face more intricate problems than those dealt with at plant level (a six-month course).

Husk Power Systems is more than a technical innovation, however valuable it is in this respect. It integrates, into the economic life of the communities involved, a local, abundant and underutilized raw resource. It also promotes local talent. And, providing an essential service, it transforms the economic, social and health conditions of the communities it serves.

Within four years, about 80 plants and networks have been set up with cumulative improvements in service and costs. The pace of development is accelerating and inroads have been made into a neighboring state, Uttar Pradesh, as well as in East Africa; there is also interest in Bangladesh. The main lesson of the endeavor is about how to create a system providing an essential service, adapted to the needs of poor people, out of the material and labor resources that are readily available locally.

32. Heat pumps for decarbonizing buildings

Dominique Bureau

Buildings are responsible for more than a third of CO_2 emissions in the European Union or North America. Heating systems and water heaters mainly contribute to direct and indirect emissions of the sector as long as they rely on fossil fuel combustion.

Several ways are available to cut down these emissions. They are more or less cost effective depending on the context. In the first place, energy efficiency of buildings is an important issue. Most of the building stock being inefficient, its renovation is a critical element of the clean energy transition in developed countries. However, while raising thermal standards is quite easy for new buildings, refurbishing existing buildings is more difficult. Then, another lever is the switch to fuels that emit less CO_2 – coal or fuel oil to gas boilers, for example. With this approach, heat flows still follow the spontaneous direction of heat transfers, from the warmer to the colder environment.

Heat pumps move energy in the opposite direction. They draw heat from a colder spot than the building to be heated. The physical functioning is similar to that of a refrigerator. Their underlying principles were established in the nineteenth century by Nicolas Léonard Sadi Carnot and William Thomson (later Lord Kelvin). In particular, the second law of thermodynamics says that transferring energy in this direction needs additional external power. Hence, one may wonder why this is an energy-efficient solution for decarbonizing buildings.

The main reason is that most of the energy used in the heat pump cycle is coming from the external environment, air, water or ground. This energy is free, renewable, and does not contribute to global warming. Only the additional energy necessary to run the device involves direct and environmental costs.

Engineers measure the efficiency of heating systems by their coefficient of performance (COP), that is, the ratio between transferred energy and consumed energy for running electrically powered heat pumps. This ratio is equal to 1 for a conventional electrical resistance heater. It reaches 3–4 for heat pumps. Compared to a standard heating system using fossil fuel combustion, heat pumps thereby allow reductions in energy consumption in the range 65–75 per cent. Moreover, in countries where electricity is mostly decarbonized, they reduce CO_2 emissions by 90–100 per cent. Achieving such performances has required a lot of innovations, some of them quite recent.

If the principles of heat pumps are the same as those of refrigerators, the obstacles to be removed to obtain competitive systems are not small. Flows of energy are higher and the factors that affect the COP, such as weak temperature difference between sources, need optimization, the results of which depend on the context and resources availability.

Typically, tapping the atmosphere is simpler but higher performances are obtained with water or ground heat. Indeed, pioneering installations from the 1990s were using water. But access to lakes and rivers is limited, hence is generally not an option for the residential market.

Reversibility of (mostly air–air) heat pumps increases their value by providing two alternative services: air heating and air conditioning. In regions where both heat in winter and cooling in summer are necessary, reversible heat pumps can play a significant role in total final energy consumption. Thus, some further explanation on reversibility seems warranted here.

In both cases, heating and cooling, the heat pump thermodynamic cycle is the same: thanks to the working coolant fluid used, the source of heat is at a lower temperature than the sink of heat. The difference is that for a heating service, the heat source is outdoor and the heat sink indoor (place to be heated), while for a cooling service, the heat source is indoor (place to be cooled, inside the home as inside a refrigerator) and the heat sink outdoor. It is the same second law of thermodynamics behind both services, in terms of thermodynamic work to be supplied (mostly by electricity) compared to heat transfers from the hot source.

Since investment costs for heat pumps are higher than for conventional heating systems, improving efficiency and reducing capital expenditures remain the two key factors for enhanced deployment. As mentioned above, heat pump technology has been in constant evolution for 40 years, with many developments. They benefited from spillovers from technologies in air conditioning. Incremental innovation has also been recurrent in all segments of the heat pump industry, characterized by numerous international manufacturers and suppliers. Among the main players are: Daïkin, Mitsubishi Electric and Panasonic from Japan; Midea, Haier and Gree from China; Atlantic, NIBE, BDR Thermea, Ingersoll Rand, Viessmann, Stiebel Eltron, Vaillant from Europe; United Technologies-Carrier from the US, and so on.[1] The average COP, in standardized conditions, for aerothermal heat pumps on the French new residential market went from 3 in 1997 to 4.2 in 2015.[2]

Breakthroughs were obtained both at lab and firm levels:

- in the 1980s and 1990s: heating curve regulation, heat pump compressor with variable speed, electronic expansion valves;
- in the 2000s: compactness of heat exchangers, vapor injection;
- over the last decade: auto-diagnosis, real-time metering, better predictions, refrigerant fluids with lower global warming potential through greenhouse impact in (rarer) cases of leakage (hydrofluoroolefins, propane, CO_2 and mixed), recovery of heat from garbage.

Expected in the next few years:

- self-settings and self-regulation for better use and increased performance;
- expanded skilled workforce for installation and maintenance, allowing for better availability of equipment and longer lifespan;
- coupling with heat storage associated with solar thermal or solar PV.

While air-source technologies have been historically dominant and ground-source technologies have been largely developed over the last decade, more recent developments are worth mentioning:

- hybrid heat pumps that include fossil fuel heating as a back-up in case of extreme low temperatures (that can lower heat pump performance);
- heat pumps dedicated to water heating uses (cleaning and cooking);
- higher temperature applications (temperature can reach 80°C in residential applications).

At the same time, total investment costs (equipment + installation) have been trimmed, by about 25 per cent since 2010 for air-source technologies. Installation costs count for 20 per cent for aerothermal pumps but for 30–50 per cent for geothermal ones. Efficiency and quality of service provided by the firms involved are thus crucial for the growth of the markets.

The dynamics of future deployment of these technologies will depend both on public policies and market efficiency. Public policies have been devised and implemented in many countries to reduce by wide margins the levels of energy consumption in buildings and to promote renewable sources of energy. Although not specifically targeted at heat pumps, all these policies have had a major impact on the market even when oil price decreases pushed in the opposite direction. One in two single-family houses has been equipped with a heat pump in France since 2014. In 2019, the market for renovation overtook the market for new buildings.

In Europe, the market has also been expanding over the last decade, from 734 000 sales in 2009 to 1 300 000 in 2018 (21 countries). According to the European Heat Pump Association (EHPA), heat pumps sold in 2018 contrib-

uted to 68 228 jobs, 128 TWh of renewable energy produced by the heat pump
stock, 32.98 Mt of greenhouse gas emissions avoided and 164 TWh of final
energy saved.

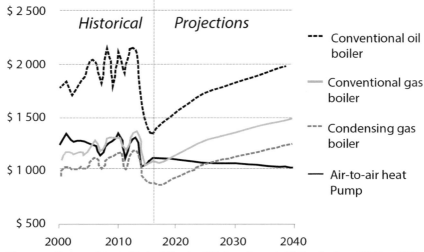

Note: Data consistent with the following IEA hypotheses in 2040: oil price at USD_{2017} 112/
barrel, natural gas at USD_{2017} 9/MBtu, CO_2 price at USD_{2017} 43/ton.
Source: IEA (2018), Figure 9.9.

*Figure 32.1   Annualized household heating costs (Europe):
                  competitiveness of electric space heating*

While heat pumps have existed for decades, recent history has witnessed
significant technological innovations. And further performance improvements
and cost decreases are possible to reduce the overall costs of the use of this type
of equipment by households and increase their competitiveness (Figure 32.1).
As a result, it is no wonder that heat pumps can become a major technology for
heating (and cooling too, notably as global warming implies hotter summers)
in future scenarios featuring climate policies, and a key enabler for building
decarbonization, based on decarbonized electricity. In the International Energy
Agency (IEA) "2 Degrees" scenario (2DS), the worldwide share of heat pump
equipment in buildings in 2050 is thrice its share in 2014. In the "Beyond 2
Degrees" scenario (B2DS), this share reaches 43 per cent of all space and
water heating equipment (Figure 32.2).

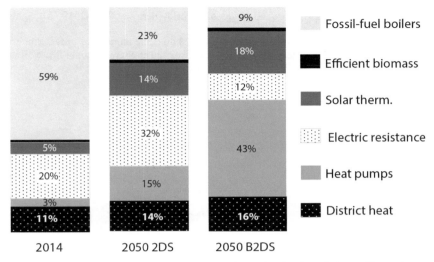

			Fossil-fuel boilers
			Efficient biomass
			Solar therm.
			Electric resistance
			Heat pumps
			District heat

2014 | 2050 2DS | 2050 B2DS

Note: Heating in buildings represents space and water heating; it excludes cooking and other end uses. Efficient gas technologies include gas condensing boilers, gas instantaneous equipment and gas heat pumps. Traditional use of solid biomass is not included.
Source: Author's figure based on IEA (2017)

Figure 32.2   Evolution of space and water heating equipment shares in buildings in IEA Energy Technology Perspectives 2017 global scenarios

NOTES

1. In 2018, the global market size was USD58.6 billion with an estimated compound annual growth rate of 8.5 per cent from 2019 to 2025. More than 75 per cent of the market is for residential applications; the remaining for both industrial and commercial applications (Grand View Research, 2020).
2. See Uniclima (2020), with similar results at the global level.

REFERENCES

European Heat Pump Association (EHPA) (2019), "Market data", accessed 17 August 2020 at www.ehpa.org/market-data/.
Grand View Research (2019), "Heat pump market size, share & trends analysis report by technology", accessed August 17, 2020 at https://www.grandviewresearch.com/industry-analysis/heat-pump-market.
International Energy Agency (IEA) (2017), *Energy Technology Perspectives 2017*, accessed 17 August 2020 at https://webstore.iea.org/download/direct/1058. All rights reserved.

International Energy Agency (IEA) (2018), *World Energy Outlook 2019*, accessed 17 August 2020 at https://www.iea.org/reports/world-energy-outlook-2019. All rights reserved.
Uniclima (2020), "Bilan 2019 et perspectives 2020 du génie climatique", press conference, Paris, 11–17 February, accessed 17 August 2020 at www.uniclima.fr/userfiles/Doc/presse/2020_02_04_DP_UNICLIMA_RESULTATS.pdf.

33. The rise of supercapacitors: making electric vehicles as convenient as ordinary ones

Claude Henry

Harold Kroto, at the University of Sussex, UK, had discovered chain-like carbon molecules in interstellar gas clouds. Would it be possible to vaporize carbon on Earth to produce similar molecules and find out what they are exactly made of? To try to answer this question, Kroto headed to Rice University (Houston, Texas), where Robert Curl and Richard Smalley had a very powerful laser that could vaporize almost any known material. He didn't know that his visit would bring to the three of them a Nobel Prize in chemistry.

In a series of experiments performed in the autumn of 1985, they simulated the physicochemical reactions that take place in interstellar clouds by applying the power of their laser to the most common form of carbon, graphite. The results were stunning: hitherto unobserved on Earth, and altogether remarkable, carbon molecules were detected. Because of their size, they are usually called nanoparticles. Since then, lots of nanoparticles have been engineered from various physical elements, not only carbon; some of them are endowed with astonishing mechanical, electrical and chemical properties. As far as mechanical strength is concerned, it can be two orders of magnitude greater than it is for steel. Electrical properties beat those of previously known electrically efficient materials. The high level of chemical activity is linked to the high surface area to volume ratio that small size entails. In short, one might say that ordinary materials, when embodied at very small scales, display remarkable properties that cannot be anticipated at larger scales.

This has been the launching pad for the explosive expansion of nanotechnologies, with myriad research and development initiatives aiming at all sorts of applications, some useful, some detrimental. Would supercapacitors emerge as among the most useful ones?

As a battery, a supercapacitor is made of two electrodes both in contact with an electrolyte, often a liquid, selected for its capacity to conduct and store electricity. In a supercapacitor – this is the main difference with a battery – no chemical reaction takes place; storage is electrostatic. That creates advantages and disadvantages.

The main advantages are the following:

- Supercapacitors are able to charge and discharge in a matter of seconds, that is, much faster than batteries.
- They can run without significant degradation up to 1 million cycles (charge–discharge) instead of a few thousand.
- They are safer in so far as no explosion is to be feared and they contain far less harmful chemicals and toxic material.
- Rare earths – mostly mined in China at the cost of devastating pollution – do not enter their fabrication, except for relatively abundant cerium and lanthanum compounds.
- They are much lighter.
- They can operate within far larger temperature ranges, circa –40°C to +60°C.

The main disadvantage is that supercapacitors currently commercialized cannot match batteries in terms of energy density, that is, in the ability of delivering energy at a regular pace for relatively long durations.

Being able to discharge quickly, supercapacitors in a vehicle can deliver bursts of power for acceleration. This is, for instance, the case in some Toyota models. PSA Groupe (formerly PSA Peugeot Citroën) integrates supercapacitors in stop-start fuel-saving systems. Mazda makes use of supercapacitors to capture and store energy during deceleration. In these functions, supercapacitors appear complementary to batteries. Complementarity might also manifest itself in a different way: progress is made in associating battery and supercapacitor, the latter assisting the former so that the time required to charge the battery is cut to minutes.

From complements to replacements? That doesn't look unrealistic any longer. A number of university and industry labs are working on new classes of either electrodes or electrolytes in supercapacitors in order to enhance their performance, particularly their energy density.

Astonishing results have been obtained using various advanced graphene-based nanomaterials – particularly bright grandchildren to Kroto, Curl and Smalley – as main components in electrodes (Li et al., 2019; Yang et al., 2017). Graphene derivatives have been selected not only for their exceptional electrical, thermal and mechanical properties – which translate into supercapacitor performances – but also for available inexpensive production processes. New electrolytes have also been engineered that can store energy more efficiently (Mao et al., 2019).

Actual leaps in energy density have been achieved. "They put", anticipates Dexter Johnson (2015) in the Institute of Electrical and Electronics Engineers' magazine, *Spectrum*, "storage capacity parity with Li-ion batteries within reach. And when you have a supercapacitor that has the storage capacity of a Li-ion battery and the ability to charge in mere moments, all-electric vehicles might just be a lot more attractive". That would be good for the climate, and much more.

REFERENCES

Johnson, D. (2015), "Supercapacitors take a huge leap in performance", *IEEE Spectrum*, 28 May.
Li, Q., M. Horn and Y. Wang et al. (2019), "A review of supercapacitors based on graphene and redox-active organic materials", *Materials*, **12** (5), 703.
Mao, X., P. Brown and C. Červinka et al. (2019), "Self-assembled nanostructures in ionic liquids facilitate charge storage at electrified interfaces", *Nature Materials*, **18** (8), 1350–7.
Yang, H., S. Kannappan, A. Sumuthira Pandian and J.-H. Jang (2017), "Graphene supercapacitor with both high power and energy density", *Nanotechnology*, **28** (44), 445401.

34. From scooter to boat: innovations in electric transport in cities of Southeast Asia[1]

Pippo Ranci

FIGHT LOCAL POLLUTION AND CONGESTION AND YOU WILL REDUCE GHG EMISSIONS

It is a lucky circumstance that greenhouse gas (GHG) emissions go largely together with local pollution. While it is difficult to convince people to accept a burden on their life today only because this will improve the world in the future, it is much easier to gather support for innovations that produce an immediate reduction of pollution and congestion in densely populated cities. Large cities in Southeast Asia provide encouraging examples of such developments.

Congestion and pollution from road traffic represent an urgent issue in Southeast Asia and China. India and China alone account for 37 out of the world's 50 most polluted cities. While in developed countries personal transportation is dominated by cars, in the developing world two-wheelers account for the majority of vehicles on the road, and three-wheelers are also widely diffused. This is why electrification of these light vehicles is a priority to reduce congestion and pollution. It will also provide powerful advances towards a reduction of GHG emissions.

One key to progress is a fast diffusion of information and communication technologies. New apps and new systems can reduce congestion through diffusion of vehicle sharing. This provides a benefit, even if traditional fossil fuel-powered vehicles remain. On the other side, diffusion of electric vehicles can radically reduce emissions, even if the traditional model of individual ownership and use is maintained.

The combination of a technology-based sharing system and diffusion of e-vehicles can provide a really effective and fast change. Innovative electric urban transport services are spreading fast in Southeast Asian cities and promise to change the habits and preferences of millions of people, improve their lives, foster economic development, and contribute to mitigating climate change.

I shall summarily illustrate a limited number of case histories in the areas of light vehicles, cars, and boats, with a paragraph focusing on the alternative charging systems and the role of integrated systems.

TRANSFORMATION OF THE RICKSHAW AND OTHER LIGHT VEHICLES

We start from the lightest of all vehicles – the push scooter that has long been a toy for children. Now endowed with a small battery-powered electric engine, it has become a short-distance individual vehicle that, well before coming back into fashion in the West, has started contributing to the revolution in Southeast Asian cities described here. The Neuron Mobility company is offering e-push scooters in Singapore, Bangkok and Chiang Mai (Thailand), Cyberjaya (Malaysia), and Brisbane (Australia). Singapore-based GrabWheels also operates this service in university campuses in Jakarta (Indonesia): you can share the scooter and use it at will. You can also take it home, accept a part-time job as a GrabFood delivery rider, and turn your expenditure into an income.

Our next step is the electric bicycle. E-bikes are spreading both as individually owned vehicles and as a sharing service. Mobycy operates e-scooter- and e-bike-sharing services in five Indian cities.

Third step, the rickshaw. Sasiranga De Silva, a 33-year-old engineer and university lecturer, set about finding the most effective way of tackling the harmful gases and noise that make life a misery for commuters in his native city of Colombo, Sri Lanka. He decided to focus on tuk tuks, the three-wheel auto rickshaws used by millions of people across the world, particularly in Asia and Africa. There are around 1 million tuk tuks in Sri Lanka, providing essential, affordable transport for many of the country's 21 million people. De Silva developed an affordable conversion kit to allow tuk tuks to run on electric power. His innovation won a US$20 000 grant from the UN Environment Programme (UNEP, 2018) as part of the Asia Pacific Low Carbon Lifestyles Challenge. De Silva, who will also receive business and marketing training as part of his prize, says his conversion kit, based around a rechargeable lithium-ion battery, will reduce noxious emissions and also save tuk tuk drivers money over time. Presently, they generally pay US$4000 to buy their vehicle. The converter kit could be priced at US$2000 and save drivers US$1000 a year (UNEP, 2019).

De Silva's conversion kit may be important, yet e-rickshaws have existed for a long time in Southeast Asia. In Nepal, an e-rickshaw system called SAFA Tempo was introduced in 1996, as a replication of e-tuk tuks already operating in India and in Sri Lanka at the time. Today, 700 SAFA Tempos run on the bumpy streets of Kathmandu, generally run by women, providing passenger services: one of the many projects managed by the US non-profit Winrock International.

In India, electric rickshaws are operated in 71 cities, and their diffusion is increasing. In 2015, the amended Motor Vehicles Act carried a definition of the e-rickshaw as "special 3 wheeled vehicle of power not exceeding 4000 Watts" and the Government of India's Smart Cities Mission, based on proposals by city governments, included financing for e-rickshaw purchase and deployment in 29 cities and for e-rickshaw charging infrastructure development also in 13 other cities.[2]

ELECTRIC CARS, OWNED OR SHARED

Ola Cabs is an Indian transportation network company offering services that include peer-to-peer ridesharing, ride service hailing, taxi and food delivery. Founded in 2010, it is now valued higher than $6 billion. It is the leader of hail-ride taxis, the Uber model, in India. In 2015, it spun out Ola Electric, an e-mobility system company, with the collaboration of the government, since the country has set a goal to gradually convert the fleet to electric. Ola Electric plans to initially place 10 000 e-vehicles in one year.

Other car-sharing companies, like Haupcar in Thailand, are introducing e-cars in their fleet. Given the relatively high cost of an e-car, electrification is easier in the sector of car sharing than in the ordinary car market. In Singapore, the BlueSG company was created in 2017 and offers an e-car sharing service in 300-locations.

The business models are many, and they change according to experience and opportunities. The Malaysian company COMOS launched an e-vehicle sharing programme in 2015. As growth came too slow, the company shifted its focus to conventional car rental, then it embarked on an e-bike sharing programme at universities and in green tourism.

THE RECHARGING CHALLENGE AND THE GROWING ROLE OF INTEGRATED SYSTEMS

Any electric vehicle relies on a battery, and one crucial element of its performance is the capacity of the battery, in terms of driving range, related to its weight and volume, and to its cost. Although two- and three-wheelers have an advantage over cars in terms of size of the battery needed, and they are used within the urban area only, their recharging is an issue.

In general, a large organization is necessary for serving a variety of e-vehicles, and here is where the ingenious inventor is not sufficient. Only a large company will be able to cover the area with a charging network. The task has an easy solution in the case of sharing, since pick-up sites may be charging points as well. This is the case of Singapore's car-sharing company BlueSG, and it may become a model for the sharing of e-bikes and other light e-vehicles.

In the general case of owned vehicles, there is a basic alternative. A provider may choose a proprietary method that will not be available to drivers who have preferred a competing brand. Alternatively, open methods may develop and be available to vehicles of different brands: competition will be eased.

Here is where a body representing the public interest, like a local or national administration, plays a crucial role. A public initiative and a clear discipline (including the rights and conditions for individual recharging at home and private recharging sites for large fleets) is a recognized necessity, and government action is present in various countries. It is crucial that this happens at an early time in the development of the service.[3]

A recharging network can be based on plug-in recharging or on battery swapping. Both types have been introduced and are developing. First, with regard to plug-in recharging, India's Ather Energy is offering three models of e-scooter for individual purchase accompanied by access rights to a network of recharging stations, presently being expanded to 30 Indian cities, where the onboard navigator indicates the nearest station, fast service is based on a proprietary method fit for Ather vehicles, and an ordinary socket for charging is also offered to all electric vehicles. Second, with regard to battery swapping, the Taiwanese electric scooter company Gogoro has developed fast-swapping batteries, which can be replaced at gas stations and close to convenient stores. More than 300 stations will open soon, and the autonomy on one charge is about 100 km. However, lack of uniformity may provide the benefits of competition, yet it will also increase costs and possibly slow down diffusion.

While recharging is usually provided by using electricity supplied by the local network, a charging network using solar energy is now offered by ChargeGrid, a spinoff of Magenta Power, a rooftop solar developer based in Mumbai (India) and now growing through an alliance with Hindustan Petroleum Corporation Limited (HPCL), a big Indian oil and gas company. It offers fully automated, unmanned stations, remotely monitored through an advanced system.

In general, the need for easy and performing services is opening the way to integrated companies, offering many services through a proprietary, versatile app. An example of a company built around an app is Bykea, started in 2016 and operating in the main Pakistani cities: Karachi, Lahore and Islamabad–Rawalpindi. It offers on-demand rides, express parcel services, bills and ticket payments.

ELECTRIC BOATS

The city government of Kaohsiung, a city in Southern Taiwan with a 2.8 million population, has introduced hybrid electric ferry boats for passenger services, to reduce pollution. If successful, the initiative will be extended to the rest of the diesel fleet to ease pollution around Taiwan's largest harbour.

An advanced version of the electric ship is the solar-powered ferry, like the one operating between Vaikom and Thavanakkadavu in the Indian state of Kerala. Inaugurated in 2017, it was built by NavAlt Solar & Electric Boats in Kochi, India. NavAlt is a joint venture firm between Navgathi Marine Design & Constructions, Alternative Energies (France) and EVE Systems (France). Its cost is 60 percent higher than a diesel-powered boat with the same functional features and safety standards. Considering the fuel savings, the new model has a payback period of less than three years, and it eliminates pollution. Thus, substitution of diesel-fuelled ships looks promising in many densely populated cities built along a river or along the seashore. The sales of electric and hybrid vessels are expected to increase significantly over the next decade, climbing to over US$20 billion worldwide by 2027 – according to a report by IDTechEx, a UK-based tech consultancy firm (Gear, 2020).

Innovation is easier where electrification involves few, relatively large, centralized decisions, and yet it can also be targeted to the numerous, small independent operators. A Singapore-based renewables start-up is on a mission to replace polluting diesel-powered boats with solar-charged electric vessels in Southeast Asia, inspired by Swedish furniture retailer IKEA's approach to part distribution and assembly.

Southeast Asia simply could not function without this life-supporting mode of transport. The Philippines is made up of 7641 islands, while 13 466 islands make up the Indonesian Archipelago. One of the most important rivers in the world, the Mekong, is home to 60 million people spread across Myanmar, Vietnam, Laos, Cambodia and Thailand who live along its tributaries and depend on the river for food, water and jobs.

Many of the region's boat users are fishermen; one-fifth of the world's fish catch comes from Southeast Asia, and Indonesia, Thailand, Vietnam and the Philippines make the list for the world's top ten fish producers. Another big part of the region's boat fleet is devoted to tourism; popular travel destinations such as Krabi, Phuket, Boracay and Bali use smaller vessels for island-hopping tours.

Heavy, diesel-powered wooden boats are the primary form of transport for navigating the waterways of developing Southeast Asia. Referred to as *rua hang yao* in Thailand, *thuyền gỗ* in Vietnam, *bangkas* in the Philippines and *jukungs* in Indonesia, these vessels are typically made of timber from fully grown trees and crafted by local boat builders. Motor engines, fuelled by diesel, are then fitted so that the boats can traverse long distances. Increasing boat numbers have sparked concerns over fuel leaks and noise pollution, which harm marine life and affect fisheries and the quality of tourist sites. Responding to this need, renewable energy solutions such as solar-powered boats look promising in Southeast Asia.

Hans van Mameren, a septuagenarian Dutchman who runs Singapore-based renewable energy consultancy Energy Renewed, has an ambitious plan to electrify 1 million diesel boats in Southeast Asia. He spent 50 years in the shipping business before launching his clean energy venture in 2017. Van Mameren's new company will supply the parts for the boats and instructions for how to assemble the kit, but, ultimately, the vessels will be put together by local boat builders who can sell off the completed boats and turn a profit. Currently, Energy Renewed's team of engineers in Singapore is working on a prototype for their electric boat assembly kit, and they plan to go to market by the end of 2020. Two prototypes have been designed, one for a catamaran and another for a longboat.

Describing local boat builders as "craftsmen", van Mameren is confident that locals who use wooden boats can easily translate their traditional boat building skills into the modern composite boat building that is needed for electric boats. His assembly kits will come with an instruction manual in the local language, and he also intends to organize training sessions to familiarize local boat builders with the assembly procedure.

Van Mameren also thinks that his idea, while expensive at the outset, will generate savings over the long term. According to his calculations, Indonesian fishermen in the divers' paradise of Raja Ampat, West Papua, spend about half of their incomes on fuel. So, instead of selling the assembly kit at prices that are beyond the incomes of local boat folk, he intends to work with local dealers to lease his electric boat assembly kits at prices lower than what they would spend on fuel.

Perhaps the biggest appeal of van Mameren's solution is its capacity to double as a rural electrification scheme. If he can secure partners to install solar panels on his customers' homes, he thinks that locals are very likely to embrace his renewable energy solution. Besides creating the boat assembly kit, van Mameren's bigger ambition is to work with solar technology specialists to install solar panels in villages where his electric boats operate. These panels will supply clean energy to charge the boats and also provide electricity for daily consumption – an important bonus for those living off-grid. "Most fishermen load ice blocks from the main ports and ferry them back to their villages to preserve their catch. If they have electricity in their villages, they can power small refrigerating units and preserve their fish there", said van Mameren (Kong, 2019).

A WARNING AND A TENTATIVE CONCLUSION

Although most of the information presented above is drawn from official or fully reliable research sources, some use of other websites, apparently reliable, has been made. It is also certain that many other initiatives, not mentioned here, are at least as worth mentioning as the ones described here.

This chapter shows cases of private for-profit or non-profit initiatives and state activities, variously combined, targeted to overcome situations of urban traffic congestion and pollution and reduce damage and suffering of large populations. In so doing they contribute to abating CO_2 emissions and mitigating climate change.

Southeast Asia is engaged in a race against time. Other parts of the world are living through similar challenges and may have something to teach and much to learn. Information is precious and collaboration, including freer trade, will be very useful.

NOTES

1. The author gratefully acknowledges information and analysis provided by Pradyumna Bhagwat of the European University Institute and Salvatore Vinci of IRENA.
2. A description of the diffusion of e-rickshaws in India (including an impressive map, p. 5), and of the promotion of e-rickshaws by the federal government and by many state governments may be found in Shandilya, Saini and Ghorpade (2019).
3. Please refer to note 2.

REFERENCES

Gear, L. (2020), "Electric leisure & sea-going boats and ships 2021–2040", *Idtechex.com*, accessed 27 August 2020 at https://www.idtechex.com/en/research-report/electric-leisure-and-sea-going-boats-and-ships-2021-2040/739.

Kong, Y.X. (2019), "An idea to electrify 1 million boats in Southeast Asia – inspired by IKEA", *Eco-business.com*, 26 August, accessed 18 August 2020 at https://www.eco-business.com/news/an-idea-to-electrify-1-million-boats-in-southeast-asia-inspired-by-ikea/?sw-signup=true.

Shandilya, N., V. Saini and A.R. Ghorpade (2019), *Handbook: E-rickshaws Deployment in Indian Cities*, New Delhi: ICLEI South Asia.

United Nations Development Programme (UNEP) (2018), "Twelve Asian entrepreneurs awarded for forward-thinking environmental solutions", 25 March [press release], accessed 17 August 2020 at https://www.unenvironment.org/news-and-stories/press-release/twelve-asian-entrepreneurs-awarded-forward-thinking-environmental.

UNEP (2019), "Taming the sputtering tuk tuk: Sri Lankan innovator develops affordable electric conversion kit", accessed 17 August 2020 https://www.unenvironment.org/news-and-stories/story/taming-sputtering-tuk-tuk-sri-lankan-innovator-develops-affordable-electric.

35. The third attempt at the electric car might be the successful one

Geoffrey Heal

Battery electric vehicles (BEVs) have lost the fight with internal combustion engines (ICEs) twice – once at the beginning of the twentieth century, when both ICE vehicles and BEVs competed, and also again at the end of that century, when General Motors released its EV1 in 1996, only to pull it from the market in 1999. In 2003, Elon Musk and partners bet on the BEV for a third time, and so far, this third bet has proven lucky.

In 2006, Musk set out his business plan:

- build sports car;
- use that money to build an affordable car;
- use *that* money to build an even more affordable car;
- while doing above, also provide zero-emission electric power-generation options.

The really smart part of this was to start by building a sports car and then the Tesla Model S, both of which could be sold to the high end of the market where buyers were not price sensitive and where the novelty and environmental friendliness of an electric vehicle was a major selling point. Rich environmental buyers would happily spend the extra for a Tesla Roadster or Model S, generating the cash that would fund the development of less expensive vehicles such as the Model 3 and Model Y. In the process, Musk and Tesla transformed EVs from utilitarian to aspirational vehicles.

Musk is a larger-than-life character, self-confident and abrasive, a successful serial entrepreneur who is seeking to revolutionize transport both on Earth and in space. Musk's earlier ventures included co-founding PayPal and Zip2, an internet mapping company: sale of these provided some of the capital to start Tesla. He co-founded Tesla and founded and owns SpaceX, the most successful commercial launcher of space rockets. SpaceX has reduced the cost of launching satellites into orbit by about 90 percent, largely by pioneering the use of reusable rockets.

Tesla states that its mission is to "accelerate the world's transition to a sustainable future," and is working on this by producing BEVs and solar cells for electric power generation. Musk commented in an interview in 2017 that "my original interest in electric cars and solar energy, which goes back to when I was in university, was not based on environmental concern, it was based on sustainability, in the sense of ensuring that civilization can continue to progress" (Smith, 2017). This theme recurs in his comments about SpaceX: Musk wants to colonize planets to ensure the survival of the human race. He feels that we may do irreparable harm to Earth.

Musk personifies Tesla: when there is a major announcement, the launch of a new product, Musk appears on stage alone. As far as the public is concerned, there is no one else senior at Tesla. This monopolizing the limelight is perhaps connected with the high turnover of senior management at Tesla: Tesla lost 44 percent of Musk's direct reports in a nine-month period in comparison with 9 percent at other high-profile Silicon Valley companies (Mitchell, 2020).

Tesla went public in 2010 and since then its market capitalization has fluctuated widely, reaching as high as $400 billion, at which point it was the most valuable car company in the US or the EU, in spite of producing fewer than half a million vehicles annually. For comparison, GM, VW and Toyota produce in the order of 10 million cars per year.

Betting on a company making only BEVs in 2003 was risky in the extreme. At that point, lithium-ion batteries cost over $1000 per kWh, and the Tesla Model S uses an 80 kWh battery – bigger in the long-range version. At 2003 prices, the battery alone would have cost $80 000! It's no wonder that BEVs were not taken seriously then. Today, Tesla claims to buy its battery packs for about $100 per kWh, so the battery is under $10 000. Tesla has played a major role in reducing battery prices, benefiting its competitors as well as itself. There are other risks associated with focusing on the lithium-ion battery technology: it could be replaced by hydrogen fuel cells or even by supercapacitors, which are used successfully in hybrid racing vehicles. It is still too early to know what electric vehicle technology will look like ten years from now.

Musk has not yet achieved one key point on his famous four-bullet-point business plan (see above): Tesla has not yet produced "an even more affordable car." To be fair, the Model 3 is more affordable than the Model S, but the least expensive version is listed on Tesla's website at $33 690, *including* potential tax incentives and fuel savings of $6300. So, the cash cost is over $40 000. The mid-range versions of the Model 3 cost just under $50 000. According to the Kelley Blue Book vehicle valuation and automotive research company, the average new car price in the US in May 2019 was $36 718, so the Model 3 is really not in the "affordable" segment of the market.

While Tesla is still a small company, with sales of under half a million units annually, it has had a profound impact on the automobile market. It has shown that BEVs can be cool and profitable, two facts that no car maker believed prior to the release of the Model S. This car received rave reviews from the automobile press and from bodies like Consumer Reports in the US, which ranked it as one of the best cars ever made. Their summary is that "The fully electric Model S is a remarkable car that combines performance, agility, styling, high-tech, no emissions and low operating costs. It's one of the best cars we've ever tested" (Consumer Reports, 2020). It rapidly took market share from Audi, BMW, Jaguar, Lexus and Mercedes in the top end of the automobile markets of the US, the EU and China, become the best-selling luxury car in the US, and was instrumental in forcing other high-end manufacturers to offer BEVs in competition with the Model S. Tesla's Model 3 has now replaced the Model S as the best-selling luxury car in the US. Without Musk's audacious bet in 2003, there probably wouldn't be electric vehicles today.

REFERENCES

Consumer Reports (2020), "Tesla Model S", 2020, accessed March 2, 2020 at https://www.consumerreports.org/cars/tesla/model-s/2020/overview/.
Mitchell, R. (2017), "If Elon Musk is your boss, get your resume ready," *The Telegraph*, May 24, accessed March 2, 2020 at https://www.latimes.com/business/story/2019-08-15/elon-musk-tesla-executive-turnover.
Smith, A. (2017), "Who is Elon Musk? Tech billionaire, SpaceX cowboy, Tesla pioneer – and real life Iron Man," *The Telegraph*, May 24, accessed August 26, 2020 at https://www.telegraph.co.uk/technology/0/elon-musk-tech-billionaire-spacex-cowboy-real-life-iron-man/.

36. Solar cookstoves for adaptation to degrading natural conditions

Claude Henry

As a contribution to the Global Burden of Disease Study, *The Lancet* published "A comparative risk assessment of disease and injury attributable to 67 risk factors" (Lim et al., 2012), which produced the following podium: (1) high blood pressure; (2) tobacco smoking, including second-hand smoke; and (3) household air pollution from solid fuels. Indeed: "In developing countries, especially in rural areas, 2.5 billion people rely on biomass, such as firewood, charcoal, agricultural waste and animal dung, to meet their energy needs for cooking. In many countries, these resources account for over 90% of household energy consumption" (International Energy Association [IEA], 2006). And the side-effects are devastating:

- Millions of premature deaths each year, and tens of millions of debilitating ailments; the victims are mainly women and children.
- Wasted time and energy in collecting and transporting fuelwood, often at distances of 5–10 km, again involving mainly women and children. It is hard work and, in certain regions, frequently puts women at risk of aggression. Moreover, it forecloses opportunities of education or of more productive activities.
- Emissions of greenhouse gases (GHGs) (CO_2, methane, N-compounds) and of black carbon. Black carbon, a volatile by-product of incomplete combustion, is emitted on a large scale (about 25 percent of black carbon from all sources worldwide); it is a powerful absorber of direct solar radiation wherever it settles, particularly on ice, on which it accelerates melting.
- Severe degradation of local forest ecosystems.

Obviously, the consequences for people and for natural capital are harsh.

Several types of stoves, along with the corresponding fuels are now on offer that are vastly more energy efficient and cleaner than the traditional devices (IEA, 2006; Reddy, 2012). The more affordable ones, which are also closer to the cooking habits of the households concerned, are improved biomass-fired stoves; the fuels are conditioned and the stoves designed in ways that reduce the side-effects – in particular, black carbon emissions – instead producing a stable solid carbon residue called biochar, which contributes to carbon sequestration and can be used to improve soil fertility. Other systems function with gas, liquid fuels, solar heat or electricity.

A diversified offer of affordable efficient stove-fuel systems is a precondition for adoption in a broad range of circumstances; it is not a sufficient one. Several factors weigh on the decisions made by households – who tend to be rather conservative in matters of cooking – mainly:

- households' incomes, taking into account extra income generation allowed by better stoves;
- prices of stoves and fuels, adjusted for public or private financial support, as the case may be;
- quality of stoves, in particular their reliability in use (a condition for allowing the cook to save time for other activities) and their compatibility with cooking traditional meals (from traditional bread in India, all sorts of tortillas in Mexico, to millet/sorghum galettes in Western African countries, ugali bread and sucuma vegetables in Eastern Africa etc.);
- integration in the local economy: local production of stoves increases their appeal to consumers.

Efforts in these directions should be informed by the build-up of knowledge about how households make their decisions (Malla and Timilsina, 2014).

With about 12 million users worldwide, the thermal solar cookstove appears as the "Petit Poucet" in the family of clean stoves. Charles Perrault's French fairytale character, Petit Poucet (Little Thumb), was, however, not merely small but also far-sighted. In a world where essential natural resources are fast degrading, it is indeed far-sighted to plan for tapping an inexhaustible resource – sun rays. Moreover, recent technical advances and diversification of models, from very simple and cheap to rather sophisticated ones (see, for instance, solarcookers.org), will boost solar cookers' appeal provided their promoters fully take into account the lessons drawn from other clean stoves' challenges (see above). Facing increasingly harsh conditions – when survival concerns supersede the conservatism of cooking habits – users will appreciate solar cookstoves' advantages.

Living in the Andean high plains, Angelina Orella has switched to a solar stove. Her assessment is shared by her fellow villagers: "Now I cook everything with the solar cooker. Ten years ago, there was enough wood around the house for cooking. Now the wood is far away". Moreover, with heat-retention baskets, insulated with llama wool, Angelina keeps the evening meal warm. Before switching to a solar stove, she followed a training program that covers not only food preparation and kitchen organization, but also the interdependence between the village and its natural environment. The program is provided by CEDESOL (Centro de Desarrollo de Energía Solar, Cochabamba, Bolivia), a non-profit voluntary organization. The support provided in this way is no less crucial than the technical performance of the stoves.

In some districts of Kenya, the effects of deforestation and of weather disorders linked to climate change are strong incentives for adopting solar cookstoves. A joint program with Amsterdam Free University ushered in the production of "box cookers" that trap sunlight though a glass top; they can trap even diffuse light on cloudy days. A non-profit organization called Farmers With A Vision (Busia County, Kenya) takes charge of training, maintenance and even access to microcredit; as in Bolivia, technology is embedded in a "sociosystem", as one would speak of ecosystems (for other interesting cases in Sub-Saharan Africa, see Batchelor et al., 2018). Natural Capital Partners, however, a for-profit corporation, offers similar support to about 100 000 rural households struggling with the effects of poverty and climate change in Henan, one of the least developed Chinese provinces.

Solar cookstoves have a specific role to play in another kind of impoverished environment – refugee camps. Depending on the way they have been introduced, their potential has been realized – in particular in Chad, Uganda, Nepal – or rather less so, as in Burkina Faso or India. Here also, the way the sociosystem is organized and sustained proves decisive (Barbieri, 2017).

Whither a new frontier? It has been suggested that photovoltaic is the future of solar cookstoves, as they might be more convenient and versatile than thermal ones. Currently, their cost would be prohibitive. However, that might change with the spectacular advances in radiation capture (PV cells) and electricity storage (batteries and supercapacitors).

REFERENCES

Barbieri, J., F. Riva and E. Colombo (2017), "Cooking in refugee camps and informal settlements – a review of available technologies and impacts on the socio-economic and environmental perspective", *Sustainable Energy Technologies and Assessments*, **22**, 194–207.

Batchelor, S., E. Brown and J. Leary et al. (2018), "Solar electric cooking in Africa: where will the transition happen first?", *Energy Research & Social Science*, **40**, 257–72.

International Energy Association (IEA) (2006), "Energy for cooking in developing countries", in (IEA), *World Energy Outlook 2006*, Paris: IEA.

Lim, S.S., T. Vos and A.D. Flaxman et al. (2012), "A comparative risk assessment of burden of disease and injury attributable to 67 risk factors and risk factor clusters in 21 regions, 1990–2010: a systemic analysis for the Global Burden of Disease Study 2010", *The Lancet*, **380** (9859), 2224–60.

Malla, S. and G.R. Timilsina (2014), "Household cooking fuel choice and adoption of improved cookstoves in developing countries: a review", *Policy Research Working Paper*, No. 6903, Washington, DC: World Bank.

Reddy, S.B.N. (2012), *Understanding Stoves: For Environment and Humanity*, 's-Hertogenbosch: MetaMeta.

37. Carbon capture from ambient air: a brake on climate change?

Claude Henry

Within the next ten years, it could prove a perilous disaster to go on increasing the stock of greenhouse gases (GHGs) in the atmosphere. Humankind, however, has not yet curbed increasing volumes of emissions, and doesn't seem determined to do so. How to avoid being squeezed? The only way, which doesn't itself tinker with essential climate mechanisms – as geoengineering projects might do (Barrett, 2012) – is to capture CO_2 from the atmosphere, and then dispose of it in various available ways. Capturing CO_2 from air and storing it – direct air capture and storage, or DACS – would be an essential complement to avoiding doom on the planet; a complement, definitely not a substitute for reducing the emissions. Driving DACS costs down is thus worth research and development efforts on par with the Apollo Program, as was already laid down 20 years ago in a visionary paper (Lackner et al., 1999). This is all the more justified as, climate change being a public bad, DACS is a public good,[1] for the provision of which you cannot rely on market mechanisms for raising adequate financial resources, even if you can rely on them to organize some form of competition, via reverse auctions, between providers.[2]

It is often argued that more broadly switching to a sustainable global development trajectory requires an "Apollo Program" of sorts. As long as sustainable development is considered in its globality, Richard Nelson, who along with Kenneth Arrow pioneered the economics of innovation, strongly disagrees: development stems from a broad diversity of decentralized endeavors. Nelson (with Sarewitz), however, also argues that there is one domain of R&D that calls for an Apollo Program, and that is CO_2 capture and storage (Sarewitz and Nelson, 2008).

Nature itself captures CO_2 from ambient air. Silicates of calcium or of magnesium are significantly more reactive with ambient CO_2 than are other minerals, the reaction forming stable solid carbonates; hence, the name mineral carbonation. They are found at higher densities in several kinds of rocks, particularly basalt and peridotite (Krevor et al., 2009). Natural weathering of such rocks fosters mineral carbonation. Peridotite is particularly productive; unfortunately, while abundant deep underground, it is relatively rare on or near the surface of the Earth, with a remarkably high presence in the Sultanate of Oman, which contains about 30 percent of the area where peridotite is apparent on Earth. According to geologists Peter Kelemen and Jürg Matter, who have extensively investigated the area: "In situ, carbonation of peridotite could consume > 1 billion tons of CO_2 per year in Oman alone, affording a low-cost, safe, and permanent method to capture and store atmospheric CO_2." (Kelemen and Matter, 2008, p. 17295). This presupposes fracturing the rock to increase the contact area between air and rock.

As reachable perdotite is relatively rare, carbonation of basalt is the practical alternative, either with CO_2 in ambient air, or CO_2 dissolved in sea water, as basalt is relatively abundant near land surface and on sea floor. Promising preliminary results have been obtained in Iceland. A project supported by the EU (CarbFix project) and started in 2012 near Reykjavik, has indeed shown the capacity and efficiency of basalt to turn CO_2 into veins of stable solid calcite and magnesite. CO_2 obtained from a nearby geothermal plant is dissolved in water and then pumped into sea floor basalt. The nice surprise has been the speed of the process: 95 percent of the CO_2 injected solidified within two years, whereas a decade was expected. An assessment of the results has been published in *Science* (Matter et al., 2016).

This project is an experience in CO_2 storage, not in capture. A second CarbFix project in Iceland. CarbFix2, deals with both aspects of the problem. It is realized by the Swiss company Climeworks, initially established in 2009 by Christoph Gebald and Jan Wurzbacher as a Swiss Federal Institute of Technology in Zurich (ETHZ) spin-off. Climeworks develops, builds and operates direct air capture (DAC) plants that capture CO_2 from air. Climeworks plants consist of modular "CO_2 collectors". One key element of Climeworks' technology is a filter material, which selectively captures CO_2. In a first step, air is drawn into the CO_2 collector using a fan. CO_2 is then captured on the surface of the filter material ("adsorption"). In a second step, when the filter material is fully saturated, the CO_2 collector is closed and the temperature increased to between 80°C and 100°C. The CO_2 thereby releases ("desorption") at a purity of over 99 percent and can be collected. The CO_2 that has been collected in this way is pumped into underground basalt, with results similar to those obtained in the first CarbFix project.[3]

Climeworks already has 14 plants in operation across Europe. Most of them do not pump the CO_2 underground for mineralization. Instead, the CO_2 is re-used for various applications, such as for the fertilization of greenhouses, for the carbonation of drinks or for the production of renewable synthetic fuels, as is the case in the plant Climeworks has built in Italy. The idea has been promoted for some years by George Olah, a Nobel laureate who is a legend in the chemistry of hydrocarbons. Olah, Surya Prakash and Goeppert (Loker Hydrocarbon Research Institute, University of Southern California):

> have proposed and developed a feasible anthropogenic chemical recycling of carbon dioxide [that can] be converted by feasible chemical transformations into liquid fuels such as methanol, dimethyl ether... The required energy for the synthetic carbon cycle can come from any alternative energy source such as solar, wind, geothermal, and even hopefully safe nuclear energy. (Olah, Surya Prakash and Goeppert, 2011, p. 12881)

This way of storing CO_2 would not reduce the amount already present in the atmosphere, but it would at least close the open carbon cycle associated with the burning of fuels made from fossil oil.

Anders Eldrup, then CEO of the Danish power utility DONG Energy (now called Oersted), had not heard of Olah et al. However, he came to concur with them. During the winter 2009–10, the Danish wind farms produced such an excess of electricity, which by all means had to be evacuated through the interconnectors to Norway and Sweden, that the price became negative. With the multiplication of offshore wind farms in Danish and British waters, it is anticipated that imbalances between production and consumption of electricity might result in negative prices for about 1000 hours/year. Anders Eldrup came to the view that, rather than excess electricity generating losses, it should be used to produce hydrogen. Similar conditions will prevail in the USA, in places across Texas and Midwestern states, where the development of wind farms is massive. In many other places, solar energy would do the job. Then, with CO_2 and cheap hydrogen at hand, it will be economical to produce the synthetic fuels envisaged by Olah et al., not only providing substitutes for fossil fuels but also, these fuels being a safe means of storage, contributing to mitigating the intermittency and volatility of renewables. Moreover, they could easily be fed into existing energy infrastructure, far more energy being carried economically in this way than along power lines.

What about DACS costs? High costs make CO_2 capture from ambient air impracticable, I remember Robert Sokolow, the eminent Princeton physicist and energy expert, saying five or six years ago. More recently, he has co-signed a paper (Creutzig et al., 2019) that sounds far less pessimistic. There are good reasons for that. From systematic observations at a Carbon Engineering pilot plant in Canada – Carbon Engineering is a company cofounded in 2009 by David Keith, professor of applied physics at the School of Engineering and Applied Science, Harvard University – it appears that "depending on financial assumptions, energy costs, and the specific choice of inputs and outputs, the levelized cost per ton CO_2 captured from the atmosphere ranges from 94 to 232 \$/t-CO_2", capture and storage included (Keith et al., 2018, p. 1). In a recent report (National Academies, 2019), a group of experts from the National

Academies of Sciences, Engineering and Medicine, refer to a similar range in their conclusions. It is interesting to note that the $150/t-$CO_2$ Swedish tax rate sits well inside this range, implying that it pays to avoid the tax by pumping CO_2 out of the atmosphere. According to a fairly comprehensive review article (Fasihi, Efimova and Breyer, 2019), it appears that with cheap renewable energy – you can take maximum advantage of locating your plant anywhere you see fit, as CO_2 concentration in the atmosphere is the same everywhere – the 2018 figures become: $85–110 in 2030 and $40–55 in 2050. Carbon capture will be performed in numerous relatively small units; such modularity allows for economies of scale and ongoing integration of technical improvements.

Who will pay? Capturing CO_2 from ambient air is a public good, as it mitigates a public bad, climate change. Only relatively small quantities of CO_2 may be sold for private uses. There is no customer for the bulk of the gas that is captured. Everybody benefits from the capture, but only philanthropists or public authorities might be motivated to contribute to the cost. Some form of public cooperation must be organized, which does not exist yet. "It may pay for us to develop carbon capture and storage as a hedge against future climate change risks" (Barrett, 2012, p. 33). Rather than waiting for severe disruptions, it would be more rational to set a Climate Apollo Program in motion right now, so as to start without delay a cumulative process of technical improvements and cost reductions characteristic of emerging technologies – think of photovoltaics or of offshore wind – in order to actually achieve what looks both necessary and possible: an affordable insurance mechanism against insuperable losses.

If voluntary finance is not easily forthcoming, compulsory finance should specifically be raised. That might be from carbon taxation or from a direct implementation of the polluter-pays-principle. Considering the extremely perilous situation we are in, Myles Allen – professor of geosystem science at Oxford University and pioneer of the studies assessing the overall limit of CO_2 emissions compatible with an Earth mean temperature increase kept under 2°C – urges that, for every ton of CO_2 emitted, one ton be captured and stored, with the emitter covering the expense (Allen, 2015).

NOTES

1.　From a public good, for example, a body of knowledge or a climate condition, nobody can be excluded, and nobody's use is curtailed by anybody else's use. In such a situation, absent some form of binding cooperation, nobody feels compelled to pay for the provision of the public good.
2.　"Reverse auctions provide a powerful means of price discovery. They have demonstrated their usefulness in renewable electricity generation… In a reverse auction for DAC, companies interested in developing or advancing direct air

capture are offered an opportunity to competitively bid for projects, where the bid is expressed in terms of a CO_2 price the bidder is willing to accept" (Lackner and Azarabadi, 2019).

3. According to specialists at the US Geological Survey: "The technology offers virtually unlimited capacity to permanently store CO_2 via a process that takes little effort to either verify or monitor" (Krevor et al., 2009, p. 1).

REFERENCES

Allen, M. (2015), "Paris emissions cuts aren't enough – we'll have to put carbon back in the ground", *The Conversation*, December 12.

Barrett, S. (2012), "Climate treaties and backstop technologies", *CESifo Economic Studies*, **58**, 31–48.

Creutzig, F., C. Breyer and J. Hilaire et al. (2019), "The mutual dependence of negative emission technologies and energy systems", *Energy & Environmental Science*, **12**, 1780–804.

Fasihi, M., O. Efimova and C. Breyer (2019), "Techno-economic assessment of CO_2 direct air capture plants", *Journal of Cleaner Production*, **224**, 957–80.

Keith, D., G. Holmes, D. St. Angelo and K. Heidel (2018), "A process for capturing CO_2 from the atmosphere", *Joule*, **2**, 1–22.

Kelemen, P. and J. Matter (2008), "In situ carbonation of peridotite for CO_2 storage", *Proceedings of the National Academy of Sciences*, **105**, 17295–300.

Krevor, S.C., C.R. Graves, B.S. van Gosen and A.E. McCafferty (2009), "Mapping the mineral resource base for mineral carbon-dioxide sequestration in the conterminous United States", *US Geological Survey Digital Data Series*, **414**, 1–14.

Lackner, K. and H. Azarabadi (2019), "Buying down the cost of air capture" [unpublished paper], Center for Negative Carbon Emissions, Arizona State University.

Lackner, K., P. Grimes and H.-J. Ziock et al. (1999), "Carbon dioxide extraction from air: is it an option", in *Proceedings of the 24th Annual Technical Conference on Coal Utilization and Fuel Systems, March 8–11, 1999, Clearwater Florida*, pp. 885–96.

Matter, J., M. Stute and S. Snaebjörnsdottir et al. (2016), "Rapid carbon mineralization for permanent disposal of anthropogenic carbon dioxide emissions", *Science*, **352**, 1312–14.

National Academies of Sciences, Engineering, Medicine (2019), *Negative Emissions Technologies and Reliable Sequestration: A Research Agenda*, Consensus Study Report, Washington, DC: National Academies Press.

Olah, G.A., G.K. Surya Prakash and A. Goeppert (2011), "Anthropogenic chemical carbon cycle for a sustainable future", *Journal of the American Chemical Society*, **133**, 12881–98.

Sarewitz, D. and R. Nelson (2008), "Three rules for technological fixes", *Nature*, **456**, 871–8.

38. Ecological engineering in coastal protection

Claude Henry

Bangladesh is suffering from the effects of sea storms more than any other country on Earth and the threats from sea-level rises are daunting. In the delta formed by the confluence of the Ganges, Brahmaputra and Meghna Rivers, these threats are mitigated by one of the largest and lushest mangroves in the world, called the Sundarbarns, an UNESCO World Heritage site. The Sundarbarns are "so thick that history has hardly ever found the way in", writes Salman Rushdie in *Midnight's Children*. History may soon find its way *against* the Sundarbarns: there are advanced plans for building a large coal-fired power plant less than 15 km from the forest; both pollution and traffic of ships bringing coal from India would upset the fragile ecological balance there. In June 2019, UNESCO has declared the Sundarbarns "World Heritage in Danger". Yet another blunder in coastal protection?

In many places all around the world, the game is over; mangroves are gone. Consider, for example, Central America's Pacific Coast. There mangroves are indeed mostly gone; beaches, fields, roads, homes and finally people have followed suit. Even the very industrial shrimp farms that displaced mangroves now come under threat. In Africa, Nigeria has the largest mangrove ecosystem, the third largest worldwide. It protects the country's vast coastal areas against the increasingly damaging intrusions from the Atlantic Ocean; it also provides essential biological resources to millions of mostly poor people. Yet, large tracts among the most valuable ones in the Niger Delta have been lost to unbridled oil exploration and extraction. These losses are no exceptions. According to the United Nations Environmental Programme report on the state of mangroves worldwide (UNEP, 2014): "The deforestation of the planet's mangroves is exceeding average forest loss by a rate of three to five times, resulting in damages of up to $42 billion annually and exposing ecosystems and coastal habitats to an increased risk of devastation from climate change" (UN News, 2014).

Of particularly high value for a country made up of more than 18 000 islands (6000 without permanent residents), mangrove forests have been severely depleted along Indonesian coastlines. The district of Probolinggo, East Java, had mangrove-lined beaches, of which only a few patches remained at the beginning of this century. Amat Samsuri, a resident in a coastal village of the district, had been familiar with mangroves since childhood. He had noticed that where the mangrove was still in place, so were fishes and shrimps – which had almost completely disappeared elsewhere – and sediments were trapped by the remaining trees – on the other hand, erosion was severe elsewhere. He started replanting, progressively identifying favorable density and mix of plants, and recognizing the importance of maintenance during the first two or three years of growth.

After ten years of solitary work – but for a brother's occasional help – he was able to gather a team of voluntary coworkers, secure some support from local authorities, and finally the recognition and the support of Mangroves for the Future (MFF). From its creation in 2007 as a joint venture between the International Union for Conservation of Nature (UICN) and the United Nations Development Programme (UNDP), MFF has supported – with money, technical and managerial assistance – about 400 projects in South and Southeast Asia, aiming at coastal ecosystems restoration and resilience building; in line with the Stockholm Resilience Centre, they see resilience as preparedness in the face of complex, changing and only partially known circumstances, on the basis of both local knowledge and applications of fast-developing applied ecological science (Lewis, 2005; Romañach et al., 2018).

Mangroves and other coastal forests, marshes, coral and oyster reefs, are ecosystems that, in addition to a variety of ecological services they provide (Donato et al., 2011; Gittman et al., 2016), are partners in the protection of coasts. By dissipating at least part of the energy carried by the waves, they reduce the constant erosion of the coast and, in rough weather, the force of the impacts of a storm either on natural structures or on artificial protection barriers. In the Netherlands, where huge artificial structures are essential for protecting the polders that lie beneath sea level, mangroves, marshes and shellfish beds are now engineered in front of these structures. They also trap sediments: as they slow down the water, sediments settle. Sedimental accretion in mangrove forests more or less keeps pace with sea-level rises. Oyster reefs have the additional advantage of growing biologically. According to Harold van Waveren, chair of the Crisis Management Group at the Rijkswaterstaat (Directorate-General for Public Works and Water Management):

> We can't just keep building higher levees, because we will end up living behind 10-meter walls…Protection against climate change is only as strong as the weakest link in the chain, and the chain in our case includes not just the big gates and dams at the sea but a whole philosophy of spatial planning, crisis management, children's education, online apps and public spaces. (Kimmerman, 2017)

That philosophy of building with nature and of deep social involvement is at the core of the renewed 2008 Delta Programme of protection against the sea (see the Deltares web page). Ecological engineering and the famed Dutch civil engineering go hand in hand, with salt marshes along the Waddenzee coastline in the north of the country; willow mangroves in front of the Dordrecht dykes – a link in the infrastructures protecting Rotterdam; and shell beds in the Oosterschelde coastal bay in the south of the country. And, as Ayana Elizabeth Johnson shows in Johnson (2019), New York City seems intent on going the Dutch way.

REFERENCES

Donato, D.C., J. Boone Kauffman, D. Murdiyarso and S. Kurnianto (2011), "Mangroves are among the most carbon-rich forests in the tropics", *Nature Geoscience*, **4**, 293–7.

Gittman, R., C.H. Peterson and C.A. Currin et al. (2016), "Living shorelines can enhance the nursery role of threatened estuarine habitats", *Ecological Applications*, **26**, 249–63.

Johnson, A.E. (2019), "The concrete jungle has 578 miles of shoreline at risk", *The New York Times*, May 27.

Kimmerman, M. (2017), "The Dutch have solutions to rising seas. The world is watching", *The New York Times*, June 15.

Lewis, R.R. (2005), "Ecological engineering for successful management and restoration of mangrove forests", *Ecological Engineering*, **24**, 403–18.

Romañach, S.S., D.L. Deangelis, H. Lye Koh and Y. Li (2018), "Conservation and restoration of mangroves: global status, perspectives and prognosis", *Ocean & Coastal Management*, **154**, 72–82.

United Nations Environmental Programme (UNEP) (2014), *The Importance of Mangroves to People: A Call to Action*, Nairobi: UNEP.

UN News (2014), "New UN report warns of 'devastating' effects from ongoing destruction of mangrove forests", September 29.

39. Better to corrupt plastics than the environment

Pippo Ranci

Plastics have entered the everyday life of humans everywhere and help solve innumerable problems, yet they are a curse on the environment. They remain in the streets and parks and beaches, wherever humans do not dispose of waste properly. This is not an easy exercise for many societies, since it requires an organized and costly system of waste collection, reuse or appropriate incineration. Plastic objects and microplastics are littering the soil and the water, suffocating and poisoning marine life.

Europe is the second largest plastics producer in the world, after China, and out of the 27 million tonnes of plastic waste produced each year in Europe, only a third is recycled. Every year, 150 000–500 000 tonnes of macroplastics and 70 000–130 000 tonnes of microplastics are dumped into the seas around Europe. The majority of these plastics enter the Mediterranean Sea, posing a major threat to marine life. Large plastic pieces injure, suffocate and often kill marine animals, including protected and endangered species, such as sea turtles. The microplastics, smaller and more insidious fragments, have reached record levels in the Mediterranean Sea: their concentration is almost four times higher than in the "plastic island" found in the North Pacific Ocean. Plastic debris in the marine environment contains organic contaminants, of which 78 percent are toxic. By entering the food chain, these fragments threaten an increasing number of animal species as well as human health (Alessi and Di Carlo, 2018).

There are three defence strategies, and they are all necessary:

• reduce the use of plastics in many uses (packaging and wrapping, dishes and cutlery, toys);
• organize reuse or recycling of plastics after use;
• develop production and use of biodegradable or compostable plastics to displace traditional plastics.[1]

We look into the third.

BIODEGRADABLE, PLEASE, WHEREVER POSSIBLE

One of the most common uses of plastics is for making containers of all sorts. If these could dissolve at the end of their useful life, the environment would be better. A neat representation of this concept can be found in a few lines written by Primo Levi, a chemist, writer and survivor of the Auschwitz Nazi extermination camp, in his book *The Periodic Table*. He recounts how some starving detainees in the camp tried to steal anything usable from the lab where they were forced to work, and they could not steal liquids for lack of containers. Here wit and chemistry make the memory of tragedy bearable:

> The great problem of packaging, which every experienced chemist knows, was well known to God Almighty, who solved it brilliantly, as he is wont to, with cellular membranes, eggshells, the multiple peel of oranges, and our own skins, because after all we too are liquids. Now, at that time there did not exist polyethylene, which would have suited me perfectly since it is flexible, light and splendidly impermeable: but it is also a bit too incorruptible, and not by chance God Almighty himself, although he is a master of polymerisation, abstained from patenting it: He does not like incorruptible things. (Levi, 1975 [1984], p. 140)[2]

One clarification is necessary. Plastics generally originate from fossil hydrocarbons. Their threat to the environment does not depend on their origin; it depends on the way they are disposed of. Plastic objects and materials pose no threat to the environment if they can be transformed into compost or other useful substances through biodegradation or anaerobic digestion, without substantial emissions. Many, but not all, bioplastics (i.e., plastics from plant material) are biodegradable, and so are a few oil-derived plastics.

Examples of new plastic materials made of agricultural products or by-products can now be found on various websites, such as that of the Ellen MacArthur Foundation. This is a path leading to establishing a circular economy.

OUR SHOPPING SKIN

One of the first and most successful applications of biodegradable plastics is the shopping bag for food. You buy food and go home, empty the bag and then use it for fruit skins, eggshells and all food scrap and leftovers. Organic waste is easier to collect when it is stored in a compostable bag and the bag itself can be processed (composted) together with its contents. Even if dispersed, these bags will not stay in the environment for long.

The biodegradable shopping bag is now familiar in countries such as France and Italy, thanks to a helping hand from government regulations imposing it or taxing the traditional shopping bag. The cycle could be completed and made easier if all food wrappings and price labels were made of biodegradable material: technically, this is quite possible. It would increase the production costs somewhat, while making correct disposal easier and cheaper. A regulatory or tax incentive could provide the impulse, and probably prove economically sound if total costs, rather than mere business costs, were considered.

Further developments are in their early phase in various sectors. Take the introduction of biodegradable dishes and cutlery in catering and in picnic equipment: again, only a matter of direct private costs versus the social cost of the full cycle. Or the introduction of biodegradable plastics into agriculture, given the vast and increasing use of mulching film to keep moisture and nourishment in the ground and facilitate the growth of vegetables and flowers: the black sheets with round holes would last as long as they are useful, then be hoed into the soil and disappear.

The share of biodegradable plastics in all plastics is still minute. Its growth potential is not negligible, but it will not be easy to achieve, since biodegradable plastic is inferior in terms of strength, hardness and tenacity. An overall replacement of traditional plastics cannot be imposed, and a piecemeal replacement calls for a mix of selective obligations and incentive measures. Its success will depend on compliance by, and persuasion of, small farmers, artisans and consumers: a set of decentralized small decisions. One chapter of this story is the many lives of a firm in Italy.

MANY LIVES OF A FIRM

Montecatini is an attractive small medieval town near Florence, turned into a spa for its thermal springs. In 1888, its name was given to a new company mining copper and sulphur in the nearby hills. Montecatini became the largest chemical company in Italy.

In 1966, it was taken over by Edison, a company that had pioneered electricity in Italy since 1881 and found itself without a mission but rich in cash, after the Italian government had nationalized electricity in 1962. The new company Montedison had a difficult life. In 1986, Raul Gardini, the strong man of the Ferruzzi family, took control as a step in his campaign to build an industrial empire out of the family's agricultural origins. Then he became involved in risky finance and there were stories of corruption, but his passion for marrying agriculture to the chemical industry left a durable mark in the company.

Old Montecatini had left a precious heritage in its research department in Novara, near Milan, where Giulio Natta had discovered isotactic polypropylene, awarding him a Nobel Prize in 1963. In the Novara site, a spin-off lab was set up in 1989 to develop chemicals made of renewable raw materials from agriculture, and then established as a company named Novamont.

Skilfully managed by chemical scientist Catia Bastioli, Novamont grew into a leader in the new market of biodegradable bioplastics. Since 1990, their Mater-Bi, a bioplastic material produced out of starch, vegetable oils, sugar and other inputs, has enabled compostable shopping bags to displace traditional plastic bags in food shops in Italy and other European countries, and biodegradable mulch film to compete with traditional plastic film for agricultural use in Europe and in North America. Disposable carrier bags are "a kind of waste that presents extremely critical issues", hence the interest in "transforming [them] into an opportunity" (Bastioli, 2013).

Novamont's ambitions go far beyond shopping bags. The company is trying to increase the renewable content of Mater-Bi. It is also developing a variety of materials in the Mater-Bi family, such as biolubricants, biochemicals and cosmetic ingredients (whose flow of polluting microplastics into the water system could be eliminated). Other innovative products made from Mater-Bi belong to the categories of food service and packaging: multi-layer compostable film can combine compostability and gas-barrier properties. Now Novamont is a worldwide company, operating through own distributors in more than 40 countries all over the world.

Its activities are expanding into the exploitation of marginal land and of deindustrialized areas, building an integrated agro-industrial bioeconomy without subtracting agricultural land to food production, using compost as an organic soil improver, and introducing new compostable herbicides that will displace the toxic ones. Together with Turin Polytechnic and the Bologna University, Novamont has set up a new foundation with the purpose of experimenting with techniques for soil revitalization in arid or even sterile areas.

NEW PATHS IN BIOCHEMISTRY

An article published in the world-level scientific journal *Nature* illustrates research under way to depolymerize PET (polyethylene terephthalate, one of the most abundant plastic materials) and make it easily recyclable (Tournier et al., 2020). The French green chemistry firm Carbios, set up in 2011, along with the Toulouse Biotechnology Institute, succeeded in finding an enzyme in leaf compost that performs very efficiently in a most valuable operation and which could provide a way out from the present plastic waste nightmare.

Similar biochemical solutions for many types of plastic materials are the object of a massive research effort by many companies worldwide. Since 2017, Carbios itself linked up with large consumers of plastic bottles (such as soft-drinks producers) and with Danish chemical company Novozymes specializing in enzymes, so that its pathbreaking innovations are headed for large-scale production and utilization.

NOTES

1. We shall use "compostable" as a synonym for "biodegradable", although some compostable materials do not biodegrade naturally but only under appropriate conditions.
2. I owe this citation from Levi to Catia Bastioli's preface in her handbook (Bastioli, 2014).

REFERENCES

Alessi, E. and G. Di Carlo (2018), *Out of the Plastic Trap: Saving the Mediterranean from Plastic Pollution*, Rome: WWF Mediterranean Marine Initiative, accessed 18 August 2020 at http://awsassets.panda.org/downloads/a4_plastics_med_web.pdf.

Bastioli, C. (2013), Speech at the 'Bioplastics: a case study of bioeconomy in Italy in the light of Horizon 2020' conference, at the European Parliament, Brussels, 6 March.

Bastioli, C. (2014), *Handbook of Biodegradable Polymers*, Shrewsbury, UK: Smithers Rapra Technology.

Levi, P. (1975 [1984]), *The Periodic Table* [originally published as *Il Sistema periodico*], New York: Schocken Books.

Tournier, V., C.M. Topham and A. Gilles et al. (2020), "An engineered PET depolymerase to break down and recycle plastic bottles", *Nature*, **580**, 216–19.

40. Drip irrigation: Daniel Hillel's legacy

Claude Henry

Did a vigorous solitary tree in the middle of a dry patch of land in Palestine (later to become Israel) inspire the most significant modern innovation in irrigation methods? Did Simcha Blass or Daniel Hillel catch sight of the tree and then have a look underground, discovering a pipe that was leaking drop after drop at the roots of the tree? The answers are somewhat contradictory. It is clear, however, that in the late 1950s and in the 1960s, both men, working in arid conditions in Israel, pioneered drip irrigation (also called micro-irrigation), taking advantage of another innovation at the time – cheap plastic tubes.

In November 2012, Daniel Hillel received the World Food Prize at the University of Iowa. In an interview with *The Wall Street Journal* (October 15, 2012) he recalled the early days of drip irrigation in the Negev Desert: "We realized through drip irrigation, by applying water to the rooting zone of crops very gradually, drop by drop, the soil is never saturated nor ever allowed to desiccate. Consequently, the system becomes more sustainable, water is used more efficiently and farmers could get much more crop per drop" (Rai, 2012). Less water and richer harvests, it was indeed a revolution in agriculture.

Simcha Blass had his own system patented in the traditional way. Daniel Hillel made his freely available, contributing personally to the adoption of drip irrigation in more than 30 countries, including neighbors of Israel such as Jordan and Egypt. Drip irrigation is by no means convenient for all crops; even for suitable crops, it is not universally adopted by farmers, but it is nevertheless practiced on a large scale in countries on all continents, including parts of China, India and the USA.

Drip irrigation systems can be very simple and inexpensive, with only basic components that can be made from recycled materials and function under Newton's law of gravity; in this way they are affordable to poor farmers in countries like Bangladesh, Burma or Zimbabwe. They can also be sophisticated, with all sorts of monitoring devices.

Technical sophistication is not an aim in itself, but it is efficient in suitable circumstances. Farmers in the High Plains of Texas privately own, according to the law of the state, the portion of the Ogallala Aquifer beneath their land (whatever that might mean); they interpret such ownership as a right to pump at will. Farmers in Nebraska use the water they extract from the same aquifer (it extends from Texas up to the Canadian border) in a radically different way: they put to good use a sophisticated irrigation system designed by the German engineering firm Siemens. Sensors are scattered across the fields that capture information about two key parameters: soil moisture on the ground and temperatures at the top of plants; this information is transmitted to a central computer that processes it in order to fine-tune the amount of water delivered to the plants. Pioneered by a few farmers in central Nebraska, the system has been tested and validated by experts in irrigation from the College of Agricultural Sciences and Natural Resources at the University of Nebraska. It has then been picked up by numerous farmers all over the state. The college has acted as mediator in adoption.

Beyond innovation in monitoring systems, social and organizational innovation also plays a critical role, to ensure that the total withdrawals from aquifers, even through very efficient irrigation techniques, do not in the end exceed the carrying capacity of the natural resources. Institutions to manage water as a common good, as existed traditionally in water-scarce communities around the Mediterranean (oases and their water rights schemes, for instance), had been challenged greatly by the capacity of individual farmers to drill their own wells and use diesel pumps at a low price, leading to rapid depletion of these resources. Re-establishing the social capital of groups of water users at the local level is a complex challenge: it took drip irrigation tomato producers in the Sahel region in Tunisia some time to complement the technical innovation they had adopted with a governance institution to limit the amount of water they were allowed to use, but it now ensures much more predictability and thus mid- to long-term economic profitability. The Tunisian government had established the legal status of *groupements d'agriculteurs* to enable such an institution to flourish, but it takes local social innovators to make them real.

In Iran, a lonely innovator demonstrated the value of drip irrigation in desperate circumstances. In this country, farmers irrigating their fields without restraint and engineering firms, owned by the Islamic Revolutionary Guards Corps, damming every other river (at least those that are not yet completely dry), are busily helping climate change to condemn the country to aridity. The fate of Lake Urmia, the Iranian counterpart of the Great Salt Lake in Utah, is reminiscent of the destruction of the Aral Sea during the rush to cotton in Central Asia under Soviet rule, with the same dust storms evolving from the parched lands. Most of Iran is now in the grip of what looks like a never-ending drought. Water management routines, which essentially boil down to depleting aquifers, don't prepare the country to face a trend that will become all the more severe as climate change advances. Actual desertification is on the march in Kerman province in Southeast Iran, which is sometimes referred to as "pistachio land". Farmers there used to waste (subsidized) water by lavishly flooding their trees in the middle of the day. One of them became the laughing stock of his neighbors when some years ago he invested in a relatively costly drip irrigation system. His orchards are now the sole green spot in a landscape of dead trees: he is the only one who can survive on today's meager water allocations.

REFERENCE

Rai, N. (2012), "Drip, drip, drip: Daniel Hillel talks about how he helped revolutionize the way farmers water their crops", *The Wall Street Journal*, October 15.

41. Making the case for agroecological innovation: the need for technical but also political entrepreneurs

Sébastien Treyer

In many regions around the world, local farmers supported by their producers' organizations, international non-governmental organizations (NGOs) and local and international researchers have been able to demonstrate, at the scale of their territory, the performance of agroecological innovation to jointly reach economic, social and environmental objectives. Instead of relying on ever greater use of chemical inputs (pesticides, fertilizers), agroecological innovation – that is, not about keeping traditional farming systems in a state of low productivity, as is often pretended – aims at changing the whole system of practices by using more ecological knowledge of the functioning of agroecosystems: it thus enables the mobilization and optimization of natural cycles in the ecosystems in order to maximize expected benefits: improved income for the farmers, enhanced resilience in the face of economic and climatic shocks, and better environmental quality (biodiversity, carbon storage in soils, reduced pollution of water and air).

Examples are numerous. Integrated pest management, relying on predators and changes in the agricultural landscape to control pests, rather than using pesticides. Or the constitution of a complex agricultural landscape with different layers of vegetation, associated on the same plot, or in a complex pluriannual crop sequence, optimizing the synergies: for instance, nitrogen-fixating legumes that provide nitrogen to the associated cereals, instead of specialized fields of monoculture that seek to avoid any competition with other plants, but increases vulnerability to invasions by pests and weeds. Overall, integrating ecology into agronomy is a very knowledge-intensive innovation pathway, and could be accelerated by recent advances in information technology and big data, as well as in ecology or even metagenomics: understanding the genetic diversity across a whole ecosystem could be very useful to better understand and optimize its functioning.

This is particularly true in arid and semi-arid areas, where the protection against soil degradation is vital, and where the recomplexification of the agricultural landscape is absolutely crucial to maintaining organic matter in soils, thus better retaining water for the plants in the agroecosystem. Although such cases are numerous and well documented, their economic performance is often questioned when discussing national agricultural policies: yields of individual crops might indeed be lower in an agroecological system than in a high-input intensified one, whereas if you count all the different types of vegetal production associated on the same plot, the overall yield of the agroecological system might actually be higher. When considering future scenarios for farm development in a tropical context in Africa that would be characterized both by a low level of input use and a low level of productivity, decision-makers from national governments as well as from development partners are prone to consider only one scenario: specialization in one type of crop, with the example of Southern American monocultures in mind, looking for high yields through intensification in inputs and technical capital. But other scenarios are possible, inspired instead by Central American or Southeast Asian agroforests, very complex systems that are less input intensive and more labour and knowledge intensive, and able to reach very high levels of productivity.

But political decision-makers and development planners are focusing mainly on one indicator to assess economic profitability and return on investment: yields of a dominant crop, as if monoculture was the only model, and yields taken as a proxy for livelihood, well-being and food security of the farmers, which is very questionable. We need to understand that this lens is too narrow with which to assess even the economic profitability dimension of agricultural development, as it does not account for the other crops in a complex despecialized farming landscape, even less as an assessment of the value and real economic profit of the whole system, or its resilience, if input charges are reduced and if diversification is used as a risk reduction strategy. But to properly assess the performances of such systems on the relevant variety of indicators, what is needed is local and site-specific knowledge, which seems much more complicated to collect and compile than statistics on yields for one crop. On top of the usual and common imbalance between new entrants and incumbents, this complexity in technical and economic assessment contributes to explaining the asymmetry of political weight in major policy decisions respectively of agroecological options and models and of business as usual scenarios – that is, input-intensive green revolution packages.

For arid regions, a network of NGOs, the Centre d'Actions et de Réalisations Internationales (CARI), particularly originating from projects in the Sahel region of Africa, has designed and implemented a scientific and political strategy to redress this imbalance. They are busy gathering, harmonizing scientific and grassroots data on the performance of agroecological innovations across different countries and regions, making them scientifically robust by also assessing their limits, and promoting them through a dedicated advocacy strategy at subnational, national, regional as well as global scales (United Nations Framework Convention on Climate Change, United Nations Convention to Combat Desertification fora, for instance). Former Food and Agriculture Organization director-general Graziano da Silva acknowledged that agroecology is a crucial innovation option for our future, in order to attain food security, prosperity and sustainability. Political entrepreneurship proves critical at all these scales.

In Bolivia, former president Evo Morales had taken the political position not to choose between agriculture industrialization and specialization, occurring mostly in the lowlands, and support for complex agroecological farming systems, mostly in the Andean part of the country, where another network of NGOs called the Centro de Investigación y Promoción del Campesinado (CIPCA) is very active. This ends up in a competition between the two types of strategies of transformation for the agricultural sector, for resources like land and water, market access, as well as for political attention. In such a situation, federative organization, coalition building and sense of political strategy are at the heart of the ability for entrepreneurs to develop if they want to contribute to the transformation towards sustainability, on top of being able to mobilize research to demonstrate the technical performance of an alternative pathway for agricultural systems.

In such a tense strategic context, where asymmetry in political weight, in access to financial but also scientific resources, linking innovative groups of farmers with groups of consumers that are looking for a new role in the food system appears to be a particularly promising political strategy. Slow Food, an international network able to attract a lot of media and political attention, linking consumers and producers locally and globally, has developed Terra Madre, a network of farmers' projects enabling them to attract funding for their agroecological innovations, as well as cities developing innovative food policies. Such strategic coalitions are necessary to open up the political space for agroecological innovation pathways.

42. Radical transformation in global supply chains: can new business models be based on biodiversity in the agrifood industry?

Sébastien Treyer

The food industry has been struggling for years with its impact on the environment. The impacts of input-intensive agricultural production on nature and the environment have been made obvious since the 1960s. *Silent Spring* by Rachel Carson from 1962 is still an extremely vivid account of the impacts of pesticides on nature, resonating with today's scientific reports on the effects on pollinators. The algae blooms in Brittany's coastal waters have been linked for a long time to a structural excess of intensive farming of pigs and chickens that has brought jobs and prosperity to a region previously suffering from underdevelopment, and emigration to other French regions. This has been well known for decades, but the trends of environment degradation have still not been reversed. One obvious explanation of the inability to change is that the downward trends in prices that farmers are being paid for their products make it nearly impossible to ask them to change their practices, because their economic viability is so close to a survival threshold. This is now all well known, and the food industry knows it must do something.

What is also well known in the public debate is that power and value are not fairly allocated along the supply chain: farmers have much less power and a small share of the value compared to upstream players (the input industry) or downstream players (processing and retailing) because their negotiation power is scattered and thus weak. That gives enormous responsibility to the large companies of the food industry: they are in power; they have the tools at hand to foster change in the whole supply chain.

The different phases of the sustainability strategy in a company like Danone are extremely interesting in this regard. In the late 2000s, this large company in the dairy industry developed a specific innovation and exploration fund, called the Livelihoods Funds, where impact investment[1] projects were explored to finance sustainable agricultural practices, landscapes and food supply chains, particularly aiming at finding solutions for carbon storage and biodiversity protection, as well as supporting smallholder farmers and food-insecure people. These explorations were significant, exploring rediversification in breeds of cattle, in sourcing strategies among a diversity of farms, in particular with regard to their size. This sometimes led to innovations that could be brought into the main business model of the company (sourcing from local smallholder livestock producers in India, for instance), but they stood in sharp contrast to the core business model at the level of the whole commercial company, driven, for instance, by the harsh competition on international milk powder markets. In such a context, massification and economies of scale seem to be a law of nature, and not an economic strategy, which makes it paradoxical to look for a business model where rediversification and destandardization would be the main motto.

However, in the early 2010s, the orientation to sustainability in the company strategy made it manifest that diversity (of animal breeds, in agroecosystems, in the size of farms from which to source) was going to be a cornerstone of a pathway to sustainability. The tension between the existing business model and the need to rediversify at all levels of the food chain was then completely explicit.

After 2015, like other main players in the industry, Danone was faced with the need to take ambitious initiatives against climate change, and recently also for biodiversity, as well as for nutrition and food security. Barilla, for instance, took important steps towards sustainable and diversified diets, also exploring more responsible supply chains and how one of its food brands, like Wasa, could become carbon neutral. Some coalitions, like the Food and Land Use Coalition (FOLU), launched in New York in September 2019, gathered main players of the industry around commitments like stopping sourcing from deforestation and shifting to more sustainable diets. These steps taken to reduce greenhouse gas emissions are already an important challenge, and monitoring the results of this initiative is particularly crucial, to make the companies accountable for their commitments, and to learn from where they might also be facing obstacles to reaching their objectives.

On top of the carbon-neutrality challenge, the year 2019 made it very clear, with the International Science-Policy Platform on Biodiversity and Ecosystem Services (IPBES) report on the state of biodiversity degradation, that biodiversity and climate change both needed to be integrated in ambitious transformations of the business models of the food system: this sector represents one of the major drivers of biodiversity degradation, not only through land use change, but also through the homogenization, specialization and simplification of agricultural landscapes. While carbon optimization of the dairy industry would mainly lead to drastic reduction of greenhouse gas emissions through substituting animal proteins with vegetal proteins (soy milk instead of cow milk), Danone's strategy for sustainability, inspired by the Livelihoods experience, insists a lot on biodiversity and rediversification of products, thus betting much more on grasslands and extensive ruminant production systems, than on substitution by vegetal proteins. These grasslands are crucial for biodiversity in different contexts – in particular, in Europe they can deliver important eco-system services, including carbon storage in soils. This strategy can also lead to more economic space for smallholder livestock producers. The crucial challenge of such a strategy is that it ultimately entails deintensification or exten-sification, and despecialization. How would it be realistically made consistent with the current trends and state of competition in the agrifood industry? The Covid-19 health crisis might actually make this rediversification strategy more attractive, both because it could enable better prevention of pandemics linked to biodiversity degradation, and because it could reinforce the resilience of the supply chains. But the situation remains very uncertain.

This is the crude challenge that a number of players in the industry, gath-ered together under a coalition named One Planet Business for Biodiversity (OP2B), in New York in September 2019, are putting at the centre of the trans-formation towards a new business model. Of course, a business strategy based on diversification can be profitable: betting on economies of scope rather than on economies of scale, for instance. But how resilient is such a strategy in a context of always harsher competition and the race to the bottom of prices on international commodity markets like the milk market? For a smaller company or for segments of the products, the strategy could be to move upmarket, looking for a bonus on prices through a specific segment of the market. But how to carry out such a strategy to move the mainstream strategy of the whole company upmarket, without losing an important share of the consumers who are neither necessarily ready nor wealthy enough to pay for higher prices to access dairy products?

In a crucial period for biodiversity, with an important meeting of the UN Convention on Biological Diversity, its 15th conference of the parties, planned in China for early 2021, this coalition of companies has planned to come up with performance indicators that would be both realistic and ambitious, driven by the objective to rediversify their portfolio of products as well as the raw materials they source from.

We are witnessing interesting times for the agrifood industry, where busi-ness as usual will soon no longer be possible, and radically disruptive business models need to be invented. But will this really be possible? We at least need to learn from this experiment, because of the boldness of the bet that is being made. And if it happens that such transformative commitments appear to be out of reach for large companies under the pressure of their shareholders, this would then pave the way for even more radical questioning about corporate purpose.

Maybe this is where the paradox of the quest for such a new business model needs to be connected with the prospect of making Danone a benefit corporation, so that it is not only shareholders who are the ultimate decision-makers about such strategic choices, and that social or environmental impact can be put higher in the performance evaluation of the company, at the same level as profitability. Exploring new business models to stay within planetary boundaries, both on climate change and biodiversity, might lead to a magnitude of transformation in economic strategies that the current legal status of companies cannot permit. The radical changes in business models that are needed for sustainability might necessitate evolutions in the structure of capitalism, which begins, for instance, with an evolution in the legal definition of corporate purpose, as has already been discussed in France with a view to integrating social and environmental interactions as a *raison d'être* in a company's statutes.

NOTE

1. Impact investing aims to generate specific beneficial social or environmental effects in addition to financial effects.

REFERENCE

IPBES (2019), *Global Assessment Report on Biodiversity and Ecosystem Services of the Intergovernmental Science-Policy Platform on Biodiversity and Ecosystem Services*, edited by E.S. Brondizio, J. Settele, S. Díaz and H.T. Ngo. Bonn: IPBES Secretariat.

43. Ethan Brown – the protein revolutionary

Geoffrey Heal

Meat, and beef in particular, is something that the environmental movement loves to hate. Cattle produce methane, a powerful greenhouse gas, and need vast areas for grazing, much of which is created by clearing forests, in the process destroying habitat and releasing stored carbon from the soil into the air. In recent years, the animal rights movement has added its growing voice to the anti-meat clamor. However, protein is an essential element of our diets, and meat is a tasty, convenient and culturally sanctified way of delivering it. Displacing animal products from diets seemed a pipe dream.

No more. Beyond Meat and Impossible Foods (and others) are transforming protein possibilities, providing foods that look and taste like meat, and have the same protein content, but are based entirely on plants. With sales growing rapidly, Beyond Meat has a stock market value of over $5 billion, having peaked at near $12 billion.

Ethan Brown, Beyond Meat's founder, is a passionate vegan, and deeply concerned about climate change. Ending the use of animal protein speaks to both these issues: it ends factory farming and the associated animal suffering, and removes a major source of greenhouse gases. He was driven to found Beyond Meat by a sense of obligation to contribute on these issues: he felt his life would be a lie unless he could resolve the conflict between eating well and doing well by the planet.

Brown emphasizes that Beyond Meat's products *are* meat, but plant-based meat rather than animal-based meat. As he explains, animals are bioreactors that take proteins from plants and rearrange them into muscle tissue: Beyond Meat's technology also takes proteins from plants and rearranges them into something very close to muscle tissue, and does this rearrangement at a vastly lower environmental cost. His aim is to make products that are indistinguishable from animal meat, but are healthier, providing protein without the harmful chemicals in red meat, such as cholesterol, and with more fiber. Beyond Meat has signed up a number of elite athletes who eat only its products, and Brown dreams of making the National Basketball Association (NBA) vegan! For 2 million years, humans and their predecessors took protein from animals, and

Brown wants our generation and his company to break that tradition and free us from dependence on animal meat.

Little in Brown's background makes him an obvious choice for such a pivotal role in human history. His father, a professor at the University of Maryland, also owned a dairy farm, where Brown spent much of his time as a youth. After graduating, Brown worked in cleantech,[1] developing fuel cells, and after completing an MBA at Columbia went back into cleantech. But all this time he was thinking about the conflict between eating well and doing well by the planet, and he began his venture into commercializing this concern by importing textured soy protein from Taiwan and selling it to Whole Foods. Then he learned about research at the University of Missouri on making protein from plants take the form of meat. He licensed this research and developed it further at the University of Maryland, and this is what in 2009 led to Beyond Meat. For the first few years he funded this venture himself, even selling his home to raise money, and then venture capital firm Kleiner Perkins and other outsiders – including Bill Gates – invested.

Ethan Brown did in fact bring several important qualities to the problem of replacing meat. One was an obsession with solving this problem, and a willingness to do whatever was needed. He is an intense and focused person, and the focus is on replacing animal meat. A second was a good enough education in science and technology to understand the scientific issues involved, and the third was a business background: as an MBA student at Columbia, he took a course on starting a new venture. Obsession, focus, understanding, business skills, and of course a receptive market: these were enough to generate the explosion of creativity that is Beyond Meat. Their research labs are in Manhattan Beach, California, and he has christened their research program the Manhattan Beach Project, riffing off the development of the atomic bomb during World War II to give a sense of urgency and importance. The Manhattan Beach Project could change the world as much as the Manhattan Project did to produce the first nuclear weapons, though in a more constructive direction.

It is worth emphasizing the receptiveness of the market for Beyond Meat and its competitors: in both the US and Europe, vegetarian and vegan diets grew rapidly in popularity from around 2000 on. Millennials and subsequent generations are increasingly "flexitarian," that is, they are reducing the amount of meat they eat and moving to largely vegan diets. The environmental community is also increasingly aware of the environmental impact of food choices and looking to minimize these. Both groups form natural markets for Beyond Meat's products.

Beyond Meat is now well established, with its products available at most major fast food chains and many retail grocery outlets. But it has to face serious competitors. Impossible Foods is one, targeting the same market sector. Good Catch aims to do for fish what Beyond Meat has done for meat. Perhaps more threatening, Tyson Foods is now selling plant-based chicken substitutes, and could easily move into other meats too. So too could several other large food conglomerates, so establishing a brand name and market position is key to Beyond Meat's long-run financial success.

Both Beyond Meat and Impossible Foods are planning to sell their products in China. This makes strategic sense: it's a huge meat market and also has an indigenous tradition of plant-based meat substitutes, many of which have been sold in Chinese restaurants in the West for many years. Indeed, Ethan Brown's first venture was importing textured soy protein from Taiwan. But China already has domestic competitors to the US start-ups, including Whole Perfect Foods and Zhenmeat, so establishing a profitable presence in China will be a challenge for the US companies.

In terms of Brown's original goals of reducing the animal welfare and environmental impacts of our food, the company has already succeeded. According to a study commissioned by Beyond Meat with the Center for Sustainable Systems at the University of Michigan, a plant-based burger generates 90 percent less greenhouse gas emissions, requires 45 percent less energy, has 99 percent less impact on water scarcity, and 93 percent less impact on land use than a quarter-pound of traditional U.S. beef. And in 2013, People for the Ethical Treatment of Animals (PETA) named Beyond Meat its company of the year. Brown and his colleagues have shown that plant-based protein can sell and be profitable, bringing about an irreversible change in the food industry.

NOTE

1.   Technologies that either reduce or optimize the use of natural resources whilst simultaneously reducing the negative effect that technology has on the plant and its ecosystems.

44. How to make a sustainable living in a tropical forest: the case of Suruí Indians in the Amazon rainforest – success under threat

Claude Henry

The community of Suruí Indians have benefited – until now – from a 1988 revision of the Brazilian Constitution that recognized the rights of Indians on their original lands, including the right to exclude intruders. However, the way, from complete isolation – despite former US President Theodore Roosevelt trekking the region in 1914, where he almost died from an infectious disease – to this recognition, has been long and paved with horrendous episodes. Isolation ceased with the construction in the 1960s of the first road through the Amazon rainforest, the Trans-Amazonian Highway. The first contacts between the Suruí and the outside world have been devastating: transmissible diseases, against which they were defenseless, and bloody confrontations with would-be settlers, lured from all over Brazil by fraudulent property titles on Amazonian land, decimated the community, from 3000 to a few hundred members. Under similar circumstances, many Indian communities were wiped out. With characteristic energy and under an exceptionally visionary leadership, the Suruí bounced back. When in 1988 their exclusive rights on their lands were confirmed, they proved able to make a living from them in the following sustainable ways:

- Harvesting timber and non-timber products according to exacting rules. They refrain from prematurely felling trees commanding high prices like the Brazil nut tree, which grows perfectly straight up to 60 meters. Their tenure security made the Suruí confident enough to devise and implement a 50-year plan for harvesting and regenerating the forest, reforesting those parts of their lands that, during the extremely difficult pre-1988 period, had been devastated by illegal logging and criminal fires.
- Sharing the cost of storing carbon with the outside world. The Suruí started to reforest on their own, but that effort could not go very far without financial resources from the outside. Chief Almir Suruí – who manages to

combine a deep attachment to the ancestral knowledge and traditions of his community, with a university education (in biology) and a keen interest in advanced technologies, and who is highly regarded by both the members of his community and many partners in Brazil and abroad – considers it legitimate to seek contributions from outside the Suruí community. The whole world is indeed benefiting from the conservation and regeneration of the Amazon rainforest. Seen from the sky, the Suruí lands appear as a green oasis surrounded by parched and ocher earth, which itself was once forest. The bulk of Suruí lands are in the state of Rondônia that, before the August 2019 fires, had already lost half its forest cover. Having been granted verified access to the markets for carbon offsets, the Suruí community agreed in September 2013 an initial transaction amounting to 120 000 tons of carbon offsets bought by the Brazilian company Natura Cosméticos, which is Latin America's largest cosmetic company and which aims at complete carbon neutrality. Other transactions followed.

- Protecting the forest against further degradation. Illegal logging, criminal forest fires and mining encroachments are ongoing threats that are essential to detect and repress as quickly as possible, before damage becomes too great. Detection is the task of the Suruí themselves; they use advanced positioning systems under a specific application of Google Earth Outreach, which Chief Almir likes to demonstrate himself to visitors. With Google Earth on his smartphone, he would zoom on the Suruí lands and check for anomalies. That day he spotted in a remote location the campsite of *garimpeiros*, illegal and sometimes aggressive gold prospectors. In this way, as soon as suspicious activities are detected, federal or state police agents can be sent exactly to the right place.

Criminal activities have always been a lingering threat. There is even a contract on Chief Almir's head. The threat has been taken seriously not only by the Suruí themselves but also, at least until recently, by the federal authorities, which assigned bodyguards from the police special forces. Nobody has forgotten the assassination on his doorstep, in the neighboring state of Acre, of Chico Mendes, the legendary defender of the forest and of the poor. And everybody knows how frequently environmental activists are murdered in the Amazon.

However, do federal and state authorities still bother? Police increasingly tend to ignore calls for help. Authorities keep denying evidence. For instance, echoing denials at federal level, retired police colonel Rocha, governor of the state of Rondônia, declared: "If we look at the situation in other countries, their forests are burning much more than in Brazil. You go to London or other countries, and what do you see? Smoke from burning, from industry. How can they demand of us what they haven't done themselves?" (Phillips, 2019). Despite this curious assessment, the firefighters based in Rondônia's capital

Porto Velho – a small band of dedicated albeit ill-equipped men and women – have in desperation attended dozens of fires a day for more than three weeks in August 2019.

Since January 1, 2019, when Jair Bolsonaro became president of Brazil, criminals have developed a sense of impunity. President Bolsonaro sees the conservation of the Amazon rainforest as a hindrance to development – that is, agrobusiness, logging and mining industries – and sees Indian indigenous people as *Untermenschen* (inferior people) who, as he once said, "smell, are undereducated and don't speak our language" (Watson, 2018). He has already transferred key decisions concerning the forest and its inhabitants to the Ministry of Agriculture, controlled by the agrobusiness lobby. He thinks the Holocaust can be forgiven, as he said at a meeting with evangelical leaders on April 13, 2019. He thus might also think that he would be forgiven for transposing into the Amazon rainforest Hitler's *Endlösung der Judenfrage* (Final Solution to the Jewish Question). Those who right now destroy the forest and confront the Indian communities are just anticipating systematic annihilation.

Can't the Brazilian people understand that everybody would miss the Suruí entrepreneurship? When you enter their forest, coming from the parched land around, you almost immediately switch from a dry to a humid atmosphere; the neighboring farms and ranches would not survive the permanent drought that would result from the disappearance of the Suruí and their forest. With the disappearance of a significant proportion of the Amazon rainforest, drought would extend to the whole of Brazil, depriving water from, in particular, the 19 million inhabitants of the São Paulo conurbation. And, last but not least, the whole world would lose an essential carbon sink and biodiversity reservoir. The Suruí are not only innovators in sustainability, they are also canaries in a mine approaching explosion.

REFERENCES

Phillips, T. (2019), "Chaos, chaos, chaos: a journey through Bolsonaro's Amazon inferno", *The Guardian*, September 9.
Watson, F. (2018), "Bolsonara's election is catastrophic news for Brazil's indigenous tribes", *The Guardian*, October 31.

45. Migrants to repopulate depopulated villages – Riace in Calabria, Italy and its mayor Mimmo Lucano

Pippo Ranci

"CLIMATE MIGRANTS"

According to a recent World Bank report (2018), in only three regions – Sub-Saharan Africa, South Asia and Latin America, which together represent 55 percent of the developing world's population – climate change will push over 143 million people – or around 2.8 percent of the population of these three regions – to migrate within their countries by 2050. These flows will be additional with respect to the well-known, and generally cross-border, flows of refugees and migrants fleeing war, poverty and oppression. It can be imagined that a share of these climate-induced migrations may well turn from internal to cross-border, according to the local conditions and developments. Climate mitigation and policies to prevent migration may reduce these impressive flows but will not eliminate them. Adaptation must be faced in various ways, including an acceptable settlement of migrants.

In this chapter we tell an unusual story of migrants from various Mediterranean and African countries settling in an area called Locride, on the southeastern coast of Calabria, Italy.

CALABRIA

Calabria is one of the poorest regions in Italy, although it is rich in history. Inhabited by Italic populations, from the eighth century BC it was an important centre of Greek civilization (Magna Graecia) and then of the Roman empire until the fifth century AD. Occupied and influenced by Byzantines, Normans and Arabs, it lived through centuries of decadence under French and Spanish rule. Life did not improve under a Piedmont-dominated kingdom of Italy, when poverty pushed hundreds of thousands of people each year to look for a better life in North and South America, then in Western Europe. After

World War II, the main destination was Northern Italy. The population of the Calabrian diaspora is estimated as two to three times the population of Calabria itself. The southeastern coast of Calabria can be reached from Libya and from the Eastern Mediterranean easily. It is geographically suited to uncontrolled immigration.

The social fabric has been torn between institutions loyal to a foreign or anyway extraneous political centre and local mafias who imposed their burden and paralysed economic growth and social progress. Migrations left many houses empty and agricultural land abandoned.

RIACE AND MAYOR LUCANO

In the midst of Locride lies Riace, a village that came to world fame as the place where two Greek bronze statues of warriors from the middle of the fifth century BC were found on the seabed in 1972. It was a village of 1600 residents according to the 2001 census, down from a level of 2400 in the 1921 census.

In 1998, a boat carrying Kurdish refugees landed on the Riace shore. Others followed, and although most of them went on towards other Italian and European destinations, many settled. In a decade, thousands of migrants arrived (an estimate is 6000), of whom 450 settled, bringing new life to the village.

This settlement has been mainly due to the courageous and stubborn action of Domenico (Mimmo) Lucano. Lucano was born nearby, moved early in his life to Riace, then to Rome as a university student and to Northern Italy as a teacher. He moved back to Riace, was a human rights activist from the 1990s and became mayor of Riace in 2004. In this role he supported the settling of migrants and refugees in the small municipality, where the population was old on average and many homes, abandoned by people who had migrated away from Italy in the previous decades, were available.

Lucano was active in having the old buildings restored and made available to the incoming population of mainly young people. He organized their activity in opening or reopening artisan and textile shops, in providing food and lodging to visitors in the homes. He secured government and private funds for training. With the arrival of new children, the planned closure of the local school could be avoided. The village flourished again as old activities were resumed by the new residents.

Economically, the new life was largely based on subsidies to specific projects and to the ordinary public cash support to immigrants (35 euros/day) that would have been paid out even if the migrants had been kept under custody and de facto prevented from doing any useful activity, as happens in many refugee camps in the world.

In order to get the new activities started, a local pseudo-currency was introduced by the Riace municipality, together with a number of municipalities of the area. The municipal administrations were in charge of handing out the 35-euro subsidy, but government funds were often late, sometimes by six or seven months. Lucano printed a local currency, carrying images of historic revolutionaries like Che Guevara and of mafia victims like Peppino Impastato: the shopkeepers accepted the notes. The initiative, although clearly useful, was criticized.

Waste collection contracts had been traditionally awarded to local small companies set up by the local mafia. Lucano chose a couple of new cooperatives who employed the migrants. They were flexible enough to use donkeys to do their job along the narrow streets where no van could enter.

Old buildings were adapted for hosting up to 100 visitors. A new farm, with livestock both for production and for teaching, was set up and managed by migrants themselves according to biological methods.

CELEBRITY AND CONTRAST

Lucano's innovative approach to dealing with refugees in the context of the European migrant crisis gained worldwide attention. Lucano came third in the 2010 competition for the World Mayor Prize run by the World Mayor Foundation, ahead of mayors in many important cities. Yet, as the saying "*nemo propheta in patria*" (no man is a prophet in his own land) goes, Lucano met strong local opposition, of three types.

First, he was dangerously opposed by the local mafia. In 2009, shortly after his first re-election as mayor, he was shot at through the window of a restaurant and two of his dogs were poisoned. Second, his administration of the Riace municipality was censured on the grounds of administrative irregularities. These accusations were not completely groundless: the permanent emergency created by the number and movement of the migrants, the innovative activities, the rigidity of the legal frame and slowness of the public administration, the difficult local relations in an area traditionally dominated by the mafias, made it almost impossible for him to avoid incurring some irregularities, at least formal. Third and most effective, he has been the target of denigration and obstruction by the Interior Minister and political leader Matteo Salvini during his tenure from June 2018 to September 2019. Lucano was taken to court more than once on the basis of various accusations, including accounting irregularities, the waste collection service assigned without a regular tender, and even accusations of attempts to celebrate marriages between a migrant and a local resident with the purpose of granting the migrant an Italian citizenship. Although the judiciary rejected some of these accusations, Lucano was suspended from office and arrested on the basis of recent legislation, introduced by the Salvini-dominated government, that makes favouring illegal immigration a criminal offence. His house arrest was converted into an order to stay away from Riace.

Inquiries and trials have been ongoing for long. No accusation was made, though, regarding pursuit of his personal interests: in fact, all the time it has been evident that he systematically sacrificed them to his humanitarian mission and, possibly, his ambition to lead a new model of immigrant integration.

The Salvini-dominated government[1] reduced or eliminated the financial provisions on which the Riace experiment was based and ordered the Riace municipality to give back all the transfer payments that had been used irregularly. Most initiatives had to be discontinued, many social enterprises were forced to close. Under the new conditions created by the anti-immigration legislation, many migrants who had settled in Riace left for other destinations. The whole experiment was destroyed.[2]

A film on Lucano's life had been commissioned by the Italian state television. It was produced in 2017, but its circulation was forbidden by government in 2018.

HOPE SUPPRESSED, FOR THE TIME BEING

New municipal elections were held in May 2019. A new mayor was elected from a local, right-wing list, with a programme of going "back to normal life", of keeping the number of new settlers low and of taking primary care of services to the residents.

Two aspects of the Riace model have attracted the attention of some experts, however. While most public refugee camps allow permanence for a limited time, usually six months, integration requires a longer stay, and Riace provided acceptance without a time limit. Moreover, distribution of cash (even through the expedient of the local currency) is more conducive to integration than distribution of food. Both aspects have been seen as important and positive in research referred to other situations (Taylor, 2016).

WILL THE MODEL SURVIVE?

The repressive attitude of government started changing in September 2019 following a political turnaround that led to a new coalition government that excluded Salvini's Lega. New developments are possible.

Whatever happens to Riace, a number of local initiatives, similar to the Riace experiment, have been undertaken in other locations. Interestingly enough, in September 2019, the government of Molise, the smallest region in Southern Italy, announced subsidies to people who moved into municipalities having fewer than 2000 residents and who started a new business.[3]

The "Riace model" is not unique. In 2015, the arrival of only ten Syrian children with their families saved the primary school of the German village Golzow, near the Polish border, from having to close down the first grade, and produced a successful case of integration, initial opposition notwithstanding. This tiny episode made news since Golzow (820 inhabitants) and its primary school were well known as the backdrop for "The Children of Golzow," an epic Communist-era documentary that followed a cohort of first graders through decades of life behind the Iron Curtain.[4]

The problem of settling waves of immigrants, moving for various reasons, among which is climate change, will remain, in Italy and elsewhere, on a level that requires new and creative solutions. The simple idea of migrants settling in depopulated regions, where a local culture can be revived through cross-fertilisation, will deserve further attention.

NOTES

1. The cabinet led by Giuseppe Conte, appointed 1 June 2018 and dissolved 5 September 2019, was formed by a coalition of Movimento 5 Stelle and Lega. The leader of the latter party, Matteo Salvini, held the position of Interior Minister and was very active in opposing Italian acceptance of migrants.
2. After a lower court decision and an appeal by the Ministry, on 7 June 2020 the Council of State has finally decided that the closure of the Centres of the Protection System for Refugees and Asylum Seekers (SPRAR), including the one of Riace, that was decided by the Interior Ministry in 2018, was illegal. On 7 July 2020 the Court for the Revision of measures restricting personal freedom (Tribunale del Riesame) has decided that the measures applied to mayor Lucano were unfounded.
3. Silvia Marchetti (2019), "These Italian towns in Molise will pay you $27,000 to move there", *CNN Travel*, 12 September, accessed 19 August 2020 at https://edition.cnn.com/travel/article/molise-italy-pay-to-move/index.html.
4. Katrin Bennhold (2019), "Syrian children saved a German village. And a village saved itself", *The New York Times*, 19 September, accessed 19 August 2020 at https://www.nytimes.com/2019/09/19/world/europe/germany-golzow-syria-refugees.html.

REFERENCES

Taylor J.E. (2016), "Research: refugees can bolster a region's economy", *Harvard Business Review*, 5 October.
World Bank (2018), *Groundswell: Preparing for Internal Climate Migration*, Washington, DC: World Bank.

46. How Loos-en-Gohelle, a derelict mining town in the north of France, has become a standard in sustainable development

Michel Berry

Jean-François Caron was elected mayor of Loos-en-Gohelle in 2001 as a member of the Green Party. An election on this ticket is very unusual in the Nord-Pas-de-Calais region, a mining area that used to employ as many as 220 000 people. He succeeded his father as mayor, and this, in the world of 'mining paternalism', gave him a sort of endorsement. Previously, Caron had also been in charge of an important group project aimed at developing the town. These unique circumstances set the stage for one of the most surprising transformations of a town and a region ever seen.[1]

BOUNCE BACK OR DIE

Jean-François Caron likes to say that he represents the generation of beneficiaries of 'non-sustainable development'. Initially, a great deal of wealth was created in the mining area, but when the mines closed the inhabitants had to deal with the after-effects. When he was elected mayor, the level of nitrates in the water tables was twice the amount permitted by the French government (99 mg per litre compared to 50 mg), and there had been a subsidence of up to 15 metres as a result of mining (Loos had nine pits in its region). The streams ran in the opposite direction to their original courses, and the low levels of the town kept changing. The surrounding countryside was spoiled because its sole purpose had been to service industrial activity for which the region and the population were merely adjustment variables.

Added to this, the population had a large identity problem. For a very long period of time, the miners had been the jewel in the working-class crown, but when the mines closed the inhabitants of the Nord-Pas-de-Calais became known as the 'freaks of France'. In 2008, in Paris, at a football cup final at the Parc des Princes stadium, there was a banner saying 'Northerners = half-bloods, paedophiles, alcoholics'. When the media latched on to this, it merely reinforced the negative image, which the mining town inhabitants found unbearable. From that moment onwards, whenever a television journalist made a documentary about Northern France, it featured people who spoke the local dialect (and therefore it was decided that the viewer needed subtitles), children whose noses were running, and broken window panes. Repairing this lost dignity was an essential part of the new mayor's strategy.

Furthermore, the mining population had been living for a long period of time in a state of submission. Nine geographical groups incorporated nationalized mines in Northern France known as 'Les Houillères'. Each group had its own maternity unit, stadium, churches, housing, associations, and social security offices, with the exception of cemeteries. A miner was liable to lose part of his salary if he did not maintain his garden, as gardening was judged to be a beneficial activity, because if a miner was gardening he was not in the local *bistrot* or trade union office. Central mining cooperatives issued families with booklets of coupons, and each purchase made using these booklets was immediately deducted from the miner's salary. These extreme conditions ensured a compliant population who found it difficult to adapt to changes in society.

A number of political and administrative strategies were put forward. Some considered reducing the size of the local population by moving inhabitants to Fos-sur-Mer, for example, a steel and oil industry site in the south of France. Thousands of people relocated there, but this did not solve the problem in the north. Other strategies of reindustrialization – for example, promoting the car industry – were implemented in order to reproduce events from the region's industrial past, but this was not in keeping with the region's mining history.

As far as Jean-François Caron was concerned, they either had to bounce back, or go under. Loos-en-Gohelle was the first town in the Nord-Pas-de-Calais region to see the situation from a different angle. Caron was convinced that the way forward for the town and the region (of which he was also vice-president) was with renewable energy and the internet. He organized conferences about employment possibilities to explain the details of these future changes. He had been working with Jeremy Rifkin[2] since 2010. Rifkin's plans were in step with the Nord-Pas-de-Calais region's ideas, which declared that renewable energy and optimized management of production and consumption, with local loops, had to be at the heart of the new model, which is less driven by production and is more economic in terms of energy. The model also stated that those involved with the development of public policy had to be fully integrated into this movement.

However, this new model and the path necessary to achieve it were not yet clear. How could one convince a population, which was used to being helped and which lacked self-confidence, to try to develop its own future? Jean-François Caron devised an approach based on three priorities: involving the inhabitants; enhancing the mining heritage; and using 'applied' renewable energy. In other words, adopting an experimental approach that allowed for errors.

DEMOCRACY INVOLVING THE POPULATION

Since his election as mayor, Caron has been working on perfecting a concept of democracy in which the population of Loos was truly involved. This approach is different from the model of 'participative democracy' (which has become increasingly fashionable in France) whereby people are asked for their opinions, and what they want, leaving politicians to decipher the population's 'wish list'. In this situation, everyone loses out, as all the needs are naturally impossible to meet: citizens become frustrated as they feel that their requests have not been heard, and policies are undermined as they appear to have betrayed the citizens. Democracy where the population is involved consists instead of organizing meetings on subjects that directly concern the population, letting the citizens express their wishes and recriminations, and then discussing possible solutions with them, and, above all, getting them involved in the process.

Setting this up is slow and requires patience. Jean-François Caron advises his teams about how to handle the first half-hour of these meetings and to say nothing while people get their complaints off their chests. After this, it is possible to talk about more concrete problems, and to begin a constructive process. In the long run, this process has surprising results, and the inhabitants can become clear about numerous subjects, and even be rude. As Jean-François Caron writes: 'the more we work with our citizens, the more their feedback helps us improve the process, and the more pertinent the projects become. This is how Loos has become noted in the product-service and cooperation system due to its ability to be close to its citizens and processes and to find a series of solutions'.

The number of social associations has doubled, and the number of people taking part in neighbourhood celebrations or in trips for local children to discover the seaside has multiplied tenfold. '50–50' joint projects have been put in place; in other words, if the inhabitants take initiatives, the town contributes by creating a charter defining the roles. For example, Loos town hall built a children's educational garden, but it is the parents' or grandparents' responsibility – and not the municipality's – to maintain the garden. Also, a skatepark was designed and built with help and input from teenagers, encouraging them to become aware about regulatory matters and to appreciate the costs of such a project. Farm roads have been resurfaced with help from local farmers who supplied the skips to transport the construction waste. Since then, the farmers have been more careful to avoid making ruts in the roads they use. The main idea behind these actions is that, in change management, the 'soft' side, with its psycho-sociological dimensions, is more important than the 'hard', tech-nological side, and that involvement in taking action is a powerful motor for triggering the process of change.

ENHANCING THE MINING HERITAGE

In the 1980s, the authorities who had taken the decision to close the pits wanted to make all trace of them disappear. According to Jean-François Caron, this marked a period of rejecting the region's history when some people even said they were sorry for having existed. Loos refused to take this point of view and declared that one could not build any future if one denied one's past. Many of Loos' inhabitants have Polish, Hungarian or North African surnames, and the mines played a crucial role in their lives and the construction of their identi-ties. Telling them that they were now the 'wretched of the Earth' and nobodies, while at the same time telling them to be creative and enterprising, would have been pointless. On the contrary, 'we realized that we had to enhance our past in order to plan for the future'. This was the thinking behind the creation in 1984 of a series of storytelling and 'sound and light' shows called the 'Gohelliades', based on the theme 'The People and Riches of the Gohelle region – Land and Industry – Art and Tradition'.[3]

In Loos, there were two large slag heaps that some officials had wanted to eradicate. The municipality of Loos replied that these were wonderful slag heaps, the highest in Europe at 146.50 metres, the same height as the Great Pyramid of Giza: 'if we marvel at the Egyptian pyramids, why should we look down on these symbols of human-made activity?' This remark was the starting point for the creation of the 'The Chain of Slag Heaps', an association that, in 2012, resulted in the coal-mining region's inclusion in UNESCO's list of World Heritage sites.

Long before he became mayor, Jean François Caron was interested, with other young people in Loos, in the revitalization of these slag heaps, remarking that very interesting flora and fauna had been found specifically in this indus-trial area. Subsequently, in 1987, they created the 'Association des Naturalistes de la Gohelle', whose role was to persuade the *département* to pass biotope legislation making people change the way in which they looked at the slag heaps and then trying to save them. When Jean-François Caron became mayor, he decided to make the heaps more accessible physically and organised activ-ities in order to discover the flora and fauna. He also wanted to integrate them into a new urban park that, like the slag heaps themselves, would enhance the image of the mining area.

The 11/19 Pit, at the foot of the slag heaps, was 1000 metres deep. It was renamed Base 11/19 and became the site of the new model for economic development. Alongside, new associations emerged, including 'The Chain of Slag Heaps', which protects the mining heritage and its biodiversity, and 'Common Culture', an association encouraging artistic creation and shows. In 2002, Jean-François Caron encouraged the development of the 'Creation of the Development of Eco-enterprises (Cd2e) association. He realized that 'the region receives a great deal of money in order to restore its degraded environment; however, the area does not have companies which can meet such needs. Therefore, we should create a system of "group intelligence", organizing technological, technical and legal monitoring, and locating research laboratories in the region'.

SUSTAINABLE DEVELOPMENT

The Cd2e association's primary concern is to promote eco-construction and eco-materials with two objectives: first, to assist and promote companies; and second, to advise local authorities and help construction projects. Over the years, the association has expanded its aid into the water and energy sectors, and even the circular economy. It currently employs about 20 people and has at its disposal a list of more than 500 regional companies that are in eco-construction and 150 in eco-materials.

There is a 'theatre of eco-materials' available as a form of demonstration to professionals (such as architects, consultants and company managers), and also to researchers and the general public who can come to discover and touch the basic materials of eco-construction. The 'Apprentis d'Auteuil' association, which helps to integrate young people into society, has opened a training facility in Loos for 350 apprentices in the eco-construction sector. LumiWatt, a platform for the development of photovoltaic activities in zones of moderate sunshine, is testing about 30 innovative technologies in collaboration with various engineering and architecture schools in the region.

Because miners did not have to pay for the coal to heat their homes, insulation was not a major concern. It has now become extremely expensive to heat their homes because of fuel costs. Eco-construction and thermal retrofitting have therefore become a priority, and the inhabitants of renovated accommodation can easily tell the difference with regard to their previous expenses and living conditions, and this, of course, is a powerful tool for change. All social housing in Loos will have to be built according to the rules of eco-construction. This amounts to about 10 per cent of all housing in Loos; in other words, between 250 and 300 eco-built and eco-fitted forms of accommodation.

In ten years, the 11/19 site has been totally transformed. While enhancing its historical heritage, the town of Loos-en-Gohelle has taken up the challenge of economic renewal by making the Base 11/19 a flagship zone for sustainable development in the Nord-Pas-de-Calais region.

Transformation has been taking place on all fronts. Water costs twice the average price in France even though it was twice as polluted as anywhere else. Over the past 15 years, all municipal buildings have been fitted with rainwater storage systems, and no drinking water whatsoever is used by municipal services. Thanks to rainwater harvesting, Loos can now go without water for three weeks as a result of its municipal watering, cleaning and sanitation requirements. Even though the price of water has not yet changed (it is fixed by a public service delegation and is based on the scale of the metropolitan area that includes several towns), consumption for municipal use has dropped considerably.

The town wants to develop a new agricultural and foodstuffs model. An initial reason for action is to supply school canteens in Loos and its surrounding area with organic products. To do so, the town is developing short-circuits in order to purchase directly from local growers. Five of them have already changed to organic farming. Their farming area represents 10 per cent of the town's total area, compared to 4 per cent as a national average. Loos is also working with school caterers to create meals requiring them, for example, to use a vegetable-processing plant to handle local produce and not to be supplied by large food manufacturers.

Loos has been called 'the town with the solutions' and was cited as a reference at the UN COP21 climate change conference. The terrorist attacks in Paris on 13 November 2015 unfortunately cancelled the scheduled meeting at Loos of 500 high-ranking civil servants from all over the world. Nonetheless, Loos' experience has received a great deal of media attention, and Jean-François Caron has become known in energy, ecological and social transition circles. He now wants to go a stage further and change scale.

CHANGING SCALE

A virtuous circle was created at Loos: feelings of trust encouraged group initiatives, and these in turn led to results that maintained and bolstered the level of trust. Apart from questions about ecology and sustainable development, the process that has been implemented has had beneficial effects on good manners. There is no damage or degradation to urban property, unlike in neighbouring towns, and the number of lawsuits between neighbours has also greatly diminished. Jean-François Caron was re-elected mayor in 2008 with a majority of 82.1 per cent, and again in 2014 with 100 per cent: a first for a politician, and a dream come true for an ecologist! This is even more surprising in the light of the fact that just a few kilometres from Loos in another mining town, Hénin-Beaumont, a National Front mayor was elected. This juxtaposition highlights the contrast in the ability of the people in one town to live together in a climate of trust, and in a nearby town, for its inhabitants to have feelings based on distrust. Despite this, a number of people in neighbouring towns and villages have begun to adopt the same methods that are in place in Loos-en-Gohelle. Mayors come to meet Jean-François Caron to ask him for advice about managing an 'eco-district', carrying out renewable energy strategies, developing eco-materials, creating food short-circuits, or even putting together the necessary specifications for calls for tender. The greatest number of requests concerns how to put participatory processes in place.

Sharing their experience is now the challenge for the Loos teams. A major difficulty, however, is that one cannot simply copy the solutions that have been put in place at Loos, because each region has its own history, resources, traditions and specific means of organizing its executive.

The way forward in terms of action to be taken emerged from work with the research intervention laboratory, Analyse du Travail et des Mutations dans l'Industrie et les Services (ATEMIS), and a person in charge of telling the story of the town's transformation. We can refer to it as the operation's 'source code'. Just like in open source, lines of code cannot be copied word for word, but serve as a basis for writing one's own, unique version. The key elements of this source code are:

- involving the inhabitants, which requires teaching team members and time;
- finding a 'shining star', a reference that encourages everyone to move forward to reach the goals achieved by this star, and to put down markers to chart the way forward (such as roofing the town's church with solar panels, or suppling organic meals for school canteens, etc.);
- addressing problems in a systemic way, which means fundamentally changing management methods used by the municipal team, which itself is ordinarily strictly separated into specific areas; and
- encouraging people to think 'outside the box', and go against one-track thinking, but without panicking the inhabitants: for example, making a slag heap a work of art was a necessary transgression to move forward.

Once the source code was formalized, the Agence de l'environnement et de la maîtrise d'énergie (ADEME)[4] was able to evaluate the town as a 'national demonstrator of changing management methods' with the aim of creating a sustainable city. Then, the source codes for Loos were compared to those of three other pilot towns, Grande Synthe (near Calais), Malaunay (in Normandy) and Le Méné (in Brittany).

Because these source codes were consistent, a project emerged. In order to refine the guidelines for action to be taken in very different contexts, a new workshop was created that brought together about 15 regions as diverse as the City of Paris (with its 'resilience strategy' and group of elected representatives responsible for the environment), L'Île-Saint Denis (part of the Plaine

Commune area), Montreuil, and the city of Caen (with the intermediary of a district transition group). This workshop is a sort of 'transitions exercise gym' where small and large regions can discuss how it is possible to manage best subsidiarity (where issues are dealt with at the most immediate or local level) and cooperation on various scales in the different and multi-layered regional frameworks. This work between regions, which are on a par, is of interest to a wide range of people, including elected representatives, officers and entrepreneurs.

A 'Third Space' has now been launched to bring together state-run institutions, authorities, companies, transition networks, consultancies and think-tanks, in order to develop a so-called 'Transitions Factory' on a national level.

Several regions are now working together to devise ways in which transition can take place as a sharing process rather than according to a 'top-down' process that is very popular in France. Drawing on local specificities and bringing together local people seems to be the most certain way to involve everyone in the process of ecological transition.

NOTES

1. This chapter comes from J.-F. Caron's talk at the École de Paris du management on 13 May 2016 entitled 'Can the unique success of Loos-en-Gohelle be repeated elsewhere?', and from J. Denantes' (2019) report in *La Jaune et la Rouge*, No. 749, pp. 82–85, entitled "Un entrepreneur de territoire dans le bassin houiller du Pas-de-Calais", accessed 19 August 2020 at https://www.lajauneetlarouge.com/wp-content/uploads/2019/10/La_jaune_et_la_rouge_749_82-85.pdf.
2. Jeremy Rifkin is an American economic and social theorist writer, public speaker, political advisor and activist. He is the author of 21 books about the impact of scientific and technological changes on the economy, the workforce, society, and the environment.
3. The 'Gohelle' region is a small, traditional area in the Pas-de-Calais *département* in Northern France. Its centre is the city of Lens (4 km from Loos). For the most part, it is a low-lying, large floodplain with different strata of rocks (sandstone, schist and limestone). There are numerous seams of coal that were full of shafts and very deep tunnels (several hundreds of metres deep) during the industrial era and until the end of the twentieth century, as in the entire mining area of the Nord-Pas-de-Calais region to which Gohelle belongs.
4. ADEME is a public agency that takes part in the implementation of public policy in the sectors of the environment, energy and sustainable development. It offers companies, local authorities, public authorities and the general public expertise and advice. Furthermore, it helps to finance projects and research for implementing projects in its fields of activity. It has more than 1000 staff.

PART VI

Investors

47. Introduction to Part VI

Nicholas Stern and Charlotte Taylor

In recent decades, the finance sector has become divorced from the real economy. Finance has become a dominant sector in and of itself, rather than playing its 'notional' role of intermediation between savers and investors, or its role in risk management for insurance, pensions and so on. This separation of finance from 'real investment' fosters asset bubbles and emboldens a focus on short-termism. Short-termism in turn places pressure on investors or corporations to act without due consideration for the impacts of their operations on the environment or wider society, particularly over the longer term. It also diminishes willingness to take risks through the kinds of innovation or investment that may have longer-term pay-offs.

Climate change, along with increasing water scarcity, destructuration of fertile soils and biodiversity collapse, pose major threats to financial stability because of potential consequences for economies, firms and financial institutions. These risks arise in three ways: physical losses due both to extreme weather events and to adverse impacts of gradual climate change; transition risks due to changes in climate policies, technology and consumer and investor preferences that reprice assets; and legal risks related to fiduciary responsibilities. Financial losses from climate events have risen sharply in recent years.

The nature of climate change means we cannot disregard or downplay the long-term impacts. And, whilst action across the whole world economy is urgent, we cannot focus only on short-term responses. We need all tools, resources and ideas, implemented over many decades, to tackle the intense climate challenge and manage the rapid and radical transition to a zero-carbon world. Policy-makers must recognize the urgency and scale of the challenge and work decisively to bring the finance sector back towards the real economy through providing clear, credible and long-term strategies and policies.

Supporting and managing the transition will require significant investment and strong innovation. Infrastructure investment will involve a doubling of the existing stock over the next 15 years or so. Much of this investment will have to happen one way or another, but to meet the climate change objectives and the Sustainable Development Goals (SDGs), all of it has to be sustainable from now on. How this infrastructure and other capital investment happens will be a key determinant of our ability to manage or avoid the extreme risks of climate change. Following the growth and infrastructure models of the past and locking in high-carbon and polluting investments would put us in great danger. On the other hand, we can set off on a new and very attractive direction for growth and development, including cities where we can move and breathe and ecosystems that are robust and fruitful.

The potential economic and social benefits of these investments in the short, medium and long term are immense. In the shorter term, since the world economy is demand constrained, with very low interest rates, the extra investments would both boost demand and sharpen supply. Investment in sustainable infrastructure and human capital can foster great advances in health and well-being across the world. In the medium term, this investment would unleash waves of innovation and discovery. In the long term, investment would protect lives and livelihoods by avoiding the worst impacts of climate change; there is no long-run feasible high-carbon growth story – it self-destructs. Growth, poverty reduction, and strong action on climate change are, therefore, complementary, interwoven and very attractive. We must not pretend that the transition will be easy: the necessary change must be rapid and radical. But it can be managed so that there are opportunities for all, and the prize is immense.

Unleashing this new form of growth, however, requires widespread structural changes to many systems across the whole economy and across the world. The financial system will be a fundamental and early driver. It must now change so that all its investments are sustainable and Paris aligned.

This part of the book draws attention to many of the positive signals we are already receiving from the financial sector; the movement has started and is gathering momentum. Jeremy Oppenheim and Catharina Dyvik highlight examples of real innovation and leadership in sustainable finance, showing important cases and examples in regulation, fiduciary duty, infrastructure and new technology, new products, data and tools, and transparency. Considering the Chinese context, Ma Jun describes the rapid proliferation of innovative green financial products, and praises the positive, proactive role that the Chinese government and regulators have played in designing and developing a thriving green financial system.

Despite the range of promising initiatives highlighted, including the Task Force on Climate-related Financial Disclosures (TCFD), the Network for Greening the Financial System (NGFS), the Green Bond Pledge, the Transition Pathway Initiative (TPI), the World Benchmarking Alliance, and ShareAction's asset owners disclosure project, we cannot yet claim that movement embodies the pace that is necessary. Given that time is absolutely of the essence, Oppenheim and Dyvik emphasize their unease that the actions they describe are not happening at the necessary scale, speed or ambition required. If done well, strategic action would enable us to get ahead of possible market disruption and embrace the opportunities presented by climate action. Delay or inaction, on the other hand, leaves us vulnerable to fast-worsening outcomes. Further, on the critical aspect of investment and disinvestment decisions, Alain Grandjean questions whether the current 'greening' of the financial system extends beyond the rhetoric to tangible choices being made by financial investors.

Whilst being realistic on current actions and intentions, we cannot afford to be negative and dismissive. Ma Jun echoes the sentiment that still stronger measures to further promote green finance are required. In response, he proposes actions that China could implement to take on this challenge. Many of the recommendations would create precedent for interventions that can be replicated in other economies: greening institutional investors; mainstreaming environmental risk analysis; and harmonizing green finance standards, are examples. Additionally, a series of interventions that can be made by public authorities to accelerate the effective consideration of climate issues in investment decisions are proposed by Grandjean: banning public banks from financing fossil fuels; greening monetary policy; and penalizing banks that finance the fossil fuel economy. Furthermore, the story, presented by Stephen Heintz, of how the Rockefeller Brothers Fund came to their decision to join 800 other individual and institutional investors, in the Divest-Invest movement, shows how much the landscape is evolving. The combination of the Fund's commitment to fully divest from fossil fuel exposure, along with an impact investment target, which was increased from 10 to 20 percent in 2016, embodies both sides of the new growth story.

It is, of course, not enough for the financial system to simply cease financing unsustainable investments; it must be transformed to mobilize the trillions that will be needed for sustainable investments and climate resilience. This will require unlocking a number of finance pools to work together: domestic public resources; international public finance; and private finance. Here, the role of national and multilateral development banks will be crucial, providing risk management and reduction, and precious patient capital at a time of mounting uncertainty. It will be vital for these institutions to better use their balance sheets and access to concessional finance to build the pipelines of assets where private actors fear to tread. The presence of a multilateral development bank or a national finance institution in a project or transaction itself reduces risks of unreliable government policies and actions. They can bring equity, guarantees and long-term loans. Further, creating the power of the example is key, particularly in developing and emerging markets, and they can back innovation and creativity.

Since it is the aggregate emissions that are fundamental, it is important for all the major countries and regions to be on board. International collaboration could greatly enhance the work of different types of financial institution.

Change is urgent everywhere, but in the context of income, technology, innovations and history, rich countries have an obligation to support and share technologies with their developing counterparts. It's important to continue to drive down costs across the board, as we have already seen in solar and wind energy, storage of electricity, LED light bulbs and so on. Collaboration can bring the necessary scale and confidence in future markets.

The rich countries must also play a strong role in driving down the cost of capital by helping with the policies and institutions that can bring through the right investment, and by helping advance the multilateral development banks (MDB), development finance institutions (DFI) and bilateral support for the right kind of finance, at the right scale, at the right time.

A positive feedback loop between international climate agreements and the confidence necessary for sustainable investment and innovation points to the critical moment presented by the 26th session of the Conference of the Parties to the United Nations Framework Convention on Climate Change (UNFCCC COP26) in 2021 and the actions that should follow.

We must emphasize again that seizing the opportunity requires radical and rapid change. Most of what we currently do will have to be done differently (technologies, institutions, business models, city planning processes, natural resource management, etc.). Managing that change in a cohesive, inclusive and just way is not only a moral obligation but also necessary for a successful transition. We have in our hands a much more attractive, sustainable, inclusive and resilient form of growth and development. With low interest rates, excess global savings and new, changing technologies, we can finance the transition to a zero-carbon economy. The challenge is to translate investment opportunities into real projects and programmes, finance them and thus scale up action with ambition and urgency.

48. Unleashing the power of financial markets for the green transition

Jeremy Oppenheim and Catharina Dyvik

We are living through one of the warmest decades ever recorded, with climate-related natural disasters increasing in frequency and intensity. We are also losing biodiversity at unprecedented rates, with over a million species on the verge of extinction. Recent Australia and Amazon forest fires remind us that deforestation, often caused by agricultural and infrastructure expansion, is also a major driver of global heating and environmental degradation.

According to the scientific community, limiting global warming and mitigating the effects of climate change will require a rapid and far-reaching transformation across the real economy if we are to reach the net-zero emissions target by 2050. To do so, we need to green our energy systems, decarbonize our heavy industries, integrate resilience into our building design, modernize our transport systems and shift how we produce our food. This will require strong and coordinated political leadership, changing consumer habits and bold businesses figuring out how to create value through sustainability. But none of this will happen – or happen fast enough – unless it is combined with rapid and widespread action from the financial sector.

There has been growing momentum and countless new initiatives over the past years that are committed to "greening" the financial system. But it is not happening at the necessary scale, speed or ambition required. The financial system is only responding at the margin. We continue to invest in high-carbon industries, with greenhouse gas emissions at record highs in 2018 and coal finance still on the rise.

Global climate finance flows dropped 11 per cent in 2018 to $546 billion[1] largely due to falling spending on wind and solar and despite unprecedented efforts to install new renewable capacity. By comparison, the largest global banks have poured nearly $2 trillion into fossil fuel financing since the Paris Agreement was adopted, with financing on the rise each year.

INVESTING IN THE NEW CLIMATE ECONOMY

To achieve net-zero emissions by 2050, a lot more capital will need to shift into the new climate economy, which is low carbon, captures negative externalities from high-emissions industries like coal or livestock, and which creates value from more circular and sustainable activities:

First, we need to invest roughly $2.5 trillion more each year in sustainable, low-carbon infrastructure – of which clean energy counts for about $1 trillion. This means a massive focus on energy efficiency, roll-out of renewable technologies, and decommissioning early energy infrastructure not compatible with Paris.[2]

Second, we must commit up to $350 billion more each year to transform global food and land use systems – which represent at least a third of the most cost-effective climate mitigation solutions and are also essential to strengthening food security and biodiversity.[3]

Finally, we will need to make infrastructure more climate resilient, which adds about 3 per cent to the upfront costs, to protect our economic and natural infrastructure against the inevitable physical impact of climate change.[4] The lion's share of this needs to go to emerging markets, who are typically on the front line of climate change and much less equipped to handle its effects.

REIMAGINING HOW WE INVEST

Investing in the low-carbon economy has traditionally been more capital intensive than continuing as usual. For example, building a wind farm has typically required higher upfront costs than building or expanding a gas facility or thermal coal power plant, resulting in a barrier to scaling up renewables. This is especially the case in emerging markets where the fiscal and social constraints are very real, and where workforces are still dependent on the coal sector for power generation. Due to significant reductions in the cost of cleantech[5] inputs (especially for solar and wind), this is gradually changing, and it is becoming an easier sell to repurpose outstanding capital towards low-carbon, resilient assets.

When we also analyse the lifetime costs of the various energy-generating technologies, renewables are rapidly becoming more competitive. Considering all plant-level costs, such as initial investments, operation costs and fuel costs during the power plant's lifetime, renewables are requiring much less ongoing expenditure compared with the "fuel" cost of a gas plant.

But it is not only this cheaper renewable technology and lower ongoing "fuel" expenditure cost that is accelerating the low-carbon transition, but also new and smarter delivery models. For example, "infra-light" solutions that are more distributed, digitized and service based can increase productivity, increase resilience to climate change and reduce upfront investment costs.[6]

Supporting such new models will require financial innovation by structuring vehicles that allow various forms of capital (including more risk-averse institutional investor capital) to invest in nascent business models, new technology solutions and aggregated pools of smaller high-impact projects. Blended finance solutions that use development capital to mitigate investor risks, as well as commercial insurance solutions, can play a crucial role to make this work.[7]

Energy-efficiency assets, for example, would normally be considered too small-scale or illiquid for institutional investors. Through innovative products such as green mortgages or other government-funded programmes, actors can be incentivized to pursue energy efficiency improvements. Pools of such assets can then be aggregated and structured into bonds that fit well for large investors such as pension funds.

Critically, investing "in line with Paris" does not mean jeopardizing returns or mandates. On the contrary, picking "winning" companies that are well equipped to manage climate-related physical and transition risks generates better performance. And it is becoming increasingly evident that incorporating environmental and social considerations is key to mitigating financial risk.

In fact, incorporating sustainability considerations into investment decisions is now slowly becoming recognized as aligned with the objectives of savers in the broader society and long-term asset owners' "fiduciary duties" (e.g., responsibilities when managing money on behalf of others). It should really be no surprise that a recent survey suggests that close to 70 per cent of UK pension plan holders want their investments to consider the impact on people and planet alongside financial performance.[8]

TODAY'S SUSTAINABLE FINANCE MARKET

With such a strong business case, is anything happening today? Newspaper headlines suggest that the finance industry is getting on with it. The macro figures for total global sustainable finance assets under management have been reported at $31 trillion for 2018 – up over 30 per cent from 2016.[9]

The mainstream media frequently report on ambitious climate finance targets from development banks, they write about investment banks that are expanding their sustainable finance practices, they highlight new climate and resilience initiatives, and they write about acquisitions of climate risk analytics companies.

Green and sustainable labelled products continue to rise with the addition of new instruments like "transition bonds", which help companies shift away from "brown" industries or high-carbon practices (e.g., oil & gas companies investing in renewables or cattle companies intensifying to avoid deforestation). "Sustainability-linked loans" and insurance products that incentivize better environmental outcomes are also becoming more common, especially in consumer facing industries like food and fashion. "Resilience products" that support climate adaptation are still nascent, but we expect these to become more popular as the impacts of climate-related natural disasters are felt around the world, including resilience bonds and parametric insurance products triggered by events like cyclones or droughts.

BUT IS IT ENOUGH?

Financing for coal, the most polluting of fossil fuels and still the largest source of energy to generate electricity worldwide, has continued to expand despite more banks and financial institutions taking steps to eliminate their involvement. Carve-outs and loopholes still exist, with large international banks still offering coal-related advisory, insurance and corporate finance services. All this has corresponded with the highest ever greenhouse gas emissions recorded in the year 2018.

Many of the market's largest players are sitting on the side-lines. Huge variation remains between investors across geographies, and the numbers and sustainability headlines may be somewhat misleading. We know that many leading investors are still grappling to understand their full exposure to climate change, and how they should position themselves ahead.

In some geographies, investors' interest has been driven heavily by pro-climate regulatory pressures (e.g., in France, the Netherlands and the UK). For others, it is more of a relatively recent realization that they need to "future-proof" portfolios for imminent shifts across demography, consumer preferences, technology and climate-related risks. But a recent report from a global credit rating agency states that banks and other investors are still dramatically underestimating climate-related risks.[10] Very few have a Paris-aligned strategy or "net-zero" ambition.

The first and most common sustainable investment strategy globally continues to be negative or exclusionary screening on the basis of environmental, social and governance (ESG) factors – especially in Europe where this accounts for more than 60 per cent of the total "sustainable finance" universe. Arguably, this kind of negative screening strategy (which excludes certain industries or companies by divesting) does little to directly support investments in a new climate economy and also removes investors' ability to engage with – or pressure – companies to become more green. But it can send a very strong signal for companies to start acting for climate.

The second strategy is ESG integration, which incorporates considerations and tools in decision-making, and this is becoming more popular. The third category with more active strategies, often called "impact" or "thematic" investing, counts for only a small fraction of the total (current size of the impact investing market roughly at $500 billion).[11]

PERCEIVED TRADE-OFFS

For the large majority, climate issues are still not considered material and do not feature in short-term investment decisions. Why? They are not convinced that pursuing green initiatives will deliver and that there is no trade-off between investment performance and sustainable investing. Certainly not in the short-run that drives their own private incentives.

Among hedge fund managers, an overwhelming 60 per cent still do not consider ESG factors when selecting equities for their portfolios. Despite the urgency of the climate situation, the prevailing belief in international finance is that portfolios will have time to gradually evolve. This leaves all mainstream portfolios exposed to the risk of a sudden shift in sentiment – a Minsky moment[12] – by the financial community once climate risk comes to the fore due to some unpredicted event.

As is often the case, finance is characterized by binary risk exposure: a problem can be neglected until it is too late. Even though capital markets are supposed to look to future cash flows, the combination of discounting methodologies, short-term incentives and the unfamiliar, non-linear nature of climate-related risks makes it almost inevitable that, absent strong regulation, market actors will only respond when it is too late. The ability of cash-rich, carbon-intensive incumbents to reward financial intermediaries with rich fees only compounds the problem.

WHAT NEEDS TO CHANGE?

Multiple market factors, information failures and policy distortions within the capital markets create a bias towards the status quo – in this case, an economy addicted to fossil fuels and a financial sector that has largely only responded in an ad hoc way to the climate crisis. Given that the low-carbon transition is one that is relatively capital intensive, it becomes a huge problem as money won't flow at the speed and scale required. As a result, the finance system is itself a brake rather than an accelerator of the required transition. We could drive real change by tackling the following six systemic barriers:

1. *Regulatory disincentives:* Many of the regulatory requirements we have today on liquidity, reserves and capital provisioning for banks and other financial institutions were introduced or significantly tightened after the global financial crisis to safeguard the stability of the financial system.

This was deemed necessary. But these tight regulations are by now seen by many to restrict the flexibility of banks (Basel III)[13] and insurers (Solvency II in Europe)[14] to invest in the low-carbon economy that we need as the regulations create hurdles to invest in green infrastructure especially in emerging markets.

Regulators have more work to do ahead to find the right path. Our existing risk assessment frameworks tend to be backward-looking and therefore do not adequately capture climate-related risks, which will require more sophisticated forward-looking analysis and longer time horizons.

One option that has been discussed is to have a differentiated capital weighting system that assigns a higher or lower risk weight for provisioning depending on sustainability merits in anticipation of future negative and sudden price developments.

Fiscal policy including how governments apply taxes and subsidies at the real asset level is also extremely important, and it can have an outsized impact and affect investment strategies for example by introducing meaningful carbon pricing and phasing out fossil fuel subsidies.

Other options include tariffs and exemptions for water supply, tax breaks for geographical diversification of farming, and exemptions from land use fees for road and rail infrastructure.

2. *Fiduciary duty and traditional mindsets:* Institutional investors often justify climate-inaction by citing their fiduciary duty to maximize returns. Their ability to factor in non-financial metrics (e.g., in relation to climate) remains unclear or secondary.

    While efforts have been taken in Europe to clarify investor duties (both by the UK Prudential Regulation Authority and at the EU level), the US is arguably still lagging behind. Most recently, even efforts to clarify potential conflicts of interests between retirement advisers and their clients through the Department of Labor fiduciary rule have been halted in the US.

    The lack of clarity on fiduciary duty further translates to how asset managers execute their investment mandates as they are rewarded on the wrong metrics in an increasingly competitive low-fee environment, typically leading to short-term performance bias. The lack of clarity on the scope of fiduciary duty and existing loopholes can further reinforce the old mindset: that taking non-financial metrics into account when assessing portfolio opportunities reduces the investable universe and risks limiting returns.

3. *Low or no asset allocation for infrastructure and climate-tech:* Traditional asset allocation strategies (and regulations) tend to restrict institutional investors from pursuing "alternative assets" like infrastructure that are arguably well suited for patient and long-term capital. Less familiarity

with this asset class often leads to a high perception of risk and reduces investor appetite for infrastructure. And even for traditional infrastructure investors, setting meaningful allocations for emerging markets is challenging due to high perceived risks and lack of historical performance data.

If you factor in that investments are required in newer, asset-light climate and technology solutions, then we are in relatively niche territory. This is especially true around cleantech innovations, which are more capital intensive than, for example, the next social media app and, as a result, suffer from a deep "valley of death" as they move beyond the demonstration phase.

Generating investable products for institutional investors through aggregation and implementing other derisking measures (including policy support, innovative public–private partnerships or blended finance platforms) can help address the challenges of investing in the low-carbon economy.

Infrastructure is an arena in which the multilateral development banks (MDBs) are playing a critical role. However, their balance sheets are stretched, and they need to further explore opportunities to use guarantees, first-loss provisions and other blended finance tools to crowd-in the private sector. In part, the MDB role will be around financial innovation; but it is just as critical that they support governments on their policy reform agenda needed to implement low-carbon, climate-resilient growth pathways.

4. *Confusing taxonomy and unknown product quality:* With growing volumes of "ESG", "sustainable", "impact", "green" and "ethical" products on the market, it is not easy for investors to navigate the shades of green versus brown. Asset managers have been able to label funds and define their investment processes as they see fit, making it challenging to compare and understand the real impact of products.

The industry has to date relied on voluntary commitments without a true standardization of practices. While voluntary taxonomies have worked relatively well in Europe to date, it may be less effective in the US where you may have a higher perception of liability risk. The EU's efforts to implement a taxonomy and regulation for low-carbon benchmarks will be a huge step forward in this respect, which hopefully will be harmonized across more geographies including the US.

Other more "traditional" products are also limited in emerging markets, preventing capital to flow cross-border, such as long-dated foreign exchange hedging instruments or sufficiently developed bond markets that enable price discovery (e.g., green bond issuance in local currency).

5. *Limited data and tools:* Financial information providers are ramping up efforts on climate alongside some new specialized players, but we do not yet have fully sophisticated data and tools, which is limiting investors' ability to accurately assess exposure of portfolios, to evaluate performance and to forecast properly in terms of climate.

There is more confidence on how to gather data points on the *physical* risk side (e.g., bottom-up estimates around probability and potential damage – for example, caused by floods). Investors are slowly getting sensitized to these risks – for example, through rising insurance claims in the context of more intense hurricane seasons and, perhaps more powerfully, through the recent PG&E bankruptcy. The latter case in which a major utility is being held responsible for major property losses as a result of the wildfires in California could be a game changer in terms of investor awareness and willingness to price physical climate risk.

On the *transition* side, frameworks and tools feel more nascent (e.g., how a company is placed to handle climate-driven industry disruption). Figuring out how to identify which companies are ahead of the curve and robust enough to manage the transition is now climbing upwards on many investors' agendas to avoid being left with stranded assets. Such examples include recent bankruptcies in the US coal sector where the transition to a clean economy is starting to price them out of the market.

Investors' own models and decision-frameworks have not been designed to incorporate or consider "difficult-to-quantify" and non-linear climate risks. For many, climate issues are still not considered material enough, or not near term enough to feature in investment decisions and valuation models. That investors are stuck with "short-term thinking" is a big problem.

A further challenge is that climate effects should not be analysed by sector teams of a specialized fund manager in isolation; it cuts across industries and its disruptive impact on business is amplified by other mega trends such as artificial intelligence, automation and so on. It could affect multiple economic sectors simultaneously, from real estate through agriculture to the energy system to global supply chains and consumer goods industries.

6. *Significant information gaps and lack of transparency:* For consumers and the broader public, it is challenging to get good information and transparency on how financial players are using their financial strength (by investing) and power (as major shareholders and bond-holders) to influence the behaviour of carbon-intensive sectors.

To some extent, investing in green assets remains a small marketing gig or nice-to-have story for financial firms, with relatively little information on how this compares to overall operations. Today it is hard to hold the financial firms accountable for their climate announcements and commitments, and to differentiate laggards from the future winners – those that are at the forefront to pick assets that will capitalize from the transitions.

Each of these barriers is challenging on an individual basis. However, when piled together, they translate into a set of deep cultural norms and incentives (both implicit and explicit) to move cautiously towards the new low-carbon world. There is great innovation taking place in the financial industry, but much of the best talent is focused on fintech (financial technology) or algorithmic trading rather than the challenge of financing a climate-friendly future.

EXAMPLES OF REAL INNOVATION AND LEADERSHIP

Despite these systemic barriers, there are still many extraordinary sustainable finance pioneers who are trying to tackle these capital market-specific constraints to accelerate Paris-aligned investment. We highlight a handful of these entrepreneurs, leaders and innovators below to show that change really is possible, but this list is by no means representative of all the people working very hard on this agenda and who deserve to be celebrated for their efforts to shift the finance system to become more sustainable:

1. *On regulation:* Frameworks can become powerful tools to incentivize or accelerate Paris alignment – for example, by making the Task Force on Climate-related Financial Disclosures (TCFD) mandatory. To get the attention of capital markets, former Bank of England Governor Mark Carney, recently appointed as the new UN Special Envoy for Climate Action and Finance, has courageously used his power to call for more disclosure, implemented widespread regulatory reform and has now rallied more than 50 central banks to join forces through the Network for Greening the Financial System (NGFS). This is under the mandate of protecting stability through a more "orderly transition" and preparing the financial sector for the new climate economy. We have already seen TCFD become a powerful mechanism for forcing investors to internalize climate risk assessments despite being voluntary, and calls for it to become mandatory in key financial markets.

2. *On fiduciary duty:* Convinced that climate change poses a financial risk to its pension scheme, the HSBC UK pension fund decided that it had to take action and "walk the talk" to fulfil its fiduciary responsibility. Knowing that more than 90 per cent of the market tends to stick with the default option, HSBC, as an early mover, shifted its employee default pension scheme (on which staff are automatically enrolled) towards a climate-tilted

option (a global equities index fund designed to reduce exposure to companies deemed to be at risk from a shift towards low-carbon-based energy, and increase exposure to those companies deemed likely to benefit).

Another example of an asset owner revisiting its fiduciary duty would be the Rockefeller Brothers Fund, who pursued a rapid divestment strategy – getting out of the most intensive sources of emissions (coal and tar sands) within a year already back in 2014. Since then, the Fund has further reduced its exposure to other fossil fuel activities.

3. *On infrastructure and new tech:* The Canadian pension fund CDPQ is a good example of a pension fund not afraid of infrastructure. It directly holds roughly 5 per cent in infrastructure versus a global average of around 1 per cent. Along with a few other primarily Scandinavian and Canadian asset owners, CDPQ has also just committed to decarbonize its entire investment portfolio as part of the new "Net-Zero Asset Owner Alliance", recognizing their important collective role in accelerating the global energy transition, but also capturing opportunities to earn solid returns by investing in low-carbon solutions.[15]

There are a range of blended finance vehicles that are excellent examples of creating structures that combine commercial capital with development finance to mobilize finance for infrastructure in emerging markets by overcoming certain investor risks (e.g., by providing development guarantees, insurance or downside protection through subordinate debt or equity in a fund).

An example is the structure developed by the Inter-American Development Bank (IDB) to accumulate a portfolio of standardized energy-efficiency receivables from Mexican energy service companies. The investments will be securitized through the issuance of green bonds in the local debt capital markets, supported by funding from the Green Climate Fund, the Clean Technology Fund and a guarantee mechanism from the IDB.

Another example of pioneering blended activity is the MacArthur Foundation, which together with its partners Rockefeller Foundation and Omidyar, is demonstrating real leadership with the 2019 launch of a catalytic capital consortium dedicating $150 million through subordinated debt, equity and guarantees to various private sector vehicles to help address financing gaps for high-impact issues.

From the private equity and asset management world, we are also seeing a growing trend of sustainability and cleantech becoming linked to long-term success. Examples include Lombard Odier, which has committed to integrate sustainability across 90 per cent of its mainstream assets and is now managing a number of forward-leaning sustainability-themed long/short equity funds, and Generation Investment Management, co-founded by Al Gore and David Blood, which has just raised another $1 billion of private equity to back later-stage start-ups that work across environmental solutions, healthcare and financial inclusion.

4. *On products:* We should highlight green bonds as an example of a product that has come far on the journey both in terms of standardization due to organizations such as the Climate Bonds Initiative working on common principles, and in terms of growth in the number of issuances from sovereigns, municipalities, corporates and banks worldwide supported by initiatives such as the "Green Bond Pledge" spearheaded by the former UN climate chief, Christiana Figueres. Green bonds, although the cumulative total issued as of mid-2019 is still minuscule at $650 billion compared to the total bond market, which exceeds $100 trillion,[16] have been instrumental not only to mainstream green finance but also to drive innovation of other products, which can help to drive capital towards low-carbon assets (e.g., green loans).

5. *On data and tools:* When it comes to investor tools and data, we are seeing a lot of innovation emerging in the climate analytics and robotics space – with deep data analytics skills bridging climate science and asset valuations.

On the *physical* risk side, a few interesting examples include "hotspot mapping" of companies' physical risk exposure (e.g., Moody's Four Twenty Seven),[17] expanding datasets to also cover physical risk (e.g., S&P's Trucost), and offerings using artificial intelligence and satellite technology to provide a picture of asset-level risk from flood, fire, heat, drought, cold, wind and hail events (e.g., Jupiter Intelligence).

On the *transition* risk side, there are a number of initiatives for investors worth following that are seeking to provide portfolio-level analysis (e.g., Paris Agreement Capital Transition Assessment – PACTA), company-level assessments (e.g., Transition Pathway Initiative –TPI) and benchmarks (e.g., World Benchmarking Alliance) to measure how assets are on the path to cope with the transition to a Paris-aligned world.

On the *financial tool* side, external providers are expanding their support with climate-risk scenario modelling (e.g., Ortec Finance), and new technology solutions are being offered to retail and institutional investors to customize portfolios to match their environmental strategies (e.g., robo-advisor OpenInvest).

6. *On transparency:* There are a number of attempts to increase visibility and transparency through developing league tables and disclosure projects (such as ShareAction's Asset Owners Disclosure Project – AODP).[18] We are also seeing some financial actors that have decided to go public with their own analysis and results in anticipation of more publicly available rankings (e.g., Legal & General Investment Management).

Positive efforts on transparency also include initiatives that are seeking to educate and increase awareness within the broader public, such as the UK-based "Make My Money Matter" campaign, which, importantly, is seeking to mobilize actors to demand that their capital is clearly and transparently invested in a way that is aligned with values, that limits harm and supports the SDGs.

CALL TO ACTION

This chapter has summarized a few of the systemic barriers that compound to prevent the capital shifts we need to see in order to accelerate the transition to a low carbon economy. And while it is possible to get disheartened by the size of the task at hand, pressure for action can only increase, giving courage to political leaders for bold policy, giving mandate for regulators to change rules, pressuring CEOs to transform their business models, driving more innovation for technology solutions and incentivizing investors to reallocate capital flows towards a low-carbon pathway.

The areas of change and examples of pioneering leaders highlighted in this chapter are a good start, but we need to go faster and scale up this agenda. Critical areas to deepen and accelerate change further include to:

- challenge asset owners, asset managers and investment consultants on the focus on quarterly earnings, past track-records and historic data instead of forward-looking and longer-term climate and tech-risk-adjusted projections;
- have finance ministers across all geographies incorporate climate resilience in macro-fiscal and financial frameworks (including working with the insurance industry for new solutions and International Monetary Fund incorporating climate in its Article IV surveillance mechanisms);
- strengthen the mandate, resources and capabilities of the multilateral development banks as a joined-up system, to crowd private capital into low-carbon, climate-resilient infrastructure across the developing world; and
- increase public awareness of the power of their personal finances to push for climate (e.g., unleashing the "Millennials" and "Generation Z" to demand more transparent, user-friendly financial products in line with their values).

We must remind ourselves that finance markets can only go so far without the right regulatory and policy context. Carbon pricing and the right sectoral policies are key – and a lot can be achieved through policy frameworks that have built-in ratcheting mechanisms (e.g., tightening regulations on the power sector or in the auto industry, predictably increasing carbon pricing across the economy), resetting expectations for investors. Fortunately, we now have finance ministers, central banks, regulators, credit rating agencies – and importantly, investors and business – all elevating and accelerating efforts on climate (although some a bit naive, or marketing driven, so far).

We are observing the start of an acceleration of action that is exciting and could lead to new norms in capital markets. We may not be that far away from a positive Minsky moment when investors shift rapidly out of high-carbon or climate-exposed assets and future-proof their portfolios. That would change the game.

NOTES

1. Climate Policy Initiative (2019), *Global Landscape of Climate Finance 2019*, accessed 31 August 2020 at https://climatepolicyinitiative.org/publication/global -landscape-of-climate-finance-2019/.
2. New Climate Economy (2016), *The Sustainable Infrastructure Imperative*, accessed 31 August 2020 at https://newclimateeconomy.report/2016/; New Climate Economy (2018), *Unlocking the Inclusive Growth Story of the 21st Century*, accessed 31 August 2020 at https://newclimateeconomy.report/2018/.
3. Food and Land Use Coalition (2019), *Growing Better: Ten Critical Transitions to Transform Food and Land Use*, accessed 31 August 2020 at https://www .foodandlandusecoalition.org/global-report/.
4. Global Commission for Adaptation (2019), *Adapt Now: A Global Call for Leadership on Climate Resilience*, accessed 31 August 2020 at https://cdn.gca.org/ assets/2019-09/GlobalCommission_Report_FINAL.pdf.
5. Any product, process or service that reduces negative environmental impacts through energy efficiency improvements, sustainable use of resources, or environmental protection activities.
6. Blended Finance Taskforce (2019), *Better Finance, Better World*, accessed 31 August 2020 at https://www.blendedfinance.earth/better-finance-better-world.
7. See Food and Land Use Coalition (2019), note 3.
8. Department for International Development UK (DFID) (2019), *Investing in a Better World: Understanding the UK Public's Demand for Opportunities to Invest in the Sustainable Development Goals*, accessed 31 August 2020 at https:// assets.publishing.service.gov.uk/government/uploads/system/uploads/attachment _data/file/834207/Investing-in-a-better-wold-full-report.pdf.
9. Global Sustainable Investment Alliance (2019), *2018 Global Sustainable Investment Review*, accessed 31 August 2020 at http://www.gsi-alliance.org/wp -content/uploads/2019/03/GSIR_Review2018.3.28.pdf.
10. S&P Global (2020), "The big picture on climate risk", accessed 31 August 2020 at https://www.spglobal.com/en/research-insights/featured/the-big-picture-on -climate-risk.
11. Global Impact Investing Network (2019), *Annual Impact Investor Survey*, accessed https://thegiin.org/assets/GIIN_2019%20Annual%20Impact%20Investor %20Survey_webfile.pdf.

12. Minsky moment refers to the onset of a market collapse when investors after periods of steady prosperity and investment gains ("bull markets") engage in increasing (debt-financed) speculative activity that reaches an extreme that is unsustainable, leading to cash flow crisis and rapid asset price deflation.
13. Basel III – a global, voluntary regulatory framework on bank capital adequacy, stress testing, and market liquidity risk.
14. Solvency II – the EU insurance regulation covering the amount of capital insurance companies must hold to reduce the risk of insolvency.
15. The UN-convened Net-Zero Asset Owner Alliance seeks to unite investor action to align asset owners' portfolios with a 1.5°C scenario, addressing Article 2.1c of the Paris Agreement.
16. Climate Bonds Initiative (2019), *Green Bond Market Summary*, 2019, accessed https://www.climatebonds.net/resources/reports/2019-green-bond-market-summary.
17. Four Twenty Seven (2019), "Demystifying climate scenario analysis for financial stakeholders", accessed http://427mt.com/wp-content/uploads/2019/12/Demystifying-Scenario-Analysis_427_2019.pdf.
18. Example league tables: Asset Owners Disclosure Project (ShareAction – asset owner/TCFD focus), InfluenceMap (lobby focus – forthcoming investor focus), Clean Energy League Tables (BNEF – renewables focus), Global Green Economy Index (Dual Citizen LLC – country focus), BankTrack (bank/fossil fuel focus).

49. The case for fossil fuel divestment

Stephen B. Heintz

"We recognize that the world is on an unsustainable path," wrote British Petroleum (BP) chairman Helge Lund in a May 2019 *Financial Times* op-ed. The findings of climate scientists are real. The world must move to a net-zero carbon future in the decades to come. It must transition to a low-carbon future as rapidly as possible. "We say this not to protect our license to operate, nor as some elaborate form of greenwashing. Apart from being the right thing to do, it is simply in our best interests," he concludes.[1]

Published to coincide with BP's Annual General Meeting (AGM) in Aberdeen, Scotland, the op-ed from the oil and gas supermajor reads like an arms manufacturer signing onto a pacifist manifesto. Not everyone was convinced. Outside the Aberdeen Exhibition and Conference Centre on the day of the AGM, protestors held up signs reading "climate emergency" and "BP climate criminals."[2] A month later, 78 artists signed an open letter protesting against the London National Portrait Gallery's acceptance of funding from BP.[3] The letter noted that BP invests only 3 percent of its available capital in renewable energy – far less than it spends actively looking for new fossil fuel reserves at a time when most of the reserves already on its books must stay in the ground.

Since the invention of the steam engine 300 years ago, the carbon-fueled economy has delivered tremendous progress. It has helped to alleviate poverty, improve health, and advance civilization. Coal, oil, and gas have brought light to billions, but for the past 30 years we have known that burning them also has a darker side. Putting short-term profits over the long-term well-being of the planet, the fossil fuel industry has evolved from an engine of civilizational progress to its archenemy.

A decade ago, no supermajor would have conceded as bluntly as BP did that the world is on an unsustainable path. Today, the global narrative around climate change has shifted, thanks to the growing climate movement, comprising in part the scientists, activists, and other actors discussed in this book. Among them are thousands of investors who are tired of trying to influence fossil fuel companies with the shares they hold – and so instead have abandoned them.

The Rockefeller Brothers Fund (RBF) announced its own decision to divest on September 22, 2014. A day earlier, 400 000 people from across the world marched through the streets of Manhattan demanding climate action. A day after, UN Secretary-General Ban Ki-moon assembled 120 heads of state in New York for the most important climate gathering since the failed Copenhagen Conference. That gathering in 2009 had enshrined 2°C of warming as the threshold for disaster, but it had failed to extract meaningful commitments to limit carbon emissions to meet this target.

In making our announcement, the RBF joined 800 other individual and institutional investors, then controlling over $52 billion in assets, in the Divest-Invest movement. The standard pledge – no new investments in fossil fuel companies; sell existing fossil fuel assets within five years; and invest in the new energy economy – was flexible enough that different investors could tailor it to fit their different circumstances. At the RBF, we went one step further: we committed to divest from coal and tar sands, the most egregious pollutants, by the end of that year, and embark on a path to eliminate our investment exposure to the remaining fossil fuel sources.

Our decision was consistent with the Rockefeller family's long tradition of stewardship of nature and the environment. John D. Rockefeller, Jr. donated thousands of acres of land and millions of dollars to natural parks around the country, including some of the most iconic – Grand Teton National Park, the Great Smokey Mountains, and Acadia National Park. When his five sons founded the Rockefeller Brothers Fund in 1940, conservation remained a focus of their philanthropy. They were guided by the simple principle that, as current board chair Valerie Rockefeller puts it, "not only rich people should have access to beautiful natural places."

In the 1970s, as society's understanding of ecological threat evolved, so too did the RBF's environmental grantmaking. The Fund's Environmental Program, launched in 1974, expanded our focus from park land acquisition to more complex ecosystem issues at the intersection of population, food, capital, pollution, and values. The addition of Steven Rockefeller, a scholar of ethics and religion and co-author of the *Earth Charter*,[4] to the RBF board of trustees in 1977 defined the path forward, establishing the holistic approach that continues to guide our work on the environment and sustainability.

By the mid-1980s, our grantmaking pivoted again in response to a new threat. Scientists had known for over a century that greenhouse gases in the atmosphere, including carbon dioxide, absorb heat from the sun with important effects on the climate. By the time the RBF made its first grant to understand global warming in 1986, to Sweden's Beijer Institute, it was clear to scientists – but not yet to the public at large – that the combustion of coal, oil, and gas over the centuries was warming the planet. The world's bottomless appetite for carbon-based energy would exacerbate the reality of the threat at the same time that our scientific understanding of it became clearer.

The RBF established its Sustainable Development program in 2003, and by 2010, directed the program's entire budget to work on climate change. By the time we announced our decision to join the Divest-Invest pledge in 2014, the RBF was devoting more than 40 percent of its total worldwide annual grants budget to combating the crisis. "John D. Rockefeller built a vast fortune on oil. Now his heirs are abandoning fossil fuels," read *The New York Times*. The media reveled in the historical irony.

Yet, John D. Rockefeller became the wealthiest man on Earth by looking furthest into the future – not by clinging to the past. He revolutionized the energy industry at a time when oil was being extracted from whale blubber. Certainly, it should not come as a surprise that his descendants would support the next phase of energy innovation. The real irony was not that we divested from fossil fuels, the source of the Rockefeller family's wealth and the RBF endowment. It was that for years we had been spending tens of millions of dollars on efforts to mitigate the climate crisis, while at the same time *investing* in the very industry most damaging to our cause. Why hadn't we shifted our portfolio sooner?

Philanthropic foundations in the United States are required by law to pay out 5 percent of their endowment each year for charitable expenditures. If a foundation aspires to exist in perpetuity, as the RBF does, the other 95 percent goes to investments that are used to regenerate the endowment and preserve its purchasing power. The conventional logic of non-profit endowment management prescribes a church–state divide between a foundation's grantmaking and investment activities.

This logic of separation is pervasive in the non-profit world, not only at grantmaking foundations. Harvard, which has the largest endowment of any U.S. university, has long justified defiance of its students' call for divestment through appeal to this supposedly sacred principle. "The endowment is a resource, not an instrument to impel social or political change," writes Drew Gilpin Faust, the school's former president.[5]

The RBF has always had an expansive understanding of what it means to pursue its mission – advancing a more just, sustainable, and peaceful world. Our grantmaking dollars are our most important tool, but they aren't our only one. Our convening power is another tool. Our reputation, rooted in the Rockefeller name, is yet another. Why should 95 percent of our endowment be off limits? Climate change is the existential crisis of our century. We wouldn't step into the ring of the most consequential fight of our lives with one hand tied behind our back.

We began thinking about the other 95 percent in 2002, a year after I joined the RBF as president. Our first concrete step toward reconciling our investments with our mission, however, came in 2005, when we adopted proxy-voting guidelines. Over the course of a year, and under the leadership of Steven Rockefeller, board chair at the time, our Investment Committee drafted a 33-page document that detailed how we would deploy our common stock ownership as assets to advance our mission and to encourage environmental, social, and governance progress. In the case of fossil fuel companies, the idea was that more transparent and equitable corporate governance structures would push the companies to become more responsible stakeholders in society.

The fossil fuel companies had other plans. In 2008, 73 Rockefeller family members threw their weight and the history of their family name behind a shareholder resolution that called for an independent chairman role at Exxon, the largest legacy company of John D. Rockefeller's Standard Oil. Neva Goodwin and Peter O'Neill led the family's shareholder crusade, which included three other resolutions, with varied levels of family support, to address global warming and renewable energy. Unfortunately, money spoke louder than morals: Exxon had just posted the highest profits in American corporate history. At Exxon's AGM in Dallas that year, none of the resolutions passed.[6] Similar resolutions failed in subsequent years. Shareholder activism, it seemed, was not the answer.

Policymaking on the national and international levels, too, would disappoint before the decade's end. The Waxman-Markey Bill passed the House of Representatives in June 2009. Had it passed the Senate, it would have established a cap-and-trade system – a carbon-pricing scheme that RBF-supported think tanks had helped devise. Weeks and months passed as advocates pushed for Senate action, but the bill was never brought up for a vote. Not a single Republican Senator was prepared to break ranks and support climate action.

Then came December, a dark month for the climate movement. Many had hoped that the UN Climate Change Conference in Copenhagen that year would result in a legally binding treaty to reduce emissions. What it gave us instead was a document that acknowledged the scope of the problem but did nothing about it. In his poem "The Snow Man," Wallace Stevens could have been writing about Copenhagen when he famously beheld "nothing that is not there and the nothing that is."

Disappointments in Dallas, Washington, and Copenhagen were top of the mind for the RBF during Investment Committee discussions in 2009 and 2010. On the grantmaking side, our Sustainable Development program director Michael Northrop would absorb the hard knocks of 2009 by shifting focus to the subnational levels of government. How would we respond on the investment side to a crisis growing more urgent by the day? In March 2010, the RBF board of trustees approved staff's recommendation to allocate up to 10 percent of our endowment to "impact investments," with a focus on clean energy and other green business ventures. We set a high bar for these investments: they must meet standard financial return objectives while also measurably contributing to positive environmental or social impact.

It would take years before our impact investments would get off the ground. As we started, our investments were managed by an investment firm along with those of a number of other institutional investors in co-mingled funds, which meant that a dozen investors had to sign off on any change in investment strategy. A second, perhaps even more fundamental obstacle was the dearth of attractive impact investment products.

If our impact investments were slow to take off, another philanthropic investment we made in 2010 brought quick returns. In July, together with the Growald Family Fund, the RBF gave $90 000 to a year-old UK organization called Investor Watch, co-founded by Mark Campanale. It was the first foundation grant Investor Watch received for a project that sought to track the fossil fuel reserves of coal companies, and later oil and gas companies.

Soon, Campanale's project at Investor Watch would spin off into its own organization, Carbon Tracker, and fundamentally change the debate around climate change. Carbon Tracker published its groundbreaking report, *Unburnable Carbon*, in late 2011.[7] Scientists had been able to calculate, approximately, what remained of our carbon budget – that is, the amount of carbon we could burn before crossing the 2°C threshold would become a foregone conclusion. What we hadn't known at the time was how much carbon fossil fuel companies had on their balance sheets. Carbon Tracker supplied the missing piece of the puzzle: 2795 gigatons. That was nearly five times the 565 gigatons of carbon that scientists had determined we could "safely" burn.

In other words: in order to stay below 2°C warming, 80 percent of known fossil fuel reserves would have to stay in the ground. They would become, as economists say, stranded assets. But investors were still pricing these companies under the assumption that every drop of oil on their books would be brought to the market. The world's financial markets were carrying a carbon bubble that would make the housing bubble of 2008 look playful by comparison. The question was when, not if, the carbon bubble would burst.

Now there was an economic dimension to a conversation that had previously been conducted along moral lines. The moral case for divestment argues that it is wrong to abet and profit from companies whose business models are premised on the destruction of the planet. The economic argument strikes the word "profit": fossil fuel companies, it says, are simply bad investments. In a widely read 2012 *Rolling Stone* article, "Global warming's terrifying new math,"[8] Bill McKibben powerfully married the moral argument with the economic argument supported by Carbon Tracker's analysis. Later that year, he went on tour with his organization 350.org to prosecute the case.

Slowly, but surely, Carbon Tracker's "stranded assets" report and McKibben's "Do the math" tour had begun to shift the public debate.

Divestment was in the air when Ellen Dorsey, Executive Director of the Wallace Global Fund, first came to the RBF in the summer of 2013.

The Wallace Global Fund had begun its own divestment discussions in 2009, after Copenhagen and Waxman-Markey had failed in large part because the fossil fuel industry had sabotaged them. In an analogy to the South African divestment movement that had helped to end apartheid, Dorsey saw divestment from fossil fuel companies as an opportunity to take away their social license and expose them for what they were: rogue actors. She formally launched the Divest-Invest Philanthropy a year later. The RBF was not among the initial wave of 17 foundations, controlling $1.7 billion in assets, who took the three-part pledge. But the seed had been planted.

In February 2014, frustrated with the slow progress of our impact investments, the RBF engaged a new outsourced chief investment office (OCIO), Perella Weinberg Partners (PWP). They didn't yet know – and neither did we, quite yet – that divestment was where we were heading. By the time our Investment Committee convened in May, our sense of urgency had grown more acute and our thinking had evolved. Studies were indicating that the climate crisis was more dire than had previously been predicted. Dorsey wanted to make a big announcement timed to Ban Ki-moon's Climate Summit in September, and she asked whether we would join. Divestment, she explained, offered an opportunity for foundations long accustomed to funding movements to instead become part of one. And doing so made economic sense, we now knew.

Could PWP help us think through divestment in time for a September announcement? The crucial question for us was what divestment would mean for the financial health of our endowment. PWP conducted an analysis that looked back 20 years and determined how our endowment would have performed had we been divested from the 200 largest coal, oil, and gas companies during that time. The result was devastating. We called it the Doomsday Scenario.

The past does not predict the future, as any investment professional will say. Confident that Carbon Tracker's analysis was fundamentally sound, we knew that the Doomsday Scenario wouldn't come to pass. Still, divestment was an untested strategy and uncharted territory. Getting out of fossil fuels made sense over the long term, but what would it mean for an institution such as ours now – especially when energy accounted for nearly 20 percent of the global economy?

We decided to take the risk. While this was a recommendation championed by the Fund's professional staff, we owe the decision to our grantees, who had been producing cutting-edge research around climate change; to our peer institutions, who pioneered the path of divestment and showed us the way; to the Rockefeller family, who had leveraged their own investments and reputations to test the waters; and to our trustees, who had the courage to follow the arguments and examples to their logical and moral conclusions.

If our decision to divest was not easy, the hard part came next: making our intention a reality. Divestment doesn't happen overnight. In our case, we had legacy investments with fossil fuel exposure that we could not sell off quickly or easily; we initially had difficultly engaging high-quality managers, some of whom would not accept our investments that came with a fossil fuel exclusion; and finally, much to our irritation, we would sometimes come across funds with attractive renewable energy solutions that we would have to forego because fossil fuels were also in the mix.

Despite the challenges of implementation, our decision to divest has paid off. As of June 2019, almost five years after we decided to divest, our endowment has outperformed a standard 70/30 benchmark (70 percent stocks, 30 percent bonds). We are now almost fully divested, with the 1 percent of our endowment still exposed to fossil fuels on track to zero as remaining legacy investments expire in the next few years. The market for fossil-free investment opportunities has grown dramatically over the past decade, as increased demand for these products from individual and institutional investors has led to increased supply.

Opportunities for impact investing have grown in parallel. While fossil fuel supermajors continue to drill for new oil and gas reserves incompatible with a livable future, the innovative companies that will replace them are expanding renewable power supplies through massive infrastructure projects; optimizing water and agriculture resources; and developing new sustainable forestry practices. Harnessing solar energy has become cheaper and more efficient than ever, with new photovoltaic installations cresting 100 gigawatts for the first time in 2018.[9] In two-thirds of the world, wind and solar are already the cheapest forms of power.[10]

As the availability of investment products grew, our 2010 goal to allocate 10 percent of our portfolio to impact was finally in sight. So, in 2016, we increased our impact investment target to 20 percent. We have already allocated 13 percent, overwhelmingly in funds that focus on clean energy and sustainable development.

The UN estimates that the world must invest $2.4 trillion annually through 2035 to avert the worst consequences of climate change – or almost $40 trillion over the next 16 years.[11] In 2018, global investments in clean energy totaled just $334 billion.[12] Despite some fluctuation, that number has hardly budged since 2011.

Lack of clarity about how to measure impact – and what counts as impact investing at all – remains a hurdle for investors toying with this idea. At the RBF, we expect clean energy investments and all impact investments to deliver market-rate returns, and we ask managers to report regularly on their contributions toward the UN Sustainable Development Goals.

Organizations such as the US Impact Investing Alliance and the newly launched UK Impact Investing Institute are helping to bring much-needed clarity and coherence to the field.[13] For the field to advance, we need better definitions and metrics. We need case studies. We need dissemination of best practices. Most of all, we need trillions of dollars and a revolution in investing. Our economy feeds on energy to power our homes, cars, computers, machines, and other equipment. Fossil fuels are like fast food: cutting them out without replacing them with new sources of energy, like cutting out burgers and fries without finding healthier substitutes, will starve us, not save us.

Five years after our Divest-Invest pledge, the performance of our portfolio makes a strong argument that the strategy, at the very least, does not hurt an endowment's bottom line. We hope and expect that our experience, on which we provide regular updates on our website, will only strengthen the argument in the years to come. In the spring of 2020 we shared the details of our performance data for this five-year period.[14] Indeed, as an institution that exists in the public trust, we believe that transparency about divestment is an important responsibility and a service to the public. As mounting evidence busts the myth that fossil fuel divestment will be painful, more investors will divest.

The last five years have debunked a second myth, too: that divestment is painless for the fossil fuel industry. When the RBF announced its divestment decision in September 2014, it was largely seen as a symbolic gesture. Our endowment at the time stood at $851 million, hardly enough to impact the multi-trillion-dollar fossil fuel industry. Even with their combined $52 billion, the 800 individual and institutional investors who took the Divest-Invest pledge that month were, given the size of the fossil fuel industry, mosquitoes to an elephant.

By the 2015 UN Climate Change Conference in Paris, that figure had risen to over $3 trillion and by the end of 2016 it was $5 trillion. The movement has spread beyond the traditional civil society actors to local and even national governments. New York City and Ireland both made headlines in 2018 with their divestment announcements, and in June 2019, Norway announced that it would partially divest its trillion-dollar sovereign wealth fund – the largest in the world.[15] Nearly 60 000 individuals and over 1000 institutional investors with combined assets of more than $12 trillion have now pledged to fully or partially divest from fossil fuels.[16] That is more than a symbolic gesture.

Fossil fuel companies are feeling threatened and exposed. When Peabody, the world's largest coal company, declared plans for bankruptcy in 2016, it cited difficulty raising capital – in part a consequence of the divestment movement – as one of the reasons. Shell announced in 2018 that it considers divestment a "material risk" to its business.[17] BASF, the German chemical company, worries that its large carbon footprint will scare away investors.[18]

Last July, shortly after its AGM in Aberdeen, BP made a remarkable public announcement: some of its resources "won't see the light of day."[19] Declining oil prices, uncertainty about carbon demand in the future, and pressure from investors mean that carbon-heavy projects in difficult to reach places are simply bad business. "There's no doubt that some of those resources won't come out the ground," said BP's head of strategy.

Carbon Tracker's thesis of stranded assets has become mainstream in the investment community. Now those assets are really becoming stranded. In the weeks after BP's announcement, its stock slid six percentage points as investors recalibrated what they thought the company was worth and where they thought it was going. Some sold their stock, perhaps because the massive heatwave that swept across Europe that month, bringing record-shattering temperatures to regions across the continent, jogged their conscience. Others sold them, no doubt, for purely financial considerations.

Why Divest-Invest? As Helge Lund might say, apart from being the right thing to do, it is simply in your own best interest.

NOTES

1. Helge Lund, "Why BP supports a fast shift to low carbon," *Financial Times*, May 20, 2019. Accessed August 28, 2020 at https://www.ft.com/content/5fb061d4 -7a1d-11e9-8b5c-33d0560f039c.
2. Ron Bousso, "BP faces climate protests at investor meeting, Shell gets boost," *Reuters*, May 21, 2019. Accessed August 28, 2020 at https://www.reuters.com/ article/us-bp-agm-protests/bp-faces-climate-protests-at-investor-meeting-shell -gets-boost-idUSKCN1SR10X.
3. Alex Marshall, "Should oil money fund the arts? Leading British artists say no," *The New York Times*, July 5, 2019. Accessed August 28, 2020 at https://www .nytimes.com/2019/07/05/arts/bp-sponsorship-national-portrait-gallery.html.
4. An international declaration of fundamental values and principles for building a just, sustainable, and peaceful global society in the 21st century, created by a global consultation process and endorsed by organizations representing millions of people.
5. Drew Gilpin Faust, "Fossil fuel divestment statement," October 3, 2013. Accessed August 28, 2020 at https://www.harvard.edu/president/news/2013/fossil-fuel -divestment-statement.
6. Leslie Eaton and Russell Gold, "Rockefeller rebellion turns up heat on Exxon," *The Wall Street Journal*, May 24, 2008. Accessed August 28, 2020 at https://www .wsj.com/articles/SB121157457128518175.
7. Carbon Tracker, "Unburnable carbon: are the world's financial markets carrying a carbon bubble?" July 13, 2011. Accessed August 20, 2020 at https:// carbontracker.org/reports/carbon-bubble/.

8.   McKibben, Bill, "Global warming's terrifying new math," *Rolling Stone*, July 19, 2012. Accessed August 20, 2020 at https://www.rollingstone.com/politics/politics -news/global-warmings-terrifying-new-math-188550/.
9.   Joshua S. Hill, "Solar breaks the 100 gigawatt barrier in 2018, could reach as high as 140 gigawatts in 2019," *CleanTechnica*, January 23, 2019. Accessed August 28, 2020 at https://cleantechnica.com/2019/01/23/solar-breaks-the-100-gigawatt -barrier-in-2018-could-reach-as-high-as-140-gigawatts-in-2019/.
10. Lynn Doan, Brian Eckhouse, Christopher Cannon, and Hannah Recht, "What's behind the world's biggest climate victory? Capitalism," *Bloomberg*, September 15, 2019. Accessed August 28, 2020 at https://www.bloomberg.com/graphics/ 2019-can-renewable-energy-power-the-world/.
11. Devin Thorpe, "The GIIN founder provides impact investing definition," *Forbes*, June 12, 2019. Accessed August 28, 2020 at https://www.forbes.com/sites/ devinthorpe/2019/06/12/the-giin-founder-provides-impact-investing-definition/ #3839669a54d2.
12. BloombergNEF, *Clean Energy Investment Trends*, 2018, January 16, 2019. Accessed August 28, 2020 at https://data.bloomberglp.com/professional/sites/24/ BNEF-Clean-Energy-Investment-Trends-2018.pdf.
13. Jennifer Thompson, "Britain aims high with launch of Impact Investing Institute," *Financial Times*, June 3, 2019. Accessed August 28, 2020 at https://www.ft.com/ content/256f3d29-7762-37e0-86cf-7810eb527504.
14. Rockerfeller Brothers Fund, *Investing in Our Mission: A Five-year Case Study of Fossil Fuel Divestment at the Rockerfeller Brothers Fund*, May 2020. Accessed August 28, 2020 at https://www.rbf.org/sites/default/files/rbf-investing-2020 -report-final-pages.pdf.
15. Jillian Ambrose, "World's biggest sovereign wealth fund to ditch fossil fuels," *The Guardian*, June 12, 2019. Accessed August 28, 2020 at https://www.theguardian .com/business/2019/jun/12/worlds-biggest-sovereign-wealth-fund-to-ditch-fossil -fuels.
16. As of March 2020. See DivestInvest's website, https://www.divestinvest.org/, for real-time updates on divestment commitments.
17. Bill McKibben, "At last, divestment is hitting the fossil fuel industry where it hurts," *The Guardian*, December 16, 2018. Accessed August 28, 2020 at https://www.theguardian.com/commentisfree/2018/dec/16/divestment-fossil-fuel -industry-trillions-dollars-investments-carbon.
18. Brad Plumer, "Companies see climate change hitting their bottom lines in the next 5 years," *The New York Times*, June 4, 2019. Accessed August 28, 2020 at https:// www.nytimes.com/2019/06/04/climate/companies-climate-change-financial -impact.html.
19. Kelly Gilblom, "BP says some of its oil 'won't see the light of day'," *Bloomberg*, July 2, 2019. Accessed August 28, 2020 at https://www.bloomberg.com/news/ articles/2019-07-02/bp-says-some-of-its-oil-won-t-see-the-light-of-day.

50. How can finance be used to combat climate change?

Alain Grandjean

On 23 September 2014, United Nations Secretary-General Ban Ki-moon invited world leaders (representatives of governments, finance, business and civil society) to New York for a climate summit as part of the preparations for COP21, which would take place in Paris in December 2015. This meeting was a notable success; coalitions of investors[1] were formed and made commitments to measure the carbon footprint of their portfolios and gradually reduce it. A little later, it was in Montreal that other investors became involved.[2] This is when "green finance" was born, and we will argue here that green finance requires serious regulation for its promises to be fulfilled.

THE FIGHT AGAINST – AND ADAPTATION TO – CLIMATE CHANGE GENERATES SIGNIFICANT INVESTMENTS

Investment needs (particularly in infrastructure) are regularly estimated at all levels. In 2014, the report from the Global Commission on the Economy and Climate[3] estimated these needs at 90 trillion dollars worldwide over the period 2015–30, while insisting that taking climate into account would only cost an additional 5 per cent. In 2016, the European Commission estimated the needs in transport, "low-carbon" energy production, networks, building renovation and industry for the period 2021–30.[4] Adding the European Investment Bank (EIB) estimates[5] for water management and flood protection, waste management, resilient urban infrastructure and research and development in transport and renewable energy, it amounts to more than 1300 billion euros per year (more than 8 per cent of the European Union's 2017 GDP). As for the financing gap, that is, the difference between the amount of the investments made and the amount of those that would need to be made, it is, for these sectors, more than 300 billion euros per year. This is in addition to the transformation that is needed in our agricultural model, the sustainable management of forests and natural areas, pollution control activities and investment in a circular economy. In addition to these amounts, there is also the need to adapt our infrastructures and buildings to "embedded" climate change (regardless of any possible future reduction in our greenhouse gas emissions), which will already have a very negative impact on our living conditions.

THE PRICE OF CARBON: THE DUAL NEED TO INCREASE IT BUT TO ACT ON OTHER LEVERS WITHOUT DELAY

We will not return here to the need to raise the price of carbon. The current level of carbon tax or price of quotas in regions such as the European Union, where a market for quotas is in place, is generally far too low (with the exception of certain Nordic countries that have introduced a much higher carbon tax alongside quotas). To take just one example, an official committee chaired by Alain Quinet[6] estimated that the target price to put the French economy on a path compatible with the Paris Agreement was 250 euros per tonne of CO_2 in 2030 and almost 800 euros in 2050. This is far from the current case (less than 50 euros for the carbon tax, and less than 30 euros for the quota price). Setting up carbon taxes[7] at a high enough level in each country is still essential, of course, but obviously very politically difficult: the climate emergency therefore requires taking additional measures that are accessible.

In the strictly financial world, several specific levers can be used. We will refer here to those that are currently being debated and which seem to us to be discriminatory, but we will begin by showing the limits of market players' action and of their enthusiasm for green finance.

Better Informed Markets: The Illusory Mantra of Green Finance

According to the prevailing and completely theoretical representation of the economy, markets are efficient as soon as they are properly informed. This representation is largely misconceived: in practice, financial markets are not efficient.[8]

Mark Carney, then Chairman of the Financial Stability Board, was officially asked by the G20 Finance Ministers in 2015 whether the climate risk could be systemic in nature. His answer, given in a speech called "Breaking the tragedy of the horizon" at the headquarters of the insurer Lloyd's of London, was affirmative and unambiguous.[9] He classified climate risks into three categories: transition risks (related to the "decarbonization" of the economy that can cause carbon assets to lose value and turn them into stranded assets),[10] physical risks related to climate change itself, and legal risks (resulting from victims' legal actions against those responsible for climate change). But he concluded this brilliant speech by emphasizing the need for financial investors to be better informed about these risks, thus simply endorsing the prevailing thesis mentioned above.

Since then, several initiatives have been carried out or are underway to meet this expectation. Following Mark Carney's speech, an international working group chaired by Michael Bloomberg, the Task Force on Climate-related Financial Disclosures (TCFD), produced a first set of general and sectoral recommendations in June 2017,[11] followed by a second report in June 2019. In December 2016, the European Commission launched a working group, the High-Level Expert Group, which issued its conclusions[12] in January 2018. The Commission's Action Plan on Sustainable Finance, adopted in March 2018, was based on its conclusions. The concrete initiatives concerned only information management and this on four subjects: the establishment of a clear and detailed Community classification system – or taxonomy – for sustainable activities, aimed at creating a common language for all actors in the financial system; the definition of standards for green bonds; for low-carbon indices;[13] and for the "metrics" to be used.

It is not possible today to make an exhaustive assessment of these various initiatives because the process is ongoing and its implementation is still partial. They have certainly had the merit of causing investors to take an interest in a subject that seemed unrelated to their profession until recently – on the grounds, also doctrinal, that finance would be neutral, which is obviously wrong.[14] Some of these investors are making green finance (notably through the issuance of "green bonds") an area for development. However, we do not see how and why an investor, whose decisions are driven by the expected financial return, would integrate a risk that he or she always perceives as long term (even if he or she might think that this term is close given the observed climate change). This is what Mark Carney made explicit when he spoke of the "tragedy of the horizon". To put it even more broadly, it is not market finance, which is short term in essence, that will in itself "save the world".

There are also a number of factual elements that show that, beyond the rhetoric, inaction is quite general. To date, portfolios have not been significantly reallocated to "low carbon". The share of "green" assets – or so-called greens[15] – remains low.[16] Investment in fossil fuels remains at very high levels. As Philippe Zaouati[17] (CEO of Mirova, the socially responsible investment fund of Natixis, the corporate and investment bank of the Banque Populaire et Caisse d'Epargne group) observes, passive management[18] (the majority of asset managers) "remains from 95% to 98% indexed on past indices and not on indices compatible with a 2°C trajectory". In addition, in the insurance sector, a recent study by the think tank Shift Project[19] shows the schizophrenia that prevails in this sector. Admittedly, "[i]nstitutions publish reports on climate risk, which are highly documented and well argued". But "when these same institutions (or others) publish a report on the insurance sector and on its risks in general, based on global analyses, the climate risk very often disappears from the radar. There is talk of 'macroeconomic', 'systemic' or 'holistic' risk, but there is no mention of climate".[20] This means that in fact these institutions do not consider that at this stage this risk is "material"; in other words, that the risks may result in a financial loss in the time frame of their analysis.

The Need for Public Intervention in the Financial Sector

These findings should encourage public authorities and regulators, who are responsible for the general interest, to move from information recommendations to active public policies and binding rules (and in practice regulations). We will not focus here on the obvious need to reduce and then eliminate fossil fuel subsidies,[21] which amounted to 340 billion dollars in 2017 for 76 countries, by implementing support policies in accordance with the countries and the specific constraints of the citizens concerned. Three other options are to be considered.

Ban public banks from financing fossil fuels
The action of public banks is by definition directly controlled by public authority, which can therefore ask them to stop financing activities related to fossil fuels. The effect is twofold, involving first their own financing, but second, the financing of private banks when they participate in syndications with them. This is particularly the case for development banks.

In 2015 the Canfin-Grandjean report,[22] submitted to the President of the French Republic in preparation for COP21, recommended in particular that "each development bank should set itself a '2°C roadmap' showing its contribution to the 2°C trajectory and the carbon content of its portfolio of financed projects as well as its approach to making its portfolio of operations resilient". It is possible to go further today. The EIB announced on Thursday 14 November 2019 that it would no longer finance new fossil fuel projects, including gas, from 2022 onwards and that it would commit to dedicating 50 per cent of its financing to environmental projects by 2025. The EIB is thus paving the way for a significant reduction in fossil fuel financing.

The greening of monetary policy
In 2012, the European Central Bank (ECB) saved the eurozone. The bank's president, Mario Draghi, announced at that time that the ECB would buy, without limit, sovereign bonds from the euro area, thus putting an end to the speculation that was endangering it. This programme of "Outright Monetary Transactions" was not provided for in the Treaties; it was challenged in the German Constitutional Court and before the European Court of Justice, but

was validated by these two bodies.[23] This is proof that necessity prevails and that it is possible to be imaginative in monetary matters.

This operation was followed in 2015 by so-called "non-conventional" QE (quantitative easing) operations, which were supposed to facilitate the exit from creeping deflation. The limits and disadvantages of QE are today under discussion: it has no effect on the real economy; negative interest rates are favourable to speculative transactions and a "zombie" economy. But QE could be a powerful lever for the ecological transition and the recovery of the – green – economy, particularly because of the priority given by the new European Commission to the fight against climate change and to a Green Deal.[24] It should also be noted that, contrary to popular belief, the ECB has full legitimacy to take action on the climate.[25] Article 127(1) of the Treaty on the Functioning of the European Union (TFEU) states that "without prejudice to the objective of price stability, the ESCB [European System of Central Banks] shall support the general economic policies in the Union with a view to contributing to the achievement of the objectives of the Union as laid down in Article 3 of the Treaty on European Union". For its part, Article 3 of the TEU explicitly includes the objective of "sustainable development of Europe, based" – among other factors – on "a high level of protection and improvement of the quality of the environment". Thus, sufficient elements of legality for the ECB to develop green monetary policies are already included in the TFEU.

How do we proceed in practice? We know that public institutions cannot benefit from financing from the ESCB, with the notable exception of public investment banks. These banks may have access, under the same conditions as private banks, to the ECB's counter (Article 123(2) of the TFEU). National and European authorities could therefore launch ambitious investment pro-grammes[26] financed by a network of public banks (the EIB, the European Bank for Reconstruction and Development [EBRD] and national banks such as Kreditanstalt für Wiederaufbau [KfW] in Germany and the Banque Publique d'investissement [BPI] and la Banque Postale in France), which would them-selves be financed by the issuance of bonds acquired by the ECB in significant volumes.[27] This proposal[28] would not require a reversal of the ban on monetary financing for states and could be compatible with the continuity of the prin-ciple of central bank independence, which is essential for such a proposal's crucial acceptance by German population.[29]

In parallel with this climate-focused buyback operation, the ECB should stop holding "carbon assets" in the securities it buys or accepts as collateral. Altogether, it would thus launch a real "green-QE", an operation that guaran-tees the financing of green and stops the financing of fossil fuels.

Penalize banks that finance the fossil fuel economy

However, this "green-QE" will not have a direct effect on private banking operations. It should be recalled that investments in fossil fuels remain considerable. The International Energy Agency (IEA)[30] estimated these investments at a total of 800 billion dollars for 2018, slightly higher than in 2017. The players in the sector are very powerful: according to Moody's Investors Services, the profits in 2018 of the five Western majors (Royal Dutch Shell, ExxonMobil, Chevron, Total and British Petroleum) were 89 billion dollars. Saudi Aramco's profits amounted to 110 billion dollars. Although these companies are powerful, and unfortunately helped by massive public subsidies, they need bank financing (for all their operations, not just investments), which they can nowadays (far too) easily find. In 2018, the world's 33 largest banking institutions provided them with a total of 600 billion dollars in financing.[31]

It is therefore advisable to strongly encourage banks to move out of financing the fossil fuel economy. This can be done, for example, by introducing a penalty factor, a "brown penalizing factor" in the calculation of the equity ratio, the risk-weighted assets (RWAs),[32] which would reduce their profitability on equity if they continue to participate in financing carbon assets (both directly and in loans to investors). This idea was endorsed by the governor of the Banque de France in April 2019.[33]

The idea was analysed by researchers Jakob Thomä and Kyra Gibhardt.[34] Natixis, decided in 2019 to simulate what could be achieved by a system called the Green Weighting Factor (with a bonus for green financing and a penalty for fossil fuel financing), thus anticipating a decision that could be taken at European level. It should be recalled that while the Basel Committee is a forum for drawing up proposals on banking regulation, it is the states and the European Union that decide on their transcription into regulations – which have sole legal force. In this case, the transcription of the Basel III agreements into a regulatory package[35] was adopted by the European Parliament in April 2019. The next version of this package could and should therefore include consideration of the climate crisis.

This approach could also be applied to insurance companies, with Pillar 1 of the Solvency II framework being devoted to the capital requirements of these companies. Insurance companies are also big investors. How they are going to be regulated is of primary importance to the climate.

CONCLUSION

Financial investors are becoming aware of climate change and are beginning to consider that it could have an impact on their profession. However, they have not significantly changed their investment or disinvestment decisions, which are crucial in the current battle. Public authorities, particularly at European level, can accelerate the effective consideration of climate issues in these decisions. These authorities have powerful levers in their hands. It is up to them to use these as soon as possible.

NOTES

1. Like the Portfolio Decarbonization Coalition; see https://unepfi.org/pdc/, accessed 24 August 2020.
2. See the Montréal Carbon Pledge at https://montrealpledge.org/, accessed 24 August 2020.
3. This commission was chaired by Felipe Calderon, Nicholas Stern and Ngozi Okonjo-Iweala. It has been continued in the "New Climate Economy" project. See https://newclimateeconomy.net, accessed 24 August 2020.
4. "Commission staff working document. Impact assessment. Accompanying the document Proposal for a Directive of the European Parliament and of the Council amending Directive 2012/27/EU on Energy Efficiency" (2016), Table 22, accessed 20 August 2020 at https://eur-lex.europa.eu/legal-content/EN/TXT/?uri =CELEX%3A52016SC0405.
5. European Investment Bank, *Restoring EU Competitiveness 2016 Updated Version*, accessed 20 August 2020 at https://www.eib.org/attachments/efs/restoring_eu _competitiveness_en.pdf.
6. See https://www.strategie.gouv.fr/publications/de-laction-climat, accessed 24 August 2020.
7. See, for example, the report published in 2017 by Nicholas Stern and Joseph Stiglitz, at https://www.carbonpricingleadership.org/report-of-the-highlevel -commission-on-carbon-prices, accessed 24 August 2020.
8. See, for example, Nicolas Bouleau's uncompromising analysis at http://www .nicolasbouleau.eu/critique-de-lefficience-des-marches-financiers/, accessed 24 August 2020.
9. See https://www.fsb.org/wp-content/uploads/Breaking-the-Tragedy-of-the -Horizon-%E2%80%93-climate-change-and-financial-stability.pdf – and here, its translation into French: https://alaingrandjean.fr/2015/11/11/mettre-fin-a-la -tragedie-des-biens-lointains-changement-climatique-et-stabilite-financiere/, both accessed 24 August 2020.
10. What they are, in fact, if we take climate change seriously. See Claude Henry's article on this subject, at https://www.lemonde.fr/idees/article/2018/09/05/claude -henry-trois-mesures-pour-sortir-du-desastre-ecologique_5350348_3232.html, accessed 24 August 2020.
11. See https://www.fsb-tcfd.org/publications/final-recommendations-report/, accessed 24 August 2020.
12. See https://ec.europa.eu/info/publications/180131-sustainable-finance-report_fr, accessed 24 August 2020.
13. We will return to this subject, whose importance is sometimes underestimated.
14. Two arguments are sufficient to demonstrate this. First, finance necessarily favours short-term profitable assets, simply because of the capitalization calculation; and second, it focuses by mimicry on the expected returns of stock market indices, which reflect the current economy, which is far too carbon intensive.
15. Are "green bonds" an illusion? This is what Ivar Ekeland and Julien Lefournier think and demonstrate in this convincing indictment, at http://www.chair-energy

-prosperity.org/publications/lobligation-verte-homeopathie-incantation/, accessed 24 August 2020.

16. In France, investments in listed green funds amount to €23 billion, or 1.3 per cent of assets under management. See https://www.novethic.fr/actualite/ finance-durable/isr-rse/verdir-le-systeme-financier-une-nouvelle-mission-pour -les-banques-centrales-147174.html, accessed 24 August 2020.

17. In an interview on 9 July 2019, entitled "Philippe Zaouati: l'impact réel de la finance durable est très faible" [Philippe Zaouati: the real impact of sustainable finance is very low]. See https://www.rsedatanews.net/article/article-finance -responsable-esg-isr-philippe-zaouati---20190709-2236, accessed 24 August 2020.

18. Passive management for a fund consists of investing in a portfolio of assets, "replicating" an index such as the MSCI World, the Euro Stoxx 600, or the CAC 40. This method reduces management costs and aligns the manager's practice with the market "trend".

19. See https://theshiftproject.org/wp-content/uploads/2019/07/2019-07 _Observatoire-173_Deux-sons-de-cloche-sur-la-mat%C3%A9rialit%C3%A9-du -risque-climat_The-Shift-Project.pdf, accessed 20 August 2020.

20. Ibid., p. 11.

21. See http://www.oecd.org/environment/fossil-fuel-support-is-rising-again-in-a -threat-to-climate-change-efforts.htm – and the IEA-OECD report on the subject at http://www.oecd.org/fossil-fuels/publication/, both accessed 24 August 2020.

22. See https://alaingrandjean.fr/wp-content/uploads/2015/06/Rapport-CANFIN -GRANDJEAN-FINAL-18062015.pdf, accessed 24 August 2020.

23. See https://www.lesechos.fr/2016/06/omt-la-bce-reste-sous-la-surveillance -appuyee-du-juge-allemand-209962, accessed 24 August 2020.

24. See, for example, https://www.lemonde.fr/international/article/2019/07/16/devant -le-parlement-europeen-ursula-von-der-leyen-promet-un-green-deal-pour-l-ue _5489898_3210.html, accessed 24 August 2020.

25. See https://alaingrandjean.fr/2019/05/14/mandat-bce-politique-monetaire -ecologique/.

26. This public investment expenditure, even financed by public banks, will weigh on the public deficit, as calculated today. I have shown in my last book that it is possible to interpret European procedures intelligently to get around this apparent difficulty. See Alain Grandjean, Marion Cohen and Kevin Puisieux, *Agir sans Attendre: Notre Plan de Climat* [Act Without Delay: Our Climate Plan], published by Les Liens qui Libèrent, 2019.

27. If necessary, and in order to avoid any legal challenge, paragraph 2 of Article 123 could be supplemented by the following sentence: "By way of derogation from the above, the European Central Bank is authorized to acquire, in significant volumes and on preferential terms, debt instruments issued by the European Investment Bank in support of investments in the ecological transition".

28. For more details on this proposal, see https://lvsl.fr/que-faut-il-changer-dans-les -traites-europeens-en-matiere-monetaire/ – and http://www.bsi-economics.org/ 950-role-politique-monetaire-, accessed 24 August 2020.

29. It is imperative to take into account the sociological realities on these subjects, even if nothing is to be expected from the Bundesbank's leaders – see the interview with its current chief Jens Weidmann: https://www.lalibre.be/economie/ conjoncture/la-politique-monetaire-ne-doit-pas-servir-les-objectifs-climatiques -bundesbank-5db85c9a9978e218e3854e91, accessed 24 August 2020.

30. See https://webstore.iea.org/world-energy-investment-2019, accessed 24 August 2020.
31. See https://www.banktrack.org/article/banking_on_climate_change_fossil_fuel _finance_report_card_2019, accessed 24 August 2020.
32. The regulator requires banks to hold a minimum capital based on the amount of their risk-weighted RWAs.
33. See https://www.novethic.fr/actualite/finance-durable/isr-rse/les-banques-de -france-et-d-angleterre-appellent-a-plus-de-regulation-du-secteur-financier-face -au-risque-climatique-145673.html, accessed 24 August 2020.
34. See Jakob Thomä, Kyra Gibhardt, "Quantifying the potential impact of a green supporting factor or brown penalty on European banks and lending", *Journal of Financial Regulation and Compliance*, 8 July 2019.
35. The CRR 2 (Capital Requirements Regulation 2) and CRD 5 (Capital Requirements Directive 5).

51. China's pioneering green finance
Ma Jun

Five years ago, few would have expected China to become a pioneer in green finance. It had only one green financial product then: a modest-sized green credit. Today, it is one of the largest markets for green bonds as well as having an array of other green finance products, such as green funds, insurance products, exchange-traded funds (ETFs) and asset-backed securities (ABSs).

China's rapid transformation has drawn much attention from the international community, with many people wondering what "secrets" powered China's progress. This chapter provides an overview of what China has achieved in developing its green finance system, highlights the key features of the Chinese approaches and explores areas of the Chinese green finance market that can be further improved.

CLOSING THE GREEN FINANCING GAP

The Paris Agreement and the UN 2030 Agenda set unprecedented global ambitions for sustainable development in the coming decade while calling for cooperation among diverse actors, both public and private, and mobilization of massive financial resources. As much as USD2.5 trillion may be needed globally each year to finance the Sustainable Development Goals (SDGs).

As China pursues its economic priorities, it has also begun feeling the heavy toll of environment degradation. Some studies estimated that the economic losses that China suffers each year from pollution and shrinking biodiversity could be as much as 6 percent of its GDP. In the last five years, the government has placed preserving and restoring the environment at the forefront of its policy initiatives, including bold commitments to curbing greenhouse gas emissions in the coming decades.

However, fiscal resources alone are far from sufficient to address these environmental challenges. In 2015, I estimated that China would need RMB4 trillion annual green investment to achieve its environmental protection goals, and only 10–15 percent of that could be met by public finance. To close this gap, the private sector would have to play a bigger role, thus the introduction of a green financial system is essential.

INTRODUCTION OF A POLICY FRAMEWORK

In 2015, China kicked off its work on green finance by introducing a comprehensive policy framework. Led by the People's Bank of China (PBOC, the central bank), seven ministries devised the "Guidelines for Establishing the Green Financial System" over a year. The purpose was to enable the financial system to mobilize trillions of yuan for sustainable investment in sectors such as renewable energy, energy efficiency, clean transportation, green buildings and environmental remediation. With 35 concrete policy measures, these guidelines laid out a clear roadmap and sent a strong signal to all stakeholders on the expected products and regulatory requirements.

Under the guidelines, green taxonomies were developed to differentiate green activities and assets from non-green ones, so that both regulators and investors knew where the green funds should go and avoid "greenwashing." To date, China has launched three different but complementary sets of taxonomies, covering green credit, green bonds and green industries.

A major effort by the policy-makers, including the PBOC and China Securities Regulatory Commission (CSRC), was setting up the regulatory regime for a green bond market. These included the definition of green bonds, verification requirements, reporting of the use of proceeds and environmental benefits, as well as incentives for green bond issuances. Regulators have also facilitated the development of the green bond verification market.

Meanwhile, to enhance the transparency of green financial activities, the CSRC released a timetable for introducing mandatory environmental, social and governance (ESG) disclosure requirements for all listed companies in China, as early as 2020. Companies will have to report environmental performance indicators and need to understand how ESG factors impact their financial performances. Such disclosure requirements, including those from the CSRC, banking and environmental regulators, have improved information flows that enable investors to identify green and non-green assets.

To promote the introduction of green financial products, various policy incentives were introduced at national and local levels. For example, the PBOC included green finance performances in its Macro-Prudential Assessments of banks. The central bank also accepted green assets as eligible collaterals for relending facilities, providing low-cost funding through banks to green projects. Many local governments give interest subsidies and guarantees for green loans. In Jiangsu, the provincial government promotes green bonds by subsidizing 30 percent of the interest payments. These incentives significantly raised companies' and investors' interests in green financial products.

PROLIFERATION OF GREEN FINANCE PRODUCTS

Over the past five years, green credit rapidly expanded while innovative green financial products also mushroomed in China, including green bonds, insurance, funds, ETFs, ABSs, and various emission trading rights.

Green credit was the first green financial product in China, dating back to 2012, when the term was defined by the *Green Credit Guidelines* of the China Banking Regulatory Commission (CBRC). Banks were also mandated to report their green credit on a biannual basis from the end of 2013. By the end of 2019, outstanding green loans of 21 major banks amounted to RMB10.6 trillion, more than doubling from the end of 2013. These loans supported many green projects such as transport, renewable energy, water treatment and solid waste treatment.

With the *Green Bond Endorsed Projects Catalogue* and the PBOC's guidelines on green financial bonds coming into effect at the end of 2015, China's green bond market took off in 2016 with RMB211 billion issued, accounting for 40 percent of the global total, which made China the largest issuer of that year. Since then, China has remained a top green bond issuer. In 2019, Chinese companies and institutions issued more than 200 green bonds, raising RMB350 billion in total. In 2016–19, the total issuance of green bonds by Chinese issuers in both domestic and international markets exceeded RMB1.1 trillion.

Over 60 percent of the green bonds issued in China received third-party green verifications, a ratio consistent with the global average. The average maturity of green bonds issued in 2019 was 4.8 years, up from 4.3 years in 2018, suggesting that the green bond market was helping address the maturity-mismatch problem between medium- and long-term green projects and bank financing, typically of short duration.

Many other green instruments were developed over the past few years. By the end of 2019, 781 green funds had been set up in China to provide mainly equity investments in environment-related companies and projects. Some Chinese investors are now looking to launch green-tech funds with foreign partners. Mandatory environmental pollution liability insurance schemes were introduced in many provinces on a pilot basis, covering over 20 industries with high environmental risks, including chemical, power, pharmaceutical, printing and dyeing. Insurance companies have also introduced policies that cover risks associated with the performance of green buildings as well as solar and wind power equipment. A growing number of green ETF products were launched to meet the demand from both institutional and individual investors. There were 32 securities/notes issued in 2019 backed by green assets such as receivables of solar and water treatment companies and green building operators.

China now has seven regional carbon markets and is preparing to launch a nationwide Emissions Trading System (ETS) covering 6 billion tons of emissions annually from around 8000 large companies. The national ETS will start with the thermal power industry, responsible for about 3 billion tons of emissions each year. China's national ETS may become the world's largest carbon market in a few years and could be linked with other national and transnational markets. In Guangdong and Hong Kong, the Greater Bay Area Green Finance Alliance is now contemplating a "carbon connect" scheme to enable foreign investors to access Guangdong-based carbon market with greater convenience.

BENEFITS OF GREEN FINANCE IN NUMBERS

Green finance has proven to support China' economy, rather than restraining growth or job creation, which was a concern of some policy-makers in the early days of the concept. This is also why a growing number of local governments in China are eager to promote green finance. Huzhou, a green finance pilot zone in Zhejiang province, reported that its outstanding green loans grew 31 percent per annum in the past three years, surpassing most other regions and other types of financing. In part due to its green finance innovation, Huzhou's GDP growth was among the top in Zhejiang while its energy intensity dropped rapidly.

According to the China Banking and Insurance Regulatory Commission (CBIRC), in 2018, the environmental benefits of green loans extended by 21 major Chinese banks included cutting energy consumption by the equivalent of burning 247 million tons of standard coal, reducing carbon emission by 518 million tons, chemical oxygen demand (COD) by 4.6 million tons, sulfur dioxide by 6.9 million tons, while saving 1 billion tons of water.

The development of green finance could also help contain financial risks. Statistics from the PBOC show that by the end of 2018, the average rate of non-performing green loans was only 0.48 percent, which was 1.81 percentage points lower than average corporate loans. Some institutes, including the Industrial and Commercial Bank of China (ICBC) and Tsinghua University, have developed models for environmental stress tests, enabling banks to quantify the credit risks arising from exposures to polluting and high-carbon sectors. These methodologies can help convince banks to reduce their "brown" exposure and increase lending to green sectors, limiting future financial risks while enhancing risk-adjusted returns. PBOC Deputy Governor Chen Yulu, while speaking at the recent China Finance Forum, stated that the Chinese central bank "would analyze the impact of climate change on the financial industry and implications for prudential regulation."

SECRETS OF THE CHINESE APPROACH

China has clearly grown more aggressively than most other countries in developing a green financial system, albeit starting from a low base with limited capacity. Many friends from abroad have asked me the "secrets" that made China a global green finance leader in only a few years. I reason that China's achievements were enabled by these five main factors:

1. First, China started its green finance agenda by building a political consensus. In many countries, green finance is promoted by one particular arm of the government or an industry body, such as a central bank, a financial regulator, an association or non-governmental organization (NGOs). China backed green finance with a political push from the very top. In 2014, a 14-action roadmap for developing the green finance system was endorsed by the Central Leading Group for Financial and Economic Affairs. Most of these 14 actions were also included in the "Integrated Reform Plan for Promoting Ecological Civilization" issued by the CPC Central Committee and the State Council, the highest decision-making bodies in China. The political backing by China's president and premier carried enormous weight in mobilizing policies and resources and facilitating inter-departmental consensus on green finance.

2. Second, China's approach to designing the green financial system was top-down and not purely market led. The successful development of green finance requires essential ingredients including:
   (a) green taxonomies and definition of green activities;
   (b) environmental information disclosure by corporations and financial institutions;
   (c) rules and standards for green finance products;
   (d) incentives to corporations and financial institutions.

   Due to the many deficiencies of the market, such as its inability to account for environmental externalities, asymmetrical access to information, and market participants' lack of analytical capacities, the market and the private sector are often unable to effectively organize or produce those essential ingredients, certainly not in a short period of time. For example, if developing green taxonomy is left to the market, financial institutions may produce many competing versions without a common language. Indeed, the lack of such a common language has constrained the development of green finance in many markets. Recognizing the need for the government or regulator to address the market's deficiencies, China took the top-down approach – its *Guidelines on Establishing a Green Financial*

System (2016) spelled out 35 actions on how these ingredients should be developed and coordinated.

3. Coordination among key ministries, the division of labor and an implementation timetable are keys to success. China recognized at the policy-design stage that green finance was not merely the responsibility of the central bank or a financial regulator. Rather, it requires policy support and resources from many other government agencies and regulators, including fiscal support, environmental regulation, and industrial policies. That is why seven ministries, namely the PBOC, the Ministry of Finance, the National Development and Reform Commission, the Ministry of Environmental Protection (now Ministry of Ecology and Environment), the CSRC, the China Banking Regulatory Commission and the China Insurance Regulatory Commission (now collectively known as CBIRC), jointly developed the green finance guidelines in 2016. More importantly, to ensure the policy documents receive more than just cursory note or lip service, these guidelines were followed by a policy document on "Division of Labor (DOL) for Implementing the Guidelines." This DOL laid out the specific tasks of each of the seven ministries and deadlines for delivering the several dozen specific policy actions promised in the guidelines. Due in part to this DOL, the implementation of the green finance guidelines has been one of the most effective undertaking compared to other policies.

4. China defined roles of industrial bodies such as national and local Green Finance Committees (GFCs). In 2015, the PBOC launched the GFC of China Society for Finance and Banking. The GFC, with 240 financial institutions, environment-related companies and research bodies as members, quickly became the main disseminator of green finance knowledge, the organizer of green finance product innovation, the key source of policy recommendations, and the coordinator for capacity-building and international collaboration. Each year, the GFC Annual Meeting recognizes nearly 20 innovations in green finance research, products or tools. The WeChat news portal maintained by GFC, with daily publications, is now the most important information platform for green finance policies, product innovations, and business opportunities. At the local level, about 20 regional GFCs play similar roles promoting green finance market development.

5. China encourages regional innovation in green finance. Since China's economy has vast regional differences, it is imperative to encourage local players to innovate in their approaches. In June 2017, the State Council approved pilot programs on green finance reform and innovation in five provinces and eight cities. In the last two years, many valuable experiences and innovations were identified. For example, Huzhou, one of the pilot cities, launched a Green Credit Online Service Platform providing

instant e-matching of green projects with green funds from banks (including over 100 green credit products) and investors. The PBOC organizes annual meetings of these pilot cities, summarizes the best practices and promotes them throughout the country.

In conclusion, green finance aims to use financial resources to address the market's salient failure to account for environmental and climate externalities in today's economy. The development of the green financial system itself can also be hindered by the limitations of the market. For example, the taxonomies, product guidelines, and disclosure requirements for green finance are largely public goods, and the technical capacities for analyzing environmental and climate risks are also semi-public goods in nature. These features of the green financial system imply that governments and regulators must take a proactive role in leading the design of the system and mobilize resources to develop the green finance market. A bottom-up approach with the government "hands off", until recently preferred in many countries, may ultimately work as the private sector gains more environmental awareness and willingness to assume responsibilities, but the world doesn't have the luxury to wait another five to ten years given today's growing climate crisis, perhaps the biggest in human history.

LOOKING INTO THE FUTURE

Despite the notable progress China has made in the past few years, the green finance capacity within its financial system remains grossly insufficient to meet the huge demand for green and low-carbon investment. According to a recent study we conducted for Chongqing municipality, a provincial-level region with a population of 30 million, its demand for green and low-carbon investment amounts to RMB300 billion per year. Applying this estimate to the entire country, it implies that China will need to invest at least RMB10 trillion per year in green and low-carbon projects, three times the green finance demand that I estimated five years ago. China needs to, and will very likely, take more aggressive measures to further promote green finance in the following areas:

- First, greening institutional investors. Many institutional investors have not yet developed strong preferences for green investments for the lack of both awareness and capacity. Regulators, research institutions, NGOs, and institutional investors should work together to raise the awareness of the benefits of ESG investing, encourage ESG disclosure on investments, develop ESG products, and educate investors.
- Second, mainstreaming environmental risk analysis. The Central Banks and Supervisors Network for Greening the Financial System (NGFS) is

planning to publish a handbook (with a collection of methodologies) to promote the use of Environmental Risk Analysis (ERA) by financial institutions. China should make full use of these technical resources and local research capacities to enable banks, asset managers and insurance companies to conduct stress tests and scenario analysis. The Chinese central bank and financial regulators, as well as the GFC, could play a key role in mainstreaming the ERA.

- Third, introducing stronger incentives for green finance. While most existing incentives for green finance have been focusing on subsidies, including subsidies for interests for green loans or green bonds, the discussion on the possibility of introducing regulatory incentives has also been popular in some large economies, like the EU and China. Statisticians in the Chinese banking system have already demonstrated that green loans are much less likely to default. Their argument is, if this is the case in many other economies, we should encourage financial regulators to make some adjustments – for example, reducing the risk weights for green loans. Some banks are already exploring this possibility internally – for example, Natixis – even before regulators are determined to make the change without violating current regulatory requirements. Chinese regulators could encourage large Chinese banks, which are authorized to use internal risk models, to learn from Natixis's experience in introducing differentiated risk weights for green and brown assets (lower for green and higher for brown assets) without altering the overall regulatory risk weights. Once a few banks' pilot programs prove successful and data issues are largely resolved, this practice could be applied to the rest of the Chinese banking system.
- Fourth, greening investments under the Belt & Road Initiative (BRI). In 2018, China GFC and the City of London jointly launched the Green Investment Principles (GIP) for the BRI, with 36 global institutions signed up to date. The GIP's three working groups are taking specific actions to promote environmental impact assessment tools, disclosure mechanisms and innovative green finance products. Further, we suggest the China authorities consider setting up a "green light system" for outbound investments, that is, introducing a mandatory requirement for environmental impact assessment for overseas investments.
- Fifth, promoting the harmonization of green finance standards in China and Europe. Both China and the EU have developed their green or sustainable finance taxonomies, and the world's green finance community is concerned about the transaction costs and risks of greenwashing associated with a proliferation of inconsistent and incomparable taxonomies. Many smaller markets are mulling whether to develop their own taxonomies. We believe that China and the EU should take the lead in exploring ways to harmonize their taxonomies, initially for facilitating cross-board green

capital flows. In the longer run, such joint work may also serve as the basis for developing harmonized global standards.

- Sixth, supporting green finance innovation in new sectors. In the past, most green finance activities took place in sectors such as renewable energy, waste treatment, and green transportation involving typically large banks and project owners. The vast potential of greening small and medium-sized enterprises (SMEs), consumption, agriculture, and buildings haven't been tapped into. Regulators, financial institutions, research bodies and NGOs should devote more resources to innovating green products in these areas. In particular, the application of digital technologies to labeling and verifying green consumer goods, green SMEs and sustainable agricultural products may significantly reduce the costs of offering green finance services and rapidly expand the market.

PART VII

Communicators

52. Introduction to Part VII
Johan Rockström

We simply have to admit it. Just as Georgina Mace highlights at the outset of her chapter on biodiversity, we have, despite the fact that biodiversity loss is perceived as a concern and has many advocates, largely failed to touch the hearts of citizens at large. The role that nature and climate – in essence, a stable planet – plays in our lives and the lives of our children on Earth has failed to become a driving force behind individual and global action for most people, in most parts of the world.

Despite significant progress in our awareness, understanding, and policy engagement in actions to solve global environmental challenges, manifested not least in UN conventions such as the Convention on Biodiversity (UNCBD) and the Framework Convention on Climate Change (UNFCCC) adopted almost 30 years ago, we now face a planetary emergency. The aggregate human pressures on the planet fuelling this emergency are not only continuing to rise, they are reaching dangerous levels, putting us at risk of triggering irreversible loss of ecological functions and a manageable climate (Steffen et al., 2018). Perhaps a central reason for this failure to reach only a minority (< 20 percent) of citizens in countries around the world is our tendency to communicate the climate and nature crises as environmental problems, instead of talking about humans and solutions (Pihl et al., 2019).

The coronavirus crisis is a devastating global health shock causing the most abrupt slowdown of the world economy since the global recession in the 1930s. It is also a major moment of learning and reckoning for all citizens in the world. If the world, from political leaders to city dwellers, is able to rise so fast, mobilizing collective action and trillions of US dollars in financial bail-out programmes to address one crisis – COVID-19 – why are we not able to rise in the face of the global climate crisis and nature crisis?

These crises, unlike the coronavirus crisis, are putting the future of humanity on Earth at risk. As proposed by François Gemenne and Anneliese Depoux, we need to focus much more on communicating the direct impacts of climate change on human well-being and health. After all, how many recall today that over a time span of only a few excessively hot months in the summer of 2003, 70 000 Europeans (Robine et al., 2008), predominantly elder and weak citizens, died as a result of the most devastating heatwave on record, very likely amplified by human-caused global warming (Stott, Stone and Allen, 2004). This was a terrible shock, hitting in particular the big cities of Europe.

The grand challenge is how do we tip the scales in the world towards global sustainability? How do we rapidly reach a point of no return, embarking on journeys that not only imminently – in the next few years – bend the global curves of negative change (on climate and biodiversity, water and air, soils and toxic waste), but also follow deep transformation pathways that, for example, cut emissions in half, globally, every decade? Communicating science on risk and solutions, continues, and will continue to be, of critical importance. Philippe Cury and Daniel Pauly remind us that committed science that actively communicates is a necessity to avoid the looming collapse of marine fisheries, and Edward Maibach shows how connecting science with innovative ways of reaching citizens can make a big difference. Importantly, Jean Jouzel points out the importance of robust science, such as the Intergovernmental Panel on Climate Change (IPCC), as a basis for credible communication on climate risks. This is a necessarily slow variable, a foundation to build on, in efforts of achieving societal system change towards sustainability.

We must admit that our sustainability-science communication, activism, and engagement on environmental risks, while having made important progress over the past decades, have not altered the course of the world (despite the existential risks we face). Emissions continue to rise (Jordan, 2019) despite temporary falls (e.g. after the financial crisis and the coronavirus crisis), and natural capital continues to be lost at a catastrophic pace. Even in the most environmentally engaged societies, it is always a committed minority, never an engaged majority, representing < 20 percent of the global population, who drive the environmental agenda (Pihl et al., 2019). I would argue that a reason for this inability to engage the broader citizenry is not poor ways of communicating, but rather communicating the wrong narrative. We have focused on sharing knowledge on why we need to protect the environment and conserve nature as a responsibility and a moral obligation. For a long time, taking care of the environment was achieved by raising awareness. Take economics as an example, where the progress of ecological economics tended to translate to different forms of "willingness to pay" for nature. In short, saving the planet was a moral obligation associated with a significant degree of personal sacrifice. With such a melody determining the development symphony, it is perhaps not so surprising that only a minority of souls have been touched.

This core narrative has been changing within the environmental movement, evolving over the last decades, culminating in the Paris climate agreement negotiations. The Paris Agreement heralded a new and more mature narrative, convincingly walking the talk in the real world. The Paris Agreement cemented the narrative of global sustainability as the prerequisite for prosperity and equity for all humans in the world. This was made possible by mounting evidence that decarbonizing the world's energy system will neither threaten the global economy nor lead to unemployment, while instead saving millions of lives through improved air quality and take the world into a new era of technology, mobility, and life quality (Luderer et al., 2019). The emerging narrative, backed by science, can be summarized like this: there is no contradiction between profit and sustainability, and that democracies, prevention of conflicts, migration, security, and social justice are better protected in a sustainable world, than in a world that runs on fossil fuels and destroys its natural capital. The new narrative is maturing and increasingly fed with empirical evidence (Clark, Feiner and Viehs, 2015).

But we are running out of time. This makes communication so fundamental. We have only a decade to decisively turn things around (United Nations Environment Programme [UNEP], 2019). The coronavirus crisis may help us, providing the direly needed evidence that sustainability and resilience are investments to reduce risks of future pandemics.

And there is reason for a certain degree of optimism. Why? Not only is science clearer than ever before in terms of immediate and long-term global risks to human development. And not only do we have overwhelming evidence that "yes we can" and "yes we gain" from transitions to circular, zero-carbon, ecosystem-conserving, economic development (Geels et al., 2017; New Climate Economy, 2018). We also know that engaged and concerned citizens across the world, while still constituting a minority, are no longer the isolated few. Opinion polls by Yale University show consistently that 60 or so percent of US citizens are concerned about climate change and want to see climate action (Gustafson et al., 2019). Similar or higher numbers are found in European and Asian countries (Global Challenges Foundation, 2018). And, green political parties and movements across the world often receive double-digit percentages of votes by citizens in elections.

We may be at a pivotal moment: with the right story (facing catastrophic risks with attractive and fair solutions) at the right time (the coronavirus crisis and the super-year 2020 when global curves of negative impact on the planet must bend), with a relatively large engagement and recognition across the world of why a stable climate and functioning nature is worth having.

As shown by Everett Rogers in his famous 1962 book *Diffusion of Innovations* (with the 5th edition published in 2003), behavioural change processes among people are largely determined by the bell-shaped distribution of groups of people. Every population will always have a small minority (2.5 percent) of "innovators", whom we can think of as the "die-hard" environmentalists. Then we have the 13.5 percent "early adopters", essentially the seriously concerned and receptive citizens who do not stand on the barricades. This makes some 15 percent sustainability-engaged core citizens in any given society. A significant minority. A voice that is often heard. At the other extreme end of the population distribution is, according to Everett Rogers, the 16 percent "laggards". Here we find the sceptics and denialists, and the actors with clear vested interests in remaining in an unsustainable world order (e.g. oil industrialists, coal miners). In between these two extremes, we have the majority. I call these the "indifferent majority". They do not question sustainability science. But they do not lift a finger to support the transition to a sustainable world. In short, they live their day-to-day lives and try to do this with a minimum of friction, that is, move along the path of least resistance. When they go to the supermarket they choose the cheapest tomatoes. They do not care whether they are ecological or not. If the sustainable option would be the best option, then they would take it.

Everett splits the majority into two parts – the "Early" and the "Late" majority – recognizing that also in the indifferent majority, there is a sequence in behavioural change. This theoretical framework suggests that in any given society there is an indifferent majority (68 percent) who do not care too much but would not object to a sustainable life as long as it makes social sense. True, while Everett's thesis applied to entrepreneurs and innovators, I am suggesting the same population dynamics applies for transitions to sustainable lifestyles. This may not be the case. Social science studies are needed. But the applicability is not far-fetched, I would argue, as sustainability has so much to do with novelty, innovation, and system change. If I am right? Then the focus of science communication, if we want to rapidly "tip the scales" to sustainability, should be on the "early majority", that is the 34 percent of any population who are quite indifferent but certainly willing to move.

My gut feeling, at the height of the corona crisis, is that this "early majority" is more receptive to change than ever before. Why are they so important? Well, there is evidence that large enough minorities can "tip over" majorities (Pihl et al. 2019). The Pareto principle (Pareto, 2014), the 20/80 law of the vital few, states that 80 percent of the effects come from 20 percent of the causes, or phrased another way, a large enough minority (20 percent) can tip the logic of the majority. This principle, originating from assessments of unequal distribution of wealth, has proven significant in understanding societal change. It is only when a large enough minority reacted against slavery, passive smoking, apartheid, or rules forbidding marriage equality, that these engrained social habits and cultural rules could be overturned and penetrate the indifferent majority.

Today, while difficult to assess, I think the proportion of citizens convinced that the sustainable narrative is our preferred path to the future is or has reached well beyond the < 5 percent "early innovators", and in some regions – for example in Europe – is approaching the 20 percent Pareto threshold (e.g. in Germany, the UK, and the Nordic countries).

This would suggest that our sustainability communication, in order to have the largest possible impact in the shortest amount of time, should focus on the receptive half of the indifferent majority. And who knows, it may be enough to add perhaps only another 5 percent or so of convinced citizens to cross the social tipping point of desired change (to reach the Pareto threshold). This feels at least quite doable.

For the early majority, the environmental storyline does not work. Urging them to "stop flying", "turn vegan", or "use only public transport" will not tip the scales. Certainly, it is not only about communicating benefits and solutions, it is also, as pointed out by Genevieve Guenther, about communicating *fear* of climate breakdown and *outrage* that powerful actors are blocking the passage of effective climate policy. And no doubt, it is a *fight* against powerful vested interests, as manifested by Michael Mann's tireless efforts of communicating the scientific facts of rapidly rising global climate risks. And, as so powerfully argued by Asmeret Asefaw Berhe, the voices of the marginalized and most threatened by the interconnected health, biosphere, and climate crises, need to be heard, loud and clear.

While all this is correct and important to incorporate in the wide narrative of sustainable development, it seems to me that we have a unique window of opportunity right now. Crossing a social tipping point feels like a real option, making the path towards a fair and safe sustainable future for all humans on Earth inevitable. The collection of writings in this book should be a battle cry to amplify the positive story of the benefits and opportunities that a transition to sustainability offers, and to target this communication at the receptive, while indifferent, majority. Potentially our best friends.

REFERENCES

Clark, G.L., Feiner, A. and Viehs, M. (2015). From the stockholder to the stakeholder: how sustainability can drive financial outperformance. *SSRN Electronic Journal*. Accessed 3 May 2020 at http://dx.doi.org/10.2139/ssrn.2508281.

Geels, F., Sovacool, B., Schwanen, T. and Sorrell, S. (2017). Sociotechnical transitions for deep decarbonization. *Science*, **357** (6357), 1242–4.

Global Challenges Foundation (2018). *Attitudes to Global Risk and Governance Survey 2018*. Stockholm: Global Challenges Foundation. Accessed 3 May 2020 at https://globalchallenges.org/wp-content/uploads/ComRes2018.pdf.

Gustafson, A., Bergquist, P., Leiserowitz, A. and Maibach, E. (2019). A growing majority of Americans think global warming is happening and are worried. *Yale Program on Climate Change Communication*, February 21.

Jordan, R. (2019). Global carbon emissions growth slows, but hits record high. *Stanford News*, December 3. Accessed 3 May 2020 at https://news.stanford.edu/2019/12/03/global-carbon-emission-increase/.

Luderer, G., Pehl, M. and Arvesen, A. et al. (2019). Environmental co-benefits and adverse side-effects of alternative power sector decarbonization strategies. *Nature Communications*, **10**, article 5229.

New Climate Economy (2018). *Unlocking the Inclusive Growth Story of the 21st Century: Accelerating Climate Action in Urgent Times*. Washington, DC: New Climate Economy c/o World Resources Institute.

Pareto, V. (2014). *Manual of Political Economy*. Oxford: Oxford University Press.

Pihl, E., Martin, M.A. and Blome, T. et al. (2019). *10 New Insights in Climate Science 2019*. Stockholm: Future Earth & The Earth League.

Robine, J.M., Cheung, S.L.K. and Le Roy, S. et al. (2008). Death toll exceeded 70,000 in Europe during the summer of 2003. *Comptes rendus biologies*, **331** (2), 171–8.

Rogers, E.M. (2003). *Diffusion of Innovations*. 5th ed. New York: Simon & Schuster.

Steffen, W., Rockström, J. and Richardson et al. (2018). Trajectories of the Earth System in the Anthropocene. In *Proceedings of the National Academy of Sciences of the United States of America*, **115** (33), 8252–9.

Stott, P., Stone, D. and Allen, M. (2004). Human contribution to the European heat-wave of 2003. *Nature*, **432**, 610–14.

United Nations Environment Programme (UNEP) (2019). *Emissions Gap Report 2019*. Nairobi: UNEP.

53. Communicating climate change science to diverse audiences

Asmeret Asefaw Berhe

BACKGROUND

As impacts of climate change continue to receive widespread global attention, the calls for better science communication around issues of climate change have been growing. Scientists and other practitioners are being urged to effectively communicate the science of climate change, the impacts that are likely to be felt by different segments of the human community, and the dangers of doing nothing to mitigate impacts of climate change in a manner that is accessible to a wide segment of society. In recent years, the calls have also been growing to ensure that we employ equity-oriented approaches, and value and include traditionally underserved and minoritized communities in our science communication efforts (Dawson, 2014; Streicher, Unterleitner and Schulze, 2014). Doing so requires that we employ a climate change science communication strategy that centers on equity and inclusion of people from all walks of life; and that we intentionally and explicitly address historic inequities with access to science and all other scholarly opportunities (Canfield et al., 2020).

An inclusive climate science communication strategy is one that values and explicitly acknowledges historical, socio-economic, and political factors that are the root causes of the climate crisis, and aims to ensure that the same factors don't guide the communication or policy decisions around climate change mitigation and adaptation efforts. It requires that we explicitly acknowledge the root causes of the current environmental crisis, including human-induced climate change; that is, to name a few causes, unsustainable extraction of global natural resources; excesses and wasteful cultures associated with capitalistic economies; patriarchal systems that have limited women's education and professional aspirations; colonial regimes and associated political institutions that have continued to exploit a segment of the human population for the benefit of a few, and so on. Beyond acknowledging the relevant root causes of the ongoing climate crisis, an effective climate science communication strategy also recognizes that we must be cognizant of the need to reach audiences where they are, including when we communicate technical information to audiences with no technical background; to help our audience establish personal, moral, and/or emotional connections with the topics we are communicating; and to aim for participatory communication models that recognize marginalized and minoritized communities likely have relevant knowledge that should be considered (ibid.). Here I draw upon my experience communicating the science of soils and, in particular, the role of soils in the maintenance of the Earth's climate and contemporary climate change. I highlight how diversity in the messenger and tailoring our messages to our audience helps in science communication.

COMMUNICATING THE ROLE OF SOILS IN CLIMATE CHANGE

My personal work on science communication has largely been focused on topics of soil science, land degradation, and climate change science. Specifically, I have worked to improve societal understanding of the role of soils in regulating the Earth's climate, and how soil is and should be an integral component of any climate change mitigation strategy. This has meant that I have to communicate some complex concepts in soil and climate sciences to audiences that have varied from elementary school children to scholars and entrepreneurs across the world. Some key lessons I have learned in my experience include the need to explain why I think everyone should care about continuing degradation of the soil resource globally and the benefits of improving soil health, rates and sources of global climate change, and the relationship between the two global and very pressing contemporary phenomena – human-caused climate change and soil degradation. Below, I highlight some of what I have learned in my efforts to effectively communicate scientific concepts and ideas with diverse audiences.

Communicating Climate Change Science

Climate change impacts are felt differently by different segments of society and individuals with diverse backgrounds, ranging from land managers, residents of small island nations or coastal communities, consumers of products that rely on fossil fuels, educators, policy-makers, and more. Members of the scientific community are currently being called into action to educate the population on the science of climate change and engage in intellectual and political exercises to get climate change onto the movement agendas of the highest levels of national, regional, and international political organizations. A combination of coordinated and grassroots communication strategies is striving to ensure that all stakeholders understand the impacts of climate change and implications of not acting in a timely manner. Climate change communication is usually highlighted as being a difficult problem that is complicated by: the distant nature of the problem (in space and time for most individuals and communities), complexity of the scientific concepts behind the issue, and the lack of relevant education by most of the audiences we are trying to reach; varying levels of uncertainty in the data or expected outcomes being communicated (Ballantyne, 2016); and because of the ongoing, concerted efforts to deny the causes and consequences of human-caused climate change. An effective climate change communication strategy then needs to not just educate diverse populations about the problem, but also seek their engagement to overcome the above-listed hurdles.

Communicating the Role of Soils

A major and common challenge around communicating the role of soils in climate change is the fact that most adults have never learned about the science of soils, let alone how it is related to maintenance of the Earth's climate and contemporary climate change. Almost all people understand that virtually all their food is grown in soil, but only a very small percentage of the population (in particular, in urban areas) can articulate any other ecological role of soil. Soil is then widely perceived as just a few feet of unconsolidated mixture of mineral and organic matter with limited roles or benefits in the Earth system that are restricted to the agricultural or food production sectors. And this lack of familiarity with soil science is further compounded by deep-seated ignorance and dismissal about the resource base that is routinely treated as being useless stuff, which we can afford to take for granted. I regularly ask students and other audiences that I engage with what is the first thing that comes to their mind when they think of soil. The overwhelming response that I get is that soil is dirt. People use the words 'soil' and 'dirt' interchangeably. For all essential purposes, soil is treated as dirt and hence as something that is not clean, is worthless, and a nuisance. Communicating the role of soils in climate change then requires reminding folks first how the ground they walk on supports life in the Earth system, how precious the soil resource is, and about how contemporary land use systems have already caused significant degradation of soil globally. Afterwards, we can have a discussion about embracing sustainable land stewardship practices and consumers' willingness to compensate land managers for the cost of sustainably managing land to ensure the food and nutritional security of the growing human population and effective climate change mitigation.

Most audiences I engage with, at times even scientific audiences outside earth and environmental sciences, are surprised to learn that soil stores twice as much carbon as all the plants on Earth plus the atmosphere combined and has the power to shape our planet's destiny. It is not common knowledge that the ongoing climate crisis is partly a result of large amounts of carbon released to the atmosphere from the terrestrial biosphere by human activity that includes deforestation and changes in land use across the globe (Amundson et al., 2015). Once I highlight how much carbon is stored in soil, I then proceed with communicating the role of soils in climate change by highlighting that small changes in the amount of carbon stored in soil, and fluxes of carbon to and from soil and the atmosphere can have a big impact in maintenance of the Earth's climate.

Similar to the discussions around climate change, at times science communication around soil carbon sequestration and generally the role of soils in climate change is complicated by varying levels of uncertainty associated with different estimates of the potential for soil to sequester atmospheric carbon dioxide; the fast-changing pace of science in this pressing area of research; and disagreements in the scientific literature, public and professional society meetings and even social media between those who advocate soil C sequestration as being a critical component of any effective climate change mitigation strategy and those that argue that the role of soils is limited, and hence we should stop highlighting the role of soils in climate change too much. This kind of debate is, of course, how science advances in our professional spaces of education and research. But, it takes a different note when we carry it into the public sphere where we give our audiences the impression that: there are still too many uncertainties and we don't know much about the processes of carbon sequestration in soil; that soil carbon sequestration is not likely to have a too significant contribution to climate change mitigation (Schlesinger and Amundson, 2019); it is not realistic to expect land managers to carry out large-scale regenerative agriculture (Amundson and Biardeau, 2018); or that the focus on soil carbon sequestration is only limited to climate change mitigation and that if we address fossil fuel emissions we might as well forget about other benefits of soil carbon sequestration (Schlesinger and Amundson, 2019). Of course, none of these points is 100 percent true. Yes, there are challenges to scaling up what we have learned from small-scale studies to a global scale, and we do recognize that determining rates of carbon sequestration that can be achieved with climate-smart land management practices can vary across the word (Paustian et al., 2016). We do understand a whole lot about the process of carbon sequestration and even its limits under a variety of soil, climate, and management conditions. We also recognize that the benefit of carbon sequestration is not limited to climate change mitigation (Chabbi et al., 2017; Rumpel, Lehmann and Chabbi, 2018). We have known for decades, if not longer, that carbon sequestration in soil is key to soil health, for water and nutrient storage and availability in soils, the ability of soils to withstand erosion, the ability to support plant productivity, and so on. Hence, even if the benefits to climate change mitigation are limited, any amount of additional atmospheric carbon dioxide that is removed from the atmosphere and sequestered in the soil system has multiple beneficial contributions to improving soil health.

In my science communication efforts on this topic then, I have chosen to highlight the overarching benefits of soil carbon sequestration to improve soil health and contribute to climate change mitigation. Without shying away from acknowledging the uncertainties, I have sought to shine a light on why investing in scientific and policy solutions that can simultaneously seek to address the global problems of soil degradation and climate change is a win–win strategy that would address two of the most challenging environmental issues of our times.

DIVERSITY IN SCIENCE COMMUNICATION

Messenger Matters

An important variable to consider in any scientific communication strategy is that personal connections with our audience are key. As in any science communication, but especially science communication that affects the health and welfare of communities, the identity of the messenger, prevailing socio-political issues, and history, matter – a lot. Histories of colonialism, slavery, racial and gender-based oppression, and other injustices perpetuated by certain segments of society on others globally mean that marginalized and minoritized communities will rightfully be weary of who is framing and communicating issues of concern to them. They will wonder if the messenger has their welfare at heart. Even if the messenger does have their welfare at heart, do they trust the messenger, do they have any reason to? Hence, it is important that we establish trust with the communities we wish to communicate with ahead of time and give them reasons to trust us. Scientific debates sometimes tend to be polarizing, and especially if any issues with science-denial or distrust of authority figures are involved, it could quickly segregate our target audiences based on whether or not they are familiar with the processes of scientific reasoning or if they value scientific evidence. While these issues are ongoing then, the last thing we need is for our audience to also be wondering if the messenger shares cultural and other personal values with them. Even when communicating empirical data then, community representation and establishing trust with our audiences makes it more likely that they would believe the message we are delivering to them (Kahan, 2010).

Reflecting on Issues Relevant to Specific Audiences

Effective science communication strategy that is meant to reach a diverse audience has to center equity and inclusion (Canfield et al., 2020). We must be able to focus on relevant history and ensure that we are telling inclusive stories that represent the communities we are trying to engage. An inclusive science communication strategy includes appropriate language, visual representations of the values of the messenger and inclusion, and explicit discussions about the rationale for action. For example, using examples of polar bears dying in the Arctic in our attempt to communicate climate change impacts to communities in Sub-Saharan Africa that are struggling with drought and other climate change effects on their food production system will obviously be off the mark. Similarly, attempts to communicate issues of how climate change is affecting the cost of fresh fruits and vegetables in the Central Valley of California to audiences living in urban deserts in the inner-cities of Detroit or Chicago is not likely to get the kind of desired attention from communities that are already struggling to get access to basic life-sustaining supplies. All the above-mentioned issues are important in their own right and are even inter-related. But, if we start with a framing that suggests that we care more about issues affecting people that are far removed from the specific community we are communicating with, or even worse non-human life forms, or if we fail to acknowledge that we care about the same things our audiences also care about, we are likely going to lose their interest. And they may tune out, thinking that climate change has nothing to do with them, and that they might not be affected, at least not anytime soon and it is a bigger issue to communities somewhere else that should care and do something about it now.

Furthermore, engaging a diverse audience in effective science communication requires that we are willing to practice participatory and inclusive approaches that consider the backgrounds, experiences, and traditional knowledge of our audiences. An inclusive science communication strategy stays away from using a deficit model that considers our audiences, especially those from underserved and minoritized communities, as lacking and less than others in their understanding of the science or ability to pursue science-informed policy goals (National Academies of Sciences, Engineering and Medicine, 2017). We must make it clear that we value and understand the traditional knowledge different communities have amassed over generations. If we demonstrate that we are open to learning from each other, it is then easier to earn trust that we aim to build a supportive community around a set of shared values around climate change and related fields. Moreover, if we establish trust with our audience, then it becomes easier to convince our audiences that, when traditional knowledge doesn't cover certain topics in a manner that science does, or if certain scientific concepts become too complicated they can trust the scientific approach (see Chapter 44 by Claude Henry in this book).

A science communication strategy that aims to engage a wide and diverse audience would also be served well if we acknowledge, advocate for, and practice any number of the proven benefits of diversity in all aspects of scholarly endeavors and science communication work. For example, we can highlight that we aim to ensure equity and inclusion in our communication because we acknowledge that involvement of diverse teams (across any number of diversity axes, including race, gender, religion, geographic origin, etc.) typically leads to excellence (Milem, 2003). Furthermore, we can explicitly recognize that the solutions that we desire to produce from the communication efforts and beyond have a far better chance of succeeding if they incorporate issues and ideas from all stakeholders; and that doing so opens opportunities for broader societal access to science education (National Academies of Sciences, Engineering and Medicine, 2017).

REFERENCES

Amundson, R., Berhe, A.A. and Hopmans, J.W. et al. 2015. Soil and human security in the 21st century. *Science*, **348** (6235), 1261071.
Amundson, R. and Biardeau, L. 2018. Opinion: soil carbon sequestration is an elusive climate mitigation tool. *Proceedings of the National Academy of Sciences*, **115** (46), 11652–6.
Ballantyne, A.G. 2016. Climate change communication: what can we learn from communication theory? *Wiley Interdisciplinary Reviews: Climate Change*, **7** (3), 329–44.
Canfield, K.N., Menezes, S. and Matsuda, S.B. et al. 2020. Science communication demands a critical approach that centers inclusion, equity, and intersectionality. *Frontiers in Communication*, **5** (2). https://doi.org/10.3389/fcomm.2020.00002.
Chabbi, A., Lehmann, J. and Ciais, P. et al. 2017. Aligning agriculture and climate policy. *Nature Climate Change*, **7** (5), 307–9.
Dawson, E. 2014. Reframing social exclusion from science communication: moving away from 'barriers' towards a more complex perspective. *Journal of Science Communication*, **13** (2), 1–5.
Kahan, D. 2010. Fixing the communications failure. *Nature*, **463** (7279), 296–7.
Le Quéré, C., Andrew, R.M. and Friedlingstein, P. et al. 2018. Global carbon budget 2018. *Earth System Science Data*, **10** (4), 2141–94.
Milem, J.F. 2003. The educational benefits of diversity: evidence from multiple sectors. In M.J. Chang, D. Witt, J. Jones and K. Hakuta (eds), *Compelling Interest: Examining the Evidence on Racial Dynamics in Higher Education*, Stanford, CA: Stanford University Press, pp. 126–69.
National Academies of Sciences, Engineering and Medicine. 2017. *Communicating Science Effectively: A Research Agenda*. Washington, DC: National Academies Press.
Paustian, K., Lehmann, J. and Ogle, S. et al. 2016. Climate-smart soils. *Nature*, **532** (7597), 49–57.

Rumpel, C., Lehmann, J. and Chabbi, A. 2018. '4 per 1,000' initiative will boost soil carbon for climate and food security. *Nature*, **553** (7686), 27.

Schlesinger, W.H. and Amundson, R. 2019. Managing for soil carbon sequestration: let's get realistic. *Global Change Biology*, **25** (2), 386–9.

Streicher, B., Unterleitner, K. and Schulze, H. 2014. Knowledge rooms – science communication in local, welcoming spaces to foster social inclusion. *Journal of Science Communication*, **13** (2), C03.

54. Global marine fisheries: avoiding further collapses

Philippe Cury and Daniel Pauly

SCIENTIFIC RESEARCH IS NOT ONLY ABOUT DISCOVERIES

Ernst Mayr, who had a long and a fruitful life working on evolution, wrote, from his farm in New Hampshire, a letter to the geneticist W. Provine:

> In your work…please always remember that a scientist's achievement may lie in many different areas: as an innovator (new discoveries, new theories, new concepts), as a synthesizer (bringing together scattered information, sharing relationships and interactions, particularly between different disciplines, like genetics and taxonomy), as a disseminator (presenting specialized information and theory in such a way that it becomes accessible to non-specialists) as a compiler or cataloguer, as an analyst (dissecting complex issues, clarifying matters by suggesting new terminologies, etc.), and in other ways. (Cited in Provine, 2005, p. 412, Figure 2)

A scientific career is not uniform, and along their respective scientific careers the authors have worked along the lines suggested by E. Mayr (Cury, 2018, Grémillet, 2019). However, they have also involved themselves in several aspects of scientists' work not included in the letter in question, including communicating with mass media, and with various fisheries stakeholders, including non-governmental organizations (NGOs), politicians and the public at large. These stakeholders are all important, but are usually neglected when dealing with fisheries, which are often viewed the sole concerns of the fishing industry and its lobbyists. This was particularly important for both of us, as innovators, synthesizers, disseminators and communicators to address the major global challenges and transformations that the oceans are facing at an unprecedented speed and strength. Thus, we will use this account on the parlous state of fisheries globally to present some of our work – not because this work was better than our colleagues' work, but because it illustrates what one (or two in this case) could contribute in the various roles outlined above.

The approaches we used fit into three groups. The first group of approaches refers to the creation of global databases, as required to tackle issues of sustainability in the global ocean. The second group was to develop approaches that would empower our colleagues, especially in developing countries, to participate in sustainability debates, by providing them with software, models and concepts that allowed them to work even in situations where there were "no data", as the mindless phrase goes. The third group of approaches consists of our involvement with civil society, as alluded to above. These three groups and the themes they imply are further developed below.

GLOBAL MARINE PATTERNS: THE ELEPHANT IN THE ROOM

Often, drastic ecosystem changes occurred a long time ago, but we have only anecdotes to work with (Pauly, 1995). Thus, the development of concepts for the integration of this knowledge of the past into current scientific models of fisheries has the effect of adding history to a discipline that has suffered from a lack of historical perspective, but which enriched debates about biodiversity. This requires us to identify global patterns that are shaping marine life and to move beyond ecological anecdotes, that is, to properly describe the elephant in the room, something enormous that people choose to ignore because dealing with it is uncomfortable.

Fishing is our last industrial activity exploiting a wild, renewable resource. The oceans, long perceived as an environment preserved from human action, do not seem to have escaped the general pattern of resource depletion. Here we explore a long depletion process that went unnoticed through the example of how we (still) operate when we exploit a wild, renewable resource.

Since the deployment of steam-driven trawlers around the British Isles in the 1880s, human have been able to extract from the sea far more than it could locally produce (Roberts, 2007). Thus, industrial fishing can hardly exploit a fishing ground for long; rather, new fishing grounds must be found as the previous ones are depleted (Pauly, 2019). This dynamic is well documented for the period following World War II, which saw a rapid rebuilding of the fleets in major fishing countries, particularly in Western Europe, then the Soviet Union, in East Asia (Japan, South Korea, Taiwan and later China) and a rapid expansion offshore and toward the southern hemisphere.

This expansion led to a major increase in global catch, convincing policy-makers that more boats automatically lead to more catch. In 1975, catches in the North Atlantic, where industrial fishing began to decline, but this was masked, at global levels, by the large catches of distant-water fisheries in the Global South, often in the waters of former European colonies (e.g., West Africa and South East Asia).

The net result of this continuing geographic expansion, which went along with fishing into deeper waters and targeted previously spurned fish, led, in spite of numerous local collapses (e.g., Northern cod off Eastern Canada), to the net increase of global catches until 1996, the year of global peak catches (Figure 54.1). Since 1996, the global catch extracted from the world's oceans is declining, despite a tremendous increase in fishing effort, notably in East Asia, driven by politicians who still believe in the magic that more boats is synonymous with more catch.

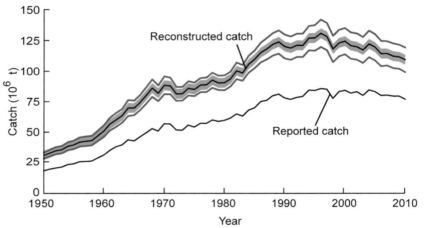

Note: Note the difference between the reported catch, assembled by the Food and Agriculture Organization of the United Nations (FAO) from the submission of their member countries, and the reconstructed catch, which includes all industrial, artisanal, subsistence recreational fisheries known to exist, in the waters of all countries and their overseas territories and in the high seas (see www.seaaroundus.org).
Source: Adapted from Pauly and Zeller (2016).

Figure 54.1   *Trajectories of reported and reconstructed marine fisheries catches, 1950–2010*

The issue that declining fisheries catches poses could be largely resolved by the introduction of stock-rebuilding programs, such as legislated and implemented in the US, in the Exclusive Economic Zones (EEZs) of maritime countries, and by drastically reducing or abolishing subsidies to fisheries that largely fund their expansion. This would help in repairing the considerable damage so far inflicted on the marine ecosystem within which fisheries are embedded. Notably, the populations of large predatory fishes (shark, tuna, cod) that regulate the functioning of marine ecosystems need to be rebuilt. The point here is that we should be able to *reverse* present trends, characterized by fish catches consisting of smaller and smaller fish, a process known as "fishing down marine food webs" (Pauly et al., 1998; Figure 54.2), rather than aim for an ill-defined "sustainability".

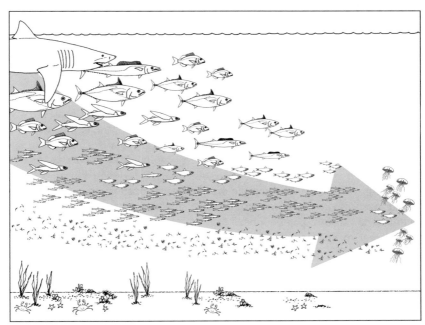

Note: When a previously pristine ecosystem becomes accessible to exploitation, it is usually the largest, longest-living fish at the top of the food chain (top left) that are affected most, because their longevity makes them more vulnerable to overfishing, whether they are sought by fishers or bycatch. In either case, the fishery then turns to medium-sized fish, often the prey of larger fish, which then benefit from an increase in abundance due to less predation. When the populations of medium-sized fish are finally depleted, the focus is then on small fish and invertebrates (shrimp, squid, etc.). Changes in the structure of the marine food web that these sequential decreases (arrow) produce, combined with the destruction of sedentary fauna by bottom trawling, lead to conditions favorable to blooms (i.e., population explosions) of harmful algae and jellyfish (see also www.fishingdown.org).
Source: Concept: Daniel Pauly; artist: Ms. Rachel "Aque" Atanacio.

Figure 54.2 *Schematic representation of fishing down*

By exploiting new fishing grounds, targeting new fish species in deeper waters (Morato et al., 2006), fisheries were able to hide the ever-stronger decline of their resource base. The ocean illustrates, in fact, how our interactions with nature's bounty resemble a "Ponzi scheme", so named after the swindler who invented this special technique in the 1920s. His method, which promised huge, steady profits from investments, was actually unsustainable, being based on using newly acquired money to stimulate profits for the initial investors. One of the most blatant Ponzi schemes in the history of finances was that developed by the Bernie Madoff, who caused the largest losses experienced by any group of investors.

Yet, the most incredible speculative operation of all time is occurring for everyone to see – the unsustainable exploitation of our natural resources. Rather than extracting, in a sustainable manner, the interest from a capital invested in profitable ventures, we live off this capital, seemingly freed from all constraints. Like Madoff, who reached a point where he could no longer find more credulous people to fleece, the fisheries reached their peak in 1996, when fishing fleets could no longer find new fishing grounds into which to expand. Thus, catches have been decreasing since by over a million tonnes per year, demonstrating the erosion of natural capital. It is time to recapitalize marine life.

In addition to re-establishing the profitability of unsubsidized fisheries, the world must also re-establish some of the fish abundance that enables marine mammal and seabird populations to thrive. Thus, in the case of seabirds, it was shown that overexploitation of forage fish (e.g., sardine, anchovy, herring, sprat) is one of the key drivers of seabird population declines, range shifts, and extinction. The global and substantial overlap and competition between small pelagic fisheries and seabirds represents 48 percent of all marine areas, notably in the Southern Ocean, Asian shelves, Mediterranean Sea, Norwegian Sea and Californian coast (Grémillet et al., 2018). A threshold in prey (fish and krill, termed "forage fish") abundance, equivalent to one-third of the maximum prey biomass, was found below that which causes consistently reduced and more variable seabird breeding success (Cury et al., 2011). This empirically derived guiding principle embraces the ecosystem approach to management aimed at sustaining the integrity of predator–prey interactions and marine food webs. Following this simple threshold in fish population management is straightforward to implement and thus contributes to ensuring the survival of seabirds.

EMPOWERING TOOLS AND CONCEPTS

The rebuilding of fish populations can be guided by "historical marine ecology", an approach for the interpretation of historical data that followed up on the realization that "shifted baselines" are often used to assess change (Pauly, 1995). This occurs when, for example, a generation of, say, fisheries scientists, strive to evaluate the changes that have occurred in an ecosystem using only the changes that they themselves witnessed, while not considering the changes that their predecessors witnessed. This now well-established phenomenon leads to changes being underestimated. Only by anchoring earlier states into historical data – as done in the new discipline of historical marine ecology – can this insidious underestimation of losses, and our resulting accommodation of it, be prevented (Figure 54.3).

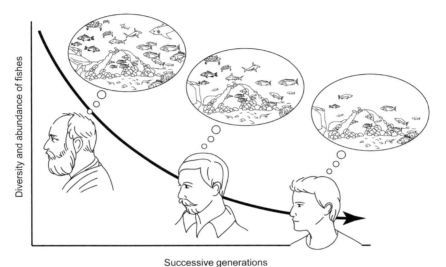

Note: The concept of "shifting baselines" reflects the gradual loss of our benchmarks in the perception of the actual productivity of the marine world due to the progressive impoverishment of the ecosystem itself. A middle-aged fisher and even more so younger fishers, lack what older fishers – for example, in the Gulf of California (Mexico) – had, thanks to their traditional knowledge: a vision of the great wealth of fish species and their ecology.
Source: Based on an original paper by Sáenz-Arroyo et al. (2005).

Figure 54.3 The concept of "shifting baselines"

The geographic expansion alluded to above and the fact that countries or regions such as the US, Japan or the EU consume four to five times more fish than is caught in their 200-mile EEZs are reflections of a huge geopolitical imbalance, with the countries of the Global South losing out. Because this losing out also manifests itself in access to knowledge about the ecology of the fish populations exploited by both local fisheries and the distant water fleets of wealthier countries, a set of tools has been made available to researchers in developing and developed countries that now help assess fisheries also in the data-sparse regions of the world.

One of these tools is FishBase (www.fishbase.org), a freely accessible online encyclopaedia of all fishes in the world, and which contains, for most commercially exploited fish species, the essential parameters (on growth, reproduction, etc.) required for managing their populations. Another similar database, SeaLifeBase (www.sealifebase.org) does the same for invertebrates such as lobster, shrimp, clams and the like. FishBase is now known throughout the world and it has saved the fisheries departments of many countries years of work devoted to estimating parameter values that were already available, if in obscure publications.

Another tool is Ecopath, an ecosystem modelling software initially developed by NOAA in Hawaii, and which was subsequently modified for general use and disseminated throughout the world (Christensen and Pauly, 1992). Now called Ecopath with Ecosim (or EwE), this has become the only ecosystem modelling software with as many implementations in developing as in developed countries (http://sirs.agrocampus-ouest.fr/EcoBase/).

Finally, there is the huge database of the Sea Around Us (www.seaaroundus .org), covering fish catches from 1950 to the near present, and which provides detailed catch data and related indicators for all maritime countries of the world. These data complement the statistics sent annually to the FAO in Rome by its member countries, which are harmonized and disseminated by FAO as "official data".

The Sea Around Us adds (1) discarded bycatch (not included in FAO statistics); (2) small-scale fisheries, not well covered by countries' official catch statistics; and (3) estimates of illegal catches to these official catches, besides allocating them to the EEZs of maritime countries and other geographies. Due to their completeness and versatility, the Sea Around Us data are increasingly used by members of civil society, notably the staff of environmental NGOs, to evaluate policies with particular emphasis on the competition between (often distant water) industrial fleets vs artisanal and subsistence fisheries that, in many developing countries, ensure local (sea-)food security.

These tools, by providing data even for countries deemed data-poor, allow their fisheries development to be projected via scenario, our next topic.

SCENARIO BUILDING: ENVISAGING OUR COMMON FUTURE

Climate change is altering the abundance and distribution of marine species, with consequences for ocean ecosystem structure and functioning, seafood supply and conservation. Quantifying future trends based on integrated models of marine socio-ecological systems is critical to inform ongoing global assessments on climate change and biodiversity, including the Intergovernmental Panel for Climate Change (IPCC) and Intergovernmental Science-Policy

Platform on Biodiversity and Ecosystem Services (IPBES), and guide viable pathways toward achieving key policy objectives, such as the United Nations Sustainable Development Goals (SDGs) of Agenda 2030.

We both started to develop ecosystem models more than 20 years ago; at the time, it seemed unreasonable to spend time constructing such models and many colleagues thought that we were wasting our time. Still, we invested in the development, parameterization and calibration of integrated socio-ecosystem models (Pauly et al., 2003; Pauly, Christensen and Walters, 2000; Shin and Cury, 2001, 2004). Once constructed, these models helped us devise new paths towards sustainability; they also helped us not only to formulate ways to mitigate present actual and future trends, but also to identify alternative pathways.

Models are, as well, important tools to communicate as they formalize in an integrated manner the natural constraints of our actions and impacts. For the first time in our human life, scientific research has demonstrated this ability to forecast within several decades the environmental future of our oceans. Models consequently represent incredible tools for policy actions by defining limits and consequences of our actions. In a manner similar to that of Hollywood screenwriters, scientists can produce today scenarios of projected futures, this time based on past environmental knowledge and a range of predictive models. Therein, each scenario represents an outline of societal choices and synthesizes our desires and beliefs in a particular operating mode. Policy-makers thus have a tool that can thus help them to make science-based decisions in a complex and changing world.

PUBLIC AWARENESS

When policy-makers are convinced that actions are needed, they must have the public agreeing to their decision; this is why it is crucial to involve and inform the public about the present state of the environment. Another positive development is that more marine scientists (except perhaps fisheries scientists in the employ of governments) are now willing to engage with the public and share their dismay at the demolition of marine ecosystems for short-term gain. Jointly with the increasing influence of environmental NGOs with a marine focus and the growth of a cadre of knowledgeable journalists, this has led to the emergence of a public unwilling to entrust publicly owned marine resources to the exclusive use of the owners of fishing fleets.

Scientists should realize that writing articles in peer-reviewed journals is a must for their career but that policy-makers and the rest of the world will read about scientific findings only after they are translated into popularized books or other accessible media. Most often, writing books for a large audience is not considered by academics, as scientific evaluation does not take them into consideration. However, books can change our way of thinking and even our life! Communicating results to a large audience is not simply an added value of a scientific career but a responsibility for scientists when considering urgency in a global emerging challenge.

Philippe Cury was approached in 2007 by Ronald Blunden, the French editor working for Calmann-Lévy, who told him that during his last scuba dive in the Mediterranean Sea, he saw very few fishes. He was disappointed and wanted to do something for the ocean. With a scientific journalist, Yves Miserey, *Une mer sans poissons* [A Sea Without Fish], was published within a few months in 2008, as editors are always in a rush. This book is based on scientific evidence and raised important issues related to the history of exploitation of marine resources, a first in France, which tends to systematically ignore overexploitation. The book was successful and translated into Chinese, Japanese, in even Catalan. The impact was great. Invitations by four successive French ministers, Prince Albert II of Monaco and Mr. Yohei Sasakawa, chairman of the Nippon foundation, followed, and by many institutions and policy-makers to discuss fisheries issues. Later, in 2013, we jointly wrote a book whose French title was, translated, *Eat Your Jellyfish! Reconciling the Cycles of Life and the Arrow of Time* (Cury and Pauly, 2013; Figure 54.4). This title was misleading; only the subtitle was informative, and we ended up being invited by a radio show to demonstrate how to cook jellyfish!

Daniel Pauly, besides scientific articles, likes writing essays on various oceans-related topics; one first collection of such essays (Pauly, 1994) also didn't make it to the intended public, because its initial publisher, which had promised to sell it for about $20 was bought by a more greedy publisher, who sold it (or not) for nearly $200. Still, he produced another collection of essays, some autographical (Pauly, 2019).

Writing such books teaches you a lot – for example, how to present scientific results to the public without distorting their meaning, and still not losing the readers. Writing books also enlarges one's audience (Cury and Pauly, 2013). Books are powerful, as they can change the world with their content. Social media have different targets and dynamics. Although YouTube and TED talks can expand one's audience, we are not fully convinced that they will survive the test of time and influence people in the long run as some books do. We believe in the magic of books. Scientists too often ignore that they have good stories, potentially of interest to laypersons – if told well. However, too few scientists are involved in communicating to the public; young scientists should communicate ecology, which is both intrinsically interesting and a matter of great urgency, given the currently and worsening biodiversity crisis.

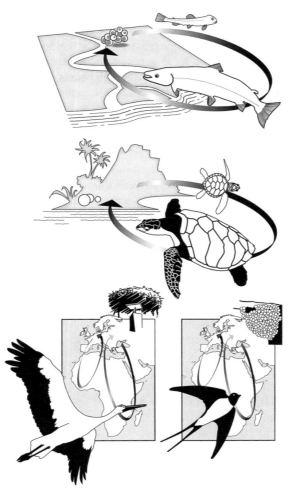

Note: For each species of large animals studied, biologists have found a tendency for the adults to undertake large-scale breeding migrations to return where they were born, completing their life cycle. This "obstinacy" makes sense: the site in question is undoubtedly favorable to the reproduction of certain members of their species (= their parents) and, consequently, they do not need to run the risk of finding an alternative site to reproduce themselves. In Cury and Pauly (2013), this behavior is contrasted with the unidirectional arrow-like changes that we impose on nature, as illustrated by Figure 54.2.
Source: © Odile Jacob, 2013.

Figure 54.4   *Obstinate nature is a universal pattern in nature as animals always return to their parents' breeding environment to reproduce*

CONCLUSION: DO IT NOW!

Scientific research is key to understanding our complex, connected and rapidly changing world. Most local issues can be related to global ones. Thus, scientists must make efforts to identify their elephants in the room, that is, to develop a sustainability science that can tackle global environmental objectives. Expertise to address key challenges such as climate change or loss of biodiversity is strongly needed in the marine environment. Such expertise should connect to policy-makers and the public at large to empower citizens. UN initiatives such as the IPCC and IPBES have been able to merge a huge multidisciplinary expertise around the issues of global warming and biodiversity losses, respectively, and synthesize knowledge and information into a comprehensive framework for policy-makers. This was made possible by addressing scientific questions relevant to society and developing large databases and ecosystem models to capture the dynamics of the different components – for example, marine ecosystems.

Overfishing appears to be easier to fix than mitigating the effect of climate change. What we lack, however, is a clear vision of the fisheries we want for the future (see, e.g., Pauly et al., 2003; Cury and Pauly, 2013, Zeller and Pauly, 2019). Such vision is required to define ecological but also socially acceptable solutions. For example, in our opinion, a transition is required towards small-scale sustainable fisheries that are selective, protect biodiversity, are energy efficient and create jobs (Pauly, 2018). It is time to make fisheries really sustainable and to stop trusting that Ponzi will find a way.

What we both learnt from those many years of research is "Do it now!" Chance is that if you do not do what you think could change things around, nobody else will do it.

REFERENCES

Christensen, V. and Pauly, D. (1992). ECOPATH II: a software for balancing steady-state ecosystem models and calculating network characteristics. *Ecological Modelling*, **61**, 169–85.

Cury, P. (2018). Obstinate nature. *ICES Journal of Marine Science*, **76** (2), 384–91.

Cury, P., I.L. Boyd and S. Bonhommeau et al. (2011). Global seabird responses to forage fish depletion – one-third for the birds. *Science*, **334**, 1703–6.

Cury, P. and Y. Miserey (2008). *Une mer sans poissons* [A Sea Without Fish]. Paris: Calmann-Lévy.

Cury, P. and D. Pauly (2013). *Mange tes méduses! Réconcilier les cycles de la vie et la flèche du temps* [Eat Your Jellyfish! Reconciling the Cycles of Life and the Arrow of Time]. Paris: Odile Jacob.

Grémillet, D. (2019). *Daniel Pauly, un océan de combats* [Daniel Pauly, An Ocean of Struggles]. Marseille: Éditions Wildproject.

Grémillet, D., A. Ponchon and M. Paleczny et al. (2018). Persisting worldwide seabird–fishery competition despite seabird community decline. *Current Biology*, **28**(24), 4009–13.

Morato, T., R. Watson, T.J. Pitcher and D. Pauly (2006). Fishing down the deep. *Fish and Fisheries*, **7** (1), 24–34.

Pauly, D. (1994). *On the Sex of Fish and the Gender of Scientists: Essays in Fisheries Science*. London, Chapman & Hall.

Pauly, D. (1995). Anecdotes and the shifting baseline syndrome of fisheries. *Trends in Ecology & Evolution*, **10** (10), 430.

Pauly, D. (2018). A vision for marine fisheries in a global blue economy. *Marine Policy*, **87**, 371–4.

Pauly, D. (2019). *Vanishing Fish: Shifting Baseline and the Future of Global Fisheries*. Vancouver: Greystone Books.

Pauly, D., J. Alder and E. Bennett (2003). The future for fisheries. *Science*, **302**, 1359–61.

Pauly, D., V. Christensen and J. Dalsgaard et al. (1998). Fishing down marine food webs. *Science*, **279**, 860–63.

Pauly, D., V. Christensen and C.J. Walters (2000). Ecopath, Ecosim and Ecospace as tools for evaluating ecosystem impact of fisheries. *ICES Journal of Marine Science*, **57**, 697–706.

Pauly, D. and D. Zeller (2016). Toward a comprehensive estimate of global marine fisheries catches. In D. Pauly and D. Zeller (eds), *Global Atlas of Marine Fisheries: A Critical Appraisal of Catches and Ecosystem Impacts*. Washington, DC: Island Press, pp. 171–81.

Provine, W.B. (2005). Ernst Mayr, a retrospective. *Trends in Ecology & Evolution*, **20**, 411–13.

Roberts, C. (2007). *The Unnatural History of the Sea*. Washington, DC: Island Press.

Sáenz-Arroyo, A., C. Roberts and J. Torre et al. (2005). Rapidly shifting environmental baselines among fishers of the Gulf of California. *Proceedings of the Royal Society B: Biological Sciences*, **272** (1575), 1957–62.

Shin, Y.-J. and P. Cury (2001). Exploring fish community dynamics through size-dependent trophic interactions using a spatialized individual-based model. *Aquatic Living Resources*, **14**, 65–80.

Shin, Y.-J. and P. Cury (2004). Using an individual-based model of fish assemblages to study the response of size spectra to changes in fishing. *Canadian Journal of Fisheries and Aquatic Science*, **61**, 414–31.

Zeller, D. and D. Pauly (2019). Viewpoint: back to the future for fisheries, where will we choose to go? *Global Sustainability*, **2** (e11), 1–8.

55. Why are we so much more afraid of COVID-19 than of climate change? Early lessons from a health crisis for the communication of climate change

François Gemenne and Anneliese Depoux

As most countries of the world were affected by the COVID-19 in the first months of 2020, many of them took radical measures to contain the spread of the pandemic. Thousands of flights were cancelled, schools and shops were closed, industrial production was slashed, people were confined at home. The whole economy came to a standstill.

Many of these measures resulted in very significant cuts in greenhouse gas emissions and atmospheric pollution. Estimates by Carbon Brief reckon that greenhouse gas emissions in China were down 25 percent in February 2020, while fine particle levels were down 20–30 percent across the country (Myllyvirta, 2020). Global air traffic was reduced by 4.3 percent that same month – and this was before the ban on flights from Europe to the US imposed by US president Donald Trump in early March.

Paradoxically perhaps, some of these measures had a positive impact for human health. Marshall Burke, from the Earth System Science Department at Stanford University, calculated that 'reductions in air pollution in China caused by this economic disruption likely saved twenty times more lives in China than have currently been lost due to infection with the virus in that country' (Burke, 2020).

Though the global impact of the pandemic on climate change will be difficult to assess, given the far-reaching economic, political and social implications of some of the containment measures, one thing is certain: it is possible for world leaders to take urgent and radical measures in the face of an imminent threat, and for the populations to accept them. Yet we haven't been able, so far, to take similar measures to confront climate change. Until the pandemic outbreak, and despite many calls from activists and scientists alike to declare a state of 'climate emergency', emissions were still rising at a yearly increase of 1 per cent.

While we were ready to treat COVID-19 as a major emergency, obviously we were not ready, or not willing, to do the same for climate change. COVID-19 was – and rightly so – treated as a major emergency, with immediate application of radical measures, following scientific advice, to contain it. The threat of climate change has not induced such radical measures so far. To put it simply: we are much more afraid of the COVID-19 than we are of climate change. And this raises a series of questions regarding the way we communicate about climate change.

In no way are we saying here that we shouldn't be afraid of COVID-19, or that it is a minor threat. On the contrary, the radical responses implemented by many governments are impressive – albeit sometimes too tardy – and we believe this holds lessons for our communication on climate change. In the midst of the health crisis, many were prompt to point out the similarities between climate change and the pandemic. Both were global crises, requiring urgent responses on the basis of scientific advice. Therefore, many activists were quick to suggest that the measures implemented to fight against the spread of the pandemic had to be replicated to slow down climate change: 'we must respond to climate change like we're responding to coronavirus', argued Zero Hour founder Jamie Margolin in *Teen Vogue* magazine.[1] Others went a step further and claimed the pandemic was an 'ultimatum of nature', a 'revenge of the Earth' or even 'good news for the environment'. #WeAreTheProblem was a popular hashtag on social media as many countries were in lockdown, as if the pandemic was eventually a way for nature to reclaim its rights.

In this chapter, we argue that climate change and the COVID-19 pandemic are not similar crises, even though they present some striking similarities. This has important consequences for the response measures to be deployed, but also for the way we communicate about climate change. Here we try to outline some early lessons from the health crisis to improve our communication on climate change.

First, if we are we so much more afraid of COVID-19 than we are of climate change, this is probably because we're afraid of getting sick ourselves. A central element of the response lies in the proximity and immediateness of the threat. We are all afraid (or should be afraid) of contracting the virus personally, while climate change still seems perceived as a concern for others – for the next generation, or far-away countries. We are well aware that COVID-19 is a threat for ourselves, while climate change remains perceived as a threat that will mostly affect others. We are afraid of getting contaminated with the virus, while we don't see climate change as contagious. Psychological research has shown that contagion – or the threat of contagion – is a powerful driver of new social norms, which we adopt to protect ourselves (Sperber, 1996).

And perhaps we should acknowledge that we, researchers, bear some responsibility for this. Climate models are calibrated on the long run, and policy objectives target 2050 or 2100. Rather than putting forward a short-term objective, the Paris Agreement insists on a long-term objective, a maximum temperature by 2100, a date that far exceeds the lifetime of most of those who are reading the present chapter – and certainly of all those who signed the Paris Agreement itself. Similarly, while industrialized countries are badly hit by the pandemic, research has consistently stressed that countries most vulnerable to climate change impacts are developing countries, or that the poorest, most marginalized populations would be disproportionately affected by climate impacts. While these facts are indisputable, they also create a social distance between climate change and those who should act to contain it.

This suggests that we should insist more on the immediate consequences of climate change, and less on the long-term objectives. In an op-ed published in *The Guardian* in late January 2020, George Monbiot suggested dropping these long-term objectives – which he found to be counterproductive – to adopt instead a maximalist approach (Monbiot, 2020). This maximalist approach is the one adopted by most governments in the face of the COVID-19 crisis: they don't seek to reduce the infection rate by a certain percentage, but rather to 'flatten the curve' as much as possible. And this is how the radical measures of containment are justified – without these, there's a fear that the crisis would become unmanageable for hospitals and health services.

Second, the impacts of climate change on public health have not been sufficiently emphasized in public debates. Yet, there is ample scientific evidence that climate change bears some significant health impacts. Every year, the annual report of *The Lancet* Countdown initiative reviews these impacts, which range from cardiovascular troubles to allergies and infectious diseases such as dengue or malaria (Watts et al., 2019). The World Health Organization reckons that climate change could claim 250 000 additional lives per year between 2030 and 2050.[2] Research has consistently shown that the arguments about the public health impacts of climate change are amongst the most persuasive, and most likely to induce behavioural changes (Maibach et al., 2018). Yet, these arguments are not often put forward in public debates on climate change (Depoux et al., 2017), even though the COVID-19 crisis shows once again the persuasiveness of such points.

Third, it is important to acknowledge that the reason confinement measures are widely accepted – though not always perfectly applied – is also because they are temporary. If radical confinement measures, such as curfew or limitation of air travel, were permanent, then it is likely they would be less accepted by the population. In that sense, we should be very careful about treating climate change as a 'crisis': a crisis is temporary and suggests a return to normality at the end of the day. Global warming is an irreversible transformation of the Earth's climate. There will be no return to 'normal': temperature will not decrease, sea-level will not go down – at least not for a really long time – and there will be no vaccine against climate change. Thus, the measures that need to be taken to address climate change cannot be temporary: they need to become permanent features of our economy, politics and way of life. Therefore, one should not make the mistake of assuming that radical measures taken against COVID-19 could easily be replicated against climate change: the former are only accepted because they are of a temporary nature.

Furthermore, the idea that we should consider the pandemic as a 'general rehearsal' before climate change can be deeply counterproductive: if people are under the impression that the fight against climate change requires the economy to be on standstill, they are likely to reject any measure taken against climate change in the future. Surely one will not look back fondly on the confinement period as the golden age of the fight against climate change.

Finally, individual knowledge is often assumed to be a key factor in the mobilization against climate change – education, for example, is often presented as a crucial weapon in the fight (Anderson, 2012), as if action would only be taken once everyone were knowledgeable about climate change and its impacts. Yet, measures against the coronavirus pandemic have been imposed on a top-down basis, not on a bottom-up basis: people didn't decide to confine themselves spontaneously. People had little medical knowledge about the virus, and yet accepted the measures in the face of an imminent danger. This holds an important lesson for climate change: if we count on every individual to do one's part, then radical action might just never materialize. Top-down measures will be needed: despite the many actions and measures taken spontaneously by civil society, legal frameworks will need to be implemented by governments.

Climate change and the COVID-19 pandemic share many characteristics: both are of global nature, requiring radical responses on the basis of scientific assessments. In both cases, these responses are required first and foremost to protect the most vulnerable. In that regard, the confinement measures taken against COVID-19 represent a remarkable display of solidarity: whole countries were in complete lockdown to protect the elderly and those with fragile health. But this solidarity was often confined to national borders: there was no global response to the crisis, but rather a myriad of different national responses, sometimes very different from one another. Climate change will require solidarity beyond borders, not just within borders – whereas the effects of closing borders to slow down the spread of the virus can be disputed, there's no question that climate change can't be stopped at the border.

There are important lessons to take away from the COVID-19 crisis for the communication of climate change. Let's not assume, however, that the measures deployed against the pandemic can be replicated as such to fight climate change. Despite their similarities, climate change will require different solutions. But the coronavirus crisis tells us it is possible to take urgent, costly and radical measures, and gives some hints as to how these can be accepted by the population.

NOTES

1. Jamie Margolin, 'Coronavirus shows us rapid global response to climate change is possible', *Teenvogue.com*, 18 March 2020, accessed 3 September 2020 at https://www.teenvogue.com/story/coronavirus-response-climate-crisis.
2. World Health Organization (2018), 'Climate change and health', accessed 3 September 2020 at https://www.who.int/news-room/fact-sheets/detail/climate-change-and-health.

REFERENCES

Anderson, A. (2012), 'Climate change education for mitigation and adaptation', *Journal of Education for Sustainable Development*, **6** (2), 191–206.

Burke, M. (2020), 'COVID-19 reduces economic activity, which reduces pollution, which saves lives', *G-FEED.com*, accessed 15 March 2020 at http://www.g-feed.com/2020/03/covid-19-reduces-economic-activity.html.

Depoux, A., Hémono, M. and Puig-Malet, S. et al. (2017), 'Communicating climate change and health in the media', *Public Health Reviews*, **38**, article 7.

Maibach, E.W., Kreslake, J.M. and Roser-Renouf, C. et al. (2015), 'Do Americans understand that global warming is harmful to human health? Evidence from a national survey', *Annals of Global Health*, **81** (3), 396–409.

Monbiot, G. (2020), 'Let's abandon climate targets, and do something completely different', *The Guardian*, 29 January.

Myllyvirta, L. (2020), 'Analysis: coronavirus has temporarily reduced China's CO_2 emissions by a quarter', *CarbonBrief.org*, 19 February, accessed 15 March 2020 at https://www.carbonbrief.org/analysis-coronavirus-has-temporarily-reduced-chinas-co2-emissions-by-a-quarter.

Sperber, D. (1996), *La Contagion des Idées*, Paris: Odile Jacob.

Watts, N., Amann, M. and Arnell, N. et al. (2019), 'The 2019 report of *The Lancet* Countdown on health and climate change: ensuring that the health of a child born today is not defined by a changing climate. *The Lancet*, **394** (10211), 1836–78.

56. Communicating the climate emergency: imagination, emotion, action

Genevieve Guenther

Communication plays an outsize role in climate-change politics. Scientists and advocates rely on language to make climate breakdown visible, whether by projecting future catastrophes in data or by attributing our increasingly dire experience of global warming to the costs of human activities like burning fossil fuels. Yet, insofar as climate communicators want not just to educate but also to persuade voters to join the climate movement, they must do more than simply convey scientific information. As rhetoricians have known for quite literally thousands of years, communicators must appeal to the imagination, using vivid images that conjure visceral emotions, to move people to act. In the case of the climate crisis, communicators should help voters feel a complex of three specific emotions: *fear* of climate breakdown, *outrage* that powerful actors are blocking the passage of effective climate policy, and *desire* for a transformed global economy. Fear motivates us to protect ourselves and the people we love; outrage empowers us to experience the climate crisis as a political problem with clear antagonists; and desire enables us to accept the costs of decarbonization as greatly outweighed by the benefits of preserving the living world.

To begin with fear. All climate communicators need to do to frighten their audiences is tell the truth. But that truth should be centered on the ways that climate change will destroy our lives and the lives of our children, not on the destruction of "nature."[1] Because "nature" is fashioned by fossil-fuel ideology as "external" to human life, the idea of its collapse in itself lacks the power to motivate large-scale political action. People need to picture their own lives or the lives of their loved ones being ruined by climate destruction before our planetary emergency will become personal for them.

Take the point, for example, that 2°C of warming will cause terrible things to happen all over the world: between 32 and 80 million people flooded out of their homes due to sea-level rise; over 400 million people without enough water to drink; over a billion people without the coral reefs on which they relied for food and sustenance.[2] While voters need to know these facts (and facts like them) they need also to imagine their implications for their own daily lives. Climate communicators can describe what it will be like to have your home inundated with water at every high tide, over and over, compelling you move whether you can afford it or not. Or to be forced to stand in sweltering, endless lines to fill remarkably heavy water bottles at a public water truck because your taps have run dry. Or to have hunger gnawing at your ribs as you try to sleep because the fish that made the bulk of your diet spawned in coral reefs that have since disappeared. These smaller, more local narratives, conveyed with striking imagery, make the climate emergency tangible. The rhetorical power of climate communication arises from stories like these, which make people's suffering visible, especially when they're contextualized in the vast scale of the overarching crisis.

Scientists have not generally talked about climate change in this way. Science communication is not narrative and vice versa. But climate scientists have become increasingly willing to allow writers, activists, and politicians to use emotive and literary language to describe the human costs of fossil fuels.[3] Scientists should continue to support artful representations of climate horrors, and on their part embrace a risk-communication framework that includes the fat-tail effects of different degrees of warming, precisely because the damage from those effects would be so devastating even if the likelihood of their occurrence is less than 95 percent. For many years, the social science research was taken to show that scaring people about climate change was counterproductive, but in fact the original research argues that fear can be motivating when balanced by a sense of agency.

The mistaken consensus about fear in climate communication was grounded in an incomplete reading of Saffron O'Neill and Sophie Nicholson-Cole's "'Fear won't do it': promoting positive engagement with climate change through visual and iconic representations" (2009). The study on which this paper was based did establish that showing decontextualized images of the natural world ravaged by climate change to "young mothers from a deprived area, young professionals between the ages of 26 and 35, and high school students" (p. 365) ultimately distanced people in those particular groups from the human causes of climate breakdown, decreasing the issue saliency of climate change for them overall. From this and another image-based survey conducted with participants already engaged in climate advocacy, O'Neill and Nicholson-Cole surmised that "fear may be an inappropriate tool for climate change communication" (p. 376). Yet, the paper itself offers a more nuanced conclusion than this surmise alone provides, for it clarifies that it is only "*on a stand-alone basis*" that fear has "a 'negative' impact on active engagement with climate change" (ibid.; my emphasis), and it ultimately recommends that "dramatic representations [meant to frighten listeners] must be partnered with those that enable a person to establish a sense of connection with the causes and consequences of climate change...so that they can see the relevance of climate change for their locality and life and see that there are ways in which they (and others) can positively respond" (ibid.).

To show voters how they can "positively respond" to the threat of the climate crisis, climate communicators should refrain from concluding their messages with the reassurance that technical solutions to the climate crisis exist. This reassurance fails to tell audiences what they can do personally to build the political coalition that will force governments to pass adequate climate policies. Worse, it inaccurately suggests that technological progress will make everything turn out all right.[4] Communicators should instead conclude their narratives by offering suggestions for political actions that collectively will produce systems change, while acknowledging that embracing these actions will require a good deal of emotional courage to confront climate breakdown as well as faith that change through politics is possible and worthwhile fighting for.[5]

This prescription might seem to lead scientists onto the shoals of political advocacy, where the authority of scientific objectivity runs aground. But it's simply the case that this round of planetary climate change is caused by human activity, which means that politics is an element of the scientific problem. The argument that scientists should refrain from discussing the organized human behavior causing our current global warming is a political ploy to keep the scientific justification for decarbonization out of the discourse of the climate movement. And in all events, any possible method of science communication has already been politicized. Even climate scientists' efforts to be judicious and objective have been weaponized by the merchants of doubt. Take, for instance, the denialist campaign to distort the concept of scientific uncertainty.[6] For decades, deniers have argued that climate scientists are too uncertain about climate change to justify the economic costs of abatement. Their claims have confused the public and delayed the implementation of climate policy at least in part because most people are largely unfamiliar with the scientific meaning of "uncertainty." Instead of hearing that scientists have identified a range of outcomes that they can project with confidence, voters hear the message that climate scientists are unsure whether climate change is real or dangerous. So when scientists attempt to be apolitical, hedging against accusations of alarmism by highlighting the "uncertainty" of their research, they unwittingly suggest that they're unsure about their own science and thereby reinforce the deniers' production of doubt. There is no pure scientific communication in a social field where climate change is politically contested. In light of this reality, scientists can best establish their objectivity by acknowledging the political context in which their speech circulates (ironically enough). This is why social science research shows that scientists can augment the authority of their communication by "inoculating" their audiences against denialist messaging before conveying scientific facts.[7]

Inoculation works because it brings the conversation back to politics and human agency. Too often, communicators represent climate change as a disembodied force that we should fight directly, when in reality we must fight the people in power who are supporting the fossil-fuel economy and blocking decarbonization. The fight against these people is best fueled by outrage – the second of the three most powerful emotions produced by effective climate communication. While climate communicators should seek to produce such outrage, they need not be histrionic to do so. Simply describing the appalling moral choice that the powerful are making, as Greta Thunberg does with such stark clarity, is enough.[8] Nor need this moral outrage be compromised by the fact that everyone in the fossil-fuel economy produces greenhouse-gas pollution to some degree. The practices of individual subjects are constrained by their systemic contexts; living in the world as it is now means participating in networks of activity that produce carbon dioxide. Yet, even within those constraints there are degrees of responsibility, ranging from the utter innocence of the over six billion people who live on less than ten dollars a day and emit almost no CO_2, through the complacency of the top 10 percent of people who produce 50 percent of annual global emissions, to the deep and shameful complicity of, for example, the many in the news media who refuse to mention climate change even in the stories about its disasters they're already reporting.[9] It is tempting to universalize the practices that lead to climate change, or, worse, characterize climate change as an expression of "human nature." But we must resist that temptation and keep both synchronic and diachronic perspectives of the crisis in view: humanity is stratified, both within nations and across the globe, not everyone is equally responsible for climate change, fossil-fuel executives and politicians have colluded to lead us to this terrifying moment,[10] and they continue to maintain genocidal energy policies while the climate emergency becomes ever more deadly with each passing day. What these executives and politicians are doing is evil and should be described as such.

But in order to communicate this moral outrage effectively, climate communicators need to make our commitment to changing the world clear. To the greatest possible degree, we need ourselves to stop consuming fossil fuels for pleasure. (Please ask yourself: would Greta Thunberg have been as effective if she had flown around Europe making her speeches?) Communicators with low-carbon footprints are more effective for three reasons. First, social-science research shows that climate-change communicators with small carbon footprints are seen as more trustworthy by their audiences.[11] Second, by performing their personal decision to decarbonize their own lives, such communicators convey that climate change is an emergency worth giving up fossil-fuel consumption to address (thereby short-circuiting the dreaded bystander effect, in which everyone waits to see their neighbor act before acting themselves).[12] Third, and perhaps most importantly, communicators who make low-carbon choices enable people to envision meaningful fossil-free lives, not marked by austerity but filled with deep local pleasures and lofty overarching significance. We don't have to be saints to be correct about atmospheric chemistry, of course, but to move people into action, communicators must offer their audiences more than bare facts. We must show them something to hope for.

Communication meant to move people to action solicits what literary criticism calls "identification": the experience of projecting oneself on to narrative characters and envisioning a different version of oneself in an imaginary context.[13] It does not simply "frame" campaigns for climate policy in terms of the co-benefits of decarbonization.[14] The style of climate communication for which I've argued here helps audiences to identify themselves with the victims of climate change, to see fossil-fuel barons and climate-denying politicians as villains, and to understand themselves as people, connected to a cause with species-defining significance, who courageously transform their priorities and band together with others to create a new world. In other words, this style of communication activates the cultural memory of a very old and powerful literary genre: that of the epic, in which the hero draws on his skill, virtue, and cunning to fight against great odds, save his household, and found a new era. From David who ingeniously describes how to topple Goliath, to Aeneas who perseveres in his duty despite the temptations of pleasure, to the band of rebels in *Star Wars* who build a coalition of misfits to topple the Empire, models for imagining the fight to end the fossil-fuel economy against great odds are there to be deployed. Changing people's minds requires not just iterating bare facts but also offering concrete actions and inspiring the belief in personal agency that can be devoted to the collective production of a habitable world. There is no greater task for climate-change communicators now than telling the stories that will bring that world into being.

NOTES

1. See Van der Linden, Maibach and Leiserowitz (2015, p. 759): "Information about climate change risks needs to be translated into relatable and concrete personal experiences." See also Corner and Clark (2017, p. 53): "People are more likely to be willing to act on climate change if they think that it will impact them (or people they care about and who are similar to them) in the near future."
2. See Intergovernmental Panel on Climate Change (IPCC) (2018).
3. Compare, for instance, the changed reaction of the scientific community to the publication of the monograph *The Uninhabitable Earth* (2019) by the American journalist David Wallace-Wells. When in 2017 Wallace-Wells published the article that he later expanded into the book, he was criticized by many climate

scientists for using literary devices like hyperbole and amplification to frighten people with exaggerations of the dangers of climate breakdown. See Climate Feedback (2017). The publication of his book 18 months later, by contrast, went uncontested, suggesting that these same scientists no longer felt the need to attack the method of underscoring the terrors of climate change with rhetorical and literary devices.

4.   For a study showing that complacency is *increased* by communication centering on the reduction of emissions due to technological progress (what the paper calls "an optimistic message"), see Hornsey and Fielding (2016).

5.   My model of "political action" relies on a bifold conception of "politics" in democratic regimes. On the one hand, "politics" includes all actions that culminate in the passing and enforcement of legislation – everything from campaigning, lobbying, debating, and voting, to governmental procedures, to persuading, striking, organizing, and so on. On the other hand, "politics" also includes what Chantal Mouffe (2005) calls "agonism" within "a common symbolic space" (p. 20), an agonism inflected by "hegemonic practices" that bestow social power on certain identities and institutions within that space. In this conception of politics, "every hegemonic order is susceptible to being challenged by counter-hegemonic practices, ie. practices which will attempt to disarticulate the existing order and install another form of hegemony" (p. 18). Brulle and Norgaard (2019) elaborate this conception of the political in the sphere of climate action by envisioning "actions at the individual level to reshape the self and the daily habitus, at the institutional level to revise or invent new collective routines of action, and at the ideological level to support social movements that seek to advance alternative ideological frameworks to guide social action" (p. 904).

6.   See Oreskes and Conway (2010). In subsequent research, Oreskes demonstrates that the political misuse of the concept of scientific uncertainty extends back even to 1920s' US debates over making electricity a public good. See Oreskes (2015).

7.   See Cook (2019) and Cook, Lewandowsky and Ecker (2017).

8.   See Thunberg (2019).

9.   Oxfam (2015). For data on the US broadcast media's nearly ubiquitous silence on climate change in 2019, see Macdonald, Fisher and Cooper (2020).

10. See Banerjee, Cushman and Hasemyer (2015) and Supran and Oreskes (2017).

11. See Attari, Krantz and Weber (2016, 2019); Westlake (2018); and Thompson (2011).

12. See Griskevicius, Cialdini and Goldstein (2008); Cialdini (1984), Ch. 4; Cialdini and Goldstein (2004); and Darley and Latané (1968). See also Brulle and Norgaard (2019), p. 904: "Transforming existing organizational practices…is dependent on the creation of social imaginaries that generate the cultural resources to envision variations in practice."

13. The insight that stories inspire identification is ancient, advanced by Plato in Books III and X of his *Republic* as the justification for banishing poets from his ideal city, lest they inspire youth to identify with and imitate their licentious representations of the gods. This power of poetry to inspire emulation became praiseworthy in the literary theory of the Renaissance – see, for instance, Sir Philip Sidney's *The Defense of Poesie* – and continues even now to motivate justifications for literary education. For a modern, ironic reworking of the idea, see, for example, Girard (1965).

14. For an example of this approach, see Maibach et al. (2010).

REFERENCES

Attari, Shazeen Z., David H. Krantz and Elke U. Weber (2016), "Statements about climate researchers' carbon footprints affect their credibility and the impact of their advice," *Climatic Change*, **138** (1–2), 325–38.

Attari, Shazeen Z., David H. Krantz and Elke U. Weber (2019), "Climate change communicators' carbon footprints affect their audiences' policy support," *Climatic Change*, **154**, 529–45.

Banerjee, Neela, John H. Cushman Jr., and David Hasemyer (2015), *Exxon: The Road Not Taken*, Brooklyn, NY: Inside Climate News.

Brulle, Robert J. and Kari Marie Norgaard (2019), "Avoiding cultural trauma: climate change and social inertia," *Environmental Politics*, **28** (5), 886–908.

Cialdini, Robert B. (1984), *Influence: The Psychology of Persuasion*, New York: William Morrow.

Cialdini, Robert B. and Noah J. Goldstein (2004), "Social influence: compliance and conformity," *Annual Review of Psychology*, **55**, 592–621.

Climate Feedback (2017), "Scientists explain what *New York Magazine* article on 'The Uninhabitable Earth' gets wrong," 9 July, accessed 15 March 2020 at https://climatefeedback.org/evaluation/scientists-explain-what-new-york-magazine-article-on-the-uninhabitable-earth-gets-wrong-david-wallace-wells/.

Cook, John (2019), "Understanding and countering misinformation about climate change," in Innocent Chiluwa and Sergei A. Samoilenko (eds), *Handbook of Research on Deception, Fake News, and Misinformation Online*, Hershey, PA: IGI-Global, pp. 281–306.

Cook, John, Stephan Lewandowsky and Ullrich K.H. Ecker (2017), "Neutralizing misinformation through inoculation: exposing misleading argumentation techniques reduces their influence," *PLoS ONE*, **12** (5), e0175799.

Corner, Adam and Jamie Clark (2017), *Talking Climate: From Research to Practice in Public Engagement*, Cham, Switzerland: Palgrave Macmillan.

Darley, John M. and Bibb Latané (1968), "Bystander intervention in emergencies: diffusion of responsibility," *Journal of Personality and Social Psychology*, **8** (4), 377–83.

Girard, René (1965), *Deceit, Desire, and the Novel: Self and Other in Literary Structure*, Baltimore, MD: Johns Hopkins University Press.

Griskevicius, Vladas, Robert B. Cialdini and Noah J. Goldstein (2008), "Social norms: an underestimated and underemployed lever for managing climate change," accessed 23 March 2020 at https://pdfs.semanticscholar.org/8791/b3ce170ee1328adb2df83d75c36fdad326e9.pdf.

Hornsey, Matthew J. and Kelly S. Fielding (2016), "A cautionary note about messages of hope: focusing on progress in reducing carbon emissions weakens mitigation motivation," *Global Environmental Change*, **39**, 26–34.

Intergovernmental Panel on Climate Change (IPCC) (2018), *Special Report on Global Warming of 1.5°C*, Geneva: IPCC.

Macdonald, Ted, Allison Fisher and Evlondo Cooper (2020), "How broadcast TV networks covered climate change in 2019," *MediaMatters.org*, 27 February, accessed 23 March 2020 at https://www.mediamatters.org/broadcast-networks/how-broadcast-tv-networks-covered-climate-change-2019.

Maibach, Edward, Matthew Nisbet and Paula Baldwin et al. (2010), "Reframing climate change as a public health issue: an exploratory study of public reactions," *BMS Public Health*, **10** (1), 299–309.

Mouffe, Chantal (2005), *On the Political*, London: Routledge.

O'Neill, Saffron and Sophie Nicholson-Cole (2009), "'Fear won't do it': promoting positive engagement with climate change through visual and iconic representations," *Science Communication*, **30** (3), 355–79.

Oreskes, Naomi (2015), "The fact of uncertainty, the uncertainty of facts and the cultural resonance of doubt," *Philosophical Transactions of the Royal Society A: Mathematical, Physical, and Engineering Sciences*, **373** (2055), 20140455.

Oreskes, Naomi and Erik Conway (2010), *Merchants of Doubt: How a Handful of Scientists Obscured the Truth on Issues from Tobacco Smoke to Global Warming*, New York: Bloomsbury.

Oxfam (2015), "Extreme carbon inequality: why the Paris climate deal must put the poorest, lowest emitting and most vulnerable people first," Oxfam Media Briefing, 2 December, accessed 23 March 2020 at https://oi-files-d8-prod.s3.eu-west-2.amazonaws.com/s3fs-public/file_attachments/mb-extreme-carbon-inequality-021215-en.pdf.

Plato (1992), *Republic*, trans. G.M.A. Grube, Indianapolis, IN: Hackett.

Sidney, Sir Philip (2004), *The "Defense of Poesy" and Selected Renaissance Literary Criticism*, ed. Gavin Alexander, London: Penguin.

Supran, Geoffrey and Naomi Oreskes (2017), "Assessing ExxonMobil's climate change communications (1977–2014)," *Environmental Research Letters*, **12** (8), 23 August, accessed 23 March 2020 at https://iopscience.iop.org/article/10.1088/1748-9326/aa815f.

Thompson, Edward (2011), "Making our actions consistent with our scientific predictions," *Weather*, **66**, 195.

Thunberg, Greta (2019), *No One is Too Small to Make a Difference*, New York: Penguin.

Van der Linden, Sander, Edward Maibach and Anthony Leiserowitz (2015), "Improving public engagement with climate change: five 'best practice' insights from psychological science," *Perspectives on Psychological Science*, **10** (5), 758–63.

Wallace-Wells, David (2019), *The Uninhabitable Earth: Life After Warming*, New York: Tim Duggan Books.

Westlake, Steve (2018), "A counter-narrative to carbon supremacy: do leaders who give up flying because of climate change influence the attitudes and behaviour of others?" unpublished MSc dissertation, Birkbeck University, London.

57. Climate change: from research to communication

Jean Jouzel

Over the last ten years, I have probably dedicated more time to science communication than to scientific research, with a presence in various media – radio, TV, newspapers, magazines – and frequent conferences for the general public or in more specialized circles including education. I have been involved in the writing of popular books dealing with both past and future climate scenarios and of numerous – currently one per month or so – forewords of books published by colleagues, or simply dealing, in some way, with climate issues. I have inspired characters of comics and of drama. More importantly, I have had opportunities to regularly exchange and interact with policy-makers, parliamentarians, ministers (environment, research) and successive presidents of my country. And since 2010, I have been a member of the Economic, Social and Environmental Council (CESE), a constitutional consultative assembly in France.

One quote I'm proud of is the citation used by the committee of the Vetlesen Prize – considered to be the earth sciences' equivalent of a Nobel – which I received in 2012 along with Susan Solomon, an American atmospheric chemist. This committee pointed out that "[i]n the longest climate reconstruction yet from ice cores, Jouzel in a 2007 study in the journal *Science* charted temperatures in Antarctica for the last 800 000 years, over eight consecutive ice ages",[1] and added: "He has also been a leader in bringing human-caused climate change to the public's attention".

After obtaining a degree in chemistry in 1968, I started my PhD, the aim of which was to derive information about the growth of large hailstones from the internal distribution of water isotopes,[2] HDO (deuterium), $H_2^{18}O$ (oxygen 18) and HTO (tritium). Then, I had no idea that I would one day become a specialist in major climatic shifts based on analysis of Antarctic and Greenland ice, nor that I would help raise public awareness of the potential impact of human activity on changes in the Earth's climate. Indeed, I have been lucky that Claude Lorius, a French glaciologist, was regularly visiting the laboratory bringing snow samples from Antarctica for isotopic analysis. The research I was carrying out on hailstones appeared useful for snow studies: in both cases, the stable isotopic composition (deuterium or oxygen 18) is governed by the temperature of formation either of the ice layers in hailstones or of the snow in polar regions. For this reason, Claude Lorius encouraged me to also work on Antarctic snow, and rapidly on Antarctic ice. Under his mentorship and in strong collaboration with his Grenoble team, my research became, starting in the 1970s, largely dedicated to reconstructing past climate changes from ice cores using their isotopic composition as a paleothermometer.

In 1975, Lorius took the lead on a successful project to carry out deep drilling at the Antarctic site of Dome C[3] and, thanks to personal contacts, began in the 1980s a collaboration among French and Soviet teams to study the ice extracted by Soviet drillers at Vostok, another site in the heart of the Antarctic continent. Not only, and for the first time, was an ice core covering a full glacial-interglacial cycle back to 160 000 years ago, but Grenoble colleagues Dominique Raynaud, Jean-Marc Barnola and Jérôme Chappellaz, were also then able to reveal the composition of the atmosphere through an analysis of the tiny bubbles of air trapped in the ice.[4] This enabled us to establish a firm link between the temperature[5] and the concentration of greenhouse gases (carbon dioxide and methane) over this last glacial-interglacial cycle[6] and to show that their current concentration was never encountered over this entire period. This led to a series of historic publications in the journal *Nature* with, in 1987, three articles that guaranteed a very large promotion of the Vostok drilling, the results of which were called a "cornucopia".[7]

The Vostok project gave me one of the first opportunities to have contact with the media – in fact, with one of the most famous science writers at that time. I was interviewed in our Saclay laboratory by Walter Sullivan, reporter for *The New York Times*, considered the "dean" of science writers. I was very proud of this interview, which marked the beginning of more than 30 years of interactions with the media.

The Vostok records, extended in the 1990s over the last four ice ages, not only shed light on mechanisms at play during glacial-interglacial changes but also provide information relevant to the future of our climate in response to emissions of greenhouse gases resulting from anthropogenic activities. I became rapidly interested in this issue, which, at that time, was heavily discussed at the international level, leading in 1988 to the launch of the Intergovernmental Panel on Climate Change (IPCC). I should add that, in the early 1980s, my interest in future climate change benefited from a one-year stay at the NASA Goddard Institute in New York and interactions with two prominent scientists already deeply concerned by this issue: Jim Hansen, head of this institute and best known for his 1988 congressional testimony, and Wally Broecker, who, in 1975, was the first scientist to coin the term "global warming".[8]

In the early 1990s, I was involved, including in field work, in a European project aiming to drill an ice core in Central Greenland. The isotopic data measured on this ice[9] and along a second core drilled by a US team 30 km apart[10] further increased concerns about the future of our climate. The stability of the current climate, which has prevailed for around 10 000 years, appeared to be unusual. In this region, the last glacial period and the following transition are characterized by a series of rapid climate changes with large warmings, up to 15°C, occurring in a few decades or less. Such events are possibly linked with changes in oceanic circulation, an explanation popularized, in a too simplistic way, by modifications in the course of the Gulf Stream. This decadal time scale is relevant to future climate change, which somewhat questions the stability of our climate in a warming world, giving rise to the notion of climatic "surprises", as quoted in the 1995 IPCC report.[11]

Once the Greenland projects were completed, I was often solicited by the media to explain why and how these results are relevant to our future, all the more because I was a lead author of this IPCC report, selected thanks to my knowledge of past climate changes. This participation reinforced my awareness for what is central in IPCC – namely, the evolution of our climate during this century and beyond. I was also involved in the third report, again as lead author, and in the two following ones as bureau member, vice-chair of the scientific working group. As a consequence, an increasing part of media solicitations was, over all this period, associated with my involvement in the IPCC.

Quite naturally, the questions addressed by the media, initially connected with paleoclimate issues, my field of expertise, evolved towards concerns about anthropogenic climate changes, their causes and consequences and the way forward to mitigate and adapt to these changes. In turn, I have attracted media attention and acquired credibility on climate issues at large, largely thanks to the quality of the French team contributions to ice core science as fully recognized at the national level by the Gold Medal, the most prestigious scientific award in France, that we received, both Claude Lorius and myself, in 2002.

It is around that time that I started to communicate to the political world. This was not at all my decision but came from solicitations motivated by the visibility acquired thanks to my presence in the media and my scientific expertise, but also thanks to this Gold Medal award and later on, to the 2007 Nobel Peace Prize received by Al Gore and the IPCC. But I recognize that I was interested in such interactions while continuing to have media attention on scientific issues. Also I'm convinced that, as scientists, it is our role to answer questions that policy-makers are willing to raise; in this context, I am in full agreement with the IPCC's willingness to address "policy-relevant" questions without being "policy prescriptive".

It is with this spirit that I have contributed in 2006 to a parliamentary report dealing with the greenhouse effect. My next involvement was the process called "Grenelle de l'Environnement", aimed at preparing decisions to be taken at the ministerial level. I have, along with Sir Nicholas Stern, an economist, co-chaired the first group dealing with climate change and energy. I have then partipated in various committees dealing with adaptation to climate change in 2010 and with the preparation of the law on the energy transition in 2015. I have also had interactions with policy-makers in attending, as a scientific expert and member of the French delegation, all the COP meetings since 2001. At last, as mentioned above, I have been a member of CESE since 2010, where I have contributed as co-rapporteur to advice dealing with energy transition, climate adaptation, the relationship between science and society and climate justice. These various activities, clearly outside my own field of research, have also provided many opportunities to communicate to the general public and interact with the media.

In 2017, I published with Pierre Larrouturou, now a member of the French Parliament, a book entitled *Pour éviter un chaos climatique et financier* [To Avoid Climate and Financial Chaos][12] and, at his initiative, we launched the project of a Climate-Finance Pact with the aim of a creating a treaty establishing a union for climate and biodiversity. Such a more political initiative also requires communication and this also holds true for my current involvement as chairman of the support committee of Anne Hidalgo, in view of her re-election as mayor of Paris.

To sum up, I have had over more than 30 years, and still have, the opportunity to communicate to a large variety of audiences with the aim to deliver an apparently simple message – the urgency of combating climate warming – while the climatic system and how it reacts to the increasing greenhouse effect, which is linked to our activities, is awfully complex. To deliver this message, I benefit from being a climate scientist recognized for his contributions to a better understanding of climate mechanisms at play in the past and relevant to our future, such as the role of greenhouse gases and the existence of abrupt climate changes. Still, my focus is generally on the future climate and here I spend time showing and discussing data on temperature, sea-level, extreme events, and so on – well documented and increasingly convincing – and how their evolution well corresponds to projections made by climate modellers in the 1980s, giving confidence for model projections for coming decades and beyond. I don't hesitate, even if it is not my field of expertise, to discuss the consequences of climate warming and the solutions to mitigate, and to adapt to, this warming. Such communication is largely facilitated by the accessibility of IPCC reports that I amply use in my presentations and I would like to thank all those who contribute to the high quality of these reports.

NOTES

1. Jouzel, J., V. Masson-Delmotte and O. Cattini et al. (2007), "Orbital and millennial Antarctic climate variability over the past 800,000 years", *Science*, **317** (5839), 793–6.
2. Jouzel, J., L. Merlivat and E. Roth (1975), "Isotopic study of hail", *Journal of Geophysical Research*, **80** (36), 5015–30.
3. Lorius, C., L. Merlivat, J. Jouzel and M. Pourchet (1979), "A 30 000-year isotope climatic record from Antarctic ice", *Nature*, **280**, 644–8.
4. Barnola, J.M., D. Raynaud, Y.S. Korotkevich and C. Lorius (1987), "Vostok ice core provides 160,000 years records of atmospheric CO_2", *Nature*, **329**, 408–14; Chappellaz, J., J.M. Barnola and D. Raynaud et al. (1990), "Ice-core record of atmospheric methane over past 160,000 years", *Nature*, **345**, 127–31.
5. Jouzel, J., C. Lorius and J.R. Petit et al. (1987), "Vostok ice core: a continuous isotope temperature record over the last climatic cycle (160,000 years)", *Nature*, **329**, 403–8.
6. Genthon, G., J.M. Barnola and D. Raynaud et al. (1987), "Vostok ice core: climatic response to CO_2 and orbital forcing changes over the last climatic cycle", *Nature*, **329**, 414–18; Lorius, C., J. Jouzel and D. Raynaud et al. (1990), "The ice-core record: climate sensitivity and future greenhouse warming", *Nature*, **347**, 139–45.
7. Campbell, P. (1987), "The Antarctic cornucopia", *Nature*, **329**, 387.
8. Broecker, W.S. (1975), "Climatic change: are we on the brink of a pronounced global warming?", *Science*, **189**, 460–63.
9. Dansgaard, W., S.J. Johnsen and H.B. Clausen et al. (1993), "Evidence for general instability of past climate from a 250-kyr ice-core record", *Nature*, **364**, 218–20.
10. Grootes, P.M., M. Stuiver and J.W.C. White et al. (1993), "Comparison of the oxygen isotope records from the GISP2 and GRIP Greenland ice cores", *Nature*, **366**, 552–4.
11. Intergovernmental Panel on Climate Change (IPCC) (1995), *IPCC Second Assessment: Climate Change 1995: A Report of the Intergovernmental Panel on Climate Change*, Geneva: IPCC.
12. Jouzel, J. and P. Larrouturou (2017), *Pour éviter un chaos climatique et financier*, Paris: Odile Jacob.

58. Communicating biodiversity loss and its link to economics

Georgina M. Mace

Climate change and biodiversity loss are the two most important features of human-driven global environmental change. They are also closely related. Not only are they both direct consequences of human population growth, natural resource consumption and waste, but there are many interrelationships among the actions that will be necessary to address each of them. However, while biodiversity loss attracts a great deal of popular interest, it has not achieved the same degree of political attention as climate change. Biodiversity lacks effective intergovernmental commitments, something that biodiversity scientists regularly lament (Legagneux et al., 2018). Perhaps this is because the causes of biodiversity loss are complex and less clear-cut than are the causes of climate change. While it is clear that moving away from our current carbon-based economy will be difficult, it is much more tangible than the multiple actions across scales and sectors that will be required to reverse biodiversity loss (IPBES, 2019). At least we know what we must do to limit the degree of climate change. But the lack of binding commitments addressing biodiversity loss may also be due to the fact that the immediate consequences of biodiversity loss are neither evident nor obviously material compared to climate change impacts. It is accepted that climate change carries substantial economic costs, and even existential threats. By contrast, the consequences of biodiversity loss are multiple, vague and often contested. While there are very good reasons to be concerned about biodiversity loss and its potential to pose a serious risk to future generations, biodiversity can be perceived as an idle concern for amateur naturalists, or a manageable problem that technological innovation will address as necessary.

The recognition of ecosystem services and their importance for society (Daily, 1997) has to some extent transformed the way in which biodiversity is perceived in policy-making. A developing narrative about the dependence of people on nature, and assessments such as those produced by the Millennium Ecosystem Assessment (MEA, 2005), The Economics of Ecosystems and Biodiversity (TEEB, 2010), and the Intergovernmental Science-Policy Platform on Biodiversity and Ecosystem Services (IPBES,

2019) (see Glossary) have documented the value of nature to people in ever more detail along with growing evidence for the continuing loss of nature. Yet, the economic and existential risks are hard to grasp and even harder to quantify. I have spent the last 30 years researching biodiversity loss and ecosystem change, and this chapter describes the journey that I have taken to measure the rate of loss and unambiguously present the evidence for why it matters to society. I don't have an answer, but I will conclude with some suggestions and current activities that will hopefully improve the situation over the next few years.

BIODIVERSITY ASSESSMENT

Based on an early interest in natural history, and a general enthusiasm for science, I studied zoology as an undergraduate and evolutionary ecology for my PhD. In the 1970s and 1980s, ecological theory was a rapidly moving and an inspiring area of science in which to be involved, building on the great work of Robert MacArthur, Robert May, Edward Wilson and John Maynard Smith among many others. I'm not a good mathematician, but I can follow theory and think conceptually, and I am better than some at organizing data. So, I ended up doing a PhD that was largely statistical and then I went on to study at the Smithsonian Institution in Washington, DC, USA. Here I first encountered research into species conservation. At the time, a large gulf existed between conservation practice and the nascent field of conservation science. The debate about whether protected areas should be single and large, or many and small, and the genetics of small populations dominated the conservation science agenda, and while the theory was developing it had rather little connection to practice and decisions on the ground.

I continued my academic studies in comparative biology but by the mid- to late 1980s the biodiversity crisis was becoming clear. There was much interest in designing conservation programmes at a larger scale to address burgeoning species loss. I found myself to be one of a relatively small group of people actually working on the population biology of species conservation. Michael Soule called this a 'crisis science' and I was among the first members of the Society for Conservation Biology that he and others founded to develop the science to address the crisis.

I struggled with postdoc appointments while small children dominated the rest of my time, and I ended up with several short-term positions working on conservation planning for a wide range of species. I developed conservation plans for everything from gorillas, rhinos and oryx, to snails, bats and ducks, and many others besides. There were many different species in various habitats facing multiple threats, and we were trying to create practical tools to assist managers and funders to focus and prioritize conservation projects. Ultimately, this work led to what became a long-running project that I ran collaboratively with Simon Stuart of IUCN. This was to develop the international rules that are now used to list species at the highest risk of extinction – the IUCN Red List categories and criteria (IUCN, 2001). We worked through a series of drafts, undertook reviews and consultations, and eventually presented a final version of the system that was ultimately approved by the IUCN Council in 2000. This system has been in place ever since. It is well maintained by IUCN staff working with the wide network of species experts worldwide, and the combination of clear and well-established rules, an effective team maintaining and organizing the data, and a managed expert network provides an authoritative system that documents the growing numbers of threatened species in ever greater detail. The list provides one of a handful of global metrics used to track the state of biodiversity (Butchart et al., 2006, 2010).

I learned a huge amount from being involved with the IUCN and the Red List, working with government and non-government scientists and conservation practitioners, and considering the decision-making process as well as natural science. For the first time, I found myself a target of lobbying. Developing science-based criteria for threatened species turns out to have political consequences because some species are very important to certain groups of people who feel very strongly about whether or not they should be listed as threatened. It was clear that public and personal concern for species was not necessarily closely related to the urgency of conservation action, and some species that were economically important (including marine turtles and Atlantic cod) met the qualifying criteria in the IUCN Red List. The experience taught me a lot about the relationship between science and policy. With support from IUCN, we stuck to the science, but it was clear that in many cases the choice about where to place the boundary between threat categories was a compromise. Somebody was going to disagree with the outcome, and while some differences were due to different levels of risk tolerance, sometimes it was simply a case of pitting one difficult and complex species conservation issue against another.

Around the turn of the millennium the Millennium Ecosystem Assessment (MEA) was being developed. Unlike the IPCC's focus on climate, the MEA had a focus on ecosystems and ecosystem services. Over a five-year period, using assessment processes from the IPCC, the work developed to create a policy-relevant assessment of the state of the world's ecosystems and their ability to continue to support the needs of people into the future. There were many fundamental questions that had to be addressed. How to define and classify ecosystems? What are ecosystem services? How is biodiversity involved in ecosystem services? As well as this, there was a set of fundamental questions about how all this would be important to people. Who are the people that depend upon ecosystems, how should we identify the functions and structures in ecosystems upon which we depend, and most important of all, what is the value of ecosystem services? What do future generations stand to lose if we continue to allow ecosystems and biodiversity to degrade? Most contentious of all, what is the value of biodiversity?

My role in the MEA was interesting. I was recruited to contribute to the first volume (reviewing the status and trends of ecosystems) because of my work on species for the Red List. I had a broad knowledge of biodiversity and threatened species, and many contacts globally in the conservation world. I was in a great position to be a Coordinating Lead Author for the biodiversity chapter of the MEA and I organized a team of co-authors with access to the best data and knowledge covering many geographic and taxonomic groups. We just needed a clear focus for the chapter. By the time I was signed up to do this, the conceptual work to define ecosystem services had been more or less completed. Ecosystem services were organized into a classification that is still widely used today, with provisioning, regulating, cultural and supporting services all contributing to the benefits that flow to people from ecosystems. My MEA work was to pull together the biodiversity chapter to sit within this scheme. At the first meeting I was asked in which part of the ecosystem services classification I thought biodiversity should be placed. Should I go and work with the food, water and energy people? Would it be better as a regulating service alongside climate and pest regulation, or was it actually a cultural service, meeting some specific needs for societal cohesion and inspiration?

I was baffled by this discussion. To me it was clearly none of these. Ecosystems are defined by the interactions between living (biotic) and non-living (abiotic) components, and so ecosystems don't exist or function without their living components, and their living components are biodiversity. I was not sure at all how biodiversity science should sit in the conceptual framework of the MEA, but I was absolutely sure that biodiversity is not simply another ecosystem service. I argued at the time that it underpinned just about all ecosystem services. While many people wanted biodiversity to be an outcome of good ecosystem services management, I wanted it to be an input to well-functioning ecosystems from which ecosystem services could be expected to flow. Ecologists had long been interested in how diversity was maintained in ecological communities, and what the consequences of changing diversity were for essential functions such as biomass production and decomposition. There was a growing body of evidence that for many services, greater diversity underpinned stronger and more resilient ecosystem services, but that selection for a few top-performing species was key to ecosystem simplification for agriculture, fisheries and forestry (Cardinale et al., 2012). It is this tension that makes the debate about biodiversity loss in a resource-hungry world so complicated. The MEA biodiversity chapter was homeless while we debated this issue, but in the end it was one of the underpinning introductory chapters along with drivers, human well-being and vulnerable people (Mace et al., 2005).

There were for me a few interesting legacies of the MEA experience and they have persisted in my research over the 15 years since. It was through work on the MEA that I first formally encountered economists. I could see the importance of agreeing how economic valuation of ecosystem services should be undertaken, and what these values might be. But the MEA team as a whole struggled with economics and valuation. There were many different perspectives and approaches, and consensus never developed enough for a clear message to emerge. Heated debates about monetization of ecosystem service benefits focused not only on the methods for doing it but about whether it had any meaning or utility for decisions, and if so whose decisions (and for whose benefit)? While difficult and slightly frustrating I found these economics discussions to be both interesting and important, and it was somewhat frustrating that we could not find a clear role for economics in the MEA.

Second, despite the vagueness of where biodiversity should sit in the MEA, everyone thought it was important and it was always a highlight in any wider discussion or presentation. The headlines about species extinctions were unarguable and attracted a lot of attention. We did a reasonable job of pulling together a coherent global assessment of the data on biodiversity loss and at the launch of the MEA in 2005 it was our figures on extinction rates that grabbed the popular headlines. This was despite the stark warning from the overall assessment that the world was on an unsustainable development trajectory and needed to change course. The clear disconnect in my mind between the data on species extinctions and the evidence for unsustainable patterns of resource use was not apparently a problem for most people, even though it is clear that actions to reduce the former may have little to do with reversing the latter. Interestingly, almost exactly the same happened early in 2019 with the release of the IPBES Global Assessment (IPBES, 2019). Despite the carefully articulated conclusions from IPBES about actions needed to address the severe risks of losing 'natures' contributions to people', the popular headlines featured the million species at risk of extinction over coming decades, and illustrated the work with charismatic tigers, rhinos and elephants. Somehow the message that ecosystems matter materially to people for wider reasons than the loss of charismatic species was lost in popular press reports for both the MEA in 2005 and 15 years later for IPBES.

USING ECONOMIC ARGUMENTS

I encountered several groups of people who really wanted us to say something tangible about the economic value of lost biodiversity. There were various figures around at the time, including the widely cited figure of $33 trillion

(Costanza et al., 1997), but these seemed to be estimates of the marginal values of ecosystem services, and not easy to relate to biodiversity. Surely biodiversity, the sum of the diversity of life on Earth cannot be accounted for in this way? It is fundamental and its loss would be existential. I think we still struggle to conceptualize the measurement of biodiversity value (see below), but it was clear that there were ways of asking and answering the question about the value of intact nature that were both valid and useful. Andrew Balmford's work (Balmford et al., 2002), for example, had shown how intact ecosystems carried about 100 times the total social value of converted ecosystems across a wide range of ecosystem types. Similarly, there were many case studies emerging that showed how loss of certain biodiversity components would lead to the collapse of ecosystem service benefits, such as pollinators or pest-control species, and even how poor management would reduce the value of benefit flows.

Conservationists, environment policy-makers, natural resource managers and development scientists were all interested in the question of valuation of biodiversity. Yet, we had very few answers, and those that we were able to point to were all very specific, relating to a specific service (for example, pollinators or watershed management) that was difficult to generalize across places and across ecosystems and ecosystem service categories. As a result, it was difficult to construct an overarching economic case for biodiversity.

Nevertheless, it was still clear that there was not a problem communicating the biodiversity crisis. We had plenty of compelling figures and statistics documenting the ongoing loss of species, loss of biota and transformation of ecosystems. Each annual release of the IUCN Red List documented increasing rates of threat among the world's species and attracted headlines in newspapers and on broadcast media. But, slightly alarmingly, this was often the last item in a TV news broadcast and frequently presented as mildly amusing anecdotes, illustrated with a quirky story about the loss of a rare, unusual species. The dusky seaside sparrow and George, the last Hawaiian land snail, have had their 15 minutes of fame as a result. But stark as it is, this narrative is not apparently doing anything to stimulate actions at the scale and intensity needed. Meanwhile, biodiversity scientists were continuing to document the very clear evidence that the intergovernmental commitment made in 2002 to slow the rate of biodiversity loss had demonstrably failed. If anything, the evidence in 2010 was that the rate of loss was still increasing (Butchart et al., 2010) and despite new political commitments made in 2010, the situation is not improving (Green et al., 2019; Tittensor et al., 2014).

The Stern Review, published in 2006, provided a model for the kind of evidence-based analysis needed to support action. Stern's bold approach, to estimate the costs of inaction on climate change, attracted wide attention and, coming from a credible and authoritative economist, its message reached into the highest reaches of government and corporations. TEEB (2010), set up to mirror the Stern Review, was influential for business and government, but other than making the roles of ecosystem services clearer, it did not transform the seriousness of commitments made towards biodiversity at any level.

Following the global MEA, the UK government's Environment Department (Defra), undertook an ecosystem assessment in the UK. This ambitious project was ably led by Bob Watson who was then the Chief Scientific Adviser in Defra. He had wide experience of assessments from working on the IPCC and MEA. The UK National Ecosystem Assessment (UKNEA, 2011) was a two-year project to assess the state of ecosystems and ecosystem services in the UK, and their ability to support the needs of people into the future. At the very first meeting of the expert group I sat next to Ian Bateman, an environmental economist who had been recruited to the project by Bob Watson. It took no time for he and I to agree that the UK was the perfect case study to use to trial a full economic analysis of the costs and benefits of ecosystems and biodiversity. We worked together on a conceptual framework for the assessment that would improve the comprehensiveness of ecosystem service valuations (Mace and Bateman, 2011), and he recruited a team of economists to work across the different components of the work to ensure that this consistent approach was followed. Needless to say, it was not straightforward. But we did manage to map and value multiple ecosystem services at national scale and show the importance of non-market services, especially recreational values and carbon values. Market values, mainly from food production, once the effects of subsidies were removed, actually had remarkably low welfare values. Managing the UK landscape for the full suite of ecosystem services could therefore be shown to increase the social welfare value almost 100 times. Of course, there is a practical problem with this finding in that there are no mechanisms to pay landowners for these services. But the headline result remains valid and the outcome was I think a marked improvement over earlier attempts. We wrote this up for a paper published in 2013 that showed clearly that the value of UK ecosystem services was substantial but lay almost entirely outside market mechanisms (Bateman et al., 2013).

The UKNEA also did not treat biodiversity as an ecosystem service and the approach we took for economic analysis was to lay out alternative scenarios for ecosystem management and then compare both the total social value of ecosystem services alongside a measure of biodiversity conservation (bird species richness). Our models showed clearly, and not surprisingly, that land management strategies that maximized the social value of ecosystem services were almost optimal (not quite) for biodiversity conservation. So, in a situation where ecosystem services are taken seriously in land use decisions there will be almost no opportunity cost from biodiversity conservation. The problem is that land use decisions that maximize market values (food production almost entirely) has a substantial cost for both ecosystem services and biodiversity conservation. There are parallels in other contexts where enlightened political decisions recognize not only the limits of valuation, but also the risks of taking them too seriously (Box 58.1).

BOX 58.1 PRIME MINISTER ROCARD ON HOW TO EVALUATE AN ECOSYSTEM (CONTRIBUTED BY CLAUDE HENRY)

At the end of the 1980s, there was an advanced project to build a dam on the upper course of the Loire, in the middle of a long canyon known as les Gorges de la Loire, with the objective of, it was claimed, regulating the flows downstream. I was asked to build a multidisciplinary and international team (not a frequent assemblage in France at the time) of experts: Welsh and Dutch ecologists, French and English economists and hydrologists, and the well-known English landscape architect Jeremy Purseglove. We quantified in monetary terms things like damages from potential floods, incomes from agriculture and tourism that were at stake, and so on. Potential losses of biodiversity were carefully evaluated, albeit not translated into monetary evaluations. And Jeremy made eloquent drawings, with comments for interpretation, pre- and post-project, without any reference to economic values.

A report was written, bilingual, and a meeting was organized at Matignon, the residence of the Prime Minister. Rocard was a macroeconomist by training, and an imaginative maverick in politics. He enjoyed the discussion on the report, and then concluded: 'It is a comprehensive and serious piece of work, made possible by the diversity of expertises and cultures in the team. I am particularly happy that you didn't try to foul me by pretending that every aspect is susceptible to be valued in monetary terms. It would have been misleading and in any case we don't need it; it is my responsibility to make an overall assessment'. Soon he killed the project.

The UKNEA certainly attracted attention in government, as well as in business and industry. The UK government White Paper in 2011, 'The Natural Choice', drew heavily on the work. It stated:

> The Government wants this to be the first generation to leave the natural environment of England in a better state than it inherited. To achieve so much means taking action across sectors rather than treating environmental concerns in isolation. It requires us all to put the value of nature at the heart of our decision-making – in Government, local communities and businesses. In this way we will improve the quality and increase the value of the natural environment across England.

The White Paper also called for the creation of a Natural Capital Committee (NCC) that would put nature at the heart of decision-making in government and advise how to achieve this ambition to be the first generation to leave the environment in a better state.

As a member of the NCC, I was surrounded by economists of various kinds, including people with a primary interest in environmental economics but also interested in energy economics and corporate accounting. It was an extremely interesting committee and we had many lively debates about how to value and measure natural capital, including biodiversity. The NCC itself also became quite controversial; to many people, even putting a value to nature devalues it. According to *The Guardian* journalist George Monbiot, for example, nature should be beyond valuation. Or, for some people, it seemed that the interest in valuing nature being taken by the UK government was simply a prelude to selling off large tracts of forested land. Certain journalists and lobby groups alike were aghast at the work of the NCC. My own view, which I tried to explain repeatedly was that we were interested in putting a value to nature so that it could be taken seriously and invested in. We were not trying to reduce it to a marketable commodity, far from it in fact. The more I worked in the NCC, the more two overarching conclusions became clear to me. First, that broad-sense biodiversity, the diversity of life, is beyond valuation. Its roles are so fundamental and foundational that any attempt to value it is ultimately meaningless. In effect, it is of infinite value and its loss ultimately creates an existential risk, even if we are quite a long way from realizing this risk. However, there are many useful approaches to valuing nature's services or ecosystem services, the flow of benefits from which people derive health, well-being and fulfilling lives. These methods are easier for some kinds of services than others, but the more comprehensive we can be, the better because there are many win–wins in the area of ecosystem service management. There are some win–loses too – unfortunately, very often related to provisioning services or ecosystem services whereby energy and matter are removed from the ecosystem and used or transformed. Mapping, quantifying and modelling these ecosystem services locally is the science-based information needed for land management decisions, and the tools and techniques for doing this are increasingly widely available and useful. However, the sum of these values will always be a substantial underestimate of the value of nature.

A corollary of this is that ecosystems and biodiversity can usefully be considered a capital stock. So, in accounting terms, a balance sheet approach is appropriate. Ecosystems, including their biodiversity components, are assets whose condition can be measured, at least in physical terms, and this should not deteriorate over time unless for some reason a decision is made to abandon the asset. Investing in ecosystems will generally lead to an improved flow of ecosystem services, so valuing the services is one way to ensure that the ecosystem itself is being well managed. However, the sum of the value of the services is not necessarily a good indicator of the state of the asset because certain high monetary value services might dominate, at least transiently, but the ecosystem itself may be unsustainable. Apparently comprehensive valuations of all ecosystem services that an ecosystem supplies are always likely to be an underestimate of ecosystem value because of services we cannot measure or do not (yet) use.

CONCLUSIONS

There is no single answer to the question of how to value biodiversity, or how to communicate the societal consequences of ongoing biodiversity loss. There are multiple perceptions of how and why biodiversity loss matters, and few shared approaches to its valuation. Economic valuation is one of the approaches that I think is a necessary part of the solution, but it is far from being sufficient. Valuation is useful to show that biodiversity loss has material consequences and that it plays a significant role in the economy and should therefore be afforded serious consideration alongside health, infrastructure, education, justice and other essential societal concerns. I support the idea of including the natural environment and biodiversity in national accounts, although there is much work to be done to ensure this is done well (Bright et al., 2019; Mace, 2019). But the complexity and scope of biodiversity means that the values are going to be partial, inaccurate and very likely large underestimates. There is a risk that the values are easily contested and can underplay the irreplaceability of nature.

In fact, many people feel that using valuation diminishes nature by commodifying it. The moral commitment to saving species is most often applied to charismatic megafauna, such as the great whales, elephants and tigers, but in principle applies to all of life on Earth. The cultural values of biodiversity are unarguable and nearly always gather wide support, demonstrated very recently by substantial shifts in people's attitudes to plastic waste brought about by compelling images of its direct impact on ocean wildlife in a David Attenborough documentary. But these cultural values are societally driven and as such are changeable and heterogeneous, requiring a much more sophisticated approach to establishing relational values relevant to different groups of people (Pascual et al., 2017).

Despite these difficulties, the ecosystem services approach and effective policy and public communication of biodiversity loss have certainly enhanced the degree to which it is perceived to be a serious problem over the past 20 years. Biodiversity loss is now seen to be a global challenge equivalent to climate change. However, methods for communicating it, and for acting on its consequences still lag behind, and there is plenty to do. A clearer appreciation of the underpinning roles of biodiversity, including for achieving the Sustainable Development Goals, or for addressing the nexus of environmental issues such as food and energy security in a changing climate, will become increasingly important.

REFERENCES

Balmford, A., Bruner, A. and Cooper, P. et al. 2002. Economic reasons for conserving wild nature. *Science*, **297**, 950–53.

Bateman, I.J., Harwood, A.R. and Mace, G.M. et al. 2013. Bringing ecosystem services into economic decision-making: land use in the United Kingdom. *Science*, **341**, 45–50.

Bright, G., Connors, E. and Grice, J. 2019. Measuring natural capital: towards accounts for the UK and a basis for improved decision-making. *Oxford Review of Economic Policy*, **35**, 88–108.

Butchart, S.H.M., Akçakaya, H.R., Kennedy, E. and Hilton-Taylor. C. 2006. Biodiversity indicators based on trends in conservation status: strengths of the IUCN Red List Index. *Conservation Biology*, **20**, 579–81.

Butchart, S.H.M., Walpole, M. and Collen, B. et al. 2010. Global biodiversity: indicators of recent declines. *Science*, **328**, 1164–8.

Cardinale, B.J., Duffy, J.E. and Gonzales, A. 2012. Biodiversity loss and its impact on humanity. *Nature*, **486**, 59–67.

Costanza, R., d'Arge, R. and de Groot, R. et al. 1997. The value of the world's ecosystem services and natural capital. *Nature*, **387**, 253–60.

Daily, G.C. 1997. *Nature's Services*. Washington, DC: Island Press.

Green, E.J., Buchanan, G.M. and Butchart, S.H. et al. 2019. Relating characteristics of global biodiversity targets to reported progress. *Conservation Biology*, **33** (6), 1360–69.

IPBES. 2019. *Summary for Policymakers of the Global Assessment Report on Biodiversity and Ecosystem Services of the Intergovernmental Science-Policy Platform on Biodiversity and Ecosystem Services*. Bonn: IPBES.

IUCN. 2001. *IUCN Red List Categories and Criteria – Version 3.1*. Gland, Switzerland: IUCN – The World Conservation Union.

Legagneux, P., N. Casjus and K. Cazelles et al. 2018. Our house is burning: discrepancy in climate change vs. biodiversity coverage in the media as compared to scientific literature. *Frontiers in Ecology and Evolution*, **5**. https://doi.org/10.3389/fevo.2017.00175.

Mace, G.M. 2019. The ecology of natural capital accounting. *Oxford Review of Economic Policy*, **35**, 54–67.

Mace, G.M., Masundire, H. and Baillie, J. et al. 2005. Biodiversity. In R. Hassan, R. Scholes and N. Ash (eds), *Millennium Ecosystem Assessment: Ecosystems and Human Well-being: Current State and Trends, Volume 1*. Washington, DC: Island Press.

Mace, G.M. and Bateman, I.J. 2011. Conceptual framework and methodology. In UKNEA (ed.), *The UK National Ecosystem Assessment: Technical Report*. Cambridge, UK: UNEP-WCMC.

Millennium Ecosystem Assessment (MEA). 2005. *Ecosystems and Human Well-being: Synthesis*. Washington, DC: World Resources Institute.

Pascual U., Balvanera, P. and Diaz, S. 2017. Valuing nature's contributions to people: the IPBES approach. *Current Opinion in Environmental Sustainability*, **26–27**, 7–16.

Stern, N. 2006. *The Economics of Climate Change*. London: HM Treasury.

TEEB. 2010. *The Economics of Ecosystems and Biodiversity: Mainstreaming the Economics of Nature: A Synthesis of the Approach, Conclusions and Recommendations of TEEB*. Nairobi: UNEP.

Tittensor, D.P., Walpole, M. and Hill, S.L.L. 2014. A mid-term analysis of progress toward international biodiversity targets. *Science*, **346**, 241–4.

UKNEA. 2011. *The UK National Ecosystem Assessment: Technical Report*. Cambridge: UNEP-WCMC.

Glossary of abbreviations in the text

IPBES	Intergovernmental Science-Policy Platform on Biodiversity and Ecosystem Services. An independent intergovernmental body, established by UN member states in 2012 (www.ipbes.net)
IPCC	Intergovernmental Panel on Climate Change. Under the UN Framework Convention on Climate Change, the IPCC provides policy-makers with regular scientific assessments on climate change, its implications and potential future risks (www.ipcc.net)
IUCN	The International Union for Conservation of Nature. A membership union composed of both government and civil society organizations (www.iucn.org)
MEA	Millennium Ecosystem Assessment. An assessment of the consequences of ecosystem change for human well-being called for by the United Nations Secretary-General Kofi Annan in 20000. From 2001 to 2005, the MEA involved the work of more than 1360 experts worldwide (www.millenniumassessment.org)
TEEB	The Economics of Ecosystems and Biodiversity was a study led by Pavan Sukhdev from 2007 to 2011. It continues as an international initiative to draw attention to the global economic benefits of biodiversity (www.teebweb.org)

59. Helping trusted messengers find their voice on climate change

Edward Maibach

Imagine this. You're a public health professional. Your entire career has been devoted to fighting some of humanity's most terrible afflictions: cancer, HIV/AIDS, addiction, and others. One day, suddenly, you come to recognize climate change as the most terrible of all afflictions threatening human health and well-being. What would you do? I suspect you would do – or have already done – as I did: refocus your life to help to avert a sustained global public health catastrophe from climate change. Anything less would feel like a betrayal of your most deeply held values.

It took nearly two decades for me to recognize climate change for what it truly is. It should have been immediately obvious, but it wasn't. That it took so long has given me insight and empathy for how difficult it can be for people to recognize that climate change is not only a threat to plants, penguins and polar bears, but also a profound threat to us, now and for countless generations to come. Helping reveal this truth has become my life's new work.

In fact, revealing truths about health has always been the focus of my work. Some of these truths are horrible (such as the pervasive lies told by the tobacco industry that have led to countless addictions, dreaded illnesses, and early deaths), and some have been wonderful (such as the safety and effectiveness of childhood vaccines). Trained in both public health and communication science, my work has always aimed to help people – members of the public, government officials, business leaders, civic leaders and others – have the information they need to make the best possible decisions about health – their health as well as the health of others.

Breathtaking gains have been made in human health worldwide over the past century. With each passing decade we've learnt more about the conditions that foster good health – including education, a living wage, sanitation services, clean air and water, nutritious food, physical activity, and immunizations – and most nations have made great progress in ensuring their people have access to these health-enhancing conditions. However, over the past two decades, public health experts have slowly come to realize that a stable climate is also fundamental to health because climate change harms people's health, and the ecosystems on which we depend, in many ways.

Like many Americans, I took note of the 1988 U.S. Congressional testimony by Dr. James Hansen of the NASA Goddard Space Institute warning about the dangers of human-caused climate change, and read many news accounts about climate change over the next two decades. In 2006, however, I had a sudden awakening. At the urging of a family member, my wife and I enrolled in a week-long study trip in the Alps. The trip director asked us to prepare for the trip by watching *An Inconvenient Truth* (the movie about Al Gore's climate education efforts) and reading *The Weather Makers* (a book about climate change by Australian scientist Tim Flannery).

The "study" portion of the trip was a series of climate change lectures addressing its causes, impact, risks and possible solutions presented over four days by two leading experts, John Schellnhuber and Ottmar Edenhofer of the Potsdam Institute for Climate Impact Research. Although John and Ottmar didn't directly address human health in their lectures, in the closing moments of their final lecture I had a moment of epiphany. In that instant, the horrible truth became clear: the long arc of human history would cease bending toward longevity, prosperity, and justice unless climate change was stopped – or greatly limited.

BEGINNING AGAIN WITH A SEARCH FOR ACTIONABLE INSIGHTS

The fierce urgency of that realization compelled me to search for ways to help. Conversations with myriad experts over the next few months revealed several insights that suggested how I might be helpful. At that time in America there was a profound lack of will – both political will and public will – to address climate change. The lack of public will – that is, the lack of public demand on government and business leaders to embrace climate solutions – was enabling a lack of political will. In turn, the lack of political action – and industry action – reinforced the apathy of the American people who were largely taking their cues about climate change from what political "elites" were (or more likely weren't) saying.

Neither of these "deficits of will" was happenstance. Rather, they were the product of well-funded, sustained, strategic communication and lobbying by the fossil fuel industry and their allies to convince Americans – especially our leaders – that climate change was either not real, not human-caused, not serious, and/or not solvable without causing arguably worse problems (like "killing the American economy"). The parallels between this situation and the tobacco use epidemic were uncanny. Indeed, research by science historians and others soon proved these parallels were not a coincidence. To forestall enactment of climate policies that could threaten the fossil fuel industry's profit margins, the industry was actively using the kinds of misinformation, influence peddling and other dirty tricks that were developed and perfected by the tobacco industry.

In response, my mission became to conduct social science research and use the findings of such research to counteract the corrosive influence of climate misinformation campaigns in America. To that end, my colleagues Anthony Leiserowitz (Yale) and Connie Roser-Renouf (George Mason University) and I started the Climate Change in the American Mind polling project. Through these polls we sought to reveal opportunities to promote public understanding of climate change and to build public will for climate solutions. Started in 2008, the project is now in its 12th year, and we've conducted more than two dozen polls. These polls have proven to be incredibly productive in that they've yielded many actionable insights that, in turn, have influenced many public education campaigns.

An important premise of our polling project was that all successful public health campaigns – arguably, all successful communication campaigns – feature *simple clear messages, repeated often, by a variety of trusted voices*. Through our polling, we've sought to better understand what the public knows and doesn't know about climate change, and who they trust as messengers, with the specific aim of improving existing public information campaigns and enabling the development of effective new initiatives – *featuring simple clear messages, repeated often, by a variety of trusted voices*.

At least two important insights were revealed by our first poll in 2008. A solid majority of Americans understood and accepted the reality of climate change, although many fewer understood or accepted that human activity is the cause, and most saw it as a distant problem – distant in time (not yet), space (not here), and species (not us). The survey also revealed that two-thirds of Americans trust TV weathercasters as a source of information about climate change. Both insights proved to be directly actionable.

HELPING TV WEATHERCASTERS FIND THEIR VOICE AS LOCAL CLIMATE EDUCATORS

Seeing climate change as a distant problem is not only factually incorrect – in that climate change is already harming people in every region of the world – it's also highly consequential in that problems seen as distant tend to receive little public attention or concern. We inferred that public information campaigns that emphasize the "here, now, us" qualities of climate change could help enhance public understanding and build public will. Moreover, because TV weathercasters are excellent communicators who have frequent and broad access to the public at relevant times (e.g., before, during and after weather events that are influenced by climate change), we inferred that they likely have considerable potential to educate the American public about the "here, now, us" qualities of climate change.

Several other colleagues and I harnessed these insights in a public education initiative called Climate Matters. Launched in 2010 as a year-long pilot-test at a local television station (WLTX) in Columbia, South Carolina, the concept was simple: TV weathercasters routinely have opportunities to teach their viewers about the ways that climate change is already changing the weather and other climate-sensitive conditions in their community, such as spring "bud burst" and "first frost" in fall. They can also present projections to reveal what is likely to occur in the future – for example, the projected annual increase in dangerously hot days in their community, 25 and 50 years from now.

We worked with the station's chief meteorologist, Jim Gandy, to prepare the educational campaign. Specifically, we identified 12 weather events that Jim felt were likely to occur over the next year (e.g., extreme precipitation events) – weather events that, if they occurred, would create a "news hook" for Jim to explain on-air how the event was part of a larger pattern of weather changes in Columbia caused by global climate change. By the end of the year-long pilot-test – which proved to be highly successful – Jim had aired 13 such stories, each approximately two minutes long. As compared to viewers of the other local TV stations, WLTX viewers came to see climate change as more of a "here, now, us" problem.

Concurrently, we surveyed TV weathercasters across America to determine their interest in educating viewers about the local implications of climate change. About half said they were interested in doing so, but relatively few actually were. Most of the weathercasters who expressed an interest in educating their viewers about climate change pointed to a handful of barriers that were preventing them from doing so on-air. Happily, the most common barriers to on-air climate reporting were problems that we felt we could help weathercasters overcome, including lack of time to prepare the stories, lack of access to broadcast quality graphics, and lack of access to climate experts.

In 2012, using this information – both the successful pilot-test of Climate Matters and the survey data showing high levels of weathercaster interest in reporting on climate change as a local problem – we began to offer weathercasters in other cities localized climate reporting resources. The response has been dramatic and remarkable. As of today (March 18, 2020), more than 800 TV weathercasters (out of the approximately 2000 weathercasters in America) are participating in the program. There is at least one participating weathercaster in every American state, and in 88 percent of U.S. TV markets. Participating weathercasters receive reporting resources via email approximately once per week – in English and/or Spanish. On-air reporting about climate change by weathercasters has increased more than 50-fold since 2012.

And most importantly, a growing set of evaluation studies shows that Climate Matters is making a difference: public understanding of climate change as a "here, now, us" problem is increasing most rapidly in media markets where Climate Matters materials are being used most.

The Climate Matters model is an approach to public education that may be worth replicating in other parts of the world. Indeed, it's already been adapted and is being used in Melbourne, Australia. At the very least, localized climate reporting can help people better understand the specific impacts that their community is already experiencing, and the best available projections about what the future may hold for their community. This enhanced understanding has great potential to help people, organizations and communities make better decisions about how to respond so that people and ecosystems aren't needlessly harmed.

HELPING HEALTH PROFESSIONALS FIND THEIR VOICE AS CLIMATE AND CLEAN ENERGY EDUCATORS

Our polling research and other studies conducted since 2010 strongly suggest that health professionals have a necessary and unique role to play in educating Americans about climate change, and in advocating for climate solutions. Few Americans are aware of the many ways that climate change harms the health of people living in the U.S., nor are they aware that some groups of people are more likely to be harmed than others – for example, young children, older adults, people who already suffer from various chronic illnesses, and people in low-income communities. Not surprisingly, most members of the public place high trust in health professionals as sources of information about the health relevance of climate change. Perhaps most importantly, a broad cross-section of Americans respond positively to information about the health harms of climate change and air pollution, and the health benefits of clean energy. Even Americans who are skeptical of climate change tend to respond positively to information about the health harms of fossil fuel use – because it is consistent with their pre-existing belief that fossil fuel use produces air and water pollution and is bad for people's health, unlike clean, renewable energy.

To determine if these insights were actionable, in 2014 and 2015 we surveyed the members of three U.S. medical societies: the National Medical Association (African-American physicians), the American Thoracic Society, and the American Academy of Allergy, Asthma and Immunology. A large majority of physicians in all three societies supported the idea of their medical society becoming more active in educating the public and policy-makers about the health implications of climate change and climate solutions. Many survey participants also said that they would like to become personally involved in such efforts.

In partnership with these and several other national medical societies, in 2017 we launched a formal collaboration called the Medical Society Consortium for Climate and Health. The mission of the Consortium is "to organize, empower and amplify the voice of America's doctors to convey how climate change is harming our health and how climate solutions will improve it." Membership in the Consortium has grown rapidly – currently including 26 national medical societies that collectively represent well over half of all American physicians, and 44 other "affiliate" member organizations that represent state medical groups, nursing societies, public health societies, health care delivery organizations, and climate science organizations. The Consortium has had considerable success in generating media coverage of climate change as a health issue: more than 1000 news stories, op-eds and letters to the editor have already been published, and interest in such stories by news media outlets appears to be escalating.

The Consortium and its member societies have also been active in conducting direct outreach to members of Congress, for example, bringing physicians to Capitol Hill to meet with their elected federal representatives. Moreover, the early successes of the Consortium have inspired the formation of several state-focused initiatives called [State] Clinicians for Climate Action. These state-focused organizations are conducting direct outreach to governors and state legislators, and in some cases local government officials.

The Consortium has also helped create broader health coalition efforts. In 2019, for example, the Consortium helped pull together more than 150 other health organizations to write, endorse and issue a Climate, Health and Equity Policy Action Agenda. The agenda identifies ten policies that protect human health and the Earth's climate, and calls on government, business, and civil society leaders, elected officials, and candidates for office to recognize climate change as a health emergency and to work across government agencies and with communities and businesses to prioritize the recommended policies. This policy action agenda is an important step forward because it represents a consensus view from a wide cross-section of the American health community about the policy actions they are asking government and business leaders to take, as well as the actions that they are asking themselves and all other health organizations to take.

My colleagues and I aspire to leverage these important actions by the American medical community – and the broader health community in the U.S. – to inspire health professionals in other nations to use their trusted voices to advocate for policies that will advance climate, health and equity goals in their nations. Ultimately, my vision is a global climate, health and equity campaign, led by health professionals, to support, defend and strengthen the goal of the

Paris Agreement – limiting global warming to no more than 2°C, ideally no more than 1.5°C – because, arguably, it is humanity's most important public health goal.

CONCLUSION

"No one can do everything, but everyone can do something." This saying – attributed to various people, although I first heard it from primatologist and conservation champion Jane Goodall – holds much meaning for me. The work I've described here was not mine alone – indeed, I've collaborated with dozens or perhaps hundreds of people on this work. The question I urge you to consider is: What "something" can you start – or support – that is likely to be most helpful in averting a sustained global public health catastrophe from climate change? I urge you to give that "something" your best shot.

60. From climate scientist to climate communicator: a process of evolution

Michael E. Mann

I was never trained in the art of science communication. Instead, I was forced to learn to communicate to the public and policymakers through trial by fire. Back in the late 1990s, while I was still a junior postdoctoral researcher, I found myself under attack over a graph my co-authors and I had published. I'm speaking of the now iconic "Hockey Stick" graph (Mann, Bradley and Hughes, 1998). The curve told an unmistakable story, namely that the current warming spike is unprecedented as far back as we can go. Our continued burning of fossil fuels is the culprit. That made the Hockey Stick a threat to fossil fuel interests profiting from our societal addiction to oil, coal, and natural gas.

As detailed in my book *The Hockey Stick and the Climate Wars* (2012), fossil fuel interests, and front groups and politicians doing their bidding, attacked both the Hockey Stick and me. Despite the numerous independent confirmations of my findings by the U.S. National Academy of Sciences and dozens of other assessments, the effort to discredit this research – and to discredit me personally – has continued. Whether I liked it or not, I would ultimately have to enter the fray. In order to defend myself and my science, I would be forced out of the comfort of the laboratory into the rough-and-tumble of the public sphere.

As scientists in the public sphere, what *is* our role? There is a wide range of views among my colleagues. At one end, you have scientists like the distinguished former director of the NASA Goddard Institute for Space Studies, James Hansen. Hansen has engaged in civil disobedience, facing arrest along with actress Daryl Hannah in 2009 to protest mountaintop removal coal mining. He was arrested again in Washington, D.C. in 2010, protesting the construction of the Keystone XL pipeline, a project that would open the floodgates for the distribution of dirty "tar sands" oil from Canada to the world, something Hansen declared would be "game over" for stabilizing greenhouse gas levels below dangerous limits. Hansen has publicly campaigned for a carbon tax.

One colleague, Ken Caldeira of Stanford University, expressed concern "about the presentation of such a prescriptive and value-laden work" by Hansen. Yet, Caldeira himself has publicly advocated for a dramatic scaling up of nuclear energy. One might argue that too is rather prescriptive and value laden. It would appear that what is merely policy informative to one person is policy prescriptive to another. Is this going too far as a scientist? Should we avoid commenting on the societal implications of our science? Does speaking out jeopardize our credibility?

There was a time when I believed that to be the case. Back in 2003, when asked in a Senate hearing to comment on a matter of policy, I readily responded that "I am not a specialist in public policy" and it would not "be useful for me to testify on that." But, because I have been educated, if unwillingly, in the realities of the public debate, I have arrived now at a very different viewpoint. If we scientists choose *not* to engage on the societal implications of our scientific research, I now feel, we leave a vacuum that will be filled by those whose agenda is one of short-term self-interest at the expense of the greater public good. There is a great opportunity cost to society if scientists refuse to engage in the larger conversation – if we do not do all we can to assure that the policy debate is informed by an honest assessment of the threat.

Yet, it is not an uncommon view among scientists that we compromise our objectivity if we choose to wade into policy matters or the societal implications of our work. It has been argued (e.g., *Unscientific America* by Chris Mooney and Sheril Kirshenbaum, 2009) that the greatest scientific communicator of the modern era, Carl Sagan, was blackballed from the National Academy of Sciences, in essence, because many of his fellow scientists looked down on his efforts to popularize science and to speak to its societal implications.

It would indeed be problematic if scientists' views on policy somehow influenced the way go about doing their science. But there is nothing inappropriate at all, in my view, about drawing upon our expertise as scientists to speak out about the very real implications of our research. My colleague Stephen Schneider of Stanford University, who passed away in 2010, used to like to say that being a scientist-advocate is not an oxymoron. Just because we are scientists does not mean that we should check our citizenship at the door, he used to explain (his final book, *Science as a Contact Sport: Inside the Battle to Save Earth's Climate*, is a must-read for anyone interested in the nexus of science and policy). The *New Republic* once called him a "scientific pugilist" for being a forceful advocate for action, I myself have sometimes been characterized this way. But fighting for scientific truth and an informed discourse is nothing to apologize for.

The great physicist Albert Einstein understood the ethical obligations of being a scientist. Einstein wrote a letter to Franklin Delano Roosevelt (FDR) warning of the danger were the Nazis to develop atomic warfare before we did, leading to the famous Manhattan Project and the development of the atomic bomb by America. The unfortunate reality is that FDR did not immediately heed Einstein's warning. It largely fell on deaf ears. In his exasperation,

Einstein actually wrote *four* letters to FDR, each more urgent that the previous, urging the president to act. One could well say that Einstein was an advocate. One might well label him an activist, or even an agitator.

How will history judge us if we see the threat unfolding but fail to communicate the urgency of acting on what may well be the greatest challenge human civilization has yet encountered. I surely don't want that to be our legacy. I believe that it is our moral obligation to ensure that we, as a civilization, do not leave behind a degraded planet for our children and grandchildren. So, today I expend much of my effort seeking to inform the public discourse over climate change and what we can do to avert a crisis. It's a very different life from the one I thought I'd signed up for when I chose to double major in applied math and physics in college, and to study theoretical physics in graduate school. Little did I know then that I might find myself at the center of one of the most contentious political debates in modern history.

Had it not been for the Hockey Stick, I would likely have spent my career pursuing my true passion – scientific research. It's why I got into science in the first place. I enjoy crunching numbers, seeking patterns, solving problems, and sharing my findings with fellow scientists at conferences and by publishing them in the peer-reviewed literature. That, and teaching students and training postdoctoral researchers – the life of a typical academic scientist – is what I had set out to do.

But I ended up on a very different trajectory, one that would place me at the fractious climate debate just as it was ramping up in the late 1990s. To survive, I had to learn how to communicate effectively. Only then could I possibly hope to combat a well-oiled fossil fuel disinformation campaign focused on discrediting me and my research.

Those early experiences were mostly a matter of defense, with me responding to attacks on the editorial pages of right-leaning newspapers, congressional witch-hunts and legal assaults by fossil fuel industry-affiliated groups. But over time I understood that I had an opportunity to speak to much more important larger issues – the reality, and threat of climate change, and the opportunity we still have to avert a catastrophe. I had been given an opportunity to influence the societal conversation about the greatest challenge we face as a civilization – a great privilege indeed. And the more effective I became as a communicator, the more opportunities I would be granted by media organizations to get my message out. To borrow a sports metaphor, I came to understand that the best defense is indeed a good offense.

My life today is very different from the academic scientist career I had envisioned. While I still do research and attend scientific meetings, publish scientific articles, teach and advise graduate students and postdoctoral researchers, much of my time these days is spent on public engagement and communication. That takes many forms.

I do hundreds of media interviews a year, making regular appearances on national television and radio shows, and doing about 50 speaking engagements, panel discussions, and events a year. I've given congressional testimony on numerous occasions and have appeared in various documentaries and films. I've authored or co-authored four books (currently working on a fifth). I have a regular column in *Newsweek* magazine, and write dozens of op-eds and commentaries a year in venues such as *The New York Times*, *The Washington Post*, *USA Today*, *The Wall Street Journal* and *The Guardian*, as well as science-focused publications like *Scientific American* and *New Scientist*. Recognizing the importance of social media in reaching younger audiences in particular, I am also active on social media, including Twitter (with more than 120 000 followers), Facebook and now Instagram.

I've also advised politicians and celebrities from California Governor Jerry Brown to actor Leonardo DiCaprio to science celebrity Bill Nye "The Science Guy". I view the relationships I've developed with these thought leaders as my greatest opportunities to influence the public discourse. Leonardo DiCaprio's Oscar acceptance speech several years ago was devoted primarily to raising awareness about the climate crisis. It was heard by 34.5 million people and resulted in the largest increase in public engagement with climate change ever as measured by Google searches on the topic. I assisted DiCaprio with his 2015 speech at the United Nations, another galvanizing moment for public and policymaker engagement on climate change. I embrace the conclusion of a recent PLOS study that "the scientific community must adapt to the 21st century dynamic communication landscape and ready itself for the next opportunity to harness the agents of change" (Leas et al., 2016).

What all these activities mean is that I no longer devote the bulk of my time and effort to actually doing scientific research – the very thing that attracted me to the world of science from my youngest days. But it's a sacrifice I'm happy to make. I've been given a precious opportunity to work to ensure that our civilization is informed about the threat posed by climate change and the options we still have to do something about it. I wouldn't trade that opportunity for anything.

REFERENCES

Leas, E.C., B.M. Althouse and M. Dredze et al. (2016), "Big data sensors of organic advocacy: the case of Leonardo DiCaprio and climate change", *PLoS ONE*, **11** (8), e0159885.

Mann, M.E. (2012), *The Hockey Stick and the Climate Wars*, New York: Columbia University Press.

Mann, M.E., R.S. Bradley and M.K. Hughes (1998), "Global-scale temperature patterns and climate forcing over the past six centuries", *Nature*, **392**, 779–87.

Mooney, C. and S. Kirshenbaum (2009), *Unscientific America: How Scientific Illiteracy Threatens our Future*, New York: Basic Books.

Schneider, S. (2009), *Science as Contact Sport: Inside the Battle to Save Earth's Climate*, Washington, D.C.: National Geographic.

61. Communicating science beyond the ivory tower

David R. Montgomery

In college I never imagined that I'd spend a lot of time later in life writing about soil. Soil, after all, was the stuff that my professors told me to look past to study the more interesting rocks below. As it turned out, I gravitated toward the interface between geology and the living world, to the form of the land itself and geomorphology – the science of landscape evolution.

So, it became important to know what set the properties of the soil because that influenced how erosion shaped the land – what kind of landslides to expect where and how they'd behave, whether the soil would blow away with the wind if stripped of vegetation, or erode off in a few rainstorms if plowed. Understanding the soil came along for the ride in learning about the land.

Little did I know that years later soil would take me on an intellectual journey to explore how the way that people treated the land shaped how the land would treat their descendants. Eventually I came to see how reversing soil degradation could help address some of the largest and most daunting challenges humanity faces today – feeding the world, cooling the planet, and saving biodiversity. Now, in writing about what I learned along the way, I try to share insight and build support for changes I see as necessary to avoid calamity. But I didn't set out to become a writer.

For a decade after graduate school I did extensive fieldwork on erosion, rivers, landslides, and mountain range evolution that took me around the world, to Asia, South America, the Himalayas and Tibet. I studied sediment-choked rivers on the flanks of active volcanoes in the Philippines, floodplain sedimentation in the jungles of the upper Amazon, how wood-choked rivers in the rainforests of the Olympic Peninsula created ideal salmon habitat, and how clearcuts that harvested most trees in an area caused landslides on the steep rain-soaked slopes of the Pacific Northwest. I learned to work with new forms of digital topography and helped discover giant ancient floods that ripped through parts of Tibet and Alaska.

But it was understanding the ways that the changing nature of the landscape affected salmon populations in Europe, New England, and the Pacific Northwest that pulled me into writing for the general public. I began studying the effects of land use on river systems and the salmon that lived in them after taking a two-year temporary position at the University of Washington, where I still teach three decades later. After being invited by the governor's office to participate in an independent science panel to evaluate statewide salmon recovery plans, I started asking – and reading – about what had happened to salmon in Europe and New England. I thought it logical to assess whether there were lessons from the experience of those regions that would prove useful in the Pacific Northwest.

I did not plan on writing a book about it. Then I met an editor who was visiting an author on the faculty in the department where I'd just gotten tenure. She was not shy about looking for potential new authors and over lunch I pitched her a popular-science book about the environmental history of soil erosion. "You want to write a book about dirt? What else you got?" came her terse reply.

I responded with an apparently more appealing idea that became my first general-audience book, *King of Fish: The Thousand-Year Run of Salmon* (2003). In it I told the environmental history behind the decimation of Atlantic salmon runs and how the Pacific Northwest was repeating mistakes without learning clear lessons from the long history back east. Along the way, I learned that I liked writing for non-scientists. It was liberating as a writer not to be limited to the rigid hypothesis, methods, results, discussion, and conclusions format I'd become accustomed to following. Science, history, and experience could tell an engaging story if synthesized and woven together in a more reader-friendly way.

Soon after the book came out, an editor with another publisher asked me what my next one would tackle. I took a chance and once again suggested a history of how soil erosion affected human societies in the past. Little did I know that one of the editor's personal interests lay in archaeology. He was hooked, and soon so was I, spending nights and weekends for the next several years researching and writing *Dirt: The Erosion of Civilizations* (2007). In my travels, I'd noticed that impoverished peoples often inhabited regions with degraded soil, but I did not fully appreciate the global story until I dug into the archaeological literature and recognized a repeated pattern. Societies that did not take care of their land did not last.

Yet, curiously, there was a surprising villain to the tale – the plow. How did this icon of agriculture turn bad? Tillage leaves the land bare and vulnerable to erosion by wind and rain. And over time soil organic matter falls on newly tilled fields. While nature takes centuries to make an inch of topsoil, plowed fields can lose as much in decades. Over and over again throughout history farming practices degraded the fertility of the land – with devastating consequences.

Writing *King of Fish* and then *Dirt* gave me a new window into natural resources management. I not only learned that I like delving into history, but I became intrigued by parallels in the broad arc of these environmental stories of natural resource mismanagement. A disturbing conclusion emerged regarding how societies can inadvertently degrade resources they value and depend on. A lot of the science we do know does not get used in setting policies and making decisions at a societal level. And all too often a short-term focus leads to policies and behaviors that cause damage over the long run.

Somewhat demoralized, but interested in developing as a writer, I next decided to indulge a personal interest in the tangled history of science and religion in regard to what shaped the world we know. Exploring the origin of the world's flood stories in *The Rocks Don't Lie* (2012), I looked into how geologists and theologians viewed the story of Noah's Flood. The historical dance of reason and faith turned out far more interesting than I'd suspected – some of humanity's oldest stories reflect our innate curiosity about what shaped the world we know. While our understanding of the nature of our world keeps changing, our fascination with it doesn't diminish.

But in the back of my mind I continued to wrestle with the problem that soil is a fundamental resource we take for granted and have destroyed time and again. I knew we couldn't afford to do so once again on a global scale – and that we were on track to doing just that. Identifying problems wasn't enough; identifying solutions was essential.

Inspiration came from an unexpected quarter. As I was finishing writing *Dirt*, my biologist wife was turning our back yard into a garden. Over the course of a few years she turned what started out as khaki, organic-matter-poor dirt with nary a worm into dark, rich soil supporting an explosion of life above ground. Looking into how her intensive composting and mulching pulled off this biological alchemy, she and I wrote *The Hidden Half of Nature* (Montgomery and Biklé, 2016), which explored the new microbial science behind how soil life supports the botanical world, and the parallels between the human gut and the rhizosphere – the life-filled zone around the roots of plants. New science pointed to a new way of seeing how cultivating beneficial life below ground holds the key to rapidly rebuilding soil fertility, and how cultivating beneficial life in our bodies could help stem the rising tide of chronic diseases.

Of course, this brought up more questions about soil. What would it take to restore healthy soil on working farms, and could it be done at scale? Could we reverse the historical pattern of soil degradation that had cursed ancient societies? These are questions I then set out to answer in *Growing a Revolution* (2017). Visiting farms around the world that had already brought degraded soils back to enviable productivity, I found that the common element among them was adopting practices based on three simple principles that radically reversed conventional agricultural philosophy through the combination of minimal disturbance of the soil (not tilling), keeping the ground covered with living plants (planting cover crops between cash crops), and growing a diversity of cash and cover crops. Some farmers and ranchers accelerated the process by also adopting regenerative grazing practices based on frequent movement of compact herds across the land – much like native herbivores once moved across the plains. I was particularly impressed by how practices based on these principles rapidly made a positive difference on both conventional and organic farms. But while the general principles translated from one region to another, farmers used a wide range of specific practices to implement them, adapting specific practices so as to be appropriate for their crops, climate, and tools.

This is not really a new thing. For centuries, farmers around the world have adopted practices to maintain or enhance the fertility of their land. Cover crops, planting legumes, and crop rotations are not new ideas (United States Department of Agriculture [USDA], 1938). What is new is the idea of coupling these practices to minimal soil disturbance, such as with no-till farming. This parallels other approaches rooted in a philosophy of improving soil health, like agroforestry, permaculture, and biodynamic practices. What is becoming clear is that we face a serious problem in how the dominant, now-conventional style of monoculture-oriented, tillage intensive, and chemistry-centric farming degrades the soil over the long run.

According to a United Nations report, global land degradation already negatively impacts the well-being of at least 3.2 billion people – more than a third of humanity (IPBES, 2018). Decades ago, Pimentel et al. (1995) estimated that a third of the world's cropland had been degraded since World War II, and that we lose another 0.5–1 percent (about 12 million ha) each year. More recently, a 2015 United Nations Food and Agriculture Organization report on the status of the world's soil resources related that soil erosion results in an ongoing annual loss of 0.3 percent of global crop yields, enough to reduce global harvests almost 10 percent by 2050 (FAO, 2015).

Of course, the problem is not just soil erosion. North American farmland has already lost half its soil organic matter (Baumhardt, Stewart and Sainju, 2015). While estimates of how much carbon can be returned to the soil in the form of organic matter through new agricultural practices vary greatly, doing so would benefit various efforts to rebuild soil fertility and soil organic matter (and thereby reduce atmospheric CO_2 levels) (e.g., Lal et al., 2018), conserve terrestrial biodiversity, and improve farm profitability (LeCanne and Lundgren, 2018). Disagreements over just how much wider adoption of regenerative farming could contribute should not be taken as a reason to delay wider implementation of practices that can deliver improvements to each of these challenges.

Too often we think of science as new technologies and products to sell, and overlook opportunities to use new science to rethink our fundamental assumptions and reshape conventional practices. To me, the overarching revelation of *The Hidden Half of Nature* and *Growing a Revolution* lay in how an entirely different agricultural strategy comes into focus when we look to the role of soil life in rebuilding soil health.

What emerged from this journey of personal discovery was a new framing of an old problem as recent science pulled together from disparate disciplines pointed the way to a more sustainable agriculture. Here was a new philosophy of agriculture that could reverse the environmental damage of conventional methods. It was a new story for agriculture.

Like it or not, there is tremendous value to the stories that frame how we see the world. For we are hard-wired to relate to the world through stories. I suspect that many thousands of years of campfires drilled it deep into the fabric of our brains.

New stories can help us rethink public myths like the oft-repeated proclamations that organic farming can't feed the world and that we'll all starve if we don't use a lot of synthetic nitrogen fertilizer. If we neglect the state of the soil, these bits of conventional wisdom sound entirely reasonable. Yet they ring hollow once you see the way that rebuilding soil fertility can change the equation – and the answer.

Do we need more scientists to try their hand at communicating to the general public? The web-based media don't really do it. Their format is too brief and content generally too shallow. Television and movies usually go sensationalist when they engage in science-themed shows about supervolcanoes!, mega-quakes!, and killer landslides! And, of course, industry tends to spin science in their favor when they can – or can get away with it. So does that mean we should just rely on journalists to convey science to the general public? Unfortunately, they all too often allow myths to pass as gospel and miss the significance of ideas behind the science.

While I've heard it said that communicating science to the public is too important to be left to scientists, I believe that communicating science to the general public is too important to be left to journalists and spin-meisters. Given the global environmental crossroads humanity is fast approaching we need more scientists to tell the story of what science means, why it's important, and what it means for what we should do. And while scientists should not decide policy, we should not be so shy about expressing our opinions in the policy arena. Although lots of scientists actively avoid making policy recommendations, scientists should not forfeit their voice in policy debates just because they're scientists.

Any credible, sober assessment of humanity's current trajectory would conclude that our global society needs to change a lot of things this century, and do so profoundly in agriculture and energy in particular. While scientists tend to specialize in a narrow disciplinary focus these days, there remains a huge need to synthesize and translate science we already know for the general public and policymakers – and do it in a readily digestible form at more than a superficial level. Unfortunately, too many scientists shy away from engagement in policy discussions, choosing to stay in their lane and considering such input as out of bounds.

It seems to me that the people who know the most about an issue probably have advice worth listening to in regard to deciding what to do about it. The voices of independent scientists should be amplified and brought into public discourse about policy and not squelched or muzzled as a matter of course. Those who understand how the world really works need to help both frame the issues of importance and publicly guide us to solutions that work, for us all – and for the future.

REFERENCES

Baumhardt, R.L., B.A. Stewart and U.M. Sainju, 2015. North American soil degradation: processes, practices, and mitigating strategies. *Sustainability*, **7**, 2936–60.

Food and Agricultural Organization of the United Nations (FAO), 2015. *Status of the World's Soil Resources*. Edited by L. Montanarella et al. Rome: Food and Agricultural Organization of the United Nations.

Intergovernmental Science-Policy Platform on Biodiversity and Ecosystem Services (IPBES), 2018. *Summary for Policymakers of the Thematic Assessment Report on Land Degradation and Restoration of the Intergovernmental Science-Policy Platform on Biodiversity and Ecosystem Services*. Edited by R. Scholes et al. Bonn: IPBES Secretariat.

LaCanne, C.E. and J.G. Lundgren, 2018. Regenerative agriculture: merging farming and natural resource conservation profitably. *PeerJ*, **6**, e4428.

Lal, R., P. Smith and H.F. Jungkunst et al., 2018. The carbon sequestration potential of terrestrial ecosystems. *Journal of Soil and Water Conservation*, **73**, 145A–152A.

Montgomery, D.R., 2003. *King of Fish: The Thousand-Year Run of Salmon*. Boulder, CO: Westview Press.

Montgomery, D.R., 2007. *Dirt: The Erosion of Civilizations*. Berkeley, CA: University of California Press.

Montgomery, D.R., 2012. *The Rocks Don't Lie: A Geologist Investigates Noah's Flood*. New York: W.W. Norton.

Montgomery, D.R., 2017. *Growing a Revolution: Bringing Our Soil Back to Life*. New York: W.W. Norton.

Montgomery, D.R. and A. Biklé, 2016. *The Hidden Half of Nature: The Microbial Roots of Life and Health*. New York: W.W. Norton.

Pimentel, D., C. Harvey and P. Resosudarmo et al., 1995. Environmental and economic costs of soil erosion and conservation benefits. *Science*, **267**, 1117–23.

United States Department of Agriculture (USDA), 1938. *Soils and Men: Yearbook of Agriculture 1938*. Washington, D.C.: United States Government Printing Office.

Index